Lecture Notes in Computer Science   14245

Formal Methods

Subline of Lecture Notes in Computer Science

More information about this series at https://link.springer.com/bookseries/558

Panagiotis Katsaros · Laura Nenzi
Editors

Runtime Verification

23rd International Conference, RV 2023
Thessaloniki, Greece, October 3–6, 2023
Proceedings

 Springer

Editors
Panagiotis Katsaros (iD)
Aristotle University of Thessaloniki
Thessaloniki, Greece

Laura Nenzi (iD)
University of Trieste
Trieste, Italy

ISSN 0302-9743   ISSN 1611-3349   (electronic)
Lecture Notes in Computer Science
ISBN 978-3-031-44266-7   ISBN 978-3-031-44267-4   (eBook)
https://doi.org/10.1007/978-3-031-44267-4

Preface

This volume contains the refereed proceedings of the 23rd International Conference on Runtime Verification (RV 2023), which was held during October 3–6, 2023, at the Aristotle University of Thessaloniki, in Greece. The RV series is a sequence of annual meetings that bring together scientists from both academia and industry interested in investigating novel lightweight formal methods to monitor, analyze, and guide the runtime behavior of software and hardware systems. Runtime verification techniques are crucial for system correctness, reliability, and robustness; they provide an additional level of rigor and effectiveness compared to conventional testing and are generally more practical than exhaustive formal verification. Runtime verification can be used prior to deployment, for testing, verification, and debugging purposes, and after deployment for ensuring reliability, safety, and security, for providing fault containment and recovery, and for online system repair.

RV started in 2001 as an annual workshop and turned into a conference in 2010. The workshops were organized as satellite events of established forums, including the conference on Computer-Aided Verification and ETAPS. The proceedings of RV from 2001 to 2005 were published in Electronic Notes in Theoretical Computer Science. Since 2006, the RV proceedings have been published in Springer's Lecture Notes in Computer Science. Previous RV conferences took place in Istanbul, Turkey (2012); Rennes, France (2013); Toronto, Canada (2014); Vienna, Austria (2015); Madrid, Spain (2016); Seattle, USA (2017); Limassol, Cyprus (2018); and Porto, Portugal (2019). The conferences in 2020 and 2021 were held virtually due to COVID-19, whereas in 2022 RV took place in Tbilisi, Georgia.

This year we received 39 submissions, 28 as regular contributions and 11 as short, tool, or benchmark papers. Each of these submissions went through a rigorous single-blind review process as a result of which all papers received three review reports. The committee selected 20 contributions, 13 regular and 7 short/tool/benchmark papers, for presentation during the conference and inclusion in these proceedings. The evaluation and selection process involved thorough discussions among the members of the Program Committee (PC) and external reviewers through the EasyChair conference manager, before reaching a consensus on the final decisions.

The conference featured two keynote speakers:

- Corina Păsăreanu, KBR – NASA Ames and Carnegie Mellon University, US
- Saddek Bensalem, Université Grenoble Alpes, VERIMAG, France

Both keynote talks focused on the runtime monitoring of autonomous systems with machine learning components and the monitoring of the learning components themselves, an area that poses important new challenges for the RV community.

These latest developments are presented in the two invited papers that were submitted by the keynote speakers and their collaborators:

- "Assumption Generation for Learning-Enabled Autonomous Systems" by Corina Păsăreanu, Ravi Mangal, Divya Gopinath, and Huafeng Yu
- "Customizable Reference Runtime Monitoring of Neural Networks using ResolutionBoxes" by Changshun Wu, Yliès Falcone, and Saddek Bensalem

The conference also included four tutorials:

- "Instrumentation for RV: From Basic Monitoring to Advanced Use Cases" by Yliès Falcone and Chukri Soueidi
- "Runtime Monitoring DNN-based Perception" by Chih-Hong Cheng, Michael Luttenberger, and Rongjie Yan
- "Monitorability for Runtime Verification" by Klaus Havelund and Doron Peled
- "Learning-Based Approaches to Predictive Monitoring with Conformal Statistical Guarantees" by Francesca Cairoli, Luca Bortolussi and Nicola Paoletti

RV 2023 is the result of the combined efforts of many individuals to whom we are deeply grateful. In particular, we thank the PC members and sub-reviewers for their accurate and timely reviewing, all authors for their submissions, and all attendees of the conference for their participation. We also thank Thao Dang and Volker Stolz, chairs of RV 2022, for their help and the RV Steering Committee for their support.

August 2023   Panagiotis Katsaros
                                                                Laura Nenzi

Organization

Program Committee

Giorgio Audrito	University of Turin, Italy
Benoit Barbot	Univ. Paris-Est Creteil, France
Saddek Bensalem	Univ. Grenoble Alpes, VERIMAG, France
Domenico Bianculli	University of Luxembourg, Luxembourg
Borzoo Bonakdarpour	Michigan State University, USA
Chih-Hong Cheng	Fraunhofer IKS and TU München, Germany
Michele Chiari	TU Wien, Austria
Thao Dang	CNRS/VERIMAG, France
Jyotirmoy Deshmukh	University of Southern California, USA
Alexandre Donzé	Decyphir, Inc., USA
Georgios Fainekos	Toyota NA R&D, USA
Yliès Falcone	Univ. Grenoble Alpes, CNRS, Inria, Grenoble INP, France
Lu Feng	University of Virginia, USA
Adrian Francalanza	University of Malta, Malta
Sylvain Hallé	Université du Québec à Chicoutimi, Canada
Klaus Havelund	California Institute of Technology, USA
Panagiotis Katsaros	Aristotle University of Thessaloniki, Greece
Anna Lukina	TU Delft, The Netherlands
Anastasia Mavridou	KBR Inc, NASA Ames Research Center, USA
Stefan Mitsch	Carnegie Mellon University, USA
Laura Nenzi	University of Trieste, Italy
Dejan Nickovic	Austrian Institute of Technology AIT, Austria
Gordon Pace	University of Malta, Malta
Nicola Paoletti	King's College London, UK
Doron Peled	Bar-Ilan University, Israel
Giles Reger	Amazon Web Services, USA and University of Manchester, UK
Jose Ignacio Requeno	Complutense University of Madrid, Spain
Indranil Saha	Indian Institute of Technology Kanpur, India
Cesar Sanchez	IMDEA Software Institute, Spain
Gerardo Schneider	Chalmers — University of Gothenburg, Sweden
Julien Signoles	CEA LIST, France
Oleg Sokolsky	University of Pennsylvania, USA
Volker Stolz	Høgskulen på Vestlandet, Norway
Hazem Torfah	Chalmers University of Technology, Sweden
Dmitriy Traytel	University of Copenhagen, Denmark
Stavros Tripakis	Northeastern University, USA

Masaki Waga   Kyoto University, Japan
Wenhua Yang   Nanjing University of Aeronautics and Astronautics,
                                China

Steering Committee

Saddek Bensalem   VERIMAG, France
Yliès Falcone   Univ. Grenoble Alpes, France
Giles Reger   Amazon Web Services, USA and University of
                                Manchester, UK
Oleg Sokolsky   University of Pennsylvania, USA
Klaus Havelund   Jet Propulsion Laboratory, USA
Howard Barringer   University of Manchester, UK
Ezio Bartocci   Technical University of Vienna, Austria
Insup Lee   University of Pennsylvania, USA
Martin Leucker   University of Lübeck, Germany
Grigore Rosu   University of Illinois, Urbana-Champaign, USA

Additional Reviewers

Abusdal, Ole Jørgen   Hildebrandt, Thomas
Araujo, Hugo   Hsu, Tzu-Han
Balakrishnan, Anand   Kuipers, Tom
Cairoli, Francesca   Mukhopadhyay, Shilpa
El-Hokayem, Antoine   Nouri, Ayoub
Esposito, Marco   Schneider, Joshua
Ganguly, Ritam   Soueidi, Chukri
Godbole, Adwait

Contents

Tutorials

Invited Papers

Assumption Generation
for Learning-Enabled Autonomous
Systems

Corina S. Păsăreanu[1,2]([✉]), Ravi Mangal[2], Divya Gopinath[1], and Huafeng Yu[3]

[1] KBR, NASA Ames, Mountain View, USA
`pcorina@cmu.edu`
[2] Carnegie Mellon University, Pittsburgh, USA
[3] Boeing Research and Technology, Arlington, USA

Abstract. Providing safety guarantees for autonomous systems is difficult as these systems operate in complex environments that require the use of learning-enabled components, such as deep neural networks (DNNs) for visual perception. DNNs are hard to analyze due to their size (they can have thousands or millions of parameters), lack of formal specifications (DNNs are typically learnt from labeled data, in the absence of any formal requirements), and sensitivity to small changes in the environment. We present an assume-guarantee style compositional approach for the formal verification of system-level safety properties of such autonomous systems. Our insight is that we can analyze the system *in the absence* of the DNN perception components by automatically synthesizing *assumptions* on the DNN behaviour that *guarantee* the satisfaction of the required safety properties. The synthesized assumptions are the *weakest* in the sense that they characterize the output sequences of all the possible DNNs that, plugged into the autonomous system, guarantee the required safety properties. The assumptions can be leveraged as run-time monitors over a deployed DNN to guarantee the safety of the overall system; they can also be mined to extract local specifications for use during training and testing of DNNs. We illustrate our approach on a case study taken from the autonomous airplanes domain that uses a complex DNN for perception.

1 Introduction

Autonomy is increasingly prevalent in many applications, such as recommendation systems, social robots and self-driving vehicles, that require strong safety guarantees. However, this is difficult to achieve, since autonomous systems are meant to operate in uncertain environments that require using machine-learnt components. For instance, deep neural networks (DNNs) can be used in autonomous vehicles to perform complex tasks such as perception from high-dimensional images. DNNs are massive (with thousands, millions or even billions of parameters) and are inherently opaque, as they are trained based on data, typically in the absence of any specifications, thus precluding formal reasoning over

P. Katsaros and L. Nenzi (Eds.): RV 2023, LNCS 14245, pp. 3–22, 2023.
https://doi.org/10.1007/978-3-031-44267-4_1

their behaviour. Current system-level assurance techniques that are based on formal methods, either do not scale to systems that contain complex DNNs [27,30], provide no guarantees [24], or provide only probabilistic guarantees [16,29] for correct operation of the autonomous system. Falsification techniques [9,11] can be used to find counterexamples to safety properties but they cannot guarantee that the properties hold.

Moreover, it is known that, even for well-trained, highly-accurate DNNs, their performance degrades in the presence of distribution shifts or adversarial and natural perturbations from the environment (e.g., small changes to correctly classified inputs that cause DNNs to mis-classify them) [17]. These phenomena present safety concerns but it is currently unknown how to provide strong assurance guarantees about such behaviours. Despite significant effort in the area, current formal verification and certification techniques for DNNs [15,23] only scale to modest-sized networks and provide only partial guarantees about input-output DNN behaviour, i.e. they do not cover the whole input space. Furthermore, it is unknown how to relate these (partial) DNN guarantees to strong guarantees about the safety of the overall autonomous system.

We propose a compositional verification approach for learning-enabled autonomous systems to achieve *strong* (i.e., non-probabilistic) assurance guarantees. The inputs to the approach are: the design models of an autonomous system, which contains both conventional components (controller and plant modeled as labeled transition systems) and the learning-enabled components (DNN used for perception), and a safety property specifying the desired behaviour of the system.

While the conventional components can be modeled and analyzed using well-established techniques (e.g., using model checking for labeled transition systems, as we do in this paper), the challenge is to reason about the perception components. This includes the complex DNN together with the sensors (e.g., cameras) that generate the high-dimensional DNN inputs (e.g., images), which are subject to random perturbations from the environment (e.g., change in light conditions), all of them difficult, if not impossible, to model precisely. To address this challenge, we take an abductive reasoning approach, where we analyze the system *in the absence* of the DNN and the sensors, deriving conditions on DNN behaviour that guarantee the safety of the overall system. We build on our previous work on automated assume-guarantee compositional verification [14,28], to automatically generate *assumptions* in the form of labeled transition systems, encoding sequences of DNN predictions that guarantee system-level safety. The assumptions are the weakest in the sense that they characterize the output sequences of all the possible DNNs that, plugged into the autonomous system, satisfy the property. We further propose to mine the assumptions to extract local properties on DNN behavior, which in turn can be used for the separate testing and training of the DNNs.

We envision the approach to be applied at different development phases for the autonomous system. At design time, the approach can be used to uncover problems in the autonomous system *before* deployment. The automatically generated assumptions and the extracted local properties can be seen as *safety requirements* for the development of neural networks. At run time, the assumptions can be deployed as safety monitors over the DNN outputs to *guarantee the safety behaviour* of the overall system.

We summarize our contributions as follows: (1) Analysis with strong safety guarantees for autonomous systems with learning-enabled perception components. The outcome of the analysis is in the form of *assumptions* and *local specifications* over DNN behavior, which can be used for training and testing the DNN and also for run-time monitoring to provide the safety guarantees. (2) Demonstration of the approach on a case study inspired by a realistic scenario of an autonomous taxiing system for airplanes, that uses a complex neural network for perception. (3) Experimental results showing that the extracted assumptions are small and understandable, even if the perception DNN has large output spaces, making them amenable for training and testing of DNNs and also for run-time monitoring. (4) Probabilistic analysis, using empirical probabilities derived from profiling the perception DNN, to measure the probability that the extracted assumptions are violated when deployed as run-time safety monitors. Such an analysis enables developers to estimate how restrictive the safety monitors are in practice.

2 Preliminaries

Labeled Transition Systems. We use finite labelled transition systems (LTSs) to model the behaviour of an autonomous system. A *labeled transition system* (LTS) is a tuple $M = (Q, \Sigma, \delta, q_0)$, where

- Q is a finite set of *states*;
- Σ, the *alphabet* of M, is a set of observable actions;
- $\delta \subseteq Q \times (\Sigma \cup \{\tau\}) \times Q$ is a *transition relation*;
- $q_0 \in Q$ is the initial state.

Here τ denotes a local, unobservable action. We use $\alpha(M)$ to denote the alphabet of M (i.e. $\alpha(M) = \Sigma$). A trace $\sigma \in \Sigma^*$ of an LTS M is a sequence of observable actions that M can perform starting in the initial state. The *language* of M, denoted $L(M)$, is the set of traces of M. Note that our definition allows non-deterministic transitions.

Given two LTSs M_1 and M_2, their *parallel composition* $M_1 \| M_2$ synchronizes shared actions and interleaves the remaining actions. We provide the definition of $\|$ (which is commutative and associative) in a process-algebra style. Let $M = (Q, \Sigma, \delta, q_0)$ and $M' = (Q', \Sigma', \delta', q'_0)$ be two LTSs. We say that M *transits to* M' with action a, written as $M \xrightarrow{a} M'$, iff $(q_0, a, q'_0) \in \delta$, $\Sigma = \Sigma'$, $Q = Q'$, and $\delta = \delta'$. Let $M_1 = (Q_1, \Sigma_1, \delta_1, q_{1,0})$ and $M_2 = (Q_2, \Sigma_2, \delta_2, q_{2,0})$. $M_1 \| M_2$ is an LTS $M = (Q, \Sigma, \delta, q_0)$ such that $Q = Q_1 \times Q_2$, $q_0 = (q_{1,0}, q_{2,0})$, $\Sigma = \Sigma_1 \cup \Sigma_2$ and δ is defined as follows:

$$\frac{M_1 \xrightarrow{a} M'_1, a \notin \Sigma_2}{M_1 \| M_2 \xrightarrow{a} M'_1 \| M_2} \qquad \frac{M_1 \xrightarrow{a} M'_1, M_2 \xrightarrow{a} M'_2, a \neq \tau}{M_1 \| M_2 \xrightarrow{a} M'_1 \| M'_2}$$

We also use LTSs to represent safety properties P. P can be synthesized, for example, from a specification in a temporal logic formalism such as (fluent) LTL [12]. The language of P describes the set of allowable behaviours for M; $M \models P$ iff $L(M{\downarrow}_{\alpha(P)}) \subseteq L(P)$ where $\alpha(P)$ is the alphabet of P. The ${\downarrow}_{\Sigma}$ operation hides (i.e., makes unobservable by replacing with τ) all the observable actions of an LTS that are not in Σ. The verification of property P is performed by first building an *error* LTS, P_{err}, which is the complement of P trapping possible violations with an extra error state err, and checking reachability of err in $M \parallel P_{err}$.

Weakest Assumption. A component (or subsystem) M, modeled as an LTS, can be viewed as *open*, interacting with its *context* (i.e., other components or the external world) through an interface $\Sigma_I \subseteq \alpha(M)$. For a property P, the weakest assumption characterizes *all* the *contexts* in which M can be guaranteed to satisfy the property. We formalize it here, generalizing [14] to consider a subset of Σ_I.

Definition 1. (Weakest assumption). *For LTS M, safety property P ($\alpha(P) \subseteq \alpha(M)$) and $\Sigma \subseteq \Sigma_I$, the weakest assumption A_w^{Σ} for M with respect to P and Σ is a (deterministic) LTS such that $\alpha(A_w^{\Sigma}) = \Sigma$ and for any other component N, $M{\downarrow}_{\Sigma} \parallel N \models P$ iff $N \models A_w^{\Sigma}$.*

Prior work [14] describes an algorithm for building the weakest assumption for components and safety properties modeled as LTSs. We modify it for our purpose in this paper.

3   Compositional Verification of Learning-Enabled Autonomous Systems

We present a compositional approach for verifying the safety of autonomous systems with learning-enabled components. We model our system as a parallel composition of LTSs; however our approach is more general, and can be adapted to reasoning about more complex, possibly unbounded, representations, such as transition systems with countably infinite number of states and hybrid systems, by leveraging previous work on assuming-guarantee reasoning for such systems [4,13]. We focus on cyber-physical systems that use DNNs for vision perception (or more generally, perception from high-dimensional data). These DNNs are particularly difficult to reason about, due to large sizes, opaque nature, and sensitivity to input perturbations or distribution shifts.

Let us consider an autonomous system consisting of four components; systems with more components can be treated similarly. The system contains a *Perception* component (i.e., a DNN) which processes images ($img \in Img$) and produces estimates ($s_{est} \in Est$) of the system state, a *Controller* that sends commands[1] ($c \in Cmd$) to the physical system being controlled in order to

---

[1] We use "commands" instead of "actions" since we already use actions to refer to the transition labels of LTSs.

maneuver it based on these state estimates, the *Dynamics* modeling the evolution of the actual physical system states ($s \in Act$) in response to control signals, and the *Sensor*, e.g., a high-definition camera, that captures images representing the current state of the system and its surrounding environment ($e \in Env$). There may be other sensors (radar, LIDAR, GPS) that we abstract away for simplicity.

Suppose that each of these components can be modeled as an LTS. The alphabet of observable actions for each component is as follows: $\alpha(Perception) = Img \cup Est$, $\alpha(Controller) = Est \cup Cmd$, $\alpha(Dynamics) = Act \cup Cmd$, and $\alpha(Sensor) = Act \cup Env \cup Img$. We can write the overall system as $System = Sensor \parallel Perception \parallel Controller \parallel Dynamics$.

Although simple, the type of system we consider resembles (semi-)autonomous mechanisms that are already deployed in practice, such as adaptive cruise controllers and lane-keeping assist systems, which similarly use a DNN for visual perception to provide guidance to the software controlling electrical and mechanical subsystems of modern vehicles. An example of such a system designed for autonomous taxiing of airplanes on taxiways is illustrated in Fig. 1. Section 4 includes a detailed explanation of this system.

We aim to check that the overall system satisfies a *safety property* P. For the example described in the next section, one such safety property is that the airplane does not go off the taxiway, which can be expressed in terms of constraints on the allowed actual system states. In order to check this property, one could run many simulations, using, e.g., XPlane [1]. However, simulation alone may not be enough to achieve the high degree of confidence in the correctness of the system necessary for deployment in a safety-critical

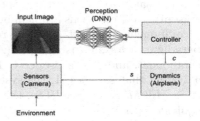

Fig. 1. Autonomous system using a DNN for perception

setting (e.g., an airplane in our case). We therefore aim to formally verify the property, i.e., we aim to check that $System \models P$ holds.

Formally verifying *System* presents serious scalability challenges, even ignoring the learning-enabled aspect, since the conventional components (*Controller* and *Dynamics*) can be quite complex; nevertheless they can be tackled with previous techniques, possibly involving abstraction to reduce their state spaces [13]. The DNN component makes the scalability problem extremely severe. Further, the perturbations from the external world can not be modeled precisely.

Assume-Guarantee Reasoning. To address the above challenges, we decompose *System* into two subsystems—$M_1 = Controller \parallel Dynamics$, i.e., the conventional components, which can be modeled and analyzed using established model-checking techniques, on one side, and $M_2 = Perception \parallel Sensor$, i.e., the perception components, which are challenging to analyze precisely, on the other side. The *interface* between M_1 and M_2 consists of the updates to the actual system states, henceforth called *actuals* (performed by the *Dynamics* component)

Algorithm 3.1: Computing Weakest Assumption

Inputs: LTS model M, property P, and interface alphabet $\Sigma \subseteq \Sigma_I$
Output: Assumption A_w^Σ for M with respect to P, Σ

1   BuildAssumption(M, P, Σ):
2     $M' := (M \,\|\, P_{err})\!\downarrow_\Sigma$
3     $M'' :=$ BackwardErrorPropagation(M')
4     $A_{err}^\Sigma :=$ Determinization(M'')
5     $\hat{A}_{err}^\Sigma :=$ CompletionWithSink(A_{err}^Σ)
6     $A_w^\Sigma :=$ ErrorRemoval($\hat{A}_{err}^\Sigma$)
7   **return** A_w^Σ

---

and to the estimated system states, henceforth called *estimates* (performed by the *Perception* component); let us denote it as $\Sigma_I = Act \cup Est$. We then focus the analysis on M_1.

Formally checking that system-level property P holds on M_1 in isolation does not make too much sense, as M_1 is meant to work together with M_2 and will not satisfy P by itself (except in very particular cases). Assume-guarantee reasoning addresses this problem by checking properties using *assumptions* about a component's context (i.e., the rest of the system). In the assume-guarantee paradigm, a formula is a triple $\langle A, M, P \rangle$, where A is an assumption, M is a component, and P is a property. The formula is true if whenever M is part of a system that satisfies A, the system also guarantees P, i.e., $\forall M'$, $M \,\|\, M' \models A \Rightarrow M \,\|\, M' \models P$. For LTSs, this is equivalent to $A \,\|\, M \models P$; $\langle true, M, P \rangle$ is equivalent to $M \models P$.

Using these triples we can formulate rules for compositional, assume-guarantee reasoning. The simplest such rule allows us to prove that our *System*, composed of M_1 and M_2, satisfies property P, by checking that M_1 satisfies P under an assumption A and discharging A on M_2:

$$\frac{\langle A, M_1, P \rangle \quad \langle true, M_2, A \rangle}{\langle true, M_1 \| M_2, P \rangle}$$

We then seek to automatically build an assumption A such that $\langle A, M_1, P \rangle$ holds; one such assumption is the weakest assumption described in Sect. 2 for some alphabet $\Sigma \subseteq \Sigma_I$; i.e., by definition $\langle A_w^\Sigma, M_1, P \rangle$ is true. If we can also show that $\langle true, M_2, A_w^\Sigma \rangle$ is true, then, according to the rule, it follows that the autonomous system satisfies the property.

M_1 *Analysis and Assumption Generation.* We first check that M_1 does not violate the property assuming *perfect perception* by using a simple abstraction that maps each actual to the corresponding estimate. This mimics a DNN that is perfectly accurate. This allows us to uncover and fix all the errors that are due to interactions in the controller and dynamics, independent of errors in perception.

We then build the weakest assumption for M_1 with respect to property P and interface alphabet $\Sigma \subseteq \Sigma_I$. We use Algorithm 3.1 which adapts the algorithm from [14] for our purpose. The function BuildAssumption has as parameters an LTS model M (M_1 in our case), a property P, and an interface alphabet Σ. The first step builds $M \parallel P_{err}$ (P_{err} is the complement of P) and applies projection with Σ to obtain the LTS M'. The next step performs backward propagation of *err* over transitions that are labeled with either τ or actuals (i.e., actions in *Act*) thus pruning the states where the *context* of M can not prevent it from entering the *err* state. The resulting LTS is further processed with a *determinization step* which performs τ elimination and subset construction (for converting the non-deterministic LTS into a deterministic one). Unlike regular automata algorithms, Determinization treats sets that contain *err* as *err*. In this way, if performing a sequence of actions from Σ does not *guarantee* that M is safe, it is considered as an error trace. Subsequently, the resulting deterministic LTS A_{err}^{Σ} is *completed* such that every state has an outgoing transition for every action. This is done by adding a special *sink* state and transitions leading to it. These are missing transitions in A_{err}^{Σ} and represent behaviors that are never exercised by M; with this completion, they are made into sink behaviors and no restriction is placed on them. The assumption A_w^{Σ} is obtained from the complete LTS by removing the *err* state and all the transitions to it.

This procedure is similar to the one in [14] with the difference that the backward error propagation step is performed not only over τ transitions but also over transitions labeled with actuals. Intuitively, this is because the actuals are updated by M_1 (via the *Dynamics* component in our system) and are only read by M_2; thus, the assumption should restrict M_1 by blocking the estimates that lead to error but not by refusing to read the actuals. Another difference is that we allow the assumption alphabet to be smaller than Σ_I (this is needed as explained later in this section).

By construction, $A_w^{\Sigma_I}$ captures *all* the traces over $\Sigma_I^* = (Act \cup Est)^*$ that ensure that M_1 does not violate the prescribed safety property, i.e. $A_w^{\Sigma_I} \parallel M_1 \models P$ and therefore $\langle A_w^{\Sigma_I}, M_1, P \rangle$.

Theorem 1. *Let $A_w^{\Sigma_I}$ be the LTS computed by BuildAssumption(M_1, P, Σ_I), then $A_w^{\Sigma_I}$ is the weakest, i.e., $\forall M_2.M_2 \models A_w^{\Sigma_I}$ iff $M_1 \parallel M_2 \models P$.*

Proof. (Sketch) '$\Rightarrow$' similar to [14]. '$\Leftarrow$' by contradiction. Assume $M_2 \not\models A_w^{\Sigma_I}$ although $M_1 \parallel M_2 \models P$. Then there is a trace $\sigma \in L(M_2 \downarrow_{\Sigma_I})$ that is also in $L(A_{err}^{\Sigma_I})$. From the construction of the assumption, either (1) σ or (2) $\sigma.a$ is in $L((M_1 \parallel P_{err}) \downarrow_{\Sigma_I})$, where $a \in Act$ represents an update to the actuals by M_1 and . denotes concatenation. Case (1) is similar to [14]. Case (2) is new. By construction, σ must end in an estimate (due to our special backward error propagation). Furthermore, for our system, actuals and estimates are alternating; thus, M_2 must perform a read of the actuals after the estimate and that actual must be a; thus $\sigma.a$ is also in $L(M_2 \downarrow_{\Sigma_I})$, and can be used to build a counterexample for $M_1 \parallel M_2 \models P$, which is a contradiction.

Note that since we checked that the system satisfies the property assuming the DNN is *perfectly accurate*, it follows that property violations can happen *only when the DNN is inaccurate*. As a result, the assumption will only place restrictions on *the incorrect outputs* of the DNN.

To complete the assume-guarantee proof, we also need to formally check $\langle true, M_2, A_w^\Sigma \rangle$. However, this may be infeasible in practice (as explained before). Instead, we show how the assumption can be leveraged for monitoring (at run-time) the outputs of the DNN, to *guarantee* that the overall system satisfies the required property. This is achieved by blocking the behaviours that violate the assumption. We also show how automatically generated assumptions can be leveraged for extracting *local DNN specifications* and how both the assumptions and the local specifications can be leveraged for training and testing the DNN.

A_w^{Est} **for Run-Time Monitoring.** The assumptions $A_w^{\Sigma_I}$ can potentially be used as a monitor deployed at run-time to ensure that the autonomous system guarantees the desired safety properties. One difficulty is that Σ_I refers to labels in both Est and Act which represent the estimated and actual values of the system states, respectively. However the autonomous system may not have access to the actual system state—the very reason it uses a DNN is to get the estimated values of the system state.

While in some cases, it may be possible to get the actual values through alternative means, e.g., through other sensors, we can also set the alphabet of the assumption to be only in terms of the estimates received from the DNN, i.e., $\Sigma = Est$, and build a run-time monitor solely based on A_w^{Est}.

Since A_w^{Est} is modeled only in terms of the Est alphabet, it follows that it can be deployed as a run-time monitor on the outputs of a DNN that is used by the autonomous system. If an assumption is violated, the system will go to a fail-safe mode (modeled as $Q = -1$ in our case study). This could involve e.g., calling the human operator to take over control of the airplane.

A_w^{Est} **for Testing and Training DNNs.** The extracted assumptions over alphabet Est can also be used for testing a candidate DNN to ensure that it follows the behaviour prescribed by the assumption. For many autonomous systems (see e.g., the airplane taxiing application in Sect. 4), the perception DNN is trained and tested based on images obtained from simulations which naturally come in a sequence, and therefore, can be easily checked against the assumption by evaluating if the sequence of DNN predictions represents a trace in $L(A_w^{Est})$. The assumption can also be used during the training of the DNN as a specification of desired output for unlabeled real data, thus reducing the burden of manually labeling the input images. We leave these directions for future work.

$A_w^{\Sigma_I}$ **for Synthesizing Local Specifications.** We also propose to analyze the (complement of the) weakest assumption generated over the full interface alphabet $\Sigma_I = Act \cup Est$ to synthesize local, non-temporal specifications for the DNN. These specifications can be used as formal *documentation* of the expected DNN behavior; furthermore, they can be leveraged to train and test the DNN. Unlike the temporal LTS assumptions, evaluating the DNN with respect to local spec-

---

Algorithm 3.2: Synthesizing Local Specifications

Inputs: $A_{err}^{\Sigma_I} = (Q, \Sigma_I, \delta, q_0)$
Output: Local specifications Φ

1 SynthesizeSpec($A_{err}^{\Sigma_I}$):
2      $\Phi := \{\}$
3   **foreach** $q \in Q$ **do**
4   **if** $\exists a.(q, a, err) \in \delta$ **then**
5            $E := \{a \mid (q, a, err) \in \delta\}$
6            $E' := Est - E$
7   **foreach** $(q', a', q) \in \delta$ **do**
8               $\phi := (s = a') \Rightarrow \bigvee_{a \in E'}(s_{est} = a)$
9               $\Phi := \Phi \cup \phi$

10   **return** Φ

---

ifications does not require sequential data, making them more natural to use when evaluating DNNs.

Algorithm 3.2 describes a procedure for synthesizing such local specifications. The input to the algorithm is *the complement* of the assumption, i.e., the output of line 4 in Algorithm 3.1, which encodes the error traces of the assumption. We aim to extract local specifications from the error transitions. We first note that in $A_{err}^{\Sigma_I}$, only transitions corresponding to estimates (i.e., labeled with elements from Est) can lead to the err state; this is due to our special error propagation. Furthermore, actuals and estimates are alternating, due to the nature of the system. Algorithm 3.2 exploits this structure in $A_{err}^{\Sigma_I}$ to synthesize local specifications.

For each state q in $A_{err}^{\Sigma_I}$ (line 3) that can directly transition to the err state (line 4), the algorithm first collects all the actions a that lead to err (line 5). As described earlier, these actions belong to Est. Next, for each incoming transition to q (line 7), we construct a local specification ϕ (line 8). Each incoming transition to q corresponds to an action $a' \in Act$ as described earlier. The local specification expresses that for an actual system state s with value a', the corresponding estimated system state (s_{est}) should have a value in E' to avoid err.

We can argue that if $M_2 = Perception \parallel Sensor$ satisfies these local specifications then it also satisfies the assumption (proof by contradiction). Intuitively, this is true because the local specifications place stronger requirements on M_2 compared with the assumption $A_w^{\Sigma_I}$.

Theorem 2. *For $A_{err}^{\Sigma_I}$ and $M_2 = Perception \parallel Sensor$, if M_2 satisfies local specifications $\Phi = $ SynthesizeSpec($A_{err}^{\Sigma_I}$), then $\langle true, M_2, A_w^{\Sigma_I} \rangle$ holds.*

Proof. (Sketch) Assume that $\langle true, M_2, A_w^{\Sigma_I} \rangle$ does not hold, i.e., there is a counterexample trace σ of M_2 that violates the assumption; this is a trace in $A_{err}^{\Sigma_I}$. Due to our error propagation, it must be the case that the last action in this trace is an estimate $s_{est} \in Est$. Let q_i be the state in $A_w^{\Sigma_I}$ that is reached by simulating σ on $A_w^{\Sigma_I}$ prior to the last, violating estimate s_{est}. Since M_2 satisfies the local specification for q_i it means there can be no s_{est} leading to err from q_i, a contradiction.

Furthermore, if $\langle true, M_2, A_w^{\Sigma_I} \rangle$ holds, then, according to the assume-guarantee reasoning rule, it follows that the $System = M_1 \parallel M_2$ satisfies the required properties. While it may be infeasible to *formally prove* such properties for M_2, these local specifications can be used instead for testing and even training the DNN. Given an image img labeled with the underlying actual a' (i.e., the *Sensor* produces img when the actual state is a'), we can test the DNN against the local specification $s = a' \Rightarrow \bigvee_{a \in E'} (s_{est} = a)$, by checking if the DNN prediction on img satisfies the consequent of the specification. Compared with the standard DNN testing objective that checks if the state estimated by the DNN *matches* the underlying actual system state, our local specifications yield a relaxed testing objective. Similarly, these specifications can also be used during training to relax the training objective. Instead of requiring the DNN to predict the actual system state from the image, under the relaxed objective, any prediction that satisfies the corresponding local specification is acceptable. Such a relaxed objective could potentially lead to a better DNN due to the increased flexibility afforded to the training process, but we leave the exploration of this direction for future work.

4   The TaxiNet System

We present a case study applying our compositional approach to an experimental autonomous system for center-line tracking of airplanes on airport taxiways [3, 29]. The system uses a DNN called TaxiNet for perception. TaxiNet is a regression model with 24 layers including five convolution layers, and three dense layers (with 100/50/10 ELU [5] neurons) before the output layer. TaxiNet is designed to take a picture of the taxiway as input and return the plane's position with respect to the center-line on the taxiway. It returns two outputs; cross track error (`cte`), which is the distance in meters of the plane from the center-line and heading error (`he`), which is the angle in degrees of the plane with respect to the center-line. These outputs are fed to a controller which in turn manoeuvres the plane such that it remains close to the center of the taxiway. This forms a closed-loop system where the perception network continuously receives images as the plane moves on the taxiway. The architecture of the system is the same as in Fig. 1. For this application, state s captures the position of the airplane on the surface in terms of `cte` and `he` values.

Safety Properties. We aim to check that the system satisfies two safety properties, as provided by the industry partner. The properties specify conditions for safe operation in terms of allowed `cte` and `he` values for the airplane by using taxiway dimensions. The first property states that the airplane shall never leave the taxiway (i.e., $|\text{cte}| \leq 8$ meters). The second property states that the airplane shall never turn more than a prescribed degree (i.e., $|\text{he}| \leq 35$ degrees), as it would be difficult to manoeuvre the airplane from that position. Note that the

```
Controller = S0,
S0=(turn → est[cte:CTERange][he:HERange] → S1[cte][he]),
S1[cte:CTERange][he:HERange] =
  if (cte==1 && he==0) then (cmd[0] → S0)
  else if (cte==1 && he==1) then (cmd[2] → S0)
  else if (cte==1 && he==2) then (cmd[1] → S0)
  else if (cte<1 && (he==0 || he==1)) then (cmd[2] → S0)
  else if (cte<1 && he==2) then (cmd[0] → S0)
  else if (cte>1 && (he==0 || he==2)) then (cmd[1] → S0)
  else if (cte>1 && he==1) then (cmd[0] → S0).
```

```
Dynamics = (start[1][0] → S0[1][0]),
S0[cte:CTERange][he:HERange] = (turn → cmd[c:CmdRange] → S1[cte][he][c]),
S1[cte:CTERange][he:HERange][c:CmdRange] =
  if ((he==1 && c==1)||(he==2 && c==2)) then (err → ERROR)
  else if ((cte==0 && he==0 && c==1)||(cte==2 && he==0 && c==2)) then (err →
      ERROR)
  else if ((cte==0 && he==1 && c==0)||(cte==2 && he==2 && c==0)) then (err →
      ERROR)
  else if (he==0 && c==0) then (act[cte][0] → S0[cte][0])
  else if ((he==0 && c==1) || (he==1 && c==0)) then (act[cte-1][1] → S0[cte
      -1][1]) //move left one position
  else if ((he==0 && c==2) || (he==2 && c==0)) then (act[cte+1][2] → S0[cte
      +1][2]) //move right one position
  else if ((he==1 && c==2) || (he==2 && c==1)) then (act[cte][0] → S0[cte][0])
  .
```

Fig. 2. *Controller* and *Dynamics* in the process-algebra style FSP language [26] for the LTSA tool. Identifiers starting with lowercase/uppercase letters denote labels/processes (states in the underlying LTS), respectively; → denotes labeled transitions between states. Both labels and processes can be indexed.

DNN output values are normalized to be in the safe range; however, this does not preclude the overall system from reaching an error state.

Component Modeling. We build a discrete-state model of $M_1 = Controller \parallel Dynamics$ as an LTS. We assume a discrete-event controller and a discrete model of the aircraft dynamics. The *Controller* and the *Dynamics* operate over discretized actual and estimated values of the system state. We use a fixed discretization for he and experiment with discretizations at different granularities for cte, as defined by a parameter MaxCTE. For instance, when MaxCTE = 2, the discretization divides the cte and he as follows.

$$\underline{cte} = \begin{cases} 0 \text{ if cte} \in [-8, -2.7) \\ 1 \text{ if cte} \in [-2.7, 2.7] \\ 2 \text{ if cte} \in (2.7, 8] \end{cases} \qquad \underline{he} = \begin{cases} 1 \text{ if he} \in [-35, -11.67) \\ 0 \text{ if he} \in [-11.67, 11.66] \\ 2 \text{ if he} \in (11.66, 35.0] \end{cases}$$

For simplicity, we use cte and he to denote both the discrete and continuous versions in other parts of the paper (with meaning clear from context).

Figure 2 gives a description of the *Controller* and *Dynamics* components. We use act[cte][he] to denote actual states s in the *Act* alphabet and est[cte][he] to denote the estimated states s_{est} in *Est*. While we could express the safety properties as property LTSs, for simplicity, we encode them here as the ERROR states in the LTS of the *Dynamics* component, where an error for either cte or he indicates that the airplane is off the taxiway or turned more than the prescribed angle, respectively. Tools for analyzing LTSs, such as LTSA [32], can check reachability of error states automatically.

The *Controller* reads the estimates via est-labeled transitions. The *Controller* can take three possible actions to steer the airplane—GoStraight, TurnLeft, and TurnRight (denoted by cmd[0], cmd[1], and cmd[2] respectively). The *Dynamics* updates the system state, via act-labeled transitions; the initial state is act[1][0]. Action turn is meant to synchronize the *Controller* and the *Dynamics*, to ensure that the estimates happen after each system update.

We analyze $M_1 = Controller \parallel Dynamics$ as an *open* system; in M_1 the estimates can take *any* values (see transition labeled est[cte : CTERange] [he : HERange] in the *Controller*), irrespective of the values of the actuals. Thus, we implicitly take a *pessimistic view* of the *Perception* DNN and assume the worst-case—the estimates can be arbitrarily wrong—for its behavior. It may be that a well-trained DNN with high test accuracy may perform much better in practice than this worst-case scenario. However, it is well known that even highly trained, high performant DNNs are vulnerable to adversarial attacks, natural and other perturbations as well as to distribution shifts which may significantly degrade their performance. We seek to derive strong guarantees for the safety of the overall system even in such adversarial conditions, hence our *pessimistic* approach.

Note also that when using an optimistic *Perception* component, LTSA reports no errors, meaning that the system is safe assuming no errors in the perception.

Assumption Generation. We build an assumption, using the procedure described in Algorithm 3.1, that *restricts* M_1 in such a way that it satisfies the safety properties. At the same time, the assumption does not restrict M_1 unnecessarily, i.e., it allows M_1 to operate normally, as long as it can be prevented (via parallel composition with the assumption) from entering the error states.

For the assumption alphabet, we consider $\Sigma_I = $ act[CTERange][HERange] $\cup$ est[CTERange][HERange] which consists of actual and estimated values exchanged between M_1 and M_2. As mentioned in Sect. 3, while the resulting assumption $A_w^{\Sigma_I}$ can be leveraged for synthesizing local specifications, using it as run-time monitor can be difficult since the actual values of the system state may not be available at run-time with the system accessing the external world only through the values that are estimated by the DNN. We therefore define a second alphabet, $\Sigma =$ est[CTERange][HERange], which consists of only the estimated values, and build a second assumption A_w^{Est}. We describe these two assumptions in more detail below.

Assumption A_w^{Est}. Figure 3 shows the assumption that was generated for the alphabet Σ consisting of only the estimated values (est[CTERange][HERange]).

In the figure, each circle represents a state. The initial state (0) is shown in red. Let us look at some of the transitions in detail. The initial state has a transition leading back to itself with labels est[0][2], est[1][0], est[2][1]. This indicates that if the DNN keeps estimating either [0][2] or [1][0] or [2][1] for

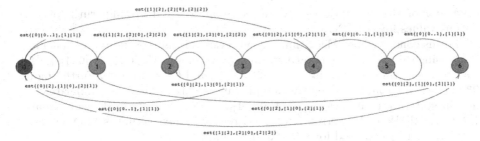

Fig. 3. Assumption A_w^{Est} for TaxiNet when MaxCTE = 2.

```
Assumption_TaxiNet_Err = Q0,
    Q0  = (est{[0][0..1], [1][1]} → Q1
          |est{[0][2], [1][0], [2][1]} → Q8
          |est{[1][2], [2].{[0], [2]}} → Q9),
    Q1  = (act[2][2] → Q3),
    Q3  = (est{[0][0..2], [1][0..1], [2][1]} → ERROR
          |est{[1][2], [2].{[0], [2]}} → Q4),
    Q4  = (act[2][0] → Q5),
    Q5  = (est{[0][0..1], [1][1]} → ERROR
          |est{[0][2], [1][0], [2][1]} → Q4
          |est{[1][2], [2].{[0], [2]}} → Q6),
    Q6  = (act[1][1] → Q7),
    Q7  = (est{[1][2], [2].{[0], [2]}} → ERROR
          |est{[0][0..1], [1][1]} → Q8
          |est{[0][2], [1][0], [2][1]} → Q9),
    Q8  = (act[1][0] → Q0),
    Q9  = (act[0][1] → Q10),
    Q10 = (est{[0][2], [1].{[0], [2]}, [2][0..2]} → ERROR
          |est{[0][0..1], [1][1]} → Q11),
    Q11 = (act[0][0] → Q12),
    Q12 = (est{[1][2], [2].{[0], [2]}} → ERROR
          |est{[0][2], [1][0], [2][1]} → Q11
          |est{[0][0..1], [1][1]} → Q13),
    Q13 = (act[1][2] → Q14),
    Q14 = (est{[0][0..1], [1][1]} → ERROR
          |est{[0][2], [1][0], [2][1]} → Q1
          |est{[1][2], [2].{[0], [2]}} → Q8).
```

Fig. 4. $A_{err}^{\Sigma_I}$ for TaxiNet when $\Sigma_I = Est \cup Act$ and MaxCTE = 2. We show it in textual form for readability.

cte and he, then the system continues to remain safe, regardless of the actuals. Intuitively, this is true because the system starts in initial actual state [1][0] and all three estimates ([0][2], [1][0], [2][1]) lead to the same action issued by the controller, which is GoStraight, ensuring that the system keeps following the straight line, never going to error.

The assumption can be seen as a *temporal specification* of the DNN behaviour which was derived automatically from the behaviour of M_1 with respect to the desired safety properties.

Assumption $A_w^{\Sigma_I}$. The code for $A_{err}^{\Sigma_I}$, generated for the purpose of synthesizing local specifications using the alphabet Σ_I with both actual and estimated values (act[CTERange][HERange], est[CTERange][HERange]), is shown in Fig. 4. Recall that this code is the result of step 4 in Algorithm 3.1; thus it encodes the *error* *behaviour* of the perception in terms of estimated and ground-truth (actual) output values for the DNN.

Let us consider how Algorithm 3.2 synthesizes local, non-temporal specifications using this code. For instance, in state Q3, estimates $\{[0][0..2], [1][0..1], [2][1]\}$ lead to error, thus only estimates $[1][2]$, $[2][0]$, and $[2][2]$ are safe. Furthermore, Q3 is reached (from Q1) when the actual state is $[2][2]$. Following similar reasoning, in state Q5, estimates $[0][2]$, $[1][0]$, $[1][2]$, $[2][0..2]$ are safe (since estimates $\{[0][0..1], [1][1]\}$ lead to error) and Q5 is reached when actual is $[2][0]$. Similar patterns can be observed for Q7, Q10, Q12, and Q14.

From Q3, we can infer the following local specification for the DNN: $(\mathtt{cte}^* = 2 \wedge \mathtt{he}^* = 2) \Rightarrow ((\mathtt{cte} = 1 \wedge \mathtt{he} = 2) \vee (\mathtt{cte} = 2 \wedge \mathtt{he} = 0) \vee (\mathtt{cte} = 2 \wedge \mathtt{he} = 2))$. Here '*' denotes actual state values. This specification gets translated back to the original, continuous DNN outputs as follows: $(\mathtt{cte}^* \in [2.7, 8) \wedge \mathtt{he}^* \in (11.66, 35.0]) \Rightarrow ((\mathtt{cte} \in [-2.7, 2.7] \wedge \mathtt{he} \in (11.66, 35.0]) \vee (\mathtt{cte} \in [2.7, 8) \wedge \mathtt{he} \in [-11.67, 11.66]) \vee (\mathtt{cte} \in [2.7, 8) \wedge \mathtt{he} \in (11.66, 35.0]))$. This specification can be interpreted as follows. For an input image that has ground truth $\mathtt{cte}^* \in [2.7, 8) \wedge \mathtt{he}^* \in (11.66, 35.0]$, the output of the DNN on that image should satisfy $(\mathtt{cte} \in [-2.7, 2.7] \wedge \mathtt{he} \in (11.66, 35.0]) \vee (\mathtt{cte} \in [2.7, 8) \wedge \mathtt{he} \in [-11.67, 11.66]) \vee (\mathtt{cte} \in [2.7, 8) \wedge \mathtt{he} \in (11.66, 35.0])$.

Thus, the specification tolerates some DNN output values that are different than the ground truth, as they do not affect the safety of the overall system. The industry partner is using these specifications to help elicit DNN requirements, which are always a challenge in learning-enabled system development. The specifications can also be used to support sensitivity analysis of the DNN. The requirements and sensitivity analysis are important contributors in the assurance of learning-enabled safety-critical systems.

5   Evaluation

Assumptions for Increasing Alphabet Sizes. Our approach is general, and is not dependent on the granularity of discretization used for the system states

Table 1. Effect of discretization granularity on assumptions.

MaxCTE	Assump. size	M_1 size	Time (sec.)	Memory (KB)
2	7	99	0.079	9799
4	13	261	0.126	10556
6	19	495	0.098	9926
14	43	2151	0.143	13324
30	91	8919	0.397	31056
50	151	23859	2.919	45225
100	301	92709	81.529	132418

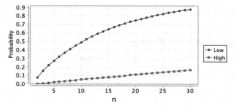

Fig. 5. Probability of the assumption being violated. n indicates horizon length. Low and High correspond to lower and higher accuracy DNNs.

(cte and he); however, this granularity defines the size of the interface alphabet and can thus affect the scalability of the approach (Table 1).

We experimented with generating assumptions A_w^{Est} for the TaxiNet case study, under different alphabet sizes; i.e., different values of MaxCTE defining the granularity for cte; the granularity of he stays the same. Figure 5 shows the results; we used an implementation in LTSA on a MacBook Air with a 1.4 GHz Intel Core i5 processor and 8 GB memory.

We first note that the generated assumptions are much smaller than the corresponding M_1 components. For instance, for MaxCTE = 2, M_1 has 99 states (and 155 transitions) while the assumption is much smaller (7 states); it appears for this problem, the assumption size is linear in the size of the interface alphabet, making them good candidates for efficient run-time monitoring. The results indicate that the assumption generation is effective even when the size of the interface alphabet—corresponding to the number of possible DNN output values—is large. For instance, when MaxCTE = 100, it means that cte has 101 intervals while HE has 3 intervals, thus the DNN can be seen as having $101 * 3 = 303$ possible discrete output values. The generated assumption has 301 states and the assumption generation is reasonably fast. The results indicate that our approach is promising in handling practical applications, even for DNNs (classifiers) with hundreds of possible output values.

In case assumption generation no longer scales, we can group multiple DNN output values into a single (abstract) value, guided by the logic of the downstream decision making components (similar to how we group together multiple continuous DNN output values into discrete values representing intervals in the TaxiNet example). Incremental techniques, that use learning and alphabet refinement [10] can also help alleviate the problem and we plan to explore them in the future.

Assumptions as Run-time Safety Monitors. The goal of this evaluation is to: (i) check that the TaxiNet system augmented with the safety monitor is guaranteed to be safe, (ii) quantify the permissiveness of the monitor, i.e., the probability of the the assumption being violated during system operation.

To this end, we devised an experiment that leverages probabilistic model checking using the PRISM tool [25]. We built PRISM models for the TaxiNet *Controller* and *Dynamics* components that are equivalent to the corresponding LTSs encoded in the FSP language. We also had to encode the *Sensor* and *Perception* components since our goal is to study the behavior of the overall system. For this purpose, we use our prior work [29] to build a conservative probabilistic abstraction of $M_2 = Sensor \parallel Perception$ that maps every actual system state value to a probability distribution over estimated system state values; the probabilities associated with the transitions from actual to estimated values are empirically derived from running the DNN on a representative data set provided by the industrial partner (11,108 images).

PRISM Results. We first double-checked that the PRISM model of the Tax-iNet system, augmented with the run-time monitor[2], does not violate the two safety properties, which PRISM confirmed, validating the correctness of our approach.

The run-time monitor blocks the system when the assumption is violated (see $Q = -1$ in Appendix, with no out-going transitions). While blocking the system is always safe, it comes at a cost, as it prevents the system from performing its normal operation. We analyzed a PCTL [25] property, $P =?[F(Q = -1)]$, that asks for the probability of the system reaching $Q = -1$, thereby quantifying the permissiveness of the run-time monitor. The results are shown in Fig. 5 for two different versions of the DNN that vary in their accuracies. Our comparison shows that, as expected, using a DNN with better accuracy leads to less likelihood of the monitor to block the system.

6 Related Work

There are several approaches for formally proving safety properties of autonomous systems with low-dimensional sensor readings [7,8,19–22,31]; however, they are intractable for systems that use rich sensors producing high-dimensional inputs such as images. More closely related works aim to build models based on the analysis of the perception components. However, they either do not provide guarantees [24] or do not scale to large networks [30].

The most closely related approach is the one in [16], which builds abstractions of the DNN components as guided by system-level safety properties. The method does not provide strong system-level guarantees; instead it only provides a probabilistic result that measures empirically how *close* a real DNN is to the abstraction. Another difference is that the approach in [16] uses the training data to help discover the right abstraction, whereas we do not rely on any data.

In recent work [29], we built a probabilistic abstraction of the camera and perception DNN for the probabilistic analysis of the same TaxiNet case study. The approach facilitates obtaining *probabilistic* guarantees with respect to the satisfaction of safety properties of the entire system. Another recent work leverages assume-guarantee contracts and probabilistic model checking to evaluate probabilistic properties of the end-to-end autonomy stack [18]. In contrast, we focus here on obtaining strong (non-probabilistic) safety guarantees.

The work in [27] aims to verify the safety of the trajectories of a camera-based autonomous vehicle in a given 3D-scene. Their abstraction captures only one environment condition (i.e., one scene) and one camera model, whereas our approach is not particular to any camera model and implicitly considers all the possible environment conditions.

Our work is also related to safe shielding for reinforcement learning [2]. That work does not consider complex DNNs as part of the system and therefore does

---

[2] We provide the code of the monitor in the appendix.

not discuss suitable techniques for them. Nevertheless, we note that our assumptions are monitoring the outputs of the DNN instead of the actions of the controller (as in shielding), and can thus be used to prevent errors earlier. Further the local specifications enable DNN testing and training.

7   Conclusion

We presented a compositional approach for the verification of autonomous systems that use DNNs for perception. We demonstrated our approach on the TaxiNet case study. While our approach opens the door to analyzing autonomous systems with state-of-the-art DNNs, it can suffer from the well known scalability issues associated with model checking. We believe we can address this issue via judicious use of abstraction and compositional techniques. Incremental, more scalable, techniques for assumption generation can also be explored, see. e.g. [6].

In future work we plan to investigate systems with multiple machine learning components (e.g., both camera and LIDAR) and decompose the global assumption into assumptions for each such component. These assumptions can then be used to guide the development of the components and can be deployed as monitors.

Appendix: **PRISM** Encoding for TaxiNet with Safety Monitor

We show the PRISM code for M_2 and the safety monitor in Fig. 6. We use the output of step 4 in procedure BuildAssumption(Algorithm 3.1) as a safety monitor, i.e., the assumption LTS has both *err* and *sink* states, with a transition to *err* state interpreted as the system aborting. The encoding closely follows the transitions of the assumption computed for M_1 over alphabet $\Sigma = Est$.

Variable pc encodes a program counter. M_2 is encoded as mapping the actual system state (represented with variables cte and he) to different estimated states (represented with variables cte_est and he_est). The transition probabilities are empirically estimated based on profiling the DNN; for simplicity we update cte_est and he_est in sequence. The monitor maintains its state using variable Q (initially 0); it transitions to its next state after cte_est and he_est have been updated; the abort state (Q $= -1$) traps behaviours that are not allowed by the assumption; there are no outgoing transitions from such an abort state.

```
// M₂ = Sensor || Perception
[] cte=1 & pc=1 → 0.962: (cte_est'=1) & (pc'=2) + 0.002: (cte_est'=0) & (pc
   '=2) + 0.036: (cte_est'=2) & (pc'=2);
[] cte=0 & pc=1 → 0.681: (cte_est'=1) & (pc'=2) + 0.319: (cte_est'=0) & (pc
   '=2);
[] cte=2 & pc=1 → 0.398: (cte_est'=1) & (pc'=2) + 0.602: (cte_est'=2) & (pc
   '=2);

[] he=0 & pc=2 → 0.675: (he_est'=0) & (pc'=3) + 0.304: (he_est'=1) & (pc'=3)
   + 0.021: (he_est'=2) & (pc'=3);
[] he=1 & pc=2 → 0.043: (he_est'=0) & (pc'=3) + 0.957: (he_est'=1) & (pc'=3);
[] he=2 & pc=2 → 0.377: (he_est'=0) & (pc'=3) + 0.107: (he_est'=1) & (pc'=3)
   + 0.516: (he_est'=2) & (pc'=3);
```

```
// Safety Monitor
[] Q=0 & pc=3 & ((cte_est=0 & he_est=2)|(cte_est=1 & he_est=0)|(cte_est=2 &
   he_est=1)) → 1: (Q'=0) & (pc'=4);
[] Q=0 & pc=3 & ((cte_est=0 & he_est<2)|(cte_est=1 & he_est=1)) → 1: (Q'=1) &
   (pc'=4);
[] Q=0 & pc=3 & ((cte_est=1 & he_est=2)|(cte_est=2 & (he_est=0|he_est=2))) →
   1: (Q'=4) & (pc'=4);

[] Q=1 & pc=3 & ((cte_est=0)|(cte_est=1 & he_est<2)|(cte_est=2 & he_est=1)) →
   1: (Q'=-1) & (pc'=6);
[] Q=1 & pc=3 & ((cte_est=1& he_est=2)|(cte_est=2 & (he_est=0|he_est=2))) →
   1: (Q'=2) & (pc'=4);

[] Q=2 & pc=3 & ((cte_est=0 & he_est<2)|(cte_est=1 & he_est=1)) → 1: (Q'=-1)
   & (pc'=6);
[] Q=2 & pc=3 & ((cte_est=0 & he_est=2)|(cte_est=1 & he_est=0)|(cte_est=2 &
   he_est=1)) → 1: (Q'=2) & (pc'=4);
[] Q=2 & pc=3 & ((cte_est=1 & he_est=2)|(cte_est=2 & (he_est=0|he_est=2))) →
   1: (Q'=3) & (pc'=4);
...
```

Fig. 6. TaxiNet M_2 and safety monitor in PRISM.

References

1. X-plane flight simulator. https://www.x-plane.com/
2. Alshiekh, M., Bloem, R., Ehlers, R., Könighofer, B., Niekum, S., Topcu, U.: Safe reinforcement learning via shielding. In: McIlraith, S.A., Weinberger, K.Q. (eds.) Proceedings of the Thirty-Second AAAI Conference on Artificial Intelligence, (AAAI-18), the 30th Innovative Applications of Artificial Intelligence (IAAI-18), and the 8th AAAI Symposium on Educational Advances in Artificial Intelligence (EAAI-18), New Orleans, Louisiana, USA, 2–7 February 2018, pp. 2669–2678. AAAI Press (2018). https://www.aaai.org/ocs/index.php/AAAI/AAAI18/paper/view/17211
3. Beland, S., et al.: Towards assurance evaluation of autonomous systems. In: IEEE/ACM International Conference On Computer Aided Design, ICCAD 2020, San Diego, CA, USA, 2–5 November 2020, pp. 84:1–84:6. IEEE (2020)
4. Bogomolov, S., Frehse, G., Greitschus, M., Grosu, R., Pasareanu, C., Podelski, A., Strump, T.: Assume-guarantee abstraction refinement meets hybrid systems. In: Yahav, E. (ed.) HVC 2014. LNCS, vol. 8855, pp. 116–131. Springer, Cham (2014). https://doi.org/10.1007/978-3-319-13338-6_10
5. Clevert, D., Unterthiner, T., Hochreiter, S.: Fast and accurate deep network learning by exponential linear units (elus). In: Bengio, Y., LeCun, Y. (eds.) 4th International Conference on Learning Representations, ICLR 2016, San Juan, Puerto

Rico, 2–4 May 2016, Conference Track Proceedings (2016). http://arxiv.org/abs/1511.07289

6. Cobleigh, J.M., Giannakopoulou, D., PÅsÅreanu, C.S.: Learning assumptions for compositional verification. In: Garavel, H., Hatcliff, J. (eds.) TACAS 2003. LNCS, vol. 2619, pp. 331–346. Springer, Heidelberg (2003). https://doi.org/10.1007/3-540-36577-X_24

7. Dawson, C., Gao, S., Fan, C.: Safe control with learned certificates: a survey of neural lyapunov, barrier, and contraction methods for robotics and control. IEEE Trans. Rob. **39**(3), 1749–1767 (2023). https://doi.org/10.1109/TRO.2022.3232542

8. Dawson, C., Lowenkamp, B., Goff, D., Fan, C.: Learning safe, generalizable perception-based hybrid control with certificates. IEEE Rob. Autom. Lett. **7**(2), 1904–1911 (2022)

9. Dreossi, T., Donzé, A., Seshia, S.A.: Compositional falsification of cyber-physical systems with machine learning components. J. Autom. Reason. **63**, 1031–1053 (2019)

10. Gheorghiu, M., Giannakopoulou, D., Pǎsǎreanu, C.S.: Refining interface alphabets for compositional verification. In: Grumberg, O., Huth, M. (eds.) TACAS 2007. LNCS, vol. 4424, pp. 292–307. Springer, Heidelberg (2007). https://doi.org/10.1007/978-3-540-71209-1_23

11. Ghosh, S., Pant, Y.V., Ravanbakhsh, H., Seshia, S.A.: Counterexample-guided synthesis of perception models and control. In: 2021 American Control Conference (ACC), pp. 3447–3454. IEEE (2021)

12. Giannakopoulou, D., Magee, J.: Fluent model checking for event-based systems. In: Paakki, J., Inverardi, P. (eds.) Proceedings of the 11th ACM SIGSOFT Symposium on Foundations of Software Engineering 2003 held jointly with 9th European Software Engineering Conference, ESEC/FSE 2003, Helsinki, Finland, 1–5 September 2003, pp. 257–266. ACM (2003). https://doi.org/10.1145/940071.940106

13. Giannakopoulou, D., Pasareanu, C.S.: Abstraction and learning for infinite-state compositional verification. In: Banerjee, A., Danvy, O., Doh, K., Hatcliff, J. (eds.) Semantics, Abstract Interpretation, and Reasoning about Programs: Essays Dedicated to David A. Schmidt on the Occasion of his Sixtieth Birthday, Manhattan, Kansas, USA, 19–20 September 2013, EPTCS, vol. 129, pp. 211–228 (2013). https://doi.org/10.4204/EPTCS.129.13

14. Giannakopoulou, D., Pasareanu, C.S., Barringer, H.: Assumption generation for software component verification. In: 17th IEEE International Conference on Automated Software Engineering (ASE 2002), Edinburgh, Scotland, UK, 23–27 September 2002, pp. 3–12. IEEE Computer Society (2002). https://doi.org/10.1109/ASE.2002.1114984

15. Gopinath, D., Katz, G., Pǎsǎreanu, C.S., Barrett, C.: DeepSafe: a data-driven approach for assessing robustness of neural networks. In: Lahiri, S.K., Wang, C. (eds.) ATVA 2018. LNCS, vol. 11138, pp. 3–19. Springer, Cham (2018). https://doi.org/10.1007/978-3-030-01090-4_1

16. Hsieh, C., Li, Y., Sun, D., Joshi, K., Misailovic, S., Mitra, S.: Verifying controllers with vision-based perception using safe approximate abstractions. IEEE Trans. Comput.-Aided Des. Integr. Circ. Syst. **41**(11), 4205–4216 (2022)

17. Huang, X., et al.: A survey of safety and trustworthiness of deep neural networks: verification, testing, adversarial attack and defence, and interpretability. Comput. Sci. Rev. **37**, 100270 (2020)

18. Incer, I., et al.: Pacti: scaling assume-guarantee reasoning for system analysis and design. arXiv preprint arXiv:2303.17751 (2023)

19. Ivanov, R., Carpenter, T., Weimer, J., Alur, R., Pappas, G., Lee, I.: Verisig 2.0: verification of neural network controllers using taylor model preconditioning. In: Silva, A., Leino, K.R.M. (eds.) CAV 2021. LNCS, vol. 12759, pp. 249–262. Springer, Cham (2021). https://doi.org/10.1007/978-3-030-81685-8_11
20. Ivanov, R., Carpenter, T.J., Weimer, J., Alur, R., Pappas, G.J., Lee, I.: Verifying the safety of autonomous systems with neural network controllers. ACM Trans. Embed. Comput. Syst. (TECS) **20**(1), 1–26 (2020)
21. Ivanov, R., Jothimurugan, K., Hsu, S., Vaidya, S., Alur, R., Bastani, O.: Compositional learning and verification of neural network controllers. ACM Trans. Embed. Comput. Syst. (TECS) **20**(5s), 1–26 (2021)
22. Ivanov, R., Weimer, J., Alur, R., Pappas, G.J., Lee, I.: Verisig: verifying safety properties of hybrid systems with neural network controllers. In: Proceedings of the 22nd ACM International Conference on Hybrid Systems: Computation and Control, pp. 169–178 (2019)
23. Katz, G., et al.: The marabou framework for verification and analysis of deep neural networks. In: Dillig, I., Tasiran, S. (eds.) CAV 2019. LNCS, vol. 11561, pp. 443–452. Springer, Cham (2019). https://doi.org/10.1007/978-3-030-25540-4_26
24. Katz, S.M., Corso, A.L., Strong, C.A., Kochenderfer, M.J.: Verification of image-based neural network controllers using generative models. J. Aeros. Inf. Syst. **19**(9), 574–584 (2022)
25. Kwiatkowska, M., Norman, G., Parker, D.: PRISM 4.0: verification of probabilistic real-time systems. In: Gopalakrishnan, G., Qadeer, S. (eds.) CAV 2011. LNCS, vol. 6806, pp. 585–591. Springer, Heidelberg (2011). https://doi.org/10.1007/978-3-642-22110-1_47
26. Magee, J., Kramer, J.: Concurrency: State Models and Java Programs. John Wiley and Sons Inc., Hoboken (2000)
27. Habeeb, P., Deka, N., D'Souza, D., Lodaya, K., Prabhakar, P.: Verification of camera-based autonomous systems. IEEE Trans. Comput.-Aided Des. Integr. Circ. Syst. (2023). https://doi.org/10.1109/TCAD.2023.3240131
28. Pasareanu, C.S., Giannakopoulou, D., Bobaru, M.G., Cobleigh, J.M., Barringer, H.: Learning to divide and conquer: applying the l* algorithm to automate assume-guarantee reasoning. Formal Methods Syst. Des. **32**(3), 175–205 (2008). https://doi.org/10.1007/s10703-008-0049-6
29. Pasareanu, C.S., et al.: Closed-loop analysis of vision-based autonomous systems: A case study. In: Enea, C., Lal, A. (eds.) Computer Aided Verification - 35th International Conference, CAV 2023, Paris, France, 17–22 July 2023, Proceedings, Part I. Lecture Notes in Computer Science, vol. 13964, pp. 289–303. Springer, Heideleberg (2023). https://doi.org/10.1007/978-3-031-37706-8_15
30. Santa Cruz, U., Shoukry, Y.: Nnlander-verif: a neural network formal verification framework for vision-based autonomous aircraft landing. In: NASA Formal Methods Symposium, pp. 213–230. Springer, Heidelberg (2022). https://doi.org/10.1007/978-3-031-06773-0_11
31. Seshia, S.A.: Introspective environment modeling. In: Finkbeiner, B., Mariani, L. (eds.) RV 2019. LNCS, vol. 11757, pp. 15–26. Springer, Cham (2019). https://doi.org/10.1007/978-3-030-32079-9_2
32. Yang, Y., Zu, Q., Ke, W., Zhang, M., Li, X.: Real-time system modeling and verification through labeled transition system analyzer. IEEE Access **7**, 26314–26323 (2019). https://doi.org/10.1109/ACCESS.2019.2899761

Customizable Reference Runtime Monitoring of Neural Networks Using Resolution Boxes

Changshun Wu[1], Yliès Falcone[2], and Saddek Bensalem[1]

[1] University Grenoble Alpes, VERIMAG, Grenoble, France
{changshun.wu,saddek.bensalem}@univ-grenoble-alpes.fr
[2] Univ. Grenoble Alpes, Inria, CNRS, LIG, 38000 Grenoble, France
ylies.falcone@univ-grenoble-alpes.fr

Abstract. Classification neural networks fail to detect inputs that do not fall inside the classes they have been trained for. Runtime monitoring techniques on the neuron activation pattern can be used to detect such inputs. We present an approach for monitoring classification systems via data abstraction. Data abstraction relies on the notion of box with a resolution. Box-based abstraction consists in representing a set of values by its minimal and maximal values in each dimension. We augment boxes with a notion of resolution and define their clustering coverage, which is intuitively a quantitative metric that indicates the abstraction quality. This allows studying the effect of different clustering parameters on the constructed boxes and estimating an interval of sub-optimal parameters. Moreover, we automatically construct monitors that leverage both the correct and incorrect behaviors of a system. This allows checking the size of the monitor abstractions and analysing the separability of the network. Monitors are obtained by combining the sub-monitors of each class of the system placed at some selected layers. Our experiments demonstrate the effectiveness of our clustering coverage estimation and show how to assess the effectiveness and precision of monitors according to the selected clustering parameter and monitored layers.

Keywords: Runtime monitoring · Neural networks · Resolution boxes

1 Introduction

Today's systems rely on so-called learning-enabled components (LECs). Prototyping such systems may seem quick and easy, but prototypes are not safe and incur a high cost, referred to as technical debt [19]. Traffic violations, accidents, and even human casualties have resulted from faults of LECs. Therefore, such systems are not trustworthy [10]. The safety-critical nature of such systems

Support from the European Union's Horizon 2020 research and innovation programme under grant agreement No. 956123 - FOCETA and the French national program "Programme Investissements d'Avenir IRT Nanoelec" (ANR-10-AIRT-05).

P. Katsaros and L. Nenzi (Eds.): RV 2023, LNCS 14245, pp. 23–41, 2023.
https://doi.org/10.1007/978-3-031-44267-4_2

involving LECs raised the need for formal methods [20]. Verification techniques for data-driven learning components have been actively developed in the past 3–4 years (cf. [9] for a survey). However, their scalability should be significantly improved to meet industrial needs. To favor scalability, and because some essential properties of LECs cannot be guaranteed statically at design time, some research efforts in the last few years have focused on using dynamic verification techniques such as testing [17, 21–23] and runtime monitoring [3, 4, 7, 14].

We contribute to the research efforts on monitoring LECs. One challenge is the absence of a behavioral specification of components. This implies a change of paradigm: to move from behavior-based verification to data-based verification. Henceforth, existing approaches essentially proceed in two steps. First, one characterizes the seen data (e.g., via probability distribution) or the compact patterns generated from them (via Boolean or high-dimension geometry abstraction). Then, one uses the established characterizations as references to check the system decisions on new inputs by checking the similarity between the produced patterns at runtime and the reference patterns. Existing approaches can be split in two categories depending on the abstractions used to record the reference patterns: Boolean abstraction [3, 4] and geometrical-shape abstraction [3, 7, 14].

We focus on the monitoring approaches based on geometrical-shape abstraction and make two main contributions. First, we extend the approach in [7], which only leverages the good reference behaviors of the network. We leverage both the good and bad reference behaviors for two reasons: i) the monitored systems are learned from massive data and bad reference behaviors often contain useful information, as we demonstrate in the experiments; ii) the geometrical-shape abstractions of the good and bad reference behaviors may intersect or not. Thus, a new generated pattern can belong to both abstractions. Hence, the verdicts produced by [7] based only on good behaviors may be partial. We use both the good and bad network behaviors, i.e., correct and incorrect decisions respectively as references to build box abstractions. Using these references, a runtime monitor assigns verdicts to a new input as follows. If the input generates patterns (e.g., values at close-to-output layers) that fall only within the good references, then the input is accepted. If the input generates patterns captured by both the good and bad references, it marks the input as uncertain. Otherwise, the input is rejected. Moreover, introducing uncertainty verdicts allows identifying suspicious regions when the abstractions of good and bad references overlap. By reducing the abstraction size, one may remove the overlapping regions and obtain suitable abstraction size. Otherwise, it indicates that the network does not have a good separability: the correctly classified and mis-classified samples are tangled. This provides feedback to the network designer. It also permits comparing the regions of patterns and thus enables the study of the relationship between good and bad behavior patterns of the network.

Second, in order to reduce the white space in an abstraction (a box) for a dataset, the authors in [7] proposed to first partition the dataset into a set of smaller subsets via applying a parameterised clustering algorithm and then build an abstraction for each obtained cluster. However, the approach in [7] completely ignores how to tune the clustering parameter and compare the sizes of the single abstraction and a set of smaller abstractions before and after the partition. Thus, we introduce the notion of *box with resolution* which consists intuitively in tiling the space of a box. By doing this, one can measure the clustering coverage which is an indicator of the coarseness of the abstraction and the precision of the boxes. In choosing the box resolution, there is a tradeoff between the precision of the related abstractions and the related overhead (i.e., augmenting the precision augments the overhead). To control the precision, we discuss how to tune the clustering parameters by observing the clustering coverage and the number of uncertainties. We achieve better precision and recall in all cases.

Paper Organization. Sect. 2 introduces preliminary concepts and notation. Section 3 defines boxes with a resolution. Section 4 presents our monitoring framework. Section 5 presents the results of our experimental evaluations. Section 6 positions our work and details the improvements over state of the art.

2   Preliminaries

For a set E, $|E|$ denotes its cardinality. $\mathbb{N}$ and $\mathbb{R}$ are the sets of natural and real numbers. For $x \in \mathbb{R}$, $\lceil x \rceil$ denotes the least integer strictly greater than x. To refer to integer intervals, we use $[a \cdots b]$ with $a, b \in \mathbb{N}$ and $a \leq b$. To refer to real intervals, we use $[a, b]$ with $a, b \in \mathbb{R} \cup \{-\infty, \infty\}$ and if $a, b \in \mathbb{R}$, then $a \leq b$. For $n \in \mathbb{N} \setminus \{0\}$, $\mathbb{R}^n \stackrel{\text{def}}{=} \underbrace{\mathbb{R} \times \cdots \times \mathbb{R}}_{n \text{ times}}$ is the space of real coordinates of dimension n and its elements are called n-dimensional vectors. We use $\mathbf{x} = (x_1, \ldots, x_n)$ to denote an n-dimensional vector and $\theta_i : \mathbb{R}^n \to \mathbb{R}$ the projection on the i-th dimension for $i \in [1 \cdots n]$, i.e., $\theta_i(\mathbf{x}) = x_i$.

Feedforward Neural Networks. A neuron is an elementary mathematical function. A *(forward) neural network* is a sequential structure of $L \in \mathbb{N} \setminus \{0\}$ layers, where, for $i \in [1 \cdots L]$, the i-th layer comprises d_i neurons and implements a function $g^{(i)} : \mathbb{R}^{d_{i-1}} \to \mathbb{R}^{d_i}$. The inputs of neurons at layer i comprise (1) the outputs of neurons at layer $(i - 1)$ and (2) a bias. The outputs of neurons at layer i are inputs for neurons at layer $i + 1$. Given a network input $\mathbf{x} \in \mathbb{R}^{d_0}$, the output at the i-th layer is computed by the function composition $f^{(i)}(\mathbf{x}) \stackrel{\text{def}}{=} g^{(i)}(\cdots g^{(2)}(g^{(1)}(\mathbf{x})))$. For networks used for classification tasks, aka classification networks, *the decision* $\mathsf{dec}(\mathbf{x})$ of classifying input $\mathbf{x}$ into a certain class is given by the index of the neuron of the output layer whose value is maximum, i.e., $\mathsf{dec}(\mathbf{x}) \stackrel{\text{def}}{=} \mathrm{argmax}_{1 \leq i \leq d_L} \theta_i(f^{(L)}(\mathbf{x}))$. We only consider well-trained networks (weights and bias related to neurons are fixed). Our method is applicable to networks with various neuron activation functions.

Abstraction for High-level Features. As runtime monitoring requires intensive usage of the high-level features (here, the features are neuron values at some layers in form of high dimensional vectors), affordable computational complexity of *storage, construction, membership query,* and *coarseness control* is paramount. While there are other candidate abstractions using different geometry shapes (e.g., zonotope [15], polyhedra [5]), our study of these alternative shapes along with the complexity considerations, led us to follow [7] and use box abstraction.

Box Abstraction [7]. A box is a set of contiguous n-dimensional vectors constrained by real intervals. The *box abstraction* of $X \subseteq \mathbb{R}^n$ is defined as $B(X) \overset{\text{def}}{=} \{(x_1,\ldots,x_n) \in \mathbb{R}^n \mid \bigwedge_{i \in [1-n]} a_i \leq x_i \leq b_i\}$, where $a_i = \mathsf{min}(\{\theta_i(\mathbf{x})\})$ and $b_i = \mathsf{max}(\{\theta_i(\mathbf{x})\})$, for $\mathbf{x} \in X$ and $i \in [1 \cdots n]$. A box is equivalently encoded as the list of intervals of its bounds on each dimension, i.e., $B(X) = [[a_1, b_1], \cdots, [a_n, b_n]]$. Moreover, given two n-dimensional boxes $B(X') = [[a'_1, b'_1], \ldots, [a'_n, b'_n]]$ and $B(X) = [[a_1, b_1], \cdots, [a_n, b_n]]$, $B(X')$ is said to be a *sub-box* of $B(X)$ if the vectors of $B(X')$ are all in $B(X)$, i.e., if $\forall i \in [1 \cdots n] : a_i \leq a'_i \wedge b'_i \leq b_i$. For two datasets X' and X, if $X' \subseteq X$, then $B(X')$ is a sub-box of $B(X)$. Furthermore, the *emptiness check* of a box as well as the *intersection* between two n-dimensional boxes is a box and can be easily computed using their lower and upper bounds on each dimension.

Example 1. Consider a set of vectors (dataset) $X = \{(0.1, 0.5), (0.1, 1.0), (0.2, 0.8), (0.6, 0.2), (1.0, 0.3)\}$. Its box abstraction is the set $\{(x_1, x_2) \in \mathbb{R}^2 \mid x_1 \in [0.1, 1.0], x_2 \in [0.2, 1.0]\}$, also encoded as $[[0.1, 1.0], [0.2, 1.0]]$.

Remark 1. An n-dimensional box can be represented by $2 \times n$ bounds. The complexity of building a box for a set of n-dimensional vectors of cardinal m is $O(m \times n)$, while the membership query of a vector in a box is $O(n)$.

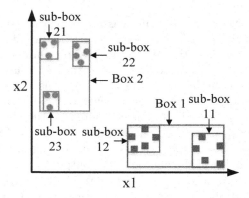

Fig. 1. Box abstractions for two sets of points (the green and red one) built without and with clustering. (Color figure online)

Box with Clustering. In certain cases (e.g., with boxes 1 and 2 in Fig. 1), the box of a set X is s.t. most of the elements of X end up close to the boundaries of the box (there is "white space"). Consequently, more elements not originally present in the set end up in the box. This situation is not desirable for our monitoring purpose. To remedy this, one can apply a clustering algorithm to determine a partition of the set based on an appropriate similarity measure such as distance (e.g., k-means clustering [13]), density (DBSCAN [18]), connectivity (hierarchical clustering [16]), etc. Finding the best clustering algorithms for monitoring remains an open question out of the scope of this paper. We adopt k-means even though other clustering algorithms are usable with our framework.

By grouping the close points in a cluster and computing the boxes on each cluster separately permits abstracting these sets more precisely as the union of the boxes (sub-boxes in Fig. 1) computed for the clusters.

3   Boxes with a Resolution

Applying clustering algorithm before computing abstractions for a set of points was first proposed in [7]. However, neither the effect of using clustering algorithms in monitoring nor the relationship between the clustering parameters and the monitor performance were studied in [7]. Moreover, going back to Fig. 1, with boxes, we observe that it is difficult to *quantify* the precision of the abstraction provided by boxes.

To address the aforementioned problems, we introduce *box with a resolution*, which is essentially a box divided into a certain number of cells of the same size. Moreover, we use the ratio between the number of cells covered by the set of boxes computed for the partition of points to the total number of cells. This ratio serves to measure the relative coarseness of the box abstractions computed with and without clustering.

We refer to this metric as the *clustering coverage*. In this section, we compute efficiently (an approximation) of the clustering coverage.

We consider a set X of n-dimensional vectors, its n-dimensional box (abstraction) $B(X) = [[a_1, b_1], \cdots, [a_n, b_n]]$, its *partition* $\pi(X) = \{X^1, \ldots, X^k\}$ obtained with clustering, and the set of boxes computed for the partitioned dataset $\mathcal{B}_X = \{B^1, \ldots, B^k\}$ where $B^i = B(X^i)$ for $i \in [1 \cdots k]$. We refer informally to $B(X)$ as the global box and to $B^1, \ldots, B^k$ as the local boxes. We measure their relative sizes. Local boxes often exist on different dimensions, i.e., some of their intervals is of length 0.

Box Covered Space. The box covered space associated with $B(X)$ is a box of (possibly) lower dimension used for measuring the spaced covered.

Definition 1 (Box covered space). *The covered space of $B(X)$ is defined as* $CovB(X) \stackrel{\text{def}}{=} [[a_i, b_i] \text{ if } a_i \neq b_i \mid [a_i, b_i] \in B(X)]$.

Example 2. For $X = \{(1.5, 2.0, 1), (1.8, 2.3, 1)\}$ and $B(X) = [[1.5, 1.8], [2.0, 2.3], [1, 1]]$, we have: $CovB(X) = [[1.5, 1.8], [2.0, 2.3]]$.

Adding Resolution. Let $|CovB(X)|$ denote the length of $CovB(X)$ – it is the number of dimensions on which the box abstraction of X exists. We divide each interval/dimension of $CovB(X)$ into $|X|$ subintervals of the same length. Consequently, the space enclosed in $CovB(X)$ is equally divided into $|X|^{|CovB(X)|}$ subspaces. Each such a subspace is called a *box cell*. Each box cell can be encoded (as a box) by $|CovB(X)|$ intervals and can be indexed by coordinates of size $|CovB(X)|$. We can hence reuse the notions and notation related to boxes. We use $\mathcal{C}_X$ to denote the set of cells obtained from $CovB(X)$.

Definition 2 (Covered cells). *A box cell $c \in \mathcal{C}_X$ is said to be* covered *by a box $b \in \mathcal{B}_X$ if $c \cap b \neq \emptyset$. The set of covered cells by a box b, $\{c \in \mathcal{C}_X \mid c \cap b \neq \emptyset\}$, is denoted by $CovCell(b)$.*

Using the intervals defining a local box b and the global box $B(X)$, we can compute the number of covered cells in $b \in \mathcal{B}$, denoted by $|CovCell(b)|$. For $b \in \mathcal{B}$, let $b = [[a'_1, b'_1], \ldots, [a'_n, b'_n]]$, we have: $|CovCell(b)| = \prod_{i=1}^{n} n_i$, with $n_i = \min(|X|, \lceil \frac{|X| \times (b'_i - a_i)}{(b_i - a_i)} \rceil) - \lceil \frac{|X| \times (a'_i - a_i)}{(b_i - a_i)} \rceil + 1$, if $b'_i \neq a'_i$; otherwise 1.

Definition 3 (Sub-box coverage). *The sub-box coverage of $b \in \mathcal{B}_X$ to $B(X)$ is defined as: $covge_X(b) = \frac{|CovCell(b)|}{|X|^{|CovB(X)|}}$.*

Example 3. Consider set X in Example 1. Its covered space is $CovB(X) = [[0.1, 1.0], [0.2, 1.0]]$. For $X^1 = \{(0.1, 0.5), (0.1, 1.0), (0.2, 0.8)\}$, the coverage of $B(X^1) = [[0.1, 0.2], [0.5, 1.0]]$ is $covge_X(B(X^1)) = \frac{|CovCell(B(X^1))|}{|X|^2} = 4/25$.

Clustering Coverage Estimation. We extend the notion of sub-box coverage to set $\mathcal{B}_X$ of local boxes. We note it $covge_X(\mathcal{B}_X)$ and define it as the ratio between the total number of cells covered by the union of boxes in $\mathcal{B}_X$ to the whole number of cells in $CovB(X)$: $covge_X(\mathcal{B}_X) = covge_X(\cup_{b \in \mathcal{B}_X})$.

The exact value of $covge_X(\mathcal{B}_X)$ can, in theory, be easily computed. However, in practice the computation may be very expensive with high dimensionality due to the large number of cells and intersections between boxes. Henceforth, we only estimate the coverage value by considering the pair-wise intersections of boxes. This is a reasonable approximation because the set of sub-boxes considered is built from a partition of the input dataset after applying a clustering algorithm: in principle a good clustering implies few elements in the intersections between the clusters, especially if the number of clusters is important.

For $\mathcal{B}_X$, we define $\mathcal{B}_X^{int} = \{b_i \cap b_j \mid i \in [1 \cdots k - 1], j \in [i + 1 \cdots k]\}$ as the set of pair-wise intersections of boxes in $\mathcal{B}_X$.

Proposition 1 (Clustering coverage estimation). *The clustering coverage is lower and upper bounded by r_l and r_u, respectively, where:*

$$r_u = \sum_{b \in \mathcal{B}_X} covge_X(b) \quad and \quad r_l = r_u - \sum_{b \in \mathcal{B}_X^{int}} covge_X(b).$$

Example 4. Considering the set X in Example 1, we assume that it is partitioned into two clusters $X^1 = \{(0.1, 0.5), (0.1, 1.0), (0.2, 0.8)\}$ and $X^2 = \{(0.6, 0.2), (1.0, 0.3)\}$ along with two smaller boxes $B(X^1) = [[0.1, 0.2], [0.5, 1.0]]$ and $B(X^2) = [[0.6, 1.0], [0.2, 0.3]]$, then the clustering coverage is 0.28 because: $r_l = r_u = \frac{|CovCell(B(X^1))| + |CovCell(B(X^2))|}{5^2} = \frac{4+3}{25} = 0.28$.

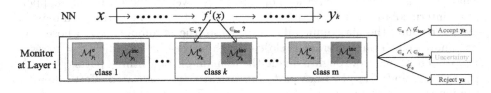

Fig. 2. Framework of runtime monitoring of neural networks.

Remark 2. Clustering coverage allows to better assess the amount of "blank space" between the points in a given set. On the one hand, obtaining smaller clusters (equivalence classes) before applying abstraction technique augments the precision of the abstraction. On the other hand, having too small clusters: (1) augments the computational overhead, and (2) induces some overfitting for the monitor. We further demonstrate the effect of clustering in our experiments.

4 Runtime Monitoring of NNs Using Resolution Boxes

The frameworks defined in [4,7] *only* utilize the high-level features obtained from the layers close to the output layer. Moreover, to build the monitor, [4,7] only consider "good behaviors", i.e., the features of correctly classified inputs as reference. Our framework shown in Fig. 2 is inspired from [4,7] but additionally makes use of the "bad behaviors", i.e. the ones of misclassified inputs. This has two advantages. First, it allows refining the monitor output by adding a notion of *uncertainty* to the previous monitor verdicts, i.e., *accept* and *reject*. Second, when the monitor produces "uncertainty" as output, it avoids falsely accepted samples.

4.1 Clustering Parameter Selection Using Coverage

Using the clustering coverage estimation, we show how to adjust the clustering parameter of the k-means clustering algorithm[1]. The *clustering parameter* τ serves as a threshold for determining the number k of clusters as follows.

---

[1] Recall that the k-means algorithm divides a set of N samples from a set X into k disjoint clusters $\mathbb{C} = \{C^1, \ldots, C^k\}$, each cluster C^j denoted by the mean μ_j of the samples in the cluster, and aims to choose centroids that minimise inertia. .

Essentially, the algorithm starts by grouping the inputs into one cluster[2] and iteratively incrementing the number of clusters. At each step k, it computes the so called $inertia^k = \sum_{j=1}^{k} \sum_{i=1}^{|C^j|} \|x_i - \mu_j\|^2$, computes the improvement over the previous step and compares it to the threshold τ. That is, it checks whether $1 - \frac{inertia^{k+1}}{inertia^k} < \tau$ and stops if the answer is positive.

Our experiments suggested (see Sect. 5.1) that the difference of clustering coverage between the parameters τ in the regions close to two endpoints is very small, that is the higher variations of clustering coverage with τ mainly happen in an intermediate interval of $[0, 1]$. Thus, it is of interest to identify such regions by determining the maximum value $\tau_{\max}$ (resp. the minimum $\tau_{\min}$) whose corresponding clustering coverage is close enough to the one for which $\tau = 1$ (resp. $\tau = 0$). Then, one can roughly divide the domain of τ into three parts: $[0, \tau_{\min}]$, $[\tau_{\min}, \tau_{\max}]$, and $[\tau_{\max}, 1]$. Each part demonstrates the correlated effect on partitioning the dataset in terms of space coverage. Based on this, one can fine-tune the value of τ according to the monitor performance (see Sect. 5.2). We believe that this can also be used with other geometrical shape abstractions for initial clustering parameter selection, especially when the enclosed space is hard to calculate in high-dimensional space, e.g., zonotope and polyhedra. For identifying such regions, we use binary searches of the values of $\tau_{\min}$ and $\tau_{\max}$ with two user-specified thresholds.

Algorithm 1. Construct abstraction for class y at layer ℓ

Input: $y \in \mathcal{Y}$ (output class), ℓ (monitored layer), $D = \{(\mathbf{x}^1, y^1), \ldots, (\mathbf{x}^m, y^m)\}$ (training data), τ (clustering parameter)

Output: $\mathcal{M}_{y,\ell} = (\mathcal{M}_{y,\ell}^c, \mathcal{M}_{y,\ell}^{inc})$ (a pair of two sets of abstractions)

1: $V_{y,\ell}^c \leftarrow \{f^\ell(\mathbf{x}) \mid (\mathbf{x}, y') \in D \wedge y' = y \wedge y = \mathbf{dec}(\mathbf{x})\}$

   (* collect the neuron values at layer ℓ for inputs correctly classified in y *)

2: $V_{y,\ell}^{inc} \leftarrow \{f^\ell(\mathbf{x}) \mid (\mathbf{x}, y') \in D \wedge y' \neq y \wedge y = \mathbf{dec}(\mathbf{x})\}$

   (* collect the neuron values at layer ℓ for inputs incorrectly classified as class y *)

3: $\mathbb{C}_{y,\ell}^c, \mathbb{C}_{y,\ell}^{inc} \leftarrow \mathbf{cluster}(V_{y,\ell}^c, \tau), \mathbf{cluster}(V_{y,\ell}^{inc}, \tau)$

   (* divide collected vectors into clusters *)

4: $\mathcal{M}_{y,\ell}^c, \mathcal{M}_{y,\ell}^{inc} \leftarrow \emptyset, \emptyset$ (* sets of abstractions for class y *)

5: **for** $C \in \mathbb{C}_{y,\ell}^c, C' \in \mathbb{C}_{y,\ell}^{inc}$ **do**

6:    $A_{y,\ell}^C, A_{y,\ell}^{C'} \leftarrow \mathbf{abstract}(C), \mathbf{abstract}(C')$

   (* abstractions for clusters C and C' *)

7:    $\mathcal{M}_{y,\ell}^c, \mathcal{M}_{y,\ell}^{inc} \leftarrow \mathcal{M}_{y,\ell}^c \cup \{A_{y,\ell}^C\}, \mathcal{M}_{y,\ell}^{inc} \cup \{A_{y,\ell}^{C'}\}$

8: **end for**

9: **return** $\mathcal{M}_{y,\ell} = (\mathcal{M}_{y,\ell}^c, \mathcal{M}_{y,\ell}^{inc})$

4.2 Monitor Construction

We construct and attach monitors to specific chosen layers. For a given layer ℓ and each output class $y \in \mathcal{Y}$, we construct a monitor $\mathcal{M}_{y,\ell}$, which has two parts,

---

[2] The starting point of searching a fine k can be optimized, details are omitted for space reasons.

Table 1. Data and patterns related to the network in Fig. 3.

true-label	x_1	x_2	v_1	v_2	y_1	y_2	prediction
class 1	0.1	0	0.08	0.06	**0.078**	0.062	class 1
class 1	0.2	0.1	0.18	0.16	**0.222**	0.162	class 1
class 1	0.8	0.3	0.7	0.6	**0.69**	0.61	class 1
class 1	0.9	0.4	0.8	0.7	**0.79**	0.71	class 1
class 2	0.3	0.25	0.29	0.28	**0.289**	0.281	*class 1*
class 2	0.4	0.35	0.39	0.38	**0.389**	0.381	*class 1*
class 2	0.5	0.8	0.56	0.62	0.566	**0.614**	class 2
class 2	0.6	0.9	0.66	0.72	0.666	**0.714**	class 2

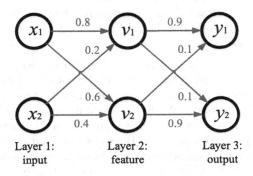

Layer 1: input   Layer 2: feature   Layer 3: output

Fig. 3. An example of neural network.

$\mathcal{M}^{c}_{y,\ell}$ and $\mathcal{M}^{inc}_{y,\ell}$, both of which are sets of abstractions used as references of high-level features for inputs correctly and incorrectly classified as y, respectively.

Algorithm 1 constructs the monitor in three steps: i) extract the values of high-level features at monitored layer ℓ (lines 1 and 2); ii) apply clustering algorithm to the obtained features and partition them into local distributed clusters (line 3), see Sect. 4.1; iii) construct an abstraction for each cluster. The union of abstractions computed as such forms $\mathcal{M}^{c}_{y,\ell}$.

Example 5. Consider the network in Fig. 3 and the data used to build its monitor given by columns 1–3 in Table 1. We consider output class 1 at layer 2. Algo. 1:

1. extracts the features (values of v_1 and v_2 in Table 1) generated at layer 2 and classify them into two sets $V^{c}_{1,2} = \{(0.078, 0.062), (0.222, 0.162), (0.69, 0.61),$ $(0.79, 0.71)\}$ and $V^{inc}_{1,2} = \{(0.289, 0.281), (0.389, 0.381)\}$ according to whether their inputs are correctly classified or not.
2. partitions set $V^{c}_{1,2}$ into two clusters $\mathbb{C}^{c}_{1,2} = \{C_1, C_2\}\}$ with $C_1 = \{(0.078,$ $0.062), (0.222, 0.162)\}$, $C_2 = \{(0.69, 0.61), (0.79, 0.71),$ and keeps $V^{inc}_{1,2}$ as a single cluster $\mathbb{C}^{inc}_{1,2} = \{C_3\}$ with $C_3 = \{(0.289, 0.281), (0.389, 0.381)\}$;

3. builds the box abstractions for each cluster obtained at step 2: $A_{1,2}^{C_1} = B(C_1)$
$= [[0.078, 0.222], [0.062, 0.162]]$, $A_{1,2}^{C_2} = B(C_2) = [[0.69, 0.79], [0.61, 0.71]]$, and
$A_{1,2}^{C_3} = B(C_3) = [[0.289, 0.389], [0.281, 0.381]]$.

Finally, the monitor for class 1 is the pair of sets: $\mathcal{M}_{1,2} = (\mathcal{M}_{1,2}^c, \mathcal{M}_{1,2}^{inc})$, where
$\mathcal{M}_{1,2}^c = \{A_{1,2}^{C_1}, A_{1,2}^{C_2}\}$ and $\mathcal{M}_{1,2}^{inc} = \{A_{1,2}^{C_3}\}$.

4.3   Monitor Execution

After constructing the monitor, it is deployed in the network and works as follows. For each new input, it gets the value $\mathbf{v}$ at monitored layer ℓ ($\mathbf{v} \leftarrow f^\ell(\mathbf{x})$)
and determines its memberships to abstractions from $\mathcal{M}_{y,\ell}^c$ and $\mathcal{M}_{y,\ell}^{inc}$ according
the network prediction of class y. Out of the four possibilities, we distinguish
three outcomes: i) "uncertainty", if $\mathbf{v}$ is contained by both abstractions from
$\mathcal{M}_{y,\ell}^c$ and $\mathcal{M}_{y,\ell}^{inc}$; ii) "accept", if $\mathbf{v}$ is only contained by some abstraction from
$\mathcal{M}_{y,\ell}^c$; iii) "reject", otherwise.

Example 6. Consider the network in Fig. 3 and the monitor constructed in
Example 5. Since there is no overlap between the built abstractions, the monitor has only two possible outcomes: accept and reject. Assume $\mathbf{x}^1 = (0.15, 0.1)$
and $\mathbf{x}^2 = (0.6, 0.5)$ are input. We first collect its output at watched layer 2:
$f^2(\mathbf{x}^1) = (0.14, 0.13)$ and $f^2(\mathbf{x}^2) = (0.58, 0.56)$. Then, the network outputs the
predictions: $\mathbf{dec}(\mathbf{x}^1) = 1$, $\mathbf{dec}(\mathbf{x}^2) = 1$. Based on the predicted classes, the monitor checks whether its produced feature is in some abstractions: $f^2(\mathbf{x}^1)$ is in
abstraction $A_{1,2}^{C_1}$, while $f^2(\mathbf{x}^2)$ is outside any abstraction in $\mathcal{M}_{1,2}^c$. The monitor
accepts $\mathbf{x}^1$ and rejects $\mathbf{x}^2$.

4.4   Dealing with Uncertainty Verdicts

We note that using "uncertainty" provides a new dimension to verify the quality
of the built monitor for a given network, since it measures the "overlap" between
the abstractions of correct and incorrect behaviors. The more "uncertainty" a
monitor produces as verdict, the worse the abstraction is. The reason for a high
level of uncertainty can be twofold, as illustrated in Fig. 4: i) the abstraction
built is too coarse (shown on the left); ii) the network intrinsically has a bad
separability of classification, i.e., good and bad features are entangled (on the
right).

   In the following, we give a sufficient condition for the non-existence of uncertainty verdict of a monitor and discuss how to distinguish the types of uncertainties.

Proposition 2. *A monitor $\mathcal{M}_{y,\ell} = (\mathcal{M}_{y,\ell}^c, \mathcal{M}_{y,\ell}^{inc})$ for an output class y built at
layer ℓ never produces a "uncertainty" verdict if $\mathcal{M}_{y,\ell}^c \cap \mathcal{M}_{y,\ell}^{inc} = \emptyset$.*

   The above condition states that there exists no box in $\mathcal{M}_{y,\ell}^c$ which intersects
with a box in $\mathcal{M}_{y,\ell}^{inc}$. The condition can be verified in time $O(k_1 \times k_2 \times n)$, provided
that $\mathcal{M}_{y,\ell}^c$ and $\mathcal{M}_{y,\ell}^{inc}$ contain k_1 and k_2 n-dimensional boxes, respectively.

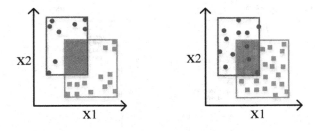

Fig. 4. Uncertainty sources.

When there exists a box in $\mathcal{M}^c_{y,\ell}$ overlapping with a box in $\mathcal{M}^{\text{inc}}_{y,\ell}$, we define a two-step method to roughly conclude the possibility of the overlapping region. Deep exploration of such an overlapping region is out of the scope of this paper.

- Step 1. Check if the features to be abstracted are well partitioned using two criteria: i) whether the clustering parameter τ is small enough (compared to a user-guided threshold 0.05 or 0.01), since a small value of τ implies that partitioning the features into more clusters does not improve the clustering effect significantly; ii) whether the average number of features per cluster is small enough, which can be directly seen when the partition is fine.
- Step 2. Stab at overlapping region in two steps. Considering a pair of overlapping boxes $B(X^c)$ and $B(X^{\text{inc}})$ for two clusters of good and bad features X^c and X^{inc}, respectively, let $X^c_o = X^c \cap B(X^c) \cap B(X^{\text{inc}})$ and $X^{\text{inc}}_o = X^{\text{inc}} \cap B(X^c) \cap B(X^{\text{inc}})$ be the corresponding sets of good and bad features located in the overlapping region.
  - Step 2.1. Calculate the ratios between the numbers of good and bad features inside the overlapping region to the total numbers of good and bad features, i.e., $r_c = |X^c_o|/|X^c|$ and $r_{\text{inc}} = |X^{\text{inc}}_o|/|X^{\text{inc}}|$. If any of the ratios is greater than a user-guided threshold (e.g., 10%), we say that the features are potentially entangled. This requires further analysis (step 2.2). Otherwise, we conclude that the overlapping region is due to coarse abstractions and a more precise abstraction should be used.
  - Step 2.2. Label features in X^c_o and X^{inc}_o as 0 and 1, respectively. Consider a good (bad) feature $\mathbf{x}$ in the overlapping region, then explore the k neighbors of $\mathbf{x}$ to see if the label of $\mathbf{x}$ will be inverted by its neighbors; if there are only a few points (say 5%, perhaps outliers) whose labels are inverted, then we conclude that the overlapping region is not an entangled area, else it is.

To sum up, the possibility of overlapping between $\mathcal{M}^c_{y,\ell}$ and $\mathcal{M}^{\text{inc}}_{y,\ell}$ can be determined in two steps: first verify if the features to be abstracted are fine-partitioned and then explore how many overlapping regions between $\mathcal{M}^c_{y,\ell}$ and $\mathcal{M}^{\text{inc}}_{y,\ell}$ can be considered as entangled areas.

34   C. Wu et al.

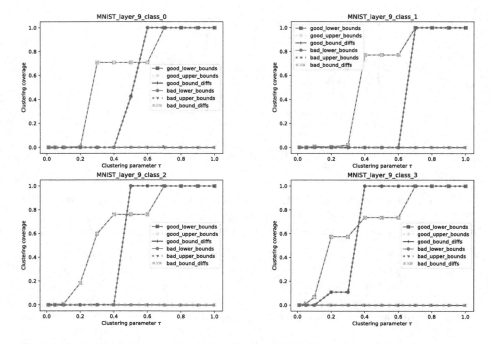

Fig. 5. Clustering coverage estimations for the high-level features obtained at the output layer for benchmark MNIST.

5   Experimental Evaluation

First, we show that our estimation of clustering coverage is precise, i.e., the difference between the estimated lower and upper bounds is zero or negligible. Second, we assess the monitor performance under different settings of clustering parameter τ and chosen monitoring layers. We built monitors on benchmark MNIST [12] using its $60,000$ training samples and tested the monitors' performance via its $10,000$ test samples and $10,000$ samples from the test set of F_MNIST [25]. For consistency, we used the common network in [4] and [7], whose accuracies on training and test sets are 99% and 98.52%, respectively. The monitors are placed at the last four layers (layers 6, 7, 8, and 9). For parameter τ, we tried out the 12 values in $\mathbb{T} = \{1.0, 0.9, 0.8, 0.7, 0.6, 0.5, 0.4, 0.3, 0.2, 0.1, 0.05, 0.01\}$. Since a monitor is built for each output class at each monitored layer, 480 monitors were constructed and tested. For space reasons, further evaluation results confirming our conclusions can be found in [24].

5.1   Clustering Coverage Estimation

Figure 5 contains 4 graphs which result from the clustering coverage estimation for partitioning the high-level features at the output layer by using the clustering parameters in $\mathbb{T}$. Each graph contains six curves which represent the lower bounds, the upper bounds, the bound differences of clustering coverage for the partitions corresponding to the good and bad features used to construct the corresponding monitor reference.

We observed that the relative difference between estimated lower and upper bounds is zero or extremely small – less than 1‰, as shown in Fig. 5. Moreover, as we stated in previous section, the clustering coverage lines close to two endpoints are flat, which indicates that the difference of clustering coverage between the parameters τ in such regions is zero or very small.

5.2   Assessing Monitor Precision

Evaluating Monitors for Classification Systems. Since we create monitors for image classification systems, we use two sorts of images to construct the test dataset. The first sort is referred to as known inputs; these are the images belonging to one of classes of the system (i.e., from MNIST). The second sort is referred to as unknown inputs; these are the images not belonging to any class of the system (i.e., from F_MNIST). In testing a monitor, one can choose the ratio between known and unknown inputs depending on the criticality and the purpose of the classification system. Once the test data is prepared, we feed it to the network and evaluate the performance of every monitor by considering different kinds of outcomes as indicated in the confusion matrix shown in Table 2.

Comparison with [7]. Controlling the coarseness of built abstractions with regard to effectiveness is crucial. However, how to control the size of sub-box abstractions via clustering parameter is ignored in [7]. This paper addresses it as follows. First, we introduce the notion of clustering coverage to measure, in terms of covered space, the relative size of sub-box abstractions w.r.t the global one. Second, we leverage the network bad behaviors, which introduces a new monitor outcome of uncertainty. The number of uncertainty outcomes (MN and MP in Table 2) is an hint on the coarseness of built abstractions. Furthermore, we provide the following improvements: 1) the object of study, novelty detection, is refined to each output class of a given network, since the original definition of novelty, *true positive* in [7], includes not only unknown inputs, but also known inputs which belong to one of output classes but misclassified and whose feature is outsize abstraction; 2) we use a clustering parameter that is specific to each output class at each monitored layer, and possibly to each set of good and bad features; while [7] uses a uniform clustering parameter for all output classes and monitored layers. This enables precise control on the numbers of FN and FP, e.g., see Fig. 6: a higher F1 score can be always achieved via selecting a group of clustering parameters customized to each output class.

In the sequel, we discuss in details three topics: i) relationship between monitor effectiveness and clustering parameter; ii) how to tune the clustering parameter; iii) how to select the best layers to monitor.

Monitor Effectiveness vs Clustering Parameter. We now evaluate the monitor effectiveness according to the clustering parameter τ. For space reasons, in Fig. 7,

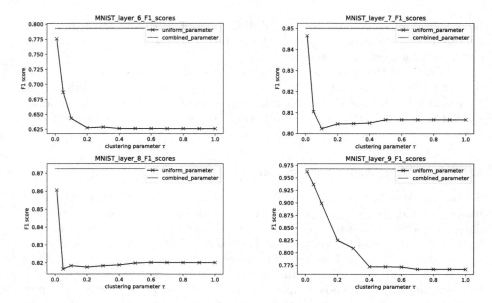

Fig. 6. Comparison of F1 scores obtained via setting uniform (as in [7]) and combined parameters on benchmark MNIST.

Table 2. Confusion matrix – outcomes given monitor verdict and real nature.

real nature	verdict		
	negative (accept)	**positive** (reject)	**uncertainty**
negative (labelled y)	true negative (TN)	false positive (FP)	missed negative (MN)
positive (labelled non-y)	false negative (FN)	true positive (TP)	missed positive (MP)

we only present the results of 72/480 monitors, representing 12 values of τ for 6 output classes (more results in [24]). Monitors watch the last layer of the network. Each curve depicts the number of outcomes indicated in Table 2. By changing the value of τ, one can directly control the sensitivity of the monitor to report an abnormal input. This encourages (i) clustering the high-level features into smaller clusters before computing a global abstraction for them and (ii) selecting a clustering parameter specific for each output-class monitor.

Moroever, we make the following observations. 1) The number of TN is only affected when the value of τ is very small, in most cases less than 0.1. Consequently, the abstractions for good high-level features are too coarse in most cases. 2) In most cases, the number of uncertainties is zero or close to zero by setting a small value of τ. This indicates that the network has a good separability of classification and also that the abstractions for good and bad features are precise enough. However, the capability of reducing uncertainty to zero may stem from over-precise abstractions. 3) In terms of errors, the number of FP is very small, meaning that the probability of mis-classifying negative samples is very low, while the number of FN is very high. However, the number of FN

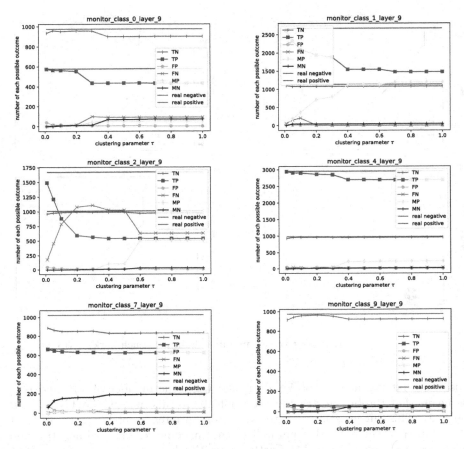

Fig. 7. Numbers of outcomes in Table 2 for 10 monitors built at the output layer for MNIST.

can be greatly reduced. This indicates that the detection of positive samples is insufficient due to the coarseness of abstraction. 4) The number of TP can be always augmented by shrinking the abstraction. 5) The monitors for different output classes have different degrees of sensitivity to parameter τ. For example, the performance of monitors for classes 9 does not depend on τ.

Clustering Parameter Tuning. The monitor effectiveness depends on the clustering parameter. One can adjust τ to improve the monitor detection capability of positive samples, i.e., abnormal inputs. In doing so, one can observe: i) the clustering coverage estimation to decide whether the "white space" has been sufficiently removed; ii) the numbers of uncertainties to determine if they can be reduced to zeros, indicating whether the good and bad features can be well separated by box abstractions; iii) the number changes of TN and TP when τ is decreased after reducing the numbers of uncertainties into zeros (i.e., abstractions for good and bad features are non-overlapping). For instance, if one

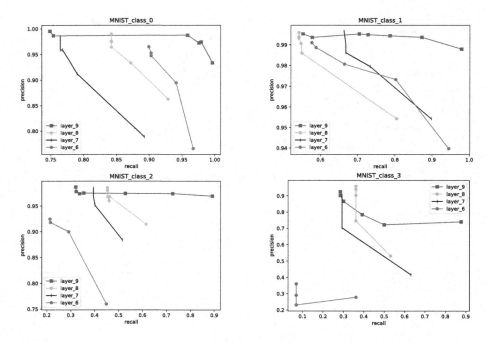

Fig. 8. Precision-Recall curves for monitors built on benchmark MNIST.

observes that the number of TN decreases while the number of TP increases, it means that the box abstractions are not able to distinguish the TN and TP samples. This suggests investigating the appropriateness of boxes to abstract the features or the network separability, since in some regions real negative and positives samples are entangled. Furthermore, the dependence to τ differs among classes, so it is desirable to fine-tune τ for each class separately. This also applies to the monitors built in different layers because their features completely differ.

Monitor Precision vs Monitored Layer. We use precision and recall to study the relationship between the monitor effectiveness and the monitored layer. We use precision-recall curves to show the tradeoff between precision and recall for different values of τ. *Precision or positive predictive value (PPV)* is defined as the number of TP over the total number of predictive positive samples, i.e., $precision = \frac{TP}{TP+FP}$, while *recall or true positive rate (TPR)* is defined as the number of TP over the total number of real positive samples, i.e., $recall = \frac{TP}{TP+FN+MP}$. A large area under the curve indicates both a high recall and high precision. High precision indicates a low false positive rate, and high recall indicates a low false negative rate. High scores for both show that the classifier is returning accurate results (high precision), as well as returning a majority of all positive results (high recall). Based on this, by examining the precision-recall curves shown in Fig. 8, we can see that for MNIST, it is better to monitor the output layer, as one can mostly achieve high precision and recall.

5.3   Discussion and Lessons Learned

Our experiments were conducted on a Windows PC (Intel Core i7-7600U CPU @2.80 GHz, with 8 GB RAM) and the implementation is available[3]. The one-step construction and test of 480 monitors on benchmark MNIST took, respectively, $2,473$ and 85 seconds.[4]

We also experimented on F_MNIST and CIFAR10 [11] and report the results in [24]. The overall results on different benchmarks confirm that it is necessary to partition (e.g., clustering here) the high-level used features before computing a global abstraction for them, since on all tried benchmarks there exist many uncertainties. Results also suggest that the clustering parameter should be customized for each output-class of a network at different layers, even for the good and bad features of the same output-class. However, we point out that the optimal monitored layer is not always the output layer, since we observed on benchmark F_MNIST that in most cases the monitor's performance at the fourth to the last layer is superior than that ones at the last three layers by observing their precision-recall curves. Until now, no general law can be given to predict such optimal monitored layer and we believe that it makes the method presented in this paper important to best configure monitors for a given classification system. Last but not least, the success of using abstraction-based monitors relies on three pivotal factors: i) accuracy and separability of classification of the monitored network, which determines the reliability of the system itself and can not be improved by added monitors; ii) sufficiency of data for constructing a monitor, else the abstraction will be not representative so that the monitor is not reliable; iii) implementation error of network and monitors since the construction and membership query of box abstractions demand precise computation.

6   Related and Future Work

We compare with the approaches aiming at assessing the decisions of neural networks to improve the confidence (in safety-critical scenarios).

Anomaly detection is a statistical approach that has been extensively studied in the areas of statistics and traditional machine learning; see [1,2,8] for surveys. All recent approaches consist essentially in computing a confidence score over the network decisions. Whenever a decision has a score lower than the required threshold, it is rejected and the input declared abnormal. For instance, in the context of deep learning, [6] is a well-known method that calculates a confidence score (i.e., softmax prediction probability) in terms of sample distribution.

---

[3] https://gricad-gitlab.univ-grenoble-alpes.fr/rvai-public/decision-boundary-of-box-based-monitors.

[4] To save computation cost (and favor reproducibility), we proceed 3 steps: 1) high-level features extraction, which can be one-time generated in seconds and used multiple times afterwards; 2) feature partition with many values of τ, during the experiment, which took the most time due to the search of the fine k. But, this can be very efficient if the options are tried out in descending order; 3) monitor creation and test, which can be done immediately.

Some recent approaches in formal methods build runtime monitors to supervise the network decision [3,4,7,14]. Such runtime monitoring approaches fundamentally differ from the traditional ones for software and hardware systems: a network input is declared abnormal when the network decision is rejected by the monitor following some references. The monitor verdict is based on the membership test of the induced neuron activation pattern in a pre-established sound over-approximation of neuron activation patterns recorded from network correct decisions constructed from re-applying the training dataset on a well trained network. The approach in [4] uses boolean abstraction to approximate and represent neuron activation patterns from correctly classified training data and is effective on reporting network misclassifications. However, the construction and membership test of boolean formula are computationally expensive, especially when dealing with patterns at layers with many neurons, e.g., running out of 8 GB memory when building such formula for a layer of 84 neurons. To reduce the complexity of abstraction methods, [7] introduces *box abstraction*, which can be easily computed and membership tested. It shows how to partition the obtained patterns into smaller clusters first and then constructing abstractions on these smaller clusters. Furthermore, [14] extends [7] by *active* monitoring of networks that detects unknown input classes and adapts to them at runtime; however [14] requires human interactions and retraining the network.

Our approach complements and generalises the frameworks in [4,7] by observing and recording the neuron activation patterns at hidden and output layers from both correct and incorrect classifications of known classes of inputs. Additional patterns from misclassified known classes of inputs introduces "uncertainty", which provides insights to the precision of the abstraction-based monitor and the separability of network. Moreover, boxes with a resolution allow defining clustering coverage as a metric to quantify the precision improvement in terms of the spaces covered by the box abstraction constructed with and without clustering. Hence, one can compare the effectiveness of different clustering parameters and tune the parameter of the monitoring approach.

In the future, we aim to study combinations of monitors. Beyond boxes, several candidate abstractions remain to be studied for monitoring purposes. In terms of monitoring, updating at operation time the abstractions would permit monitors that continuously learn operation-time inputs. Moreover, reacting to abnormal inputs remains to be studied. More generally, we believe that LECs need different interacting and complementary methods and toolsets to provide comprehensive solutions affording the needed confidence, e.g., testing and monitoring for design time, monitoring and enforcement for operation time.

References

1. Chalapathy, R., Chawla, S.: Deep learning for anomaly detection: a survey. arXiv preprint arXiv:1901.03407 (2019)
2. Chandola, V., Banerjee, A., Kumar, V.: Anomaly detection: a survey. ACM Comput. Surv. (CSUR) **41**(3), 1–58 (2009)

3. Cheng, C.H.: Provably-robust runtime monitoring of neuron activation patterns. arXiv preprint arXiv:2011.11959 (2020)
4. Cheng, C.H., Nührenberg, G., Yasuoka, H.: Runtime monitoring neuron activation patterns (2019)
5. Cromwell, P.R.: Polyhedra. Cambridge University Press, Cambridge (1997)
6. Hendrycks, D., Gimpel, K.: A baseline for detecting misclassified and out-of-distribution examples in neural networks. arXiv preprint arXiv:1610.02136 (2016)
7. Henzinger, T.A., Lukina, A., Schilling, C.: Outside the box: abstraction-based monitoring of neural networks. In: ECAI 2020, pp. 2433–2440. IOS Press (2020)
8. Hodge, V., Austin, J.: A survey of outlier detection methodologies. Artif. Intell. Rev. **22**(2), 85–126 (2004)
9. Huang, X., et al.: A survey of safety and trustworthiness of deep neural networks: verification, testing, adversarial attack and defence, and interpretability. Comput. Sci. Rev. **37**, 100270 (2020)
10. Intelligence, F.C.F.A.: Research challenge ii: Dependability, finnish center for artificial intelligence (2018)
11. Krizhevsky, A., Hinton, G., et al.: Learning multiple layers of features from tiny images (2009)
12. LeCun, Y., Bottou, L., Bengio, Y., Haffner, P.: Gradient-based learning applied to document recognition. Proc. IEEE **86**(11), 2278–2324 (1998)
13. Lloyd, S.: Least squares quantization in pcm. IEEE Trans. Inf. Theory **28**(2), 129–137 (1982)
14. Lukina, A., Schilling, C., Henzinger, T.A.: Into the unknown: active monitoring of neural networks. arXiv preprint arXiv:2009.06429 (2020)
15. McMullen, P.: On zonotopes. Trans. Am. Math. Soc. **159**, 91–109 (1971)
16. Murtagh, F., Contreras, P.: Algorithms for hierarchical clustering: an overview. Wiley Interdisc. Rev. Data Min. Knowl. Disc. **2**(1), 86–97 (2012)
17. Pei, K., Cao, Y., Yang, J., Jana, S.: Deepxplore: automated whitebox testing of deep learning systems (2017)
18. Schubert, E., Sander, J., Ester, M., Kriegel, H.P., Xu, X.: DBSCAN revisited, revisited: why and how you should (still) use DBSCAN. ACM Trans. Database Syst. (TODS) **42**(3), 1–21 (2017)
19. Sculley, D., et al.: Hidden technical debt in machine learning systems (2015)
20. Seshia, S.A., Sadigh, D.: Towards verified artificial intelligence. CoRR arXiv:1606.08514 (2016)
21. Sun, Y., Huang, X., Kroening, D., Sharp, J., Hill, M., Ashmore, R.: Testing deep neural networks. arXiv preprint arXiv:1803.04792 (2018)
22. Tian, Y., Pei, K., Jana, S., Ray, B.: Deeptest: automated testing of deep-neural-network-driven autonomous cars (2018)
23. Wicker, M., Huang, X., Kwiatkowska, M.: Feature-guided black-box safety testing of deep neural networks (2018)
24. Wu, C., Falcone, Y., Bensalem, S.: Customizable reference runtime monitoring of neural networks using resolution boxes. CoRR abs/2104.14435 (2021). https://arxiv.org/abs/2104.14435v2
25. Xiao, H., Rasul, K., Vollgraf, R.: Fashion-mnist: a novel image dataset for benchmarking machine learning algorithms. arXiv preprint arXiv:1708.07747 (2017)

Regular Papers

Scalable Stochastic Parametric Verification with Stochastic Variational Smoothed Model Checking

Luca Bortolussiⓘ, Francesca Cairoli$^{(\boxtimes)}$ ⓘ, Ginevra Carbone, and Paolo Pulcini

Department of Mathematics and Geoscience, University of Trieste, Trieste, Italy
francesca.cairoli@units.it

Abstract. Parametric verification of linear temporal properties for stochastic models requires to compute the satisfaction probability of a certain property as a function of the parameters of the model. Smoothed model checking (smMC) [8] infers the satisfaction function over the entire parameter space from a limited set of observations obtained via simulation. As observations are costly and noisy, smMC leverages the power of Bayesian learning based on Gaussian Processes (GP), providing accurate reconstructions with statistically sound quantification of the uncertainty. In this paper we propose Stochastic Variational Smoothed Model Checking (SV-smMC), which exploits stochastic variational inference (SVI) to approximate the posterior distribution of the smMC problem. The strength and flexibility of SVI, a stochastic gradient-based optimization making inference easily parallelizable and enabling GPU acceleration, make SV-smMC applicable both to Gaussian Processes (GP) and Bayesian Neural Networks (BNN). SV-smMC extends the smMC framework by greatly improving scalability to higher dimensionality of parameter spaces and larger training datasets, thus overcoming the well-known limits of GP.

1 Introduction

Parametric verification of logical properties aims at providing meaningful insights into the behaviour of a system, checking whether its evolution satisfies or not a certain requirement while varying some parameters of the system's model. The requirement is typically expressed as a temporal logic formula. Stochastic systems, however, require the use of probabilistic model checking (PMC) techniques as the satisfaction of a property is itself a stochastic quantity, facing significant scalability issues. To ameliorate such problems, statistical model checking (SMC) uses statistical tools to estimate the satisfaction probability of logical properties from trajectories sampled from the stochastic model. These estimates are enriched with probabilistic bounds of the estimation errors. If the number of sampled trajectories is sufficiently large, the satisfaction probability, estimated as the average of satisfaction on individual runs, will converge to the true probability. However, if the parameters of the stochastic model vary, the

P. Katsaros and L. Nenzi (Eds.): RV 2023, LNCS 14245, pp. 45–65, 2023.
https://doi.org/10.1007/978-3-031-44267-4_3

dynamics of the system will also vary. Therefore, SMC has to be performed from scratch for each set of parameter values, making SMC computationally unfeasible for stochastic parametric verification at runtime. This includes, for instance, estimating a satisfaction probability from the current state of the system, considering the current state as the varying parameter, or estimating the effect on future behaviour of tuning some control parameter. In other words, we can easily express runtime verification (RV) of a stochastic system, whose goal is to monitor how the future satisfaction of a given requirement behaves w.r.t. the current state of the system, as a parametric verification problem. The current state of the system, which changes over time, can be represented as a varying parameter. Therefore, RV inherits the computational unfeasibility of stochastic parametric verification.

Population continuous-time Markov chains (CTMC) offer a very expressive formalism to describe the dynamical behaviour of stochastic processes. Moreover, the satisfaction probability of a signal temporal logic (STL) requirement over parametric stochastic models, in particular CTMCs, has been proved to be a smooth function of the parameters of the model [8]. This result enables the use of machine learning techniques to infer an approximation of this function from a limited pool of observations. Observations, computed via SMC for a small number of parameter values, are noisy and may be computationally demanding to obtain. This calls for Bayesian approaches, where predictions are efficiently computed and enriched with a probabilistic quantification of the predictive uncertainty. In this regard, in [8] the authors present smoothed model checking (smMC), a fully Bayesian solution based on Gaussian Processes (GP). Since the observation process is non-Gaussian, outputs are in fact realizations of a Bernoulli distribution, exact GP inference is unfeasible. The authors thus resort to the Expectation Propagation (EP) algorithm to approximate the posterior inference. Unfortunately, the cost of EP is cubic in the number of observations used to train the GP, making smMC applicable only to models with a low dimensional parameter space as they require a limited number of training observations. In [26], this scalability problem is tackled by using a sparse variational approach to GP inference that builds on [30]. Variational inference (VI) is used to perform approximate inference of a GP classification (GPC) problem, whereas sparsification is used to reduce the computational complexity, by performing inference on a limited set of observations, called inducing points. However, the objective function used in [26] presents limitations that severely affect the overall performance in terms of both accuracy and efficiency. More precisely, it leaves no room for an optimal selection of the inducing variables and it does not allow for mini-batch optimization, a popular technique used to improve the efficiency of gradient-descent methods over large-scale problems. Moreover, in [26] the observation process is modeled by a Bernoulli likelihood instead of a binomial as in [8]. The latter can condense the satisfaction of the M simulations into a single observation, whereas the former must considers them as M different observations. This has a strong effect on the dimension of the training set which is of paramount importance for the sake of scalability. While smMC in [8] and in [26] renders parametric verification feasible at runtime, the number of parameters that are allowed to vary is still limited (up to a 4-dimensional parameter space with a reasonable computational budget). Finding an effective solution that makes smMC scale to large datasets, thus to large parameter spaces, remains an open issue.

Main Contributions. The main contribution is to tackle the scalability issues of smMC by leveraging stochastic variational inference (SVI), instead of EP or VI, to solve the smMC Bayesian inference problem. More precisely, we propose a novel approach for scalable stochastic parametric verification, called Stochastic Variational Smoothed Model Checking (SV-smMC), that leverages Stochastic Variational Inference (SVI) to make the smMC Bayesian inference scale to large datasets. The variational rationale is to transform the inference problem into an optimization one. The approach is stochastic in the sense that stochastic gradient descent (SGD) is used in the gradient-based optimization of a suitable variational objective function. SVI is extremely flexible and it is thus applied both to Gaussian Processes (GP) and to Bayesian Neural Networks (BNN). The main advantage of SVI, compared to the VI used for example in [26], is the use of mini-batches that makes inference easily parallelizable, enabling also GPU acceleration. Moreover, in SVI the inducing variables are optimally selected during inference so that sparsification causes a less pronounced drop in the reconstruction accuracy w.r.t. [26]. As a result, SV-smMC can face extremely large datasets. This result has significant implications for RV as it enables us to consider variability both in the rate parameters and in the initial state of the stochastic system. One can also take into account the variability solely in the state space, thereby accommodating larger state spaces that are commonly encountered in complex systems.

Overview of the Paper. This paper is structured as follows. We start by presenting the background theory in Sect. 2, comprised of the formal definition of the smMC Bayesian inference problem (Sect. 2.3). In Sect. 3 the theoretical details of SV-smMC are presented both for the GP version (Sect. 3.1) and for the BNN version (Sect. 3.2). Section 4 compares the performances of SV-smMC against those of smMC on three stochastic models with increasing parametric complexity. Two of these case studies are taken from [8] to make a fair comparison of the performances. Moreover, in order to have a better quantification of the scalability of the proposed solution, we test SV-smMC on a pool of randomly generated stochastic processes over parameter spaces of increasing dimension for multiple randomly generated temporal properties. Finally, Sect. 5.1 briefly discuss how to obtain local statistical guarantees over the prediction error.

2   Background

2.1   Population Continuous Time Markov Chain

A population of interacting agents can be modeled as a stochastic system evolving continuously in time over a finite or countable state space $\mathcal{X}$. Assuming the system is Markovian, meaning the memory-less property holds, we can rely on the formalism of population Continuous Time Markov Chains (CTMC) $\mathcal{M}$. A population is specified by n different species $\{S_1, \ldots, S_n\}$ subject to a dynamics described by r different rules (reactions) $\{R_1, \ldots, R_r\}$. The respective CTMC is described by:

- a state vector, $X(t) = (X_1(t), \ldots, X_n(t))$, taking values in $\mathcal{X} \subseteq \mathbb{N}^n$ and counting the number of agents in each species at time t;
- a finite set of reactions $R = (R_1, \ldots, R_r)$ describing how the state of the population changes in time. A general reaction R_i is identified by the tuple (τ_i, ν_i), where:
    - $\rho_i : \mathcal{X} \times \Theta_i \to \mathbb{R}_{\geq 0}$ is the *rate function* of reaction R_i that associates with each reaction the rate of an exponential distribution, as a function of the global state of the model and of parameters θ_i, and
    - ν_i is the *update vector*, giving the net change of agents due to the reaction, so that the firing of reaction R_i results in a transition of the system from state $X(t)$ to state $X(t) + \nu_i$.

Reaction rules are easily visualised in the chemical reaction style, as

$$R_i : \sum_{j \in \{1, \ldots, n\}} \alpha_{ij} S_j \xrightarrow{\rho_i(X, \theta_i)} \sum_{j \in \{1, \ldots, n\}} \beta_{ij} S_j.$$

The stoichiometric coefficients $\alpha_i = [\alpha_{i1}, \ldots, \alpha_{in}], \beta_i = [\beta_{i1}, \ldots, \beta_{in}]$ can be arranged so that they form the update vector $\nu_i = \beta_i - \alpha_i$ for reaction R_i.

The parameters $\theta = (\theta_1, \ldots, \theta_r)$ have a crucial effect on the dynamics of the system: changes in θ can lead to qualitatively different dynamics. We stress such crucial dependency by using the notation $\mathcal{M}_\theta$. The trajectories of such a CTMC can be seen as samples of random variables $X(t)$ indexed by time t over a state space $\mathcal{X}$. A parametric CTMC (pCTMC) is a family $\mathcal{M}_\theta$ of CTMCs where the parameters θ vary in a domain Θ. For simplicity, but without loss of generality, for the rest of the paper we fix the initial state of the pCTMC and consider only the rate parameters as varying conditions. We stress that all the results remain valid if the initial state of the system varies, e.g. when it represents the current state in an RV framework.

Running Example. A well-known example of pCTMC is the SIR model describing the spread of an epidemic in a population of fixed size N. Let S, I and R denote respectively the species of susceptible, infected and recovered individuals. The stochastic dynamics is described by an infection reaction $R_1 : S + I \to 2I$ happening with rate function $\beta X_S X_I / N$, and a recovery reaction $R_2 : I \to R$ happening with rate function γX_I. The rate parameters, $\theta = (\beta, \gamma)$, and the initial state of the population, $X(0) = (X_S(0), X_I(0), N - X_S(0) - X_I(0))$, play a crucial role in shaping the future dynamics of the system, ultimately determining whether and when the disease will be eradicated.

2.2   Signal Temporal Logic

Properties of CTMC trajectories can be expressed via Signal Temporal Logic (STL) [21] formulas. STL allows the specification of properties of dense-time, real-valued signals, and the automatic generation of monitors for testing properties on individual trajectories. The rationale of STL is to transform real-valued signals into Boolean ones, using formulae built on the following *STL syntax*:

$$\varphi := true \mid \mu \mid \neg\varphi \mid \varphi \wedge \varphi \mid \varphi \, \mathcal{U}_I \varphi, \tag{1}$$

where $\mathcal{U}_I$ is the until operator, $I \subseteq \mathbb{T}$ is a temporal interval, either bounded, $I = [a, b]$, or unbounded, $I = [a, +\infty)$, for any $0 \leq a < b$. Atomic propositions μ are (non-linear) inequalities on population variables. From this essential syntax it is easy to define other operators: $false := \neg true$, $\varphi \vee \psi := \neg(\neg\varphi \wedge \neg\psi)$, eventually $F_I := true \, \mathcal{U}_I \varphi$ and globally $G_I := \neg F_I \neg\varphi$. Monitoring the satisfaction of a formula is done recursively on the parsing tree structure of the STL formula. See [21] for the details on STL Boolean semantics and on Boolean STL monitors.

Running Example (Continued). In the context of the previously described SIR model, we can define an STL property to monitor the termination of the epidemic in a time between 100 and 120 time units from the epidemic onset. Formally, $\varphi = (X_I > 0) \, \mathcal{U}_{[100,120]} \, (X_I = 0)$. Because of the stochastic nature of the system, even when both the rate parameters and the initial state are fixed, the satisfaction of this property is a random variable over Boolean truth values.

2.3   Smoothed Model Checking

Probabilistic Model Checking (PMC). Verification of temporal properties is of paramount importance, especially for safety-critical processes. When the system evolves stochastically, probabilistic model checking [2] comes into play. For linear time properties, like those of STL, the goal is to compute the probability $Pr(\varphi|\mathcal{M})$ that a stochastic system $\mathcal{M}$ satisfies a given STL formula φ. Exact computation of $Pr(\varphi|\mathcal{M})$ suffers from very limited scalability and furthermore requires the full knowledge of the stochastic model.

Statistical Model Checking (SMC). Statistical model checking [33] fights the two aforementioned issues: instead of analyzing the model, it evaluates the satisfaction of the given formula on a number of observed runs of the system, and derives a statistical estimate of $Pr(\varphi|\mathcal{M})$, valid only with some confidence. Given a CTMC $\mathcal{M}_\theta$ with fixed parameters θ, time-bounded CTMC trajectories are sampled by standard simulation algorithms, such as SSA [13], and monitoring algorithms for STL [21] are used to assess if the formula φ is satisfied for each sampled trajectory. This process produces samples from a Bernoulli random variable equal to 1 if and only if φ is true. SMC [34,37] then uses standard statistical tools, either frequentist [34] or Bayesian [37], to estimate from these samples the satisfaction probability $Pr(\varphi|\mathcal{M}_\theta)$ or to test if $Pr(\varphi|\mathcal{M}_\theta) > q$ with a prescribed confidence level.

Satisfaction Function for pCTMCs. Building on [8], our interest is in parametric verification [16], i.e. to quantify how the satisfaction of STL formulae depend on the unknown parameters of the pCTMC. We define the *satisfaction function* $f_\varphi : \Theta \to [0,1]$ associated to φ as

$$f_\varphi(\theta) = Pr(\varphi = true | \mathcal{M}_\theta).$$ (2)

In practice, for every $\theta \in \Theta$, $f_\varphi(\theta)$ quantifies the probability that a realization of $\mathcal{M}_\theta$ satisfies φ. An accurate estimation of the satisfaction function f_φ over the entire parameter space Θ by means of SMC would require a prohibitively large number of evaluations. In particular, SMC must be run from scratch for every parameter $\theta \in \Theta$. In [8] – Theorem 1 – it has been shown that $f_\varphi(\theta)$ is a smooth function of the model parameters and thus machine learning techniques can be used to infer this function from a limited set of observations and this is exactly the goal of smoothed model checking (smMC).

Smoothed Model Checking. Given a pCTMC $\mathcal{M}_\theta$ and an STL formula φ, the goal of smMC is to find a statistical estimate of the satisfaction function of (2) from a set of noisy observations of f_φ obtained at few parameter values $\theta_1, \theta_2, \ldots$. The task is to construct a statistical model that, for any value $\theta^* \in \Theta$, computes efficiently an estimate of $f_\varphi(\theta^*)$ together with a credible interval associated with the prediction. More precisely, given an input point θ, our observations are obtained by evaluating a property φ on few trajectories sampled from the stochastic model $\mathcal{M}_\theta$ via SSA. Thus, given a set of N_t parameter values, $\Theta_t = \{\theta_1, \ldots, \theta_{N_t}\}$, we simulate, for each parameter θ_i, M_t trajectories, obtaining M_t Boolean values $\ell_i^j \in \{0,1\}$ for $j = 1, \ldots, M_t$. We condense these Boolean values in a vector $L_i = [\ell_i^1, \ldots, \ell_i^{M_t}]$. The noisy observations form the *training set*

$$D_t = \{(\theta_i, L_i) \mid i = 1, \ldots, N_t\}.$$ (3)

In practice, smMC can be framed as a *Bayesian inference problem* that aims at inferring an accurate probabilistic estimate of the unknown satisfaction function $f_\varphi : \Theta \to [0,1]$. In the following, let $f : \Theta \to [0,1]$. The main ingredients of a Bayesian approach are the following:

1. Choose a *prior* distribution, $p(f)$, over a suitable function space, encapsulating the beliefs about function f prior to any observations being taken.
2. Determine the functional form of the observation process by defining a suitable *likelihood* function that effectively models how the observations depend on the uncertain parameter θ. Our observation process can be modeled by a binomial over M_t trials with parameter $f_\varphi(\theta)$. Given the nature of our training set, defined in (3), we define the probabilistic likelihood as

$$p(D_t | f) = \prod_{i=1}^{N_t} Binomial(L_i \mid M_t, f(\theta_i)).$$

3. Leverage Bayes' theorem to define the *posterior* distribution over functions given the observations

$$p(f|D_t) = \frac{p(D_t|f)p(f)}{p(D_t)}.$$

Computing $p(D_t) = \int p(D_t|f)p(f)df$ is almost always computationally intractable as we have non-conjugate prior-likelihood distributions. Therefore, we need algorithms to accurately approximate such posterior distribution.
4. Evaluate such posterior at points θ_*, resulting in a predictive distribution $p(f_*|\theta_*, D_t)$, whose statistics are used to obtain the desired estimate of the satisfaction probability together with the respective credible interval.

Two main ingredients are essential to define the smMC solution strategy:

(i) the probabilistic model chosen to describe the distribution over functions f,
(ii) the approximate inference strategy.

Running Example (Continued). For visualization purposes, consider a one-dimensional configuration, where $\beta = 0.12$ and γ varies in the interval $[0.005, 0.2]$. The exact satisfaction function $f_\varphi(\gamma)$ is unknown, but we can obtain noisy observations via SMC. We randomly sample N_t values of γ and, for each value of γ, we simulate M_t trajectories and evaluate the STL satisfaction of each realization. The purple bars in Fig. 1 represent the SMC 95% confidence intervals around the empirical mean of the satisfaction probability.

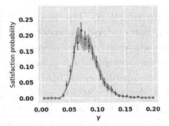

Fig. 1. Bayesian inference of the satisfaction function $f_\varphi(\gamma)$.

SmMC learns a probabilistic model of the satisfaction function over γ, i.e. infers the posterior distribution (point 3). Estimating the satisfaction probability at a new point γ_* reduces to evaluating the posterior predictive distribution in γ_* (point 4). Figure 1 shows the 95% credible intervals of the posterior predictive distribution over a grid of test parameters.

Previous Works and Limitations. The smMC technique presented in [8] uses Gaussian Processes (GP) as probabilistic model – ingredient (*i*) – and the Expectation Propagation (EP) algorithm to approximate the posterior distribution – ingredient (*ii*). EP [22,27] is an iterative algorithm that aims at matching the product of non-Gaussian likelihoods with a product of univariate Gaussian distributions. If the prior is Gaussian, this results in a closed-form analytic expression of the approximate posterior. However, the resulting analytic expression involves the inversion of the covariance matrix estimated at all pairs of parameter values. Therefore, this solution scales as $\mathcal{O}(N_t^3)$, it is thus unfeasible for large datasets. On the other hand, the rationale of VI, used in [26], is to directly approximate the non-Gaussian posterior with a parametric distribution (typically a Gaussian) building an optimization problem to search for the variational parameters that best fit the data. However, computing the optimization loss requires the derivation of the analytical form of a Gaussian with the inversion of a covariance matrix. Therefore, the cost is still cubic in the number of parameter values. Moreover, if the observation process is modeled by a Bernoulli, as in [26], meaning if Boolean values ℓ_i^j are considered as individual observations instead of condensing them in a vector L_i, inference scales as $\mathcal{O}\left((N_t M_t)^3\right)$. In order to mitigate such scalability issues, the authors of [26] propose a sparsification technique. Sparsification reduces the computational complexity to $\mathcal{O}\left((m M_t)^3\right)$, where m is the number of sparse observations, known as inducing variables, considered. Nonetheless, sparsification strongly reduces the reconstruction accuracy, especially if the m sparse observations are randomly selected. The objective function used in [26] does not explicitly depend on the inducing variables, forcing them to be fixed a priori, leaving no room for an optimal selection of such points. Moreover, the variational optimization problem of [26] cannot be framed in terms of stochastic gradient descent optimization. These issues strongly limit the scalability capabilities of the proposed solution.

Our Contribution. The main contribution of this paper, explained in the next section, is to introduce stochastic variational inference (SVI) as an efficient and scalable alternative for ingredient (*ii*). The rationale is to frame Bayesian inference as an optimization problem, typical workaround of variational approaches, and define an objective function that enables optimization in terms of stochastic gradient descent (SGD) so that smMC becomes efficient and scalable even on extremely large datasets. Furthermore, our objective function explicitly depends on the inducing variables that can be considered as additional variational parameters to be optimized with SGD. Therefore, our sparsification strategy allows for an optimal selection of sparse observations. SVI is then applied on two different probabilistic models, i.e. on two alternatives for ingredient (*i*): Gaussian Processes (GP) and Bayesian Neural Networks (BNN).

3   Stochastic Variational Smoothed Model Checking

The goal of Stochastic Variational Smoothed Model Checking (SV-smMC) is to make smMC scale to high-dimensional models. SV-smMC proposes stochastic variational inference as ingredient (*ii*) to efficiently compute the approximate posterior distribution $p(f|D_t)$ so that inference scales well to large datasets D_t.

The core idea behind variational approaches is to translate the posterior inference into an optimization problem, where a parametric distribution is proposed as a candidate approximator of the unknown posterior distribution. The optimization problem aims at minimizing the difference, measured by the Kullback-Leibler (KL) divergence, between these two distributions. However, as the posterior is unknown, various model-specific strategies can be developed to derive from the KL formula a lower bound of the marginal log-likelihood of our data. This lower bound, known as evidence lower bound (ELBO), is used as new objective function as it does not depend explicitly on the unknown posterior.

This bound is then optimized with respect to the parameters of the proposed variational distribution. The latter is typically chosen to have nice statistical properties, making predictions feasible and efficient. Owing to the work of [15], in order to scale VI over very large datasets, the (black-box VI) optimization task can be phrased as a stochastic optimization problem [36] by estimating the gradient of the ELBO with Monte Carlo methods. Moreover, the dataset can be divided into mini-batches. As for ingredient (i), SV-smMC can use two alternative probabilistic models to define distributions over function f. The first one is based on Gaussian Processes (GP), whereas the second one is based on Bayesian Neural Networks (BNN). SVI is applied to both probabilistic models with the proper model-specific adjustments to the variational formulation. Below, we provide an intuitive presentation of the approximate inference processes, whereas more formal details are provided in Appendix A in [6].

3.1   Gaussian Processes over Non-Gaussian Likelihoods

Gaussian Processes (GP) are a well-known formalism to define distributions over real-valued functions of the form $g : \Theta \to \mathbb{R}$. A GP distribution is uniquely identified by its mean $\mu(\theta) = \mathbb{E}[g(\theta)]$ and its covariance function $k_\gamma(\theta, \theta')$ and characterized by the fact that the distribution of g over any finite set of points $\hat{\theta}$ is Gaussian with mean $\mu(\hat{\theta})$ and variance $k_\gamma(\hat{\theta}, \hat{\theta})$. In the following, we let g_t, μ_t and $K_{N_t N_t}$ denote respectively the latent, the mean and the covariance functions evaluated on the training inputs Θ_t.

The GP prior over latent functions g evaluated at training inputs Θ_t – step 1 – is defined as $p(g|\Theta_t) = \mathcal{N}(g|\mu_t, K_{N_t N_t})$. The posterior over latent variables $p(g_t|D_t)$ – step 3 – is not available in closed form since it is the convolution of a Gaussian and a binomial distribution. Hence, we have to rely on SVI for posterior approximation (details later). Once we obtain a tractable posterior approximation, in order to make predictions over a test input θ_*, with latent variable g_*, we have to compute an empirical approximation of the predictive distribution

$$p(f_*|\theta_*, D_t) = \int \Phi(g_*) p(g_*|\theta_*, D_t) dg_*, \qquad (4)$$

in which the outputs of the latent function $g : \Theta \to \mathbb{R}$ are mapped into the $[0, 1]$ interval by means of a so-called link function Φ, typically the inverse logit or the inverse probit function [5], so that $f : \Theta \to [0, 1]$ is obtained as $f = g \circ \Phi$.

Stochastic Variational Inference. Here we outline an intuitive explanation of the SVI steps to approximate the GP posterior when the likelihood is non-Gaussian. For a more detailed mathematical description see Appendix A in [6]. The main issue with GP inference is the inversion of the $N_t \times N_t$ covariance matrix $K_{N_t N_t}$. This is the reason why variational approaches to GP start with sparsification, i.e. with the selection of $m \ll N_t$ inducing points that live in the same space of Θ_t and, from them, define a set of inducing variables u_t. The covariance matrix over inducing points, K_{mm}, is less expensive to invert and thus it acts as a low-rank approximation of $K_{N_t N_t}$. We introduce a Gaussian variational distribution

$q(u_t)$ over inducing variables whose goal is to be as similar as possible to the posterior $p(u_t|D_t)$. A classical VI result is to transform the expression of the KL divergence between the variational distribution $q(u_t)$ and the posterior $p(u_t|D_t)$ into a lower bound over the marginal log-likelihood $\log p(D_t)$. As our likelihood – step 2 – factors as $p(D_t|g_t) = \prod_{i=1}^{N_t} p(L_i|g_i)$ and because of the Jensen inequality we obtain the following ELBO (see Appendix A.1 in [6] for the mathematical details):

$$\log p(D_t) \geq \sum_{i=1}^{N_t} \mathbb{E}_{q(g_i)}[\log p(L_i|g_i)] - KL[q(u_t)\|p(u_t)] := \mathcal{L}_{GP}(\nu, \gamma), \quad (5)$$

where L_i denotes the set of observed Boolean tuples corresponding to points in θ_i in D_t, $p(u_t)$ denotes the prior distribution over inducing variables and ν denotes the hyper-parameters introduced to describe the sparsification and the variational distribution. The distribution $q(g_t)$ is Gaussian with an exact analytic derivation from $q(u_t)$ that requires $\mathcal{O}(m^2)$ computations (no matrix inversion involved here). The SVI algorithm then consists of maximizing $\mathcal{L}_{GP}$ with respect to its parameters using gradient-based stochastic optimization. We stress that, at this step, the selection of inducing variable is optimized, resulting in a more effective sparsification. Computing the KL divergence in (5) requires only $\mathcal{O}(m^3)$ computations. Most of the work will thus be in computing the expected likelihood terms. Given the ease of parallelizing the simple sum over N_t, we can optimize $\mathcal{L}_{GP}$ in a stochastic fashion by selecting mini-batches of the data at random.

Predictive Distribution. The predictive posterior $p(g_*|\theta_*, D_t)$ is now approximated by a variational distribution $q(g_*)$, which is Gaussian and whose mean and variance can be analytically computed with cost $\mathcal{O}(m^2)$. From the mean and the variance of $q(g_*)$, we obtain the respective credible interval and we can use the link function Φ to map it to a subset of the interval $[0, 1]$, in order to obtain the mean and the credible interval of the posterior predictive distribution $p(f_*|\theta_*, D_t)$ of equation (4).

3.2 Bayesian Neural Networks

The core idea of Bayesian neural networks (BNNs) [5,14,18,31], is to place a probability distribution over the weights $\mathbf{w}$ of a neural network $f_\mathbf{w} : \Theta \to [0, 1]$, transforming the latter into a probabilistic model.

The Bayesian learning process starts by defining a prior distribution $p(\mathbf{w})$ over $\mathbf{w}$ – step 1 – that expresses our initial belief about the values of the weights. As we observe data D_t, we update this prior to a posterior distribution $p(\mathbf{w}|D_t)$ – step 3 – using Bayes' rule. Because of the non-linearity introduced by the neural network function $f_\mathbf{w}(\theta)$ and since the likelihood $p(D_t|\mathbf{w})$ – step 2 – is binomial, the posterior $p(\mathbf{w}|D_t)$ is non-Gaussian and it cannot be computed analytically. In order to predict the satisfaction function over an unobserved input θ_*, we marginalize the predictions with respect to the posterior distribution of the parameters, obtaining

$$p(f_*|\theta_*, D_t) = \int f_{\mathbf{w}}(\theta_*)p(\mathbf{w}|D_t)d\mathbf{w}. \tag{6}$$

The latter is called *posterior predictive* distribution and it can be used to retrieve information about the uncertainty of a specific prediction f_*. Unfortunately, the integration is analytically intractable due to the non-linearity of the neural network function [5, 20] so we empirically estimate such quantity.

Stochastic Variational Inference. The rationale of SVI for BNNs is to choose a parametric variational distribution $q_\psi(\mathbf{w})$ that approximates the unknown posterior distribution $p(\mathbf{w}|D_t)$ by minimizing the KL divergence $KL[q_\psi(\mathbf{w})||p(\mathbf{w}|D_t)]$ between these two distributions. Since the posterior distribution is not known, the classic variational approach is to transform the minimization of the KL divergence into the maximization of the Evidence Lower Bound (ELBO) [17], defined as

$$\mathcal{L}_{BNN}(\psi) := \mathbb{E}_{q_\psi(\mathbf{w})}\left[\log\ p(D_t|\mathbf{w})\right] - KL\left[q_\psi(\mathbf{w})||p(\mathbf{w})\right] \leq \log\ p(D_t), \tag{7}$$

see Appendix A.2 in [6] for the mathematical details. The first term is the expected log-likelihood of our data with respect to values of $f_{\mathbf{w}}$ sampled from $q_\psi(\mathbf{w}|D_t)$, whereas the second term is the KL divergence between the proposal distribution and the prior. The distribution q_ψ should be a distribution easy to sample from and such that the KL divergence is easy to compute. A common choice for q_ψ is the Gaussian distribution (where ψ denotes its mean and variance). KL divergence among two Gaussian distributions has an exact analytical form, hence the ELBO of (7) can be computed and it can be used as the objective function of a maximization problem over ψ.

Predictive Distribution. The predictive distribution (6) is a non-linear combination of Gaussian distributions, and thus it is not Gaussian. However, samples can be easily extracted from $q_\psi(\mathbf{w})$, which allows us to obtain an empirical approximation of the predictive distribution. Let $[w_1, \ldots, w_C]$ denote a vector of C realizations of the random variable $\mathbf{w} \sim q_\psi(\mathbf{w})$. Each realization w_i induces a deterministic function f_{w_i} that can be evaluated at θ_*, the unobserved input, providing an empirical approximation of $p(f_*|\theta_*, D_t)$.

Running Example (End). The SIR model is rather simple with a two-dimensional parameter space and a two-dimensional state space. However, if one is interested in estimating the satisfaction function w.r.t. both states and rate parameters (a typical RV framework) we notice how EP inference already reaches its computational bottleneck, VI fails, whereas, SV-smMC easily succeeds (see Sect. 4.3 below).

4   Experiments

4.1   Case Studies

We briefly introduce the case studies used to investigate the scalability and the accuracy of SV-smMC. In order to make a fair comparison, we start by reproducing the case studies presented in [8], Network Epidemics and Prokaryotic Gene Expression, and then add a third biological model, Three-layer Phosphorelay. Finally, to have a better and unbiased quantification of the performances and of the scalability of SV-smMC, we test it over randomly generated pCTMC with parameter spaces of increasing dimensions.

- **Network Epidemics (SIR)**: see running example.
- **Prokaryotic Gene Expression (PGE)**: model of LacZ, X_{LacZ}, protein synthesis in E. coli. The dynamics is governed by 11 parameters k_1, k_2, ..., k_{11}. We choose an STL property for monitoring bursts of gene expression, rapid increases in LacZ counts followed by long periods of lack of protein production: $\varphi = F_{[1600,2100]}(\Delta X_{LacZ} > 0 \land G_{[10,200]}(\Delta X_{LacZ} \leq 0))$, where $\Delta X_{LacZ}(t) = X_{LacZ}(t) - X_{LacZ}(t-1)$.
- **Three-layer Phosphorelay (PR)**: network of three proteins $L1$, $L2$, $L3$ involved in a cascade of phosphorylation reactions (changing the state of the protein), in which protein Lj, in its phosphorylated form Ljp, acts as a catalyser of phosphorylation of protein $L(j+1)$. There is a ligand B triggering the first phosphorylation in the chain. The dynamics depends on 6 parameters k_p, k_1, k_2, k_3, k_4, k_d. The chosen STL property models a switch in the most expressed protein between $L1p$ and $L3p$ after time 300: $\varphi = G_{[0,300]}(L1p - L3p \geq 0) \land F_{[300,600]}(L3p - L1p \geq 0)$.
- **Random pCTMC**: we randomly generate pCTMC over parameter spaces of increasing dimension. The number of interacting species n and the type and the number of reactions are randomly determined. The STL properties considered captures different behaviours: $\varphi_1 = G_{[0,T]}(S_i \leq S_j)$, $\varphi_2 = F_{[0,T]}(S_i \leq S_j)$ and $\varphi_3 = F_{[0,T]}(G(S_i < \tau))$, where τ and T are two fixed hyper-parameters and the species to be monitored, S_i and S_j, are randomly sampled for each property.

Details about the dynamics, i.e. about the reactions, the selected initial states and the chosen parametric ranges, are provided in Appendix B in [6].

4.2   Experimental Details

Dataset Generation. The training set D_t is built as per (3). The test set, used to validate our results, can be summarized as $D_v = \{(\theta_j, (\ell_j^1, \ldots, \ell_j^{M_v})) \mid j = 1, \ldots, N_v\}$, where M_v is chosen very large, $M_v \gg M_t$, so that we have a good estimate of the true satisfaction probability over each test input. Input data, i.e. the parameter values, are scaled to the interval $[-1, 1]$ to enhance the performances of the inferred models and to avoid sensitivity to different scales in the parameter space. In the first three case studies, the biology-inspired ones, we choose different subsets of varying parameters and train a separate model on each of these choices. In other words, we fix some of the parameters and let only the remaining ones vary. In particular, in SIR we consider the following configurations: (a) fix γ and let β vary, (b) fix β and let γ vary, (c) vary both β and γ; in PGE we consider the following configurations: (d) k_2 is the only parameter allowed to vary, (e) we let k_2 and k_7 vary; in PR we consider the following configurations: (f) only k_1 varies, (g) only k_p, k_d vary, (h) only k_1, k_2, k_3 vary, (i) only k_1, k_2, k_3, k_4 vary, (l) all six parameters are allowed to vary.

On the other hand, to better analyze the scalability of SV-smMC we randomly generate pCTMC over parameter spaces Θ of dimension 2, 3, 4, 8, 12, 16 and 20. For each dimension, we generate three different models and each model is tested over the three random properties φ_1, φ_2, φ_3 defined above. Table 2 in Appendix B in [6] shows the chosen dimensions for each generated dataset. In general, the number of observed parameters N_t and the number of observations per point M_t increase proportionally to the dimensionality of Θ.

Experimental Settings. The CTMC dynamics is simulated via StochPy SSA[1] simulator for biology inspired models, whereas GillesPy2[2] is used to generate and simulate random pCTMC. The Boolean semantics of pcheck library[3] is used to check the satisfaction of a certain formula for a specific trajectory. GPyTorch [12] library is used to train the VI-GP and SVI-GP models, whereas Pyro [4] library is used to train the SVI-BNN models, both built upon PyTorch [25] library. Instead, EP-GP is implemented in NumPy[4]. The experiments were conducted on a shared virtual machine with a 32-Core Processor, 64 GB of RAM and an NVidia A100 GPU with 20GB, and 8 VCPU. Code and data are available at: https://github.com/ailab-units/SV-smMC.git.

Training and Evaluation. We apply Stochastic Variational Inference on both Gaussian Processes (SVI-GPs) and Bayesian Neural Networks (SVI-BNNs) and compare them to the baseline smMC approaches, where Gaussian Processes were inferred using either Expectation Propagation (EP-GPs) [8] or Variational Inference (VI-GPs) [26]. All models (EP-GP, VI-GP, SVI-GP and SVI-BNN) are Bayesian and trained over the training set D_t. Once the training phase is over, for each pair $\left(\theta_j, (\ell_j^1, \ldots, \ell_j^{M_v})\right) \in D_v$ in the test set, we obtain a probabilistic estimate of the satisfaction probability $f(\theta_j)$ (defined in Sect. 3). We compare such distribution to the satisfaction probability $f_\varphi(\theta_j)$ estimated as the mean $\bar{L}_i$ over the Bernoulli trials $(\ell_j^1, \ldots, \ell_j^{M_v})$ and we call the latter SMC satisfaction probability. We stress that SMC estimates provably converge to the true satisfaction probabilities, meaning that the width of confidence intervals converges to zero in the limit of infinite samples, while Bayesian inference quantifies the

---

[1] https://github.com/SystemsBioinformatics/stochpy

[2] https://github.com/StochSS/GillesPy2.

[3] https://github.com/simonesilvetti/pcheck.

[4] Our implementation builds on https://github.com/simonesilvetti/pyCheck/blob/master/smothed/smoothedMC.py.

predictive uncertainty. Consequently, regardless of the number of samples, SMC and Bayesian estimates have different statistical meanings.

Evaluation Metrics. To define meaningful measures of performance, let's clarify the notation. For each point in the test set, $j \in \{1, \ldots, N_v\}$, let $\bar{L}_j$ and σ_j denote respectively the average and the standard deviation over the M_v Bernoulli trials $(\ell_j^1, \ldots, \ell_j^{M_v})$. The inferred models, on the other hand, provide a posterior predictive distribution $p(f_j | \theta_j, D_t)$, let q_ϵ^j denote the ϵ-th quantile of such distribution. The metrics used to quantify the overall performances of the models over each case study and each configuration are the following:

(i) the *root mean squared error* (RMSE) between SMC and the expected satisfaction probabilities, i.e. the root of the average of the squared residuals

$$\mathrm{RMSE} = \frac{1}{N_v} \sum_{j=1}^{N_v} \left(\bar{L}_j - \mathbb{E}_{p(f | \theta_j, D_t)}[f(\theta_j)] \right)^2.$$

This measure evaluates the quality of reconstruction provided by the mean of the posterior predictive distribution;

(ii) the *accuracy* over the test set, i.e. the fraction of non empty intersections between SMC confidence intervals and estimated $(1 - \epsilon)$ credible intervals:

$$\mathrm{Acc} = \frac{1}{N_v} \cdot \left| \left\{ j \in \{1, \ldots, N_v\} : \left[-\frac{z\,\sigma_j}{\sqrt{M_v}}, \frac{z\,\sigma_j}{\sqrt{M_v}} \right] \cap \left[q_{\epsilon/2}^j, q_{1-\epsilon/2}^j \right] \neq \emptyset \right\} \right|.$$

In particular, we set $z = 1.96$ and $\epsilon = 0.05$ in order to have the 95% confidence intervals and the 95% credible intervals respectively;

(iii) the *average width* of the estimated credible intervals

$$\mathrm{Unc} = \frac{1}{N_v} \sum_{j=1}^{N_v} \left(q_{1-\epsilon/2}^j - q_{\epsilon/2}^j \right),$$

which quantifies how informative the predictive uncertainty is and allows us to detect over-conservative predictors.

A good predictor should be balanced in terms of low RMSE, high test accuracy, i.e. high values for Acc, and narrow credible intervals, i.e. low values for Unc.

Implementation Details. Both SVI-GP and SVI-BNN models are trained for $2k$ epochs with mini-batches of size 100 and a learning rate of 0.001. In SVI-GP the prior is computed on a maximum of $1k$ inducing points selected from the training set. SVI-BNNs have a fully connected architecture with 3 layers and Leaky ReLU nonlinear activations. To evaluate SVI-BNNs we take $1k$ samples from the posterior distribution evaluated over test inputs.

Prior Tuning. Choosing an adequate prior is of paramount importance. In this paper we leverage model-specific strategies to pick reasonable ones, however, no guarantees can be provided about the adequacy of such priors. For GP, the prior is strongly related to the chosen kernel and adapted to data by type II maximum likelihood maximization. In EP-GP the optimal kernel hyperparameters are searched beforehand (as in [8]), whereas in SVI-GP the kernel hyperparameters are optimized on the fly, i.e. the variational loss is maximized also w.r.t. the kernel hyperparameters. In SVI-BNN, a deterministic NN (with the same architecture of the BNN) is trained and the learned weights are used to center the prior distribution which is Gaussian with standard deviation equal to $1/m$ (m is the layer-width).

4.3   Experimental Results

Computational Costs. The cost of EP-GP inference is dominated by the cost of matrix inversion, which is cubic in the number of points in the training set. The cost of VI-GP is cubic in the number of randomly selected inducing points and linear in the total number of observations, i.e. the number of training points times the number of observations per point. The cost of SVI-GP inference is cubic in the number of optimally selected inducing points, which is chosen to be sufficiently small, and linear in the number of training instances. The cost of SVI-BNN is linear in the number of training points but it also depends on the architectural complexity of the chosen neural network. Stochastic variational models are trained by means of SGD, which is a stochastic inference approach. Thus, at least on simple configurations, it is likely to take longer than EP in reaching convergence. The computational advantage becomes significant as the complexity of the case study increases, i.e., when the training set is sufficiently large. EP faces memory limits, becoming unfeasible on configurations with parameter space of dimension higher than four. As a collateral advantage, SVI-GP optimizes the kernel hyperparameters on the fly during the training phase, whereas in EP-GP the hyperparameters search is performed beforehand and it is rather expensive. Compared to our SV-smMC approaches, VI-GPs do not allow for GPU acceleration, as a consequence the training times over one-dimensional case studies go from the 40 min of our SVI-based approaches to 3 h.

For the randomly generated pCTMC we let the dimension of the training set grow linearly with the dimension of the parameter space ($N_t = 5000 \cdot r$) and so does the training time of SVI-GP and SVI-BNN (see Fig. 2). On the other hand, Fig. 2 shows how the training time of EP-GP grows much faster with respect to r and becomes soon unfeasible ($r > 4$). SV-smMC is trained leveraging GPU acceleration. Its convergence times are comparable to EP's on simple configurations and they outperform EP on more complex ones. Evaluation time for EP-GPs and SVI-GPs is negligible as it is computed from the analytic posterior. The evaluation time for SVI-BNNs with $1k$ posterior samples is in turn negligible.

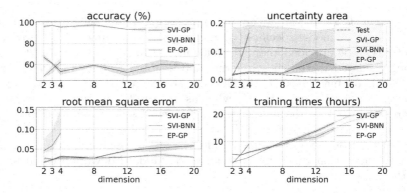

Fig. 2. Quantitative analysis of the scalability performances over randomly generated pCTMC with parameter spaces of increasing dimension (x-axis). For each dimension, we plot the 95% confidence interval of Acc, RMSE and Unc over each test set corresponding to that dimension.

Table 1. Root Mean Square Error ($\times 10^{-2}$), test accuracy (%) and average uncertainty width for EP-GP, VI-GP, SVI-GP and SVI-BNN. SVI-BNNs are evaluated on $1k$ posterior samples. For each case study, we highlight the minimum MSE, the highest accuracy values and the lowest and highest uncertainty values. Uncertainty is compapurple to the average uncertainty width of the test set.

Configuration	RMSE				Accuracy				Uncertainty				
	EP-GP	VI-GP	SVI-GP	SVI-BNN	EP-GP	VI-GP	SVI-GP	SVI-BNN	Test	EP-GP	VI-GP	SVI-GP	SVI-BNN
(a) SIR β	1.41	2.11	**1.38**	1.43	**100.00**	96.3	98.80	**100.00**	0.044	0.044	0.060	0.032	0.097
(b) SIR γ	1.02	2.12	**0.84**	0.96	77.80	59.8	77.30	**92.60**	0.018	0.018	0.041	0.012	0.058
(c) SIR β, γ	1.25	–	1.20	**0.99**	72.75	–	85.75	**92.25**	0.019	0.042	–	0.019	0.047
(d) PGE k_2	**5.34**	6.06	5.83	5.51	93.75	95.75	94.00	**97.50**	0.039	0.030	0.057	0.037	0.080
(e) PGE k_2, k_7	6.48	–	3.44	**2.06**	78.25	–	89.25	**95.00**	0.043	0.021	–	0.056	0.093
(f) PR k_1	2.25	1.76	1.99	**1.78**	99.70	99.80	99.20	**100.00**	0.058	0.059	0.066	0.046	0.100
(g) PR k_p, k_d	2.95	–	2.31	**1.89**	99.25	–	96.25	**99.75**	0.055	0.108	–	0.037	0.093
(h) PR k_1, k_2, k_3	6.97	–	2.30	**2.01**	99.80	–	93.70	**100.0**	0.050	0.340	–	0.030	0.121
(i) PR $k_1, \ldots, k_4$	10.63	–	**2.44**	2.67	99.02	–	93.65	**99.92**	0.050	0.682	–	0.030	0.150
(l) PR $k_p, k_1, \ldots, k_4, k_d$	–	–	1.87	**1.56**	–	–	97.02	**99.80**	0.049	–	–	0.028	0.087

Performance Evaluation. The evaluation metrics are the root mean square error (RMSE), the accuracy (Acc) and the width of the uncertainty quantification area (Unc). Results over the randomly generated pCTMC are summarized in Fig. 2, whereas results over the biological case studies are summarized in Table 1. For completeness, we compare our SV-smMC with the VI-GPs approach presented in [26]. However, using a Bernoulli likelihood instead of a Binomial creates an extremely inefficient computational bottleneck that makes VI-GP feasible only over the one-dimensional scenario, where it is outperformed by all methods (see Table 1). Figure 2 shows, for each dimension, the 95% confidence interval of Acc, RMSE and Unc over each test set corresponding to that dimension. More precisely, each dimension has nine associated datasets, three models with three properties each, so that nine different smMC models have been trained. Notice

how the width of the inferred credible intervals is compared against the width
of SMC confidence intervals.

In addition, Fig. 7–Fig. 10 in Appendix D of [6] show the results over one-
dimensional configurations - (a), (b), (d) and (f) respectively - whose results over
the test set are easy to visualise. In particular, we show the mean and the 95%
credible intervals of the estimated satisfaction probability $f(\theta_j)$ for EP-GPs,
SVI-GPs and SVI-BNNs. Figure 11–Fig. 13 in Appendix D of [6] compare the
results of EP-GPs, SVI-GPs and SVI-BNNs over two-dimensional configurations
- (c), (e) and (g). In particular, we compare the SMC estimate of the satisfaction
probability $f_\varphi(\theta_j)$ to the average satisfaction probability $\mathbb{E}[f(\theta_j)]$ estimated by
EP-GPs, SVI-GPs and SVI-BNNs over each input θ_j of the test set.

We now compare the performances obtained by the variational approaches
of SV-smMC to those of the smMC baseline based on EP-GP. Table 1 and Fig. 2
show how the RMSE of SV-smMC solutions is almost always lower than that
of smMC. In addition, the baseline solution presents an RMSE that grows proportionally to the complexity and the dimensionality of the underlying configuration. On the contrary, SV-smMC solutions do not reflect such behaviour, as
the value of the RMSE is almost constant across all the different configurations.
About the informativeness of uncertainty estimations, we notice how SVI-BNN
tends to produce credible intervals that are always larger than the one of SVI-
GP, which, in turn, tends to underestimate the underlying uncertainty. This
phenomenon appears in all the different configurations and it is easily observable in Fig. 2. We argue that SVI-GP tends to provide overconfident predictions
due to the sparsification strategies used during inference. Such behaviour is well-
known and discussed in [10, 28]. SVI-BNN does not present such behaviour as
it does not undergo any sparsification. On the other hand, the baseline smMC
tends to have tight uncertainty estimates on low-dimensional configurations,
but it becomes excessively over-conservative in high-dimensional configurations,
making the predicted credible intervals almost uninformative. All models reach
extremely high accuracies over the test set. SVI-BNN reaches the best performances over all the configurations: the average accuracy is around 95% and it is
always higher than 71%. This result is not surprising given that SVI-BNN shows
low RMSEs (overall average around 0.02) and slightly over-conservative credible
intervals (overall average uncertainty width around 0.1). The SVI-GP accuracy,
on the other hand, fluctuates around 60% as it tends to provide over-confident
credible intervals with an overall average RMSE comparable to that of SVI-BNN
but with overall average uncertainty width of around 0.03.

Related Work. A number of recent works tackle the problem of parametric verification of a stochastic process, we here present the most relevant. In [1] the
parameter space of a pCTMC is explicitly explored, while [11] assumes a probability distribution over the parameters and proposes a sampling-based approach.
In [19] conformal predictions are used over the expected value of the stochastic
process rather than its distribution and [7] presents a frequentist, rather than
Bayesian, approach based on quantile regression. The conformal recalibration

is constant over the entire state space, whereas our Bayesian quantification of uncertainty is point-specific.

Discussion. To summarize, we can see how, in general, SV-smMC solutions scale a lot better to high-dimensional problems compared to smMC, both in terms of feasibility and in terms of quality of the results. SVI-BNN reaches the highest accuracy and provides rather conservative predictions. SVI-GP, on the other, reaches low RMSEs and tends to provide overconfident predictions. Therefore BNNs should be preferred in the verification of safety-critical systems, whereas GPs can be a good solution when overconfidence is more tolerable. Finally, we see how EP-GP is competitive only on extremely simple configurations. As the dimensionality increases, so does the error: the RMSE increases and the credible intervals become excessively broad. Moreover, we soon reach the memory-bound wall that makes EP-GP solution unfeasible on configurations with more than four parameters.

We conclude by suggesting how smMC, either the original EP-based version or the novel SVI-based version, may be enriched with *probabilistically approximately correct statistical guarantees over the generalization error* holding pointwise at any prediction point without affecting the scalability at runtime. See Sect. 5.1 for an intuition of the solution based on Conformal Predictions [32]. A detailed presentation of such an extension is left for future work.

5   Conclusions

This paper presents SV-smMC, an extension of Smoothed Model Checking, based on stochastic variational inference, that scales well to high dimensional parameter spaces and that enables GPU acceleration. In addition, this paper offers a comparison of the performances of stochastic variational inference over two different Bayesian approaches - namely Gaussian processes (SVI-GP) and Bayesian neural networks (SVI-BNN) - against those of the baseline smMC, based on the expectation propagation technique. In particular, our experiments show that the posterior predictive distribution provided by SVI-BNN provides the best overall results in terms of the estimated satisfaction probabilities. On the other hand, thanks to GPU acceleration, SVI-GP is able to achieve competitive performances with a significant speed-up in computational time. Furthermore, we show how variational approaches are able to overcome the computational limitations of the expectation propagation algorithm over large datasets.

SV-smMC can be naturally extended with active learning ideas, following the line of [3,9,29], solving efficiently parameter synthesis and design tasks.

5.1   Statistical Guarantees

The Bayesian quantification of uncertainty, despite being based on statistically sound operations, offers no guarantees per se as it strongly depends on the chosen prior. Additionally, in smMC, either EP- or SVI-based, we further add the error of approximate inference on top of this. Here we briefly discuss how smMC, in all its versions, can be enriched with *probabilistically approximately correct statistical guarantees over the generalization error* holding point-wise at any prediction point. This result is obtained by combining Bayesian estimates of uncertainty with Inductive Conformal Prediction [32,35], a framework that can be applied on top of any deterministic regressor to enrich its predictions with statistically valid quantification of the predictive uncertainty. The rationale is to transform point-wise predictions made by the expectation over the posterior $q(f)$ into statistically valid prediction intervals. ICP is non-informative to check how the uncertainty distributes over Θ as the interval width is constant over the entire parameter space Θ. Normalized Inductive Conformal Predictions (NICP) [23,24] consider locally weighted residuals to overcome this limitation, so that prediction intervals are tighter for parameters that are deemed easy to predict and vice-versa. Retrieving such guarantees does not affect the scalability at runtime. Our intuition is to exploit the Bayesian quantification of uncertainty of smMC as the normalizing function of a NICP approach, that in turn will provide us with point-specific statistical guarantees over the error coverage. More details and some preliminary results can be found in Appendix C in [6].

Acknowledgments. This work has been partially supported by the PRIN project "SEDUCE" n. 2017TWRCNB and by the PNRR project iNEST (Interconnected North-Est Innovation Ecosystem) funded by the European Union Next-GenerationEU (Piano Nazionale di Ripresa e Resilienza (PNRR) - Missione 4 Componente 2, Investimento 1.5 - D.D. 1058 23/06/2022, ECS_00000043).

References

1. Badings, T.S., Jansen, N., Junges, S., Stoelinga, M., Volk, M.: Sampling-based verification of ctmcs with uncertain rates. In: Shoham, S., Vizel, Y. (eds.) Computer Aided Verification: 34th International Conference, CAV 2022, Haifa, Israel, 7–10 August 2022, Proceedings, Part II, pp. 26–47. Springer, Heidelberg (2022). https://doi.org/10.1007/978-3-031-13188-2_2
2. Baier, C., Katoen, J.P.: Principles of Model Checking. MIT press, Cambridge (2008)
3. Bartocci, E., Bortolussi, L., Nenzi, L., Sanguinetti, G.: System design of stochastic models using robustness of temporal properties. Theor. Comput. Sci. **587**, 3–25 (2015). https://doi.org/10.1016/j.tcs.2015.02.046
4. Bingham, E., et al.: Pyro: Deep universal probabilistic programming. J. Mach. Learn. Res. **20**, 28:1–28:6 (2019). https://jmlr.org/papers/v20/18-403.html
5. Bishop, C.M.: Pattern Recognition and Machine Learning. Springer, Heidelberg (2006)
6. Bortolussi, L., Cairoli, F., Carbone, G., Pulcini, P.: Stochastic variational smoothed model checking. arXiv preprint arXiv:2205.05398 (2022)
7. Bortolussi, L., Cairoli, F., Paoletti, N.: Conformal quantitative predictive monitoring of stl requirements for stochastic processes. In: 26th ACM International Conference on Hybrid Systems: Computation and Control (2023)
8. Bortolussi, L., Milios, D., Sanguinetti, G.: Smoothed model checking for uncertain continuous-time Markov chains. Inf. Comput. **247**, 235–253 (2016)

9. Bortolussi, L., Silvetti, S.: Bayesian statistical parameter synthesis for linear temporal properties of stochastic models. In: Beyer, D., Huisman, M. (eds.) TACAS 2018. LNCS, vol. 10806, pp. 396–413. Springer, Cham (2018). https://doi.org/10.1007/978-3-319-89963-3_23

10. Candela, J.Q., Rasmussen, C.E.: A unifying view of sparse approximate gaussian process regression. J. Mach. Learn. Res. **6**, 1939–1959 (2005)

11. Češka, M., Dannenberg, F., Paoletti, N., Kwiatkowska, M., Brim, L.: Precise parameter synthesis for stochastic biochemical systems. Acta Informatica **54**, 589–623 (2017)

12. Gardner, J.R., Pleiss, G., Bindel, D., Weinberger, K.Q., Wilson, A.G.: Gpytorch: blackbox matrix-matrix gaussian process inference with gpu acceleration. In: Proceedings of the 32nd International Conference on Neural Information Processing Systems, pp. 7587–7597. NIPS'18, Curran Associates Inc., Red Hook (2018)

13. Gillespie, D.T.: Exact stochastic simulation of coupled chemical reactions. J. Phys. Chem. **81**(25), 2340–2361 (1977)

14. Goan, E., Fookes, C.: Bayesian neural networks: an introduction and survey. In: Mengersen, K.L., Pudlo, P., Robert, C.P. (eds.) Case Studies in Applied Bayesian Data Science. LNM, vol. 2259, pp. 45–87. Springer, Cham (2020). https://doi.org/10.1007/978-3-030-42553-1_3

15. Hoffman, M.D., Blei, D.M., Wang, C., Paisley, J.: Stochastic variational inference. J. Mach. Learn. Res. **14**, 1303–1347 (2013)

16. Jansen, N., et al.: Accelerating parametric probabilistic verification. In: Norman, G., Sanders, W. (eds.) QEST 2014. LNCS, vol. 8657, pp. 404–420. Springer, Cham (2014). https://doi.org/10.1007/978-3-319-10696-0_31

17. Jordan, M.I., Ghahramani, Z., Jaakkola, T.S., Saul, L.K.: An introduction to variational methods for graphical models. Mach. Learn. **37**(2), 183–233 (1999)

18. Lampinen, J., Vehtari, A.: Bayesian approach for neural networks-review and case studies. Neural Netw. **14**(3), 257–274 (2001)

19. Lindemann, L., Qin, X., Deshmukh, J.V., Pappas, G.J.: Conformal prediction for stl runtime verification. arXiv preprint arXiv:2211.01539 (2022)

20. MacKay, D.J.: A practical bayesian framework for backpropagation networks. Neural Comput. **4**(3), 448–472 (1992)

21. Maler, O., Nickovic, D.: Monitoring temporal properties of continuous signals. In: Lakhnech, Y., Yovine, S. (eds.) FORMATS/FTRTFT -2004. LNCS, vol. 3253, pp. 152–166. Springer, Heidelberg (2004). https://doi.org/10.1007/978-3-540-30206-3_12

22. Minka, T.P.: Expectation propagation for approximate bayesian inference. arXiv preprint arXiv:1301.2294 (2013)

23. Papadopoulos, H., Haralambous, H.: Reliable prediction intervals with regression neural networks. Neural Netw. Off. J. Int. Neural Netw. Soc. **24**(8), 842–51 (2011)

24. Papadopoulos, H., Vovk, V., Gammerman, A.: Regression conformal prediction with nearest neighbours. J. Artif. Intell. Res. **40**, 815–840 (2014)

25. Paszke, A., et al.: Pytorch: an imperative style, high-performance deep learning library. In: Advances in Neural Information Processing Systems, pp. 8024–8035 (2019)

26. Piho, P., Hillston, J.: Active and sparse methods in smoothed model checking. In: Abate, A., Marin, A. (eds.) QEST 2021. LNCS, vol. 12846, pp. 217–234. Springer, Cham (2021). https://doi.org/10.1007/978-3-030-85172-9_12

27. Rasmussen, C.E.: Gaussian processes in machine learning. In: Bousquet, O., von Luxburg, U., Rätsch, G. (eds.) ML -2003. LNCS (LNAI), vol. 3176, pp. 63–71. Springer, Heidelberg (2004). https://doi.org/10.1007/978-3-540-28650-9_4

28. Rasmussen, C.E., Candela, J.Q.: Healing the relevance vector machine through augmentation. In: Proceedings of the 22nd international conference on Machine learning (2005)
29. Silvetti, S., Policriti, A., Bortolussi, L.: An active learning approach to the falsification of black box cyber-physical systems. In: Polikarpova, N., Schneider, S. (eds.) IFM 2017. LNCS, vol. 10510, pp. 3–17. Springer, Cham (2017). https://doi.org/10.1007/978-3-319-66845-1_1
30. Titsias, M.: Variational learning of inducing variables in sparse gaussian processes. In: Artificial Intelligence and Statistics, pp. 567–574. PMLR (2009)
31. Titterington, D.: Bayesian methods for neural networks and related models. Stat. Sci. **19**, 128–139 (2004)
32. Vovk, V., Gammerman, A., Shafer, G.: Algorithmic Learning in a Random World, vol. 29. Springer, Heidelberg (2005). https://doi.org/10.1007/978-3-031-06649-8
33. Younes, H.L.S., Simmons, R.G.: Probabilistic verification of discrete event systems using acceptance sampling. In: Brinksma, E., Larsen, K.G. (eds.) CAV 2002. LNCS, vol. 2404, pp. 223–235. Springer, Heidelberg (2002). https://doi.org/10.1007/3-540-45657-0_17
34. Younes, H.L., Simmons, R.G.: Statistical probabilistic model checking with a focus on time-bounded properties. Inf. Comput. **204**(9), 1368–1409 (2006)
35. Zeni, G., Fontana, M., Vantini, S.: Conformal prediction: a unified review of theory and new challenges. ArXiv arXiv:2005.07972 (2020)
36. Zinkevich, M., Weimer, M., Li, L., Smola, A.: Parallelized stochastic gradient descent. Adv. Neural Inf. Process. Syst. **23** (2010)
37. Zuliani, P., Platzer, A., Clarke, E.M.: Bayesian statistical model checking with application to simulink/stateflow verification. In: Proceedings of the 13th ACM International Conference on Hybrid Systems: Computation and Control, pp. 243–252 (2010)

Monitoring Blackbox Implementations of Multiparty Session Protocols

Bas van den Heuvel$^{(\boxtimes)}$ ⬡, Jorge A. Pérez ⬡, and Rares A. Dobre

University of Groningen, Groningen, The Netherlands
vdheuvel.bas@gmail.com

Abstract. We present a framework for the distributed monitoring of networks of components that coordinate by message-passing, following multiparty session protocols specified as global types. We improve over prior works by (i) supporting components whose exact specification is unknown ("blackboxes") and (ii) covering protocols that cannot be analyzed by existing techniques. We first give a procedure for synthesizing monitors for blackboxes from global types, and precisely define when a blackbox correctly *satisfies* its global type. Then, we prove that monitored blackboxes are *sound* (they correctly follow the protocol) and *transparent* (blackboxes with and without monitors are behaviorally equivalent).

Keywords: distributed monitoring · message-passing · concurrency · multiparty session types

1 Introduction

Runtime verification excels at analyzing systems with components that cannot be (statically) checked, such as closed-source and third-party components with unknown/partial specifications [2,12]. In this spirit, we present a monitoring framework for networks of communicating components. We adopt *global types* from *multiparty session types* [17,18] both to specify protocols and to synthesize monitors. As we explain next, rather than process implementations, we consider *"blackboxes"*—components whose exact structure is unknown. Also, aiming at wide applicability, we cover networks of monitored components that implement global types that go beyond the scope of existing techniques.

Session types provide precise specifications of the protocols that components should respect. It is then natural to use session types as references for distributed monitoring [3,7,14,20,21,24]. In particular, Bocchi *et al.* [6,7,9] use multiparty session types to monitor networks of π-calculus processes. Leveraging notions originally conceived for static verification (such as *global types* and their *projection* onto *local types*), their framework guarantees the correctness of monitored networks with statically and dynamically checked components.

This research has been supported by the Dutch Research Council (NWO) under project No. 016.Vidi.189.046 (Unifying Correctness for Communicating Software).

P. Katsaros and L. Nenzi (Eds.): RV 2023, LNCS 14245, pp. 66–85, 2023.
https://doi.org/10.1007/978-3-031-44267-4_4

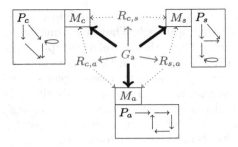

Fig. 1. Monitoring setup based on the global type (multiparty protocol) G_a (1). Each protocol participant has a blackbox (an LTS), attached to a monitor (e.g. P_c and M_c). The monitors are synthesized from G_a (thick arrows). Relative types (e.g. $R_{c,s}$) obtained by projection from G_a (thin gray arrows) are used in this synthesis (dotted arrows).

However, existing monitoring techniques based on multiparty session types have two limitations. One concerns the class of protocols they support; the other is their reliance on fully specified components, usually given as (typed) processes. That is, definitions of networks assume that a component can be inspected—an overly strong assumption in many cases. There is then a tension between (i) the assumptions on component structure and (ii) the strength of formal guarantees: the less we know about components, the harder it is to establish such guarantees.

Our Approach. We introduce a new approach to monitoring based on multiparty session types that relies on minimal assumptions on a component's structure. As key novelty, we consider *blackboxes*—components with unknown structure but observable behavior—and *networks* of monitored blackboxes that use asynchronous message-passing to implement multiparty protocols specified as global types.

As running example, let us consider the global type G_a (inspired by an example by Scalas and Yoshida [23]), which expresses an authorization protocol between three participants: server (s), client (c), and authorization service (a).

$$G_a := \mu X.s!c\{\mathsf{login}\langle\rangle.c!a\{\mathsf{pwd}\langle\mathsf{str}\rangle.a!s\{\mathsf{succ}\langle\mathsf{bool}\rangle.X\}\},\mathsf{quit}\langle\rangle.\mathsf{end}\} \qquad (1)$$

This recursive global type (μX) specifies that s sends to c ($s!c$) a choice between labels login and quit. In the login-branch, c sends to a a password of type $\langle\mathsf{str}\rangle$ and a notifies s whether it was correct, after which the protocol repeats (X). In the quit-branch, the protocol simply ends (end). As explained in [23], G_a is not supported by most theories of multiparty sessions, including those in [6,7,9].

Figure 1 illustrates our approach to monitoring global types such as G_a. There is a blackbox per participant, denoted P_s, P_c, and P_a, whose behavior is given by a labeled transition system (LTS). Each blackbox implements a participant as dictated by G_a while coupled with a monitor (M_s, M_c, and M_a in Fig. 1). Monitors are *synthesized* from G_a by relying on *relative types* [15], which provide local views of the global type: they specify protocols between *pairs* of participants; hence, in the case of G_a, we have three relative types: $R_{c,s}$, $R_{c,a}$, and $R_{s,a}$.

Introduced in [15] for type-checking communicating components, relative types are instrumental to our approach. They give a fine-grained view of protocols that is convenient for monitor synthesis. Relative types explicitly specify *dependencies* between participants, e.g., when the behavior of a participant p is the result of a prior choice made by some other participants q and r. Treating dependencies as explicit messages is key to ensuring the distributed implementability of protocols that usual multiparty theories cannot support (e.g., G_a (1)). Our algorithm for monitor synthesis mechanically computes these dependencies from relative types, and exploits them to coordinate monitored blackboxes.

A central ingredient in our technical developments is the notion of *satisfaction* (Definition 13), which defines when a monitored blackbox conforms to the role of a specific protocol participant. Building upon satisfaction, we prove *soundness* and *transparency* for networks of monitored blackboxes. Soundness (Theorem 17) ensures that if each monitored blackbox in a network behaves correctly (according to a global type), then the entire network behaves correctly too. Transparency (Theorem 23) ensures that monitors do not interfere with the (observable) behavior of their contained blackboxes; it is given in terms of a (weak) behavioral equivalence, which is suitably informed by the actions of a given global type.

Related Work. The literature on distributed runtime verification is vast. In this setting, the survey by Francalanza *et al.* [12] proposes several classification criteria. Phrased in terms of their criteria, our work concerns distributed monitoring for asynchronous message-passing. We work with blackboxes, whose monitors are minimally intrusive: they do not alter behavior, but do contribute to coordination.

The works by Bocchi *et al.* [6,7,9] and by Scalas and Yoshida [23], mentioned above, are a main source of inspiration to us. The work [23] highlights the limitations of techniques based on the projection of a global type onto local types: many practical protocols, such as G_a, cannot be analyzed because their projection onto local types is undefined. With respect to [6,7,9], there are three major differences. First, Bocchi *et al.* rely on precise specifications of components (π-calculus processes), whereas we monitor blackboxes (LTSs). Second, we resort to relative types, whereas they rely on local types; this is a limitation, as just mentioned. Third, their monitors drop incorrect messages (cf. [1]) instead of signaling errors, as we do. Their framework ensures transparency (akin to Theorem 23) and safety, i.e., monitored components do not misbehave. In contrast, we establish soundness, which is different and more technically involved than safety: our focus is on monitoring blackboxes rather than fully specified components, and soundness concerns correct behavior rather than the absence of misbehavior.

We mention runtime verification techniques based on *binary* session types, a sub-class of multiparty session types. Bartolo Burló *et al.* [3] monitor sequential processes that communicate synchronously, prove that ill-typed processes raise errors, and consider also probabilistic session types [4,5]. Other works couple monitoring session types with *blame assignment* upon protocol violations [14,19,21,24]. Jia *et al.* [21] monitor asynchronous session-typed processes. Gommerstadt *et al.* [13,14] extend [21] with rich refinement-based contracts. We do not consider blame assignment, but it can conceivably be added by enhancing error signals.

Let ℓ and T denote a label and a data type, respectively.

$$\begin{array}{llll} \text{Actions} & \alpha, \beta ::= \tau \text{ (silent)} \mid m \text{ (message)} \mid \mathsf{end} \text{ (end)} & & \\ \text{Messages} & m, n ::= p!q(\ell\langle T\rangle) \text{ (output)} & \mid p!q(\!(\ell)\!) & \text{(dep. output, only for networks)} \\ & \quad\mid p?q(\ell\langle T\rangle) \text{ (input)} & \mid p?q(\!(\ell)\!) & \text{(dep. input)} \end{array}$$

Given α, the *recipient in* α is defined as follows:

$$\begin{aligned} &\mathrm{recip}(p!q(\ell\langle T\rangle)) := \mathrm{recip}(p!q(\!(\ell)\!)) := q \\ &\mathrm{recip}(p?q(\ell\langle T\rangle)) := \mathrm{recip}(p?q(\!(\ell)\!)) := \mathrm{recip}(\tau) := \mathrm{recip}(\mathsf{end}) := \text{undefined} \end{aligned}$$

Let $D, E, \ldots$ denote sets of participants; $I, J, \ldots$ denote non-empty sets of labels; $X, Y, \ldots$ denote recursion variables.

$$\begin{array}{lll} \text{Networks} & \mathcal{P}, \mathcal{Q} ::= [\langle p : P : \vec{m}\rangle : M : \vec{n}] & \text{(monitored blackbox)} \\ & \quad\mid \mathcal{P} \mid \mathcal{Q} & \text{(parallel composition)} \\ & \quad\mid \mathsf{error}_D & \text{(error signal)} \end{array}$$

$$\begin{array}{llll} \text{Monitors} & M ::= p!q\{\!\{i\langle T_i\rangle.M\}\!\}_{i\in I} \text{ (output)} & \mid p!D(\ell).M & \text{(dep. output)} \\ & \quad\mid p?q\{\!\{i\langle T_i\rangle.M\}\!\}_{i\in I} \text{ (input)} & \mid p?q\{\!\{i.M\}\!\}_{i\in I} & \text{(dep. input)} \\ & \quad\mid \mu X.M \mid X \text{ (recursion)} & \mid \mathsf{end} & \text{(end)} \\ & \quad\mid \mathsf{error} \text{ (error)} & \mid \checkmark & \text{(finished)} \end{array}$$

The set of *subjects of a network* is as follows:

$$\mathrm{sub}([\langle p : P : \vec{m}\rangle : M : \vec{n}]) := \{p\} \quad \mathrm{sub}(\mathcal{P}|\mathcal{Q}) := \mathrm{sub}(\mathcal{P}) \cup \mathrm{sub}(\mathcal{Q}) \quad \mathrm{sub}(\mathsf{error}_D) := D$$

Fig. 2. Actions, messages, networks, and monitors.

Outline. Section 2 defines networks of monitored blackboxes and their behavior. Section 3 defines how to synthesize monitors from global types. Section 4 defines correct monitored blackboxes, and establishes soundness and transparency. Section 5 concludes the paper. We use colors to improve readability.

The full version of this paper [16] includes an appendix with additional examples (including the running example from [7]), a description of a practical toolkit based on this paper, and omitted proofs.

2 Networks of Monitored Blackboxes

We write $P, Q, \ldots$ to denote *blackbox processes* (simply *blackboxes*) that implement protocol *participants* (denoted $p, q, \ldots$). We assume that a blackbox P is associated with an LTS that specifies its behavior. Transitions are denoted $P \xrightarrow{\alpha} P'$. Actions α, defined in Fig. 2 (top), encompass messages m, which can be labeled data but also *dependency messages* (simply *dependencies*). As we will see, dependencies are useful to ensure the coordinated implementation of choices. Messages abstract away from values, and include only their type.

A silent transition τ denotes an internal computation. Transitions $p!q(\ell\langle T\rangle)$ and $p?q(\ell\langle T\rangle)$ denote the output and input of a message of type T with label ℓ

between p and q, respectively. If a message carries no data, we write $\ell\langle\rangle$ (i.e., the data type is empty). Dependency outputs are used for monitors, defined below.

We adopt minimal assumptions about the behavior of blackboxes:

Definition 1 (Assumptions). *We assume the following about LTSs of blackboxes:*

- *(**Finite** τ) Sequences of τ-transitions are finite.*
- *(**Input/Output**) There are never input- and output-transitions available at the same time.*
- *(**End**) There are never transitions after an* end*-transition.*

Example 2. The blackboxes P_c, P_s, P_a implement c, s, a, respectively, in G_a (1) with the following LTSs:

$$P_c^l \xleftarrow[c!a(\text{pwd}\langle\text{str}\rangle)]{c?s(\text{login}\langle\rangle)} P_c \xrightarrow{c?s(\text{quit}\langle\rangle)} P_c^q \xrightarrow{\text{end}} P_c^e$$

$$P_s^l \xleftarrow[s?a(\text{succ}\langle\text{bool}\rangle)]{s!c(\text{login}\langle\rangle)} P_s \xrightarrow{s!c(\text{quit}\langle\rangle)} P_s^q \xrightarrow{\text{end}} P_s^e$$

$$
\begin{array}{ccccccc}
P_a^{l_s} & \xleftarrow{a?s(\!(\text{login})\!)} & P_a & \xrightarrow{a?s(\!(\text{quit})\!)} & P_a^{q_s} & \xrightarrow{a?c(\!(\text{quit})\!)} & P_a^{q_c} \\
\downarrow{\scriptstyle a?c(\!(\text{login})\!)} & & \downarrow{\scriptstyle a!s(\text{succ}\langle\text{bool}\rangle)} & & & & \downarrow{\scriptstyle \text{end}} \\
P_a^{l_c} & \xrightarrow{a?c(\text{pwd}\langle\text{str}\rangle)} & P_a^p & & & & P_a^e
\end{array}
$$

All three LTSs above respect the assumptions in Definition 1. On the other hand, the following LTS violates all three assumptions; in particular, there are an input- and an output-transition simultaneously enabled at Q:

$$\tau \circlearrowleft Q^p \xleftarrow{c!a(\text{pwd}\langle\text{str}\rangle)} Q \underset{\text{end}}{\overset{c?s(\text{quit}\langle\rangle)}{\rightleftarrows}} Q^q$$

Blackboxes communicate asynchronously, using buffers (denoted $\vec{m}$): ordered sequences of messages, with the most-recently received message on the left. The empty buffer is denoted ε. When a blackbox does an input transition, it attempts to read the message from its buffer. An output transition places the message in the recipient's buffer; to accommodate this, we mark each blackbox with the participant they implement. The result is a *buffered blackbox*, denoted $\langle p : P : \vec{m}\rangle$.

By convention, the buffer of p contains output messages with recipient p. We allow the silent reordering of messages with different senders; this way, e.g., given $q \neq r$, $\vec{m}, q!p(\ell\langle T\rangle), r!p(\ell'\langle T'\rangle), \vec{n}$ and $\vec{m}, r!p(\ell'\langle T'\rangle), q!p(\ell\langle T\rangle), \vec{n}$ are the same.

Having defined standalone (buffered) blackboxes, we now define how they interact in *networks*. We couple each buffered blackbox with a *monitor* M, which has its own buffer $\vec{n}$. The result is a *monitored blackbox*, denoted $[\langle p : P : \vec{m}\rangle : M : \vec{n}]$.

Monitors define finite state machines that accept sequences of incoming and outgoing messages, as stipulated by some protocol. An *error* occurs when a message exchange does not conform to such protocol. Additionally, monitors support the dependencies mentioned earlier: when a blackbox sends or receives a message, the monitor broadcasts the message's label to other monitored blackboxes such that they can receive the chosen label and react accordingly.

Networks, defined in Fig. 2 (bottom), are compositions of monitored blackboxes and *error signals*. An error signal error_D replaces a monitored blackbox when its monitor detects an error involving participants in the set D. Indeed, a participant's error will propagate to the other monitored blackboxes in a network. Output and (dependency) input monitors check outgoing and incoming (dependency) messages, respectively. Output dependency monitors $p!D(\ell).M$ broadcast ℓ to the participants in D. Recursive monitors are encoded by recursive definitions $(\mu X.M)$ and recursive calls (X). The end monitor waits for the buffered blackbox to end the protocol. The error monitor denotes an inability to process received messages; it will be useful when the sender and recipient of an exchange send different dependency messages. The finished monitor $\checkmark$ is self-explanatory.

We now define the behavior of monitored blackboxes in networks:

Definition 3 (LTS for Networks). *We define an LTS for networks, denoted* $\mathcal{P} \xrightarrow{\alpha} \mathcal{Q}$*, by the rules in Fig. 3 (Page 7) with actions* α *as in Fig. 2 (top). We write* $\mathcal{P} \Rightarrow \mathcal{Q}$ *to denote a sequence of zero or more* τ*-transitions* $\mathcal{P} \xrightarrow{\tau} \ldots \xrightarrow{\tau} \mathcal{Q}$*, and we write* $\mathcal{P} \nrightarrow$ *to denote that there do not exist* $\alpha, \mathcal{Q}$ *such that* $\mathcal{P} \xrightarrow{\alpha} \mathcal{Q}$*.*

Figure 3 gives four groups of rules, which we briefly discuss. The Transition group [BUF-*] defines the behavior of a buffered blackbox in terms of the behavior of the blackbox it contains; note that input transitions are hidden as τ-transitions. The Transition group [MON-*] defines the behavior of a monitored blackbox when the behavior of the enclosed buffered blackbox concurs with the monitor; again, input transitions are hidden as τ-transitions.

When the behavior of the buffered blackbox does not concur with the monitor, the Transition group [ERROR-*] replaces the monitored blackbox with an error signal. Transition [PAR-ERROR] propagates error signals to parallel monitored blackboxes. If a network parallel to the monitored blackbox of p has an outgoing message with recipient p, Transition [OUT-MON-BUF] places this message in the buffer of the monitored blackbox as a τ-transition. Transition [PAR] closes transitions under parallel composition, as long as the recipient in the action of the transition (recip(α)) is not a subject of the composed network (sub($\mathcal{Q}$), the participants for which monitored blackboxes and error signals appear in $\mathcal{Q}$). Transition [CONG] closes transitions under $\equiv$, which denotes a congruence that defines parallel composition as commutative and associative.

Figure 4 shows transitions of correct/incorrect communications in networks.

$$[\text{BUF-OUT}] \quad \frac{P \xrightarrow{p!q(\ell\langle T\rangle)} P'}{\langle p : P : \vec{m}\rangle \xrightarrow{p!q(\ell\langle T\rangle)} \langle p : P' : \vec{m}\rangle}$$

$$[\text{BUF-IN}] \quad \frac{P \xrightarrow{p?q(\ell\langle T\rangle)} P'}{\langle p : P : \vec{m}, q!p(\ell\langle T\rangle)\rangle \xrightarrow{\tau} \langle p : P' : \vec{m}\rangle}$$

$$[\text{BUF-IN-DEP}] \quad \frac{P \xrightarrow{p?q(\!(\ell)\!)} P'}{\langle p : P : \vec{m}, q!p(\!(\ell)\!)\rangle \xrightarrow{\tau} \langle p : P' : \vec{m}\rangle}$$

$$[\text{BUF-TAU}] \quad \frac{P \xrightarrow{\tau} P'}{\langle p : P : \vec{m}\rangle \xrightarrow{\tau} \langle p : P' : \vec{m}\rangle}$$

$$[\text{BUF-END}] \quad \frac{P \xrightarrow{\text{end}} P'}{\langle p : P : \vec{m}\rangle \xrightarrow{\text{end}} \langle p : P' : \vec{m}\rangle}$$

$$[\text{MON-OUT}] \quad \frac{\langle p : P : \vec{m}\rangle \xrightarrow{p!q(j\langle T_j\rangle)} \langle p : P' : \vec{m}\rangle \quad M = p!q\{\!\{i\langle T_i\rangle.M_i\}\!\}_{i\in I} \quad j \in I}{[\langle p : P : \vec{m}\rangle : M : \vec{n}] \xrightarrow{p!q(j\langle T_j\rangle)} [\langle p : P' : \vec{m}\rangle : M_j : \vec{n}]}$$

$$[\text{MON-IN}] \quad \frac{M = p?q\{\!\{y.M_i\}\!\}_{y\in Y} \quad x \in Y \quad n' \in \{q!p(x), q!p(\!(x)\!)\}}{[\langle p : P : \vec{m}\rangle : M : \vec{n}, n'] \xrightarrow{\tau} [\langle p : P : n', \vec{m}\rangle : M_j : \vec{n}]}$$

$$[\text{MON-TAU}] \quad \frac{\langle p : P : \vec{m}\rangle \xrightarrow{\tau} \langle p : P' : \vec{m}'\rangle \quad M \neq \checkmark}{[\langle p : P : \vec{m}\rangle : M : \vec{n}] \xrightarrow{\tau} [\langle p : P' : \vec{m}'\rangle : M : \vec{n}]}$$

$$[\text{MON-OUT-DEP}] \quad \frac{}{[\langle p : P : \vec{m}\rangle : p!(D \cup \{q\})(\ell).M' : \vec{n}] \xrightarrow{p!q(\!(\ell)\!)} [\langle p : P : \vec{m}\rangle : p!D(\ell).M' : \vec{n}]}$$

$$[\text{MON-OUT-DEP-EMPTY}] \quad \frac{}{[\langle p : P : \vec{m}\rangle : p!\emptyset(\ell).M' : \vec{n}] \xrightarrow{\tau} [\langle p : P : \vec{m}\rangle : M' : \vec{n}]}$$

$$[\text{MON-REC}] \quad \frac{[\langle p : P : \vec{m}\rangle : M\{\mu X.M/X\} : \vec{n}] \xrightarrow{\alpha} [\langle p : P' : \vec{m}'\rangle : M' : \vec{n}']}{[\langle p : P : \vec{m}\rangle : \mu X.M : \vec{n}] \xrightarrow{\alpha} [\langle p : P' : \vec{m}'\rangle : M' : \vec{n}']}$$

$$[\text{MON-END}] \quad \frac{\langle p : P : \vec{m}\rangle \xrightarrow{\text{end}} \langle p : P' : \vec{m}\rangle}{[\langle p : P : \vec{m}\rangle : \text{end} : \varepsilon] \xrightarrow{\text{end}} [\langle p : P' : \vec{m}\rangle : \checkmark : \varepsilon]}$$

$$[\text{ERROR-OUT}] \quad \frac{\langle p : P : \vec{m}\rangle \xrightarrow{p!q(j\langle T_j\rangle)} \langle p : P' : \vec{m}\rangle \quad \begin{array}{l} M = p!r\{\!\{i\langle T_i\rangle.M_i\}\!\}_{i\in I} \implies (r \neq q \vee j \notin I) \\ M \notin \{\mu X.M', p!D(\ell).M'\} \end{array}}{[\langle p : P : \vec{m}\rangle : M : \vec{n}] \xrightarrow{\tau} \text{error}_{\{p\}}}$$

$$[\text{ERROR-END}] \quad \frac{\langle p : P : \vec{m}\rangle \xrightarrow{\text{end}} \langle p : P' : \vec{m}\rangle \quad \vec{n} = \varepsilon \implies M \notin \{\mu X.M', p!D(\ell).M', \text{end}\}}{[\langle p : P : \vec{m}\rangle : M : \vec{n}] \xrightarrow{\tau} \text{error}_{\{p\}}}$$

$$[\text{ERROR-IN}] \quad \frac{M = p?q\{\!\{y.M_y\}\!\}_{y\in Y} \quad x \notin Y \quad n' \in \{q!p(x), q!p(\!(x)\!)\}}{[\langle p : P : \vec{m}\rangle : M : \vec{n}, n'] \xrightarrow{\tau} \text{error}_{\{p\}}}$$

$$[\text{ERROR-MON}] \quad \frac{}{[\langle p : P : \vec{m}\rangle : \text{error} : \vec{n}] \xrightarrow{\tau} \text{error}_{\{p\}}}$$

$$[\text{PAR-ERROR}] \quad \frac{}{\text{error}_D \mid [\langle p : P : \vec{m}\rangle : M : \vec{n}] \xrightarrow{\tau} \text{error}_{D\cup\{p\}}}$$

$$[\text{OUT-MON-BUF}] \quad \frac{\mathcal{P} \xrightarrow{n'} \mathcal{P}' \quad n' \in \{q!p(x), q!p(\!(x)\!)\}}{\mathcal{P} \mid [\langle p : P : \vec{m}\rangle : M : \vec{n}] \xrightarrow{\tau} \mathcal{P}' \mid [\langle p : P : \vec{m}\rangle : M : n', \vec{n}]}$$

$$[\text{PAR}] \quad \frac{\mathcal{P} \xrightarrow{\alpha} \mathcal{P}' \quad \text{recip}(\alpha) \notin \text{sub}(\mathcal{Q})}{\mathcal{P} \mid \mathcal{Q} \xrightarrow{\alpha} \mathcal{P}' \mid \mathcal{Q}}$$

$$[\text{CONG}] \quad \frac{\mathcal{P} \equiv \mathcal{P}' \quad \mathcal{P}' \xrightarrow{\alpha} \mathcal{Q}' \quad \mathcal{Q}' \equiv \mathcal{Q}}{\mathcal{P} \xrightarrow{\alpha} \mathcal{Q}}$$

Fig. 3. LTS for Networks (Definition 3).

$$[\langle c : P_c : \varepsilon\rangle : c?s\{\!\{\mathsf{quit}\langle\rangle.\mathsf{end}\}\!\} : \varepsilon] \quad _\tau \quad [\langle c : P_c : \varepsilon\rangle : c?s\{\!\{\mathsf{quit}\langle\rangle.\mathsf{end}\}\!\} : s!c(\mathsf{quit}\langle\rangle)]$$
$$|\ [\langle s : P_s : \varepsilon\rangle : s!c\{\!\{\mathsf{quit}\langle\rangle.\mathsf{end}\}\!\} : \varepsilon] \xrightarrow{\quad} |\ [\langle s : P_s^{\mathsf{q}} : \varepsilon\rangle : \mathsf{end} : \varepsilon]$$

$$\downarrow \tau$$

$$[\langle c : P_c^{\mathsf{e}} : \varepsilon\rangle : \checkmark : \varepsilon] \xleftarrow[\ \mathsf{end}\ ]{\ \mathsf{end}\ } [\langle c : P_c^{\mathsf{q}} : \varepsilon\rangle : \mathsf{end} : \varepsilon] \quad _\tau \quad [\langle c : P_c : s!c(\mathsf{quit}\langle\rangle)\rangle : \mathsf{end} : \varepsilon]$$
$$|\ [\langle s : P_s^{\mathsf{e}} : \varepsilon\rangle : \checkmark : \varepsilon] \qquad |\ [\langle s : P_s^{\mathsf{q}} : \varepsilon\rangle : \mathsf{end} : \varepsilon] \xleftarrow{\quad} |\ [\langle s : P_s^{\mathsf{q}} : \varepsilon\rangle : \mathsf{end} : \varepsilon]$$

$$[\langle c : P_c : \varepsilon\rangle : c?s\{\!\{\mathsf{login}\langle\rangle.M_c^!\}\!\} : s!c(\mathsf{quit}\langle\rangle)] \quad _\tau \quad \mathsf{error}_{\{c\}} \qquad _\tau$$
$$|\ [\langle s : P_s^{\mathsf{q}} : \varepsilon\rangle : \mathsf{end} : \varepsilon] \xrightarrow{\quad} |\ [\langle s : P_s^{\mathsf{q}} : \varepsilon\rangle : \mathsf{end} : \varepsilon] \xrightarrow{\quad} \mathsf{error}_{\{c,s\}}$$

Fig. 4. The LTS for Networks at work: transitions of correctly/incorrectly communicating monitored blackboxes of participants of G_{a} (1). Top: s sends to c label quit, monitor of c reads message, blackbox of c reads message, both components end. Bottom: monitor of c expects login message but finds quit message so signals error, error propagates to s.

3 Monitors for Blackboxes Synthesized from Global Types

In theories of multiparty session types [17,18], *global types* conveniently describe message-passing protocols between sets of participants from a vantage point. Here we use them as specifications for monitors in networks (Algorithm 2); for a local view of such global protocols we use *relative types* [15], which describe the interactions and dependencies between *pairs* of participants.

Definition 4 (Global and Relative Types).

Global types $\quad G, G' ::= p!q\{i\langle T_i\rangle.G\}_{i \in I}$ *(exchange)* $\mid$ end *(end)*
$$\mid \mu X.G \mid X \qquad \text{(recursion)}$$

Relative types $\quad R, R' ::= p!q\{\!\{i\langle T_i\rangle.R\}\!\}_{i \in I} \quad$ *(exchange)* $\mid$ end $\qquad$ *(end)*
$$\mid (p!r)!q\{\!\{i.R\}\!\}_{i \in I} \quad \text{(output dep.)} \mid \mu X.R \mid X \text{ (recursion)}$$
$$\mid (p?r)!q\{\!\{i.R\}\!\}_{i \in I} \quad \text{(input dep.)}$$

We write $\mathsf{part}(G)$ *to denote the set of participants involved in exchanges in* G.

The global type $p!q\{i\langle T_i\rangle.G_i\}_{i \in I}$ specifies that p sends to q some $j \in I$ with T_j, continuing as G_j. A relative type specifies a protocol between a pair of participants, say p and q. The type $p!q\{\!\{i\langle T_i\rangle.R_i\}\!\}_{i \in I}$ specifies that p sends to q some $j \in I$ with T_j, continuing as R_j. If the protocol between p and q depends on a prior choice involving p or q, their relative type includes a *dependency*: $(p!r)!q\{\!\{i.R_i\}\!\}_{i \in I}$ (resp. $(p?r)!q\{\!\{i.R_i\}\!\}_{i \in I}$) specifies that p forwards to q the $j \in I$ sent to (resp. received from) r by p. For both global and relative types, tail-recursion is defined with recursive definitions μX and recursive calls X, and end specifies the end of the protocol.

Relative types are obtained from global types by means of projection:

Definition 5 (Relative Projection). *The* relative projection *of a global type onto a pair of participants, denoted* $G \rangle (p, q)$, *is defined by Algorithm 1.*

Algorithm 1: Relative Projection of G onto p and q (Def. 5).

```
1  def G ⟩ (p, q) as
2  │  switch G do
3  │  │  case s!r{i⟨T_i⟩.G_i}_{i∈I} do
4  │  │  │  ∀i ∈ I. R_i := G_i ⟩ (p, q)
5  │  │  │  if (p = s ∧ q = r) then  return p!q{|i⟨T_i⟩.R_i|}_{i∈I}
6  │  │  │  else if (q = s ∧ p = r) then  return q!p{|i⟨T_i⟩.R_i|}_{i∈I}
7  │  │  │  else if ∀i,j ∈ I. R_i = R_j then  return ∪_{i∈I} R_i
8  │  │  │  else if s ∈ {p, q} ∧ t ∈ {p, q} \ {s} then  return (s!r)!t{|i.R_i|}_{i∈I}
9  │  │  │  else if r ∈ {p, q} ∧ t ∈ {p, q} \ {r} then  return (r?s)!t{|i.R_i|}_{i∈I}
10 │  │  case μX.G′ do
11 │  │  │  R′ := G′ ⟩ (p, q)
12 │  │  │  if (R′ contains an exchange or a recursive call on any Y ≠ X) then
      │  │  │      return μX.R′
13 │  │  │  else  return end
14 │  │  case X do  return X
15 │  │  case end do  return end
```

The projection of an exchange onto (p, q) is an exchange if p and q are sender and recipient (lines 5 and 6). Otherwise, if the protocol between p and q does not depend on the exchange (the projections of all branches are equal), the projection is the union of the projected branches (line 7). The union of relative types, denoted $R \cup R'$, is defined only on identical relative types (e.g., $p!q\{|i\langle T_i\rangle.R_i|\}_{i\in I} \cup p!q\{|i\langle T_i\rangle.R_i|\}_{i\in I} = p!q\{|i\langle T_i\rangle.R_i|\}_{i\in I}$; see [16] for a formal definition). If there is a dependency and p or q is sender/recipient, the projection is a dependency (lines 8 and 9). Projection is undefined if there is a dependency but p nor q is involved.

The projection of $\mu X.G'$ is a relative type starting with a recursive definition, provided that the projection of G' onto (p, q) contains an exchange or nested recursive call (line 12) to avoid recursion with only dependencies; otherwise, the projection returns end (line 13). The projections of recursive calls and end are homomorphic (lines 14 and 15).

Example 6. The relative projections of G_a (1) are:

$$R_{c,s} := G_\mathsf{a} \rangle (c, s) = \mu X.s!c\{|\mathsf{login}\langle\rangle.X, \mathsf{quit}\langle\rangle.\mathsf{end}|\}$$

$$R_{c,a} := G_\mathsf{a} \rangle (c, a) = \mu X.(c?s)!a\{|\mathsf{login}.c!a\{|\mathsf{pwd}\langle\mathsf{str}\rangle.X|\}, \mathsf{quit}.\mathsf{end}|\}$$

$$R_{s,a} := G_\mathsf{a} \rangle (s, a) = \mu X.(s!c)!a\{|\mathsf{login}.a!s\{|\mathsf{succ}\langle\mathsf{bool}\rangle.X|\}, \mathsf{quit}.\mathsf{end}|\}$$

Hence, the exchange from s to c is a dependency for the protocols of a.

Not all global types are sensible. A valid global type may, e.g., require a participant p to have different behaviors, depending on a choice that p is unaware of (see, e.g., [8]). In the following, we work only with *well-formed* global types:

Definition 7 (Well-formedness). *We say a global type G is* well-formed *if and only if, for all pairs of participants $p \neq q \in \mathrm{part}(G)$, the projection $G \rangle (p, q)$ is defined, and all recursion in G is non-contractive (e.g., $G \neq \mu X.X$) and bound.*

Algorithm 2: Synthesis of Monitors from Global Types (Definition 9).

```
1  def gt2mon(G, p, D) as
2    switch G do
3      case s!r{i⟨Tᵢ⟩.Gᵢ}ᵢ∈ₗ do
4        deps := {q ∈ D | q depsOn p in G}
5        if p = s then  return p!r{{i⟨Tᵢ⟩.p!deps(i).gt2mon(Gᵢ, p, D)}}ᵢ∈ₗ
6        else if p = r then  return p?s{{i⟨Tᵢ⟩.p!deps(i).gt2mon(Gᵢ, p, D)}}ᵢ∈ₗ
7        else if p ∉ {r, s} then
8          depOnₛ := (s ∈ D ∧ p depsOn s in G)
9          depOnᵣ := (r ∈ D ∧ p depsOn r in G)
10         if (depOnₛ ∧ ¬depOnᵣ) then  return p?s{{i.gt2mon(Gᵢ, p, D)}}ᵢ∈ₗ
11         else if (depOnᵣ ∧ ¬depOnₛ) then  return p?r{{i.gt2mon(Gᵢ, p, D)}}ᵢ∈ₗ
12         else if (depOnₛ ∧ depOnᵣ) then
13           | return p?s{{i.p?r{{i.gt2mon(Gᵢ, p, D)}} ∪ {{j.error}}ⱼ∈ₗ\{i}}}ᵢ∈ₗ
14         else return gt2mon(Gₖ, p, D)  (arbitrary k ∈ I)
15     case μX.G' do
16       D' := {q ∈ D | G ⟩ (p, q) ≠ end}
17       if D' ≠ ∅ then  return μX.gt2mon(G', p, D')
18       else return end
19     case X do  return X
20     case end do  return end
```

Our running example G_a (1) is well-formed in the above sense; also, as explained in [23], G_a is *not* well-formed in most theories of multiparty sessions (based on projection onto local types). As such, G_a goes beyond the scope of such theories.

Synthesizing Monitors. Next, we define a procedure to synthesize monitors for the participants of global types. This procedure detects dependencies as follows:

Definition 8 (Dependence). *Given a global type G, we say p depends on q in G, denoted $p\,\mathsf{depsOn}\,q\,$in$\,G$, if and only if*
$G = s!r\{i\langle T_i\rangle.G_i\}_{i\in I} \wedge p \notin \{s, r\} \wedge q \in \{s, r\} \wedge \exists i, j \in I.\ G_i \rangle (p, q) \neq G_j \rangle (p, q).$

Thus, $p\,\mathsf{depsOn}\,q\,$in$\,G$ holds if and only if G is an exchange involving q but not p, and the relative projections of at least two branches of the exchange are different.

Definition 9 (Synthesis of Monitors from Global Types). *Algorithm 2 synthesizes the monitor for p in G with participants D, denoted $\mathsf{gt2mon}(G, p, D)$.*

Initially, $D = \mathsf{part}(G) \setminus \{p\}$. The monitor for p of an exchange where p is sender (resp. recipient) is an output (resp. input) followed in each branch by a dependency output, using Dependence to compute the participants with dependencies (lines 5 and 6). If p is not involved, we detect a dependency for p with Dependence. In case p depends on sender/recipient but not both, the monitor is a dependency input (lines 10 and 11). If p depends on sender *and* recipient, the monitor contains two consecutive dependency inputs (line 13); when the two received labels differ, the monitor enters an error-state. When there is no dependency for p, the monitor uses an arbitrary branch (line 14). To synthesize a monitor for $\mu X.G'$, the algorithm uses projection to compute D' with participants having exchanges with p in G' (cf. Algorithm 1 line 12). If D' is non-empty, the monitor starts with a recursive definition (line 17) and the algorithm continues with D'; otherwise, the monitor is end (line 18). The monitors of X and end are homomorphic (lines 19 and 20).

Example 10. Let us use $G = p!q\{\ell\langle T\rangle.\mu X.p!r\{\ell'\langle T'\rangle.X, \ell''\langle T''\rangle.\mathsf{end}\}\}$ to illustrate Algorithm 2. We have $G \rangle (p,q) = p!q\{\ell\langle T\rangle.\mathsf{end}\}$: the projection of the recursive body in G is $(p!r)!q\{\ell'\langle T'\rangle.X, \ell''\langle T''\rangle.\mathsf{end}\}$, but there are no exchanges between p and q, so the projection of the recursive definition is end. Were the monitor for p synthesized with $q \in D$, Dependence would detect a dependency: the recursive definition's monitor would be $p!r\{\ell'\langle T'\rangle.p!\{q\}(\ell').X, \ell''\langle T''\rangle.p!\{q\}(\ell'').\mathsf{end}\}$. However, per $G \rangle (p,q)$, p nor q expects a dependency at this point of the protocol. Hence, the algorithm removes q from D when entering the recursive body in G.

Example 11. The monitors of c, s, a in G_a (1) are:

$$M_c := \mathrm{gt2mon}(G_\mathsf{a}, c, \{s,a\})$$
$$= \mu X.c?s \left\{\!\!\left\{ \begin{array}{l} \mathsf{login}\langle\rangle.c!\{a\}(\mathsf{login}).c!a\{\!\{\mathsf{pwd}\langle\mathsf{str}\rangle.c!\emptyset(\mathsf{pwd}).X\}\!\}, \\ \mathsf{quit}\langle\rangle.c!\{a\}(\mathsf{quit}).\mathsf{end} \end{array}\!\!\right\}\!\!\right\}$$

$$M_s := \mathrm{gt2mon}(G_\mathsf{a}, s, \{c,a\})$$
$$= \mu X.s!c \left\{\!\!\left\{ \begin{array}{l} \mathsf{login}\langle\rangle.s!\{a\}(\mathsf{login}).s?a\{\!\{\mathsf{succ}\langle\mathsf{bool}\rangle.s!\emptyset(\mathsf{succ}).X\}\!\}, \\ \mathsf{quit}\langle\rangle.s!\{a\}(\mathsf{quit}).\mathsf{end} \end{array}\!\!\right\}\!\!\right\}$$

$$M_a := \mathrm{gt2mon}(G_\mathsf{a}, a, \{c,s\})$$
$$= \mu X.a?s \left\{\!\!\left\{ \begin{array}{l} \mathsf{login}.a?c \left\{\!\!\left\{ \begin{array}{l} \mathsf{login}.a?c\{\!\{\mathsf{pwd}\langle\mathsf{str}\rangle.a!\emptyset(\mathsf{pwd}). \\ \quad\quad a!s\{\!\{\mathsf{succ}\langle\mathsf{bool}\rangle.a!\emptyset(\mathsf{succ}).X\}\!\}\}\!\}, \\ \mathsf{quit}.\mathsf{error} \end{array}\!\!\right\}\!\!\right\}, \\ \mathsf{quit}.a?c\{\!\{\mathsf{quit}.\mathsf{end}, \mathsf{login}.\mathsf{error}\}\!\} \end{array}\!\!\right\}\!\!\right\}$$

4 Properties of Correct Monitored Blackboxes

Given a global type G, we establish the precise conditions under which a network of monitored blackboxes correctly implements G. That is, we define how the monitored blackbox $\mathcal{P}$ of a participant p of G should behave, i.e., when $\mathcal{P}$ *satisfies* the role of p in G (Satisfaction, Definition 13). We then prove two important properties of networks of monitored blackboxes that satisfy a given global type:

Soundness: The network behaves correctly according to the global type (Theorem 17);

Transparency: The monitors interfere minimally with buffered blackboxes (Theorem 23).

As we will see in Sect. 4.2, satisfaction is exactly the condition under which a network $\mathcal{P}$ is sound with respect to a global type G.

4.1   Satisfaction

Our aim is to attest that $\mathcal{P}$ satisfies the role of p in G if it meets certain conditions on the behavior of monitored blackboxes with respect to the protocol. As we have seen, the role of p in G is determined by projection. Satisfaction is then a relation $\mathcal{R}$ between (i) monitored blackboxes and (ii) maps from participants $q \in \mathrm{part}(G) \setminus \{p\}$ to relative types between p and q, denoted RTs; $\mathcal{R}$ must contain $(\mathcal{P}, \mathtt{RTs})$ with relative projections of G. Given any $(\mathcal{P}', \mathtt{RTs}')$ in $\mathcal{R}$, the general idea of satisfaction is (i) that an output to q by $\mathcal{P}'$ means that $\mathtt{RTs}'(q)$ is a corresponding exchange from p to q, and (ii) that if there is a q such that $\mathtt{RTs}'(q)$ is an exchange from q to p then $\mathcal{P}'$ behaves correctly afterwards.

In satisfaction, dependencies in relative types require care. For example, if $\mathtt{RTs}'(q)$ is an exchange from p to q and $\mathtt{RTs}'(r)$ is a dependency on this exchange, then $\mathcal{P}'$ must first send a label to q and then send *the same label* to r. Hence, we need to track the labels chosen by the monitored blackbox for later reference. To this end, we uniquely identify each exchange in a global type by its *location* $\vec{\ell}$: a sequence of labels denoting the choices leading to the exchange. Projection then uses these locations to annotate each exchange and recursive definition/call in the relative type it produces. Because projection skips independent exchanges (Algorithm 1, line 7), some exchanges and recursive definitions/calls may be associated with multiple locations; hence, they are annotated with *sets* of locations, denoted $\mathbb{L}$. Satisfaction then tracks choices using a map from sets of locations to labels, denoted Lbls. Projection with location annotations is formally defined in [16], along with a corresponding definition for unfolding recursion.

Before defining satisfaction, we set up some useful notation for type signatures, locations, relative types, and maps.

Notation 12. *Let $\boldsymbol{P}$ denote the set of all participants, $\boldsymbol{R}$ the set of all relative types, $\boldsymbol{N}$ the set of all networks, and $\boldsymbol{L}$ the set of all labels.*

Notation $\mathbb{P}(S)$ denotes the powerset of S. Given a set S, we write $\vec{S}$ to denote the set of all sequences of elements from S. We write $\mathbb{L} \sqcap \mathbb{L}'$ to stand for $\mathbb{L} \cap \mathbb{L}' \neq \emptyset$. We write $\mathbb{L} \leq \mathbb{L}'$ if every $\vec{\ell}' \in \mathbb{L}'$ is prefixed by some $\vec{\ell} \in \mathbb{L}$.

In relative types, we write $\Diamond$ to denote either ! or ?. We write $\mathrm{unfold}(R)$ for the inductive unfolding of R if R starts with recursive definitions, and for R itself otherwise. We write $R \triangleq R'$ whenever $\mathrm{unfold}(R) = \mathrm{unfold}(R')$.

We shall use monospaced fonts to denote maps (such as RTs and Lbls). We often define maps using the notation of injective relations. Given a map M, we write $(x, y) \in \mathtt{M}$ to denote that $x \in \mathrm{dom}(\mathtt{M})$ and $\mathtt{M}(x) = y$. We write $\mathtt{M}[x \mapsto y']$ to denote the map obtained by adding to M an entry for x pointing to y', or updating an already existing entry for x. Maps are partial unless stated otherwise.

Definition 13 (Satisfaction). *A relation $\mathcal{R}$ is sat-signed if its signature is $\boldsymbol{N} \times (\boldsymbol{P} \rightarrow \boldsymbol{R}) \times (\mathbb{P}(\vec{\boldsymbol{L}}) \rightarrow \boldsymbol{L})$. We define the following properties of relations:*

- *A sat-signed relation $\mathcal{R}$ holds at p if it satisfies the conditions in Fig. 5.*
- *A sat-signed relation $\mathcal{R}$ progresses at p if for every $(\mathcal{P}, \mathtt{RTs}, \mathtt{Lbls}) \in \mathcal{R}$, we have $\mathcal{P} \xrightarrow{\alpha} \mathcal{P}'$ for some α and $\mathcal{P}'$, given that one of the following holds:*

Given $(\mathcal{P}, \mathtt{RTs}, \mathtt{Lbls}) \in \mathcal{R}$, all the following conditions hold:

1. **(Tau)** If $\mathcal{P} \xrightarrow{\tau} \mathcal{P}'$, then $(\mathcal{P}', \mathtt{RTs}, \mathtt{Lbls}) \in \mathcal{R}$.
2. **(End)** If $\mathcal{P} \xrightarrow{\text{end}} \mathcal{P}'$, then, for every $(q, R) \in \mathtt{RTs}$, $R \doteq \text{end}$, $\mathcal{P}' \not\rightarrow$, and $(\mathcal{P}', \emptyset, \emptyset) \in \mathcal{R}$.
3. **(Output)** If $\mathcal{P} \xrightarrow{p!q(j\langle T_j \rangle)} \mathcal{P}'$, then $\mathtt{RTs}(q) \doteq p!q^{\mathbb{L}}\{\!|i\langle T_i \rangle.R_i|\!\}_{i \in I}$ with $j \in I$, and $(\mathcal{P}', \mathtt{RTs}[q \mapsto R_j], \mathtt{Lbls}[\mathbb{L} \mapsto j]) \in \mathcal{R}$.
4. **(Input)** If there is $(q, R) \in \mathtt{RTs}$ such that $R \doteq q!p^{\mathbb{L}}\{\!|i\langle T_i \rangle.R_i|\!\}_{i \in I}$, then $\mathcal{P} = [\langle p : P : \vec{m} \rangle : M : \vec{n}]$, and, for every $j \in I$,
   $([\langle p : P : \vec{m} \rangle : M : q!p(j\langle T_j \rangle), \vec{n}], \mathtt{RTs}[q \mapsto R_j], \mathtt{Lbls}[\mathbb{L} \mapsto j]) \in \mathcal{R}$.
5. **(Dependency output)** If $\mathcal{P} \xrightarrow{p!q(j)} \mathcal{P}'$, then $\mathtt{RTs}(q) \doteq (p\lozenge r)!q^{\mathbb{L}}\{\!|i.R_i|\!\}_{i \in I}$ with $j \in I$, there is $(\mathbb{L}', j) \in \mathtt{Lbls}$ such that $\mathbb{L}' \pitchfork \mathbb{L}$, and $(\mathcal{P}', \mathtt{RTs}[q \mapsto R_j], \mathtt{Lbls}) \in \mathcal{R}$.
6. **(Dependency input)** If there is $(q, R) \in \mathtt{RTs}$ s.t. $R \doteq (q\lozenge r)!p^{\mathbb{L}}\{\!|i.R_i|\!\}_{i \in I}$, then $\mathcal{P} = [\langle p : P : \vec{m} \rangle : M : \vec{n}]$, and either of the following holds:
   - (Fresh label) there is no $\mathbb{L}' \in \text{dom}(\mathtt{Lbls})$ such that $\mathbb{L}' \pitchfork \mathbb{L}$, and, for every $j \in I$,
     $([\langle p : P : \vec{m} \rangle : M : q!p(j), \vec{n}], \mathtt{RTs}[q \mapsto R_j], \mathtt{Lbls}[\mathbb{L} \mapsto j]) \in \mathcal{R}$;
   - (Known label) there is $(\mathbb{L}', j) \in \mathtt{Lbls}$ such that $\mathbb{L}' \pitchfork \mathbb{L}$ and $j \in I$, and
     $([\langle p : P : \vec{m} \rangle : M : q!p(j), \vec{n}], \mathtt{RTs}[q \mapsto R_j], \mathtt{Lbls}) \in \mathcal{R}$.

Fig. 5. Satisfaction: conditions under which $\mathcal{R}$ holds at p (Definition 13).

- $\mathtt{RTs} \neq \emptyset$ *and, for every* $(q, R) \in \mathtt{RTs}$, $R \doteq \text{end}$;
- *There is* $(q, R) \in \mathtt{RTs}$ *such that (i)* $R \doteq p!q^{\mathbb{L}}\{\!|i\langle T_i \rangle.R_i|\!\}_{i \in I}$ *or* $R \doteq (p\lozenge r)!q^{\mathbb{L}}\{\!|i.R_i|\!\}_{i \in I}$, *and (ii) for every* $(q', R') \in \mathtt{RTs} \setminus \{(q, R)\}$, *either* $R' \doteq \text{end}$ *or* $\text{unfold}(R')$ *has locations* $\mathbb{L}'$ *with* $\mathbb{L} \leq \mathbb{L}'$.
- *A sat-signed relation* $\mathcal{R}$ *is a* satisfaction *at* p *if it holds and progresses at* p.

We write $\mathcal{R} \models^{\mathtt{Lbls}} \mathcal{P} \triangleright \mathtt{RTs} @ p$ *if* $\mathcal{R}$ *is a satisfaction at* p *with* $(\mathcal{P}, \mathtt{RTs}, \mathtt{Lbls}) \in \mathcal{R}$, *and* $\mathcal{R} \models \mathcal{P} \triangleright \mathtt{RTs} @ p$ *when* $\mathtt{Lbls}$ *is empty. We omit* $\mathcal{R}$ *to indicate such* $\mathcal{R}$ *exists.*

Satisfaction requires $\mathcal{R}$ to hold at p: each $(\mathcal{P}, \mathtt{RTs}, \mathtt{Lbls}) \in \mathcal{R}$ enjoys the conditions in Fig. 5, discussed next, which ensure that $\mathcal{P}$ respects the protocols in $\mathtt{RTs}$.

(Tau) allows τ-transitions without affecting $\mathtt{RTs}$ and $\mathtt{Lbls}$. (End) allows an end-transition, given that all relative types in $\mathtt{RTs}$ are end. The resulting state should not transition, enforced by empty $\mathtt{RTs}$ and $\mathtt{Lbls}$.

(Output) allows an output-transition with a message to q, given that $\mathtt{RTs}(q)$ is a corresponding output by p. Then, $\mathtt{RTs}(q)$ updates to the continuation of the appropriate branch and $\mathtt{Lbls}$ records the choice under the locations of $\mathtt{RTs}(q)$.

(Input) triggers when there is $(q, R) \in \mathtt{RTs}$ such that R is a message from q to p. Satisfaction targets the behavior of $\mathcal{P}$ on its own, so we simulate a message sent by q. The resulting behavior is then analyzed after buffering any such message; $\mathtt{RTs}(q)$ is updated to the continuation of the corresponding branch. As for outputs, $\mathtt{Lbls}$ records the choice at the locations of $\mathtt{RTs}(q)$.

(Dependency Output) allows an output-transition with a dependency message to q, given that $\mathtt{RTs}(q)$ is a corresponding dependency output by p with locations $\mathbb{L}$. The message's label should be recorded in $\mathtt{Lbls}$ at some $\mathbb{L}'$ that shares a location with $\mathbb{L}$: here $\mathbb{L}'$ relates to a past exchange between p and some r in G from which the dependency output in $\mathtt{RTs}(q)$ originates. This ensures that the dependency output is preceded by a corresponding exchange, and that the dependency output carries the same label as originally chosen for the preceding exchange. Afterwards, $\text{RTs}(q)$ is updated to the continuation of the appropriate branch.

(Dependency Input) triggers when there is $(q, R) \in \text{RTs}$ such that R is a dependency exchange from q to p, forwarding a label exchanged between q and r. As in the input case, a message from q is simulated by buffering it in $\mathcal{P}$. In this case, $\text{RTs}(r)$ could be a dependency exchange from r to p, originating from the same exchange between q and r in G. To ensure that the buffered messages contain the same label, we distinguish "fresh" and "known" cases. In the fresh case, we consider the first of the possibly two dependency exchanges: there is no $\mathbb{L}' \in \text{dom}(\text{Lbls})$ that shares a location with the locations $\mathbb{L}$ of $\text{RTs}(q)$. Hence, we analyze each possible dependency message, updating $\text{RTs}(q)$ appropriately and recording the choice in Lbls. The known case then considers the second dependency exchange: there is a label in Lbls at $\mathbb{L}'$ that shares a location with $\mathbb{L}$. Hence, we buffer a message with the same label, and update $\text{RTs}(q)$ accordingly.

Satisfaction also requires $\mathcal{R}$ to progress at p, for each $(\mathcal{P}, \text{RTs}, \text{Lbls}) \in \mathcal{R}$ making sure that $\mathcal{P}$ does not idle whenever we are expecting a transition from $\mathcal{P}$. There are two cases. (1) If all relative types in RTs are end, we expect an end-transition. (2) If there is a relative type in RTs that is a (dependency) output, we expect an output transition. However, $\mathcal{P}$ may idle if it is waiting for a message: there is $(q, R) \in \text{RTs}$ such that R is a (dependency) input originating from an exchange in G that precedes the exchange related to the output.

Definition 14 (Satisfaction for Networks). *Let us write* $\text{RTsOf}(G, p)$ *to denote the set* $\{(q, G \rangle (p, q)) \mid q \in \text{part}(G) \setminus \{p\}\}$. *Moreover, we write*

- $\mathcal{R} \vDash [\langle p : P : \varepsilon \rangle : M : \varepsilon] \triangleright G @ p$ *if and only if* $M = \text{gt2mon}(G, p, \text{part}(G) \setminus \{p\})$ *and* $\mathcal{R} \vDash [\langle p : P : \varepsilon \rangle : M : \varepsilon] \triangleright \text{RTsOf}(G, p) @ p$. *We omit* $\mathcal{R}$ *to say such* $\mathcal{R}$ *exists.*
- $\vDash \mathcal{P} \triangleright G$ *if and only if* $\mathcal{P} \equiv \prod_{p \in \text{part}(G)} [\langle p : P_p : \varepsilon \rangle : M_p : \varepsilon]$ *and, for every* $p \in \text{part}(G)$, $\vDash [\langle p : P_p : \varepsilon \rangle : M_p : \varepsilon] \triangleright G @ p$.

Example 15. The following satisfaction assertions hold with implementations, relative types, and monitors from Examples 2 and 6 and 11, respectively:

$$\vDash [\langle c : P_c : \varepsilon \rangle : M_c : \varepsilon] \triangleright \{(s, R_{c,s}), (a, R_{c,a})\} @ c$$
$$\vDash [\langle s : P_s : \varepsilon \rangle : M_s : \varepsilon] \triangleright \{(c, R_{c,s}), (a, R_{s,a})\} @ s$$
$$\vDash [\langle a : P_a : \varepsilon \rangle : M_a : \varepsilon] \triangleright \{(c, R_{c,a}), (s, R_{s,a})\} @ a$$
$$\vDash [\langle c : P_c : \varepsilon \rangle : M_c : \varepsilon] \| [\langle s : P_s : \varepsilon \rangle : M_s : \varepsilon] \| [\langle a : P_a : \varepsilon \rangle : M_a : \varepsilon] \triangleright G_{\mathsf{a}}$$

We also have: $\nvDash [\langle c : P_c : \varepsilon \rangle : \mu X.c?s\{\{\text{quit}\langle\rangle.\text{end}\}\} : \varepsilon] \triangleright G_{\mathsf{a}} @ c$. This is because $R_{c,s}$ specifies that s may send login to c, which this monitor would not accept.

4.2 Soundness

Our *first result* is that satisfaction is sound with respect to global types: when a network of monitored blackboxes satisfies a global type G (Definition 14), any path of transitions eventually reaches a state that satisfies another global type reachable from G. Hence, the satisfaction of the individual components that a network comprises is enough to ensure that the network behaves as specified by the global type. Reachability between global types is defined as an LTS:

Definition 16 (LTS for Global Types). *We define an LTS for global types, denoted $G \xrightarrow{\ell} G'$, by the following rules:*

$$\frac{j \in I}{p!q\{i\langle T_i\rangle.G_i\}_{i\in I} \xrightarrow{j} G_j} \qquad \frac{G\{\mu X.G/X\} \xrightarrow{\ell} G'}{\mu X.G \xrightarrow{\ell} G'}$$

Given $\vec{\ell} = \ell_1, \ldots, \ell_n$, we write $G \xrightarrow{\vec{\ell}} G'$ to denote $G \xrightarrow{\ell_1} \ldots \xrightarrow{\ell_n} G'$.

Theorem 17 (Soundness). *If $\models \mathcal{P} \triangleright G$ (Definition 14) and $\mathcal{P} \Rightarrow \mathcal{P}_0$ then there exist $G', \vec{\ell}, \mathcal{P}'$ such that $G \xrightarrow{\vec{\ell}} G'$, $\mathcal{P}_0 \Rightarrow \mathcal{P}'$, and $\models \mathcal{P}' \triangleright G'$.*

We sketch the proof of Theorem 17 (see [16] for details). We prove a stronger statement that starts from a network $\mathcal{P}$ that satisfies an intermediate G_0 reachable from G. This way, we apply induction on the number of transitions between $\mathcal{P}$ and $\mathcal{P}_0$, relating the transitions of the network to the transitions of G_0 one step at a time by relying on Satisfaction. Hence, we inductively "consume" the transitions between $\mathcal{P}$ and $\mathcal{P}_0$ until we have passed through $\mathcal{P}_0$ and end up in a network satisfying G' reachable from G_0. We use an auxiliary lemma to account for global types with *independent exchanges*, such as $G' = p!q\{\ell\langle T\rangle.r!s\{\ell'\langle T'\rangle.\mathsf{end}\}\}$. In G', the exchange involving (p, q) is unrelated to that involving (r, s), so they occur concurrently in a network implementing G'. Hence, the transitions from $\mathcal{P}$ to $\mathcal{P}_0$ might not follow the order specified in G_0. The lemma ensures that concurrent (i.e., unrelated) transitions always end up in the same state, no matter the order. This way we show transitions from $\mathcal{P}$ in the order specified in G_0, which we restore to the observed order using the lemma when we are done.

Theorem 17 implies that any $\mathcal{P}$ that satisfies some global type is *error free*, i.e., $\mathcal{P}$ never reduces to a network containing error_D (stated and proved formally in the full version of this paper [16]).

4.3   Transparency

The task of monitors is to observe and verify behavior *with minimal interference*: monitors should be *transparent*. Transparency is usually expressed as a bisimulation between a monitored and unmonitored component [1,7,11,22].

Our *second result* is thus a transparency result. For it to be informative, we assume that we observe the (un)monitored blackbox as if it were running in a network of monitored blackboxes that adhere to a given global protocol. This way, we can assume that received messages are correct, such that the monitor does not transition to an error signal. To this end, we enhance the LTS for Networks:

1. As in Satisfaction, we consider (un)monitored blackboxes on their own. Hence, we need a way to simulate messages sent by other participants. Otherwise, a

$$[\text{BUF-MON}] \quad \frac{\alpha = p?q(x), n' = q!p(x) \text{ or } \alpha = p?q(\!(x)\!), n' = q!p(\!(x)\!) \quad \Omega(\alpha) = \Omega'}{[\langle p : P : \vec{m} \rangle : M : \vec{n}] \underset{\Omega}{\overset{\alpha}{\leadsto}}_{\Omega'} [\langle p : P : \vec{m} \rangle : M : n', \vec{n}]}$$

$$[\text{BUF-UNMON}] \quad \frac{\alpha = p?q(x), m' = q!p(x) \text{ or } \alpha = p?q(\!(x)\!), m' = q!p(\!(x)\!) \quad \Omega(\alpha) = \Omega'}{\langle p : P : \vec{m} \rangle \underset{\Omega}{\overset{\alpha}{\leadsto}}_{\Omega'} \langle p : P : m', \vec{m} \rangle}$$

$$[\text{DEP}] \quad \frac{P \xrightarrow{p!q(\!(\ell)\!)} P'}{P \underset{\Omega}{\overset{\tau}{\leadsto}}_{\Omega} P'} \qquad [\text{NO-DEP}] \quad \frac{P \xrightarrow{\alpha} P' \quad \alpha \notin \{p?q(x), p?q(\!(x)\!), p!q(\!(\ell)\!)\} \quad \Omega(\alpha) = \Omega'}{P \underset{\Omega}{\overset{\alpha}{\leadsto}}_{\Omega'} P'}$$

Fig. 6. Enhanced LTS for Networks (Definition 19).

blackbox would get stuck waiting for a message and the bisimulation would hold trivially. We thus add a transition that buffers messages. Similar to Satisfaction (Input) and (Dependency Input), these messages cannot be arbitrary; we parameterize the enhanced LTS by an *oracle* that determines which messages are allowed as stipulated by a given global type.

2. Besides observing and verifying transitions, our monitors additionally send dependency messages. This leads to an asymmetry in the behavior of monitored blackboxes and unmonitored blackboxes, as the latter do not send dependency messages. Hence, we rename dependency output actions to τ.

We now define the enhanced LTS for networks, after setting up some notation.

Notation 18. *Let A denote the set of all actions. Given $\Omega : \mathbb{P}(\vec{A})$, we write $\alpha + \Omega$ to denote the set containing every sequence in Ω prepended with α. We write $\Omega(\alpha) = \Omega'$ iff $\alpha + \Omega' \subseteq \Omega$ and there is no Ω'' such that $\alpha + \Omega' \subset \alpha + \Omega'' \subseteq \Omega$.*

Definition 19 (Enhanced LTS for Networks). *We define an enhanced LTS for Networks, denoted $P \underset{\Omega}{\overset{\alpha}{\leadsto}}_{\Omega'} P'$ where $\Omega, \Omega' : \mathbb{P}(\vec{A})$, by the rules in Fig. 6. We write $P \underset{\Omega}{\Longrightarrow}_{\Omega} P'$ whenever P transitions to P' in zero or more τ-transitions, i.e., $P \underset{\Omega}{\overset{\tau}{\leadsto}}_{\Omega} \cdots \underset{\Omega}{\overset{\tau}{\leadsto}}_{\Omega} P'$. We write $P \underset{\Omega}{\overset{\alpha}{\Longrightarrow}}_{\Omega'} P'$ when $P \underset{\Omega}{\Longrightarrow}_{\Omega} P_1 \underset{\Omega}{\overset{\alpha}{\leadsto}}_{\Omega'} P_2 \underset{\Omega'}{\Longrightarrow}_{\Omega'} P'$, omitting the α-transition when $\alpha = \tau$. Given $\vec{\alpha} = \alpha_1, \ldots, \alpha_n$, we write $P \underset{\Omega_0}{\overset{\vec{\alpha}}{\Longrightarrow}}_{\Omega_n} P'$ when $P \underset{\Omega_0}{\overset{\alpha_1}{\Longrightarrow}}_{\Omega_1} P_1 \cdots P_{n-1} \underset{\Omega_{n-1}}{\overset{\alpha_n}{\Longrightarrow}}_{\Omega_n} P'$.*

Thus, Transitions [BUF-*] simulate messages from other participants, consulting Ω and transforming it into Ω'. Transition [DEP] renames dependency outputs to τ. Transition [NO-DEP] passes any other transitions, updating Ω to Ω' accordingly.

We now define a weak bisimilarity on networks, governed by oracles.

Definition 20 (Bisimilarity). *A relation $\mathcal{B} : N \times \mathbb{P}(\vec{A}) \times N$ is a (weak) bisimulation if, for every $(\mathcal{P}, \Omega, \mathcal{Q}) \in \mathcal{B}$: (1) For every $\mathcal{P}', \alpha, \Omega_1$ such that $\mathcal{P} \underset{\Omega}{\overset{\alpha}{\leadsto}}_{\Omega_1} \mathcal{P}'$, there exist $\vec{b}, \Omega_2, \mathcal{Q}', \mathcal{P}''$ such that $\mathcal{Q} \underset{\Omega}{\overset{\vec{b},\alpha}{\Longrightarrow}}_{\Omega_2} \mathcal{Q}', \mathcal{P}' \underset{\Omega_1}{\overset{\vec{b}}{\Longrightarrow}}_{\Omega_2} \mathcal{P}''$, and $(\mathcal{P}'', \Omega_2, \mathcal{Q}') \in \mathcal{B}$; and (2) The symmetric analog.*

We say $\mathcal{P}$ and $\mathcal{Q}$ are bisimilar with respect to Ω, denoted $\mathcal{P} \approx_\Omega \mathcal{Q}$, if there exists a bisimulation $\mathcal{B}$ such that $(\mathcal{P}, \Omega, \mathcal{Q}) \in \mathcal{B}$.

To improve readability, below we write '$\bigcup[x \in S \ldots]$' instead of '$\bigcup_{x \in S \ldots}$'.

$$\bigcup[(q, R) \in \mathtt{RTs}.\ R \doteq p!q^{\mathbb{L}}\{\!|i\langle T_i\rangle.R_i|\!\}_{i \in I}] \bigcup[j \in I]$$
$$p!q(j\langle T_j\rangle) + \mathtt{LO}(p, \mathtt{RTs}[q \mapsto R_j], \mathtt{Lbls}[\mathbb{L} \mapsto j]) \qquad\qquad \text{(Output)}$$

$$\cup \bigcup[(q, R) \in \mathtt{RTs}.\ R \doteq q!p^{\mathbb{L}}\{\!|i\langle T_i\rangle.R_i|\!\}_{i \in I}] \bigcup[j \in I]$$
$$p?q(j\langle T_j\rangle) + \mathtt{LO}(p, \mathtt{RTs}[q \mapsto R_j], \mathtt{Lbls}[\mathbb{L} \mapsto j]) \qquad\qquad \text{(Input)}$$

$$\cup \bigcup[(q, R) \in \mathtt{RTs}.\ R \doteq (q\Diamond r)!p^{\mathbb{L}}\{\!|i.R_i|\!\}_{i \in I} \wedge \not\exists \mathbb{L}' \in \mathrm{dom}(\mathtt{Lbls}).\ \mathbb{L}' \between \mathbb{L}] \bigcup[j \in I]$$
$$p?q(j) + \mathtt{LO}(p, \mathtt{RTs}[q \mapsto R_j], \mathtt{Lbls}[\mathbb{L} \mapsto j]) \qquad\quad \text{(Fresh Dependency Input)}$$

$$\cup \bigcup[(q, R) \in \mathtt{RTs}.\ R \doteq (q\Diamond r)!p^{\mathbb{L}}\{\!|i.R_i|\!\}_{i \in I} \wedge \exists(\mathbb{L}', j) \in \mathtt{Lbls}.\ \mathbb{L}' \between \mathbb{L} \wedge j \in I]$$
$$p?q(j) + \mathtt{LO}(p, \mathtt{RTs}[q \mapsto R_j], \mathtt{Lbls}) \qquad\qquad \text{(Known Dependency Input)}$$

$$\cup \bigcup[(q, R) \in \mathtt{RTs}.\ R \doteq (p\Diamond r)!q^{\mathbb{L}}\{\!|i.R_i|\!\}_{i \in I} \wedge \exists(\mathbb{L}', j) \in \mathtt{Lbls}.\ \mathbb{L}' \between \mathbb{L} \wedge j \in I]$$
$$\mathtt{LO}(p, \mathtt{RTs}[q \mapsto R_j], \mathtt{Lbls}) \qquad\qquad \text{(Dependency Output)}$$

$$\cup\ \mathtt{end} + \mathtt{LO}(p, \emptyset, \emptyset) \quad [\text{only if } \forall(q, R) \in \mathtt{RTs}.\ R \doteq \mathtt{end}] \qquad\qquad \text{(End)}$$

$$\cup\ \tau + \mathtt{LO}(p, \mathtt{RTs}, \mathtt{Lbls}) \qquad\qquad \text{(Tau)}$$

Fig. 7. Definition of the Label Oracle (Definition 21), $\mathtt{LO}(p, \mathtt{RTs}, \mathtt{Lbls})$.

Clause 1 says that $\mathcal{Q}$ can mimic a transition from $\mathcal{P}$ to $\mathcal{P}'$, possibly after τ- and [BUF]-transitions. We then allow $\mathcal{P}'$ to "catch up" on those additional transitions, after which the results are bisimilar (under a new oracle); Clause 2 is symmetric. Additional [BUF]-transitions are necessary: an unmonitored blackbox can read messages from its buffer directly, whereas a monitor may need to move messages between buffers first. If the monitor first needs to move messages that are not in its buffer yet, we need to add those messages with [BUF]-transitions. The unmonitored blackbox then needs to catch up on those additional messages.

Similar to Soundness, Satisfaction defines the conditions under which we prove transparency of monitors. Moreover, we need to define the precise oracle under which bisimilarity holds. This oracle is defined similarly to Satisfaction: it depends on actions observed, relative types (in $\mathtt{RTs}$), and prior choices (in $\mathtt{Lbls}$).

Definition 21 (Label Oracle). *The* label oracle *of participant p under $\mathtt{RTs} : P \to R$ and $\mathtt{Lbls} : \mathbb{P}(\vec{L}) \to L$, denoted $LO(p, \mathtt{RTs}, \mathtt{Lbls})$ is defined in Fig. 7.*

The label oracle $\mathtt{LO}(p, \mathtt{RTs}, \mathtt{Lbls})$ thus consists of several subsets, each resembling a condition of Satisfaction in Fig. 5. Dependency outputs are exempt: the Enhanced LTS for Networks renames them to τ, so the label oracle simply looks past them without requiring a dependency output action.

We now state our transparency result, after defining a final requirement: minimality of satisfaction. This allows us to step backward through satisfaction relations, such that we can reason about buffered messages.

Definition 22 (Minimal Satisfaction). *We write $\vdash \mathcal{P} \triangleright G @ p$ whenever there exists $\mathcal{R}$ such that $\mathcal{R} \vDash \mathcal{P} \triangleright RTsOf(G, p) @ p$ (Definition 13) and $\mathcal{R}$ is minimal, i.e., there is no $\mathcal{R}' \subset \mathcal{R}$ such that $\mathcal{R}' \vDash \mathcal{P} \triangleright RTsOf(G, p) @ p$.*

Theorem 23 (Transparency). *Suppose* $\vdash [\langle p{:}P{:}\varepsilon\rangle{:}M{:}\varepsilon]\triangleright G@p$ *(Definition 22).* *Let* $\Omega := \mathit{LO}(p, \mathit{RTsOf}(G,p), \emptyset)$. *Then* $[\langle p : P : \varepsilon\rangle : M : \varepsilon] \approx_\Omega \langle p : P : \varepsilon\rangle$.

We sketch the proof of Theorem 23 (see [16]). The minimal satisfaction of the monitored blackbox contains all states that the monitored blackbox can reach through transitions. We create a relation $\mathcal{B}$ by pairing each such state $[\langle p{:}P'{:}\vec{m}\rangle{:}M'{:}\vec{n}]$ with $\langle p{:}P'{:}\vec{n}, \vec{m}\rangle$—notice how the buffers are combined. We do so while keeping an informative relation between relative types, monitors, buffers, and oracles. This information gives us the appropriate oracles to include in $\mathcal{B}$. We then show that $\mathcal{B}$ is a weak bisimulation by proving that the initial monitored and unmonitored blackbox are in $\mathcal{B}$, and that the conditions of Definition 20 hold. While Clause 1 is straightforward, Clause 2 requires care: by using the relation between relative types, monitors, and buffers, we infer the shape of the monitor from a transition of the unmonitored blackbox. This allows us to show that the monitored blackbox can mimic the transition, possibly after outputting dependencies and/or receiving additional messages (as discussed above).

We close by comparing our Theorems 17 and 23 with Bocchi *et al.*'s safety and transparency results [7], respectively. First, their safety result [7, Thm. 5.2] guarantees satisfaction instead of assuming it; their framework suppresses unexpected messages, which prevents the informative guarantee given by our Theorem 17. Second, Theorem 23 and their transparency result [7, Thm. 6.1] differ, among other things, in the presence of an oracle, which is not needed in their setting: they can inspect the inputs of monitored processes, whereas we cannot verify the inputs of a blackbox without actually sending messages to it.

5 Conclusion

We have proposed a new framework for dynamically analyzing networks of communicating components (blackboxes), governed by global types, with minimal assumptions about observable behavior. We use global types and relative projection [15] to synthesize monitors, and define when a monitored component satisfies the governing protocol. We prove that networks of correct monitored components are sound with respect to a global type, and that monitors are transparent.

We have implemented a practical toolkit, called RelaMon, based on the framework presented here. RelaMon allows users to deploy JavaScript programs that monitor web-applications in any programming language and with third-party/closed-source components according to a global type. The toolkit is publicly available [10] and includes implementations of our running example (the global type G_a), as well as an example that incorporates a closed-source weather API.

As future work, we plan to extend our framework to uniformly analyze systems combining monitored blackboxes and statically checked components (following [15]). We also plan to study under which restrictions our approach coincides with Bocchi *et al.*'s [7].

Acknowledgments. We are grateful to the anonymous reviewers for useful remarks.

References

1. Aceto, L., Cassar, I., Francalanza, A., Ingólfsdóttir, A.: On runtime enforcement via suppressions. In: Schewe, S., Zhang, L. (eds.) 29th International Conference on Concurrency Theory (CONCUR 2018). Leibniz International Proceedings in Informatics (LIPIcs), vol. 118, pp. 34:1–34:17. Schloss Dagstuhl–Leibniz-Zentrum fuer Informatik, Dagstuhl, Germany (2018). https://doi.org/10.4230/LIPIcs.CONCUR.2018.34
2. Bartocci, E., Falcone, Y., Francalanza, A., Reger, G.: Introduction to runtime verification. In: Bartocci, E., Falcone, Y. (eds.) Lectures on Runtime Verification. LNCS, vol. 10457, pp. 1–33. Springer, Cham (2018). https://doi.org/10.1007/978-3-319-75632-5_1
3. Bartolo Burlò, C., Francalanza, A., Scalas, A.: On the monitorability of session types, in theory and practice. In: Møller, A., Sridharan, M. (eds.) 35th European Conference on Object-Oriented Programming (ECOOP 2021). Leibniz International Proceedings in Informatics (LIPIcs), vol. 194, pp. 20:1–20:30. Schloss Dagstuhl – Leibniz-Zentrum für Informatik, Dagstuhl, Germany (2021). https://doi.org/10.4230/LIPIcs.ECOOP.2021.20
4. Bartolo Burlò, C., Francalanza, A., Scalas, A., Trubiani, C., Tuosto, E.: Towards probabilistic session-type monitoring. In: Damiani, F., Dardha, O. (eds.) COORDINATION 2021. LNCS, vol. 12717, pp. 106–120. Springer, Cham (2021). https://doi.org/10.1007/978-3-030-78142-2_7
5. Bartolo Burlò, C., Francalanza, A., Scalas, A., Trubiani, C., Tuosto, E.: PSTMonitor: monitor synthesis from probabilistic session types. Sci. Comput. Program. **222**, 102847 (2022). https://doi.org/10.1016/j.scico.2022.102847
6. Bocchi, L., Chen, T.-C., Demangeon, R., Honda, K., Yoshida, N.: Monitoring networks through multiparty session types. In: Beyer, D., Boreale, M. (eds.) FMOODS/FORTE -2013. LNCS, vol. 7892, pp. 50–65. Springer, Heidelberg (2013). https://doi.org/10.1007/978-3-642-38592-6_5
7. Bocchi, L., Chen, T.C., Demangeon, R., Honda, K., Yoshida, N.: Monitoring networks through multiparty session types. Theor. Comput. Sci. **669**, 33–58 (2017). https://doi.org/10.1016/j.tcs.2017.02.009
8. Castagna, G., Dezani-Ciancaglini, M., Padovani, L.: On global types and multiparty session. Logical Methods Comput. Sci. **8**(1) (2012). https://doi.org/10.2168/LMCS-8(1:24)2012
9. Chen, T.-C., Bocchi, L., Deniélou, P.-M., Honda, K., Yoshida, N.: Asynchronous distributed monitoring for multiparty session enforcement. In: Bruni, R., Sassone, V. (eds.) TGC 2011. LNCS, vol. 7173, pp. 25–45. Springer, Heidelberg (2012). https://doi.org/10.1007/978-3-642-30065-3_2
10. Dobre, R.A., Heuvelvan den Heuvel, B., Pérez, J.A.: RelaMon: a JS toolkit for the runtime verification of web applications written in any language (2023). https://github.com/basvdheuvel/RelaMon. Accessed June 2023
11. Falcone, Y., Fernandez, J.C., Mounier, L.: What can you verify and enforce at runtime? Int. J. Softw. Tools Technol. Transfer **14**(3), 349–382 (2012). https://doi.org/10.1007/s10009-011-0196-8
12. Francalanza, A., Pérez, J.A., Sánchez, C.: Runtime verification for decentralised and distributed systems. In: Bartocci, E., Falcone, Y. (eds.) Lectures on Runtime

Verification. LNCS, vol. 10457, pp. 176–210. Springer, Cham (2018). https://doi. org/10.1007/978-3-319-75632-5_6

13. Gommerstadt, H., Jia, L., Pfenning, F.: Session-typed concurrent contracts. In: Ahmed, A. (ed.) ESOP 2018. LNCS, vol. 10801, pp. 771–798. Springer, Cham (2018). https://doi.org/10.1007/978-3-319-89884-1_27

14. Gommerstadt, H., Jia, L., Pfenning, F.: Session-typed concurrent contracts. J. Logical Algebraic Methods Program. **124**, 100731 (2022). https://doi.org/10.1016/j. jlamp.2021.100731

15. Van den Heuvel, B., Pérez, J.A.: A decentralized analysis of multiparty protocols. Sci. Comput. Program. 102840 (2022). https://doi.org/10.1016/j.scico.2022.102840

16. Van den Heuvel, B., Pérez, J.A., Dobre, R.A.: Monitoring blackbox implementations of multiparty session protocols (2023). https://doi.org/10.48550/arXiv.2306. 04204

17. Honda, K., Yoshida, N., Carbone, M.: Multiparty asynchronous session types. In: Proceedings of the 35th Annual ACM SIGPLAN-SIGACT Symposium on Principles of Programming Languages, POPL 2008, San Francisco, California, USA, pp. 273–284. Association for Computing Machinery (2008). https://doi.org/10.1145/ 1328438.1328472

18. Honda, K., Yoshida, N., Carbone, M.: Multiparty asynchronous session types. J. ACM **63**(1) (2016). https://doi.org/10.1145/2827695

19. Igarashi, A., Thiemann, P., Tsuda, Y., Vasconcelos, V.T., Wadler, P.: Gradual session types. J. Funct. Program. **29**, e17 (2019/ed). https://doi.org/10.1017/ S0956796819000169

20. Igarashi, A., Thiemann, P., Vasconcelos, V.T., Wadler, P.: Gradual session types. Proc. ACM Program. Lang. **1**(ICFP), 38:1–38:28 (2017). https://doi.org/10.1145/ 3110282

21. Jia, L., Gommerstadt, H., Pfenning, F.: Monitors and blame assignment for higher-order session types. In: Proceedings of the 43rd Annual ACM SIGPLAN-SIGACT Symposium on Principles of Programming Languages, POPL 2016, pp. 582–594. ACM, New York (2016). https://doi.org/10.1145/2837614.2837662

22. Ligatti, J., Bauer, L., Walker, D.: Edit automata: enforcement mechanisms for run-time security policies. Int. J. Inf. Secur. **4**(1), 2–16 (2005). https://doi.org/10. 1007/s10207-004-0046-8

23. Scalas, A., Yoshida, N.: Less is more: multiparty session types revisited. Proc. ACM Program. Lang. **3**(POPL), 30:1–30:29 (2019). https://doi.org/10.1145/3290343. Revised, extended version at https://www.doc.ic.ac.uk/research/technicalreports/ 2018/DTRS18-6.pdf

24. Thiemann, P.: Session types with gradual typing. In: Maffei, M., Tuosto, E. (eds.) TGC 2014. LNCS, vol. 8902, pp. 144–158. Springer, Heidelberg (2014). https:// doi.org/10.1007/978-3-662-45917-1_10

Mining Specification Parameters for Multi-class Classification

Edgar A. Aguilar[1], Ezio Bartocci[2], Cristinel Mateis[1],
Eleonora Nesterini[1,2](✉), and Dejan Ničković[1]

[1] AIT Austrian Institute of Technology, Vienna, Austria
{cristinel.mateis,dejan.nickovic}@ait.ac.at
[2] TU Wien, Vienna, Austria
{ezio.bartocci,eleonora.nesterini}@tuwien.ac.at

Abstract. We present a method for mining parameters of temporal specifications for signal classification. Given a parametric formula and a set of labeled traces, we find one parameter valuation for each class and use it to instantiate the specification template. The resulting formula characterizes the signals in a class by discriminating them from signals of other classes. We propose a two-step approach: first, for each class, we approximate its validity domain, which is the region of the valuations that render the formula satisfied. Second, we select from each validity domain the valuation that maximizes the distance from the validity domain of other classes. We provide a statistical guarantee that the selected parameter valuation is at a bounded distance from being optimal. Finally, we validate our approach on three case studies from different application domains.

Keywords: Specification mining · Signal Temporal Logic · Cyber-physical systems

1 Introduction

Formal specifications are crucial during system design, verification, and operation. They allow a precise and unambiguous exchange of requirements between engineering teams, enable rigorous verification of critical system components, and translate into test oracles and runtime monitors during system execution.

Cyber-physical systems (CPS) include physical parts whose properties are only partially known at design time. Generally, an engineer may expect a system to act a certain way without knowing the exact numerical values that characterize the system's behavior. For instance, an engineer may know that the system response to a step input is an overshoot while being unaware of its delay from

This work has received funding from the European Union's Horizon 2020 research and innovation programme under grant agreement No 956123 and it is partially funded by the TU Wien-funded Doctoral College for SecInt: Secure and Intelligent Human-Centric Digital Technologies.

P. Katsaros and L. Nenzi (Eds.): RV 2023, LNCS 14245, pp. 86–105, 2023.
https://doi.org/10.1007/978-3-031-44267-4_5

the input or its amplitude. We can express this partial knowledge about the intended property using a parameterized specification template. Characterizing the actual parameters is a challenging task that requires the help of an automated tool.

Related Work. Specification mining [3] is an emerging area of research in the field of CPS motivated by the need to analyze and explain the massive amount of data gathered from these systems while interacting with the environment. The vast majority of the available approaches employ Signal Temporal Logic (STL) [14] as the formal specification language for mining requirements in CPS [5,19]. Parametric Signal Temporal Logic (PSTL) [1] is a parametric extension of STL in which parameters replace both threshold constants in numerical predicates and time bounds in temporal operators. Some works address the problem of learning the optimal parameters for a given candidate template formula [1,2,10], while others learn both the structure and the parameters [5,6,11,16]. These approaches focus on learning an STL formula using only positive examples of trajectories [11] or positive and negative examples [2,16].

In this paper, we broaden the applicability of STL specification mining to the multi-class classification problem: we aim to find the set of parameters for given PSTL template formulas that can discriminate multiple classes of trajectories. We assume a set of labeled traces and characterize each class of traces with an STL formula. A final classifier leverages STL quantitative semantics to evaluate how robustly a trace satisfies/violates each specification and consequently predicts the trace's label. Recently, also other papers [13,15] considered a similar task. However, both works limit the space of mined specifications to STL fragments, reducing the resulting expressiveness. Moreover, they are both template-free methods; namely, they mine both the formula template and its numerical predicates. Such an approach is a double-edged sword: on the one hand, template-free methods do not require prior knowledge, but, on the other hand, they do not allow embedding information in the procedure and thus steer the search toward specific properties that are relevant in a particular application. Conversely, we aim to tackle the complementary task of mining parameters without any restrictions on STL grammar.

Our Contribution. In this paper, we propose a family of methods for mining PSTL parameters for multi-class classification. We assume a PSTL template associated with each labeled class of signals and choose the parameters in each template to maximize discrimination from the signals with the other labels. We devise a two-step approach to this problem. For each labeled class of signals, we first approximate two validity domains, one for the signals belonging to that class and one for all other signals. The *validity domain* is the region of the parameter space that instantiates satisfied specifications from a given template. In the second step, we select a parameter instantiation within the first validity domain and maximize its distance from the other one. We return both the set of instantiated STL specifications (one for each class) and a classifier that combines them. The former helps gain insights into what discriminates one class from the others. At the same time, the latter is essential to performing the classification task and, in particular, to classifying new unlabeled traces.

One of the main advantages of the proposed methods is that they do not require any assumptions regarding the monotonicity of parameters. Monotonicity is a common restriction in the specification mining literature because it significantly simplifies the geometry of the resulting validity domains and thus leads to a much more tractable problem. Additionally, we show that our selection of parameter valuations has a statistical guarantee of being optimal. We implement our approach in a publicly available prototype tool and evaluate it on three case studies from different application domains.

2 Preliminaries

A *time series* $\boldsymbol{x} = (t_1, x_1), (t_2, x_2), \ldots, (t_l, x_l)$ is a finite sequence of (time, value) pairs, where $t_1 = 0$, $t_i < t_{i+1}$ for every $i \in \{1, \ldots, l-1\}$, and $x_i \in \mathbb{R}^k$ is a vector of real values. We denote by $|\boldsymbol{x}| = l$ the length of $\boldsymbol{x}$. We will abuse notation, and also denote by $\boldsymbol{x}$ the signal $\mathbb{R}_{\geq 0} \to \mathbb{R}^k$, such that $\boldsymbol{x}(t) = x_i$ if $t \in [t_i, t_{i+1})$ with $i < l$, or $\boldsymbol{x}(t) = x_l$ if $t \geq t_l$.

The distance between a point $\boldsymbol{v} \in \mathbb{R}^k$ and a (non-empty) set $\mathcal{Q} \subset \mathbb{R}^k$ is defined as:

$$d(\boldsymbol{v}, \mathcal{Q}) = \inf\{\|\boldsymbol{v} - \boldsymbol{q}\| \mid \boldsymbol{q} \in \mathcal{Q}\}, \quad (1)$$

where $\|\cdot\|$ is the Euclidean norm in $\mathbb{R}^k$. To compute the distance from one set to another, we consider the so-called *directed Hausdorff distance* defined by:

$$D(\mathcal{V}, \mathcal{Q}) = \sup\{d(\boldsymbol{v}, \mathcal{Q}) \mid \boldsymbol{v} \in \mathcal{V}\}. \quad (2)$$

We observe that function D is not a proper distance because it is not necessarily symmetric. Intuitively, the function computes the longest distance from a point in $\mathcal{V}$ and its closest point in $\mathcal{Q}$. Figure 1 depicts how function D works and how it is related to the Hausdorff distance.

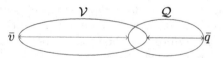

Fig. 1. The Hausdorff distance D_H between sets $\mathcal{V}$ and $\mathcal{Q}$ is defined as: $D_H(\mathcal{V}, \mathcal{Q}) := \max\{D(\mathcal{V}, \mathcal{Q}), D(\mathcal{Q}, \mathcal{V})\}$. In the above example, $D(\mathcal{V}, \mathcal{Q}) = d(\bar{v}, \mathcal{Q})$, $D(\mathcal{Q}, \mathcal{V}) = d(\bar{q}, \mathcal{V})$, and $D_H(\mathcal{V}, \mathcal{Q}) = D(\mathcal{V}, \mathcal{Q})$.

Signal Temporal Logic (STL) [14] is a specification language used to express continuous temporal properties over real-valued signals. The syntax of STL is given by the grammar:

$$\varphi := \mathbf{true} \mid f(\boldsymbol{x}) > 0 \mid \neg\varphi \mid \varphi_1 \wedge \varphi_2 \mid \varphi_1 \, \mathbf{U}_I \, \varphi_2$$

where **true** is the Boolean true constant, $f(\boldsymbol{x}) > 0$ is an atomic proposition with $f \colon \mathbb{R}^k \to \mathbb{R}$, $\neg$ is the Boolean negation, $\wedge$ is the Boolean conjunction, and $\mathbf{U}_I$ is the *until* operator defined over the interval I in $\mathbb{R}_{\geq 0}$. The interval I is generally omitted if $I = [0, \infty)$. The *finally* $\mathbf{F}$ and *globally* $\mathbf{G}$ operators can be derived as follows: $\mathbf{F}_I\varphi := \mathbf{true}\,\mathbf{U}_I\varphi$ and $\mathbf{G}_I\varphi := \neg\mathbf{F}_I\neg\varphi$.

The quantitative semantics of STL [7] is defined in terms of the *robustness function* ρ that has as arguments: the STL specification φ, the signal $\boldsymbol{x}$ and the time t. The value $\rho(\varphi, \boldsymbol{x}, t)$ is defined inductively as follows:

$$\rho(\mathbf{true}, \boldsymbol{x}, t) = +\infty$$

$$\rho(f(\boldsymbol{x}) > 0, \boldsymbol{x}, t) = f(\boldsymbol{x}(t))$$

$$\rho(\neg\varphi, \boldsymbol{x}, t) = -\rho(\varphi, \boldsymbol{x}, t)$$

$$\rho(\varphi_1 \wedge \varphi_2, \boldsymbol{x}, t) = \min\left(\rho(\varphi_1, \boldsymbol{x}, t), \rho(\varphi_2, \boldsymbol{x}, t)\right)$$

$$\rho(\varphi_1 \, \mathbf{U}_I \, \varphi_2, \boldsymbol{x}, t) = \sup_{t' \in t \oplus I} \left(\min\left(\rho(\varphi_2, \boldsymbol{x}, t'), \inf_{t'' \in (t, t')} (\rho(\varphi_1, \boldsymbol{x}, t''))\right)\right)$$

where $\oplus$ denotes the Minkowski sum. We indicate $\rho(\varphi, \boldsymbol{x}, 0)$ by $\rho(\varphi; \boldsymbol{x})$. The STL quantitative semantics is *sound*, i.e., when $\rho(\varphi, \boldsymbol{x}, t) > 0$ the signal $\boldsymbol{x}$ satisfies φ, while when $\rho(\varphi, \boldsymbol{x}, t) < 0$ it violates it.

A *PSTL template* is an STL formula where some temporal or magnitude values are replaced by parameter symbols [1]. If m is the number of different parameter symbols in a PSTL formula, we indicate by $P = \{p_1, \ldots, p_m\}$ the set of parameter symbols and with $\mathcal{W}$ the *parameter space*, that is the set of values that parameter symbols may assume. In our case, $\mathcal{W}$ is a closed hyperbox in $\mathbb{R}^m$:

$$\mathcal{W} = \prod_{i=1}^{m} [a_i, b_i], \tag{3}$$

where, for every $i \in \{1, \ldots, m\}$, a_i and b_i are scalar values in $\mathbb{R}$ and $b_i > a_i$. A *parameter valuation* $\boldsymbol{v} \in \mathcal{W}$ maps a PSTL formula φ into the STL formula φ_v obtained from φ by replacing its parameter symbols with $\boldsymbol{v}$. For example, given the template $\varphi = \mathbf{G}_{[T_1, T_2]}(x \geq k)$, where T_1 and T_2 are temporal parameters and k is a magnitude parameter, if $\boldsymbol{v} = (0, 2, 3.5)$, then the resulting STL formula φ_v is $\varphi_v = \mathbf{G}_{[0,2]}(x \geq 3.5)$. With a little abuse of notation, we will occasionally write that a signal $\boldsymbol{x}$ satisfies/violates a parameter valuation $\boldsymbol{v}$ to mean that $\boldsymbol{x}$ satisfies/violates the specification φ_v.

Given a signal $\boldsymbol{x}$ and a PSTL formula φ, the *validity domain* $\mathcal{V}(\boldsymbol{x}, \varphi) \subseteq \mathcal{W}$ is defined as the set of all parameter valuations $\boldsymbol{v}$ that generate STL formulas φ_v satisfied by the signal $\boldsymbol{x}$. In the example, if the signal $\boldsymbol{x}$ satisfies $\varphi_v = \mathbf{G}_{[0,2]}(x \geq 3.5)$, then $\boldsymbol{v} \in \mathcal{V}(\boldsymbol{x}, \varphi)$. The validity domain of a finite set $\mathcal{S}$ of signals corresponds to the intersection of all validity domains of signals in the set $\mathcal{S}$. In other words, $\boldsymbol{v} \in \mathcal{V}(\mathcal{S}, \varphi)$ if and only if φ_v is satisfied by all signals in $\mathcal{S}$.

3   Problem Description

Hypotheses. We assume that two classes of time-series are given: $\mathcal{S}_1$ and $\mathcal{S}_2$. The restriction to two classes is for the sake of a simpler description: in Sect. 4.3, we show how the proposed method is extended to an arbitrary number of classes. In addition, the user provides a PSTL template for each class of signals. We first assume the template φ is the same for both classes and then, in Sect. 4.2, we present the generalization to different templates. Finally, we assume that the lower/upper bounds on parameter values are available, so the values of a_i and b_i in Eq. (3) are known for all $i = 1, \ldots, m$.

Goal. Our goal is to discriminate classes $\mathcal{S}_1$ and $\mathcal{S}_2$ using formula φ. To do so, we need to find two parameters valuations $\boldsymbol{v}_1^*$ and $\boldsymbol{v}_2^*$ for φ such that they characterize the two sets of time series and *best* discriminate between them, where *best* refers to the following optimality criteria. We denote by $\mathcal{V}_i$ the validity domain $\mathcal{V}(\mathcal{S}_i, \varphi)$ of class $\mathcal{S}_i$ with respect to φ whenever φ is clear from the context.

Definition 1. *An optimal parameter valuation $\boldsymbol{v}_1^*$ for $\mathcal{S}_1$ with respect to $\mathcal{S}_2$ is such that (i) $\boldsymbol{v}_1^* \in \mathcal{V}_1$, and (ii) $d(\boldsymbol{v}, \mathcal{V}_2) \leq d(\boldsymbol{v}_1^*, \mathcal{V}_2)$ for all $\boldsymbol{v} \in \mathcal{V}_1$, where d is the point-set distance defined in (1).*

The first condition ensures that all time series in $\mathcal{S}_1$ satisfy the STL formula $\varphi_{\boldsymbol{v}_1^*}$, while the second one forces $\boldsymbol{v}_1^*$ to be the point in $\mathcal{V}_1$ that is the *furthest* from the other class satisfaction region. In other words, the first condition makes $\varphi_{\boldsymbol{v}_1^*}$ a characterization of time series in $\mathcal{S}_1$, while the second condition renders $\varphi_{\boldsymbol{v}_1^*}$ one of the *best* instantiations of φ for discriminating $\mathcal{S}_1$ from $\mathcal{S}_2$ (the optimal point is not necessarily unique). The definition of $\boldsymbol{v}_2^*$ for $\mathcal{S}_2$ is analogous.

In some extreme cases, we observe that the given definition of an optimal point is meaningless because the Hausdorff distance between the two validity domains is zero (for example, if the two validity domains are identical or one validity domain is a subset of the other). This eventuality may happen when the template φ is not suitable for discriminating the two classes; in this case, there is no choice of the parameter valuations that would help with the classification. The only reasonable possibility is that the user changes the PSTL template. Section 5 shows an example of this instance.

Once our procedure identifies the parameter valuations, we need to perform the classification. We remind that the validity domain of a class is the intersection of the validity domains of all signals belonging to that class. It follows that a signal $\boldsymbol{x}$ belonging to $\mathcal{S}_2$ does not necessarily violate $\varphi_{\boldsymbol{v}}$ with $\boldsymbol{v} \in \mathcal{V}_1 \setminus \mathcal{V}_2$. As a consequence, it may happen that $\boldsymbol{x}$ satisfies both $\varphi_{\boldsymbol{v}_1^*}$ and $\varphi_{\boldsymbol{v}_2^*}$. Hence, we cannot simply use the Boolean satisfaction of $\varphi_{\boldsymbol{v}_1^*}$ and $\varphi_{\boldsymbol{v}_2^*}$ to predict the signal's label. For this reason, we use the quantitative semantics of STL and classify a signal $\boldsymbol{x}$ in class 1 if $\rho(\varphi_{\boldsymbol{v}_1^*}; \boldsymbol{x}) \geq \rho(\varphi_{\boldsymbol{v}_2^*}; \boldsymbol{x})$ and in class 2 otherwise, being ρ the robustness function defined in Sect. 2.

4 Our Approach

We propose a two-step approach to address the problem of Sect. 3: for each class, we compute (i) an over-approximation $\hat{\mathcal{V}}$ of its validity domain $\mathcal{V}$, and (ii) an approximation of the *optimal* point in the validity domain. For the approximation of the validity domains, we divide the parameter space $\mathcal{W}$ into a lattice of cells. We present two methods: one in which the cell resolution is fixed and one in which it is adaptive. We first consider the case in which the same PSTL template is associated with the two different classes of signals (Sect. 4.1). Then, we extend our approach to allow two different PSTL templates (Sect. 4.2) and an arbitrary number of classes (Sect. 4.3). The proofs are shown in the Appendix.

4.1 Binary Satisfaction

Algorithm 1: Validity domain approximation with *FixedBin*
Input: PSTL template φ, set of signals $\mathcal{S}$, parameter space $\mathcal{W}$, number of trials N
Output: Approximated validity domain $\hat{\mathcal{V}}$
1 $\hat{\mathcal{V}} \leftarrow \emptyset$
2 $\mathcal{C} \leftarrow$ cell_partition($\mathcal{W}$)
3 **foreach** $C \in \mathcal{C}$ **do**
4   **for** $i = 1, \ldots, N$ **do**
5          $v \leftarrow$ uniform(C)
6   flag $\leftarrow$ true
7   **foreach** $x \in \mathcal{S}$ **do**
8   **if** $x \not\models \varphi_v$ **then**
9   flag $\leftarrow$ false
10   break
11   **if** flag **then**
12              $\hat{\mathcal{V}} \leftarrow \hat{\mathcal{V}} \cup C$
13   break
14 **return** $\hat{\mathcal{V}}$

Algorithm 2: Validity domain approximation using *AdaBin*.
Input: PSTL template φ, set of signals $\mathcal{S}$, cell C, approx. validity domain $\hat{\mathcal{V}}$, # trials N, threshold on the concentration of satisfied parameter valuation h
Output: New approximation for $\hat{\mathcal{V}}$
1 counter $\leftarrow 0$
2 **for** $i = 1, \ldots, N$ **do**
3      $v \leftarrow$ uniform(C)
4   flag $\leftarrow$ true
5   **foreach** $x \in \mathcal{S}$ **do**
6   **if** $x \not\models \varphi_v$ **then**
7   flag $\leftarrow$ false
8   break
9   **if** flag **then** counter $\leftarrow$ counter $+1$
10 **if** $\frac{\text{counter}}{N} \geq h$ **then return** $\hat{\mathcal{V}} \cup C$
11 **else if** counter $= 0$ **then return** $\hat{\mathcal{V}}$
12 **else if** size(C) $= g$ **then return** $\hat{\mathcal{V}} \cup C$
13 **else**
14      $C_1, \ldots, C_{2^m} \leftarrow$ split(C)
15   **for** $j = 1, \ldots, 2^m$ **do**
16          $\hat{\mathcal{V}} \leftarrow$ Algorithm2($\varphi, \mathcal{S}, C_j, \hat{\mathcal{V}}, N, h$)
17 **return** $\hat{\mathcal{V}}$

Fixed Granularity with Binary Satisfaction (FixedBin). We first describe how we compute the approximation $\hat{\mathcal{V}}$ of a validity domain $\mathcal{V}$ (Algorithm 1). The parameter space $\mathcal{W}$ is divided into a partition $\mathcal{C}$ of axis-aligned closed-hyperboxes having all the same size that we call *cells* (line 2). Each cell is then evaluated separately, and included in the over-approximation $\hat{\mathcal{V}}$ only if a parameter valuation $\boldsymbol{v}$ inside the cell is found such that the STL formula $\varphi_{\boldsymbol{v}}$ is satisfied by all time series in the class under study. If, after N trials, no valid parameter valuation is found, then the cell is not included in $\hat{\mathcal{V}}$.

We observe that $\hat{\mathcal{V}}$ is intended to be an over-approximation of $\mathcal{V}$. However, it is possible that a cell $C \subseteq \mathcal{W}$ is not included in $\hat{\mathcal{V}}$ even though there exists a valuation $\boldsymbol{v} \in C$ in the cell that is also included in $\mathcal{V}$. This can happen because we decide whether C shall be included in $\hat{\mathcal{V}}$ based on a finite number N of samples in C. It follows that the choice of N in Algorithm 1 affects the likelihood of a cell that has non-empty intersection with the true validity domain to be included in the over-approximation, as stated by Lemma 1.

Lemma 1 (Choice of N). *Let $\mathcal{V}$ be a validity domain and C a cell not included in the (intended) over-approximation $\hat{\mathcal{V}}$ computed with N random samples per cell. If $N \geq \log_{1-p_0}(\alpha)$ with p_0, $\alpha \in (0,1)$, then the fraction of points in C that are contained in $\mathcal{V}$ is smaller than p_0 with confidence $1 - \alpha$.*

As a concrete example, let us set $p_0 = 0.01$ and $\alpha = 0.05$. In this setting, we need to examine $N \geq \log_{(1-p_0)} \alpha = \log_{0.99}(0.05) = 298$ parameter valuations to conclude with confidence 95% that the proportion of satisfied parameter valuations in the cell is less than 1%.

Once we have computed both $\hat{\mathcal{V}}_1$ and $\hat{\mathcal{V}}_2$, we select the point $\hat{\boldsymbol{v}}_1$ in $\hat{\mathcal{V}}_1$ such that $\hat{\boldsymbol{v}}_1$ and $\hat{\mathcal{V}}_2$ have maximum distance. In other words, we select $\hat{\boldsymbol{v}}_1$ such that $d(\hat{\boldsymbol{v}}_1, \hat{\mathcal{V}}_2) = D(\hat{\mathcal{V}}_1, \hat{\mathcal{V}}_2)$, where the functions d and D are defined in (1) and (2), respectively. To prove the existence of such a point $\hat{\boldsymbol{v}}_1$, we need to show that $\hat{\mathcal{V}}_1$ is a compact set, so that the supremum in definition (2) is in fact a maximum. Since the cells used to approximate $\mathcal{V}_1$ are closed-hyperboxes, $\hat{\mathcal{V}}_1$ is also a closed set (it is finite union of closed sets). Moreover, $\hat{\mathcal{V}}_1$ is a bounded set because it is a subset of the parameter space $\mathcal{W}$ that is bounded by hypothesis. Finally, being a closed and bounded set in $\mathbb{R}^m$, $\hat{\mathcal{V}}_1$ is compact. The same reasoning is applied to the choice of $\hat{\boldsymbol{v}}_2$ in $\hat{\mathcal{V}}_2$.

The following theorem relates the selected parameter valuation to an optimal one, showing that the difference of their respective distances to the other class validity domain is upper-bounded by the cells' size. Hence, it can be arbitrarily reduced.

Theorem 1 (Optimality) . *Let $i \in \{1,2\}$, $\mathcal{V}_i$ be the validity domain for class $\mathcal{S}_i$, and $\hat{\mathcal{V}}_i$ be the approximation of $\mathcal{V}_i$ using $N \geq \log_{1-p_0}(\alpha)$ random samples per cell and the cell resolution given by vector $\boldsymbol{g} \in \mathbb{R}^m_{\geq 0}$. Let $\boldsymbol{v}_i^*$ be an optimal parameter valuation for class i and $\hat{\boldsymbol{v}}_i$ the parameter valuation found with Fixed-Bin. Then, the difference of the distances from $\hat{\boldsymbol{v}}_i$ and from $\boldsymbol{v}_i^*$ to the other class validity domain is bounded by the cell resolution:*

$$|d(\hat{\boldsymbol{v}}_i, \mathcal{V}_{(i \bmod 2)+1}) - d(\boldsymbol{v}_i^*, \mathcal{V}_{(i \bmod 2)+1})| \leq \|\boldsymbol{g}\| \qquad (4)$$

with probability $1 - p_0$ and confidence $1 - \alpha$.

In practice, the values of p_0 and α are chosen freely by the user, affecting the number of random samples N required to guarantee (4): the smaller p_0 and α are, the greater N must be.

Finally, the complexity of the algorithm is reported in the following theorem.

Theorem 2 (Complexity) . *Let n be the total number of signals and let m be the number of different parameter symbols in the PSTL template φ. Let $\boldsymbol{g} \in \mathbb{R}_{\geq 0}^m$ be the vector that contains the minimal sizes of the cells and let the parameter space be $\mathcal{W} = \prod_{i=1}^m [a_i, b_i]$ as in Eq. (3). Then, the total number L of monitors is exponential in m and linear in n. In particular,*

$$L \leq \left(\max_{i=1,\dots,m} \left\lceil \frac{b_i - a_i}{g_i} \right\rceil \right)^m \cdot (N \cdot n) = \mathcal{O}(M^m) \cdot \mathcal{O}(n),$$

where N is the maximum number of parameter valuations to be evaluated in every cell and M is a suitable positive number.

Adaptive Granularity with Binary Satisfaction (AdaBin). We present an alternative to compute over-approximations of validity domains using an adaptive cell resolution that exploits binary search (Algorithm 2).

The algorithm starts considering an initial empty approximation of the validity domain ($\hat{\mathcal{V}} \leftarrow \emptyset$), and the whole parameter space as a single cell ($C \leftarrow \mathcal{W}$). One cell at a time is then evaluated with three possible outcomes: (i) the cell is added to the approximation of the validity domain; (ii) the cell is not added to the approximation of the validity domain; (iii) the cell is split. The first two scenarios happen, respectively, when the cell presents a high concentration h of satisfied parameter valuations (line 10), or when no satisfied parameter valuations are found (line 11). Otherwise, reminding that m is the number of parameter symbols in the template φ, the cell is split into 2^m new cells generated by dividing each edge into two (at its middle point). When the minimal cell size is reached (line 12), we perform (i) if at least one satisfied parameter valuation is found. The minimal cell resolution $\boldsymbol{g}$ has to be reached by doing the same amount of splits in all parameter dimensions. Recalling the representation of parameter space $\mathcal{W}$ in Eq. (3), it follows that there must exist a natural number k such that

$$b_i - a_i = 2^k \cdot g_i \quad \forall i \in \{1, \dots, m\}. \tag{5}$$

AdaBin is introduced to speed up the approximation of the validity domains by employing the finest cell resolution only in the most uncertain areas of the parameter space, such as those on the validity domains boundaries. On the other hand, *AdaBin* may be less accurate than *FixedBin*, and the guarantee expressed by Theorem 1 does not apply. However, we observe that a reduction in the accuracy of the approximation of the validity domain does not necessarily result in a decrease in the classification accuracy.

Monotonic Variant. The *monotonic variant* of the previous methods is introduced to speed up the computation of the validity domain approximations in case the parametric STL template is monotonic with respect to all its parameters. A PSTL formula φ is *monotonically increasing* (or *decreasing*) with respect to its parameter p_i, if, for every pair of valuations w_i and w_i' such that $w_i \leq w_i'$ (or $w_i \geq w_i'$) and for every signal $\boldsymbol{x}$, $\rho(\varphi_{\boldsymbol{v},w_i}; \boldsymbol{x}) \leq \rho(\varphi_{\boldsymbol{v},w_i'}; \boldsymbol{x})$, where $\boldsymbol{v}$ corresponds to a generic valuation of the other parameters in φ.

For a PSTL formula φ that is monotonic with respect to all its parameters, we define the *lowest point* and the *highest point* of a cell C. The cells that we use to approximate the parameter space are closed hyperboxes in $\mathbb{R}^m$; hence, they are representable as $C = \prod_{i=1}^{m}[q_i, Q_i]$, where q_i, $Q_i \in \mathbb{R}$ and $q_i < Q_i$ for every $i \in \{1, \ldots, m\}$. The *lowest point* in C is the point that is the most likely to be violated, namely the vector in $\mathbb{R}^m$ whose i-th component is q_i if φ is increasing with respect to parameter p_i, or Q_i if φ is decreasing with respect to p_i. Conversely, the *highest point* of a cell C is the point which is most likely to be satisfied, being the vector in $\mathbb{R}^m$ whose i-th component is Q_i if φ is increasing with respect to parameter p_i, or q_i if φ is decreasing with respect to p_i.

The following equivalences are the bases of the monotonic variant methods, allowing for a complete evaluation of a cell through the study of only these two special parameter valuations: (i) all parameter valuations in a cell are violated if and only if its *highest point* is violated, and (ii) all parameter valuations in a cell are satisfied if and only if its *lowest point* is satisfied.

Remark 1. *If the PSTL template is monotonic with respect to all its parameters, then* (4) *holds deterministically because the statistical guarantee in Lemma 1 is not needed for the evaluation of the cell if highest and lowest points are studied.*

4.2 Different Templates

The following extension should be applied when the user wants to describe the two classes of signals with different PSTL templates. Let φ_1 represent the temporal behavior of time series in class $\mathcal{S}_1$ and φ_2 for class $\mathcal{S}_2$. The parameter valuation $\hat{\boldsymbol{v}}_1$ is chosen in $\hat{\mathcal{V}}(\mathcal{S}_1, \varphi_1)$ to maximize the distance from $\hat{\mathcal{V}}(\mathcal{S}_2, \varphi_1)$ and is used to instantiate the PSTL template φ_1 for the characterization of $\mathcal{S}_1$. Analogously, $\hat{\boldsymbol{v}}_2$ will instantiate φ_2 to characterize $\mathcal{S}_2$ by discriminating $\hat{\mathcal{V}}(\mathcal{S}_2, \varphi_2)$ from $\hat{\mathcal{V}}(\mathcal{S}_1, \varphi_2)$. In other words, the computation of $\hat{\boldsymbol{v}}_1$ and $\hat{\boldsymbol{v}}_2$ is carried out separately by applying one of the previous methods twice: once as if the only given PSTL formula were φ_1, and the other time as if the only given PSTL formula were φ_2.

4.3 Multiple Classes

In this section, we describe the generalization of our approach to the more general problem where the number of classes of time series is $k > 2$. Let us suppose to have a dataset of time series labeled with k values. The symbol $\mathcal{S}_i$ represents the class of time series labeled by i, where $i \in \{1, 2, \ldots, k\}$. The validity domain (with respect to a given PSTL formula φ) is represented by $\mathcal{V}_i$. We approximate all $\mathcal{V}_i$ separately with one of the two proposed methods. Then, for every label $i \in \{1, \ldots, k\}$, the parameter valuation $\hat{v}_i$ is chosen in $\hat{\mathcal{V}}_i$ to maximize the distance from the union set of the other validity domains. Therefore, $\hat{v}_i = \arg \max_{v \in \hat{\mathcal{V}}_i} d\left(v, \bigcup_{\substack{j=1 \\ j \neq i}}^{k} \hat{\mathcal{V}}_j\right)$, where d is the point-set distance defined in (1). Finally, for the classification purpose, in analogy with the binary case, we classify a signal x into the class i such that $i = \arg \max_{j=1,\ldots,k} \rho(\varphi_{\hat{v}_j}; x)$.

5 Application

We implemented our approach in the publicly available tool MiniPaSTeL[1] (Mining Parameters for Signal Temporal Logic), leveraging the RTAMT tool [17] for monitoring STL formulas, and applied it to three case studies. We provide the scripts and the seeds to reproduce the results we present. We run the experiments on a MacBook Pro with 16 GB RAM and M1 processor. For each application, we report the set of mined STL specifications and the misclassification rate (MCR) achieved in the classification. Moreover, each case study focuses on seeking an answer to a research question:

RQ1 [Applicability]. *Does the need for a PSTL template as input limit the applicability of our approach?* Our method requires the user to provide the PSTL template, but such a template may not be available or may be inadequate to discriminate between different classes. In such cases, we can interleave our approach with the human investigation to refine guesses for the PSTL template. The Aircraft Elevator case study illustrates how we can use the method to support the user in finding a suitable specification.

RQ2 [Performance Evaluation]. *How does our method compare to state-of-the-art?* We compare our approach to existing ones on the Naval dataset showing that it is comparable to or outperforms the state-of-the-art in terms of MCR. Moreover, we study how the MCR and the execution time vary with the number of training samples in the dataset.

RQ3 [Explainability of the Results]. *Can the user exploit the results to infer new insights into the traces?* The choice of parameter values in existing specification mining methods is generally carried out by applying off-the-shelf optimization techniques that minimize a given objective function without providing a general understanding of the values selection. Conversely, our method provides a visual understanding of how the parameters are selected by plotting (projections of) the validity domains. Thanks to that, it is possible to explain (unexpected) results, as shown in the Parking case study.

---

[1] https://github.com/eleonoranesterini/MiniPaSTeL

5.1 Aircraft Elevator

To answer **RQ1**, we consider the Simulink model of the Aircraft Elevator Control System [9], whose output signals report the position over time of the left elevator of the aircraft. We generated time series of two classes, S_1 and S_2, by varying the parameters of the system input function: Fig. 2a depicts one representative signal per class.

We explore the workflow in which an engineer uses our approach to explore manually crafted templates and find one that discriminates well between two classes of signals.

By analyzing the shape of the time series in Fig. 2a, we observe that the signals from both classes are characterized by oscillations around the same values, but with different frequencies. In particular, the red one has a higher frequency than the blue one. To leverage this difference, we may design a specification that imposes that signals oscillate around the higher (unknown) value p for a certain (unknown) amount of time T. For each class, we learn the values p and T. We expect the signals of the two classes stabilizing around the same value with the interval of time for the time series in S_1 longer than for time series in S_2. Thus, we consider the following PSTL template:

$$\varphi = \mathbf{G}\Big((x \geq p) \rightarrow (\mathbf{G}_{[0,T]}|x - p| < 0.5)\Big).$$

The formula φ expresses the behavior of signal x that remains "close" to the magnitude parameter p for T time units, immediately after the signal has become greater than p. We decided to manually set the notion of "closeness" to indicate a distance smaller than the value 0.5. This makes the validity domains 2-dimensional, giving the reader a better visual understanding of how the proposed methods work.

The parameter space is given by $\mathcal{W} = [0, 1000] \times [-1.6, 1.6]$. We impose the minimal sizes of cells in the parameter space to be $\boldsymbol{g} = (31.25, 0.1)$ to satisfy (5) for $k = 5$. We then apply *FixedBin* method to compute the parameter valuations $\hat{\boldsymbol{v}}_1$ and $\hat{\boldsymbol{v}}_2$. $\hat{\mathcal{V}}_1$, $\hat{\mathcal{V}}_2$, $\hat{\boldsymbol{v}}_1$, and $\hat{\boldsymbol{v}}_2$ are shown in Fig. 2b: $\hat{\mathcal{V}}_1$ is represented by the cyan region, $\hat{\mathcal{V}}_2$ by the red one (not visible because entirely subsumed by $\hat{\mathcal{V}}_1$), while the gray color represents their overlapping. The use of *AdaBin* method leads to the same approximations with the only difference that cells do not have all the same (minimal) size.

The mined parameter valuations are $\hat{\boldsymbol{v}}_1 = (438, 1.0)$ and $\hat{\boldsymbol{v}}_2 = (719, 1.6)$ for S_1 and S_2, respectively, yielding the following specifications:

$$S_1 : \varphi_{\hat{\boldsymbol{v}}_1} = \mathbf{G}((x \geq 1.0) \rightarrow (\mathbf{G}_{[0,438]}|x - 1.0| < 0.5))$$
$$S_2 : \varphi_{\hat{\boldsymbol{v}}_2} = \mathbf{G}((x \geq 1.6) \rightarrow (\mathbf{G}_{[0,719]}|x - 1.6| < 0.5)).$$

We note that $\hat{\boldsymbol{v}}_2$ belongs not only to $\hat{\mathcal{V}}_2$, but also to $\hat{\mathcal{V}}_1$. From Fig. 2b, we observe that this is inevitable: since $\hat{\mathcal{V}}_2$ is a subset of $\hat{\mathcal{V}}_1$, every parameter valuation $\boldsymbol{v} \in \hat{\mathcal{V}}_2$ is also in $\hat{\mathcal{V}}_1$, resulting in $d(\boldsymbol{v}, \hat{\mathcal{V}}_1) = 0$. Hence, the chosen φ cannot be instantiated to discriminate S_2 from S_1. This observation suggests the PSTL formula should be changed to better discriminate between the two sets.

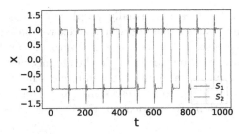

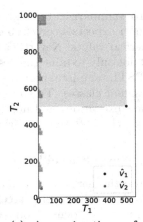

(a) The blue time series depicts one representative element in S_1, the red one in S_2.

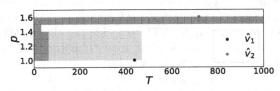

(b) Approximations of validity domains for φ (cyan for S_1 and red for S_2) using *FixedBin*.

(c) Approximations of validity domains for ψ (cyan for S_1 and red for S_2) using *AdaBin*.

Fig. 2. Time series and validity domains for the Aircraft Elevator case study.

We then observe that φ requires the signal to remain close to p for at least T time units without specifying any condition about when the signal has to fall. Therefore, $\mathcal{V}_1$ includes $\mathcal{V}_2$ because the satisfaction of *high* values of T implies the satisfaction of *low* values of T. Hence, we change the PSTL formula φ by adding the requirement that the signal has to move away from the value around which it oscillates after T_2 time units. Furthermore, to remain in the 2-dimensional parameter space for visualization reasons, we replace the parameter value p with the scalar value 1.1. As a result, the new PSTL template we define is:

$$\psi = \mathbf{G}\Big((x \geq 1.1) \to \big(\mathbf{G}_{[0,T_1]}|x - 1.1| < 0.5 \wedge \mathbf{G}_{[T_2,T_2+T_1]}|x - 1.1| > 0.5\big)\Big),$$

where T_1 is just a different symbol to indicate the parameter T in φ. In this case, both parameters T_1 and T_2 are temporal parameters, so the parameter space becomes $\mathcal{W} = [0, 1000] \times [0, 1000]$.

The approximations of validity domains with respect to the new template ψ are shown in Fig. 2c (this plot is done with *AdaBin* to show what the approximation with adaptive cell size looks like). We see that no validity domain subsumes the other one any longer, so it is possible to find parameter valuations discriminating one set of time series from the other one. The mined values are $\hat{v}_1 = (500, 500)$ and $\hat{v}_2 = (16, 47)$.

By studying the performances of φ and ψ as classifiers, we confirm the outcomes of the manual analysis carried out with the visualization of the validity domains. As expected, φ performs very poorly, with a MCR of 0.5 because all signals in S_1 are misclassified in class 2; conversely, ψ achieves a MCR of 0.

To summarize, template-based techniques are usually employed when an engineer expects a certain behavior from the system and wants to extrapolate its numerical values. Nevertheless, this case study shows how our approach can be used not only to mine the desired parameters but also to help the engineer refine the PSTL template, providing a visual understanding of the differences between two signal classes. This observation opens up to processes in which the algorithm's executions and human investigation are interleaved: the engineer steers the search while the algorithm refines it.

5.2   Naval Surveillance

We use the naval surveillance dataset [12] to compare the performance of our methods to existing ones (**RQ2**). Since, to the best of our knowledge, there are no existing works focusing on parameter mining for STL to tackle the classification task, the only meaningful comparisons that are possible are with methods mining both the template and the parameters of the STL formula.

The dataset contains 2000 2-dimensional signals describing the evolution over time of the coordinates of ships approaching a harbor; each signal contains 61 sample points. Figure 3 depicts the projection of some examples of the signal data set to the 2-dimensional spatial coordinates. The signals are partitioned into three different classes:

- *green* signals represent nominal behaviors in which ships arrive from the sea, get through the passage between the island and the peninsula, and reach the harbor.
- *red* signals describe anomalous trajectories of ships deviating to the island before heading towards the harbor (behavior relatable to human trafficking activities).
- *blue* signals depict ships that approach the passage between the island and the peninsula but that, at a certain point, turn around and go back to the open sea; this scenario could be connected to terrorist activities.

This dataset was mainly used for anomaly detection purposes, namely with the goal of discriminating the normal behavior from the two anomalous ones [4,12,16]. Similarly to authors in [15], we are rather interested in characterizing the three classes by discriminating each class from the other two. We consider the PSTL template mined in [16]: $\varphi = ((x_2 > p_2)\, \mathbf{U}_{[T_1,T_2]}\, (x_1 \leq p_1))$, where x_1 and x_2 are variables that refer to

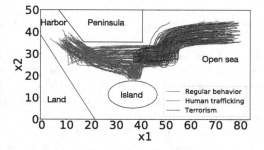

Fig. 3. Traces representing ship trajectories. The Figure has been redrawn from [12].

the first and second coordinate of the signals, respectively. For each one of the three classes, we aim to find the parameter valuations for p_1, p_2, T_1 and T_2 that produce the most appropriate instantiation of φ.

We observe that φ is monotonic with respect to all its parameters (increasing with respect to T_2 and p_1, and decreasing with respect to T_1 and p_2). Hence, we can apply the monotonic variant of our methods. The set of specifications generated using 150 training samples (50 for each class) is:

$$\text{Class 1 (green): } \varphi_{\hat{v}_1} = (x_2 > 22.44)\, \mathbf{U}_{[110,150]}\, (x_1 \leq 42.0)$$

$$\text{Class 2 (red): } \varphi_{\hat{v}_2} = (x_2 > 24.25)\, \mathbf{U}_{[20,75]}\, (x_1 \leq 42.0)$$

$$\text{Class 3 (blue): } \varphi_{\hat{v}_3} = (x_2 > 29.69)\, \mathbf{U}_{[110,300]}\, (x_1 \leq 66.37).$$

We evaluate the classification performance of our method for each class by considering the misclassification rate (MCR), namely the number of misclassified signals over the total number of signals. MCR for class i is defined as $\text{MCR}_i := \frac{|\text{FN}_i| + |\text{FP}_i|}{\sum_{j=1}^{k} |\mathcal{S}_j|}$, where FN_i and FP_i correspond to the false negatives and false positives of class i, respectively.

Table 1 summarizes the results of average MCRs on the testing set over five different runs (different training samples are drawn at every run), the number of training and testing samples used and the computational time. We use Table 1 to first study how our method scales when varying the number of training samples and then to compare our approach with previous works in the literature.

As stated by Theorem 2, the complexity of *FixedBin* increases linearly with the increasing of the number of traces in the dataset; this is consistent with the experimental results reported in the first three rows of Table 1 and (depicted in the Figure in the Appendix). In terms of MCR, we would expect the performance to improve when increasing the number of traces in the training set; we observe that this trend is confirmed (*FixedBin* achieves better results with 150 signals than with 30), but not in a monotonic way, as *FixedBin* with 90 samples outperforms the other two.

To make a fair comparison with the existing works from the literature, we installed the tools presented in [4,15,16] on our laptop and ran them with the same number of training and testing samples. For [16] we could not reproduce the results reported in the paper and the MCR we obtained is very poor; conversely, the results achieved for [4,15] are consistent with the values presented in the respective papers.

Our misclassification rates in classifying class 1 for *FixedBin* and *AdaBin* are slightly greater but still comparable with MCR_1 of [4,15], while, for the second and third classes, our methods outperform the only method that tackled the multi-class classification problem. We remark that [15] addresses the multi-class classification problem as multiple binary classification problems. This means that three different classifiers are trained: one to distinguish class 1 from classes 2 and 3 together, a second for class 2 versus classes 1 and 3, and a third for class 3 versus classes 1 and 2. This is a common approach when tackling the multi-class classification problem, but, if no rules about how to combine the classifiers are presented, the prediction of the label of a new trace might be ambiguous: a trace might be unintentionally classified in several classes at the same time. Conversely, we combine different classifiers into a unique one discriminating among the three classes simultaneously.

Table 1. Comparison of MCR values (average and standard deviation, when available) with previous works on testing set, number of training and testing samples and computational time.

	# samples (train–test)	MCR_1	MCR_2	MCR_3	Time (hours)
FixedBin	30–1970	0.04 ± 0.02	0.003 ± 0.003	0.04 ± 0.02	0.78 ± 0.02
FixedBin	90–1910	0.008 ± 0.008	0.002 ± 0.002	0.006 ± 0.006	1.71 ± 0.05
FixedBin	150–1850	0.02 ± 0.01	0.003 ± 0.002	0.02 ± 0.01	2.53 ± 0.07
AdaBin	150–1850	0.01 ± 0.02	0.002 ± 0.001	0.01 ± 0.02	3.7 ± 0.3
[4]	150–1850	0.008 ± 0.004	–	–	0.0001 ± 0.0001
[15]	150–1850	0.009 ± 0.01	0.01 ± 0.005	0.08 ± 0.07	0.53 ± 0.01
[16]	150–1850	0.52 ± 0.1	–	–	0.043 ± 0.001

Since both of our methods approximate the entire validity domain before selecting the parameter values, the computational time is higher compared to that of other tools. Nevertheless, the approaches we propose can be parallelized because the most expensive part corresponds to the computation of the different validity domains that are independent of each other. For *FixedBin*, even different cells within the same validity domain are computed independently. Surprisingly, we observe that *AdaBin* performs slower than *FixedBin*, despite evaluating a smaller number of parameters (12138 versus 65536). The reason for that might be attributed to the recursive implementation of *AdaBin*, which is generally less efficient than an iterative one (as used in *FixedBin*). However, it is important to note that this result is specific to the monotonic variants, where only one parameter is monitored for every cell. Therefore, in this setting, skipping the evaluation of one cell does not accelerate the overall process as much as in the general case.

5.3 Parking Scenario

In this case study, a vehicle is driving through a parking lot when a pedestrian walks out from behind a SUV onto the path of the ego vehicle. More specifically, the pedestrian walks in the x-direction at a speed of 1.5m/s, while the vehicle drives in an orthogonal y-direction with a constant velocity in the range [5.55, 11.11] mps (20–40 kph).

Fig. 4. Example of images extracted from the onboard camera of the vehicle. For illustration purpose, four pedestrians were placed in each scene. Left: scenario of a clear day with adult pedestrian. Right: scenario with foggy night and child.

The vehicle is equipped with an automatic emergency braking (AEB) function which brakes as hard as possible to avoid a collision with the pedestrian. We simulate the scenario with CARLA 9.13, an open-source photo-realistic driving simulator for autonomous vehicle research [8]. An RGB camera is mounted on top of the vehicle and is equipped with YOLOv7, a state of the art image detection deep neural network [18]. We use the YOLOv7 model off-the-shelf and trigger an AEB procedure when there is an output with the label "person" with over 0.94 confidence probability (the threshold was set to completely eliminate false positives).

Since the AEB functionality is triggered through visual data, we have 3 different visual variations of the scenario: Time of day {day, night}, Clarity {clear, foggy}, Pedestrian type {adult, child}. For each combination, we collected 200 batches of data (coordinates of the position, velocity and acceleration of the car and the pedestrian). Figure 4 shows two images extracted from the onboard camera for further illustration.

Suppose we are an engineer who wants to characterize the dynamics of two classes of data belonging to two opposite scenarios: an adult crossing the parking lot during the day versus a child pedestrian at night. Since each episode might end either with the vehicle braking and reaching a complete stop before hitting the pedestrian or with the vehicle crashing into the pedestrian, we start our analysis by providing the outcome of the episodes (crash or no crash) with an intuitive robustness measure. In particular, in the case of a non-crashing episode, we study the distance $d(t)$ of the car and the pedestrian over time. If we registered no crash, the car managed to stop in time, so $d(t)$ remains strictly positive throughout the whole episode. The greater the distance is, the safer the episode is (and vice versa). We translate the study of the distance between car and pedestrian as a function of the car's velocity as the following PSTL template:

$$\varphi_1 = \mathbf{G}(v_c(t) < v_{\text{no-crash}}) \rightarrow \mathbf{G}(d(t) \geq d_{\text{no-crash}}),$$

where $v_c(t)$ indicates the car's velocity at time t, while $v_{\text{no-crash}}$ and $d_{\text{no-crash}}$ are the parameters to be mined.

Conversely, we can quantify the robustness of a crashing scenario by studying how strong the impact on the pedestrian is. To do so, we can either consider the car's velocity at the moment of the crash or the distance the car would have required to stop after passing the crashing point. We opt for the latter option so that both the two measures of robustness are distances. Knowing the velocity v and the acceleration a (which is a deceleration) at the last frame before the crash, we apply basic notions of physics and estimate the distance D covered by the car before getting to a complete stop after passing the pedestrian's y-position using the following relationship: $D = \frac{v^2}{2a}$. The greater D is, the stronger the impact is, and, consequently, the unsafer the scenario is. To study the value of D as a function of the car's velocity, we consider the following PSTL template:

$$\varphi_2 = \mathbf{F}(v_c(t) > v_{\text{crash}}) \rightarrow (D \geq d_{\text{crash}}),$$

where $v_c(t)$ represents the car's velocity at time t, while v_{crash} and d_{crash} are the parameters to learn.

The quantification of the robustness of crashing and non-crashing episodes led to two PSTL templates. What would the engineer need to do now? Pick just one of the two templates? If our approach discriminated two classes using only one formula (as is always the case in the literature), the answer would be yes, but our approach allows different classes to be associated with different templates (Sect. 4.2). Guided by common sense, we judge the scenario taking place during the day and with the adult as pedestrian to be *safer* than the one by night with the child pedestrian since the greater visibility should allow the car to identify the pedestrian in advance (we will see later on that our method's output verifies the validity of this assumption). Since φ_1 describes a non-crashing episode, we associate it to the *safer* scenario - day and adult - whose class of data we indicate by $\mathcal{S}_1$. Conversely, the crashing episode template φ_2 is used for the *unsafer* scenario - night and child - indicated by $\mathcal{S}_2$.

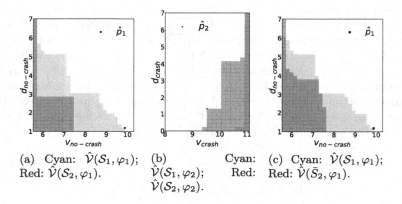

(a) Cyan: $\hat{\mathcal{V}}(\mathcal{S}_1, \varphi_1)$;
Red: $\hat{\mathcal{V}}(\mathcal{S}_2, \varphi_1)$.

(b)   Cyan:
$\hat{\mathcal{V}}(\mathcal{S}_1, \varphi_2)$;   Red:
$\hat{\mathcal{V}}(\mathcal{S}_2, \varphi_2)$.

(c) Cyan: $\hat{\mathcal{V}}(\mathcal{S}_1, \varphi_1)$;
Red: $\hat{\mathcal{V}}(\bar{\mathcal{S}}_2, \varphi_1)$.

Fig. 5. Left and Middle: Approximation of validity domains for $\mathcal{S}_1$ in cyan and $\mathcal{S}_2$ in red (gray color is given by their overlapping) with respect to φ_1 (Left) and φ_2 (Middle). Right: Approximation of validity domains of $\mathcal{S}_1$ and $\bar{\mathcal{S}}_2$ with respect to φ_1. (Color figure online)

We run the experiments with *FixedBin* (in 6.2 min) learning from the 80% of the dataset. Figure 5a depicts the approximated validity domains of $\mathcal{S}_1$ and $\mathcal{S}_2$ with respect to φ_1: parameter $\hat{p}_1$ is chosen in $\mathcal{V}(\mathcal{S}_1, \varphi_1)$ to maximize the distance from $\mathcal{V}(\mathcal{S}_2, \varphi_1)$. Similarly, Fig. 5b represents the validity domains with respect to φ_2, where $\hat{p}_2$ is extracted in $\mathcal{V}(\mathcal{S}_2, \varphi_2)$. The learned specifications are:

$$\mathcal{S}_1 : \varphi_{1,\hat{p}_1} = \mathbf{G}(v_c(t) < 9.87) \rightarrow \mathbf{G}(d(t) \geq 1.18)$$
$$\mathcal{S}_2 : \varphi_{2,\hat{p}_2} = \mathbf{F}(v_c(t) > 9.53) \rightarrow (D \geq 1.31).$$

We combine $\varphi_{1,\hat{p}_1}$ and $\varphi_{2,\hat{p}_2}$ to predict the classification of the unseen set of traces (20% of the dataset) and we achieve a MCR of 0.037. In this application, all other tools perform worse: the MCR for [4] is 0.13, for [16] is 0.5, while [15] returns failure after more than one hour and half of computation. Moreover, to answer **RQ3**, we observe that, apart from the classification itself, our approach provides additional insights into the case study thanks to the computation of the entire validity domains. For instance, by observing Fig. 5 (Left and Middle), the engineer gets the proof that S_2 actually describes an *unsafer* scenario than S_1 (for every velocity value, $d_{\text{no-crash}}$ is smaller for S_2, while d_{crash} is greater). In addition, the engineer finds out that the safety on non-crashing scenarios remains unchanged by varying the velocity in the range $[6, 7.5]$ mps ($d_{\text{no-crash}}$ remains, indeed, around 5 meters for the day-adult scenario and 3 meters for the night-child one), but it falls abruptly when the velocity overcomes the threshold of 7.5 mps (≈ 27 kph). Finally, the knowledge of the entire validity domains allows the engineer to easily add restrictions on the parameters to be learned (e.g., increasing the lower bound of $d_{\text{no-crash}}$ from one meter to two meters to enhance safety).

So far, we compared the scenarios of an adult pedestrian crossing the parking lot during the day versus a child pedestrian at night, both with a clear sky. What would happen if the latter scenario had foggy weather instead? Our human experience would consider the fog as a factor that decreases visibility and, consequently, increases the danger. To check this hypothesis, we run new experiments with the second class of data $\bar{S}_2$ representing traces collected in a foggy night and with a child pedestrian. The MCR value we obtain now is 0.15, significantly greater than before (the other tools achieved the following MCRs: 0.11 for [4], 0.5 for [16], failure for [15]). Without any additional insights, we would not be able to understand the reason behind this unintuitive result: we would have expected a decrease in the MCR due to a larger gap in safety between the two classes caused by the presence of fog. By comparing Fig. 5a with Fig. 5b, we observe that the addition of fog produces the expansion of the validity domain of $\bar{S}_2$ with respect to φ_1, meaning that the vehicle manages to stop further from the pedestrian than in the limpid scenario. Consequently, the foggy scenario is actually safer and therefore less distinguishable from S_1. By manually inspecting the CARLA simulations, we confirmed this analysis by noticing that the fog added some visual noise masking the pedestrian, but in fact also accentuated their contour. The latter effect made the pedestrians more easily recognizable for YOLO. In conclusion, thanks to the insights provided by our method, we discovered that our human intuition for which the fog renders a pedestrian less visible does not hold in the CARLA simulation environment.

6   Conclusion and Future Work

We presented a new approach to mine parameters of arbitrary PSTL templates to perform multi-class classification tasks over time series data. We proposed two variants of the mining procedure, providing a statistical guarantee of optimality for the mined parameters. We validated the applicability of our approach in three case studies by demonstrating how to leverage our method's outputs to refine the PSTL template or infer new insights into the data and by comparing our performances with the state-of-the-art.

The approach proposed in this paper is passive - the specification is mined with respect to a set of existing signals. We plan to explore the active learning approach and devise a testing strategy that can help inferring a representative specification that explains well the examples.

References

1. Asarin, E., Donzé, A., Maler, O., Nickovic, D.: Parametric identification of temporal properties. In: Khurshid, S., Sen, K. (eds.) RV 2011. LNCS, vol. 7186, pp. 147–160. Springer, Heidelberg (2012). https://doi.org/10.1007/978-3-642-29860-8_12

2. Bartocci, E., Bortolussi, L., Sanguinetti, G.: Data-Driven Statistical Learning of Temporal Logic Properties. In: Legay, A., Bozga, M. (eds.) FORMATS 2014. LNCS, vol. 8711, pp. 23–37. Springer, Cham (2014). https://doi.org/10.1007/978-3-319-10512-3_3

3. Bartocci, E., Mateis, C., Nesterini, E., Nickovic, D.: Survey on mining signal temporal logic specifications. Inf. Comput. **289**(Part), 104957 (2022). https://doi.org/10.1016/j.ic.2022.104957

4. Bombara, G., Vasile, C.I., Penedo, F., Yasuoka, H., Belta, C.: A decision tree approach to data classification using signal temporal logic. In: Proceedings of HSCC 2016, pp. 1–10. ACM (2016). https://doi.org/10.1145/2883817.2883843

5. Bortolussi, L., Gallo, G.M., Křetínský, J., Nenzi, L.: Learning model checking and the kernel trick for signal temporal logic on stochastic processes. In: TACAS 2022. LNCS, vol. 13243, pp. 281–300. Springer, Cham (2022). https://doi.org/10.1007/978-3-030-99524-9_15

6. Bufo, S., Bartocci, E., Sanguinetti, G., Borelli, M., Lucangelo, U., Bortolussi, L.: Temporal logic based monitoring of assisted ventilation in intensive care patients. In: Margaria, T., Steffen, B. (eds.) ISoLA 2014. LNCS, vol. 8803, pp. 391–403. Springer, Heidelberg (2014). https://doi.org/10.1007/978-3-662-45231-8_30

7. Donzé, A., Ferrère, T., Maler, O.: Efficient robust monitoring for STL. In: Sharygina, N., Veith, H. (eds.) CAV 2013. LNCS, vol. 8044, pp. 264–279. Springer, Heidelberg (2013). https://doi.org/10.1007/978-3-642-39799-8_19

8. Dosovitskiy, A., Ros, G., Codevilla, F., Lopez, A., Koltun, V.: CARLA: an open urban driving simulator. In: Proceedings of CoRL. PMLR, vol. 78, pp. 1–16, 2017. http://proceedings.mlr.press/v78/dosovitskiy17a.html

9. Ghidellaand, J., Mosterman, P.: Requirements-based testing in aircraft control design. In: AIAA Modeling and Simulation Technologies Conference and Exhibit, pp. 1–11 (2005). https://doi.org/10.2514/6.2005-5886

10. Hoxha, B., Dokhanchi, A., Fainekos, G.: Mining parametric temporal logic properties in model-based design for cyber-physical systems. Int. J. Softw. Tools Technol. Transf. **20**(1), 79–93 (2017). https://doi.org/10.1007/s10009-017-0447-4

11. Jha, S., Tiwari, A., Seshia, S.A., Sahai, T., Shankar, N.: TeLEx: learning signal temporal logic from positive examples using tightness metric. Formal Methods Syst. Des. **54**(3), 364–387 (2019). https://doi.org/10.1007/s10703-019-00332-1

12. Kong, Z., Jones, A., Belta, C.: Temporal logics for learning and detection of anomalous behavior. IEEE Trans. Autom. Control **62**(3), 1210–1222 (2017). https://doi.org/10.1109/TAC.2016.2585083

13. Linard, A., Torre, I., Leite, I., Tumova, J.: Inference of multi-class STL specifications for multi-label human-robot encounters. In: 2022 IEEE/RSJ International Conference on Intelligent Robots and Systems (IROS), pp. 1305–1311 (2022). https://doi.org/10.1109/IROS47612.2022.9982088

14. Maler, O., Nickovic, D.: Monitoring temporal properties of continuous signals. In: Lakhnech, Y., Yovine, S. (eds.) FORMATS/FTRTFT -2004. LNCS, vol. 3253, pp. 152–166. Springer, Heidelberg (2004). https://doi.org/10.1007/978-3-540-30206-3_12

15. Mohammadinejad, S., Deshmukh, J.V., Puranic, A.G., Vazquez-Chanlatte, M., Donzé, A.: Interpretable classification of time-series data using efficient enumerative techniques. In: Proceedings of HSCC 2020, pp. 9:1–9:10. ACM (2020). https://doi.org/10.1145/3365365.3382218

16. Nenzi, L., Silvetti, S., Bartocci, E., Bortolussi, L.: A robust genetic algorithm for learning temporal specifications from data. In: McIver, A., Horvath, A. (eds.) QEST 2018. LNCS, vol. 11024, pp. 323–338. Springer, Cham (2018). https://doi.org/10.1007/978-3-319-99154-2_20

17. Ničković, D., Yamaguchi, T.: RTAMT: online robustness monitors from STL. In: Hung, D.V., Sokolsky, O. (eds.) ATVA 2020. LNCS, vol. 12302, pp. 564–571. Springer, Cham (2020). https://doi.org/10.1007/978-3-030-59152-6_34

18. Wang, C.Y., Bochkovskiy, A., Liao, H.Y.M.: YOLOv7: Trainable bag-of-freebies sets new state-of-the-art for real-time object detectors. arXiv preprint arXiv:2207.02696 (2022)

19. Xu, Z., Julius, A.A.: Census signal temporal logic inference for multiagent group behavior analysis. IEEE Trans. Autom. Sci. Eng. 15(1), 264–277 (2018). https://doi.org/10.1109/TASE.2016.2611536

General Anticipatory Monitoring
for Temporal Logics on Finite Traces

Hannes Kallwies[1] , Martin Leucker[1] , and César Sánchez[2]([✉])

[1] University of Lübeck, Lübeck, Germany
{kallwies,leucker}@isp.uni-luebeck.de
[2] IMDEA Software Institute, Madrid, Spain
cesar.sanchez@imdea.org

Abstract. Runtime Verification studies how to check a run of a system
against a formal specification, typically expressed in some temporal logic.
A monitor must produce a verdict at each step that is sound with respect
to the specification. It is often the case that a monitor must produce a
? verdict and wait for more observations. On the other hand, sometimes
a verdict is inevitable but monitoring algorithms wait to produce the
verdict, because it seemingly depends on future inputs. Anticipation is
the property of a monitor to immediately produce inevitable verdicts,
which has been studied for logics on infinite traces.

Monitoring problems depend on the logic and on the semantics that
the monitor follows. In initial monitoring, at every instant the monitor answers whether the specification holds for the observed trace from
the initial state. In recurrent monitoring, the monitor answers at every
instant whether the specification holds at that time.

In this paper we study anticipatory monitoring for temporal logics
on finite traces. We first show that many logics on finite traces can be
reduced linearly to Boolean Lola specifications and that initial monitoring can be reduced to recurrent monitoring for Lola. Then we present an
algorithm with perfect anticipation for recurrent monitoring of Boolean
Lola specifications, which we then extend to exploit assumptions and
tolerate uncertainties.

1 Introduction

In this paper we study the anticipatory recurrent monitoring problem for runtime
verification of temporal logics on finite traces. We provide a general solution and
extend it to handle assumptions and uncertainties.

Runtime verification (RV) is a lightweight formal dynamic verification technique analyzing single executions of systems wrt. given correctness properties.
RV has been studied both in theory and practical applications [1,25]. The starting point is a formal specification of the property to monitor. A common specification language is Linear-time Temporal Logic (LTL) [30] which was originally

This work was funded in part by PRODIGY Project (TED2021-132464B-I00)
funded by MCIN/AEI/10.13039/501100011033/ and the European Union NextGenera-
tionEU/PRTR, and by a research grant from Nomadic Labs and the Tezos Foundation.

introduced for infinite runs. Since in monitoring the sequence of observations at any point in time is necessarily finite, LTL has been adapted to finite traces, including infinite extensions of the finite prefix seen so far [4], limiting the logic to use only the next-operator [22], or finite version of LTL [26], strong and weak versions of LTL [14] or the so-called mission time LTL [32]. These monitoring approaches attempt to answer the *initial monitoring problem*: whether the trace at the initial position satisfies the property. Monitoring ongoing executions requires to emit a verdict for every event observed, so an uncertain verdict "?" is temporarily produced if the trace observed is not yet guaranteed to be only extendable into a model (verdict *tt*) or only extendable into a counter-model (verdict *ff*). Consider for example $\square(p \rightarrow \diamondsuit q)$ (globally a p implies that there was once a q). The monitor emits ? until the first q or p is observed. The monitor emits *tt* if q happens no later than the first p, and *ff* if p happens strictly before the first q. In initial monitoring, once a certain verdict (*tt,ff*) is produced it remains fixed.

The seminal work by Havelund and Rosu [18] considers an alternative approach. Starting from specifications of past LTL formulas, the monitors in [18] produce at instant i a fresh verdict about whether the property holds at i, thus recurrently producing potentially different outcomes. We call this variant *recurrent monitoring*. As the current position is shifted with every new observation, recurrent monitoring performs a different evaluation at every instant. When recurrently monitoring $\square(p \rightarrow \diamondsuit q)$, the monitor emits a *ff* for each p that is before the first q, then recovers and starts emitting ? attempting to see a q before the next p (moving then to *tt*). These two approaches are unified in [19], separating the monitoring time at which the questions are answered from the time at which the verdict is referring to.

In recurrent monitoring, the output for the specification at time i is either produced, or a "?" is cast and the concrete verdict for time i is never cast. An alternative family of formalisms for runtime verification are stream-based runtime verification (SRV), pioneered by Lola [12], which produce one output stream value for each input position (delaying if necessary the production of the outcome of the monitor for input i until a later instant). We call this variant the *universal monitoring* because the monitors ultimately produce (sooner or later or even at the end of the trace) all verdicts for all positions. Even though the common use of SRV is to encode recurrent monitoring problems for past (or at least bounded future) specifications future universal monitoring can be performed at the price of (1) unbounded resources and (2) only guaranteeing all verdicts at the end of the trace. Modern SRV systems (both synchronous and asynchronous) including RTLola [7], Lola2.0 [15], CoPilot [29], TeSSLa [11] and Striver [17] follow this approach. In summary,

- *initial monitoring* attempts to answer, at every instant t, whether the observed trace satisfies the specification if evaluated at time 0.
- *recurrent monitoring* attempts to answer, at every instant t, whether the observed trace satisfies the specification if evaluated at t.

– *universal monitoring* attempts to answer, as soon as possible and for every position t, whether the observed trace satisfies the specification at t.

It is desirable that a monitor produces a verdict as soon as possible when this verdict is inevitable, a feature called anticipation. For example, a naive monitor for the initial monitoring for (XX *false*) would wait two steps until *false* is encountered to produce *ff* as verdict. An anticipatory monitor would immediately produce the correct verdict *ff* at time 0. As another example, X($p \rightarrow$ (X *false*)) would require to check whether p holds at the first instant (producing *ff* if p holds and *tt* if p does not hold), under perfect anticipation. Anticipation has been solved for LTL on ω-words [5] where all (infinite) futures are explored at every step and deciding an outcome when the opposite is impossible. Anticipation guarantees that equivalent specifications produce the same outputs for the same inputs and at the same times.

The contributions of this paper are the following. We consider many logics for finite traces (in Sect. 2) and translate them into SRV language Lola on Boolean streams (in Sect. 3), and show that initial monitoring can be reduced to recurrent monitoring for Lola. Section 4 gives a recurrent monitoring algorithm with perfect anticipation for Lola, and extends it to exploit assumptions and tolerate uncertainties. We have implemented our approach in a prototype tool and report on a preliminary empirical evaluation (Sect. 5).

2   Temporal Logics on Finite Traces

Preliminaries. We use $\mathbb{Z}$ for the set of integers and $\mathbb{T} = \{0 \ldots N - 1\}$ for the natural numbers from 0 to $N - 1$. Given a set of propositions AP the alphabet $\Sigma = 2^{AP}$ consists of subsets of atomic propositions. A word σ is an element of Σ^+, and $|\sigma|$ is the length of σ. We say that a natural number i is an index or position of a word σ whenever $0 \leq i < |\sigma|$. Given a word σ and an index i, we use $\sigma(i)$ for the letter at position i, (σ, i) is called a "pointed word", and (σ, i, j) is called a "segment". A *basic expression* is a Boolean combination of elements from AP, defined as follows:

$$\beta :: = \textit{true} \mid a \mid \beta \wedge \beta \mid \beta \vee \beta \mid \neg \beta$$

where $a \in AP$ is an atomic proposition. Given a letter s from Σ, $s \models p$ is defined as $s \models a$ whenever $a \in s$, and the usual definitions for Boolean operators.

We define non-deterministic finite automata with a forward and backwards acceptance, in terms of segments of words. An ϵ-NFA over alphabet Σ is a tuple $(Q, q_0, \delta, \delta_\epsilon, F)$ where Q is a finite set of states, q_0 is the initial state, $F \subseteq Q$ is a set of final states, $\delta \subseteq Q \times \Sigma \times Q$ is the transition relation and $\delta_\epsilon \subseteq Q \times Q$ is the epsilon transition relation. Given a word σ, two positions $0 \leq i, j < |\sigma|$ and an ϵ-NFA A, we say that A accepts (σ, i, j) in the *forward manner*, denoted $(\sigma, i, j) \models A$ if there is a sequence of states and positions $(q_0, i_0), (q_1, i_1) \ldots (q_n, i_n)$ starting at q_0 such that (1) $i_0 = i$ and $i_n = j$; (2)

$q_n \in F$; and (3) for every $0 \leq k < n$, either $(q_k, \sigma(i_k), q_{k+1}) \in \delta$ and $i_{k+1} = i_k + 1$, or $(q_k, q_{k+1}) \in \delta_\epsilon$ and $i_{k+1} = i_k$.

Similarly, A accepts (σ, i, j) in the *backwards manner*, denoted $(\sigma, i, j) \models A^{-1}$ if there is a sequence of states and positions $(q_0, i_0), (q_1, i_1) \ldots (q_n, i_n)$ starting at q_0 such that (1) $i_0 = i$ and $i_n = j$, (2) $q_n \in F$ and (3) for every $0 \leq k < n$, either $(q_k, \sigma(i_k), q_{k+1}) \in \delta$ and $i_{k+1} = i_k - 1$, or $(q_k, q_{k+1}) \in \delta_\epsilon$ and $i_{k+1} = i_k$.

2.1 Temporal Logics and Formalisms on Finite Traces

We now present several temporal logics over finite traces:

- LTL$_f$: an adaptation of LTL to finite traces [16,27], with past operators.
- RE: regular expressions [21,28] extended with past.
- RLTL$_f$: Regular Linear Temporal Logic (RLTL) [24,34,35] for finite paths.
- LDL$_f$: linear dynamic logic on finite traces [16].
- TRLTL$_f$: a slight variation of RLTL$_f$ introduced in this paper.
- Lola: a stream runtime verification language [12].

For all these formalisms we use basic expressions over AP for individual observations obtained from the environment.

LTL$_f$. Manna and Pnueli [27] already studied how to adapt LTL from infinite traces to finite traces, by observing that one can adapt the next operator (X) into a new variant (weak next) $\widehat{\mathsf{X}}\varphi$. Weak next is always true at the end of the trace in spite of the sub-formula φ, while $\mathsf{X}\varphi$ is defined to be false at the end of the trace in spite of φ. These notions are dual to the corresponding past operators $\ominus\varphi$ (which is automatically true at the first position) and $\ominus\varphi$ (which is automatically false at the first position). The syntax of LTL$_f$ is:

$$\varphi ::= \beta \mid \varphi \wedge \varphi \mid \neg\varphi \mid \mathsf{X}\varphi \mid \widehat{\mathsf{X}}\varphi \mid \varphi \, \mathcal{U} \, \varphi \mid \ominus\varphi \mid \ominus\varphi \mid \varphi \, \mathcal{S} \, \varphi$$

where β is a basic expression. The semantics of LTL$_f$ associates traces $\sigma \in \Sigma^+$ with formulae as follows:

$$
\begin{aligned}
(\sigma, i) &\models \beta && \text{iff } \sigma(i) \models \beta \\
(\sigma, i) &\models \varphi_1 \wedge \varphi_2 && \text{iff } (\sigma, i) \models \varphi_1 \text{ and } (\sigma, i) \models \varphi_2 \\
(\sigma, i) &\models \neg\varphi && \text{iff } (\sigma, i) \not\models \varphi \\
(\sigma, i) &\models \mathsf{X}\varphi && \text{iff } i + 1 < |\sigma| \text{ and } (\sigma, i+1) \models \varphi \\
(\sigma, i) &\models \widehat{\mathsf{X}}\varphi && \text{iff } i + 1 \geq |\sigma| \text{ or } (\sigma, i+1) \models \varphi \\
(\sigma, i) &\models \ominus\varphi && \text{iff } 0 > i - 1 \text{ or } (\sigma, i-1) \models \varphi \\
(\sigma, i) &\models \ominus\varphi && \text{iff } 0 \leq i - 1 \text{ and } (\sigma, i-1) \models \varphi \\
(\sigma, i) &\models \varphi_1 \, \mathcal{U} \, \varphi_2 && \text{iff } \text{for some } j \geq i \;\; (\sigma, j) \models \varphi_2 \text{ and for all } i \leq k < j, (\sigma, k) \models \varphi_1 \\
(\sigma, i) &\models \varphi_1 \, \mathcal{S} \, \varphi_2 && \text{iff } \text{for some } j \leq i \;\; (\sigma, j) \models \varphi_2 \text{ and for all } j < k \leq i, (\sigma, k) \models \varphi_1
\end{aligned}
$$

We use common derived operators like $\vee$ as the dual of $\wedge$, $\mathcal{R}$ as the dual of $\mathcal{U}$, $\Diamond$ (as $true \, \mathcal{U} \, \varphi$) and $\square$ (as $false \, \mathcal{R} \, \varphi$). Likewise for past: $\diamondsuit$ (as $true \, \mathcal{S} \, \varphi$). Note that $(\sigma, i) \models \varphi \, \mathcal{U} \, \psi$ if and only if $(\sigma, i) \models \psi \vee (\varphi \wedge \mathsf{X}(\varphi \, \mathcal{U} \, \psi))$. Also $\neg\mathsf{X}\varphi$ is equivalent to $\widehat{\mathsf{X}}\neg\varphi$, $\neg\widehat{\mathsf{X}}\varphi$ is equivalent to $\mathsf{X}\neg\varphi$, $\neg\ominus\varphi$ is equivalent to $\ominus\neg\varphi$, $\neg\ominus\varphi$ is equivalent to $\ominus\neg\varphi$. The presented logic was later re-introduced in [16] and named LTL$_f$.

RE with Past. Regular expressions [21,28] is a classical formalism to express regular sets of finite words. The syntax of RE is:

$$\rho :: = \beta \mid \rho + \rho \mid \rho \; ; \; \rho \mid \rho^* \rho$$

where β is a basic expression. For convenience, we define the semantics of regular expressions using segments (as in [24]):

$(\sigma, i, j) \models \beta$ iff $\sigma(i) \models \beta$ and $j = i + 1$

$(\sigma, i, j) \models x + y$ iff $(\sigma, i, j) \models x$ or $(\sigma, i, j) \models y$

$(\sigma, i, j) \models x \; ; \; y$ iff   for some $k < |\sigma|, (\sigma, i, k) \models x$ and $(\sigma, k, j) \models y.$

$(\sigma, i, j) \models x^* y$ iff   either $(\sigma, i, j) \models y$, or for some sequence $(i_0 = i, i_1, \ldots i_m),$
$(\sigma, i_k, i_{k+1}) \models x$ and $(\sigma, i_m, j) \models y$

We say that a finite word σ matches a regular expression ρ whenever $(\sigma, 0, |\sigma|) \models \rho$. In [34] past regular expressions were introduced in the context of regular linear temporal logic RLTL. The main idea is to define a new operator $\overline{\beta}$ for a basic expression β defined as $(\sigma, i, j) \models \overline{\beta}$ iff $\sigma(i) \models \beta$ and $j = i - 1$. Then, a pure past regular expression $\overline{\rho}$ is obtained from a regular expression ρ by replacing all basic expressions β with $\overline{\beta}$. Note that all basic steps in a pure future regular expression move forward and all basic steps in a past regular expression move backwards. It is crucial that we have first defined basic expressions (with $\wedge$, $\vee$ and $\neg$) that work on single letters and we do not allow $\wedge$ and $\neg$ in regular expressions, to allow linear translations into richer logics.

TRLTL$_f$. Regular Linear Temporal Logic (RLTL) [24] (see also [34,35]) extends the expressivity of LTL to all regular languages, introducing temporal operators that generalize both temporal operators from LTL and concatenation from regular expressions. The resulting logic has the same complexity as LTL and allows linear translations from both LTL and regular expressions. We now introduce a variation of RLTL for finite traces, called TRLTL$_f$ where we also add the capability in the regular expression layer to test previously defined formulas. RLTL$_f$ is TRLTL$_f$ without the φ? operator below, which does not add expressivity because RLTL$_f$ withour φ? can already cover all regular languages. The resulting syntax has a regular expression layer (ρ) and a temporal layer (φ), where α is only used to decide whether the regular expression is interpreted forward or backwards in the trace.

$$\rho :: = \rho + \rho \mid \rho \; ; \; \rho \mid \rho^* \rho \mid \beta \mid \varphi ? \qquad\qquad \alpha :: = \rho \mid \overline{\rho}$$
$$\varphi :: = true \mid \beta \mid \varphi \vee \varphi \mid \varphi \wedge \varphi \mid \neg\varphi \mid \alpha \; ; \; \varphi \mid \varphi |\alpha\rangle\!\rangle \varphi$$

Note that the regular expression layer is extended with a "test operator" φ? whose intention is to extend the language of atomic propositions with the capability to check previously defined expressions. We only introduce φ? to obtain an immediate subsumption from LDL$_f$ below. The semantics of the φ? operator is $(\sigma, i, i) \models \varphi$? iff $(\sigma, i) \models \varphi$.

The operator $\varphi |\alpha\rangle\!\rangle \varphi$ is called the power operator. The power expression $x |r\rangle\!\rangle y$ (read x at r until y) is built from three elements: y (the *attempt*), x (the *obligation*) and r (the *delay*). Informally, for $x |r\rangle\!\rangle y$ to hold, either the attempt holds, or the obligation is met and the whole expression evaluates successfully after the delay. In particular, for a power expression to hold, the obligation must be met after a finite number of delays. The power operator generalizes both Kleene repetition (x^*y is simply $true\,|\,x\rangle\!\rangle y$) and the LTL Until operator ($x\,\mathcal{U}\,y$ is simply $x\,|\,true\rangle\!\rangle y$). That is, conventional regular expressions can describe sophisticated delays with trivial obligations and escapes, while conventional LTL_f constructs allow complex obligations and escapes, but trivial one-step delays. The power operator extends the expressive power of LTL, for example, Wolper's expression [36] "p holds at even moments"—that cannot be expressed in LTL—is defined in TRLTL_f as $\neg(true\,|\,true\;;\;true\rangle\!\rangle\neg p)$, that is "it is not the case that after some sequence of $true\;;\;true$, there is no p".

The completeness of TRLTL_f with respect to regular languages is easily derived from the expressibility of regular expressions. Formally, the semantics of TRLTL_f ($\wedge$, $\vee$ and $\neg$ are standard as in LTL_f above):

$$(\sigma, i) \models r\;;\;\varphi \quad \text{iff for some } j\; (\sigma, i, j) \models r \text{ and } (\sigma, j) \models \varphi$$
$$(\sigma, i) \models \varphi_1\,|\,r\rangle\!\rangle\varphi_2 \text{ iff for some sequence } (i_0 = i, i_1, \ldots, i_m) : (\sigma, i_m) \models \varphi_2 \text{ and}$$
$$(\sigma, i_k, i_{k+1}) \models r \text{ and } (\sigma, i_k) \models \varphi_1 \text{ for every } k < m$$

It is easy to see that LTL_f is subsumed by TRLTL_f (using the linear translation from $\mathcal{U}$) because $X\varphi$ is $true\;;\;\varphi$. Similarly, RE (for pure past expressions or pure future expressions) can also be expressed in TRLTL_f using the linear translation for Kleene star.

LDL_f. Linear Dynamic Logic on finite traces (LDL_f) was introduced [16] as an extension of LTL_f to increase the expressivity to regular languages, inspired by dynamic logic. As RLTL, LDL_f considers a regular expression layer (extended with test) but restricts the temporal layer to a single "dynamic operator" $\langle\alpha\rangle\varphi$:

$$\varphi :: = \varphi \vee \varphi \;\;\big|\;\; \varphi \wedge \varphi \;\;\big|\;\; \neg\varphi \;\;\big|\;\; \langle\alpha\rangle\varphi \;\;\big|\;\; [\alpha]\varphi$$

The semantics of the dynamic operator are precisely $\langle\alpha\rangle\varphi = \alpha\;;\;\varphi$, while $[\alpha]\varphi$ is its dual $\neg(\alpha\;;\;\neg\varphi)$. Therefore LDL_f can be translated linearly to TRLTL_f. Note that TRLTL_f contains all oeprators from LDL_f and RLTL_f to ease the translation from both. Since the expressive power of both LDL_f and RLTL_f is the set of all regular languages they are equally expressive. We conjecture that one can have a linear translation from LDL_f into RLTL_f and vice-versa, but the proof of this conjecture is out of the scope of this paper.

The following lemma summarizes our expressivity results.

Lemma 1. *For every* LTL_f, *RE,* RLTL_f *and* LDL_f *expression there is an equivalent* TRLTL_f *expression of linear size.*

It is well-known that RE, RLTL_f (and therefore TRLTL_f) and LDL_f can express all regular languages. It is an open problem whether there is a *linear* translation from RLTL into LDL and from RLTL_f into LDL_f.

2.2 The Stream Runtime Verification Language Lola

In this section we recall the Lola stream runtime verification language [12]. A Lola specification describes a transformation from a set of input to output streams. Let $\mathbb{D}$ be an arbitrary data domain (which essentially is a collection of types and constructor symbols, with their interpretations as values and functions). We denote by $\mathcal{S}_{\mathbb{D}} : \mathbb{T} \to \mathbb{D}$ the set of streams of type $\mathbb{D}$. In this paper we restrict ourselves to Boolean streams, i.e. domain $\mathbb{B} = \{tt, ff\}$ with the usual symbols $true, false \wedge, \vee, \neg$, etc.

The output streams of a Lola specification are defined by expressions over other stream identifiers. Given a set of Boolean stream variables S, the set of Lola expressions $Expr_S$ is:

$$Expr_S = true \mid false \mid s[o|c] \mid \neg Expr_S \mid Expr_S \wedge Expr_S \mid Expr_S \vee Expr_S$$

where $s \in S$ is a stream variable, $o \in \mathbb{Z}$ is an offset, and $c \in \{tt, ff\}$ is a Boolean constant. Thus a Lola expression is either a constant or the application of a $\neg$, $\wedge$, $\vee$. The intended meaning of $s[o, c]$ is the value of stream s, o time instants from the current position, using c as default value if this position does not exist (because the offset takes the position beyond the beginning or end of the trace). For example, $s[3, tt]$ represents the value of s three instants in the future, or tt if the trace end is reached. Note that an offset 0 references the current value of other streams, and the index is guaranteed to be legal after adding 0. Since in this case the default value is not necessary we use the alternatives $s[now]$ or s for $s[0, tt]$. Further we use $true, false$ for the stream which has value tt resp. ff at all instances. In the following we assume Lola specifications to be in a so-called flat format, i.e. only the offsets $-1, 0, 1$ may be used. It is easy to see that every Lola specification can be transformed into a flat equivalent by introducing intermediate streams and splitting larger offsets in a sequence of $+1/-1$ offsets. This translation is linear (in the unary encoding of offsets).

A Lola specification $\varphi = (I, S, E)$ is given by I an ordered set of input stream identifiers, S an ordered set of output stream identifiers disjunct from I, and $E : S \to Expr_{S \cup I}$ a mapping which assigns to every output stream its defining expression. The semantics of a Lola specification $\varphi = (I = (i_1, \ldots, i_n), S = (s_1, \ldots, s_m), E)$ is a transformation from input to output streams: $[\![\varphi]\!] : (\mathcal{S}_{\mathbb{B}})^n \to (\mathcal{S}_{\mathbb{B}})^m$ with $[\![\varphi]\!](\tau_1, \ldots, \tau_n) = (\sigma_1, \ldots, \sigma_m)$ such that $\sigma_i(t) = [\![E(s_i)]\!](t)$ for all $i \in \{1, \ldots, m\}, t \in \mathbb{T}$ where the semantics of the defining expression is given as follows (for $c \in \mathbb{B}, o \in \mathbb{Z}, e_1, e_2 \in Expr_{S \cup I}$, stream σ corresponding to identifier $s \in S \cup I$):

$$[\![true]\!](t) = tt$$
$$[\![false]\!](t) = ff$$
$$[\![e_1 \wedge e_2]\!](t) = [\![e_1]\!](t) \wedge [\![e_2]\!](t)$$
$$[\![e_1 \vee e_2]\!](t) = [\![e_1]\!](t) \vee [\![e_2]\!](t)$$

$$[\![\neg e_1]\!](t) = \neg[\![e_1]\!](t)$$
$$[\![s[o|c]]\!](t) = \begin{cases} \sigma(t+o) & \text{if } t+o \in \mathbb{T} \\ c & \text{else} \end{cases}$$

The semantics of φ is well defined if no stream instant is dependent on itself. We only allow Lola specifications where this is guaranteed (which can be statically checked [12,33]).

3   Translating TRLTL$_f$ to Lola

In this section, we describe how to translate TRLTL$_f$ into Lola. More specifically, given a TRLTL$_f$ formula φ, we derive a corresponding Boolean Lola specification $\mathfrak{L}_\varphi$ with a distinguished stream for s_φ that is *true* at position i whenever the input word satisfies φ in position i. The input streams of the Lola specification are given by the atomic propositions. We will introduce one input stream variable t_p for each $p \in AP$. Given a word σ and an atomic proposition p, the input stream corresponding to t_p, $\tau_{t_p}(i)$, is true if and only if $p \in \sigma(i)$. Abusing notation, given a stream s and a set of streams S we use $s \cup S$ for $\{s\} \cup S$. We also use $(s = e) \cup E$ for $\{s = e\} \cup E$.

The idea of the translation is as follows. Given a TRLTL$_f$ formula φ we create for each sub-formula ψ a fresh new stream s_ψ that captures the truth value of ψ at each position, depending on the truth value of the streams for its sub-expressions. For atomic propositions, the definition is immediate as it has to coincide with the corresponding proposition on the input word. Boolean combinations of subformulas translate to the corresponding Boolean combinations of the corresponding streams. The syntax for sequential operators take a regular expression (with its direction of the evaluation) followed by another formula. The regular expressions are first transformed linearly into their corresponding ϵ-NFA representation. Without loss of generality we assume that final states have no successor[1]. We will introduce a fresh stream variable for each state of the ϵ-NFA mimicking the evaluation of the automata followed by the continuing expression. Whenever a testing operator $\psi?$ is used within the regular expression, we refer to the stream variable s_ψ and take a transition in the NFA only if s_ψ is true at the current position. The power operator in TRLTL$_f$ is translated similarly, according its unwinding law $\varphi | \alpha \rangle\!\rangle \psi \equiv \psi \vee (\varphi \wedge \alpha \, ; \, \varphi | \alpha \rangle\!\rangle \psi)$.

Let us now formally describe the translation, which is given inductively by providing a transformer for each operator of TRLTL$_f$. Each transformer takes a subformula φ and delivers a pair $(s_\varphi, \mathfrak{L}_\varphi)$ where s_φ is the *distinguished* stream of the Lola specification $\mathfrak{L}_\varphi$. Therefore, we give the translation of φ as $(s_\varphi, \mathfrak{L}_\varphi)$ and only need to define $\mathfrak{L}_\varphi$ as follows.

- For *true*, $\mathfrak{L}_{true}$ is $(I, \{s_{true}\}, \{s_{true} = true\})$. For atomic propositions $p \in AP$, $\mathfrak{L}_p$ is $(I, \{s_p\}, \{s_p = t_p[now]\})$. For $\vee$:

$$\mathfrak{L}_{\varphi \vee \psi} := (I, (s_{\varphi \vee \psi} \cup S_\varphi \cup S_\psi), (s_{\varphi \vee \psi} = s_\varphi \vee s_\psi) \cup E_\varphi \cup E_\psi)$$

Conjunction and negation can be processed in a similar manner. Basic expressions β are also inductively processed using conjunctions, disjunctions, complementation and atomic propositions.

- For $\alpha \, ; \, \varphi$ with forward $\alpha = \rho$, let $(Q, q_0, \delta, \delta_\epsilon, F)$ be the ϵ-NFA accepting the language defined by α, obtained using standard constructions. In the regular

---

[1] Every ϵ-NFA can be linearly transformed into such a representation by duplicating final states that have successors into two copies: one (final) with no successor and the other (non-final) with the successors.

expression, we treat any testing operator $\psi?$ as a single letter. To define $\mathfrak{L}_{\alpha;\varphi}$ we add a stream for each state of the automaton and one equation following the execution of the automaton. We use S_Q and E_Q for these sets of streams and equations. Let us first consider non-final states $(q \notin F)$, for which the automaton in state q may choose a letter a to proceed to some next state (processing an input letter), may choose an ϵ-transition to proceed to some next state or may perform a check $\psi?$ (at the current input). The equation that we add for state $q \notin F$ is:

$$s_q = \bigvee_{(q,a,q')\in\delta} (s_a \wedge s_{q'}[+1|\mathit{ff}]) \vee \bigvee_{(q,q')\in\delta_\epsilon} s_{q'} \vee \bigvee_{(q,\psi?,q')\in\delta} (s_\psi \wedge s_{q'})$$

For final states $q \in F$, the formula φ has to be checked at the current state as the only possible continuation: $s_q = s_\varphi$. Finally, we add the equation for the distinguished stream $s_{\alpha;\varphi}$ as $s_{\alpha;\varphi} = s_{q_0}$, being true whenever a succesful run of the ϵ-NFA followed by the successful evaluation of φ is achieved by starting in the initial state.

$$\mathfrak{L}_{\alpha;\varphi} = (I, (s_{\alpha;\varphi} \cup S_Q \cup S_\varphi), (\{s_{\alpha;\varphi} = s_{q_0}\} \cup E_Q \cup E_\varphi))$$

– For $\alpha \, ; \, \varphi$ with backward $\alpha = \bar{\rho}$, we follow a similar construction, except that upon reading a letter the offset used to continue is -1 instead of $+1$. For $q \notin F$:

$$s_q = \bigvee_{(q,a,q')\in\delta} (s_a \wedge s_{q'}[-1|\mathit{ff}]) \vee \bigvee_{(q,q')\in\delta_\epsilon} s_{q'} \vee \bigvee_{(q,\psi?,q')\in\delta} (s_\psi \wedge s_{q'})$$

For final states $q \in F$, $s_q = s_\varphi$ and for the resulting specification

$$\mathfrak{L}_{\bar{\rho};\varphi} = (I, (s_{\bar{\rho};\varphi} \cup S_Q \cup S_\varphi), (\{s_{\bar{\rho};\varphi} = s_{q_0}\} \cup E_Q \cup E_\varphi))$$

– For $\varphi | \alpha \rangle\!\rangle \psi$ and a forward regular expression α, let $(s_\varphi, \mathfrak{L}_\varphi)$ be the translation of φ and $(s_\psi, \mathfrak{L}_\psi)$ the translation of ψ. Let also $(Q, q_0, \delta, \delta_\epsilon, F)$ be the ϵ-NFA for α. The equations for $s_{\varphi|\alpha\rangle\!\rangle\psi}$ follow the unwinding equivalence $\varphi | \alpha \rangle\!\rangle \psi \equiv \psi \vee (\varphi \wedge \alpha \, ; \, \varphi | \alpha \rangle\!\rangle \psi)$. For $\alpha \, ; \, (\varphi | \alpha \rangle\!\rangle \psi)$ we follow the construction for the sequential operator by adding streams for each state of the automaton and equations following the transitions. Non-final states are treated exactly as before. For final states $q \in F$ and for the distinguished stream:

$$s_q = s_{\varphi|\alpha\rangle\!\rangle\psi} \qquad\qquad s_{\varphi|\alpha\rangle\!\rangle\psi} = s_\psi \vee (s_\varphi \wedge s_{q_0})$$

Finally, $\mathfrak{L}_{\varphi|\alpha\rangle\!\rangle\psi} = (I, S_{\varphi|\alpha\rangle\!\rangle\psi}, E_{\varphi|\alpha\rangle\!\rangle\psi})$ where

$$S_{\varphi|\alpha\rangle\!\rangle\psi} = s_{\varphi|\alpha\rangle\!\rangle\psi} \cup S_Q \cup S_\varphi \cup S_\psi$$
$$E_{\mathfrak{L}_{\varphi|\alpha\rangle\!\rangle\psi}} = (s_{\varphi|\alpha\rangle\!\rangle\psi} = s_\psi \vee (s_\varphi \wedge s_{q_0})) \cup E_Q \cup E_\varphi \cup E_\psi$$

It is easy to see that the resulting Lola specification is linear in the length of the formula. The following result establishes the correctness of the translation, which can be formally shown by induction, following the inductive definition of the construction.

Lemma 2 (Correctness of Translation). *Let φ be a* TRLTL_f *formula and* $(s_\varphi, \mathcal{L}_\varphi)$ *be the corresponding Lola specification. Let $\sigma \in \Sigma^+$ be a word. Then, for all $i \in \{0, \ldots, |\sigma|\}$, $(\sigma, i) \models \varphi$ if and only if $s_\varphi(i) = tt$.*

4 General Anticipatory Monitoring

In this section we develop an anticipatory algorithm for the recurrent monitoring problem of Lola specifications. Then, we will extend our algorithm to support assumptions and uncertainties. Our algorithm can be used for the initial monitoring problem as well, because, given a Lola specification $(s, (I, S, E))$ that we would like to use for initial monitoring, we can create $(r, (I, S \cup \{r\}, E'))$ where

$$E' = E \cup \{r = \textit{if false}[-1|tt] \textit{ then } s[now] \textit{ else } r[-1|\textit{ff}]\}$$

We use $r\langle i\rangle$ to denote the value of stream r at timepoint i. It is easy to see that at each point in time $r\langle i\rangle = s\langle 0\rangle$ Therefore answering the question, at position i, of whether $r\langle i\rangle$ is true or false, is equivalent to answering whether $s\langle 0\rangle$ is true of false. Thus, in the case of Lola, recurrent monitoring subsumes initial monitoring.

In the rest of the section to simplify the definitions we assume that $\varphi = (I, S, E)$ is an arbitrary well-defined Lola specification. We start with a general definition of recurrent monitors for Lola specifications.

4.1 Recurrent Monitors as Moore Machines

We first define the class of monitors for a Lola specification as Moore machines. These monitors will receive as inputs the values of the input streams and produce, at each instant, as output one Boolean verdict (or ?) per output stream.

Definition 1 (Moore Machine Monitor). *Given a Lola specification $\varphi = (I, S, E)$ a Moore Machine for φ is a tuple $M_\varphi = (P, \Sigma, \Omega, p_0, \delta_m, \omega)$ where*

- *P is a set of states and $p_0 \in P$ is the initial state;*
- *$\Sigma = 2^I$ is the input alphabet;*
- *$\Omega = S \rightarrow \{tt, \textit{ff}, ?\}$ is the output alphabet, that encodes one verdict per output stream;*
- *$\delta_m : P \times \Sigma \rightarrow P$ is the transition function;*
- *$\omega : P \rightarrow \Omega$ is the verdict function.*

A monitor M_φ for a Lola specification φ is *sound* for output stream s if after processing an input string u (of length i), it produces tt only if for all continuations of u, the value of $s\langle i\rangle$ is tt (analogous for $\textit{ff}$). Note that a sound monitor must produce ? if both tt and $\textit{ff}$ can be the result for $s\langle i\rangle$ depending on the continuation. Note also that a sound monitor is allowed to produce ?, even if the verdict is definite (in the extreme case, a monitor that always produces ? is sound).

4.2   An Anticipatory Algorithm

In general Lola specifications may contain future offsets, which potentially make stream events dependent on other streams at later instants. While in offline monitoring this is not a problem, as the full input word is already accessible, this poses a difficulty for online monitoring. The traditional online monitoring algorithm for Lola [12] tackles this problem by stalling computations, delaying the production of verdicts until the required values are available. This algorithm does not produce a value even when it is inevitable.

In this section we present an alternative recurrent monitoring for Lola as follows. A translation from Lola to DFA is presented in [8], which captures whether a sequence of input and output stream values matches a given Lola specification. Based on this construction, we transform a Lola specification into a labeled transition system, from which we build a perfect anticipatory monitor.

We will define a nondeterministic transition system, where the states encode (1) valuations of all (input and output) streams at the current instant and (2) guesses of the valuations at the next position. A valuation $v \in 2^{I \cup S}$ encodes which inputs and outputs are true, so states are pairs of valuations $2^{I \cup S} \times 2^{I \cup S}$. To encode the end of the input trace we use the symbol $\bot$, so the states are elements of $2^{I \cup S} \times (2^{I \cup S} \cup \{\bot\})$. Finally we also add an initial state $\#$ where no input letter has been received and thus no stream has a valuation yet, resulting in a state space

$$Q_\varphi \overset{\text{def}}{=} \{\#\} \cup (2^{I \cup S} \times (2^{I \cup S} \cup \{\bot\}))$$

Example 1. Consider for example the LTL formula $\varphi = \Box p \wedge \Diamond \neg p$. Following the translation from the previous section with some trivial simplifications (like inlining constant streams), the corresponding Lola specification would have an input stream s_p and four defined streams

$$s_{\neg p} = \neg s_p[now] \qquad\qquad s_{\Box p} = s_p[now] \wedge s_{\Box p}[+1 \mid tt]$$
$$s_{\Diamond \neg p} = s_{\neg p}[now] \vee s_{\Diamond \neg p}[+1 \mid ff] \qquad s_\varphi = s_{\Box p}[now] \wedge s_{\Diamond \neg p}[now]$$

Some possible states of the transition system include

$$q_1 = (\{s_{\neg p}, s_{\Diamond \neg p}\}, \{s_p, s_{\Box p}\}) \; q_2 = (\emptyset, \emptyset) \; q_3 = (\{s_p, s_{\Box p}, s_{\Diamond \neg p}, s_\varphi\}, \bot)$$

State q_1 encodes the situation where s_p and $s_{\Box p}$ are false and $s_{\neg p}$ and $s_{\Diamond \neg p}$ are true in the current instant. In the subsequent instant $s_{\Box p}$ and s_p are true but the other streams are false. Note that in fact only q_1 is compatible with the Lola specification, but the other states are a contradiction to the equations of the specification. State q_2 is a contradiction because s_p and $s_{\neg p}$ cannot be false at the same time. State q_3 is a contradiction because when s_p is true at the last position of the trace, $s_{\Diamond \neg p}$ has to be false.   □

Based on this encoding we build a nondeterministic transition system, where the transition relation maps state (u, v) to state (v, w) when the first component of the post state coincides the second component of the pre-state (unless $v = \bot$). The second component w of the post-state is not determined and different transitions can make different guesses.

Our transition system will have $\Sigma = 2^I$ as input alphabet, determining which input streams are true and which are false. Given an input $b \in 2^I$ and an element $(v, v') \in Q$ we write $v(b)$ when v coincides with b in the truth value of all input streams (i.e. $v \cap I = b$). Given $v, v', v'' \in 2^{I \cup S}$ we further say $(v, v') \models^i E$ if substituting every 0 offset with the value corresponding to v and every $+1$ offset with those corresponding to v' makes all equations E in the Lola specification φ true for position 0. We say $(v, v', v'') \models E$ if substituting all 0 offset operators with the value according v', all -1 offsets with the value according v and all $+1$ offsets with the value according v'' makes all equations in E are satisfied. Finally we write $(v, v') \models^f E$ if -1 offset operators replaced by values according to v and 0 offset operators by those according to v' makes the equations in E satisfied for the last instant before the trace end.

Definition 2 (Lola Nondeterministic Transition System). *Let* $\varphi = (I, S, E)$ *be a well-defined Lola specification. The Lola nondeterministic transition system (LNTS) for* φ *is a tuple* $\mathcal{T}_\varphi = (Q_\varphi, \Sigma, q_0, \delta)$*, where* $q_0 = \#$ *and*

- $\delta(\#, b) = \{(v, v') \mid v(b) \text{ and } (v, v') \models^i E\}$
- $\delta((u, v), b) = \begin{cases} \{(v, v') \mid (u, v, v') \models E\} \cup \{(v, \bot) \mid (u, v) \models^f E\} & \text{if } v(b) \\ \emptyset & \text{otherwise} \end{cases}$

The transition relation first checks that the guessed successor v is compatible with inputs received and then guesses a new successor state v' that satisfies all equations E of the specification (including the possibility of guessing $\bot$ denoting the end of the trace).

Given a tuple of input streams $\tau \in (\mathcal{S}_\mathbb{B})^{|I|}$ and a well-defined Lola specification φ, there is a unique state sequence $q_0, q_1, \ldots, q_{|\tau|}$ such that $q_{i+1} \in \delta(q_i, \tau(i))$ and $q_{|\tau|} = (v, \bot)$. This follows from the fact that a well-defined Lola specification has a unique valuation (given the whole input sequence).

The LNTS $\mathcal{T}_\varphi$ allows to define a sequence of stream valuations for the current time instant, which is consistent with the inputs received so far and with φ. To build an anticipatory monitor for φ we determinize $\mathcal{T}_\varphi$ by applying the following two stages:

Removing Dead States. First we remove all states from the transition system from which a state with $\bot$ in the second component is not reachable, which corresponds to a situation where a wrong guess was made and that cannot be completed, no matter of the future inputs. Dead states can be identified by a depth-first search in $\mathcal{T}_\varphi$ starting at the initial state. We therefore limit the state space Q_φ to $\{q \in Q_\varphi \mid \exists w \in \Sigma^*, (q', \bot) \in \widehat{\delta}(q, w)\}$ where $\widehat{\delta}$ is defined as $\widehat{\delta}(q, \epsilon) = q$ and $\widehat{\delta}(q, aw) = \widehat{\delta}(\delta(q, a), w)$.

Example 2. Consider again the specification for $\varphi = \Box p \wedge \Diamond \neg p$ and the states $q_1 = (\{s_{\neg p}, s_{\Diamond \neg p}\}, \{s_p, s_{\Box p}\})$ and $q_2 = (\{s_p, s_{\Box p}, s_{\Diamond \neg p}, s_\varphi\}, \{s_p, s_{\Box p}, s_{\Diamond \neg p}, s_\varphi\})$.

From s_1 the state $(\{s_p, s_{\Box p}\}, \bot)$ is reachable, because the sub-formula $s_{\Box p}$ is satisfied at the trace end iff s_p is satisfied. Thus q_1 is alive. On the other hand q_2 is dead, because s_p, $s_{\Box p}$ and $s_{\Diamond \neg p}$ being true at some instant imply that these three streams (and thus also s_φ) are also true at the next instant. Consequently q_2 is the only possible successor of q_2 and especially $(\{s_p, s_{\Box p}, s_{\Diamond \neg p}, s_\varphi\}, \bot)$ is not a valid successor.   □

Determinize. Second, we use a power set construction to determinize the resulting transition system[2]. If the monitor is in a power state which corresponds to states in the original transition system that have different values for an output stream, then the monitoring output is ? for this stream. On the other hand, if all states in the power set agree on the valuation of an output stream, the monitor yields exactly this valuation. In particular, the distinguished stream receives either the valuation ? or a definite valuation tt or $f\!f$. Formally, the resulting monitor is defined as follows, where $s(q)$ denotes the current valuation of stream $s \in I \cup S$ in state q.

Definition 3 (Anticipatory Recurrent Lola monitor). *Let* $\varphi = (I, S, E)$ *be a well-defined Lola specification and* $T_\varphi = (Q_\varphi, \Sigma, q_0, \delta)$ *be the corresponding LNTS with dead states removed. The anticipatory recurrent Lola monitor for* φ *is the Moore Machine Monitor* $M_\varphi : (P, \Sigma, \Omega, p_0, \delta_m, \omega)$ *where* $P = 2^{Q_\varphi}$, $p_0 = \{q_0\}$ *and*

- $\delta_m(p, x) = \{\delta(q, x) \mid q \in p\} \cap Q_\varphi$
- $\omega(p)(s) = \begin{cases} tt & \text{if } s(q) = tt \text{ for all } q \in p \\ f\!f & \text{if } s(q) = f\!f \text{ for all } q \in p \\ ? & \text{otherwise} \end{cases}$

An *anticipatory* monitor is a sound monitor for all output streams that produces tt if and only if the evaluation of the output stream at this position is tt for all continuations, i.e. when the verdict is inevitable and the analogous for $f\!f$. Such a monitor thus only yields ? when both results are possible in different continuations.

The following result proves the correctness of our construction.

Theorem 1. *Let* $\varphi = (I, S, E)$ *be a well-defined Lola specification and* M_φ *the monitor according to Definition 3. Then* M_φ *is an anticipatory recurrent monitor for* φ.

The proof follows because M_φ only contains states that can lead to end states, so for every power state in M_φ there is a continuation of the input streams such that the equations in φ are satisfied. On the other hand the power set contains all non-dead states which are reachable from q_0 after processing the input received. A tt (resp. $f\!f$) verdict for a specific stream is cast if and only if all states agree on that valuation and thus there is no continuation of the currently received inputs compatible with a different verdict. It is easy to see that the size of M_φ is $2^{2^{\mathcal{O}(|\varphi|)}}$.

---

[2] which can for performance reasons also be done on the fly while monitoring.

4.3   Assumptions

Assumptions are additional knowledge about the system and its environment and thus restrict the set of possible input sequences that may be passed to the monitor. A general way to formalize assumptions in Lola [20] is to introduce an output stream s_a expressing the assumption and assume the stream to be always true. We rule out those states where s_a is false, or states that inevitably lead to those states. We restrict the state space to states where the assumption stream is true $Q_a \overset{\text{def}}{=} \{(u,v) \in Q_\varphi \mid s_a \in u, \text{ and } v = \bot \text{ or } s_a \in v\}$ and refine the definition of alive states to $alive_a^\varphi = \{q \in Q_\varphi \mid \exists w \in \Sigma^*, (q', \bot) \in \widehat{\delta}_a(q,w)\}$ where $\widehat{\delta}_a$ is defined as $\widehat{\delta}_a(q,b) = \delta(q,b) \cap Q_a$ and $\widehat{\delta}_a(q,bw) = \widehat{\delta}_a(\widehat{\delta}_a(q,b),w)$, that is, $\widehat{\delta}_a$ is like $\widehat{\delta}$ but only considers successor states that satisfy the assumption. We define a recurrent Lola monitor with assumptions, which differs from the monitor of Definition 3 by considering an advanced set of dead states.

Definition 4 (Recurrent Lola monitor with Assumptions). *Let* $\varphi = (I, S, E)$ *be a well-defined Lola specification and let* $\mathcal{T}_\varphi = (Q_\varphi, \Sigma, q_0, \delta)$ *be the corresponding LNTS with dead states (not in* $alive_a^\varphi$*) removed. The anticipatory recurrent Lola monitor for* φ *under assumptions is the Moore machine* $(P, \Sigma, \Omega, p_0, \delta_m, \omega)$ *where* $P = 2^{Q_a}$ *and* $p_0 = \{q_0\}$ *and* $\delta_m(p,b) = \{\delta(q,b) \mid q \in p\} \cap Q_a$ *(and* Σ*,* Ω *and* ω *are as before).*

Note that $\omega(p)(s_a)$ is forced to be tt at all states and that the new Moore machine has fewer states compared to the previous construction.

4.4   Uncertainties

We now extend our approach to tolerate uncertain inputs, where the value of some input is not known to be true or false. Instead of input alphabet Σ we consider 2^Σ as uncertain input alphabet where each letter encodes which certain input letters are possible at the current instant. Consider $AP = \{p, q\}$ and $\Sigma = 2^{AP}$, then input $\{\emptyset, \{p,q\}\} \in 2^\Sigma$ encodes that it is uncertain if p, q hold but it is known that they have the same value.

In the recurrent monitor with assumptions (Definition 4) we just extend the transition function such that from a set of specific states it transitions to all states which are reachable with one of the possible inputs:

Definition 5 (Recurrent Lola Monitor with Uncertainty and Assumptions). *Let* $\varphi = (I, S, E)$ *be a well-defined Lola specification and* $\mathcal{T}_\varphi = (Q_\varphi, \Sigma, q_0, \delta)$ *be the corresponding LNTS. The recurrent Lola monitor under uncertainty and assumptions for* φ *is the Moore machine* $(P, 2^\Sigma, \Omega, p_0, \delta_m, \omega)$ *where* P*,* p_0*,* Ω *and* ω *are as before and* $\delta_m(p,B) = \{\delta(q,b) \mid q \in p, b \in B\} \cap Q_a$*.*

Note that δ_m considers all possible inputs, potentially leading to more successors.

5   Anticipatory Monitoring in Action

We implemented the algorithm for anticipatory Lola monitoring from Sect. 4 in Scala[3]. The tool receives a Lola specification, calculates the set of empty states and then simulates the power set monitor on the fly as described in Sect. 4 with minor obvious optimizations. It supports assumptions and uncertainty.

We illustrate monitoring of the following TRLTL$_f$ formula that includes past and future operators (encoded linearly):

$$\varphi = p \wedge \Box((\neg p); p \rightarrow \Diamond(q; p; p; p; (\neg q)^*; q))$$

The formula holds in every position where (1) p is true and (2) if for all subsequent positions matching $(\neg p); p$, the pattern $q; p; p; p; (\neg q)^*; q$ was present somewhere in the past.

Following Sect. 3 we manually transformed the formula into a Lola specification with two input streams, p and q, ten defined streams, seven future references and one past reference. A traditional universal Lola monitor [12] would only immediately yield the verdict $f\!\!f$ at all positions where there is no p in the trace. All the locations where φ holds would only be reported after the whole trace is processed, because the $\Box$ part of the formula introduces a future reference, so a monitoring algorithm without anticipation only resolves these streams once the end of the trace is reached.

We evaluated our anticipatory monitoring approach on three randomly generated traces of length 1000. For each position, first q was selected to be true with a probability of 66%. If q was false then p was set to true, otherwise p was set to true with a probability of 50%. Consequently there were no positions in the traces where p and q were simultaneously false.

We ran our monitor for each trace, one time with the additional assumption $\Box(p \vee q)$ in the specification and one time without. Further we executed the monitor under presence of the assumption, but total uncertain information about p (i.e. $p = ?$ was sent to the monitor at all instants). The numbers of tt resp. $f\!\!f$ verdicts are depicted in the following table:

Trace	Offline Monitor		Rec. Ant. Monitor		+ Assumption		+ Uncertainty	
	tt	$f\!\!f$	tt	$f\!\!f$	tt	$f\!\!f$	tt	$f\!\!f$
1	650	350	644	349	646	349	311	0
2	651	349	647	339	649	339	307	0
3	659	341	655	337	656	337	286	0

The first column shows the number of positions where φ is satisfied, which corresponds to the output an offline monitor with full knowledge of the whole

---

[3] Tool and example are available on https://gitlab.isp.uni-luebeck.de/public_repos/anticipatory-recurrent-artifact.

trace would yield. The recurrent anticipatory monitor is able to cast final verdicts as soon as it detects a sequence $q; p; p; p; (\neg q)^*; q$ in the trace, because from then on $\diamondsuit(q; p; p; p; (\neg q)^*; q)$ and thus $\square((\neg p); p \rightarrow \diamondsuit(q; p; p; p; (\neg q)^*; q))$ is satisfied. Hence the monitor only reports a few ? verdicts at the beginning of the trace.

When the assumption $\square(p \vee q)$ is present, the recurrent monitor already yields final verdicts after receiving the sequence $q; p; p; p$, because from this moment on it can conclude that whenever the premises of the implication inside the globally operator, $(\neg p); p$, holds, then there is a $(\neg p)$ in the trace and consequently q holds at this position. This however implies that the trace also contains a sequence matching $q; p; p; p; (\neg q)^*; q$. This is why the recurrent monitor with assumption yields a slightly higher number of certain verdicts.

If p is fully uncertain, the monitor can not directly check anymore whether $q; p; p; p$ is contained in the trace. Yet, again using the assumption it can conclude that if $q; (\neg q); (\neg q); (\neg q)$ holds somewhere in the trace, then also $q; p; p; p$ holds there and thus $\square((\neg p); p \rightarrow \diamondsuit(q; p; p; p; (\neg q)^*; q))$ is satisfied from that instant on. Hence, from that position on, the monitor is able to cast tt whenever q is false, because at these instants p must be true. However, it cannot give verdicts at positions where q is true, including all positions where p is false, and thus never produces ff. Note that a traditional (online or offline) Lola monitor without the ability of handling assumptions would not be able to cast any certain verdicts under presence of the mentioned uncertainty.

We ran our examples on a Linux machine with 8GB RAM and Intel Core i7-8550 U (1.80GHz) CPU. The average time spent for the emptiness check was 2227 ms without assumption and 2156 ms with assumption. The processing time per event (without I/O handling) was on average, 2.22 ms without assumption, 1.84 ms with assumption and 5.60 ms under additional presence of uncertainty.

6   Final Remarks

Anticipation states that an online monitor should emit a precise verdict as soon as possible with the information received. This was first introduced for infinite traces [4,6] for LTL and for timed, event-clock extensions of LTL, and later generalized to all formalisms definable by Büchi automata in [13]. In [23] anticipation is made more precise if part of the underlying system is known. All these works consider only initial monitoring. In [18], recurrent monitoring was studied for past-only LTL always yielding a verdict for the current position in the trace. A generalization of the concept for future LTL formulas—but without an explicit construction—was studied in [19] together with assumption and uncertainties (meaning imprecise or missing inputs).

In recent years, temporal logics for finite traces have gained importance so it is a natural question how the concept of recurrent monitoring under uncertainties and assumptions materializes in the finite setting.

In this paper we addressed this question for the Boolean fragment of the SRV language Lola, which is a very general formalism encompassing many temporal logics on finite traces. We showed how many temporal logics on finite traces can be linearly translated into $TRLTL_f$, which we then translated into Lola. The logic $TRLTL_f$ introduced here simply takes all operands from RLTL [24] and LDL_f [16]. Since LDL_f and $RLTL_f$ are both expressive equivalent to regular languages they are equivalent in terms of expressive power. We are studying whehter there are linear translations from LDL_f to $RLTL_f$ and vice-versa, following reductions from [31] in the context of Metric Dynamic Logic (MDL) [2,3]. MDL extends LDL_f with intervals and has the same expressive power.

We then presented a recurrent, anticipatory monitoring algorithm for Lola specifications, extended it to handle uncertainties and assumptions, and pointed out how to map initial monitoring into recurrent monitoring for Lola.

The approach most closely related to ours is [9], which also considers monitoring under uncertainties and assumptions. However, [9] is limited to LTL and assumptions given as fair Kripke structures only.

We restricted our algorithm to Boolean Lola, so it is a natural question how to deal with anticipation, assumptions, and uncertainties for specifications over arbitrary theories. While assumptions and uncertainties for non-Boolean theories are studied in [20], anticipation is not considered there. A solution for LTL extended with theories, presented in [10], is based on reduction to bounded model checking and thus not guaranteed to be perfect and not trace-length independent.

The problem of anticipatory general Lola monitoring can also be solved easily if the length of the trace is known a-priori using a bounded-model-checking approach, by unwinding the specification to the known length and using a symbolic tool (e.g. an SMT solver) to compute definite verdicts with anticipation. Future work includes anticipatory monitoring algorithms for richer data specifications (like numerical Lola specifications) without assuming a known bound on the length of the trace.

Future work further comprises an implementation of the translations from logics to Lola specifications that were described in this paper and a thorough empirical comparison to other monitoring approaches for these logics and Lola in practical scenarios.

Acknowledgements. We would like to thank the anonymous reviewers for the thorough analysis of the paper and their useful suggestions and future directions.

References

1. Bartocci, E., Falcone, Y.: Lectures on Runtime Verification - Introductory and Advanced Topics, LNCS, vol. 10457. Springer, Cham (2018). https://doi.org/10.1007/978-3-319-75632-5
2. Basin, D., Bhatt, B.N., Krstić, S., Traytel, D.: Almost event-rate independent monitoring. Formal Methods Syst. Design **54**, 449–478 (2019). https://doi.org/10.1007/s10703-018-00328-3
3. Basin, D., Krstić, S., Traytel, D.: Almost event-rate independent monitoring of metric dynamic logic. In: Lahiri, S., Reger, G. (eds.) RV 2017. LNCS, vol. 10548, pp. 85–102. Springer, Cham (2017). https://doi.org/10.1007/978-3-319-67531-2_6

4. Bauer, A., Leucker, M., Schallhart, C.: Monitoring of real-time properties. In: Arun-Kumar, S., Garg, N. (eds.) FSTTCS 2006. LNCS, vol. 4337, pp. 260–272. Springer, Heidelberg (2006). https://doi.org/10.1007/11944836_25
5. Bauer, A., Leucker, M., Schallhart, C.: Comparing LTL semantics for runtime verification. J. Log. Comput. 20(3), 651–674 (2010). https://doi.org/10.1093/logcom/exn075
6. Bauer, A., Leucker, M., Schallhart, C.: Runtime verification for LTL and TLTL. ACM Trans. Softw. Eng. Methodol. 20(4), 14:1-14:64 (2011). https://doi.org/10.1145/2000799.2000800
7. Baumeister, J., Finkbeiner, B., Schirmer, S., Schwenger, M., Torens, C.: RTLola cleared for take-off: monitoring autonomous aircraft. In: Lahiri, S.K., Wang, C. (eds.) CAV 2020. LNCS, vol. 12225, pp. 28–39. Springer, Cham (2020). https://doi.org/10.1007/978-3-030-53291-8_3
8. Bozzelli, L., Sánchez, C.: Foundations of Boolean stream runtime verification. Theor. Comput. Sci. 631, 118–138 (2016). https://doi.org/10.1016/j.tcs.2016.04.019
9. Cimatti, A., Tian, C., Tonetta, S.: Assumption-based runtime verification with partial observability and resets. In: Finkbeiner, B., Mariani, L. (eds.) RV 2019. LNCS, vol. 11757, pp. 165–184. Springer, Cham (2019). https://doi.org/10.1007/978-3-030-32079-9_10
10. Cimatti, A., Tian, C., Tonetta, S.: Assumption-based runtime verification of infinite-state systems. In: Feng, L., Fisman, D. (eds.) RV 2021. LNCS, vol. 12974, pp. 207–227. Springer, Cham (2021). https://doi.org/10.1007/978-3-030-88494-9_11
11. Convent, L., Hungerecker, S., Leucker, M., Scheffel, T., Schmitz, M., Thoma, D.: TeSSLa: temporal stream-based specification language. In: Massoni, T., Mousavi, M.R. (eds.) SBMF 2018. LNCS, vol. 11254, pp. 144–162. Springer, Cham (2018). https://doi.org/10.1007/978-3-030-03044-5_10
12. D'Angelo, B., et al.: LOLA: runtime monitoring of synchronous systems. In: Proceedings of the 12th International Symposium on Temporal Representation and Reasoning (TIME 2005), pp. 166–174. IEEE Computer Society (2005). https://doi.org/10.1109/TIME.2005.26
13. Dong, W., Leucker, M., Schallhart, C.: Impartial anticipation in runtime-verification. In: Cha, S.S., Choi, J.-Y., Kim, M., Lee, I., Viswanathan, M. (eds.) ATVA 2008. LNCS, vol. 5311, pp. 386–396. Springer, Heidelberg (2008). https://doi.org/10.1007/978-3-540-88387-6_33
14. Eisner, C., Fisman, D., Havlicek, J., Lustig, Y., McIsaac, A., Van Campenhout, D.: Reasoning with temporal logic on truncated paths. In: Hunt, W.A., Somenzi, F. (eds.) CAV 2003. LNCS, vol. 2725, pp. 27–39. Springer, Heidelberg (2003). https://doi.org/10.1007/978-3-540-45069-6_3
15. Faymonville, P., et al.: StreamLAB: stream-based monitoring of cyber-physical systems. In: Dillig, I., Tasiran, S. (eds.) CAV 2019. LNCS, vol. 11561, pp. 421–431. Springer, Cham (2019). https://doi.org/10.1007/978-3-030-25540-4_24
16. Giacomo, G.D., Vardi, M.Y.: Linear temporal logic and linear dynamic logic on finite traces. In: Proceedings of the 23rd International Joint Conference on Artificial Intelligence (IJCAI 2013), pp. 854–860. IJCAI/AAAI (2013). http://www.aaai.org/ocs/index.php/IJCAI/IJCAI13/paper/view/6997
17. Gorostiaga, F., Sánchez, C.: Stream runtime verification of real-time event streams with the Striver language. Int. J. Softw. Tools Technol. Transf. 23, 157–183 (2021). https://doi.org/10.1007/s10009-021-00605-3

18. Havelund, K., Roşu, G.: Synthesizing monitors for safety properties. In: Katoen, J.-P., Stevens, P. (eds.) TACAS 2002. LNCS, vol. 2280, pp. 342–356. Springer, Heidelberg (2002). https://doi.org/10.1007/3-540-46002-0_24
19. Kallwies, H., Leucker, M., Sánchez, C., Scheffel, T.: Anticipatory recurrent monitoring with uncertainty and assumptions. In: Dang, T., Stolz, V. (eds.) RV 2022. LNCS, vol. 13498, pp. 181–199. Springer, Cham (2022). https://doi.org/10.1007/978-3-031-17196-3_10
20. Kallwies, H., Leucker, M., Sánchez, C.: Symbolic runtime verification for monitoring under uncertainties and assumptions. In: Bouajjani, A., Holík, L., Wu, Z. (eds.) ATVA 2022. LNCS, vol. 13505, pp. 117–134. Springer, Cham (2022). https://doi.org/10.1007/978-3-031-19992-9_8
21. Kleene, S.C.: Representation of events in nerve nets and finite automata. In: Shannon, C.E., McCarthy, J. (eds.) Automata Studies, vol. 34, pp. 3–41. Princeton University Press, Princeton, New Jersey (1956)
22. Leucker, M.: Teaching runtime verification. In: Khurshid, S., Sen, K. (eds.) RV 2011. LNCS, vol. 7186, pp. 34–48. Springer, Heidelberg (2012). https://doi.org/10.1007/978-3-642-29860-8_4
23. Leucker, M.: Sliding between model checking and runtime verification. In: Qadeer, S., Tasiran, S. (eds.) RV 2012. LNCS, vol. 7687, pp. 82–87. Springer, Heidelberg (2013). https://doi.org/10.1007/978-3-642-35632-2_10
24. Leucker, M., Sánchez, C.: Regular linear temporal logic. In: Jones, C.B., Liu, Z., Woodcock, J. (eds.) ICTAC 2007. LNCS, vol. 4711, pp. 291–305. Springer, Heidelberg (2007). https://doi.org/10.1007/978-3-540-75292-9_20
25. Leucker, M., Schallhart, C.: A brief account of runtime verification. J. Logic Algebr. Progr. **78**(5), 293–303 (2009). https://doi.org/10.1016/j.jlap.2008.08.004
26. Manna, Z., Pnueli, A.: The Temporal Logic of Reactive and Concurrent Systems. Springer, New York (1992). https://doi.org/10.1007/978-1-4612-0931-7
27. Manna, Z., Pnueli, A.: Temporal Verification of Reactive Systems. Springer-Verlag, Cham (1995)
28. McNaughton, R.F., Yamada, H.: Regular expressions and state graphs for automata. IEEE Trans. Electron. Comput. **9**, 39–47 (1960). https://doi.org/10.1109/TEC.1960.5221603
29. Perez, I., Dedden, F., Goodloe, A.: Copilot 3. Technical report, NASA/TM-2020-220587, NASA Langley Research Center (2020)
30. Pnueli, A.: The temporal logic of programs. In: Proceedings of the 18th IEEE Symposium on the Foundations of Computer Science (FOCS 1977), pp. 46–57. IEEE Computer Society Press (1977). https://doi.org/10.1109/SFCS.1977.32
31. Raszyk, M.: Efficient, Expressive, and Verified Temporal Query Evaluation. Ph.D. thesis, ETH (2022). https://doi.org/10.3929/ethz-b-000553221
32. Reinbacher, T., Rozier, K.Y., Schumann, J.: Temporal-logic based runtime observer pairs for system health management of real-time systems. In: Ábrahám, E., Havelund, K. (eds.) TACAS 2014. LNCS, vol. 8413, pp. 357–372. Springer, Heidelberg (2014). https://doi.org/10.1007/978-3-642-54862-8_24
33. Sánchez, C.: Online and offline stream runtime verification of synchronous systems. In: Colombo, C., Leucker, M. (eds.) RV 2018. LNCS, vol. 11237, pp. 138–163. Springer, Cham (2018). https://doi.org/10.1007/978-3-030-03769-7_9
34. Sánchez, C., Leucker, M.: Regular linear temporal logic with past. In: Barthe, G., Hermenegildo, M. (eds.) VMCAI 2010. LNCS, vol. 5944, pp. 295–311. Springer, Heidelberg (2010). https://doi.org/10.1007/978-3-642-11319-2_22

35. Sánchez, C., Samborski-Forlese, J.: Efficient regular linear temporal logic using dualization and stratification. In: Proceedings of the 19th International Symposium on Temporal Representation and Reasoning (TIME 2012), pp. 13–20. IEEE Computer Society (2012). https://doi.org/10.1109/TIME.2012.25
36. Wolper, P.: Temporal logic can be more expressive. Inf. Control **56**, 72–99 (1983). https://doi.org/10.1016/S0019-9958(83)80051-5

Metric First-Order Temporal Logic with Complex Data Types

Jeniffer Lima Graf, Srđan Krstić$^{(\boxtimes)}$ ⓘ, and Joshua Schneider$^{(\boxtimes)}$ ⓘ

Institute of Information Security, Department of Computer Science, ETH Zürich,
Zürich, Switzerland
{srdan.krstic,joshua.schneider}@inf.ethz.ch

Abstract. Temporal logics are widely used in runtime verification as they enable the creation of declarative and compositional specifications. However, their ability to model complex data is limited. One must resort to complicated encoding schemes to express properties involving basic structures such as lists or trees. To avoid this drawback, we extend metric first-order temporal logic with a minimalistic, yet expressive, functional programming language. The extension features an expressive collection of types including function, record, variant, and inductive types, as well as support for type inference and monitoring.

Our monitor implementation directly parses traces in the JSON format, based on the user's type specification, which avoids a separate preprocessing step. We compare our approach to existing shallow embeddings of temporal properties in general-purpose host languages and to encodings into simple temporal logics. Specifically, our language benefits from a precise semantics and a good support for monitoring-specific static analysis.

Keywords: Monitoring · Temporal logic · Data types

1 Introduction

Runtime verification (or monitoring) verifies running systems in their operational environment. Implemented by processes, called *monitors*, it systematically validates a specification by searching for counterexamples in a trace of events recorded during system execution. The specification describes the intended system behavior and, if explicitly input to the monitor, it is written in a specification language. Logical specification languages (e.g., LTL) are widely used due to their declarative and compositional nature.

First-order language extensions, like metric first-order temporal logic (MFOTL) can express dependencies between the data values stored in events. Yet most monitors support only atomic data values making it difficult to write and maintain many practical specifications. Events may contain structured data (e.g., JSON or XML objects), which require either a non-trivial pre-processing step for the trace, or an elaborate encoding scheme for the specification, or

P. Katsaros and L. Nenzi (Eds.): RV 2023, LNCS 14245, pp. 126–147, 2023.
https://doi.org/10.1007/978-3-031-44267-4_7

even both. Understanding and maintaining both such specifications and pre-processing logic quickly becomes unfeasible, especially as they need to be kept in sync. For example, small changes in the pre-processing logic, like extracting event values in a different order, must be reflected in the first-order specification, e.g., by swapping the appropriate variables in the predicates. Ideally, trace pre-processing should not be done both to avoid the processing overhead and the need to have it in-sync with the specification. If this cannot be achieved, then pre-processing should be domain-independent—it should not rely on the meaning of the trace events.

For example, consider a web server execution trace with successful accesses by clients:

```
@100 {"url":"/login", "client":"123"}
@113 {"url":"/login", "client":"123", "session":{"id":7, "token":"..."}}
@115 {"url":"/secure", "client":"123", "session":{"id":7, "token":"..."}}
@200 {"url":"/secure", "client":"666"}
@800 {"url":"/secure", "client":"123", "session":{"id":7, "token":"..."}}
```

where each line contains a JSON object prefixed with a @*ddd* time-stamp in seconds.

Suppose that every client accessing the /secure URL must have a valid session, not older than 600 seconds, established previously by visiting /login. A way to monitor this specification is to translate JSON objects to tuples containing values of atomic data types:

```
@100 Access("/login", "123", False, -1, "")
@113 Access("/login", "123", True, 7, "...") etc.
```

The Boolean flag in each tuple indicates if there is a session, otherwise id and token fields have dummy values. The corresponding MFOTL formula formalizing the specification is $\mathsf{Access}(\text{/secure}, c, s, id, t) \rightarrow s = \mathsf{True} \land \blacklozenge_{[0,600)} \mathsf{Access}(\text{/login}, c, \mathsf{True}, id, t)$.

Such a flat structure makes writing specifications tedious as many variables must be used consistently and in a correct position. Moreover, changing the pre-processing (e.g., avoiding the Boolean flag by using separate Access and Session events) necessitates a non-trivial change in the specification.

In this paper we propose an extension of MFOTL, called CMFOTL, which supports complex data types. The extension is accompanied by a corresponding extension of MonPoly [7], an online monitor for MFOTL specifications.

Our presentation of CMFOTL diverges from MFOTL's standard single-sorted first-order logic definition [3,5,6,34]. We start by enumerating multiple primitive types (already supported by MonPoly) and then define a type language that allows for their combination via function, record, variant, and inductive type constructors. To use the newly added types, CMFOTL embeds a minimalistic, yet expressive, functional programming language. We develop a type system and a type inference algorithm for CMFOTL. We then present semantics for well-typed CMFOTL formulas. Finally, we describe a CMFOTL fragment monitorable using finite relations, which is implemented as a syntactic check in MonPoly and supported by the CMFOTL monitoring algorithm. While we rely on standard concepts from programming language theory, our particular design choices (Sect. 2) were heavily motivated by efficient monitoring. In particular, we make the following contributions:

- We extend MFOTL with complex data types (Sect. 3) to obtain CMFOTL (Sect. 4).
- We develop a type system for CMFOTL used by its type inference algorithm (Sect. 5).
- We define the semantics for well-typed CMFOTL formulas (Sect. 6).
- We bridge the gap between the loosely-typed JSON traces and our strongly-typed language by converting a user-facing signature for JSON events to a first-order signature with complex types (Sect. 7.1). Our monitoring algorithm for monitorable CMFOTL formulas directly processes JSON events (Sect. 7.2).
- We exemplify CMFOTL's expressiveness with multiple specifications and evaluate the performance of the extended MonPoly monitor (Sect. 8).

To the best of our knowledge this is the first logic-based specification language for monitoring that supports complex data types and has precisely defined semantics. Other approaches (Sect. 9) either rely on trace pre-processing [7,21] or on domain-specific languages (DSLs) [17,20], which often import unspecified host programming language semantics.

Our implementation and evaluation is publicly available [25].

2   Design Choices

The language extension we present in this paper is inspired by our work on applying runtime verification to large and complex distributed systems. In particular, we used the MonPoly monitor [7] in a previous case study to check properties of the Internet Computer (IC) [4]. The IC's execution traces were recorded in a detailed JSON format, which required us to engineer a non-trivial mapping from the source data into more abstract events with appropriate parameters. The parameters had to be atomic data (e.g., integers or strings) for compatibility with MonPoly. Writing the specifications representing IC's properties in MFOTL was an iterative process. In addition to clarifying and fixing imprecise versions of the specification, we also had to account for changes in the format and semantics of the JSON events, which would additionally prompt modifications of the event pre-processing. Synchronizing it with the actual MFOTL specifications was a manual and error-prone process, which had to be tested regularly.

To avoid pre-processing while also supporting realistic event sources, our new language provides *record types* with labeled fields, which correspond to JSON objects. *Named* record types can be defined in the language's user-facing signature, whereas *unnamed* record types can be defined directly within formulas. As JSON objects may not always conform to a rigid structure (e.g., some fields may be optional as in the JSON trace in Sect. 1), we also decided to introduce *variant types* and the *optional type* as a special case.

JSON arrays motivate the need for *list types* and more broadly *inductive types*. We chose to use an iso-recursive [16] over an equi-recursive formalism [27] for our type system due to its simpler type inference algorithm. As an example specification, consider the following execution trace of a webshop application containing information about parcels sent to customers.

```
@100 {"customer":"Alice", "parcel":{"content":[{"content":[]}]}}
@200 {"customer":"Bob", "parcel":{"content":[{"content":[{},{}]}]}}
```

One could interpret the objects in the `parcel` fields as arbitrarily nested boxes that make up the parcel. A possible specification for this trace could be that only parcels that consist of up to ten boxes (including all nested boxes) are allowed. In this example, inductive types are necessary to represent both the box objects and the array associated with the `content` field. The user must define the inductive type for the boxes in the user-facing signature. This has the benefit that it allows us to use type-specific *recursors*, which guarantee termination of the monitor's computations [19]. As a result, only total functions can be expressed and our language is not Turing-complete.

We realize the above extensions with a minimal number of syntactic constructs in the core language. We also provide syntactic sugar for writing specifications in a convenient way. Our new language CMFOTL is a many-sorted strongly-typed logic, unlike the single-sorted logic MFOTL. In practice, the type system prevents additional sources of errors when formulating specifications. We believe that the strong type discipline is not a major burden on the user, as we also provide a type inference algorithm for the new language.

CMFOTL's syntax and semantics (almost) only extend MFOTL's terms. Compared to an alternative design based on higher-order logic, this allows for efficient monitoring as it requires only simple bottom-up term evaluation. Furthermore, by retaining the well-known MFOTL formula semantics, CMFOTL's monitoring algorithm can readily reuse existing optimizations, e.g., for temporal operators.

3   Complex Data Types

MFOTL is typically presented as a single-sorted logic [6,11], i.e., there is one *domain* that variables range over. In principle, it would suffice to extend the domain and the built-in operations (function symbols) in order to add support for complex data. However, the benefits of static typing are well-known [29]. We therefore define a type language that combines standard features that are widely used in functional programming languages, specifically record (product) types, variant (sum) types, inductive types, and type classes.

We assume an infinite supply of type variables X and labels l. The latter are used for record field and variant constructor names. The syntax of types is given by the following grammar, where $A, \ldots, A$ indicates zero or more repetitions of A.

$$\tau ::= \mathsf{Int} \mid \mathsf{Float} \mid \mathsf{Str} \mid (\tau, \ldots, \tau) \Rightarrow \tau \mid \{l : \tau, \ldots, l : \tau\} \mid \langle l : \tau, \ldots, l : \tau \rangle \mid \mu X. \tau \mid X$$

The symbols Int, Float, and Str represent primitive types for integers, floating-point numbers, and strings, respectively. The function type $(\tau_1, \ldots, \tau_n) \Rightarrow \rho$ describes total functions that map tuples over types $\tau_1, \ldots, \tau_n$ into values of type ρ.

Record types are denoted by $\{l_1 : \tau_1, l_2 : \tau_2, \ldots, l_n : \tau_n\}$, where $l_1, l_2, \ldots, l_n$ is a possibly empty list of field labels, and $\tau_1, \tau_2, \ldots, \tau_n$ are the corresponding types. The order of labels is irrelevant: $\{l : \mathsf{Int}, m : \mathsf{Str}\}$ and $\{m : \mathsf{Str}, l : \mathsf{Int}\}$ denote the same type. Intuitively, the values of a record type are tuples that assign a value to each label. They can be used to describe compound objects. The empty record type $\{\}$ serves as the unit type, which has a single value. It is sometimes convenient to use records with unnamed fields that are instead distinguished by their order of appearance. We write $(\tau_1, \ldots, \tau_n)$ for such a *tuple type*, which can be de-sugared into an equivalent record type with canonical labels.

Variant types $\langle l_1 : \tau_1, l_2 : \tau_2, \ldots, l_n : \tau_n \rangle$ are dual to records. They represent the choice of one of multiple alternatives, whose order is again irrelevant. Their values can be thought of as pairs (l_i, x), where l_i is one of the *constructors* and the value x has type τ_i. The empty variant $\langle \rangle$ represents the empty type, which does not contain any values. A simple example combining variants and the unit type is the encoding of Booleans by the $\langle \mathsf{true} : \{\}, \mathsf{false} : \{\} \rangle$ type. This type plays a special role and hence we give it the name Bool.

The expression $\mu X. \tau$ denotes an inductive type. The type variable X must occur strictly positively in τ, i.e., X must not occur as a free type variable in an argument type τ_i of any function type $(\tau_1, \ldots, \tau_n) \Rightarrow \rho$ within τ [15]. Intuitively, an inductive type $\mu X. \tau$ is the least fixpoint of the type equation $X = \tau$. The variable X is bound by $\mu X. \tau$ in τ and is thus subject to α-conversion. As an example, $\mu X. \langle \mathsf{Nil} : \{\}, \mathsf{Cons} : \{\mathsf{hd} : \mathsf{Int}, \mathsf{tl} : X\} \rangle$ represents finite lists of integers. A type without free type variables is *ground*.

4   Specification Language

We now present CMFOTL, our specification language that supports complex data types from Sect. 3. It is based on MFOTL, which has two main syntactic categories: terms and formulas. Terms evaluate to values from the domain, whereas formulas assign a truth value to every time-point in a given trace. We primarily extend the term syntax with new constructs. Specifically, we add a lambda calculus and operations to work with the new data types. We remove equality and ordering relations from the formula syntax because they can now be expressed as terms. Such terms can be used within a new, more general type of atomic formula, *assertions*, which assert the truth of an arbitrary Boolean-valued term. To keep the presentation self-contained, we also recap the unmodified parts of MFOTL. New elements are indicated with a gray background .

The syntax of terms is given by the following grammar, where c, x, l range over constants, variables, and labels, respectively.

$$t ::= c \mid x \mid t : \tau \mid \lambda(x, \ldots, x).\, t \mid t(t, \ldots, t) \mid \{l : t, \ldots, l : t\} \mid t.l \mid \mathsf{mk}\, l(t)$$

$$\mid \mathsf{case}(t; l(x) \rightarrow t, \ldots, l(x) \rightarrow t) \mid \mathsf{rec}_{X.\tau}(t) \mid \mathsf{unrec}_{X.\tau}(t) \mid \mathsf{fold}_{X.\tau}(t; x \rightarrow t)$$

We provide an intuitive explanation here; the formal semantics is postponed to Sect. 6 as it depends on the type system. Constants represent operations that are built into the monitor. We fix the set of available constants in Sect. 6. The term $t : \tau$ denotes a type ascription, which enforces and documents that t has the type τ. Lambda abstractions $\lambda(x_1, \ldots, x_n).\, t$ and function applications $t_f(t_1, \ldots, t_n)$ support multiple arguments.

The term $\{l_1 : t_1, \ldots, l_n : t_n\}$ constructs a value of a record type, and $t.l_i$ is its projection to label l_i. Dually, the term $\mathsf{mk}\, l_i(t)$ constructs a value of a variant type, and $\mathsf{case}(t; l_1(x_1) \rightarrow t_1, \ldots, l_n(x_n) \rightarrow t_n)$ performs a case distinction on t. If a constructor l_i has argument type $\{\}$, we typically omit the term in $\mathsf{mk}\, l_i$ and the variable in a case branch $l_i \rightarrow t_i$. Recursive types $\mu X.\tau$ are constructed and deconstructed via the terms $\mathsf{rec}_{X.\tau}(t)$ and $\mathsf{unrec}_{X.\tau}(t)$. Recursive computations must be expressed as a fold (i.e., a *catamorphism*) $\mathsf{fold}_{X.\tau}(t_1; x \rightarrow t_2)$, where t_1 is a value of type $\mu X.\tau$ to fold and t_2 performs one step of the computation using the partial result bound to x. The last three constructs are annotated by the inductive type to facilitate type inference.

Our modified formula syntax is mostly the same as that of MFOTL. For space reasons we exclude aggregation operators [5] and (non-recursive) let bindings [34], which our implementation also supports. The complete version of CMFOTL is shown in the extended version of this paper [24]. In the grammar below, P ranges over predicate symbols, and I ranges over non-empty and possibly unbounded intervals over the natural numbers.

$$\varphi ::= \ \downarrow t \mid P(t, \ldots, t) \mid \neg\varphi \mid \varphi \wedge \varphi \mid \varphi \vee \varphi \mid \exists x.\, \varphi \mid \bullet_I\, \varphi \mid \bigcirc_I\, \varphi \mid \varphi\, \mathsf{S}_I\, \varphi \mid \varphi\, \mathsf{U}_I\, \varphi.$$

The noteworthy change over previous versions of MFOTL is the introduction of assertions $\downarrow t$, which replace and generalize equality $(t_1 = t_2)$ and inequality $(t_1 < t_2, t_1 \leq t_2)$ formulas. Atomic predicates $P(t_1, \ldots, t_n)$, Boolean operators, and existential quantification are as in first-order logic. The past and future temporal operators $\bullet_I$, $\bigcirc_I$, S_I, and U_I are as in discrete-time MTL [1]. The interval subscripts impose bounds on the elapsed time. A missing interval defaults to the maximal interval $[0, \infty]$.

Parentheses can be omitted based on operator precedence. Our convention is that the scope of binders (lambdas, branches of case, and quantifiers) extends maximally to the right. Negation has the highest precedence, followed by conjunction and disjunction, in this order. We always parenthesize temporal operators for clarity. Additional operators are defined as syntactic sugar, for example $\blacklozenge_I\, \varphi \equiv (\downarrow\mathsf{true}\, \mathsf{S}_I\, \varphi)$ and $\Diamond_I\, \varphi \equiv (\downarrow\mathsf{true}\, \mathsf{U}_I\, \varphi)$.

Free variables $\mathsf{fv}(t)$ and $\mathsf{fv}(\varphi)$ are defined as usual. Arrows $\rightarrow$ and quantifiers indicate variable bindings, e.g., $l(x)\rightarrow t$ and $\exists x.\,\varphi$ bind x in t and φ, respectively.

5   Type System

Not all terms and formulas are meaningful. For instance, it is unclear how to interpret a projection applied to a lambda term. Therefore, we introduce a type system for CMFOTL. It is based on a inductively defined *typing judgement relation*. Only terms and formulas that are well-typed, i.e., that can be assigned a type by this relation, have a semantics. Our monitor implementation first checks well-typedness of a CMFOTL formula before proceeding to monitor it. Specifically, it performs type inference, which finds the most general type (up to the names of type variables) for every (sub-)term of the formula. Like any static type system, ours serves as an additional layer of protection against runtime errors. In monitoring, such errors may be due to a malformed specification. To define the typing judgement relation we need to define type classes and type class constraints.

A *type class* [33] is a set of types that share a specific common property, e.g., the property that addition is defined. Types can be members of multiple type classes, and type classes are partially ordered by their subset relationship. Type classes allow for overloading of operations in terms. For example, it should be possible to use the addition operator $+$ both with integers and floating-point numbers.

We use the following type classes. The class Eq consists of all types that are built without function types. We restrict the equality operator to Eq type because function equality is undecidable in general. The class $\mathsf{Ord} \supset \{\mathsf{Int}, \mathsf{Float}, \mathsf{Str}\}$ consists of all types on which a total ordering $\leq$ is defined. In addition to the three primitive types, our implementation considers record and variant types whose fields or constructor arguments are recursively members of Ord to be instances of Ord (using a lexicographic ordering). The class $\mathsf{Num} = \{\mathsf{Int}, \mathsf{Float}\}$ consists of all numeric types that support the four basic arithmetic operations and modulo. The classes $\mathsf{Proj}(l : \tau)$ consists of all record types that contain a field $l : \tau$, and the classes $\mathsf{Ctor}(l : \tau)$ consist similarly of all variant types that have a constructor $l : \tau$. With these classes our type inference (Sect. 5.2) can incorporate Ohori's approach [28] for inferring polymorphic record and variant types. The classes $\mathsf{Proj}(l : \tau)$ and $\mathsf{Ctor}(l : \tau)$ are *parametric* in τ [10] and we do not require unique field or constructor names across types. Note that the field and constructor argument types τ are uniquely determined given an instance of the respective type class. This ensures that type inference yields the expected most general type without additional type annotations.

A *type class constraint* C is a (finite, possibly empty) set of type classes. It is a symbolic representation of the intersection of those classes. We say that the types in the intersection satisfy the constraint. The empty constraint is satisfied by all types. We attach type class constraints to type variables to restrict the types that they can be instantiated with. For bound type variables, we denote the constraint as part of the binder (e.g., $\mu X : \{\mathsf{Num}\}.\,\tau$).

5.1   Typing Rules

The typing judgement relation $\Gamma \vdash t :: \tau$ for terms is a ternary relation between variable contexts Γ, terms t, and types τ. A variable context is a finite mapping from variables to types. The typing judgement is defined as the least relation closed under the rules shown in Fig. 1a. Each rule consist of a possibly empty sequence of hypotheses above the line and a conclusion below the line. There is an implicit condition for all rules: any free type variables must be free in the conclusion's context or type, i.e., hidden polymorphism is not allowed. For terms with a varying number of sub-terms, such as lambda terms, there is a corresponding sequence of assumptions or variable bindings, which we abbreviate using an ellipsis ($\cdots$). The sequence should be extended to the concrete number of elements in the obvious way when applying the rule. When we write $\Gamma, x : t$ it means that the variable context contains the binding $x : t$, together with zero or more bindings for *other* variables as described by Γ. An assumption such as $\pi \in \mathsf{Proj}(l : \tau)$ means that the type π must be a member of the type class $\mathsf{Proj}(l : \tau)$. Finally, $\tau[\sigma/X]$ denotes the capture-avoiding substitution of σ for all free occurrences of the type variable X in τ.

Constants may be polymorphic. Therefore, every constant has an associated type scheme, i.e., a type that may have free type variables. When applying the CST rule, these free type variables are substituted for arbitrary types subject to any type class constraints.

The FOLD rule is best explained with an example. Recall that the inductive type $\mathsf{list} \equiv \mu X. \langle \mathsf{Nil} : \{\}, \mathsf{Cons} : \{\mathsf{hd} : \mathsf{Int}, \mathsf{tl} : X\}\rangle$ represents lists of integers. The term

$$\mathsf{fold}_{\mathsf{list}}(x; y \rightarrow \mathsf{case}(y; \mathsf{Nil} \rightarrow 0, \mathsf{Cons}(z) \rightarrow \mathsf{plus}(1, z.\mathsf{tl})))$$

computes the length of the list x. Here, the constant plus is a function that takes two numeric arguments and computes their sum. The derivation shown in Fig. 2 holds under the assumption that x has type list in Γ. It proves that the above term has type Int. Note that the type of y is equal to part of the list under the binder μX, except that X has been substituted by Int, which is the result type of the recursive computation.

The typing judgement for formulas depends on a *first-order signature* in addition to the variable context. In MFOTL, the first-order signature defines a finite set of predicate symbols and their arities, i.e., the number of arguments. To account for CMFOTL's type system, a first-order signature Δ additionally associates a sequence of types $\tau_1, \ldots, \tau_n$ with each predicate symbol of arity n. Similarly to variable contexts, we write $\Delta, R : (\tau_1, \ldots, \tau_n)$ for the first-order signature that assigns the given types to the symbol R.

Given a first-order signature Δ, a variable context Γ, and a CMFOTL formula φ, the judgement $\Delta; \Gamma \vdash \varphi$ states that φ is well-typed formula. Note that formulas do not have a value (they can only be satisfied or not) and hence we do not assign a type to them. The rules for formulas are shown in Fig. 1b.

$$\frac{\tau \text{ is an instance of } c\text{'s type scheme}}{\Gamma \vdash c :: \tau} \text{ Cst} \qquad \frac{}{\Gamma, x : \tau \vdash x :: \tau} \text{ Var} \qquad \frac{\Gamma \vdash t :: \tau}{\Gamma \vdash (t : \tau) :: \tau} \text{ Asc}$$

$$\frac{\Gamma, x_1 : \tau_1, \ldots, x_n : \tau_n \vdash t :: \rho}{\Gamma \vdash \lambda(x_1, \ldots, x_n).\, t :: (\tau_1, \ldots, \tau_n) \Rightarrow \rho} \text{ Lam}$$

$$\frac{\Gamma \vdash t_f :: (\tau_1, \ldots, \tau_n) \Rightarrow \rho \quad \Gamma \vdash t_1 :: \tau_1 \quad \cdots \quad \Gamma \vdash t_n :: \tau_n}{\Gamma \vdash t_f(t_1, \ldots, t_n) :: \rho} \text{ App}$$

$$\frac{\Gamma \vdash t_1 :: \tau_1 \quad \cdots \quad \Gamma \vdash t_n :: \tau_n}{\Gamma \vdash \{l_1 : t_1, \ldots, l_n : t_n\} :: \{l_1 : \tau_1, \ldots, l_n : \tau_n\}} \text{ Prod} \qquad \frac{\Gamma \vdash t :: \pi \quad \pi \in \mathsf{Proj}(l : \tau)}{\Gamma \vdash t.l :: \tau} \text{ Proj}$$

$$\frac{\Gamma \vdash t :: \tau \quad \sigma \in \mathsf{Ctor}(l : \tau)}{\Gamma \vdash l(t) :: \sigma} \text{ Ctor}$$

$$\frac{\Gamma \vdash t :: \langle l_1 : \tau_1, \ldots, l_n : \tau_n \rangle \quad \Gamma, x_1 : \tau_1 \vdash t_1 :: \rho \quad \cdots \quad \Gamma, x_n : \tau_n \vdash t_n :: \rho}{\Gamma \vdash \mathsf{case}(t; l_1(x_1) {\to} t_1, \ldots, l_n(x_n) {\to} t_n) :: \rho} \text{ Case}$$

$$\frac{\Gamma \vdash t :: \tau[\mu X.\tau / X]}{\Gamma \vdash \mathsf{rec}_{X.\tau}(t) :: \mu X.\tau} \text{ Rec} \qquad \frac{\Gamma \vdash t :: \mu X.\tau}{\Gamma \vdash \mathsf{unrec}_{X.\tau}(t) :: \tau[\mu X.\tau / X]} \text{ UnRec}$$

$$\frac{\Gamma \vdash t_1 :: \mu X.\tau \quad \Gamma, x : \tau[\rho / X] \vdash t_2 :: \rho}{\Gamma \vdash \mathsf{fold}_{X.\tau}(t_1; x {\to} t_2) :: \rho} \text{ Fold}$$

(a) Typing rules for terms

$$\frac{\Gamma \vdash t_1 :: \tau_1 \quad \cdots \quad \Gamma \vdash t_n :: \tau_n}{\Delta, R : (\tau_1, \ldots, \tau_n);\ \Gamma \vdash R(t_1, \ldots, t_n)} \text{ Pred} \qquad \frac{\Gamma \vdash t :: \mathsf{Bool}}{\Delta;\ \Gamma \vdash {\downarrow} t} \text{ Assert}$$

$$\frac{\Delta;\ \Gamma \vdash \varphi}{\Delta;\ \Gamma \vdash {\star} \varphi} \text{ UnForm} \quad \star \in \{\neg, {\bullet}_I, {\circ}_I\}$$

$$\frac{\Delta;\ \Gamma \vdash \varphi \quad \Delta;\ \Gamma \vdash \psi}{\Delta;\ \Gamma \vdash \varphi \star \psi} \text{ BinForm} \quad \star \in \{\wedge, \vee, \mathsf{S}_I, \mathsf{U}_I\} \qquad \frac{\Delta;\ \Gamma, x : \tau \vdash \varphi}{\Delta;\ \Gamma \vdash \exists x.\ \varphi} \text{ Exists}$$

(b) Typing rules for formulas

Fig. 1. Typing rules for CMFOTL

$$\dfrac{\dfrac{\dfrac{}{\Gamma' \vdash y :: \langle \mathsf{Nil} : \{\}, \mathsf{Cons} : \tau \rangle}\ \mathrm{V_{AR}} \quad (1)\ (2)}{\dfrac{\Gamma \vdash x :: \mathsf{list}}{}\ \mathrm{V_{AR}} \quad \Gamma' \vdash \mathsf{case}(y; \mathsf{Nil} \to 0, \mathsf{Cons}(z) \to \mathsf{plus}(1, z.\mathsf{tl})) :: \mathsf{Int}}\ \mathrm{C_{ASE}}}{\Gamma \vdash \mathsf{fold}_{\mathsf{list}}(x; y \to \mathsf{case}(y; \mathsf{Nil} \to 0, \mathsf{Cons}(z) \to \mathsf{plus}(1, z.\mathsf{tl}))) :: \mathsf{Int}}\ \mathrm{F_{OLD}}$$

$$\dfrac{}{(1):\quad \Gamma' \vdash 0 :: \mathsf{Int}}\ \mathrm{C_{ST}}$$

$$\dfrac{\dfrac{}{\Gamma'' \vdash \mathsf{plus} :: (\mathsf{Int}, \mathsf{Int}) \Rightarrow \mathsf{Int}}\ \mathrm{C_{ST}} \quad \dfrac{}{\Gamma'' \vdash 1 :: \mathsf{Int}}\ \mathrm{C_{ST}} \quad \dfrac{\dfrac{}{\Gamma'' \vdash z :: \tau}\ \mathrm{V_{AR}}}{\Gamma'' \vdash z.\mathsf{tl} :: \mathsf{Int}}\ \mathrm{P_{ROJ}}}{(2):\quad \Gamma'' \vdash \mathsf{plus}(1, z.\mathsf{tl}) :: \mathsf{Int}}\ \mathrm{A_{PP}}$$

$$\Gamma' \equiv \Gamma, y : \langle \mathsf{Nil} : \{\}, \mathsf{Cons} : \tau \rangle \qquad \Gamma'' \equiv \Gamma', z : \tau \qquad \tau \equiv \{\mathsf{hd} : \mathsf{Int}, \mathsf{tl} : \mathsf{Int}\}$$

Fig. 2. Example type derivation

5.2 Type Inference

We implemented a type inference algorithm based on the Damas–Hindley–Milner framework [13]. Our handling of type classes is similar to the approach described by Chen, Hudak, and Odersky [10]. Neither work considers a logical layer like CMFOTL's formula language, but the extension to formulas is straightforward.

The algorithm proceeds bottom-up in a syntax-directed fashion while propagating the current knowledge about the variable context and first-order signature. The signature is initially obtained from the user (see Sect. 7.1). For compound expressions, the sub-expressions (i.e., terms and/or formulas) are visited first to obtain their most general types. As is typical for type systems, there is a unique rule that applies to every syntax construct. We determine the most general instance of that rule which agrees with the sub-expressions' types through unification. A type error is reported whenever unification fails. The unification procedure must take the type class constraints of type variables into account. Additional care is required for variable binders such as lambda functions as bound variables can shadow variables of the same name in the surrounding context.

Let us revisit the list sum example from the previous subsection. Suppose that the constant '0' is the first sub-expression to be visited. It is not polymorphic and hence the type Int is returned immediately. Next, we consider $\mathsf{plus}(1, z.\mathsf{tl})$. This term is in the scope of the variables x, y, and z. Whenever the algorithm enters a scope of a binder, it adds the variable with a fresh, unrestricted type variable to the context. Let us call these τ_x, τ_y, τ_z for variables x, y, and z. The type scheme of plus is declared as $(\alpha, \alpha) \Rightarrow \alpha$ where $\alpha : \{\mathsf{Num}\}$. Whenever such a polymorphic constant is encountered, the algorithm replaces its type variables with fresh ones, say, $\tau_+ : \{\mathsf{Num}\}$ in this case. As the type of $1 :: \mathsf{Int}$ must agree with the first argument of plus, unification results in the substitution $\tau_+ \mapsto \mathsf{Int}$. This substitution is possible because Int satisfies the constraint $\{\mathsf{Num}\}$. Inferring the type of $z.\mathsf{tl}$ results in a refinement of τ_z's constraint in the variable context: it is now $\{\mathsf{Proj}(\mathsf{tl} : \mathsf{Int})\}$.

Table 1. The constants of the base model (abridged)

Constant	Type scheme	Constant	Type scheme
true , false	Bool	neg	$(\tau) \Rightarrow \tau, \tau \in \mathsf{Num}$
eq	$(\tau, \tau) \Rightarrow \mathsf{Bool}, \tau \in \mathsf{Eq}$	plus	$(\tau, \tau) \Rightarrow \tau, \tau \in \mathsf{Num}$
less	$(\tau, \tau) \Rightarrow \mathsf{Bool}, \tau \in \mathsf{Ord}$	minus	$(\tau, \tau) \Rightarrow \tau, \tau \in \mathsf{Num}$
leq	$(\tau, \tau) \Rightarrow \mathsf{Bool}, \tau \in \mathsf{Ord}$	times	$(\tau, \tau) \Rightarrow \tau, \tau \in \mathsf{Num}$
not	$(\mathsf{Bool}) \Rightarrow \mathsf{Bool}$	div	$(\tau, \tau) \Rightarrow \tau, \tau \in \mathsf{Num}$
and	$(\mathsf{Bool}, \mathsf{Bool}) \Rightarrow \mathsf{Bool}$	mod	$(\mathsf{Int}, \mathsf{Int}) \Rightarrow \mathsf{Int}$
or	$(\mathsf{Bool}, \mathsf{Bool}) \Rightarrow \mathsf{Bool}$		

Unification with the CASE rule triggers the substitution $\tau_y \mapsto \langle \mathsf{Nil} : \nu, \mathsf{Cons} : \tau_z \rangle$. At this point, there is no information about Nil's argument type. The case term itself has type Int. The most interesting step happens for the fold: To obtain a proper instance of its type rule, we unify y's type with

$$\langle \mathsf{Nil} : \{\}, \mathsf{Cons} : \{\mathsf{hd} : \mathsf{Int}, \mathsf{tl} : X\} \rangle [\mathsf{Int}/X] \equiv \langle \mathsf{Nil} : \{\}, \mathsf{Cons} : \{\mathsf{hd} : \mathsf{Int}, \mathsf{tl} : \mathsf{Int}\} \rangle.$$

This results in the substitutions $\nu \mapsto \{\}$ and $\tau_z \mapsto \{\mathsf{hd} : \mathsf{Int}, \mathsf{tl} : \mathsf{Int}\}$, where the latter satisfies constraint $\{\mathsf{Proj}(\mathsf{tl} : \mathsf{Int})\}$ from above. Since fold's most generic type is that of its last sub-term (after applying applicable substitutions), we obtain Int as the overall result.

6   Semantics

We define CMFOTL's semantics with respect to infinite *temporal structures* (i.e., traces), which associate a first-order structure with every time-point. The introduction of complex data types requires a specific domain that provides the values of all possible types. Moreover, it makes sense to provide a rigid interpretation of CMFOTL's constants so that they can be relied upon in specifications and implemented directly in the monitor. We call this fixed part of the temporal structures including the domain the *base model*. We construct the base model from a suitable subset of terms that intuitively represent *values* which cannot be simplified further by computation. As a consequence, all function values in the base model are definable and equality over functions is intensional, i.e., it depends on the functions' definitions. This is sufficient in practice because in our monitor implementation, variables of function type are instantiated only with those functions that occur in the formula or with constants of the base model; functions in the trace are not supported. Moreover, functions cannot be compared for equality as they are not part of the Eq class.

All sub-terms and variables (including bound ones) have known types after the successful completion of type inference. In this section, we use the type ascription syntax $t : \tau$ both for sub-terms and variable binders to access those types.

Moreover, we assume that all types are ground to simplify the formal semantics. This is without loss of generality because all primitive values contained in our base model are monomorphic.

The base model's *domain* $\mathcal{D}_\tau$ for type τ consists of a subset of terms (i.e., *values*) with type τ. Specifically, values are ground terms built inductively from constants, record, variant, and rec constructors, as well as lambda abstractions with an arbitrary term (i.e., not necessarily a value) for the body. Below, we use $\mathcal{D}$ when the type is clear from the context.

Table 1 shows a subset of the constants included in the base model. For the polymorphic constants, the base model specifically contains all ground instances separately (e.g., eq_{Bool}, eq_{Int}, and so forth). In addition, any integer, floating-point, or string literal can be used as a constant of the corresponding types. We also omit some string operations and conversions for lack of space. Note that the boolean operators not, and, or do not supersede the corresponding operators in CMFOTL formulas: a term is always evaluated under a concrete assignment to all of its free variables, whereas formulas can *generate* sets of assignments. We assume that for every ground instance of a function-valued constant $c :: (\tau_1, \ldots, \tau_n) \Rightarrow \rho$, there is a mapping $\boxed{c}$ from $\mathcal{D}_{\tau_1} \times \cdots \times \mathcal{D}_{\tau_n}$ to $\mathcal{D}_\rho$ which interprets the constant.

Next, we define a small-step operational semantics for well-typed terms, using call-by-value evaluation as implemented in our monitor. The single-step reduction relation $\rightsquigarrow$ is the least relation closed under the rules shown in Fig. 3. Similarly as for types, we write $t[t'/x]$ for the capture-avoiding substitution of t' for variable x in the term t. Variables that occur only on the right-hand side of $\rightsquigarrow$ are assumed to be fresh. The new terms of the form $\mathsf{mapf}_{X.\tau;\tau'}(t; x{\rightarrow}t')$ are only used for the evaluation of folds. Intuitively, they apply the operation $\mathsf{fold}_{X.\tau'}(u; x{\rightarrow}t')$ to those subterms of the value t (which has type τ) that correspond to an occurrence of the type variable X. For example, we have for $\tau \equiv \langle \mathsf{None} : \{\}, \mathsf{Some} : X \rangle$

$$
\begin{aligned}
&\mathsf{fold}_{X.\tau}(\mathsf{mk}\ \mathsf{Some}(\mathsf{rec}_{\mu X.\tau}(\mathsf{mk}\ \mathsf{None}(\{})))); x{\rightarrow}0) \\
&\rightsquigarrow (\lambda(x).\,0)\big(\mathsf{mapf}_{X.\tau;\tau}(\mathsf{mk}\ \mathsf{Some}(\mathsf{rec}_{\mu X.\tau}(\mathsf{mk}\ \mathsf{None}(\{})))); x{\rightarrow}0)\big) \\
&\rightsquigarrow (\lambda(x).\,0)\big(\mathsf{mk}\ \mathsf{Some}(\mathsf{mapf}_{X.X;\tau}(\mathsf{rec}_{\mu X.\tau}(\mathsf{mk}\ \mathsf{None}(\{})); x{\rightarrow}0))\big) \\
&\rightsquigarrow (\lambda(x).\,0)\big(\mathsf{mk}\ \mathsf{Some}(\mathsf{fold}_{X.X}(\mathsf{rec}_{\mu X.\tau}(\mathsf{mk}\ \mathsf{None}(\{})); x{\rightarrow}0))\big) \\
&\rightsquigarrow (\lambda(x).\,0)\big(\mathsf{mk}\ \mathsf{Some}((\lambda(x).\,0)(\mathsf{mapf}_{X.\tau;\tau}(\mathsf{mk}\ \mathsf{None}(\{}); x{\rightarrow}0)))\big) \\
&\rightsquigarrow (\lambda(x).\,0)\big(\mathsf{mk}\ \mathsf{Some}((\lambda(x).\,0)(\mathsf{mk}\ \mathsf{None}(\mathsf{mapf}_{X.\{\};\tau}(\{}; x{\rightarrow}0))))\big) \\
&\rightsquigarrow (\lambda(x).\,0)\big(\mathsf{mk}\ \mathsf{Some}((\lambda(x).\,0)(\mathsf{mk}\ \mathsf{None}(\{})))\big) \\
&\rightsquigarrow (\lambda(x).\,0)\big(\mathsf{mk}\ \mathsf{Some}(0)\big) \rightsquigarrow 0.
\end{aligned}
$$

The multi-step reduction relation $\rightsquigarrow^*$ is the reflexive and transitive closure of $\rightsquigarrow$.

Our type system and term semantics have two important properties: type soundness [26] and termination. These properties guarantee that our monitor does not encounter run-time errors due to the policy using undefined operations (the standard example being trying to add numbers and strings) and that it always terminates on finite traces. CMFOTL's term language is an extension of

$$\frac{\forall i.\, t_i \in \mathcal{D}}{c(t_1,\ldots) \rightsquigarrow \boxed{c}(t_1,\ldots)} \qquad \frac{t \rightsquigarrow t'}{t:\tau \rightsquigarrow t':\tau} \qquad \frac{t \in \mathcal{D}}{t:\tau \rightsquigarrow t} \qquad \frac{t \rightsquigarrow t'}{t(t_1,\ldots) \rightsquigarrow t'(t_1,\ldots)}$$

$$\frac{t_i \rightsquigarrow t_i'}{t(t_1,\ldots) \rightsquigarrow t(t_1,\ldots,t_i',\ldots)} \qquad \frac{\forall i.\, t_i \in \mathcal{D}}{(\lambda(x_1,\ldots).t)(t_1,\ldots) \rightsquigarrow t[t_1/x_1,\ldots]}$$

$$\frac{t_i \rightsquigarrow t_i'}{\{l_1:t_1,\ldots\} \rightsquigarrow \{l_1:\ldots,l_i:t_i',\ldots\}} \qquad \frac{t \rightsquigarrow t'}{t.l \rightsquigarrow t'.l} \qquad \frac{\forall i.\, t_i \in \mathcal{D}}{\{l_1:t_1,\ldots\}.l_i \rightsquigarrow t_i}$$

$$\frac{t \rightsquigarrow t'}{\mathsf{mk}\ l(t) \rightsquigarrow \mathsf{mk}\ l(t')} \qquad \frac{t \rightsquigarrow t'}{\mathsf{case}(t;l_1(x_1)\to t_1,\ldots) \rightsquigarrow \mathsf{case}(t';l_1(x_1)\to t_1,\ldots)}$$

$$\frac{t \in \mathcal{D}}{\mathsf{case}(\mathsf{mk}\ l_i(t);l_1(x_1)\to t_1,\ldots) \rightsquigarrow t_i[t/x_i]} \qquad \frac{t \rightsquigarrow t'}{\mathsf{rec}_{X.\tau}(t) \rightsquigarrow \mathsf{rec}_{X.\tau}(t')}$$

$$\frac{t \rightsquigarrow t'}{\mathsf{unrec}_{X.\tau}(t) \rightsquigarrow \mathsf{unrec}_{X.\tau}(t')} \qquad \frac{t \in \mathcal{D}}{\mathsf{unrec}_{X.\tau}(\mathsf{rec}_{X.\tau}(t)) \rightsquigarrow t}$$

$$\frac{t \rightsquigarrow t'}{\mathsf{fold}_{X.\tau}(t;x\to t'') \rightsquigarrow \mathsf{fold}_{X.\tau}(t';x\to t'')} \qquad \frac{t \rightsquigarrow t'}{\mathsf{mapf}_{X.\tau;\tau'}(t;x\to t'') \rightsquigarrow \mathsf{mapf}_{X.\tau;\tau'}(t';x\to t'')}$$

$$\frac{t \in \mathcal{D}}{\mathsf{fold}_{X.\tau}(\mathsf{rec}_{X.\tau}(t);x\to t') \rightsquigarrow (\lambda(x).t')(\mathsf{mapf}_{X.\tau;\tau}(t;x\to t'))} \qquad \mathsf{mapf}_{X.\tau';\tau}(c;x\to t') \rightsquigarrow c$$

$$\frac{}{\mathsf{mapf}_{X.X;\tau}(t;x\to t') \rightsquigarrow \mathsf{fold}_{X.\tau}(t;x\to t')}$$

$$\frac{}{\mathsf{mapf}_{X.(\tau_1,\ldots)\Rightarrow\rho;\tau}(\lambda(x_1,\ldots).t;x\to t') \rightsquigarrow \lambda(x_1,\ldots).\mathsf{mapf}_{X.\rho;\tau}(t;x\to t')}$$

$$\frac{}{\mathsf{mapf}_{X.\{l_1:\tau_1,\ldots\};\tau}(\{l_1:t_1,\ldots\};x\to t') \rightsquigarrow \{l_1:\mathsf{mapf}_{X.\tau_1;\tau}(t_1;x\to t'),\ldots\}}$$

$$\frac{}{\mathsf{mapf}_{X.\langle l_1:\tau_1,\ldots\rangle;\tau}(\mathsf{mk}\ l_i(t);x\to t') \rightsquigarrow \mathsf{mk}\ l_i(\mathsf{mapf}_{X.\tau_i;\tau}(t;x\to t'))}$$

$$\frac{\vdash \mathsf{mapf}_{X.\mu Y.\tau';\tau}(t;x\to t') :: (\mu Y.\tau')[\rho/X] \qquad X \neq Y}{\mathsf{mapf}_{X.\mu Y.\tau';\tau}(\mathsf{rec}_{Y.\tau'[\mu X.\tau/X]}(t);x\to t') \rightsquigarrow \mathsf{rec}_{Y.\tau'[\rho/X]}(\mathsf{mapf}_{X.\tau'[\mu Y.\tau'/Y];\tau}(t;x\to t'))}$$

Fig. 3. Small-step semantics for term evaluation

the simply typed lambda calculus and hence the standard technique of logical relations [29, 32] can be used to establish strong normalization into values, which implies termination and, together with type preservation, soundness. However, the fold operator and the recursion through functions in inductive types require some care. We give proofs of the following theorems in the extended version [24].

Theorem 1. $\rightsquigarrow^*$ *preserves ground types, i.e.,* $\vdash t :: \tau$ *and* $t \rightsquigarrow^* t'$ *imply* $\vdash t' :: \tau$.

Theorem 2. $\rightsquigarrow^*$ *is strongly normalizing: For every ground term* t *such that* $\vdash t :: \tau$, *there exists a unique normal form* $[\![t]\!] \in \mathcal{D}_\tau$ *such that* $t \rightsquigarrow^* [\![t]\!]$ *and there is no* u *with* $[\![t]\!] \rightsquigarrow u$.

A valuation v for a term t is a finite mapping from the term's free variables $x_i : \tau_i$ to values in the corresponding domains $\mathcal{D}_{\tau_i}$. Strong normaliza-

$v, i \models \downarrow t$ iff $[\![t]\!](v) = \text{true}$ $\qquad$ $v, i \models R(t_1, \ldots, t_n)$ iff $([\![t_1]\!](v), \ldots, [\![t_n]\!](v)) \in D_i$

$v, i \models \neg\varphi$ iff $v, i \not\models \varphi$ $\qquad$ $v, i \models \exists x : \tau.\, \varphi$ iff $v[z/x], i \models \varphi$ for some $z \in \mathcal{D}_\tau$

$v, i \models \varphi \wedge \psi$ iff $v, i \models \varphi$ and $v, i \models \psi$ $\qquad$ $v, i \models \varphi \vee \psi$ iff $v, i \models \varphi$ or $v, i \models \psi$

$v, i \models \bullet_I\, \varphi$ $\quad$ iff $i > 0, T_i - T_{i-1} \in I$, and $v, i - 1 \models \varphi$

$v, i \models \bigcirc_I\, \varphi$ $\quad$ iff $T_{i+1} - T_i \in I$ and $v, i + 1 \models \varphi$

$v, i \models \varphi\, \mathsf{S}_I\, \psi$ iff $v, j \models \psi$ for some $j \leq i, T_i - T_j \in I$, and $v, k \models \varphi$ for all k with $j < k \leq i$

$v, i \models \varphi\, \mathsf{U}_I\, \psi$ iff $v, j \models \psi$ for some $j \geq i, T_j - T_i \in I$, and $v, k \models \varphi$ for all k with $i \leq k < j$

Fig. 4. CMFOTL's formula semantics

tion allows us to lift the term semantics to an evaluation function $[\![t]\!](v) = [\![t[v(x_1)/x_1, \ldots, v(x_n)/x_n]]\!]$ returning values. Observe that for ground terms, evaluation results directly in the normal form, which justifies this mild abuse of notation.

The relation $v, i \models \varphi$ (Fig. 4) defines the satisfaction of the formula φ for a given temporal structure, valuation v, and time-point $i \in \mathbf{N}$. A temporal structure is an infinite sequence $(T_i, D_i)_{i \in \mathbf{N}}$ of finite first-order structures D_i over the signature Δ with associated time-stamps T_i. This means that each D_i assigns to every relation symbol $R : (\tau_1, \ldots, \tau_n) \in \Delta$ a finite subset of $\mathcal{D}_{\tau_1} \times \cdots \times \mathcal{D}_{\tau_n}$. Time-stamps are natural numbers $T_i \in \mathbf{N}$. They need not be unique, but we require that time-stamps are monotone ($\forall i.\ T_i \leq T_{i+1}$) and unbounded ($\forall T.\ \exists i.\ T < T_i$). Overall, the semantics is the same as MFOTL's, except for the addition of assertions.

7 Implementation

Our monitor for CMFOTL is an extension of the MonPoly tool [7], which is written in OCaml. In particular, we modified MonPoly's signature and formula parser, type inference code, and internal representation of domain values. Instead of MonPoly's first-order signature, our extension takes as input a *user-facing signature*. It allows the specification of nested and recursive structures, which are used to parse a stream of time-stamped JSON events. The events are subsequently mapped to instances of CMFOTL types based on our signature translation.

7.1 Signature Translation

We introduce the user-facing signature format and develop a translation to a first-order signature (Sect. 5.1). The user-facing signature serves two purposes: it defines the CMFOTL types used for type inference and it guides the parsing of JSON events. The syntax is geared towards usability. It consists of JSON values representing types that may refer to each other by name. Therefore, the translation to first-order signature is non-trivial in the presence of circular name references.

The user-facing signature is a sequence of record type definitions. Each definition consists of a type name followed by a *symbolic* record type. The definition may be prefixed by the keyword **event**, which marks the type as an *event type*. Only event types may occur as top-level objects in the JSON event stream. The field types γ_i of a symbolic record type must conform to the grammar

$$\gamma ::= \delta \mid \delta? \mid [\delta] \mid [\delta?]$$
$$\delta ::= name \mid \{l : \gamma, \ldots, l : \gamma\} \mid \texttt{Null} \mid \texttt{Int} \mid \texttt{Float} \mid \texttt{String} \mid \texttt{Bool}$$

where *name* refers to any type defined in the user-facing signature, including the current one. A question mark indicates an optional field and square brackets are used for arrays.

Each named type defined in the user-facing signature as $name \{l_1 : \gamma_1, \ldots, l_n : \gamma_n\}$ is translated to a CMFOTL type $\tau_{name} = [\![\{l_1 : \gamma_1, \ldots, l_n : \gamma_n\}]\!]$ according to the rules

$$[\![\delta?]\!] = \langle \textsf{None} : \{\}, \textsf{Some} : [\![\delta]\!] \rangle \quad [\![[\delta]]\!] = \mu L. \langle \textsf{Nil} : \{\}, \textsf{Cons} : \{\textsf{hd} : [\![\delta]\!], \textsf{tl} : L\} \rangle$$
$$[\![name]\!] = \tau_{name} \quad [\![\{l_1 : \gamma_1, \ldots, l_n : \gamma_n\}]\!] = \{l_1 : [\![\gamma_1]\!], \ldots, l_n : [\![\gamma_n]\!]\} \quad [\![\texttt{Null}]\!] = \{\}$$
$$[\![\texttt{Int}]\!] = \textsf{Int} \quad [\![\texttt{Float}]\!] = \textsf{Float} \quad [\![\texttt{String}]\!] = \textsf{Str} \quad [\![\texttt{Bool}]\!] = \textsf{Bool}$$

However, this translation fails if there is a circular dependency (direct or indirect) between named types, as this would result in an infinite type expression. A named type τ_1 depends directly on a named type τ_2 iff the latter occurs in τ_1's definition. We use the following algorithm to translate circular dependencies into inductive types.

1. All direct type dependencies are represented as a directed graph. We compute the graphs's strongly connected components. The edges between the strongly connected components form a tree which is processed from the leaves to the root.
2. Every component consisting of a single named type that does not refer to itself can be translated immediately as above.
3. If a component contains multiple nodes or a single component has an edge pointing to itself, it indicates the presence of one or more inductive types. We choose one node in the component based on a heuristic. The choice does not matter for correctness, but it influences the syntactic structure of the obtained types. If only one node is referenced from other components, it is selected. Otherwise, the node with the highest number of incoming edges from other components, or the single **event** type if it exists, is selected. If there is a tie, the type declared first in the signature takes precedence.
4. After selecting the node τ, all incoming edges to that node are removed from the component, and the algorithm is recursively applied to the component's subgraph. Any reference to the named type τ is translated as the type variable X_τ.
5. Finally, τ is translated to $\mu X_\tau.[\![\{l : \gamma, \ldots\}]\!]$, where $\{l : \gamma, \ldots\}$ is the definition of τ.

The resulting first-order signature consists of one unary predicate for each **event** record type. The predicate ranges over the corresponding translated type. To continue the example from Sect. 2, the user may specify the signature

```
event Send {parcel: Box, customer: string?}
Box {content: [Box]}
```

It is translated to the types $\tau_{\mathsf{Send}} = \{\mathsf{parcel} : \tau_{\mathsf{Box}}, \mathsf{customer} : \langle \mathsf{None} : \{\}, \mathsf{Some} : \mathsf{Str}\rangle\}$ and $\tau_{\mathsf{Box}} = \mu X_{\mathsf{Box}}. \{\mathsf{content} : \mu L. \langle \mathsf{Nil} : \{\}, \mathsf{Cons} : \{\mathsf{hd} : X_{\mathsf{Box}}, \mathsf{tl} : L\}\rangle\}$. The user may refer to the predicate $\mathsf{Send}(\tau_{\mathsf{Send}})$ in their specifications. For instance, the formula $\mathsf{Send}(s) \wedge \downarrow(s.\mathsf{customer} = \mathsf{mk\ None})$ detects all Send events without a customer.

The above algorithm ensures that the translations of mutually dependent types can be used directly within each other. To illustrate why this is not immediate, consider the type specifications A {x: B?} and B {y: A?}. An intuitive translation might be $\tau_A = \mu X_A. \{x : \{y : X_A?\}?\}$ and $\tau_B = \mu X_B. \{y : \{x : X_B?\}?\}$ (abbreviating the variant types for optional fields by a question mark). However, a value b of type τ_B cannot be used in the field x when constructing a value of type τ_A because the types do not match. One has to fold b first to adjust its type. Our approach yields $\tau_A = \mu X_A. \{x : \mu X_B. \{y : X_A?\}?\}$ and $\tau_B = \mu X_B. \{y : \tau_A?\}$, which are more complex expressions but do not require such conversions. The main disadvantage of our approach is that the size of the translated types has the fairly tight upper bound $n^{2^{n/3}+1}$, where n is the size of the user-facing signature (see the extended version of this paper [24] for details). This severely limits its use for complex recursive signatures. In future work, we plan to extend the type system and inference algorithm to directly support mutually recursive types.

7.2 Monitoring Algorithm

Our implementation inherits MonPoly's approach to monitoring first-order properties. The fundamental principle is to decompose the formula into sub-formulas that evaluate to *finite relations* at every time-point of the event stream. The relations are then combined from the bottom up along the formula's tree structure using a fixed set of operators, each of which corresponds to one or few MFOTL operators. Not all formulas can be decomposed readily in this way. Therefore, the monitor supports only a fragment, called the *monitorable fragment*, of the specification language. MonPoly's monitoring algorithm has been described in detail elsewhere [6] and so we focus on the necessary adjustments for CMFOTL.

Assertions $\downarrow t$ are considered monitorable on their own only if t simplifies to a ground term, which must be **true** or **false**. Otherwise, assertions must be used as part of a conjunction $\varphi \wedge \downarrow t$ such that $\mathsf{fv}(t) \subseteq \mathsf{fv}(\varphi)$ and φ is monitorable. In this case, φ is evaluated first to obtain a finite relation R. Each of R's tuple gives rise to a valuation compatible with t, such that t can be evaluated under this valuation. The tuples for which t is **true** form the relation computed for $\varphi \wedge \downarrow t$. When monitoring MFOTL using MonPoly, the formula $\varphi \wedge (x = t)$ is monitorable even if x is not free in φ. This is a useful pattern as it can be used to assign computed values to new variables. Therefore, our monitor supports it as a special case by evaluating only the term t under each of φ's valuations and assigning the result to x.

We see that it suffices to generalize the evaluation of terms. In MonPoly, domain values are represented by a single OCaml data type `cst`, which is a variant type combining integers, floats, and strings. We maintain this design and add three constructors to `cst`: one for records (represented by an association lists from field labels to `cst`), one for variant constructors (represented by a pair of the constructor name and a `cst`), and one for OCaml function closures of type `cst list -> cst`. We build a straightforward interpreter computing a `cst` value from a term and a valuation according to term semantics (Fig. 3). Note that `cst` does not mark the boundaries of inductive types. Hence, `rec` and `unrec` are ignored during monitoring.

The monitor's input is a stream of JSON values, each prefixed by a time-stamp. We parse the JSON value using the Yojson library, which returns a tree-like representation that we match recursively against the record types declared as **event** in the user-facing signature. (We currently only support records as top-level events.) Once a matching record type τ has been found, we transform the event to a `cst` value that is consistent with the type translation from the user-facing signature. We then create a first-order structure where the relation for τ is a singleton set containing the transformed value; all other relations are empty. This structure is processed by the main monitoring loop.

8   Examples and Evaluation

We illustrate CMFOTL with several examples. Some of them can also be expressed in MFOTL using a pre-processed log, as mentioned in the introduction. We compare the two languages with an earlier *encoding* approach by Zumsteg [35]. The encoding approach corresponds essentially to a fragment of CMFOTL without variant, inductive, and function types. The implementation is different, however: JSON objects are translated to graphs that can be represented by ordinary first-order structures. Our qualitative comparison is complemented by benchmark results using synthetic logs.

The first example *session* formalizes the property from the introduction (every client accessing the /`secure` URL must have a valid session, not older than 600 seconds, established previously by visiting /`login`), where we have already shown the pre-processed MFOTL version. A suitable user-facing signature for the JSON events is

```
event Access {url: string, client: string, session: Session?}
Session {id: int, token: string}
```

The session field is optional and hence it will be mapped to an option type. We must negate and rewrite the CMFOTL formula to make it conform to the monitorable fragment:

$$\text{Access}(\{\text{url} : \text{/secure}, \text{client} : \_, \text{session} : \text{mk None}\}) \lor$$
$$\exists c, s.\ \text{Access}(\{\text{url} : \text{/secure}, \text{client} : c, \text{session} : s\}) \land$$
$$\neg(\blacklozenge_{[0,600)}\ \text{Access}(\{\text{url} : \text{/login}, \text{client} : c, \text{session} : s\}))$$

Here we pattern-match on the Access predicate's arguments, which helps with monitorability: $\varphi \land \neg\psi$ is monitorable in general only if $\text{fv}(\psi) \subseteq \text{fv}(\varphi)$ [6]. Specifically, we extract the client and session fields and assign them to variables. While having well-defined semantics, the pattern matching itself is currently not supported by the implementation and must be manually translated to $\exists a.\ \text{Access}(a) \land \downarrow(a.\text{url} = \ldots) \land \ldots$.

The formula for the encoding approach is similar, except that there is no option type. We replace it with a Boolean flag in the session record indicating whether the session exists.

In the *logout* example, we check that every login is followed by a logout by the same client and with the same session within 600 seconds. This property is naturally expressed using a future operator (again showing the negation):

$$\exists c, s.\ \text{Access}(\{\text{url} : \text{/login}, \text{client} : c, \text{session} : s\}) \land$$
$$\neg(\Diamond_{[0,600)}\ \text{Access}(\{\text{url} : \text{/logout}, \text{client} : c, \text{session} : s\}))$$

This corresponds to the negated MFOTL formula $\text{Access}(\text{/login}, c, s, id, t) \land \neg \Diamond_{[0,600)}\ \text{Access}(\text{/logout}, c, s, id, t)$ for the pre-processed trace.

The last two examples cannot be expressed in MFOTL because they involve arbitrarily nested records. The *boxes* formula uses the signature from Sect. 7.1. It identifies those deliveries for which the total number of all boxes in the parcel exceeds ten:

$$\text{Send}(s) \land \downarrow(\text{fold}_{\text{Box}}(s.\text{parcel}; b \rightarrow \text{fold}_{\text{Box\_content}}(b.\text{content}; l \rightarrow$$
$$\text{case}(l; \text{Nil} \rightarrow 1,\ \text{Cons}(c) \rightarrow c.\text{hd} + c.\text{tl}))) > 10)$$

We use two nested folds because there are two nested inductive types: the Box type and the list for the content array. Our implementation provides an abbreviation mechanism for inductive types obtained from the user-facing signature. For example, Box_content refers to the translated type for the content field.

Finally, we demonstrate an application of lambda functions. Assume that the signature is **event D {lst: [int]}**. The following is the CMFOTL version of the standard functional programming example for reversing a list in linear time:

$$D(d) \land \downarrow(ys = \text{fold}_{\text{D\_lst}}(d.\text{lst}; xs \rightarrow \text{case}(xs; \text{Nil} \rightarrow (\lambda(ys).\ ys),\ \text{Cons}(c) \rightarrow$$
$$(\lambda(ys).\ c.\text{tl}(\text{rec}_{\text{D\_lst}}(\text{mk Cons}(\{\text{hd} : c.\text{hd},\ \text{tl} : ys\}))))))))(\text{rec}_{\text{D\_lst}}(\text{mk Nil}))$$

We use lambdas to pass an additional parameter (the accumulator ys) along with the fold. The fold essentially computes a function that is applied to the empty list $\text{rec}_{\text{D\_lst}}(\text{mk Nil})$.

Table 2. Benchmark results (runtime in seconds, arithmetic mean over three repetitions)

Events	session				logout				boxes	reverse
	cpx	enc	ohd	proc	cpx	enc	ohd	proc	cpx	cpx
1×10^5	0.89	1.06	19%	0.28	0.84	1.19	42%	0.18	1.46	1.48
2×10^5	2.21	2.69	22%	0.55	2.07	2.87	39%	0.35	4.11	3.78
3×10^5	4.02	4.88	21%	0.81	3.73	5.21	40%	0.53	7.41	7.11
4×10^5	6.19	7.64	23%	1.09	5.86	7.90	35%	0.71	11.91	10.90

We performed small-scale benchmarks using randomly generated traces to get a first impression of the relative performance of CMFOTL. There are at least two sources of a potential slowdown: JSON parsing and the fact that the formulas using complex data types involve additional operations to access individual fields.

Table 2 shows the results, which were obtained on a 2.5 GHz CPU (Intel Core i5-7200U) with turbo-boost disabled. The *cpx*, *enc*, and *ohd* columns display the runtime in seconds for the CMFOTL, the encoding, and the MFOTL with pre-processing approaches. The *ohd* column displays the relative overhead of *enc* compared to *cpx*. We observe that this overhead is approximately constant relative to the number of events for each of the *session* and *logout* examples. However, monitoring using pre-processed events is faster by a factor between 3 and 8 in our experiments. We point out that our measurements do not include the pre-processing itself.

9 Related Work

The type system previously used by MonPoly offers simple types and polymorphism, with type classes for numeric and ordered types only. This type system and its inference algorithm have been subsequently formalized and verified [22] within the VeriMon project [2]. Zumsteg's BSc thesis [35] added records (i.e., product types with named fields) to MonPoly's type system, but translated them back to simple types during the monitoring. Computations over inductive types can also be encoded as computation on simple types if the specification language supports a general-purpose recursion combinator [34].

BeepBeep 3 [18] is an event stream processing engine that supports multiple specification languages including the logic LTL-FO+, a first-order extension of LTL. It also supports traces consisting of arbitrary XML-based events that can be queried using XPath expressions. Unlike in CMFOTL, quantifiers in LTL-FO+ range only over the values present in the current event in the trace. There is also no support for past temporal operators, nor for metric constraints.

The ParTraP [8,9] tool has been developed to monitor medical devices. ParTraP's traces are sequences of JSON objects. Each object must carry its type and time in a hardcoded format. Our tool does not require type annotations in the trace. ParTraP also provides only local quantification over values in JSON lists that occur in the trace.

Lola [14] and its temporal extension TeSSLa [23] are specification languages that rely on stream equations for specifying properties. They are designed to focus on temporal operations on streams, whereas the streams' data is left underspecified, possibly assuming arbitrary data types. HLola [17] is a stream runtime verification tool that uses Lola as its core language and implements support for arbitrary data types. It supports input streams provided in JSON or CSV format and relies on code written in Haskell from which it inherits all available data types to describe the structure of input and output streams. Haskell's high-order functions are particularly useful for modularity and abstraction when writing specifications. However, HLola does not guarantee termination and inherits Haskell's complexity when it comes to understanding the semantics of the specifications. The latter also applies to LogFire [20], Copilot [30] and other DSL-based tools.

E-ACSL [31] and OpenJML [12] can check C and Java functions at runtime for compliance against their contracts. Both tools support contract languages that have rich types (in fact, any type supported by their respective programming language), but amount to assertions without support for temporal operators.

10   Conclusion

We proposed CMFOTL, a first-order specification language for runtime verification that supports complex data types and has simple, yet precise, semantics. We did so by extending metric first-order temporal logic with function, record, variant, and inductive types. We developed a type system and semantics for our new logic as well as a type inference algorithm, and extended MonPoly's monitoring algorithm to support our new language. Future work includes adding pattern matching, polymorphic let-bindings for terms, and support for custom variant types in the user-facing signature.

Acknowledgments. Remo Zumsteg contributed to adding product types to CMFOTL via an encoding approach. François Hublet and Dmitriy Traytel contributed to CMFOTL's type system and semantics. We thank the anonymous reviewers for helping us improve the presentation of this paper.

References

1. Alur, R., Henzinger, T.A.: Real-time logics: complexity and expressiveness. Inf. Comput. **104**(1), 35–77 (1993). https://doi.org/10.1006/inco.1993.1025
2. Basin, D., et al.: VeriMon: a formally verified monitoring tool. In: Seidl, H., Liu, Z., Pasareanu, C.S. (eds.) ICTAC 2022. LNCS, vol. 13572, pp. 1–6. Springer, Cham (2022). https://doi.org/10.1007/978-3-031-17715-6_1
3. Basin, D., et al.: A formally verified, optimized monitor for metric first-order dynamic logic. In: Peltier, N., Sofronie-Stokkermans, V. (eds.) IJCAR 2020. LNCS (LNAI), vol. 12166, pp. 432–453. Springer, Cham (2020). https://doi.org/10.1007/978-3-030-51074-9_25

4. Basin, D., et al.: Monitoring the internet computer. In: Chechik, M., Katoen, J.P., Leucker, M. (eds.) FM 2023. LNCS, vol. 14000, pp. 383–402. Springer, Cham (2023). https://doi.org/10.1007/978-3-031-27481-7_22

5. Basin, D., Klaedtke, F., Marinovic, S., Zălinescu, E.: Monitoring of temporal first-order properties with aggregations. Formal Methods Syst. Des. **46**(3), 262–285 (2015). https://doi.org/10.1007/s10703-015-0222-7

6. Basin, D., Klaedtke, F., Müller, S., Zalinescu, E.: Monitoring metric first-order temporal properties. J. ACM **62**(2), 15:1–15:45 (2015). https://doi.org/10.1145/2699444

7. Basin, D., Klaedtke, F., Zalinescu, E.: The MonPoly monitoring tool. In: Reger, G., Havelund, K. (eds.) Workshop on Competitions, Usability, Benchmarks, Evaluation, and Standardisation for Runtime Verification Tools (RV-CuBES). Kalpa, vol. 3, pp. 19–28. EasyChair (2017). https://doi.org/10.29007/89hs

8. Blein, Y., Ledru, Y., du Bousquet, L., Groz, R.: Extending specification patterns for verification of parametric traces. In: Gnesi, S., Plat, N., Spoletini, P., Pelliccione, P. (eds.) Conference on Formal Methods in Software Engineering (FormaliSE), pp. 10–19. ACM (2018). https://doi.org/10.1145/3193992.3193998

9. Ben Cheikh, A., Blein, Y., Chehida, S., Vega, G., Ledru, Y., du Bousquet, L.: An environment for the PARTRAP trace property language (tool demonstration). In: Colombo, C., Leucker, M. (eds.) RV 2018. LNCS, vol. 11237, pp. 437–446. Springer, Cham (2018). https://doi.org/10.1007/978-3-030-03769-7_26

10. Chen, K., Hudak, P., Odersky, M.: Parametric type classes. In: White, J.L. (ed.) Conference on Lisp and Functional Programming (LFP), pp. 170–181. ACM (1992). https://doi.org/10.1145/141471.141536

11. Chomicki, J.: Efficient checking of temporal integrity constraints using bounded history encoding. ACM Trans. Database Syst. **20**(2), 149–186 (1995). https://doi.org/10.1145/210197.210200

12. Cok, D.R.: OpenJML: software verification for Java 7 using JML, OpenJDK, and eclipse. In: Dubois, C., Giannakopoulou, D., Méry, D. (eds.) Workshop on Formal Integrated Development Environment (F-IDE). EPTCS, vol. 149, pp. 79–92 (2014). https://doi.org/10.4204/EPTCS.149.8

13. Damas, L., Milner, R.: Principal type-schemes for functional programs. In: DeMillo, R.A. (ed.) ACM Symposium on Principles of Programming Languages (POPL), pp. 207–212. ACM Press (1982). https://doi.org/10.1145/582153.582176

14. D'Angelo, B., et al.: LOLA: runtime monitoring of synchronous systems. In: Symposium on Temporal Representation and Reasoning (TIME), pp. 166–174. IEEE (2005). https://doi.org/10.1109/TIME.2005.26

15. Dybjer, P.: Representing inductively defined sets by wellorderings in Martin-Löf's type theory. Theor. Comp. Sci. **176**(1–2), 329–335 (1997). https://doi.org/10.1016/S0304-3975(96)00145-4

16. Gordon, M.J., Milner, A.J., Wadsworth, C.P.: Edinburgh LCF: A Mechanised Logic of Computation. Springer, Heidelberg (1979). https://doi.org/10.1007/3-540-09724-4

17. Gorostiaga, F., Sánchez, C.: HLola: a very functional tool for extensible stream runtime verification. In: TACAS 2021. LNCS, vol. 12652, pp. 349–356. Springer, Cham (2021). https://doi.org/10.1007/978-3-030-72013-1_18

18. Hallé, S., Khoury, R.: Event stream processing with BeepBeep 3. In: Reger, G., Havelund, K. (eds.) Workshop on Competitions, Usability, Benchmarks, Evaluation, and Standardisation for Runtime Verification Tools (RV-CuBES). Kalpa, vol. 3, pp. 81–88. EasyChair (2017). https://doi.org/10.29007/4cth

19. Harper, R.: Practical Foundations for Programming Languages, 2nd edn. Cambridge University Press, Cambridge (2016)
20. Havelund, K.: Rule-based runtime verification revisited. Int. J. Softw. Tools Technol. Transf. **17**(2), 143–170 (2015). https://doi.org/10.1007/s10009-014-0309-2
21. Havelund, K., Peled, D., Ulus, D.: DejaVu: a monitoring tool for first-order temporal logic. In: Workshop on Monitoring and Testing of Cyber-Physical Systems (MT@CPSWeek), pp. 12–13. IEEE (2018). https://doi.org/10.1109/MT-CPS.2018.00013
22. Kaletsch, N.: Formalizing typing rules for VeriMon. Bachelor thesis, ETH Zürich (2021)
23. Leucker, M., Sánchez, C., Scheffel, T., Schmitz, M., Schramm, A.: TeSSLa: runtime verification of non-synchronized real-time streams. In: Haddad, H.M., Wainwright, R.L., Chbeir, R. (eds.) ACM Symposium on Applied Computing (SAC), pp. 1925–1933. ACM (2018). https://doi.org/10.1145/3167132.3167338
24. Lima Graf, J., Krstić, S., Schneider, J.: Metric first-order temporal logic with complex data types. Technical report, ETH Zürich (2023), https://bitbucket.org/jshs/monpoly/src/cmfodl2/paper.pdf
25. Lima Graf, J., Krstić, S., Schneider, J.: MonPoly extended with complex data types (2023). https://bitbucket.org/jshs/monpoly/src/cmfodl2/
26. Milner, R.: A theory of type polymorphism in programming. J. Comput. Syst. Sci. **17**(3), 348–375 (1978). https://doi.org/10.1016/0022-0000(78)90014-4
27. Morris Jr, J.H.: Lambda-calculus models of programming languages. Ph.D. thesis, MIT (1969)
28. Ohori, A.: A polymorphic record calculus and its compilation. ACM Trans. Program. Lang. Syst. **17**(6), 844–895 (1995). https://doi.org/10.1145/218570.218572
29. Pierce, B.C.: Types and Programming Languages. MIT Press, Cambridge (2002)
30. Pike, L., Goodloe, A., Morisset, R., Niller, S.: Copilot: a hard real-time runtime monitor. In: Barringer, H., Falcone, Y., Finkbeiner, B., Havelund, K., Lee, I., Pace, G., Roşu, G., Sokolsky, O., Tillmann, N. (eds.) RV 2010. LNCS, vol. 6418, pp. 345–359. Springer, Heidelberg (2010). https://doi.org/10.1007/978-3-642-16612-9_26
31. Signoles, J., Kosmatov, N., Vorobyov, K.: E-ACSL, a runtime verification tool for safety and security of C programs (tool paper). In: Reger, G., Havelund, K. (eds.) Workshop on Competitions, Usability, Benchmarks, Evaluation, and Standardisation for Runtime Verification Tools (RV-CuBES). Kalpa, vol. 3, pp. 164–173. EasyChair (2017). https://doi.org/10.29007/fpdh
32. Statman, R.: Logical relations and the typed λ-calculus. Inf. Control **65**(2/3), 85–97 (1985). https://doi.org/10.1016/S0019-9958(85)80001-2
33. Wadler, P., Blott, S.: How to make ad-hoc polymorphism less ad-hoc. In: Symposium on Principles of Programming Languages (POPL), pp. 60–76. ACM Press (1989). https://doi.org/10.1145/75277.75283
34. Zingg, S., Krstić, S., Raszyk, M., Schneider, J., Traytel, D.: Verified first-order monitoring with recursive rules. In: TACAS 2022. LNCS, vol. 13244, pp. 236–253. Springer, Cham (2022). https://doi.org/10.1007/978-3-030-99527-0_13
35. Zumsteg, R.: Monitoring complex data types. Bachelor thesis, ETH Zürich (2022)

Runtime Verification Prediction for Traces with Data

Moran Omer and Doron Peled[(✉)]

Department of Computer Science, Bar Ilan University, Ramat Gan, Israel
doron.peled@gmail.com

Abstract. Runtime verification (RV) can be used for checking the execution of a system against a formal specification. First-order temporal logic allows expressing constraints on the order of occurrence of events and the data that they carry. We present an algorithm for predicting possible verdicts, within (some parametric) k events, for online monitoring executions with data against a specification written in past first-order temporal logic. Such early prediction can allow preventive actions to be taken as soon as possible. Predicting verdicts involves checking *multiple* possibilities for extensions of the monitored execution. The calculations involved in providing the prediction intensify the problem of keeping up with the speed of occurring events, hence rejecting the naive brute-force solution that is based on exhaustively checking all the extensions of a certain length. Our method is based on generating *representatives* for the possible extension, which guarantee that no potential verdict is missed. In particular, we take advantage of using BDD representation, which allows efficient construction and representation of such classes. The method is implemented as an extension of the RV tool DejaVu.

1 Introduction

Runtime verification (RV) allows verifying system executions against a specification, either online as the traces are generated or offline. Monitoring is often confined to *safety properties*, where a *failure* to satisfy the specification occurs when the inspected prefix of execution cannot be extended in any way that would satisfy the specification. The specification is typically expressed using automata or temporal logic. In particular, past time propositional temporal logic can be used to express safety properties [24], allowing an efficient RV monitoring algorithm [18]. A monitored execution trace may further consist of events that contain observed data values. To deal with observations with data, RV monitoring was extended to use first-order past temporal logic [5,15]. Other RV systems that monitor sequences of events with data include [1–4,6,11–14,16,19,25,26].

While detecting failures at run time can be used to terminate bad executions, predicting the possibility of failures before they occur can be used to employ preventing measures. We present here an algorithm for predicting a potential failure during the RV monitoring a few steps before it can potentially happen. Our prediction algorithm involves the computation of possible futures of the next k events.

The research performed by the authors was partially funded by Israeli Science Foundation grant 1464/18: "Efficient Runtime Verification for Systems with Lots of Data and its Applications".

P. Katsaros and L. Nenzi (Eds.): RV 2023, LNCS 14245, pp. 148–167, 2023.
https://doi.org/10.1007/978-3-031-44267-4_8

In online RV, it is essential to keep the *incremental complexity*, i.e., the amount of computation performed between consecutively events, as small as possible so that we keep up with the speed of reported events. This pace can be *smoothened-up* to a certain extent with the help of a buffer, but not for the long run. For predictive RV, the problem of minimizing the incremental complexity intensifies, as it involves analyzing different possibilities for the following k events. A straightforward algorithm goes through *all* possible event sequences for the next k steps, stopping when a failure occurs. This type of "brute-force" approach is immediately disqualified because of the incremental time complexity of $O(n^k)$, where n is the number of available possibilities for each event. In the case of monitoring events with data, n can be huge, or even, in principle, unbounded.

Our approach is based on using equivalence classes between data values that occur within events, which generate isomorphic extensions to the current observed trace. Then our algorithm restricts itself to using *representatives* from these equivalence classes for extending the current observed trace. This is shown to be sufficient to preserve the correctness of the prediction. In particular, we show how to take advantage of BDD representation, as is used in the DejaVu system [15] to calculate the equivalence classes and select representatives. We describe the algorithm and its implementation as an extension of the DejaVu system. We demonstrate the algorithm with experimental results and show that our method provides a substantial improvement over the straightforward prediction algorithm.

An early verdict for a finite trace against a propositional temporal specification, based on the agreement between all of its possible infinite extensions, can be calculated based on translating the specification into an automaton [21]. We show that for first-order properties of the form $\Box\varphi$, where φ is a past first-order temporal logic property, calculating such a verdict is undecidable. This further motivates our k-step predictive algorithm as a practical compromise, when an early prediction of failures is required. This also gives an explanation of the reason why systems like DejaVu [15] and MON-POLY [5] provide only the immediate *true/false* verdict per each input prefix against the past first-order LTL specification φ rather than for $\Box\varphi$.

Predictive Runtime Verification (PRV), has been proposed as an extension to standard runtime verification for propositional LTL in [27,28]. There, extensions to the currently observed trace are proposed based on static analysis or abstraction of the monitored system. A prediction of runtime verdicts based on *assumptions* about the monitored system is described in [10]. This is done using SMT-based model checking. That work also performs the prediction for a first-order LTL, but this version of the logic is restricted not to have quantifiers. This approach is orthogonal to ours, where our approach does not assume any further knowledge that can be used in generating such extensions; but combining the two approaches, when possible, can be beneficial. Predictive semantics for propositional LTL was used in [28] based on providing an early verdict for *satisfaction* of all extensions or *failure* to satisfy of all extensions for an LTL property based a on minimally observed trace. Providing such verdicts is also related to the notion of *monitorability* [7], classifying a finite trace based on all of its possible extensions as *good* or *bad* respectively. An algorithm for providing such an early verdict was given in [21].

For a past time LTL φ, one can employ an efficient algorithm that returns a *true/false* answer per each finite prefix that is monitored. Hence, the outcome can alternate between these two results. A *false* answer for a past property φ is sufficient to provide a *failure* verdict for the safety specification φ, albeit using an automata based algorithm such as [21] could have sometimes predict that *failure* is unavoidable after a shorter prefix. In [20], *anticipatory monitoring* is defined to provide the possible future verdicts after a given trace, which is also the goal of our paper. Anticipatory monitoring allows providing further information: the shortest distance to a *true* output and the longest distance to a *false* output. That work also includes a decision procedure for calculating this information for past LTL, based on a DFS on an automaton that is used to perform the monitoring. Our goal is to provide predictions for the future verdicts for traces with data with respect to a specification in first-order past temporal logic. We use here the unifying term *predictive* monitoring to refer both to the case that we calculate the possible verdicts after a bounded number of look-ahead steps as in anticipatory monitoring, for which we provide an algorithm for first-order past temporal logic, and to the case where early verdicts based on all the possible infinite extensions are sought (for an impossibility result).

2   Preliminaries

2.1   Past Time First-Order Temporal Logic

The QTL logic, used by the DejaVu tool [15, 31] and as a core subset of the logic used by the MONPOLY tool [5], is a specification formalism that allows expressing properties of executions that include data. The restriction to past time allows interpreting the formulas on finite traces.

Syntax. The formulas of the QTL logic are defined using the following grammar, where p stands for a *predicate* symbol, a is a *constant* and x is a *variable*.

For simplicity of the presentation, we define here the QTL logic with unary predicates, but this is not due to a principal restriction, and in fact QTL supports predicates over multiple arguments, including zero arguments, corresponding to propositions. The DejaVu system, as well as the method presented in this paper and its implementation [30], fully supports predicates over multiple arguments.

$$\varphi ::= \mathit{true} \mid p(\mathrm{a}) \mid p(x) \mid (\varphi \wedge \psi) \mid \neg\varphi \mid (\varphi\,\mathcal{S}\,\psi) \mid \ominus\varphi \mid \exists x\,\varphi$$

Denote by $\eta \in sub(\varphi)$ the fact that η is a subformula of φ. A QTL formula can be interpreted over multiple types (domains), e.g., natural numbers or strings. Accordingly, each variable, constant and parameter of predicate is defined over a specific type (such type declarations can appear external to the QTL formula). Type matching is enforced, e.g., for $p(a)$ ($p(x)$, respectively), the types of the parameter of p and of a (x, respectively) must be the same. We denote the type of a variable x by $type(x)$.

Propositional past time linear temporal logic is obtained by restricting the predicates to be parameterless, essentially Boolean propositions; then, no variables, constants and quantification is needed either.

Semantics. A QTL formula is interpreted over a trace (or observation), which is a finite sequence of *events*. Each event consists of a predicate symbol and parameters, e.g., $p(a), q(7)$. It is assumed that the parameters belong to particular domains that are associated with (places in) the predicates. The events in a trace are separated by dots, e.g., $p(a).q(7).p(b)$. A more general semantics can allow each event to consist of a set of predicates with parameters[1]. However, this is *not* allowed in DejaVu and in the context of this paper; for predictive RV, such generalized events can increase the complexity dramatically.

QTL subformulas have the following informal meaning: $p(a)$ is true if the last event in the trace is $p(a)$. The formula $p(x)$, for some variable x, holds if x is bound to a constant a such that $p(a)$ is the last event in the trace. The formula $(\varphi \ S \ \psi)$, which reads as φ *since* ψ, means that ψ holds in some prefix of the current trace, and for all prefixes between that one and the current trace, φ holds. The *since* operator is the past dual of the future time *until* modality. The property $\ominus \varphi$ means that φ is true in the trace that is obtained from the current one by omitting the last event. This is the past dual of the future time *next* modality. The formula $\exists x \ \varphi$ is true if there exists a value a such that φ is true with x bound to a. We can also define the following additional derived operators: $false = \neg true$, $(\varphi \vee \psi) = \neg(\neg\varphi \wedge \neg\psi)$, $(\varphi \rightarrow \psi) = (\neg\varphi \vee \psi)$, $\diamond \varphi = (true \, S \, \varphi)$ ("previously"), $\boxminus \varphi = \neg \diamond \neg\varphi$ ("always in the past" or "historically"), and $\forall x \ \varphi = \neg \exists x \ \neg\varphi$.

Formally, let *free*(η) be the set of free (i.e., unquantified) variables of a subformula η. Let γ be an assignment to the variables *free*(η). We denote by $\gamma[v \mapsto a]$ the assignment that differs from γ only by associating the value a to x; when γ assigns only to the variable x, we simply write $[v \mapsto a]$. Let σ be a trace of events of length $|\sigma|$ and i a natural number, where $i \leq |\sigma|$. Then $(\gamma, \sigma, i) \models \eta$ if η holds for the prefix of length i of σ with the assignment γ.

We denote by $\gamma|_{free(\varphi)}$ the restriction (projection) of an assignment γ to the free variables appearing in φ. Let ε be an empty assignment. In any of the following cases, $(\gamma, \sigma, i) \models \varphi$ is defined when γ is an assignment over *free*(φ), and $i \geq 1$.

- $(\varepsilon, \sigma, i) \models true$.
- $(\varepsilon, \sigma, i) \models p(a)$ if $\sigma[i] = p(a)$.
- $([x \mapsto a], \sigma, i) \models p(x)$ if $\sigma[i] = p(a)$.
- $(\gamma, \sigma, i) \models (\varphi \wedge \psi)$ if $(\gamma|_{free(\varphi)}, \sigma, i) \models \varphi$ and $(\gamma|_{free(\psi)}, \sigma, i) \models \psi$.
- $(\gamma, \sigma, i) \models \neg\varphi$ if not $(\gamma, \sigma, i) \models \varphi$.
- $(\gamma, \sigma, i) \models (\varphi \ S \ \psi)$ if for some $1 \leq j \leq i$, $(\gamma|_{free(\psi)}, \sigma, j) \models \psi$ and for all $j < k \leq i$, $(\gamma|_{free(\varphi)}, \sigma, k) \models \varphi$.
- $(\gamma, \sigma, i) \models \ominus\varphi$ if $i > 1$ and $(\gamma, \sigma, i - 1) \models \varphi$.
- $(\gamma, \sigma, i) \models \exists x \ \varphi$ if there exists $a \in type(x)$ such that $(\gamma[x \mapsto a], \sigma, i) \models \varphi$.

Set Semantics. We define an alternative semantics that is equivalent to the standard semantics presented above, but it presents the meaning of the formulas from a different point of view: the standard semantics defines whether a subformula holds given (1) an

---

[1] In the generalized semantics, the condition $\sigma[i] = p(a)$ in the definition for the $p(a)$ and $p(x)$ subformulas should be replaces with $p(a) \in \sigma[i]$ and similarly in the subsequent set semantics.

assignment of values to the (free) variables appearing in the formula, (2) a trace and (3) a position in the trace. Instead, set semantics gives the *set* of assignments that satisfy the subformula given a trace and a position in it.

Set semantics allows presenting of the RV algorithm for QTL in a similar way to the RV algorithm for propositional past time temporal logic [15]. Let $I[\varphi, \sigma, i]$ be the *interpretation function* that returns a set of assignments such that $(\gamma, \sigma, i) \models \varphi$ iff $\gamma|_{free(\varphi)} \in I[\varphi, \sigma, i]$. The empty set of assignments $\emptyset$ behaves as the Boolean constant *false* and the singleton set $\{\varepsilon\}$, which contains the empty assignment ε, behaves as the Boolean constant *true*. The union $\bigcup$ and intersection $\bigcap$ operators on sets of assignments are defined, even if they are applied to non-identical sets of variables; in this case, the assignments are extended to the union of the variables. Thus intersection between two sets of assignments A_1 and A_2 is defined like database "join" operator; i.e., it consists of the assignments whose projection on the *common* variables agrees with an assignment in A_1 and with an assignment in A_2. Union is defined as the dual operator of intersection.

Let A be a set of assignments. We denote by $hide(A, x)$ (for "hiding" the variable x) the set of assignments obtained from A after removing from each assignment the mapping from x to a value. In particular, if A is a set of assignments over only the variable x, then $hide(A, x)$ is $\{\varepsilon\}$ when A is nonempty, and $\emptyset$ otherwise. $A_{free(\varphi)}$ is the set of all possible assignments of values to the variables that appear free in φ. For convenience of the set semantics definition, we add a 0 position for each sequence σ, where I returns the empty set for each formula. The set semantics is shown in the following. For all occurrences of i, it is assumed that $i \geq 1$.

- $I[\varphi, \sigma, 0] = \emptyset$.
- $I[true, \sigma, i] = \{\varepsilon\}$.
- $I[p(a), \sigma, i] = $ if $\sigma[i] = p(a)$ then $\{\varepsilon\}$ else $\emptyset$.
- $I[p(x), \sigma, i] = \{[x \mapsto a] \mid \sigma[i] = p(a)\}$.
- $I[\neg\varphi, \sigma, i] = A_{free(\varphi)} \setminus I[\varphi, \sigma, i]$.
- $I[(\varphi \wedge \psi), \sigma, i] = I[\varphi, \sigma, i] \bigcap I[\psi, \sigma, i]$.
- $I[\ominus\varphi, \sigma, i] = I[\varphi, \sigma, i-1]$.
- $I[(\varphi \, S \, \psi), \sigma, i] = I[\psi, \sigma, i] \bigcup (I[\varphi, \sigma, i] \bigcap I[(\varphi S \psi), \sigma, i-1])$.
- $I[\exists x \, \varphi, \sigma, i] = hide(I[\varphi, \sigma, i], x)$.

2.2 Monitoring First-Order Past LTL

We review first the algorithm for monitoring first-order past LTL, implemented as part of the DejaVu tool [15]. The algorithm is based on calculating a *summary* for the current monitored trace. The summary is used, instead of storing and consulting the entire trace, for providing verdicts, and is updated when new monitored events are reported.

Consider a classical algorithm for past time propositional LTL [18]. There, the summary consists of two vectors of bits. One vector, pre, keeps the Boolean (truth) value for each subformula, based on the trace observed so far *except* the last observed event. The other vector, now, keeps the Boolean value for each subformula based on that trace *including* the last event. Given a new event e consisting of a set of propositions, which extends the monitored trace, the vector now is calculated based on the vector pre and the event e. This is summarized below:

- $\mathsf{now}(true) = True$
- $\mathsf{now}(p) = (p \in e)$
- $\mathsf{now}((\varphi \wedge \psi)) = (\mathsf{now}(\varphi) \wedge \mathsf{now}(\psi))$
- $\mathsf{now}(\neg \varphi) = \neg \mathsf{now}(\varphi)$
- $\mathsf{now}((\varphi \, \mathcal{S} \, \psi)) = (\mathsf{now}(\psi) \vee (\mathsf{now}(\varphi) \wedge \mathsf{pre}((\varphi \, \mathcal{S} \, \psi))))$.
- $\mathsf{now}(\ominus \varphi) = \mathsf{pre}(\varphi)$

When a new event appears, now becomes pre, and the now values are calculated according to the above cases.

The *first-order* monitoring algorithm replaces the two vectors of bits by two vectors of *assignments*: pre, for the assignments that satisfy each subformula given the monitored trace, except the last event, and now that for the assignments that satisfy the monitored trace. The updates in the first-order case replace, according to the set semantics, negation with complementations, conjunction with intersection and disjunction with union. We will describe how sets of assignments or, equivalently, relations, can be represented as BDDs. Then, complementation, intersection and union between relations correspond back to negation, conjunction and disjunction, respectively. Thus, the BDD-based algorithm for monitoring traces with data against a QTL specification which will be presented after explaining the BDD representation, will look similar to the RV algorithm for the propositional case without data.

BDD Representation. BDD representation, as used in the DejaVu tool allows an efficient implementation of RV for traces with data against first-order past temporal logic. We enumerate data values appearing in monitored events, as soon as we first see them. We represent enumerations as bit-vectors (i.e., Binary) encodings and construct the relations over this representation rather than over the data values themselves. Bit vectors are concatenated together to represent a tuple of values. The relations are then represented as BDDs [8]. BDDs were featured in model checking because of their ability to frequently achieve a highly compact representation of Boolean functions [9,23]. Extensive research of BDDs allowed implementing optimized public BDD packages, e.g., [29].

In order to deal with unbounded domains (where only a finite number of elements may appear in a given observed trace) and maintain the ability to perform complementation, unused enumerations represent the values that have not been seen yet. In fact, it is sufficient to use one enumeration representing these values per each variable of the LTL formula. We guarantee that at least one such enumeration exists by reserving for that purpose the enumeration $11 \dots 11$. We present here only the basic algorithm. For versions that allow extending the number of bits used for enumerations and garbage collection of enumerations, see [17].

When an event $p(a)$ is observed in the monitored execution, matched with $p(x)$ in the monitored property, a call to the procedure $hash(a)$ checks if this is the first occurrence of the value a in an event. Then a will be assigned a new enumeration $val(a)$, which will be stored under the key a. We can use a counter, for each variable x, to count the number of different values appearing so far for x. When a new value appears, this counter is incremented and converted to a binary (bit-vector) representation. The function **build**$(x, val(a))$ returns a BDD that represents an assignment for the bit vector x mapped to the enumeration corresponding to a.

For example, assume that the runtime-verifier sees the input events $open($"a"$)$, $open($"b"$)$ and that it encodes the argument values with 3 bits. We use x_1, x_2, and x_3 to represent the enumerations, with x_1 being the least significant bit. Assume that the value "a" gets mapped to the enumeration $x_3 x_2 x_1 = 000$ and that the value "b" gets mapped to the enumeration $x_3 x_2 x_1 = 001$. Then, the Boolean function representing the enumerations for $\{a, b\}$ is $(\neg x_2 \wedge \neg x_3)$, which returns 1 (*true*) for 000 and for 001.

Intersection and union of sets of assignments are translated simply into conjunction and disjunction of their BDD representation, respectively; complementation becomes BDD negation. We will denote the Boolean BDD operators as **and**, **or** and **not**. To implement the existential operators $\exists x$, we use the BDD existential operators over the Boolean variables $x_1 \ldots x_n$ that represent (the enumerations of) the values of x. Thus, if B_η is the BDD representing the assignments satisfying the subformula η in the current state of the monitor, then $\mathbf{exists}(x, B_\eta) = \exists x_1 \ldots \exists x_k B_\eta$ is the BDD that represents the assignments satisfying $\exists x \eta$. Finally, BDD($\bot$) and BDD($\top$) are the BDDs that return always 0 or 1, respectively.

The RV algorithm for a QTL formula φ based on BDDs is as follows:

1. Initially, for each $\eta \in sub(\varphi)$ of the specification φ, now(η) = BDD($\bot$).
2. Observe a new event $p(a)$ as input; $hash(a)$
3. Let pre := now.
4. Make the following updates for the formulas $sub(\varphi)$, where
   if $\psi \in sub(\eta)$ then now(ψ) is updated before now(η).
   – now(*true*) = BDD($\top$)
   – now($p(a)$) = if current event is $p(a)$ then BDD($\top$) else BDD($\bot$)
   – now($p(x)$) = if current event is $p(a)$ then $\mathbf{build}(x, val(a))$ else BDD($\bot$)
   – now($(\eta \wedge \psi)$) = $\mathbf{and}($now(η), now(ψ)$)$
   – now($\neg \eta$) = $\mathbf{not}($now(η)$)$
   – now($(\eta \mathcal{S} \psi)$) = $\mathbf{or}($now(ψ), $\mathbf{and}($now(η), pre($(\eta \mathcal{S} \psi)$)$)$$)$
   – now($\ominus \eta$) = pre(η)
   – now($\exists x \eta$) = $\mathbf{exists}(\langle x_0, \ldots, x_{k-1}\rangle$, now($\eta$)$)$
5. Goto step 2.

For a subformula η of the specification, now(η) is the BDD representation of $I[\eta, \sigma, i]$ according to the set semantics. The output of the algorithm after a given trace corresponds to the value of now(φ). Accordingly, it will be *true* if this value is BDD($\top$) and *false* if it is BDD($\bot$).

2.3 Predictive Runtime Verification

While monitoring an execution of a system against a formal specification, it is sometimes beneficial to be able to predict forthcoming possible results. The RV algorithm for QTL provides a *true*/*false* output for each prefix that is observed. The output can alternate between these truth values for subsequent prefixes. It is sometimes useful to be able to predict the possible outputs for extensions of the current trace, e.g., a possible future *false* output that corresponds to some potential problem. Then, one may apply some measures to alleviate such a situation, either by imposing some control on the system or by performing an abort.

Classical definitions for RV over temporal properties, e.g., [7,21], suggest calculating a conclusive *verdict* of *success* or *failure*, respectively, when *all* the extensions of the current trace into a full execution agree w.r.t. *satisfying* or *not satisfying*, respectively, the property. In particular, this can be useful if such a verdict can be decided based on a minimal prefix. For past temporal logic, a *true/false* output is given based on the currently monitored prefix. The outputs can alternate over subsequent prefixes. *Aniticipatory RV* [20] generalizes this, and looks at the possible outputs after a given prefix and the (minimal and maximal) distances to them (including the distance ∞) and provides an algorithm for the propositional version of the logic. We are interested here in calculating the possible outputs for all extensions of the current trace, limited to k additional events, where k is fixed, for the *first-order* past LTL QTL. We will show in Sect. 4 that making a prediction about *all* the extensions of a QTL property, without a given bound, is undecidable.

A naive k-step prediction algorithm would check, after the currently inspected trace, the possible extensions of up to k events. For each such extension, the RV algorithm is applied, continuing from the current prefix, to provide a verdict. Depending on the interpretation, a subsequent *false* output can mean a *failure* verdict, which can be sufficient to stop the generation of longer or further extensions and take some preventing action. Obviously, this method is impractical: even if the number of possible events extending a single trace by one step is finite, say n, its time complexity is $O(n^k)$. For the propositional case, this may be feasible when the specification involves only a few propositions (with m propositions, one can form $n = 2^m$ events). However, for the case of events with data, n can be enormous, or even unbounded.

2.4   Isomorphism over Relations Representing QTL Subformulas

The main challenge in predicting the future outputs for a trace is to restrict the number of cases one needs to consider when extending it. It can be argued that one can limit the number of possible events extending a trace by a single step to the values that appeared so far; in addition, for values that *did not* appear so far in the trace, a single representative is enough (but after using that representative in the current event, one needs a fresh representative for the values not seen so far, and so forth). However, in this case, the number of relevant events increases as the trace increases (although some clever use of garbage collection [17] may sometimes decrease the relevant values), which can result in a large number of values after a long trace.

Our proposed prediction method is based on calculating equivalence relations on the observed data values that guarantee the following: an extension of the currently observed trace can be simulated by an extension of the same length and with the same verdict when replacing in the next observed event an occurring data value with an equivalent one.

Let $R \subseteq \mathcal{D} = D_1 \times \ldots \times D_n$ be a relation over multiple (not necessarily distinct) domains obtained as the set semantics. Recall from sets semantics that if $R = I[\eta, \sigma, i]$ then it represents the assignments that satisfy the specification η at the ith position of the trace σ. In this context, each tuple in R is an assignment for the free variables of η. Thus, each component D_i is associated with some variable $x \in free(\eta)$. Let $f^x : D_i \mapsto D_i$ be a function over D_i, where the ith component of the relation R is associated with the variable x. We abuse notation and denote by $f^x(\tau)$ also the extension of f^x to a tuple $\tau \in \mathcal{D}$, which changes only the D_i component in the tuple according to f^x. Furthermore, denote by $f^x[R]$ the application of f^x to each tuple in R. We say that R and R' are *isomorphic* with respect to f^x if $R' = f^x[R]$ for an injective and surjective function f^x. If $R = f^x[R]$, then we say that R is an *automorphism* with respect to f^x.

Lemma 1. *If R_i and $R_i{}'$ are isomorphic (automorphic) w.r.t. f^x for $i \in \{1, 2\}$, then also the following are isomorphic with respect to f^x:*

- $\overline{R_i}$ *(the complement of R_i),*
- $R_1 \cap R_2$ *and* $R_1{}' \cap R_2{}'$ *and*
- $R_1 \cup R_2$ *and* $R_1{}' \cup R_2{}'$.

Denote by $f^x_{a \leftrightarrow b}$ the function that replaces a with b and vice versa, and does not change the other values. Denote by $R_{x=a}$ the restriction of the relation R to tuples where their x component has the value a. The following lemma provides a condition for deciding automorphism.

Lemma 2. $f^x_{a \leftrightarrow b}$ *is an automorphism over R if $R_{x=a} = R_{x=b}$.*

Denote by $E[\eta, \sigma, x]$ the equivalence relation w.r.t. the variable $x \in free(\eta)$ for a subformula η of a given specification φ, constructed from $R = I[\eta, \sigma, i]$ where $i = |\sigma|$. That is,

$$E[\eta, \sigma, x] = \{(a, b) \mid R_{x=a} = R_{x=b}\}. \tag{1}$$

Let t be some type of variables allowed in the specification. Then, let

$$\mathcal{E}[\sigma, t] = \bigcap_{x \in free(\eta) \,\wedge\, type(x)=t \,\wedge\, \eta \in sub(\varphi)} E[\eta, \sigma, x]. \tag{2}$$

We need to take care of the following special case. Let $r(a)$ appears in the specification for some constant a. Then a can only be equivalent to itself, since $I[r(a), \ \sigma.r(a), \ i] \neq I[r(a), \ \sigma.r(b), \ i]$ for any $b \neq a$ for events $r(a)$ and $r(b)$. (A similar argument holds for an event with more arguments, e.g., $r(y, a, b)$.) For simplicity, the following descriptions will refer to events with a single argument (as we did in the definition of the syntax of QTL).

Lemma 3. *Let $(a, b) \in \mathcal{E}[\sigma, t]$ and r is a predicate over a parameter of type t. Then, $f^x_{a \leftrightarrow b}$ is an isomorphism between the relations in the summary after $\sigma.\{r(a)\}$ and $\sigma.\{r(b)\}$.*

Proof. By construction, $f^x_{a \leftrightarrow b}[R]$ is an automorphism for each relation $R = I[\sigma, \eta, i]$ in the summary. The result is obtained using Lemma 1 by induction on the number of operators that need to be applied to construct the relations $I[\sigma.r(a), \eta, i+1]$ and $I[\sigma.r(b), \eta, i+1]$ in the subsequent summary, according to the set semantics, from the relations calculated for σ. Note that because of using different singleton relation for the event $r(a)$ extending the current trace and a different singleton relation for the event $r(b)$, the *automorphism* calculated from the original summary results is an *isomorphism* for the subsequently constructed relations rather than an automorphism. $\qquad \square$

Lemma 4. *Let $(a, b) \in \mathcal{E}[\sigma, t]$. Then for each finite trace $\sigma.r(a).\rho$ there exists a trace $\sigma.r(b).\rho'$ such that these traces result in the same verdict, and ρ and ρ' have the same length.*

Proof. We construct the extension ρ' as follows: for each term that appears in an event of ρ, we construct a corresponding term with the same predicate, and with a replaced with b and vice versa, and other values unchanged. Then the result is obtained by induction on the length of the considered extensions. The induction step (including the first step after σ) is obtained using Lemma 3. $\qquad\Box$

Consequently, it is redundant to generate two extensions $r(a)$ and $r(b)$ for a trace σ where $(a, b) \in \mathcal{E}[\sigma, t]$. Applying Lemma 4 repeatedly from σ results in the following recursive procedure for predicting RV. From every extension of σ up to k events, it runs on every predicate r and extends it with a single value for every equivalence class from $\mathcal{E}[\sigma, t]$. The principle algorithm then appears in Algorithm 1. In this version, the algorithm stops and produces a *failure* verdict whenever one of the extensions of the current trace *falsifies* the specification φ. Other variants can exit upon *satisfying* φ, or continue to check whether both *true* and *false* are attainable.

Algorithm 1. Pseudocode for the prediction algorithm

```
 1: procedure PREDICT(σ, k)
 2:     for each type t in the specification do
 3:         E ← 𝓔[σ, t]
 4:         while E ≠ ∅ do
 5:             let [a] ∈ E                          ▷ [a] is the eq. class containing a.
 6:             for each predicate r over parameter of type t do
 7:                 generate an event r(a)
 8:                 apply RV to update summary from σ to σ.r(a)
 9:                 if RV output is false then
10:                     exit("failure verdict")
11:                 if k > 1 then
12:                     PREDICT(σ.r(a), k − 1)
13:             E ← E \ [a]
```

An (implemented) extension of the described algorithm allows the predicates to have multiple parameters as follows. Equivalence classes are calculated independently for each parameter, and each event includes a representative for each corresponding equivalence class. Hence, in $write(f, d)$, we select a representative for f and a representative for d, making the number of cases the product of the two equivalence classes used.

The calculation of $\mathcal{E}[\sigma, t]$ involves intersecting equivalence classes of relations associated with the assignments for the free variables that satisfy subformulas of φ. Each individual equivalence class is calculated with respect to a free variable with the type t. Refining the type definitions in the formula can result in checking less representatives. Consider for example the following property $\forall f \, ((\exists d \; write(f, d)) \rightarrow$

($\neg close(f)$ S $open(f)$)). Both variables f and d can be originally defined with type strings. However, the f operator corresponds to a *file-name*, and the d operator corresponds to *data*. If we duplicate the type *string* into these two copies, we can achieve a more efficient prediction, where representatives for the file names observed would be used solely for f and representatives for the data values observed would be used for d.

Duplicating of types associated with variables, and corresponding also to constants and parameters of predicates, can be automated. First, rename the variables so that each quantified variable appears exactly once (this does not change the meaning of the formula). Now, observe the following principle: all the variables that appear within the same predicate (and in the same position, if the predicate has multiple parameters), must have the same type. Now, if the same variable appears (in the same position) in different predicates and within the same scope of quantification, then forcing variables to have the same type based on the above principle can diffuse to other occurrences of these predicates.

A graph algorithm can then be used for automating type duplication. The nodes of the graph are labeled by either variables or predicates (for predicates with multiple parameters, such a node will include the predicate *and* the position of the relevant parameter, respectively). Undirected edges will connect variables with the predicates (with positions, respectively) in which they occur. Then, all the variables in a maximal connected subgraph must have the same type, whereas a type that is shared by multiple such subgraphs can be duplicated in order to refine the calculation of the equivalences. Consider the following formula ($\exists x \diamondsuit (q(x) \vee r(x)) \wedge (\forall y \exists z (\diamondsuit r(y) \rightarrow \diamondsuit q(z)) \vee \exists u \diamondsuit p(u)))$. Then according to the constructed graph, which appears in Fig. 1, the variables x, y and z need to be of the same type, but u can have a different type.

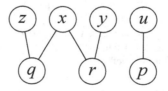

Fig. 1. Variables/Predicates dependency graph

An Example of Equivalence Class Partitioning. Consider the following property $\exists x (\diamondsuit q(x) \wedge \neg \diamondsuit r(x))$ and the trace $q(1).q(2).r(1).q(3).q(4).q(5).r(2).r(3).r(4).q(6)$

Table 1 presents relations that correspond to the subformulas in the summary. The table shows these relations in now after a trace that includes the first event, the first two events, all but the last event, and the entire trace. The letter U represents the set of all possible values for x (this can be, e.g., the natural numbers). The last column presents the equivalence relations, as defined in Eq. (1), calculated per each relation at the end of the trace.

The intersection of the equivalence relations that appear in the last column of the table gives the following equivalence classes:

$$\{\{1,2,3,4\},\{5\},\{6\},U \setminus \{1,2,3,4,5,6\}\}.$$

Table 1. Calculating relations and equivalence classes for the example property

Subformula	Event					Eq. classes
	$q(1)$	$q(2)$	... $r(4)$	$q(6)$		
$q(x)$	$\{1\}$	$\{2\}$	$\emptyset$	$\{6\}$		$\{\{6\}, U \setminus \{6\}\}$
$\diamond\, q(x)$	$\{1\}$	$\{1,2\}$	$\{1,2,3,4,5\}$	$\{1,2,3,4,5,6\}$		$\{\{1,2,3,4,5,6\}, U \setminus \{1,2,3,4,5,6\}\}$
$r(x)$	$\emptyset$	$\emptyset$	... $\{4\}$	$\emptyset$		$\{U\}$
$\diamond\, r(x)$	$\emptyset$	$\emptyset$	$\{1,2,3,4\}$	$\{1,2,3,4\}$		$\{\{1,2,3,4\}, U \setminus \{1,2,3,4\}\}$
$\neg\, \diamond\, r(x)$	U	U	$U \setminus \{1,2,3,4\}$	$U \setminus \{1,2,3,4\}$		$\{\{1,2,3,4\}, U \setminus \{1,2,3,4\}\}$
$\diamond\, q(x) \wedge \neg\, \diamond\, r(x)$	$\{1\}$	$\{1,2\}$	$\{5\}$	$\{5,6\}$		$\{\{5,6\}, U \setminus \{5,6\}\}$

This is the equivalence relation defined in Eq. (2) that is used to select the representatives for extending the trace.

3   Prediction Using BDD Representation

We saw in the previous section how to define equivalence classes on data values that would lead to extensions of the current trace with the same lengths and verdicts. We established that it is sufficient to select a single representative from each equivalence class. Calculating these equivalence classes explicitly can be complex and time consuming. Instead, we show how to take advantage of the BDD representation to calculate the equivalence classes. We encode these equivalence classes using Boolean formulas that involve the components of the summary, calculated during the RV algorithm, which are also BDDs. These formulas can be used to calculate the equivalence classes using a BDD package. Then, selecting a representative from the equivalence class and updating the remaining equivalence classes are also implemented using operators on BDDs.

Recall that the RV algorithm described in Sect. 2.2 calculates BDDs that correspond to the assignments for the subformulas after an inspected trace σ of length i. That is, for a subformula η, the BDD $\mathsf{now}(\eta)$ represents the relation $R = I[\eta, \sigma, i]$ containing the assignments to the free variables of R that satisfy η at position $i = |\sigma|$ of the trace σ. Suppose that R is such a BDD B in the summary, with the bits $x_1, \ldots, x_n$ representing (enumeration) values of the D_i component of R, and with the bits $y_1, \ldots, y_m$ representing the rest of the components.

Implementing the algorithm using BDDs, we start by translating the condition of Lemma 2 for automorphism into a check that can be automated using BDDs. Let B be the BDD representation of $R = I[\eta, \sigma, i]$, let $a_1, \ldots, a_n$ be the bit vector that represents the value (enumeration) a, and let $b_1, \ldots, b_n$ be the bit vector that represents the value b. Then $f^x_{a \leftrightarrow b}$ is an automorphism over R iff the following BDD formula evaluates to $true$[2]:

$$\forall y_1 \ldots \forall y_m ((B[x_1 \setminus a_1] \ldots [x_n \setminus a_n]) \leftrightarrow (B[x_1 \setminus b_1] \ldots [x_n \setminus b_n])) \qquad (3)$$

---

[2] $(\eta \leftrightarrow \psi)$ is a shorthand for $((\eta \to \psi) \wedge (\eta \leftarrow \psi))$. Also $B[c \setminus d]$ denotes the BDD where the value of the bit c in the BDD is set constantly to d.

Next, we generate from a BDD B, representing some relation $R = I[\eta, \sigma, i]$ in the summary, a representation of the equivalence classes of $E[\eta, \sigma, x]$. This is an implementation of Equation (1) using BDDs. The bit vectors $g_1, \ldots, g_n$ and $h_1, \ldots, h_n$ represent pairs of values g and h for the variable x such that $f_{g \leftrightarrow h}$ is an isomorphism for R. That is $R_{x=g} = R_{x=h}$ for each pair of values g and h. We denote this formula by $GH[B,x]$.

$$GH[B,x] = \forall y_1 \ldots \forall y_m (\exists x_1 \ldots \exists x_n (B \wedge (x_1 \leftrightarrow g_1) \ldots \wedge (x_n \leftrightarrow g_n)) \leftrightarrow$$
$$\exists x_1 \ldots \exists x_n (B \wedge (x_1 \leftrightarrow h_1) \ldots \wedge (x_n \leftrightarrow h_n))) \tag{4}$$

An alternative and more efficient method for obtaining the BDD $GH[B,x]$ is to employ the simplified formula, which avoids using the existential quantification.

$$GH[B,x] = \forall y_1 \ldots \forall y_m (B[x_1 \setminus g_1] \ldots [x_n \setminus g_n] \leftrightarrow B[x_1 \setminus h_1] \ldots B[x_n \setminus h_n]) \tag{5}$$

Now we can construct a BDD representation for the equivalence classes $\mathcal{E}[\sigma,t]$, as defined in Eq. (2). We need to take, for each type t the conjunction of all $GH[B_\eta, x]$, for $\eta \in sub(\varphi)$, $x \in free(\varphi)$ and $type(x) = t$, and where $B_\eta = now(\eta)$ in the summary of the RV algorithm.

$$GH = \bigwedge_{x \in free(\eta) \wedge type(x) = t \wedge \eta \in sub(\varphi)} GH[B_\eta, x] \tag{6}$$

4   Undecidability of Unbounded Prediction

We presented an algorithm for calculating the verdicts that can be obtained by extending the inspected trace, checked against a first-order past LTL specification, by up to k steps. In this section we will show that making such a prediction *without a length restriction* is undecidable[3].

The proof is by reduction from the undecidable *post correspondence problem* (PCP). An instance of the PCP problem consists of two *indexed* sets T_1 and T_2, each of $n > 0$ nonempty *words* from over some finite alphabet Σ. The problem is to decide whether there is a non-empty finite sequence $i_1, i_2, \ldots, i_k$ of indexes, where each $i_j \in [1..|T_1|]$, such that $T_1(i_1).T_1(i_2) \ldots T_1(i_k) = T_2(i_1).T_2(i_2) \ldots T_2(i_k)$ (using the concatenation operator "."). That is, whether concatenating words from T_1 and from T_2, with possible repeats, according to some common sequence of indexes, gives the same string.

For example, consider an instance of PCP where $T_1 = \{(aa,1),(abb,2),(aba,3)\}$ and $T_2 = \{(baa,1),(aab,2),(ab,3)\}$, where each pair includes a word and its corresponding index. Thus, we can write, e.g., $T_1(2) = abb$. For this instance of PCP, there is a simple solution, where each word appears exactly once; when concatenating the words with index order 3 2 1, we obtain $T_1(3).T_1(2).T_1(1) = aba.abb.aa$, and for $T_2(3).T_2(2).T_2(1) = ab.aab.baa$, resulting in the same string

$$abaabbaa. \tag{7}$$

---

[3] A proof of undecidability of first-order *future* LTL that includes *interpreted* and *uninterpreted* *relation* and *function* symbols is shown in [6]. Note that our logic is far more restrictive than that.

The reduction constructs from each instance of the PCP problem a past first-order LTL formula that is satisfiable by a trace if and only if it describes a solution to the problem. The trace simulates a concatenating of words from T_1 and T_2. The input includes, except for the sequence of letters, additional information that allows breaking the string according to the tokens of T_1 and according to the tokens of T_2.

Adjacent to each letter in the string, we add two values, from some unbounded events, which delimit the individual strings for T_1 and for T_2, correspondingly. For example, given the delimiting values p, q, r, we obtain from the above concatenated word in (7) the following sequence of triples, each consisting of a letter from Σ, and two delimiters, for T_1 and T_2:

$$
\overbrace{\underbrace{(a,p,p)(b,p,p)(a,p,q)}_{p}\underbrace{(a,q,q)(b,q,q)}_{q}\underbrace{(b,q,r)(a,r,r)(a,r,r)}_{r}}^{T_1}.
$$

$$
\underbrace{\qquad\qquad\qquad\qquad\qquad\qquad\qquad\qquad\qquad}_{T_2}
$$

(with the T_1 braces over p, q, r and the T_2 braces under p, q, r) $\qquad$ (8)

In each triple, the first component is the letter, the second is the delimiting value for T_1 and the third component is the delimiting value for T_2.

The delimiting value will appear for both strings in T_1 and of T_2 *in the same order*, to impose the restriction that the same sequence of indexes are used. Thus, in (8), p appears before q and q appears before r. A delimiting value will not repeat after having followed the letters for a single appearance of a string from T_1, and similarly for T_2, even if the same string repeats in the concatenation. The temporal specification will enforce that delimiting of a word from T_1 and delimiting of a word from T_2 with the same value (e.g., the value q) to words with the same indexes in T_1 and T_2 respectively. In the above example, the delimiting value q corresponds to words of T_1 and T_2 with the index 2.

Now, to represent such as sequence as an input trace for RV, each of the above triples will correspond to a successive triple of events, each of the form $l(x).t_1(v_1).t_2(v_2)$. Finally, the trace ends with a single parameterless event e. The predicates in the monitored events have the following roles:

e with no parameters (a proposition). It designates the end of the sequence representing a solution for the PCP problem.

$l(x)$ This is a letter within the concatenation. Since the two concatenations of words need to produce the *same* string, there is only a single $l(x)$ event in each triple.

$t_1(v_1)$ v_1 is a delimiting value for the currently observed word from T_1. Similarly,

$t_2(v_2)$ v_2 is a delimiting value for the currently observed word from T_2.

Then, the sequence (8) become the following sequence of events:

$$l(a).t_1(p).t_2(p).\ \ l(b).t_1(p).t_2(p).\ \ l(a).t_1(p).t_2(q).\ \ l(a).t_1(q).t_2(q).$$
$$l(b).t_1(q).t_2(q).\ \ l(b).t_1(q).t_2(r).\ \ l(a).t_1(r).t_2(r).\ \ l(a).t_1(r).t_2(r).\ \ e.$$

Then, we construct a QTL formula φ as the concatenation of the following conditions:

- Value v_1 (v_2, respectively) within the predicates t_1 (t_2, respectively) can only appear in adjacent triples. Once this value is replaced by a different value in the next triple, the old value never returns.
- The order between the v_1 values and the v_2 values is the same, that is, $t_1(p)$ appears before $t_1(q)$ if and only if $t_2(p)$ appears before $t_2(q)$.
- Each concatenation of letters $l(x)$ from subsequent triples, that is limited by events of the form $t_1(p)$ for some value p forms a word $T_1(i)$ for some i. Similarly, the concatenation of letters $l(x)$ limited by $t_2(q)$ forms a word $T_2(j)$ for some j. Furthermore, if $p = q$ then $i = j$.

Now, φ is satisfied by a trace σ if σ describes a solution for the PCP instance. Hence, predicting when there is a *true* outcome for an extension of the empty trace is undecidable. The undecidability proof suggests that our algorithm for predicting the verdict in k steps gives a compromise for this kind of long-term prediction.

Our undecidability proof has several additional consequences. Temporal safety [22] properties can be written as $\Box\psi$ (see [24]), where $\Box$ stands for the standard LTL operator *always*, i.e., *for each prefix*, and ψ contains only past modalities. It follows from the above construction that the satisfiability of the first-order temporal safety properties of the form $\Box\psi$ for a past ψ is undecidable: just take $\psi = \neg\varphi$ with the above constructed formula φ, which is satisfiable exactly when the instance of the PCP problem does not have a solution. For propositional LTL, it is useful to conclude a *success* (*failure*, respectively) verdict based on monitoring a *minimal* prefix of a trace, when all of its infinite extensions satisfy (does not satisfy, respectively) the property. Such an algorithm appears in [21]. It follows from our construction that this is undecidable for the first-order case. This also gives some explanation of why RV tools for first-order past LTL, such as DejaVu and MONPOLY provide a *true/false* outputs for past properties ψ, instead of checking $\Box\psi$.

5   Experiments

In order to assess the effectiveness and efficiency of our algorithm, which we term iPRV (isomorphic Predictive RV), we extended DejaVu to incorporate our prediction approach. The experiments were performed on an Apple MacBook Pro laptop with an M1 Core processor, 16 GB RAM, and 512 GB SSD storage, running the macOS Monterey operating system. We carried out a comparative analysis against the straightforward brute-force prediction method, which was also integrated into DejaVu. We expressed properties, four of them are shown in Fig. 2, using DejaVu's syntax, and evaluated the tool's performance based on time, and the number of prediction extensions (we termed *cases* or C) used. We repeated experiments with traces of diverse sizes and events order. To measure performance and the influence of the size of parameter k, we experimented with different sizes of k. We used two different approaches when conducting experiments: some experiments stopped once the expected verdict *false* was reached, while others ran until all possible extensions, either exhaustively, for brute-force, or based on representatives with our algorithm, were examined (unless a time limit was surpassed). The unstopped experiments simulated the worst-case scenario when the expected verdict was not found. All the experiments in this section, along with their specifications and the corresponding traces, including further examples, are available in our GitHub repository [30].

P1.	exists x . (@p(x) & g(x) & H (p(x) → (!@p(x) & !(@(@(p(x)))))) & H (g(x) → (!@g(x))))
P2.	forall x . (r(x) → exists y . (!q(y) S p(y)))
P3.	forall f . ((exists d . write(f,d)) → (!close(f) S open(f)))
P4.	exists x . (P q(x) & !P r(x))

1. $\varphi_1 = \exists x\, (\ominus p(x) \wedge g(x) \wedge \boxminus (p(x) \rightarrow (\neg \ominus p(x) \wedge \neg(\ominus(\ominus(p(x)))))) \wedge \boxminus (g(x) \rightarrow (\neg \ominus g(x))))$

2. $\varphi_2 = \forall x\, (r(x) \rightarrow \exists y(\neg q(y)\, S\, p(y)))$

3. $\varphi_3 = \forall f\, ((\exists d\, write(f,d)) \rightarrow (\neg close(f)\, S\, open(f)))$

4. $\varphi_4 = \exists x\, (\diamondsuit q(x) \wedge \neg \diamondsuit r(x))$

Fig. 2. Evaluated properties in DejaVu (left) and QTL (right) formalism. (The QTL operators $\boxminus$ and $\diamondsuit$ are denoted in DejaVu as **H** and **P** respectively)

Traces. Distinct trace files, τ_{min}, τ_{med}, and τ_{max}, were generated for each property, to evaluate iPRV approach. Those files contain random traces in which the order of the events along with their values were set in randomly. Moreover, the min, med, and max descriptors associated with each file represent the size of the trace. The diversity of traces enabled us to perform a thorough analysis and comparison of the performance of iPRV in comparison to the trivial brute-force approach, under different trace sizes and events order for each property.

The τ_{min} traces consist of small traces with less than 15 events each; they provide small equivalence classes. The τ_{med} traces consist of up to 150 events, while the τ_{max} trace can contain up to 1000 events.

For example, for property P4, the traces were created as a random sequence of events with predicates q and r, with data that was randomly generated within a specified range. However, a constraint was applied such that the number of all the q events does not exceed in every prefix of the generated trace the number of r events by more than 5. This guarantees the violation of property P4 for $k \geq 6$.

Results. Tables 2 and 3 summarize part of our experiment results. They illustrate the efficacy of the iPRV, our proposed prediction algorithm, in comparison to the straightforward brute-force approach. The use of the ∞ symbol indicates instances where the prediction process exceeded 1000 seconds. Additionally, C denotes the number of extensions calculated during a single prediction.

Table 2 displays the results of the experiments where the prediction process was executed until all possible outcomes were found, which simulates the worst-case scenario when the expected verdict is not found. Table 3 offers a comparative on-the-fly analysis, where the prediction process stops upon the discovery of a failure. Not surprisingly, as the prediction horizon increases from $k = 4$ to $k = 5$, both methods take more time to complete the executions. The brute-force method, in particular, struggles to complete the executions as complexity rises. From the results, we can conclude that iPRV is at least a few times faster than the brute-force method.

In few cases, in particular where the trace is short and the prediction horizon is not large, the speed improvement was not very significant, but still iPRV is faster; whereas in some comparisons it takes almost the same time. In other cases, it is four times faster and even much more. For example, in Table 2, for property P1, the iPRV method with $k = 4$ and τ_{med} took 0.05 seconds, while in the same configuration, but for the brute-force method, it took more than 131.54 seconds, which means that iPRV is approximately 2600 times faster in this case. In other cases, the brute-force method did not stop within the time frame of 1000 seconds while iPRV managed to stop with a calculation time that is significantly shorter than the 1000 seconds. In these cases, the speed improvement is several orders of magnitude (assuming, optimistically, a 1000 seconds execution time for the brute-force executions). Furthermore, the number of extensions (denoted in the table by C) required by the iPRV method to provide the prediction is significantly less than for the brute-force method. The gap between these methods intensifies as the prediction horizon k increases.

Table 2. Comparison where both methods run fully

Property	Method	Trace τ_{min}	Trace τ_{med}	Trace τ_{max}
P1	iPRV ($k = 4$)	0.06 s, 1,280 C	0.05 s, 1,168 C	0.10 s, 2,184 C
	Brute ($k = 4$)	0.07 s, 2,416 C	131.54 s, 108,496,240 C	∞
	iPRV ($k = 5$)	0.21 s, 7,816 C	0.15 s, 6,984 C	0.31 s, 13,304 C
	Brute ($k = 5$)	0.24 s, 21,568 C	∞	∞
P2	iPRV ($k = 4$)	0.09 s, 2,240 C	0.07 s, 1,856 C	0.12 s, 2,240 C
	Brute ($k = 4$)	0.81 s, 296,631 C	∞	∞
	iPRV ($k = 5$)	0.23 s, 15,292 C	0.21 s, 12,672 C	0.29 s, 15,296 C
	Brute ($k = 5$)	6.62 s, 7,103,366 C	∞	∞
P3	iPRV ($k = 4$)	0.04 s, 864 C	0.03 s, 576 C	0.04 s, 864 C
	Brute ($k = 4$)	0.05 s, 1,504 C	0.64 s, 259,840 C	∞
	iPRV ($k = 5$)	0.14 s, 5,184 C	0.10 s, 4,352 C	0.17 s, 5,184 C
	Brute ($k = 5$)	0.15 s, 10,736 C	1.21 s, 2,538,680 C	∞
P4	iPRV ($k = 4$)	0.12 s, 4,388 C	0.14 s, 4,388 C	0.19 s, 4,388 C
	Brute ($k = 4$)	0.50 s, 170,304 C	∞	∞
	iPRV ($k = 5$)	0.40 s, 37,512 C	0.45 s, 37,512 C	0.69 s, 37,512 C
	Brute ($k = 5$)	3.29 s, 3,558,752 C	∞	∞

Table 3. Comparison where both methods stopped at the expected verdict

Prop	Method	$k = 5$	$k = 10$	$k = 20$	$k = 50$	$k = 100$
P1	iPRV	0.02 s, 1 C	0.01 s, 1 C	0.03 s, 1 C	0.03 s, 1 C	0.04 s, 1 C
	Brute	0.05 s, 1 C	0.09 s, 1 C	0.14 s, 1 C	0.27 s, 1 C	0.39 s, 1 C
P2	iPRV	0.29 s, 15,296 C	∞	∞	∞	∞
	Brute	∞	∞	∞	∞	∞
P3	iPRV	0.02 s, 3 C	0.03 s, 3 C	0.08 s, 3 C	0.05 s, 3 C	0.08 s, 3 C
	Brute	1.31 s, 819 C	1.51 s, 819 C	2.29 s, 819 C	5.19 s, 819 C	10.22 s, 819 C
P4	iPRV	0.62 s, 37,512 C	4.24 s, 446,857 C	6.10 s, 668,869 C	6.87 s, 668,869 C	6.58 s, 668,869 C
	Brute	∞	∞	∞	∞	∞

6 Conclusion

In this work, we presented an algorithm for predicting the possible future outputs during RV of executions with data; the specification is written in past time first-order linear temporal logic QTL and the prediction is limited to the next (parametric) k events. This can be used for preventive actions to be taken before an unrecoverable situation occurs. For efficiency, our algorithm calculates equivalence classes of values that produce isomorphic extensions to the currently observed trace. This allows exploring only representative extensions in order to perform predictions, avoiding the inefficient naive method that checks all the possible event sequences for the next k steps. We demonstrated how to leverage from the BDDs representations for efficient construction and representation of these equivalence classes. The algorithm was implemented as an extension of the RV tool DejaVu.

We have shown that, unlike propositional temporal logic, prediction for past first-order temporal specification *without* a fixed length limit is an undecidable problem. This was proved using a reduction from the post correspondence problem (PCP). This makes the k-step prediction a decidable compromise.

The experimental results indicate that our proposed algorithm significantly outperforms the brute-force method in terms of time and the number of prediction cases calculated during the prediction process; in certain cases, our prediction method successfully concluded its prediction, while the brute-force approach persisted in running without attaining completion within a reasonable time frame.

Although our experimental results show that the speed of our algorithm is far better than the brute-force approach, prediction can still be a significant time consuming task. Whereas the incremental processing after each event in DejaVu takes typically microseconds [15], the incremental complexity for prediction for, e.g., $k = 4$ can take a significant fraction of a second, and for a larger prediction horizon it can further grow. This of course depends on the property and the observed trace. Thus, a naive use of the prediction algorithm with a not so large prediction horizon should be able, in principle, to online monitor traces with the arrival speed of a few events per second. We propose that prediction should be used in combination with other methods that allow restricting the future executions of the observed system, e.g., when an approximated model of the system is available or is obtained using learning techniques (see, e.g., [27,28]). Moreover, prediction should be delegated to a concurrent task, so that normal (prediction-less) monitoring would not be delayed, in case of a quick burst of newly observed events.

Acknowledgements. The authors would like to thank Panagiotis Katsaros for insightful comments on a preliminary draft of the paper.

References

1. Allan, C., et al.: Adding trace matching with free variables to AspectJ. In: OOPSLA 2005, SIGPLAN Notices, vol. 40, no. 10, pp. 345–364. ACM (2005)
2. Barringer, H., Goldberg, A., Havelund, K., Sen, K.: Rule-based runtime verification. In: Steffen, B., Levi, G. (eds.) VMCAI 2004. LNCS, vol. 2937, pp. 44–57. Springer, Heidelberg (2004). https://doi.org/10.1007/978-3-540-24622-0_5
3. Barringer, H., Havelund, K.: TRACECONTRACT: a scala DSL for trace analysis. In: Butler, M., Schulte, W. (eds.) FM 2011. LNCS, vol. 6664, pp. 57–72. Springer, Heidelberg (2011). https://doi.org/10.1007/978-3-642-21437-0_7
4. Barringer, H., Rydeheard, D., Havelund, K.: Rule systems for run-time monitoring: from EAGLE to RULER. In: Sokolsky, O., Taşiran, S. (eds.) RV 2007. LNCS, vol. 4839, pp. 111–125. Springer, Heidelberg (2007). https://doi.org/10.1007/978-3-540-77395-5_10
5. Basin, D.A., Klaedtke, F., Müller, S., Zalinescu, E.: Monitoring metric first-order temporal properties. J. ACM **62**(2), 45 (2015)
6. Bauer, A., Küster, J.-C., Vegliach, G.: From propositional to first-order monitoring. In: Legay, A., Bensalem, S. (eds.) RV 2013. LNCS, vol. 8174, pp. 59–75. Springer, Heidelberg (2013). https://doi.org/10.1007/978-3-642-40787-1_4
7. Bauer, A., Leucker, M., Schallhart, C.: The good, the bad, and the ugly, but how ugly is ugly? In: Sokolsky, O., Taşiran, S. (eds.) RV 2007. LNCS, vol. 4839, pp. 126–138. Springer, Heidelberg (2007). https://doi.org/10.1007/978-3-540-77395-5_11
8. Bryant, R.E.: Symbolic Boolean manipulation with ordered binary-decision diagrams. ACM Comput. Surv. **24**(3), 293–318 (1992)
9. Burch, J.R., Clarke, E.M., McMillan, K.L., Dill, D.L., Hwang, L.J.: Symbolic model checking: 10^{20} states and beyond. In: LICS, pp. 428–439 (1990)
10. Cimatti, A., Tian, C., Tonetta, S.: Assumption-based runtime verification of infinite-state systems. In: Feng, L., Fisman, D. (eds.) RV 2021. LNCS, vol. 12974, pp. 207–227. Springer, Cham (2021). https://doi.org/10.1007/978-3-030-88494-9_11
11. Colombo, C., Pace, G.J., Schneider, G.: LARVA - safer monitoring of real-time java programs (tool paper). In: SEFM 2009, pp. 33–37. IEEE Computer Society (2009)
12. Decker, N., Leucker, M., Thoma, D.: Monitoring modulo theories. J. Softw. Tools Technol. Transf. **18**(2), 205–225 (2016)
13. D'Angelo, B., et al: LOLA: runtime monitoring of synchronous systems. In: TIME 2005, pp. 166–174 (2005)
14. Hallé, S., Villemaire, R.: Runtime enforcement of web service message contracts with data. IEEE Trans. Serv. Comput. **5**(2), 192–206 (2012)
15. Havelund, K., Peled, D., Ulus, D.: First-order temporal logic monitoring with BDDs. In: FMCAD 2017, pp. 116–123 (2017)
16. Goubault-Larrecq, J., Olivain, J.: A smell of ORCHIDS. In: Leucker, M. (ed.) RV 2008. LNCS, vol. 5289, pp. 1–20. Springer, Heidelberg (2008). https://doi.org/10.1007/978-3-540-89247-2_1

17. Havelund, K., Peled, D.: BDDs on the run. In: Margaria, T., Steffen, B. (eds.) ISoLA 2018. LNCS, vol. 11247, pp. 58–69. Springer, Cham (2018). https://doi.org/10.1007/978-3-030-03427-6_8

18. Havelund, K., Roşu, G.: Synthesizing monitors for safety properties. In: Katoen, J.-P., Stevens, P. (eds.) TACAS 2002. LNCS, vol. 2280, pp. 342–356. Springer, Heidelberg (2002). https://doi.org/10.1007/3-540-46002-0_24

19. Havelund, K., Reger, G., Thoma, D., Zălinescu, E.: Monitoring events that carry data. In: Bartocci, E., Falcone, Y. (eds.) Lectures on Runtime Verification. LNCS, vol. 10457, pp. 61–102. Springer, Cham (2018). https://doi.org/10.1007/978-3-319-75632-5_3

20. Kallwies, H., Leucker, M., Sánchez, C., Scheffel, T.: Anticipatory recurrent monitoring with uncertainty and assumptions. In: Dang, T., Stolz, V. (eds.) RV 2022. LNCS, vol. 13498, pp. 181–199. Springer, Cham (2022). https://doi.org/10.1007/978-3-031-17196-3_10

21. Kupferman, O., Vardi, M.Y.: Model checking of safety properties. Formal Methods Syst. Design 19(3), 291–314 (2001)

22. Lamport, L.: Proving the correctness of multiprocess programs. IEEE Trans. Softw. Eng. 3(2), 125–143 (1977)

23. McMillan, K.L.: Symbolic Model Checking: An Approach to the State Explosion Problem. Kluwer Academic Publishers (1993)

24. Manna, Z., Pnueli, A.: The Temporal Logic of Reactive and Concurrent Systems - Specification, pp. I–XIV, 1–427. Springer, New York (1992). https://doi.org/10.1007/978-1-4612-0931-7. ISBN 978-3-540-97664-6

25. Meredith, P.O., Jin, D., Griffith, D., Chen, F., Rosu, G.: An overview of the MOP runtime verification framework. J. Softw. Tools Technol. Transf. 14, 249–289 (2011). https://doi.org/10.1007/s10009-011-0198-6

26. Reger, G., Cruz, H.C., Rydeheard, D.: MARQ: monitoring at runtime with QEA. In: Baier, C., Tinelli, C. (eds.) TACAS 2015. LNCS, vol. 9035, pp. 596–610. Springer, Heidelberg (2015). https://doi.org/10.1007/978-3-662-46681-0_55

27. Yu, K., Chen, Z., Dong, W.: A predictive runtime verification framework for cyber-physical systems. In: SERE (Companion), pp. 223–227 (2014)

28. Zhang, X., Leucker, M., Dong, W.: Runtime verification with predictive semantics. In: Goodloe, A.E., Person, S. (eds.) NFM 2012. LNCS, vol. 7226, pp. 418–432. Springer, Heidelberg (2012). https://doi.org/10.1007/978-3-642-28891-3_37

29. JavaBDD. https://javabdd.sourceforge.net

30. iPRV DejaVu tool source code. https://github.com/moraneus/iPRV-DejaVu

31. DejaVu tool source code. https://github.com/havelund/dejavu

Monitoring Hyperproperties with Prefix Transducers

Marek Chalupa$^{(\boxtimes)}$ ⓘ and Thomas A. Henzinger ⓘ

Institute of Science and Technology Austria (ISTA), Klosterneuburg, Austria
`marek.chalupa@ist.ac.at`

Abstract. Hyperproperties are properties that relate multiple execution traces. Previous work on monitoring hyperproperties focused on synchronous hyperproperties, usually specified in HyperLTL. When monitoring synchronous hyperproperties, all traces are assumed to proceed at the same speed. We introduce (multi-trace) *prefix transducers* and show how to use them for monitoring synchronous as well as, for the first time, asynchronous hyperproperties. Prefix transducers map multiple input traces into one or more output traces by incrementally matching prefixes of the input traces against expressions similar to regular expressions. The prefixes of different traces which are consumed by a single matching step of the monitor may have different lengths. The deterministic and executable nature of prefix transducers makes them more suitable as an intermediate formalism for runtime verification than logical specifications, which tend to be highly non-deterministic, especially in the case of asynchronous hyperproperties. We report on a set of experiments about monitoring asynchronous version of observational determinism.

1 Introduction

Hyperproperties [20] are properties that relate multiple execution traces of a system to each other. One of the most prominent examples of hyperproperties nowadays are the information-flow security policies [33]. Runtime monitoring [1] is a lightweight formal method for analyzing the behavior of a system by checking dynamic execution traces against a specification. For hyperproperties, a monitor must check relations between multiple traces. While many hyperproperties cannot be monitored in general [3,13,25], the monitoring of hyperproperties can still yield useful results, as we may detect their violations [24].

Previous work on monitoring hyperproperties focused on HyperLTL specifications [3,13], or other synchronous hyperlogics [2]. Synchronous specifications model processes that progress at the same speed in lockstep, one event on each trace per step. The synchronous time model has been found overly restrictive for specifying hyperproperties of asynchronous processes, which may proceed at varying speeds [7,9,12,27]. A more general, asynchronous time model allows multiple traces to proceed at different speeds, independently of each other, in order to wait for each other only at certain synchronization events. As far as we know, there has been no previous work on the runtime monitoring of asynchronous hyperproperties.

© The Author(s) 2023
P. Katsaros and L. Nenzi (Eds.): RV 2023, LNCS 14245, pp. 168–190, 2023.
https://doi.org/10.1007/978-3-031-44267-4_9

t_1 :   I(1, 1)   I(h, 1)   O(1, 1)   O(1, 1)

t_2 :   I(1, 1)   I(h, 2)   O(1, 1)   O(1, 1)

t_3 :   I(1, 1)   Dbg(1)   I(h, 2)   O(1, 1)   O(1, 1)

Fig. 1. Traces of abstract events. The event I(x, v) signals an input of value v into variable x; and O(x, v) signals an output of value v from variable x. The event Dbg(b) indicates whether the debugging mode is turned on or off.

The important class of k-safety hyperproperties [20,22] can be monitored by processing k-tuples of traces [3,22]. In this work, we develop and evaluate a framework for monitoring k-safety hyperproperties under both, synchronous and asynchronous time models. For this purpose, we introduce *(multi-trace) prefix transducers*, which map multiple (but fixed) input traces into one or more output traces by incrementally matching prefixes of the input traces against expressions similar to regular expressions. The prefixes of different traces which are consumed by a single matching step of the transducer may have different lengths, which allows to proceed on the traces asynchronously. By instantiating prefix transducers for different combinations of input traces, we can monitor k-safety hyperproperties instead of monitoring only a set of fixed input traces. The deterministic and executable nature of prefix transducers gives rise to natural monitors. This is in contrast with monitors synthesized from logical specifications which are often highly non-deterministic, especially in the case of asynchronous (hyper)properties.

We illustrate prefix transducers on the classical example of *observational determinism* [37]. Informally, observational determinism (OD) states that whenever two execution traces agree on *low* (publicly visible) inputs, they must agree also on low outputs, thus not leaking any information about *high* (secret) inputs. Consider, for example, the traces t_1 and t_2 in Fig. 1. These two traces satisfy OD, because they have the same low inputs (events I(1, ·)) and produce the same low outputs (events O(1, ·)). All other events in the traces are irrelevant to OD. The two traces even satisfy synchronous OD, as the input and output events appear at the same positions in both traces, and thus they can be analysed by synchronous-time monitors (such as those based on HyperLTL [3,13,24]), or by the following prefix transducer:

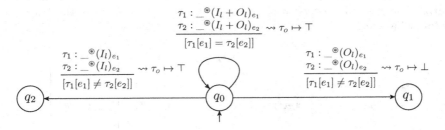

The transducer reads two traces τ_1 and τ_2 that are instantiated with actual traces, e.g., t_1 and t_2. It starts in the initial state q_0 and either repeatedly takes the self-loop transition, or goes into one of the states q_1 or q_2 where it gets stuck. The self-loop transition matches the shortest prefix of τ_1 that contains any events until a low input or output is found. This is represented by the *prefix expression* $\_^{\circledast}(I_l + O_l)$, where we use I_l (resp. O_l) to represent any low input (resp. output) event, and $\_$ stands for any event that does not match the right-hand side of $^{\circledast}$. The same pattern is independently matched by this transition also against the prefix of τ_2. Moreover, the low input or output events found on traces τ_1 and τ_2 are labeled by e_1 and e_2, resp. The self-loop transition is taken if the prefixes of τ_1 and τ_2 match the expressions and, additionally, the condition $\tau_1[e_1] = \tau_2[e_2]$ is fulfilled. The term $\tau[e]$ denotes the sequence of events in trace τ on the position(s) labeled by e. Therefore, the condition $\tau_1[e_1] = \tau_2[e_2]$ asserts that the matched input or output events must be the same (both in terms of type and values). If the transducer takes the self-loop transition, it outputs (appends) the symbol $\top$ to the output trace τ_o (as stated by the right-hand side of $\rightsquigarrow$). Then, the matched prefixes are consumed from the input traces and the transducer continues with matching the rest of the traces. The other two edges are processed analogously.

It is not hard to see that the transducer decides if OD holds for two *synchronous* input traces. State q_0 represents the situation when OD holds but may still be violated in the future. If the self-loop transition over q_0 cannot be taken, then (since we now assume synchronised traces), the matched prefixes must end either with different low input or different low output events. In the first case, OD is satisfied by the two traces and the transducer goes to state q_2 where it gets stuck (we could, of course, make the transducer total to avoid getting stuck, but in this example we are interested only in its output). In the second case, OD is violated and before the transducer changes the state to q_1, it appends $\bot$ to the output trace τ_o. OD is satisfied if τ_o does not contain (end with) $\bot$ after finishing reading (or getting stuck on) the input traces.

The transducer above works also for monitoring asynchronous OD, where the low input and output events are misaligned by "padding" events (but it requires that there is the same number and order of low input and output events on the input traces – they are just misaligned and possibly carry different values; the general setup where the traces can be arbitrary is discussed in Sect. 5). The transducer works for asynchronous OD because the prefix expressions for τ_1 and τ_2 are matched independently, and thus they can match prefixes of different lengths. For example, for $\tau_1 = t_1$ and $\tau_2 = t_3$, the run consumes the traces in the following steps:

	step 1		*step 2*		*step 3*	
t_1 :	I(1, 1)		I(h, 1)	O(1, 1)	O(1, 1)	
t_3 :	I(1, 1)	Dbg(1)	I(h, 2)	O(1, 1)	O(1, 1)	

Hitherto, we have used the output of prefix transducers to decide OD for the given two traces, i.e., to perform the monitoring task. We can also define a prefix transducer that, instead of monitoring OD for the two traces, transforms the asynchronous traces τ_1 and τ_2 into a pair of synchronous traces τ_1' and τ_2' by filtering out "padding" events:

$$\tau_1 : \_^{\circledast}(I_l + O_l)_{e_1} \rightsquigarrow \tau_1' \mapsto \tau_1[e_1] \quad \overset{\downarrow}{\underset{}{\bigcirc\!\!\!\!\bigcirc\, q_0\, \bigcirc\!\!\!\!\bigcirc}} \quad \tau_2 : \_^{\circledast}(I_l + O_l)_{e_2} \rightsquigarrow \tau_2' \mapsto \tau_2[e_2]$$

In this example, the transducer appends every event labeled by e_i to the output trace τ_i', and so it filters out all events except low inputs and outputs. It reads and filters both of the input traces independently of each other. The output traces from the transducer can then be forwarded to, e.g., a HyperLTL monitor[1].

Contributions. This paper makes the following contributions:

- We introduce multi-trace prefix expressions and transducers (Sect. 2 and Sect. 3). These are formalisms that can efficiently and incrementally process words (traces) either fully synchronously, or asynchronously with synchronization points.
- We suggest that prefix transducers are a natural formalism for specifying many synchronous and asynchronous k-safety hyperproperties, such as observational determinism.
- We design an algorithm for monitoring synchronous and asynchronous k-safety hyperproperties using prefix transducers (Sect. 4).
- We provide some experiments to show how our monitors perform (Sect. 5).

2   Prefix Expressions

In this section, we define *prefix expressions* – a formalism similar to regular expressions designed to deterministically and unambiguously match prefixes of words.

2.1   Preliminaries

We model sequences of events as *words* over finite non-empty alphabets. Given an alphabet Σ, the set of finite words over this alphabet is denoted as Σ^*. For two words $u = u_0...u_l \in \Sigma_1^*$ and $v = v_0...v_m \in \Sigma_2^*$, their concatenation $u \cdot v$, also written uv if there is no confusion, is the word $u_0...u_l v_0...v_m \in (\Sigma_1 \cup \Sigma_2)^*$. If

---

[1] One more step is needed before we can use a HyperLTL monitor, namely, to transform the trace of abstract events from the example into a trace of sets of atomic propositions. This can be also done by a prefix transducer.

$w = uv$, we say that u is a prefix of w, written $u \leq w$, and v is a suffix of w. If $u \leq w$ and $u \neq w$, we say that u is a proper prefix of w.

For a word $w = w_0...w_{k-1} \in \Sigma^*$, we denote $|w| = k$ its length, $w[i] = w_i$ for $0 \leq i < k$ its i-th element, $w[s..e] = w_s w_{s+1}...w_e$ the sub-word beginning at index s and ending at index e, and $w[s..] = w_s w_{s+1}...w_{k-1}$ its suffix starting at index s.

Given a function $f : A \rightarrow B$, we denote $Dom(f) = A$ its domain. Partial functions with domain A and codomain B are written as $A \hookrightarrow B$. Functions with a small domain are sometimes given extensionally by listing the mapping, e.g., $\{x \mapsto 1, y \mapsto 2\}$. Given a function f, $f[x \mapsto c]$ is the function that coincides with f on all elements except on x where it is c.

2.2   Syntax of Prefix Expressions

Let L be a non-empty set of labels (names) and Σ a finite non-empty alphabet. The syntax of *prefix expressions* (PE) is defined by the following grammar:

$$\alpha ::= \epsilon \mid a \mid (\alpha.\alpha) \mid (\alpha + \alpha) \mid (\alpha^{\circledast}\beta) \mid (\alpha)_l$$
$$\beta ::= a \mid (\beta + \beta) \mid (\beta)_l$$

where $a \in \Sigma$ and $l \in L$. Many parenthesis can be elided if we let '$\circledast$' (iteration) take precedence before '.' (concatenation), which takes precedence before '+' (disjunction, plus). We write $a.b$ as ab where there is no confusion. In the rest of the paper, we assume that a set of labels L is implicitly given, and that L always has „enough" labels. We denote the set of all prefix expressions over the alphabet Σ (and any set of labels L) as $PE(\Sigma)$, and $PE(\Sigma, L)$ if we want to stress that the expressions use labels from L.

The semantics of PEs (defined later) is similar to the semantics of regular expressions with the difference that a PE is not matched against a whole word but it matches only its prefix, and this prefix is the shortest one possible (and non-empty – if not explicitly specified). For this reason, we do not use the classical Kleene's iteration as it would introduce ambiguity in matching. For instance, the regular expression a^* matches all the prefixes of the word aaa. And even if we specify that we should pick the shortest one, the result would be ϵ, which is usually not desirable, because that means no progress in reading the word. Picking the shortest non-empty prefix would be a reasonable solution in many cases, but the problem with ambiguity persists. For example, the regular expression $(ab)^*(a + b)^*$ matches the word ab in two different ways, which introduces non-determinism in the process of associating the labels with the matched positions.

To avoid the problems with Kleene's iteration, we use a binary iteration operator that is similar to the *until* operator in LTL in that it requires some letter to appear eventually. The expression $\alpha^{\circledast}\beta$ could be roughly defined as $\beta + \alpha\beta + \alpha^2\beta + ...$ where we evaluate it from left to right and β must match *exactly* one letter. The restriction on β is important to tackle ambiguity, but it also helps efficiently evaluate the expression – it is enough to look at a single letter to decide whether to continue matching whatever follows the iteration, or whether to match the left-hand side of the expression. Allowing β to match a sequence of letters would require a look-ahead or backtracking and it is a subject of future extensions. With our iteration operator, expressions like $(ab)^{\circledast}(a+b)^{\circledast}$ and $a^{\circledast}$ are malformed and forbidden already on the level of syntax.

Sub-expressions of a PE can be labeled and the matching procedure described later returns a list of positions in the word that were matched for each of the labels. We assume that every label is used maximally once, that is, no two sub-expressions have the same label. Labels in PEs are useful for identifying the sub-word that matched particular sub-expressions, which will be important in the next section when we use logical formulae that relate sub-words from *different* words (traces). Two examples of PEs and their informal evaluation are:

- $(a+b)_l^{\circledast}a$ – match a or b, associating them to l, until you see a. Because whenever the word contains a, the right-hand side of the iteration matches, the left part of the iteration never matches a and a is redundant in the left-hand side sub-expression. For the word $bbbaba$, the expression matches the prefix $bbba$ and l is associated with the list of position ranges $(0,0),(1,1),(2,2)$ that corresponds to the positions of b that were matched by the sub-expression $(a+b)$.
- $(a^{\circledast}b)_{l_1}((b+c)^{\circledast}(a+d))_{l_2}$ – match a until b is met and call this part l_1; then match b or c until a or d and call that part l_2. For the word $aabbbada$, the expression matches the prefix $aabbba$. The label l_1 is associated with the range of positions $(0,2)$ containing the sub-word aab, and l_2 with the range $(3,5)$ containing the sub-word bba.

2.3 Semantics of Prefix Expressions

We first define *m-strings* before we get to the formal semantics of PEs. An m-string is a sequence of pairs of numbers or a special symbol $\bot$. Intuitively, $(p, \bot)$ represents the beginning of a match at position p in the analyzed word, $(\bot, p)$ the end of a match at position p, and (s, e) is a match on positions from s to e. The concatenation of m-strings reflects opening and closing the matches.

Definition 1 (M-strings). *M-strings are words over the alphabet $M = (\mathbb{N} \cup \{\bot\}) \times (\mathbb{N} \cup \{\bot\})$ with the partial concatenation function $\odot : M^* \times M \hookrightarrow M^*$ defined as*

$$
\alpha \odot (c,d) = \begin{cases} (c,d) & \text{if } \alpha = \epsilon \wedge c \neq \bot \\ \alpha \cdot (c,d) & \text{if } \alpha = \alpha' \cdot (a,b) \wedge b \neq \bot \\ \alpha' \cdot (a,d) & \text{if } \alpha = \alpha' \cdot (a,b) \wedge b = \bot \wedge c = \bot \\ \alpha' \cdot (c,d) & \text{if } \alpha = \alpha' \cdot (a,b) \wedge b = \bot \wedge c \neq \bot \end{cases}
$$

Every m-string is built up from the empty string ϵ by repeatedly concatenating $(p, \bot)$ or $(\bot, p)$ or (p, p). The concatenation $\odot$ is only a partial function (e.g., $\epsilon \odot (\bot, \bot)$ is undefined), but we will use only the defined fragment of the domain. It works as standard concatenation if the last match was closed (e.g., $(0,4) \odot (7, \perp) = (0,4)(7, \perp)$), but it overwrites the last match if we start a new match without closing the old one (e.g., $(0, \perp) \odot (2, \perp) = (2, \perp)$). Overwriting the last match in this situation is valid, because labels are assumed to be unique and opening a new match before the last match was closed means that the old match failed.

We extend $\odot$ to work with m-strings on the right-hand side:

$$\alpha \odot w = \begin{cases} \alpha & \text{if } w = \epsilon \\ (\alpha \odot x) \odot w' & \text{if } w = x \cdot w' \end{cases}$$

While evaluating a PE, we keep one m-string per label used in the PE. To do so we use *m-maps*, partial mappings from labels to m-strings.

Definition 2 (M-map). *Let L be a set of labels and $M = (\mathbb{N} \cup \{\perp\}) \times (\mathbb{N} \cup \{\perp\})$ be the alphabet of m-strings. An m-map is a partial function $m : L \hookrightarrow M^*$. Given two m-maps $m_1, m_2 : L \hookrightarrow M^*$, we define their concatenation $m_1 \odot m_2$ by*

$$(m_1 \odot m_2)(l) = \sigma_1 \odot \sigma_2$$

for all $l \in Dom(m_1) \cup Dom(m_2)$ where $\sigma_i = \epsilon$ if $m_i(l)$ is not defined and $\sigma_i = m_i(l)$ otherwise.

We denote the set of all m-maps $L \hookrightarrow M^*$ for the set of labels L as $\mathbb{M}_L$.

The evaluation of a PE over a word w is defined as an iterative application of a set of rewriting rules that are inspired by language derivatives [5,14]. For the purposes of evaluation, we introduce two new prefix expressions: $\perp^2$ and $[\alpha]_l$. PE $\perp$ represents a failed match and $[\alpha]_l$ is a ongoing match of a labeled sub-expressions $(\alpha)_l$. Further, for a PE α, we define inductively that $\epsilon \in \alpha$ iff

- $\alpha = \epsilon$, or
- α is one of $(\alpha_0 + \alpha_1)$ or $(\alpha_0 + \alpha_1)_l$ or $[\alpha_0 + \alpha_1]_l$ and it holds that $(\epsilon \in \alpha_0 \vee \epsilon \in \alpha_1)$.

For the rest of this section, let us fix a set of labels L, an alphabet Σ, and denote $\mathbb{E} = PE(\Sigma, L)$ the set of all prefix expressions over this alphabet and this set of labels. The core of evaluation of PEs is the *one-step relation* $\overset{a,p}{\Longrightarrow} \subseteq (\mathbb{E} \times \mathbb{M}_L) \times (\mathbb{E} \times \mathbb{M}_L)$ defined for each letter a and natural number p, whose defining rules are depicted in Fig. 2. We assume that the rules are evaluated modulo the equalities $\epsilon \cdot \alpha = \alpha \cdot \epsilon = \alpha$, and we say that α' is a *derivation* of α if $\alpha \overset{a,p}{\Longrightarrow} \alpha'$ for some a and p.

The first seven rules in Fig. 2 are rather standard. Rules for disjunction are non-standard in the way that whenever an operand of a disjunction is evaluated to ϵ, the whole disjunction is evaluated to ϵ (rule OR-END) in order to obtain the shortest match. Also, after rewriting a disjunction, operands that evaluated

---

[2] Because PEs and m-strings never interact together, we use the symbol $\perp$ in both, but formally they are different symbols.

$$\frac{}{(\epsilon, M) \xrightarrow{a,p} (\bot, \emptyset)} \text{(Eps)} \qquad \frac{}{(\bot, M) \xrightarrow{a,p} (\bot, \emptyset)} \text{(Bot)} \qquad \frac{}{(a, M) \xrightarrow{a,p} (\epsilon, M)} \text{(Ltr)}$$

$$\frac{a \neq b}{(a, M) \xrightarrow{b,p} (\bot, \emptyset)} \text{(Ltr-fail)} \qquad \frac{(\alpha, M) \xrightarrow{a,p} (\alpha', M') \quad \alpha' \neq \bot \quad \epsilon \notin \alpha'}{(\alpha\beta, M) \xrightarrow{a,p} (\alpha'\beta, M')} \text{(Concat)}$$

$$\frac{(\alpha, M) \xrightarrow{a,p} (\alpha', M') \quad \epsilon \in \alpha'}{(\alpha\beta, M) \xrightarrow{a,p} (\beta, M')} \text{(Concat-}\epsilon\text{)} \qquad \frac{(\alpha, M) \xrightarrow{a,p} (\alpha', M') \quad \alpha' = \bot}{(\alpha\beta, M) \xrightarrow{a,p} (\bot, \emptyset)} \text{(Concat-}\bot\text{)}$$

$$\frac{(\alpha_0, M) \xrightarrow{a,p} (\alpha_0', M_0') \quad (\alpha_1, M) \xrightarrow{a,p} (\alpha_1', M_1') \quad \epsilon \in \alpha_0' \vee \epsilon \in \alpha_1'}{(\alpha_0 + \alpha_1, M) \xrightarrow{a,p} (\epsilon, M_0' \odot M_1')} \text{(Or-end)}$$

$$\frac{(\alpha_0, M) \xrightarrow{a,p} (\alpha_0', M_0') \quad (\alpha_1, M) \xrightarrow{a,p} (\alpha_1', M_1') \quad \epsilon \notin \alpha_0' \wedge \epsilon \notin \alpha_1'}{(\alpha_0 + \alpha_1, M) \xrightarrow{a,p} (\alpha_0' + \alpha_1', M_0' \odot M_1') \quad \alpha_0' + \alpha_1' \text{ is reduced w.r.t } \alpha + \bot = \bot + \alpha = \alpha} \text{(Or)}$$

$$\frac{(\beta, M) \xrightarrow{a,p} (\beta', M') \quad \epsilon \in \beta'}{(\alpha^\circledast\beta, M) \xrightarrow{a,p} (\epsilon, M')} \text{(Iter-end)} \qquad \frac{(\beta, M) \xrightarrow{a,p} (\beta', \_) \quad \epsilon \notin \beta' \quad (\alpha, M) \xrightarrow{a,p} (\alpha', M')}{(\alpha^\circledast\beta, M) \xrightarrow{a,p} (\alpha'\alpha^\circledast\beta, M')} \text{(Iter)}$$

$$\frac{(\alpha, M) \xrightarrow{a,p} (\alpha', M') \quad \epsilon \notin \alpha'}{((\alpha)_l, M) \xrightarrow{a,p} ([\alpha']_l, \{l \mapsto (p, \bot)\} \odot M')} \text{(L-start)} \qquad \frac{(\alpha, M) \xrightarrow{a,p} (\alpha', M') \quad \epsilon \notin \alpha'}{([\alpha]_l, M) \xrightarrow{a,p} ([\alpha']_l, M')} \text{(L-cont)}$$

$$\frac{(\alpha, M) \xrightarrow{a,p} (\alpha', M') \quad \epsilon \in \alpha'}{((\alpha)_l, M) \xrightarrow{a,p} (\epsilon, M' \odot \{l \mapsto (p, p)\})} \text{(L-ltr)} \qquad \frac{(\alpha, M) \xrightarrow{a,p} (\alpha', M') \quad \epsilon \in \alpha'}{([\alpha]_l, M) \xrightarrow{a,p} (\epsilon, M' \odot \{l \mapsto (\bot, p)\})} \text{(L-end)}$$

Fig. 2. One-step relation for evaluating prefix expressions. The rules are evaluated modulo the equalities $\epsilon \cdot \alpha = \alpha \cdot \epsilon = \alpha$.

to $\bot$ are dropped (unless the last one if we should drop all operands). The only non-shortening rule is ITER that unrolls α if β was not matched in $\alpha^\circledast\beta$. Thus, evaluating $\alpha^\circledast\beta$ can first prolong the expression and then eventually end up again in $\alpha^\circledast\beta$ after a finite number of steps. This does not introduce any problems as the set of derivations remains bounded [16].

There are four rules for handling labellings. Rule L-LTR handles one-letter matches. Rule L-START handles the beginning of a match where the expression $(\alpha)_l$ gets rewritten to $[\alpha]_l$ so that we know we are currently matching label l in the next steps. Rules L-CONT and L-END continue and finish the match once the labeled expression evaluates to ϵ. Concatenating m-maps in the rules works well because of the assumption that no two sub-expressions have the same label. Therefore, there are no collisions and we always concatenate information from processing the same sub-expression.

The one-step relation is deterministic, i.e., there is always at most one rule that can be applied and thus every PE has a unique single derivation for a fixed letter a and position p.

Theorem 1 (Determinism of $\overset{a,p}{\Longrightarrow}$). *For an arbitrary PE α over alphabet Σ, and any $a \in \Sigma$ and $p \in \mathbb{N}$, there exist at most one α' such that $\alpha \overset{a,p}{\Longrightarrow} \alpha'$ (that is, there is at most one defining rule of $\overset{a,p}{\Longrightarrow}$ that can be applied to α).*

Proof (Sketch). Multiple rules could be applied only if they match the same structure of α (e.g., that α is a disjunction). But for such rules, the premises are pairwise unsatisfiable together.

Having the deterministic one-step relation, we can define the *evaluation function* on words $\delta : \mathbb{E} \times \Sigma^* \to \mathbb{E} \times \mathbb{M}_L$ that returns the rewritten PE and the m-map resulting from evaluating the one-step relation for each single letter of the word: $\delta(\alpha, w) = \overline{\delta}(\alpha, w, 0, \emptyset)$ where

$$\overline{\delta}(\alpha, w, p, M) = \begin{cases} (\alpha, M) & \text{if } w = \epsilon \\ \overline{\delta}(\alpha', w', p+1, M') & \text{if } w = aw' \wedge (\alpha, M) \overset{a,p}{\Longrightarrow} (\alpha', M') \end{cases}$$

We also define the *decomposition function* $\rho : \mathbb{E} \times \Sigma^* \to (\Sigma^* \times \mathbb{M}_L \times \Sigma^*) \cup \{\bot\}$ that decomposes a word $w \in \Sigma^*$ into the matched prefix with the resulting m-map, and the rest of w:

$$\rho(\alpha, w) = \begin{cases} (u, m, v) & \text{if } w = uv \wedge \delta(\alpha, u) = (\epsilon, m) \\ \bot & \text{otherwise} \end{cases}$$

Function ρ is well-defined as there is at most one u for which $\delta(\alpha, u) = (\epsilon, \_)$. This follows from the determinism of the one-step relation. Function ρ is going to be important in the next section.

Before we end this section, let us remark that thanks to the determinism of the one-step relation and the fact that there is only a finite number of derivations of any PE α, the evaluation function for a fixed PE can be represented as a *finite transducer* [16]. Given the transducer for PE α and $w \in \Sigma^*$ s.t. $(u, m, v) = \rho(\alpha, w)$, u is the prefix of w that leads the transducer to the accepting state and the transducer outputs a sequence $m_0, ..., m_k$ such that $m_0 \odot ... \odot m_k = m$. As a result, we have an efficient and incremental way of evaluating PEs. Moreover, it suggests how to compose and perform other operations with PEs.

3   Multi-trace Prefix Expressions and Transducers

In this section, we define *multi-trace prefix expressions* and *multi-trace prefix transducers*.

3.1   Multi-trace Prefix Expressions

A multi-trace prefix expression (MPE) matches prefixes of multiple words. Every MPE consists of prefix expressions associated with input words and a *condition* which is a logical formula that must be satisfied by the matched prefixes.

Definition 3 (Multi-trace prefix expression). *Multi-trace prefix expression (MPE) over trace variables V_τ and alphabet Σ is a list of pairs together with a formula:*

$$(\tau_0, e_0), \ldots, (\tau_k, e_k)[\varphi]$$

where $\tau_i \in V_\tau$ are trace variables and e_i are PEs over the alphabet Σ. The formula φ is called the condition of MPE. We require that for all $i \neq j$, labels in e_i and e_j are distinct.

If the space allows, we typeset MPEs over multiple lines as can be seen in the examples of prefix transducers throughout the paper.

MPE conditions are logical formulae over m-strings and input words[3]. Terms of MPE conditions are $l_1 = l_2$, $\tau_1[l_1] = \tau_2[l_2]$, and $\tau_1[l_1] = w$ for labels or m-string constants l_1, l_2, trace variables $\tau_1, \tau_2 \in V_\tau$, and (constant) words w over arbitrary alphabet. Labels are evaluated to the m-strings associated with them by a given m-map, $\tau[l]$ is the concatenation of sub-words of the word associated with τ on positions specified by the m-string for l, and constants evaluate to themselves. For example, if label l evaluates to $(0,1)(3,4)$ for a given m-map, then $\tau[l]$ evaluates to $abba$ if τ is mapped to $abcba$. A well-formed MPE condition is a boolean formula built up from the terms.

The satisfaction relation of MPE conditions is defined w.r.t an m-map M, and a *trace assignment* $\sigma : V_\tau \to \Sigma^*$ which is a map from a set of trace variables V_τ into words. We write $\sigma, M \models \varphi$ when σ and M satisfy condition φ. Because of the space restrictions, we refer to the extended version of this paper [16] for formal definition of the satisfaction relation for MPE conditions. Nonetheless, we believe that MPE conditions are intuitive enough from the examples.

Given an MPE α, we denote as $\alpha(\tau)$ the PE associated with trace variable τ and if we want to highlight that α has the condition φ, we write $\alpha[\varphi]$. We denote the set of all MPEs over trace variables V_τ and alphabet Σ as $MPE(V_\tau, \Sigma)$. An MPE $\alpha[\varphi]$ over trace variables $V_I = \{\tau_1, ..., \tau_k\}$ satisfies a trace assignment σ, written $\sigma \models \alpha$, iff $\forall \tau \in V_I : \rho(\alpha(\tau), \sigma(\tau)) = (u_\tau, M_\tau, v_\tau)$ and $\sigma, M_{\tau_1} \odot ... \odot M_{\tau_k} \models \varphi$. That is, $\sigma \models \alpha$ if every prefix expression of α has matched a prefix on its trace and the condition φ is satisfied.

3.2   Multi-trace Prefix Transducers

Multi-trace prefix transducers (MPT) are finite transducers [36] with MPEs as guards on the transitions. If a transition is taken, one or more symbols are appended to one or more output words, the state is changed to the target state of the transition and the matched prefixes of input words are consumed. The evaluation then continues matching new prefixes of the shortened input words.

---

[3] The conditions can be almost arbitrary formulae, depending on how much we are willing to pay for their evaluation. They could even contain nested MPEs. As we will see later, MPE conditions are evaluated only after matching the prefixes which gives us a lot of freedom in choosing the logic. For the purposes of this work, however, we use only simple conditions that we need in our examples and evaluation.

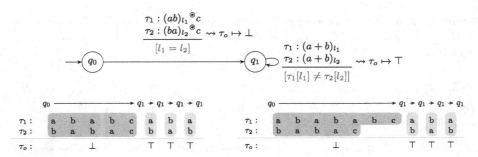

Fig. 3. The MPT from Example 1 and a demonstration of its two runs. Colored regions show parts of words as they are matched by the transitions, the sequence of passed states is shown above the traces.

Combining MPEs with finite state transducers allows to read input words asynchronously (evaluating MPEs) while having synchronization points and finite memory (states of the transducer).

Definition 4 (Multi-trace prefix transducer). *A multi-trace prefix expression transducer (MPT) is a tuple* $(V_I, V_O, \Sigma_I, \Sigma_O, Q, q_0, \Delta)$ *where*

- V_I *is a finite set of input trace variables*
- V_O *is a finite set of output trace variables*
- Σ_I *is an input alphabet*
- Σ_O *is an output alphabet*
- Q *is a finite non-empty set of states*
- $q_0 \in Q$ *is the initial state*
- $\Delta : Q \times MPE(V_I, \Sigma_I) \times (V_O \hookrightarrow \Sigma_O^*) \times Q$ *is the transition relation; we call the partial mappings* $(V_O \hookrightarrow \Sigma_O^*)$ *output assignments.*

A *run* of an MPT $(V_I, V_O, \Sigma_I, \Sigma_O, L, Q, q_0, \Delta)$ on trace assignment σ_0 is a sequence $\pi = (q_0, \sigma_0) \xrightarrow{\nu_0} (q_1, \sigma_1) \xrightarrow{\nu_1} \ldots \xrightarrow{\nu_{k-1}} (q_k, \sigma_k)$ of alternating states and trace assignments (q_i, σ_i) with output assignments ν_i, such that for each $(q_i, \sigma_i) \xrightarrow{\nu_i} (q_{i+1}, \sigma_{i+1})$ there is a transition $(q_i, \alpha, \nu_i, q_{i+1}) \in \Delta$ such that $\sigma_i \models \alpha$ and $\forall \tau \in V_I : \sigma_{i+1}(\tau) = v_\tau$ where $(\_, \_, v_\tau) = \rho(\alpha(\tau), \sigma_i(\tau))$. That is, taking a transition in an MPT is conditioned by satisfying its MPE and its effect is that every matched prefix is removed from its word and the output assignment is put to output.

The output $O(\pi)$ of the run π is the concatenation of the output assignments $\nu_0 \cdot \nu_1 \cdot \ldots \cdot \nu_{k-1}$, where a missing assignment to a trace is considered to be ϵ. Formally, for any $t \in V_O$, $\nu_i \cdot \nu_j$ takes the value

$$(\nu_i \cdot \nu_j)(t) = \begin{cases} \nu_i(t) \cdot \nu_j(t) & \text{if } \nu_i(t) \text{ and } \nu_j(t) \text{ are defined} \\ \nu_i(t) & \text{if } \nu_i(t) \text{ is defined and } \nu_j(t) \text{ is undefined} \\ \nu_j(t) & \text{if } \nu_i(t) \text{ is undefined and } \nu_j(t) \text{ is defined} \end{cases}$$

Example 1. Consider the MPT in Fig. 3 and words $t_1 = ababcaba$ and $t_2 = babacbab$ and the assignment $\sigma = \{\tau_1 \mapsto t_1, \tau_2 \mapsto t_2\}$. The run on this assignment is depicted in the same figure on the bottom left. The output of the MPT on σ is $\bot\top\top\top$. For any words that are entirely consumed by the MPT without getting stuck, it holds that τ_1 starts with a sequence of ab's and τ_2 with a sequence of ba's of the same length. Then there is one c on both words and the words end with a sequence of a or b but such that when there is a in one word, there must be b in the other word and vice versa.

Now assume that the words are $t_1 = abababcaba$ and $t_2 = babacbab$ with the same assignment. The situation changes as now the expression on trace t_1 matches the prefix $(ab)^3$ while on t_2 the prefix $(ba)^2$. Thus $l_1 = (0, 6) \neq (0, 4) = l_2$ and the match fails. Finally, assume that we remove the condition $[l_1 = l_2]$ from the first transition. Then for the new words the MPT matches again and the match is depicted on the bottom right in Fig. 3.

In the next section, we work with *deterministic* MPTs. We say that an MPT is deterministic if it can take at most one transition in any situation.

Definition 5 (Deterministic MPT). *Let* $T = (V_I, V_O, \Sigma_I, \Sigma_O, Q, q_0, \Delta)$ *be an MPT. We say that T is deterministic (DMPT) if for any state $q \in Q$, and an arbitrary trace assignment $\sigma : V_I \to \Sigma_I^*$, if there are multiple transitions $(q, \alpha_1, \nu_1, q_1), ..., (q, \alpha_k, \nu_k, q_k)$ such that $\forall i : \sigma \models \alpha_i$, it holds that there exists a proper prefix η of σ, (i.e., $\forall \tau \in V_I : \eta(\tau) \leq \sigma(\tau)$ and for some τ' it holds that $\eta(\tau') < \sigma(\tau')$), and there exist i such that $\eta \models \alpha_i$ and $\forall j \neq i : \eta \not\models \alpha_j$.*

Intuitively, an MPT is DMPT if whenever there is a trace assignment that satisfies more than one transition from a state, one of the transitions matches "earlier" than any other of those transitions.

4   Hypertrace Transformations

A *hyperproperty* is a set of sets of infinite traces. In this section, we discuss an algorithm for monitoring k-*safetyhyperproperties*, which are those whose violation can be witnessed by at most k finite traces:

Definition 6 (k-**safety hyperproperty).** *A hyperproperty S is k-safety hyperproperty iff*

$$\forall T \subseteq \Sigma^\omega : T \notin S \implies \exists M \subseteq \Sigma^* : M \leq T \wedge |M| \leq k \wedge (\forall T' \subseteq \Sigma^\omega : M \leq T' \implies T' \notin S)$$

where Σ^ω is the set of infinite words over alphabet Σ, and $M \leq T$ means that each word in M is a (finite) prefix of a word in T.

We assume *unbounded parallel input model* [25], where there may be arbitrary many traces digested in parallel, and new traces may be announced at any time. Our algorithm is basically the combinatorial algorithm for monitoring hyperproperties of Finkbeiner et al. [23,28] where we exchange automata generated from HyperLTL specifications with MPTs. That is, to monitor a k-safety hyperproperty, we instantiate an MPT for every k-tuple of input traces. An advantage of using MPTs instead of monitor automata in the algorithm of

Finkbeiner et al. is that we automatically get a monitoring solution for asynchronous hyperproperties. A disadvantage is that we cannot automatically use some of the optimizations designed for HyperLTL monitors that are based on the structure (e.g., symmetry) of the HyperLTL formula [24].

The presented version of our algorithm assumes that the input is DMPT as it is preferable to have deterministic monitors. Deciding whether a given MPT is deterministic depends a lot on the chosen logic used for MPE constraints. In the rest of the paper, we assume that the used MPTs are *known* to be DMPTs (which is also the case of MPTs used in our evaluation). We make the remark that in cases where the input MPT is not known to be deterministic and/or a check is impractical, one may resort to a way how to resolve possible non-determinism instead, such as using priorities on the edges. This is a completely valid solution and it is easy to modify our algorithm to work this way. In fact, the algorithm works also with non-deterministic MPTs with a small modification.

4.1   Algorithm for Online Monitoring of k-safety Hyperproperties

Our algorithm is depicted in Algorithm 1 and Algorithm 2 (auxiliary procedures). In essence, the algorithm maintains a set of *configurations* where one configuration corresponds to the state of evaluation of one edge of an DMPT instance. Whenever the algorithm may make a progress in some configuration, it does so and acts according to whether matching the edge succeeds, fails, or needs more events.

Now we discuss functioning of the algorithm in more detail. The input is an DMPT $(\{V_I, \{\tau_O\}, \Sigma_I, \{\bot, \top\}, Q, q_0, \Delta\})$. W.l.o.g we assume that $V_I = \{\tau_1, ..., \tau_k\}$. The DMPT outputs a sequence of verdicts $\{\top, \bot\}^*$. A violation of the property is represented by $\bot$, so whenever $\bot$ appears on the output, the algorithm terminates and reports the violation.

A configuration is a 4-tuple $(\sigma, (p_1, ..., p_k), M, e)$ where σ is a function that maps trace variables to traces, the vector $(p_1, ..., p_k)$ keeps track of reading positions in the input traces, M is the current m-map gathered while evaluating the MPE of e, and e is the edge that is being evaluated. More precisely, e is the edge that still needs to be evaluated in the future as its MPE gets repeatedly rewritten during the run of the algorithm. If the edge has MPE E, we write $E[\tau \mapsto \xi]$ for the MPE created from E by setting the PE for τ to ξ.

The algorithm uses three global variables. Variable *workbag* stores configurations to be processed. Variable *traces* is a map that remembers the so-far-seen contents of all traces. Whenever a new event arrives on a trace t, we append it to *traces(t)*. Traces on which a new event may still arrive are stored in variable *onlinetraces*. Note that to follow the spirit of online monitoring setup, in this section, we treat traces as *opaque* objects that we query for next events.

In each iteration of the main loop (line 5), the algorithm first calls the procedure `update_traces` (line 6, the procedure is defined in Algorithm 2). This procedure adds new traces to *onlinetraces* and updates *workbag* with new configurations if there are any new traces, and extends traces in *traces* with new events. The core of the algorithm are lines 9–39 that take all configuration sets and update them with unprocessed events.

Algorithm 1: Online algorithm for monitoring hyperproperties with MPTs

---

Input: an DMPT $(\{\{\tau_1, ..., \tau_k\}, \{\tau_O\}, \Sigma_I, \{\bot, \top\}, Q, q_0, \Delta\})$

Output: *false* + witness if an DMPT instance outputs $\bot$, *true* if no DMPT instance outputs $\bot$ and there are finitely many traces. The algorithm does not terminate otherwise.

```
 1   traces ← ∅                               // Stored contents of all traces
 2   onlinetraces ← ∅                      // Traces that are still being extended
 3   workbag ← ∅                           // Sets of configurations to process
 4
 5   while true do
 6       update_traces (workbag, onlinetraces, traces)
 7       workbag′ ← ∅ // The new contents of workbag
 8
 9       foreach C ∈ workbag do
10           C′ ← ∅ // The rewritten set of configurations
11
12           // Try to move each configuration in the set of configurations
13           foreach c = (σ, (p₁, ..., pₖ), M, q ──E[φ]↝ν──▸ q′)) ∈ C do
14               E′, M′ ← E, M
15               (p′₁, ..., p′ₖ) ← (p₁, ..., pₖ)
16               // Progress on each trace where possible
17               foreach 1 ≤ i ≤ k s.t. pᵢ < |traces(σ(τᵢ))| ∧ E(τᵢ) ≠ ε do
18                   E′ ← E′[τᵢ ↦ ξ] where E(τᵢ), M′ ──traces(σ(τᵢ))[pᵢ],pᵢ──▸ ξ, M″
19                   M′ ← M″
20                   p′ᵢ ← p′ᵢ + 1
21                   if ξ = ⊥ then                          // Configuration failed
22                       continue with next configuration (line 13)
23               if ∀j.E′(τⱼ) = ε then                   // All prefix expressions matched
24                   if σ, M′ ⊨ φ then                   // The condition is satisfied
25                       // Compare p′₁, ..., p′ₖ against positions in other
                            configurations from this set to see if this must be
                            the shortest match
26                       if (p′₁, ..., p′ₖ) < (p″₁, ..., p″ₖ) for all (p″₁, ..., p″ₖ) of c′ ∈ C, c′ ≠ c
                            then
27                           if ⊥ ∈ ν then                  // Violation found
28                               return false + σ
29                           // Edge is matched, no violation found, queue
                                successor edges
30                           workbag′ ←
                                workbag′ ∪ {cfgs(q′, (σ(τ₁), ..., σ(τₖ)), (p′₁, ..., p′ₖ))}
31                           // This set of configurations is done
32                           continue outer-most loop (line 9)
33                       else
34                           continue with next configuration (line 13)
35               // If the configuration has matched or it can still make a
                    progress, put it back (modified) to the set
36               if E′ has matched or
                    ¬(∀1 ≤ i ≤ k : σ(τᵢ) ∉ onlinetraces ∧ pᵢ = |traces(σ(τᵢ))|) then
37                   C′ ← C′ ∪ {(σ, (p′₁, ..., p′ₖ), M′, q ──E′[φ]↝ν──▸ q′)}
38           if C′ ≠ ∅ then
39               workbag′ ← workbag′ ∪ {C′} // Queue the modified set of
                    configurations
40
41       workbag ← workbag′
42       if workbag = ∅ and no new trace will appear then
43           return true
```

Algorithm 2: Auxiliary procedures for Algorithm 1

---

1   // Auxiliary procedure that returns a set of configurations for
      outgoing edges of q

2   **Procedure cfgs**(q, $(t_1, ..., t_k)$, $(p_1, ..., p_k)$)

3       $\sigma \leftarrow \{\tau_i \mapsto t_i \mid 1 \leq i \leq k\}$

4   **return** $\{(\sigma, (p_1, ..., p_k), (0, ..., 0), \emptyset, e) \mid e$ is an outgoing edge from q $\}$

5

6   // Auxiliary procedure to add new traces and update the current
      ones

7   **Procedure update_traces**(*workbag, onlinetraces, traces*)

8   **if** *there is a new trace t* **then**   // Update *traces* and *workbag* with the
      new trace

9   *onlinetraces* $\leftarrow$ *onlinetraces* $\cup$ $\{t\}$

10   *traces* $\leftarrow$ *traces*$[t \mapsto \epsilon]$

11   *tuples* $\leftarrow$ $\{(t_1, ..., t_k) \mid t_j \in Dom(traces), t = t_i$ for some $i\}$

12   *workbag* $\leftarrow$ *workbag* $\cup$ $\{$**cfgs**$(q_0, (t_1, ..., t_k), (0, ..., 0)) \mid (t_1, ..., t_k) \in$
       tuples$\}$

13

14   **foreach** $t \in$ *onlinetraces that has a new event e* **do**   // Update traces
      with new events

15   *traces*(t) = *traces*$(t) \cdot e$

16   **if** *e was the last event on t* **then**   // Remove finished traces from
      onlinetraces

17   *onlinetraces* $\leftarrow$ *onlinetraces* $\setminus$ $\{t\}$

The algorithm goes over every set of configurations from *workbag* (line 9) and attempts to make a progress on every configuration in the set (line 13). For each trace where a progress can be made in the current configuration (line 17), i.e., there is an unprocessed event on the trace τ_i ($p_i < |traces(\sigma(\tau_i))|$), and the corresponding PE on the edge still has not matched ($E(\tau_i) \neq \epsilon$), we do a step on this PE (line 18). The new state of the configuration is aggregated into the primed temporary variables ($E', M', ...$). If the MPE matches (lines 23 and 24), we check if other configurations from the set have progressed enough for us to be sure that this configuration has matched the shortest prefix (line 26). That is, we compare $p'_1, ..., p'_k$ against positions $p''_1, ..., p''_k$ from each other configuration in C if it is strictly smaller (i.e., $p'_i \leq p''_i$ for all i and there is j s.t., $p'_j < p''_j$). If this is true, we can be sure that there is no other edge that can match a shorter prefix and that has not matched it yet because it was waiting for events. If this configuration is the shortest match, the output of the edge is checked if it contains $\bot$ (line 27) and if so, *false* with the counterexample is returned on line 28 because the monitored property is violated. Else, the code falls-through to line 30 that queues new configurations for successor edges as the current edge has been successfully matched and then continues with a new iteration of the outer-most loop (line 32). The continue statement has the effect that all other configurations derived from the same state (other edges) are dropped and therefore progress is made only on the configuration (edge) that matched. If any progress on the MPE can be made in the future, or it has already matched but we do not know if it is the shortest match yet, the modified configuration is pushed into the set of configurations instead of the original one (line 37). If not all the configurations from C were dropped because they could not proceed, line 39 pushes the modified set of configurations back to workbag and a new iteration starts.

4.2   Discussion

To see that the algorithm is correct, let us follow the evolution of the set of configurations for a single instance of the DMPT on traces $t_1, ..., t_k$. The initial set of configurations corresponding to outgoing edges from the initial state is created and put to *workbag* exactly once on line 12 in Algorithm 2. When it is later taken from *workbag* on line 9 (we are back in Algorithm 1), every configuration (edge) is updated – a step is taken on every PE from the edge's MPE (lines 17–18) where a step can be made. If matching the MPE fails, the configuration is discarded due to the jump on line 22 or line 34. If matching the MPE has neither failed nor succeeded (and no violation has been found, in which case the algorithm would immediately terminate), the updated configuration is pushed back to *workbag* and revisited in later iterations. If the MPE has been successfully matched and it is not known to be the shortest match, it is put back to *workbag* and revisited later when other configurations may have proceeded and we may again check if it is the shortest match or not. If it is the shortest match, its successor edges are queued to *workbag* on line 30 (if no violation is found). Note that the check for the shortest match may fail because of some configuration that has failed in the current iteration but is still in C. Such configurations, however, will get discarded in the current iteration and in the next iteration the shortest match is checked again without these. This way we incrementally first match the first edge on the run of the DMPT (or find out that no edge matches), then the second edge after it gets queued into *workbag* on line 30, and so on.

The algorithm terminates if the number of traces is bounded. If it has not terminated because of finding a violation on line 28, it will terminate on line 43. To see that the condition on line 42 will eventually get true if the number of traces is bounded, it is enough to realize that unless a configuration gets matched or failed, it is discarded at latest when failing the condition on line 36 after reading entirely (finite) input traces. Otherwise, if a configuration fails, the set is never put back to *workbag* and if it gets matched, it can get back to *workbag* repeatedly only until the shortest match is identified. But if every event comes in finite time, some of the configurations in the set will eventually be identified as the shortest match (because the MPT is deterministic), and the set of configurations will be done. Therefore, *workbag* will eventually become empty.

Worth remark is that if we give up on checking if the matched MPE is the shortest match on line 26 (we set the condition to *true*) and on line 32, we continue with the loop on line 13 instead of with the outer-most loop, i.e., we do not discard the set of configurations upon a successfully taken edge, the algorithm will work also for generic *non-deterministic* MPTs.

Even though this algorithm is very close to the algorithm of Finkbeiner et al. [23,25,28] where we replace monitoring automata with prefix transducers, there is an important difference. In our algorithm, we assume that existing traces may be extended at any time until the last event has been seen. This is also the reason why we need the explicit check whether a matched configuration is the shortest match. The algorithm of Finkbeiner et al. assumes that when a new trace appears, its contents is entirely known. So their algorithm is incremental on the level of traces, while our algorithm is incremental on the level of traces *and* events.

The monitor templates in the algorithm of Finkbeiner et al. are automata whose edges match propositions on different traces. Therefore, they can be seen as trivial DMPTs where each prefix expression is a single letter or ϵ. Realizing this, we could say that our monitoring algorithm is an asynchronous extension of the algorithm of Finkbeiner et al. where we allow to read multiple letters on edges, or, alternatively, that in the context of monitoring hyperproperties, DMPTs are a generalization of HyperLTL template automata to asynchronous settings.

5   Empirical Evaluation

We conducted a set of experiments about monitoring asynchronous version of OD on random and semi-random traces. The traces contain input and output events I(t, n) and O(t, n) with t $\in$ {l, h}, and n a 64-bit unsigned number. Further, a trace can contain the event E without parameters that abstracts any event that have occurred in the system, but that is irrelevant to OD.

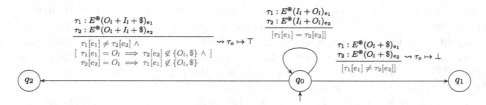

Fig. 4. The DMPT used for monitoring asynchronous OD in the experiments.

The DMPT used for monitoring OD is a modified version of the DMPT for monitoring OD from Sect. 1, and is shown in Fig. 4. The modification makes the DMPT handle also traces with different number and order of input and output events. The letter $ represents the end of trace and is automatically appended to the input traces. We abuse the notation and write $\tau_1[e_1] = O_l$ for the expression that would be formally a disjunction comparing $\tau_1[e_1]$ to all possible constants represented by O_l. However, in the implementation, this is a simple constant-time check of the type of the event, identical to checking that an event matches O_l when evaluating prefix expressions. The term $\tau_i[e_i] \notin \{O_l, \$\}$ is just a shortcut for $\tau_i[e_i] \neq O_l \wedge \tau_i[e_i] \neq \$$.

The self-loop transition in the DMPT in Fig. 4 has no output and we enabled the algorithm to stop processing traces whenever $\top$ is detected on the output of the transducer because that means that OD holds for the input traces. Also, we used the reduction of traces [24] – because OD is symmetric and reflexive, then

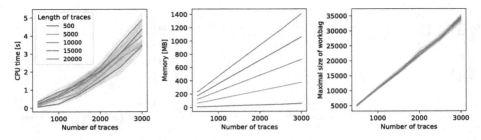

Fig. 5. CPU time and maximal memory consumption of monitoring asynchronous OD on random traces with approx. 10% of low input events and 10% of low output events. Values are the average of 10 runs.

if we evaluate it on the tuple of traces (t_1, t_2), we do not have to evaluate it for (t_2, t_1) and (t_i, t_i).

Monitors were implemented in C++ with the help of the framework VAMOS [17]. The experiments were run on a machine with *AMD EPYC* CPU with the frequency 3.1 GHz. An artifact with the implementation of the algorithm and scripts to reproduce the experiments can be found on Zenodo[4].

Experiments on Random Traces. In this experiment, input traces of different lengths were generated such that approx. 10% were low input and 10% low output events. These events always carried the value 0 or 1 to increase the chance that some traces coincide on inputs and outputs.

Results of this experiment are depicted in Fig. 5. The left plot shows that the monitor is capable of processing hundreds of traces in a short time and seem to scale well with the number of traces, irrespective of the length of traces. The memory consumption is depending more on the length of traces as shown in the middle plot. This is expected as all the input traces are stored in memory. Finally, the maximal size of the workbag grows linearly with the number of traces but not with the length of traces, as the right plot shows.

Experiments on Periodic Traces. In this experiment, we generated a single trace that contains low input and output events periodically with fixed distances. Multiple instances of this trace were used as the input traces. The goal of the experiment is to see how the monitor performs on traces that must be processed to the very end and if the performance is affected by the layout of events.

The plots in Fig. 6 show that the monitor scales worse than on random traces as it has to always process the traces to their end. For the same reason, the performance of the monitor depends more on the length of the traces. Still, it can process hundreds of traces in a reasonable time. The data do not provide a clear hint on how the distances between events change the runtime, but they do not affect it significantly. The memory consumption remains unaffected by distances.

---

[4] https://doi.org/10.5281/zenodo.8191723.

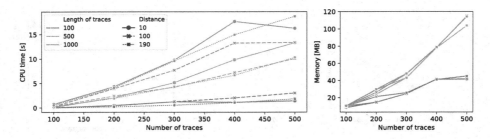

Fig. 6. The plot shows CPU time and memory consumption of monitoring asynchronous OD on instances of the same trace with low input and output events laid out periodically with fixed distances.

6   Related Work

In this section, we review the most closely related work. More exhaustive review can be found in the extended version of this paper [16].

Logics for Hyperproperties. Logics for hyperproperties are typically created by extending a logic for trace properties. Hyperlogics *HyperLTL* [19] and *HyperCTL** [19] extend *LTL* and *CTL**, resp., with explicit quantification over traces. The logic *FO[<,E]* [26] and *S1S[E]* [21] are first- and second- order logics with successors extended with the *equal level predicate* that relates the same time points on different traces.

All of the hitherto mentioned logics use *synchronous time model*. *Asynchronous HyperLTL* [9], *Stuttering HyperLTL* [12], and *Context HyperLTL* [12] are extensions of HyperLTL to asynchronous time model. Gutsfeld et al. [27] introduce *Multi-tape Alternating Asynchronous Word Automata (AAWA)* and the temporal fixpoint calculus H_μ for the specification and analysis of asynchronous hyperproperties. AAWAs are so far the only automata-based formalism for specification of asynchronous hyperproperties. Beutner et al. define *HyperATL** [11], an extension of the logic *ATL** [4] that can capture asynchronous hyperproperties via quantification over *strategies* of a scheduler. *Hypernode automata* [8] introduced by Bartocci et al. combine finite-state automata with the *hypertrace logic* which allows to describe properties that have multiple „phases". The hypertrace logic ignores stuttering and prefixing to enable asynchronous time model.

Runtime Monitoring of Hyperproperties. The first paper on runtime monitoring of hyperproperties is due to Agrawal and Bonakdarpur [3]. They consider monitoring k-safety hyperproperties specified with HyperLTL. In general, monitoring algorithms for hyperproperties can be classified as combinatorial or constraint-based [28]. Combinatorial algorithms [23, 24, 28] construct multiple instances of an monitoring automaton and therefore our algorithm fall into this category. Constraint-based algorithms [2, 13, 28, 29] translate the monitoring task into a set of constraints (e.g., SMT formulae) and apply rewriting and solving of the constraints to monitor a given hyperproperty.

Stream runtime verification (SRV) [35] specifies monitoring as transformation of streams of data, which makes SRV also related to transducers. It is common that there are multiple input and output streams in an SRV specification, and languages like TeSSLa [32] support asynchronous time model. So far as we know, no one has used SRV languages in the context of hyperproperties yet.

Automata and Regular Expressions. *Automata* and *transducers* [36] are the basis of MPTs and are well explored. *Multi-track automata* [15] are automata that read n-tuples of letters. They commonly use also a special letter λ for a gap (no letter) and thus can describe asynchronous reading of words. *Regular expressions (RE)* are an ubiquitous formalism with many uses and many restrictions/extensions. *Prefixed regular expressions (PRE)* [6] are a subset of REs with some properties similar to PEs. Semantically, *prefix-free* REs [30] are closer to PEs than PREs, because PEs give raise to prefix-free languages as follows from [31, Lemma 1] and the fact that a PE corresponds to a prefix-free transducer [16]. REs with the *shortest-match semantics* [18] are very close to PEs, however, unlike PEs, they can be ambiguous. MPTs with a single input word could be seen as a modification of *expression automata* [31], which are automata with REs on edges.

Backreferences in regular expressions refer to parts of the word that were already matched [34]. They can be even named [10], raising more similarities to our labels. In REs, backreferences bring a great power as they allow non-regular languages to be matched [10]. PEs can also recognize some non-regular patterns, however, labels are much weaker than backreferences because MPE constraints are evaluated only a posteriori, while backreferences modify the way how REs are matched.

7   Conclusion and Future Work

We introduced prefix expressions and multi-trace prefix transducers, a formalism that we see as a natural executable specification for the monitoring of synchronous and asynchronous hyperproperties. Prefix expressions are similar to regular expressions, but match only prefixes of words. The reason why we prefer prefix expressions over regular expressions (that could also be used to match prefixes) is that our prefix expressions are deterministic and unambiguous. These properties make evaluating prefix expressions efficient. The matched prefixes, more precisely their parts that were explicitly labeled, can be then reasoned about using logical formulae, which are a part of multi-trace prefix expressions that extend prefix expressions to multiple words. Multi-trace prefix expressions are used as guards on edges in multi-trace prefix transducers, which incrementally match and consume prefixes of input words and transform them into output words. Combining prefix expressions with finite state transducers allows us to read input words asynchronously (matching prefix expressions) with synchronisation points (states of the transducer).

We use prefix transducers to monitor synchronous and asynchronous k-safety hyperproperties. Our experimental evaluation of monitoring asynchronous observational determinism shows that a prefix-transducer-based monitoring algorithm can scale to thousands of traces.

Prefix transducers provide a flexible formalism for optimizing monitoring algorithms. We currently implement an asynchronous monitoring algorithm that uses prefix transducers to summarize the seen traces, similar to the constraint-based algorithms for monitoring synchronous hyperproperties [28]. We also want to analyze the transducers to avoid instantiating them on redundant tuples of traces, similar to the optimizations for HyperLTL monitors [24]. Furthermore, the evaluation of prefix transducers provides many opportunities for parallelization, ranging from parallelizing the workbag in Algorithm 1 to evaluating prefix expressions for different traces in parallel. Finally, we work on compiling prefix transducers from a high-level logical specification languages for asynchronous hyperproperties, namely [8]. All our implementation work is carried out to extend the VAMOS [17] software infrastructure for monitoring.

Acknowledgements. This work was supported in part by the ERC-2020-AdG 101020093. The authors would like to thank Ana Oliveira da Costa for commenting on a draft of the paper.

References

1. Bartocci, E., Falcone, Y. (eds.): Lectures on Runtime Verification - Introductory and Advanced Topics. LNCS, vol. 10457. Springer, Cham (2018). https://doi.org/10.1007/978-3-319-75632-5
2. Aceto, L., Achilleos, A., Anastasiadi, E., Francalanza, A.: Monitoring hyperproperties with circuits. In: Mousavi, M.R., Philippou, A. (eds.) FORTE 2022. LNCS, vol. 13273, pp. 1–10. Springer, Cham (2022). https://doi.org/10.1007/978-3-031-08679-3_1
3. Agrawal, S., Bonakdarpour, B.: Runtime verification of k-safety hyperproperties in HyperLTL. In: CSF 2016, pp. 239–252. IEEE (2016). https://doi.org/10.1109/CSF.2016.24
4. Alur, R., Henzinger, T.A., Kupferman, O.: Alternating-time temporal logic. J. ACM **49**(5), 672–713 (2002). https://doi.org/10.1145/585265.585270
5. Antimirov, V.M.: Partial derivatives of regular expressions and finite automaton constructions. Theor. Comput. Sci. **155**(2), 291–319 (1996). https://doi.org/10.1016/0304-3975(95)00182-4
6. Baeza-Yates, R.A., Gonnet, G.H.: Fast text searching for regular expressions or automaton searching on tries. J. ACM **43**(6), 915–936 (1996). https://doi.org/10.1145/235809.235810
7. Bartocci, E., Ferrère, T., Henzinger, T.A., Nickovic, D., da Costa, A.O.: Flavors of sequential information flow. In: Finkbeiner, B., Wies, T. (eds.) VMCAI 2022. LNCS, vol. 13182, pp. 1–19. Springer, Cham (2022). https://doi.org/10.1007/978-3-030-94583-1_1
8. Bartocci, E., Henzinger, T.A., Nickovic, D., da Costa, A.O.: Hypernode automata (2023). https://doi.org/10.48550/arXiv.2305.02836
9. Baumeister, J., Coenen, N., Bonakdarpour, B., Finkbeiner, B., Sánchez, C.: A temporal logic for asynchronous hyperproperties. In: Silva, A., Leino, K.R.M. (eds.) CAV 2021. LNCS, vol. 12759, pp. 694–717. Springer, Cham (2021). https://doi.org/10.1007/978-3-030-81685-8_33

10. Berglund, M., van der Merwe, B.: Regular expressions with backreferences re-examined. In: Stringology Conference 2017, pp. 30–41. Czech Technical University in Prague (2017). http://www.stringology.org/event/2017/p04.html
11. Beutner, R., Finkbeiner, B.: A temporal logic for strategic hyperproperties. In: CONCUR 2021. LIPIcs, vol. 203, pp. 24:1–24:19. Schloss Dagstuhl - Leibniz-Zentrum für Informatik (2021). https://doi.org/10.4230/LIPIcs.CONCUR.2021.24
12. Bozzelli, L., Peron, A., Sánchez, C.: Asynchronous extensions of HyperLTL. In: LICS 2021, pp. 1–13. IEEE (2021). https://doi.org/10.1109/LICS52264.2021.9470583
13. Brett, N., Siddique, U., Bonakdarpour, B.: Rewriting-based runtime verification for alternation-free HyperLTL. In: Legay, A., Margaria, T. (eds.) TACAS 2017. LNCS, vol. 10206, pp. 77–93. Springer, Heidelberg (2017). https://doi.org/10.1007/978-3-662-54580-5_5
14. Brzozowski, J.A.: Derivatives of regular expressions. J. ACM **11**(4), 481–494 (1964). https://doi.org/10.1145/321239.321249
15. Bultan, T., Yu, F., Alkhalaf, M., Aydin, A.: Relational string analysis. In: Bultan, T., Yu, F., Alkhalaf, M., Aydin, A. (eds.) String Analysis for Software Verification and Security, pp. 57–68. Springer, Cham (2017). https://doi.org/10.1007/978-3-319-68670-7_5
16. Chalupa, M., Henzinger, T.A.: Monitoring hyperproperties with prefix transducers (2023). https://doi.org/10.48550/arXiv.2308.03626
17. Chalupa, M., Muehlboeck, F., Lei, S.M., Henzinger, T.A.: VAMOS: middleware for best-effort third-party monitoring. In: Lambers, L., Uchitel, S. (eds.) FASE 2023. LNCS, vol. 13991, pp. 260–281. Springer, Cham (2023). https://doi.org/10.1007/978-3-031-30826-0_15
18. Clarke, C.L.A., Cormack, G.V.: On the use of regular expressions for searching text. ACM Trans. Program. Lang. Syst. **19**(3), 413–426 (1997). https://doi.org/10.1145/256167.256174
19. Clarkson, M.R., Finkbeiner, B., Koleini, M., Micinski, K.K., Rabe, M.N., Sánchez, C.: Temporal logics for hyperproperties. In: Abadi, M., Kremer, S. (eds.) POST 2014. LNCS, vol. 8414, pp. 265–284. Springer, Heidelberg (2014). https://doi.org/10.1007/978-3-642-54792-8_15
20. Clarkson, M.R., Schneider, F.B.: Hyperproperties. J. Comput. Secur. **18**(6), 1157–1210 (2010). https://doi.org/10.3233/JCS-2009-0393
21. Coenen, N., Finkbeiner, B., Hahn, C., Hofmann, J.: The hierarchy of hyperlogics. In: LICS 2019, pp. 1–13. IEEE (2019). https://doi.org/10.1109/LICS.2019.8785713
22. Finkbeiner, B., Haas, L., Torfah, H.: Canonical representations of k-safety hyperproperties. In: CSF 2019, pp. 17–31. IEEE (2019). https://doi.org/10.1109/CSF.2019.00009
23. Finkbeiner, B., Hahn, C., Stenger, M., Tentrup, L.: Monitoring hyperproperties. In: Lahiri, S., Reger, G. (eds.) RV 2017. LNCS, vol. 10548, pp. 190–207. Springer, Cham (2017). https://doi.org/10.1007/978-3-319-67531-2_12
24. Finkbeiner, B., Hahn, C., Stenger, M., Tentrup, L.: RVHyper: a runtime verification tool for temporal hyperproperties. In: Beyer, D., Huisman, M. (eds.) TACAS 2018. LNCS, vol. 10806, pp. 194–200. Springer, Cham (2018). https://doi.org/10.1007/978-3-319-89963-3_11
25. Finkbeiner, B., Hahn, C., Stenger, M., Tentrup, L.: Monitoring hyperproperties. Formal Methods Syst. Des. **54**(3), 336–363 (2019). https://doi.org/10.1007/s10703-019-00334-z

26. Finkbeiner, B., Zimmermann, M.: The first-order logic of hyperproperties. In: STACS 2017. LIPIcs, vol. 66, pp. 30:1–30:14. Schloss Dagstuhl - Leibniz-Zentrum für Informatik (2017). https://doi.org/10.4230/LIPIcs.STACS.2017.30

27. Gutsfeld, J.O., Müller-Olm, M., Ohrem, C.: Automata and fixpoints for asynchronous hyperproperties. In: POPL 2021, pp. 1–29 (2021). https://doi.org/10.1145/3434319

28. Hahn, C.: Algorithms for monitoring hyperproperties. In: Finkbeiner, B., Mariani, L. (eds.) RV 2019. LNCS, vol. 11757, pp. 70–90. Springer, Cham (2019). https://doi.org/10.1007/978-3-030-32079-9_5

29. Hahn, C., Stenger, M., Tentrup, L.: Constraint-based monitoring of hyperproperties. In: Vojnar, T., Zhang, L. (eds.) TACAS 2019. LNCS, vol. 11428, pp. 115–131. Springer, Cham (2019). https://doi.org/10.1007/978-3-030-17465-1_7

30. Han, Y.-S., Wang, Y., Wood, D.: Prefix-free regular-expression matching. In: Apostolico, A., Crochemore, M., Park, K. (eds.) CPM 2005. LNCS, vol. 3537, pp. 298–309. Springer, Heidelberg (2005). https://doi.org/10.1007/11496656_26

31. Han, Y.-S., Wood, D.: The generalization of generalized automata: expression automata. In: Domaratzki, M., Okhotin, A., Salomaa, K., Yu, S. (eds.) CIAA 2004. LNCS, vol. 3317, pp. 156–166. Springer, Heidelberg (2005). https://doi.org/10.1007/978-3-540-30500-2_15

32. Leucker, M., Sánchez, C., Scheffel, T., Schmitz, M., Schramm, A.: TeSSLa: runtime verification of non-synchronized real-time streams. In: SAC 2018, pp. 1925–1933. ACM (2018). https://doi.org/10.1145/3167132.3167338

33. McLean, J.: Security models and information flow. In: SP 1990, pp. 180–189. IEEE (1990). https://doi.org/10.1109/RISP.1990.63849

34. Penna, G.D., Intrigila, B., Tronci, E., Zilli, M.V.: Synchronized regular expressions. Acta Informatica **39**(1), 31–70 (2003). https://doi.org/10.1007/s00236-002-0099-y

35. Sánchez, C.: Synchronous and asynchronous stream runtime verification. In: VORTEX 2021, pp. 5–7. ACM (2021). https://doi.org/10.1145/3464974.3468453

36. Veanes, M., Hooimeijer, P., Livshits, B., Molnar, D., Bjørner, N.S.: Symbolic finite state transducers: algorithms and applications. In: POPL 2012, pp. 137–150. ACM (2012). https://doi.org/10.1145/2103656.2103674

37. Zdancewic, S., Myers, A.C.: Observational determinism for concurrent program security. In: CSFW 2003, p. 29. IEEE (2003). https://doi.org/10.1109/CSFW.2003.1212703

Compositional Simulation-Based Analysis
of AI-Based Autonomous Systems
for Markovian Specifications

Beyazit Yalcinkaya[1]([✉]), Hazem Torfah[1], Daniel J. Fremont[2],
and Sanjit A. Seshia[1]

[1] University of California, Berkeley, CA, USA
{beyazit,torfah,sseshia}@berkeley.edu
[2] University of California, Santa Cruz, CA, USA
dfremont@ucsc.edu

Abstract. We present a framework for the compositional simulation-based analysis of AI-based autonomous systems for Markovian safety specifications. Our compositional approach allows us to cut down the cost of executing a large number of long-running simulations, by decomposing a simulation-based analysis task into several shorter and more efficient ones. Results obtained from the individual analyses are then stitched together to generate a result for the overall simulation-based task. Our approach is based on a decomposition of scenarios formalized as concurrent hierarchical probabilistic extended state machines that describe sequential and parallel compositions of scenarios. We present two instantiations of our framework for falsification and statistical verification. Using case studies from the autonomous driving domain, we demonstrate the scalability of our compositional approach in comparison to a monolithic analysis approach.

Keywords: Simulation-based analysis · AI-based autonomous systems · Compositional scenarios

1 Introduction

Artificial intelligence (AI) and machine learning (ML) are starting to be used more widely in autonomous systems, in tasks that span perception, prediction, planning, and control. However, there is a growing concern about how to assure the safety of systems that use AI/ML-based components. Formal methods can play a key role in assuring the safety of AI systems [23]. However, due to the high complexity of these components, verification and testing methods must often handle them as black-box components rather than using classic model-based approaches. Simulation-based formal analysis has become commonplace

This work is partially supported by NSF grants 1545126 (VeHICaL, including an NSF-TiH grant) and 1837132, by DARPA contracts FA8750-18-C-0101 (AA), FA8750-20-C-0156 (SDCPS), and FA8750-23-C-0080 (ANSR), by Berkeley Deep Drive, by C3DTI, and by Toyota under the iCyPhy center.

P. Katsaros and L. Nenzi (Eds.): RV 2023, LNCS 14245, pp. 191–212, 2023.
https://doi.org/10.1007/978-3-031-44267-4_10

for assessing the correctness of AI-based autonomous systems. The correctness of the system is evaluated against a specification, defining the safety conditions, by searching through its behaviors in a number of simulations.

Obtaining meaningful and high-confidence verification results requires the execution of a *large number of long-running simulations*, which remains an intensive and costly process. This is a consequence of the high dimensionality of the simulation feature spaces induced by the complex environments in which the systems are executed. In many cases, however, simulation models, also called scenarios, are composed of several smaller scenarios in which a system is tested. For a better and more efficient simulation-based analysis process, we need to take advantage of this composition, transforming a large monolithic analysis process into several easier analysis tasks.

In this paper, we present a compositional approach to simulation-based analysis of autonomous systems. Our approach is based on a decomposition of scenarios where sub-scenarios can be either composed sequentially, representing the different stages of the simulation, or in parallel, representing different possibilities for a stage of the simulation. In this way, a simulation-based analysis problem is decomposed into several smaller problems, each on the sub-scenario level. Results obtained from each sub-analysis problem are stitched together to form a result for the bigger problem. Our framework assumes that the specifications are *Markovian* (memoryless). In practice, most specifications encountered in AI-based autonomous systems are Markovian, e.g., the absence of collisions, obeying traffic lights, keeping a safe distance between agents.

We present a formalization of compositional scenarios based on concurrent hierarchical probabilistic extended state machines, where each of the states of a machine represents one of the sub-scenarios. A scenario is defined in terms of a Markov decision process, representing the agents' behavior and distributions over the feature space of the environment model that the scenario represents. Based on this formalization, we present a framework that can be instantiated to a compositional algorithm for simulation-based analysis tasks of Markovian safety specifications provided there is an aggregation function that allows us to correctly stitch together the individual result to a global one. In general, it is not straightforward to do compositional statistical analysis when the interface specifications are not given. Our formalization and framework define a systematic way to solve this problem via constructing the interface specifications on the fly by computing the post-conditions of the sub-scenarios in each iteration.

We show how we can use our framework to define compositional algorithms for the tasks of falsification and statistical model checking. We evaluate our approach by applying the instantiated algorithms for these problems on benchmarks from the domain of autonomous driving. Our results show that using the compositional algorithms results in a speed up in solving the tasks in comparison to a monolithic approach. In particular, for falsification, the compositional algorithm improves by more than 50% over the monolithic approach in terms of the number of simulation steps needed to find a falsifying example. For statistical verification, in one case study, our approach outperforms the monolithic one using, on average, only half the number of simulation steps. In another case study, the compositional approach converges after a small number of steps, while the monolithic one exceeds a timeout threshold of 100 simulation runs.

To summarize, our main contributions are: (i) a formalization of compositional scenarios based on concurrent hierarchical probabilistic extended state machines and Markov-decision processes, (ii) a generic framework for the compositional analysis of AI-based autonomous systems, and (iii) experimental evaluation on two instantiations of the framework for falsification and statistical verification, showing its efficacy and scalability in comparison to monolithic simulation-based analysis methods.

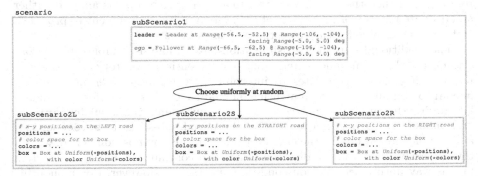

Fig. 1. A snippet of a compositional scenario where individual sub-scenarios are defined using a SCENIC program.

2   Motivating Example

Consider an autonomous driving task with two cars, Leader and Follower, where the former drives around the city and, at an intersection, turns left, right, or goes straight uniformly at random, and the latter follows Leader while keeping a safe distance. We analyze this system using the compositional scenario given in Fig. 1. The individual scenarios are defined using SCENIC [11], a probabilistic scenario-description language, which we will use in our experiments as a way to define scenarios.[1] The program defines a monolithic scenario scenario composed of four sub-scenarios, subScenario1, subScenario2L, subScenario2S, and subScenario2R. The scenario begins with the sub-scenario subScenario1, then composes it sequentially with a uniform choice among subScenario2L, subScenario2S, and subScenario2R to simulate the system in a turn left, go straight, or turn right sub-scenario at an intersection.

subScenario1 creates the cars, Leader and Follower, where Follower is defined as the *ego* vehicle. Then, it defines a distribution over possible initial position and orientation values for both cars. subScenario2L creates a box (an obstacle) after the left turn and defines position and color distributions for it. Similarly, subScenario2S and subScenario2R do the same for their own cases.

---

[1] For the full syntax of SCENIC, see [11].

Assume that the controllers of the two cars are equipped with AI-based components for lane keeping and car following. Our goal is to analyze the system composed of the two cars against a system-level specification that requires the two cars to remain within a safe distance from each other that is not larger than 15 m and not smaller than 5. The analysis can be done in two ways, using *falsification* [8], capturing cases where the specification is violated, and *statistical verification* [16], providing statistical guarantees on to what extent the system satisfies the specification. The falsification process searches for counterexamples by simulating the system and sampling initial conditions and actions for the environment. On the other hand, the statistical verification process aims to gather an adequate number of executions of the system in its environment to provide a statistical guarantee for the correctness of the system.

The traditional approach to simulation-based analysis samples initial conditions for the environment and rolls out its entire trajectory. For the scenario in Fig. 1, this translates to interpreting it *monolithically*, i.e., running `scenario`. Simulating a system using `scenario` implies that, for each simulation, SCENIC samples a sub-scenario among `subScenario2L`, `subScenario2S`, and `subScenario2R`, composes it with the initial sub-scenario `subScenario1`, and samples conditions for the environment from this composition. Then, we run the simulation with the sampled conditions and continue simulating the system in this way until a termination condition is satisfied. However, this monolithic approach does not exploit the inherent compositional structure of the program. Therefore, it suffers from long simulation runs, requires a large number of executions for statistical guarantees, and does not always provide information about the intermediate behaviors of the system during its execution.

In this paper, we propose to leverage the compositional structure. Our method uses the SCENIC program in Fig. 1 at the sub-scenario level. Specifically, both for falsification and statistical verification, we first simulate the system using `subScenario1` until the cars arrive at the intersection and save the post-condition resulting from this execution. We simulate the system in this manner until the saved post-conditions converge to a stable distribution. We refer to this distribution as the *output distribution* of `subScenario1`. We then use this output distribution to analyze `subScenario2L`, `subScenario2S`, and `subScenario2R` by sampling initial conditions for these sub-scenarios. Observe that this approach is inherently more efficient than the monolithic approach as it divides the overall analysis task into smaller ones and solves them in isolation while avoiding redundant computation: e.g., we analyze `subScenario1` only once and reuse its output distribution for the other three sub-scenarios.

3   Preliminaries

3.1   Executions and Specifications

Let S be a system defined over a set of system variables V over the domain of real numbers $\mathbb{R}$. Let $[\![V]\!]$ denote the set of valuations of V. An execution of a system is a sequence σ of valuations of the variables V, i.e., $\sigma \in [\![V]\!]^*$, where for some alphabet Σ, the set Σ^* defines the set of all finite words over Σ.

For a set of system variables V, we define a specification as a set $\varphi \subseteq [\![V]\!]^*$. A specification thus defines a valid set of executions. In our work, we are particularly interested in Markovian safety specifications, also known as memoryless safety specifications, whose satisfaction on an execution can be determined based on the current valuation of system variables independent of the valuations of the variables in previous steps of the execution. Formally, a Markovian safety specification φ can be defined in terms of a set $\varphi' \subseteq [\![V]\!]$ such that for every execution $\sigma = \sigma_1 \ldots \sigma_m \in [\![V]\!]^*$ for any $m \in \mathbb{N}^+$, $\sigma \in \varphi$ if and only if for all $i \leq m$, it holds that $\sigma_i \in \varphi'$. In the rest of the paper, a specification will always refer to a Markovian safety specification.

3.2 Markov Decision Processes

For a countable set X, let $Distr(X) \subset (X \to [0,1])$ define the set of all distributions over X, i.e., for $d \in Distr(X)$ it holds that $\Sigma_{x \in X} d(x) = 1$. For $d \in Distr(X)$, let the *support* of d be defined by $Supp(d) = \{x \mid d(x) > 0\}$. A *Markov Decision Process (MDP)* is a tuple $M = (Q, Act, \mathbf{P}, \iota, X, L)$ where Q is a set of states, Act is a finite set of actions, $\mathbf{P} : Q \times Act \to Distr(Q)$ is the transition probability function such that $\sum_{q' \in Q} \mathbf{P}(q, a)(q') \in \{0, 1\}$ for every $q \in Q$ and $a \in Act$, $\iota \in Distr(Q)$ is the initial distribution such that $\sum_{q \in Q} \iota(q) = 1$, X is a finite set of variables and $L : S \to [\![X]\!]$ is a labeling function that assigns each state a valuation of the variables in X. For a state $q \in Q$, we define $\mathsf{AvAct}(q) = \{a \mid \mathbf{P}(q, a) \neq \bot\}$, where $\bot$ is the empty distribution. W.l.o.g., $|\mathsf{AvAct}(q)| \geq 1$. If $|\mathsf{AvAct}(q)| = 1$ for all $q \in Q$, we refer to M as a *Markov chain* (MC). A *finite path* in the MDP M is a sequence $\pi = q_0 a_0 q_1 \ldots q_n \in Q \times (Act \times Q)^*$ such that for every $0 \leq i < n$ it holds that $\mathbf{P}(q_i, a_i)(q_{i+1}) > 0$ and $\iota(q_0) > 0$. We denote the set of finite paths of M by Π_M. We use $\pi_\downarrow$ to denote the last state in π. A *policy* for the MDP M is a function $\sigma : \Pi_M \to Distr(Act)$ with $Supp(\sigma(\pi)) \subseteq \mathsf{AvAct}(\pi_\downarrow)$ for every $\pi \in \Pi_M$. A policy σ of M induces a Markov chain $[\![M]\!]_\sigma$. We denote the set of policies of M by $Policies(M)$.

4 Compositional Scenarios

A scenario represents a model of an environment in which we want to deploy and analyze a system. This model is defined as a distribution over spatial and temporal configurations of the environment, including those of all objects and agents. The underlying semantics of a scenario can therefore be defined by an MDP, where the nondeterministic actions capture the nondeterministic behavior of the agents and simulator, and the probabilistic behavior reflects the distributions over the feature space and probabilistic actions of agents. For example, each of the SCENIC sub-scenarios in Fig. 1, defines an MDP. A compositional scenario is a collection of scenarios that are composed sequentially and in parallel.

A compositional scenario is therefore best modeled as a concurrent hierarchical probabilistic extended state machine (CHPESM). Concurrent, because scenarios can be executed concurrently; hierarchical, because a compositional scenario can be composed of other compositional scenarios; probabilistic because switching to the next scenario can be done probabilisticly and, also, at any time the choice of attributes and actions is done based on an underlying probability distribution over valuations of the environment's feature space. The semantics of a compositional scenario is then defined by an infinite-state MDP. In the following sections, we give an overview of the CHPESM model and show how the MDP of a compositional scenario can be obtained by computing the flattening of its CHPESM.

4.1   Concurrent Hierarchical Probabilistic Extended State Machines

We define a probabilistic extended state machine (PESM) as a tuple $M = (Q, \iota, V, F, P)$ where Q is a set of states, $\iota \in Distr(Q)$ is an initial distribution over states, V is a finite set of real-valued variables, F is a set of exit states, and $P : Q \times G(V) \to Distr(Q)$ is a probabilistic transition relation, where $G(V)$ defines the set of boolean constraints of the form $x \sim c$, so-called guards, for $x \in V$ and $\sim \in \{<, \leq, =, >, \geq\}$. Given a state and a guard, P returns a distribution over states. A transition $(q, g, d) \in P$ is enabled for a valuation $v \in \llbracket V \rrbracket$ if and only if $g(v)$ is true.

Hierarchical probabilistic extended state machines (HPESMs) are probabilistic extended state machines whose states are themselves PESMs or HPESMs [20,25]. Formally, HPESMs are defined inductively as follows. Let $\mathcal{M}$ be a set of HPESMs over variables V. A HPESM $H = (Q, \iota, V, F, P, \mathcal{M}, \mu)$, where Q, ι, V, F and P are a set of states, an initial distribution over states, a set of variables, a set of exit states, and a probabilistic transition relation as in any probabilistic extended state machine. Further, $\mu : Q \to \mathcal{M}$ is a mapping that associates each state $q \in Q$ with an HPESM from $\mathcal{M}$. For example, in Fig. 1, scenario is an HPESM with one state mapped to a PESM with states subScenario2L, subScenario2S, and subScenario2R, and subScenario1.

An HPESM H provides a compact notation for a corresponding PESM, denoted by $flat(H)$ [25]. The machine $flat(H)$ is defined inductively as follows. If H is a PESM then $flat(H) = H$. If H is not a PESM, then $flat(H) = (Q', \iota', V, F', P')$, defined as follows. $Q' = \bigcup_{q \in Q} states(flat(\mu(q)))$, with $states(.)$ being a function that returns the set of states of any PESM. For all $q \in Q$ and for all $q' \in states(flat(\mu(q)))$, $\iota'(q') = \iota(q).init(flat(\mu(q)))(q')$ with $init$ returning the initial distribution of a state machine. $P' = \{\tau = (q_1, g, d) \mid \exists q \in Q. \tau \in transitions(flat(q))$ or $\exists(q, g', d') \in P. q_1 \in exit(flat(\mu(q))) \wedge \forall q' \in Q. \forall q_2 \in states(flat(\mu(q'))). d(q_2) = d'(q') \cdot init(flat(\mu(q'))) (q_2)\}$, with $transitions$ and $exit$ functions returning the transition relation and exit states.

A concurrent hierarchical probabilistic extended finite state machine (CHPESM) [25] is defined inductively as follows. Every PESM is a CHPESM. For the inductive step, we distinguish two cases: (1) a CHPESM C is either a hierarchical composition of other CHPESMs, as previously defined for HPESMs, or (2) it is a parallel composition of CHPESMs, i.e., $C = C_1 \parallel \cdots \parallel C_n$ for CHPESMs $C_1, \ldots, C_n$.

Every CHPESM C is associated with a corresponding PESM defined again inductively as follows. If C is a basic PESM, then $flat(C) = C$. If C is a hierarchical composition then $flat(C)$ is defined as in the case of HPESMs. If $C = C_1 \parallel \cdots \parallel C_n$ for CHPESMs $C_1, \ldots C_n$ over a set of variables V, then $flat(C) = (Q, \iota, V, F, P)$ where $Q = states(flat(C_1)) \times \ldots states(flat(C_n))$, $\iota = init(flat(C_n)) \cdots \cdot init(flat(C_n)))$, $F = exit(flat(C_n)) \times \cdots \times exit(flat(C_n))$, and P a probabilistic transition relation where $((q_1, \ldots, q_n), \bigwedge_{i \leq n} g_i, d) \in P$ iff there is a transition $(q_i, g_i, d'_i) \in transitions(flat(C_i))$ for some $i \in \{1, \ldots, n\}$ and where $d((q'_1, \ldots, q'_n)) = \Pi_{j \text{ s.t. } q_j \neq q'_j} d_j(q'_j)$. We note that we choose a product based on self-composition, i.e., transitions represent the execution actions from different CHPESMs that can execute in parallel, in contrast to the usual synchronous product used in [25]. This is necessary as individual processes in our setting may evolve at their own pace.

4.2 Abstract Syntax and Semantics of Compositional Scenarios

Let $\mathcal{S}$ be a set of compositional scenarios. A compositional scenario is abstractly defined as a CHPESM $\mathcal{P} = (S, \iota, V, F, T, \mathcal{S}, \mu)$. Each state $s \in S$ represents a compositional scenario from $\mathcal{S}$. Each of the basic (i.e., non-decomposable) scenarios $s \in \mathcal{S}$ is defined over the feature space V.

The semantics of a compositional scenario $\mathcal{P}$ is defined by a (infinite-state) Markov decision process $[\![\mathcal{P}]\!] = (Q, Act, \mathbf{P}, \iota, X, L)$, obtained by first computing the flattening of the CHPESM and then refining the states of the resulting PESM to the MDPs they represent. A concrete scenario of $\mathcal{P}$ is a pair (v, π) for some $v \in [\![V]\!]$ and $\pi \in Policies([\![\mathcal{P}]\!])$, inducing a Markov chain $[\![\mathcal{P}]\!]_{v,\pi} = (Q, \mathbf{P}', \iota', X, L)$ where $\iota'(q) = 1$ if $q = (v, -)$ and $\iota(q) > 0$. For any other $q' \in Q \setminus \{q\}, \iota'(q') = 0$. An execution of $\mathcal{P}$ is a path of a Markov chain $[\![\mathcal{P}]\!]_{v,\pi}$ obtained for an initial sampled valuation $v \in [\![V]\!]$ and a policy $\pi \in Policies([\![\mathcal{P}]\!])$.

5 Compositional Simulation-Based Analysis

In this section, we present a generic compositional simulation-based analysis framework that can be instantiated to concrete algorithms for solving specific simulation-based analysis tasks. The framework assumes a compositional scenario structure, given by a CHPESM. Working on the PESM defining the flattening of the CHPESM, the algorithm decomposes a general simulation-based analysis task into smaller tasks, one for each state of the PESM, thus, executing analysis tasks on the sub-scenario level. Results obtained from the individual simulation-based analyses are stitched together providing a result for the overall analysis task. We first introduce the generic framework and then show two instantiations of the algorithm for falsification and statistical verification.

5.1　Generic Framework

We introduce a generic compositional simulation-based analysis framework in Algorithm 1. An instantiation of the framework is an algorithm that operates on an PESM $M = (S, \iota, V, F, P)$, defining a flattening of a compositional scenario. Such an instantiation is obtained by implementing three key procedures: *evaluate*, *terminate*, and *finalize*. The algorithm then iterates over all sub-scenarios defined by the states of M, starting with an initial state that is in the support of ι and following the transition relation P. For each sub-scenario, an algorithm executes a simulation-based analysis task implemented by the procedure *evaluate*. This process is repeated until a termination condition is satisfied, checked by the procedure *terminate*. Termination is decided based on the change in the outcomes of the evaluation processes at each sub-scenario. If the termination condition is satisfied, then the procedure *finalize* is called to compute a final result. This result is computed by stitching together the results computed by the evaluation process for the sub-scenario. If the termination condition is not satisfied, the algorithm continues by evaluating other sub-scenarios. In the following, we elaborate on the workflow of the framework by providing more details on the functionalities of procedures *evaluate*, *terminate*, and *finalize*.

Evaluation. An instantiation of our compositional approach executes simulation-based analysis tasks at the sub-scenario level starting with states from the initial distribution ι (line 2). The set W represents a working set including all sub-scenarios for which a task should be executed next. For each sub-scenario $s \in W$ (line 4), the procedure *evaluate* is invoked (line 5), which implements a specific simulation-based analysis process for a given task of interest (e.g., falsification, statistical verification, etc.). The *evaluate* procedure is provided with an input distribution d_{in}^s on the input sample space of s, and output distribution d_{out}^s on the output space of s, which is to be updated by the evaluation procedure. We represent d_{in}^s and d_{out}^s as multisets, so the distributions are extended by adding new elements to these multisets. Notice that other representations for these distributions are also possible depending on the specific needs of the task under consideration. Finally, while termination of *evaluate* may depend on the simulation-based analysis task at hand, it can also be stopped after a simulation budget c has been exhausted, i.e., a number of simulation steps c is reached as a sum of steps taken over all simulation runs performed by *evaluate*. The budget can also be unlimited, i.e., $c = -$. In this case, the termination of *evaluate* solely depends on the termination condition of the analysis task given by the underlying implementation of *evaluate*.

Algorithm 1. Compositional Simulation-based Analysis

Input:
     Probabilistic state machine $M = (S, \iota, V, F, P)$ /* Flattening of a CHPESM*/
     Local simulation budget $c \in \mathbb{N} \cup \{-\}$
1:   $initialize(\{d_{in}^s\}_{s \in S}, \{d_{out}^s\}_{s \in S}, r, \{D_{out}^s\}_{s \in S}, R)$
2:   $W := Supp(\iota),\ W' := \emptyset$
3:   **while** $True$ **do**
4:     **for** $s \in W$ **do**
5:       $d_{out}^s, r(s) := evaluate(s, d_{out}^s, d_{in}^s, c)$
6:       $R(s) := append(R(s), r(s))$
7:       $D_{out}^s := append(D_{out}^s, d_{out}^s)$
8:       **if** $terminate(\{D_{out}^s\}_{s \in S}, R)$ **then**
9:         **return** $finalize(M, r)$
10:      **for** $(s, g, d) \in P$ **do**
11:        **for** $s' \in Supp(d)$ **do**
12:          $W' := W' \cup \{s'\}$
13:          $d_{in}^{s'} := d_{in}^{s'} + d_{out}^s$
14:     **if** $W' \neq \emptyset$ **then**
15:       $W := W'$
16:       $W' := \emptyset$
17:     **else**
18:       $W = Supp(\iota)$

The outcome of *evaluate* is a distribution d_{out}^s on the outputs reached by the simulation process of *evaluate*, and a result of the analysis process that updates a mapping r for the specific sub-scenario s. For example, if *evaluate* implements a falsification task for some specification φ, then $r(s)$ is assigned to a valuation $v \in [\![V]\!]$, and a policy $\pi \in Policies(s)$, that falsify φ. If *evaluate* implements a statistical verification method, then $r(s)$ stores an estimate of the probability of satisfying a given specification in s. The history of results obtained for each sub-scenario, as well as the history of output distributions are stored in a list of mappings R, and a list of distributions D_{out}^s for each sub-scenario $s \in S$ (lines 6 and 7). For this we assume that the input and output distributions d_{in}^s, and d_{out}^s, the mapping r, as well as the lists D_{out}^s and R are initialized at the beginning of the algorithm (line 1). These lists are necessary for checking termination and are forwarded to the procedure *terminate*.

Termination. Termination of Algorithm 1 is checked after every evaluation process, and is done executing an implementation of the procedure *terminate* (line 8). Termination is decided based on the history of results stored in R, and obtained using *evaluate* at each sub-scenario, as well as the history of output distributions D_{out}^s for each sub-scenario s (collected in lines 7 and 6). For example, in the case of falsification, *terminate* is implemented as the procedure that returns $True$ if a falsifying valuation is found at any sub-scenario s, or, if such valuation is not found, then it might return $True$ after observing a stabilization in the output distribution computed for each sub-scenario. The latter stabilization condition can also be used as a termination condition for statistical verification (More details in the next sections). If *terminate* returns $False$, then Algorithm 1 continues by applying the *evaluate* procedure on other scenarios in the working set W that have not been processed so far. As long as termination is not satisfied, after each evaluation process, a new working set of sub-scenarios is computed that will be processed in the next iteration of the algorithm (lines 10 - 13). Here, successor sub-scenarios s' of a currently evaluated sub-scenario s, following the transition relation P, are added to the new working set W'. Furthermore, the input distribution $d_{in}^{s'}$ of a state s' is updated with the output distribution d_{out}^{s} of its predecessor s (line 13). Once all states in W have been processed, and the algorithm has not terminated, the set W is replaced with the set W' (line 15) and the evaluation process is repeated for the new working set. In case no new sub-scenarios are added, i.e., we reached and processed all exist scenarios F of M, and the termination condition has not been satisfied yet, the evaluation is restarted by re-initializing the set W with the set of initial states (line 18). When it finally comes to a termination of the algorithm, as a last step, the procedure *finalize* computes a final result for the overall simulation-based analysis task, using the results stored in r. We discuss some instantiations of the *finalize* procedure next.

Finalization. If the termination condition defined by the procedure *terminate* is satisfied, a last procedure *finalize* is applied on the PESM M and the computed mapping r. Executing an implementation of *finalize* stitches the results stored in r, which were obtained from evaluating each sub-scenario, to a general result for the general simulation-based analysis task. For example, in the case of a falsification task for a specification φ, *finalize* will return a valuation satisfying the input distributions of one of initial scenarios $s_0 \in Supp(\iota)$, and for which there is policy that leads to falsifying φ at s_0, or a later scenario, reachable via P from s_0. In the case of statistical verification, a satisfaction probability is computed by computing the minimum/maximum reachability probability computed over all probabilities and distributions computed for the sub-scenarios and with respect to the transition relation of M.

In the rest of the paper we refer to Algorithm 1 as the procedure *comp*. An instantiation of Algorithm 1, for an evaluation, termination, and finalization procedures λ_{ev}, λ_{ter}, and λ_{fin}, respectively, is denoted by $comp(\lambda_{ev}, \lambda_{ter}, \lambda_{fin})$.

5.2   Compositional Simulation-Based Falsification

In falsification we are interested in finding an evaluation of the feature space that falsifies a given property. Given a flattening of a compositional scenario $M = (S, \iota, V, F, P)$ and a system-level specification $\varphi \subseteq [\![V]\!]^*$, find $v \in [\![V]\!]$ and $\pi \in Policies([\![M]\!])$ such that $[\![M]\!]_{v,\pi} \not\models \varphi$. In this section, we show how we can define a compositional falsification approach by instantiating the procedures *evaluate*, *terminate*, and *finalize*.

– *evaluate*: we instantiate *evaluate* with a procedure λ_{ev}^{φ} that for a given scenario s, an input distribution d_{in}^{s}, output distribution d_{out}^{s}, and a simulation budget c, simulates s sampling initial inputs from the distribution d_{in}^{s}, and evaluates a simulation run based on a function $\lambda : 2^{[\![V]\!]^*} \times 2^{[\![V]\!]^*} \to \mathbb{B}$, that for a specification $\varphi \subseteq [\![V]\!]^*$ and a set of simulation runs, returns *True* if and only if a simulation run τ is a falsifying example for φ. i.e., $\tau \not\models \varphi$. Simulations are restarted as long as no falsifying example is found or until the simulation budget is exhausted. If a falsifying examples is detected, the falsification process returns the initial valuation of inputs sampled at that simulation and a simulation trace.

- *terminate*: termination is implemented by λ_{ter} returning *True* once a falsifying example is found at any sub-scenario. If no such example is found, the process terminates using the stabilization condition defined over the list of output distributions.
- *finalize*: The finalization procedure is implemented by λ_{fin} that chooses an initial valuation of the feature space and a path in M such that it leads to a non-empty r in one of the scenarios reachable via the path if they exist, otherwise it returns *False*.

Theorem 1. *For a compositional scenario M, a specification φ, and a falsification method λ, it is the case that $comp(\lambda_{ev}^{\varphi}, \lambda_{ter}, \lambda_{fin})(M, c) = \lambda(\varphi, M)$.*

Proof (Sketch). The correctness of this instantiation follows from the fact that once a sub-scenario has been falsified, then there is a valuation from its input distribution and a policy, inducing traces falsifying the specification. Since the input distribution is the union of output distributions of predecessor sub-scenarios, then we can find a valuation from the input distribution of that scenario and a policy that lead to the violation. We can extend this argument to reach a valuation from one of the initial sub-scenarios and build a policy that induces a trace, violating the specification. □

5.3   Compositional Simulation-Based Statistical Verification

Statistical verification is a method that allows estimating the correctness of a system for a given property by simulating the system for a number of runs and using methods from the area of statistical theory to provide guarantees on the correctness up to a statistical error [16]. We show that for a given statistical verification method, we can instantiate Algorithm 1 to an algorithm that performs the statistical verification compositionally, preserving the guarantees obtained by the statistical verification method.

Let $M = (S, \iota, V, F, P)$ be the flattening of a compositional scenario, $\varphi \subseteq [\![V]\!]^{*}$ a specification we are interested in verifying, and λ a statistical verification procedure that for M and φ, estimates the probability of M satisfying φ up to a statistical error. A compositional algorithm for solving the statistical verification problem can be achieved by using the following implementations of *evaluate*, *terminate*, and *finalize*.

- *evaluate*: we implement *evaluate* as a procedure λ_{ev}^{φ} that applies λ at each sub-scenario $s \in S$ for the specification φ. Simulation runs created by λ_{ev}^{φ} start from the input distribution d_{in}^{s}, using a simulation budget c.
- *terminate*: a termination procedure λ_{ter} can be implemented in several ways [16]. In general, the termination condition for a statistical verification process λ can be applied also over the sequence of results and post-conditions

computed by the individual statistical verification processes. One prominent example that we will use in our experiments, is a stabilization condition based on the convergence of the standard error of the mean of the simulation post-conditions [13].

- *finalize*: The finalization procedure λ_{fin} computes a probability based on the probabilities computed for each sub-scenario. It aggregates the probabilities starting from the exit states to the initial states. Specifically, the probability for a sub-scenario s, is computed as $f_{(s,g,d)\in P} \sum_{s'\in S} r(s').d(s')$ where f is an aggregation over probabilities (e.g., max, min, etc.).

Theorem 2. *For a compositional scenario M, a specification φ, and an statistical verification method λ, it is the case that $comp(\lambda_{ev}^{\varphi}, \lambda_{ter}, \lambda_{fin})(M, c) = \lambda(\varphi, M)$.*

Proof (Sketch). The correctness follows from the fact that the statistical verification processes have been *performed independently* and based on independent output distributions computed at each sub-scenario. The overall result is thus statistically correct up to the same statistical error for each sub-scenario.   □

6   Experimental Evaluation[2]

In this section, we present an experimental evaluation of the proposed method on two case studies from the autonomous driving domain. We first provide a high-level description of the autonomous driving tasks. Then, we present the details of the simulator setup, the controller implementations, and the system-level specification. We also explain the evaluation metrics and our baseline. Finally, we present compositional scenarios used for evaluation, details of their feature spaces, and the evaluation results.

6.1   An Autonomous Driving Task

The environment consists of several straight and curved road segments along with two intersections and obstacles (see Fig. 2). We have two cars: `Leader` (the black car) and `Follower` (the red car). They are tasked with following each other while maintaining a safe distance. `Leader` follows the yellow line in the middle of the road. At an intersection, it chooses to go left, straight, or right uniformly at random. After an intersection, `Leader` continues to follow the yellow line all while trying to avoid obstacles. `Follower` must follow the lead car while keeping a safe distance.

We use the Webots, an open-source 3D robot simulator widely used in industry, education, and research [17,24]. Both cars are modeled as a BMW X5 equipped with a camera facing the road. Using its camera input, `Leader`'s computer vision component uses a standard image processing technique to estimate the car's angle to the yellow line. This estimate is then used as an input to a

---

[2] Available at https://github.com/BerkeleyLearnVerify/compositional-analysis.

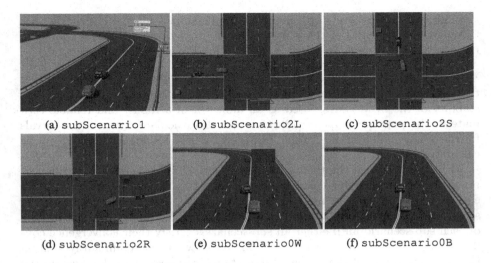

(a) subScenario1   (b) subScenario2L   (c) subScenario2S

(d) subScenario2R   (e) subScenario0W   (f) subScenario0B

Fig. 2. Snapshots of the sub-scenarios of both case studies.

PID controller which controls the steering. Follower estimates its angle to the Leader by processing its camera inputs in a similar way, and it also performs image segmentation for estimating the distance to Leader. Additionally, Leader uses a Sick LMS 291 LiDAR sensor for collision avoidance. Both cars set a target speed of 40 km/h, but Follower changes its speed by braking or speeding up to maintain a safe distance from Leader. The system-level specification formalizes the safe and specified distance between the cars with the Metric Temporal Logic (MTL) [14] property $\Box\,(\texttt{distance} \geq 5 \wedge \texttt{distance} \leq 15)$, where distance denotes the distance between the cars. Specifically, the property defines the notion of safety as keeping a distance between the cars that is not less than 5 m and not more than 15 m throughout the entire trajectory.

6.2   Evaluation Details

We evaluate our method by performing both compositional falsification and compositional statistical verification on two different compositional scenarios for the presented task. In compositional falsification, *terminate* (see line 8 in Algorithm 1) is designed to terminate the counter-example search either as soon as a falsifying example is found or until the output distributions of each sub-scenario *stabilizes* (the notion of stabilization will be defined precisely). In compositional statistical verification, the *terminate* method halts the process once the output distribution of each sub-scenario stabilizes. The notion of stabilization for each sub-scenario's output distribution is defined by the *convergence of the standard error of the mean (SEM) of the simulation post-conditions*. Specifically, at the end of each sub-scenario, we get a point in a 6D space consisting of the x-y coordinates and the orientations of both Leader and Follower. The post-conditions of sub-scenarios form a distribution, which we try to approximate through simulations. We stop generating more samples for a sub-scenario once the change in the SEM of the post-conditions drops down a threshold value Δ, i.e., the SEM converges to a stable value. The SEM $\sigma_{\bar{\mu}}$ is defined as $\sigma_{\bar{\mu}} = \frac{\bar{\sigma}}{\sqrt{n}}$, where $\bar{\sigma} = \sqrt{\frac{1}{n-1} \sum_{i=1}^{n} (x_i - \bar{\mu})^2}$ is the unbiased estimator of standard deviation, $\{x_1, x_2 \ldots, x_n\}$ is the set of n samples, and $\bar{\mu}$ is the sample mean. The stability of the SEM can be used as an indicator of a robust and reliable estimate of the population mean [13]. One can also calculate confidence intervals for the true population mean using SEM, e.g., a 95% confidence interval can be calculated as $\bar{\mu} \pm 1.96 \times \sigma_{\bar{\mu}}$.

A nuance between the theory and the practical implementation of the proposed method is that for compositional falsification, to find counter-examples earlier, we implement our method in *batched* mode. Specifically, given a batch size, we run each sub-scenario in batches and interleave the falsification process of each sub-scenario until either all sub-scenarios satisfy their convergence condition or a counter-example is found. This way we avoid redundantly waiting for the convergence of the output distributions of sub-scenarios that cannot be falsified to find counter-examples faster.

In our evaluation, we use two different sampling strategies, uniform sampling and Halton sampling [12], for both compositional falsification and compositional statistical verification. We leverage VerifAI [8,9], a toolkit for the formal design and analysis of AI/ML systems, to sample scenes from SCENIC programs according to uniform and Halton sampling. These sampling strategies are used by the *evaluate* method (see line 5 of Algorithm 1) for sampling initial conditions to simulate trajectories. Observe that both uniform and Halton sampling are *passive* sampling strategies. The usage of passive sampling strategies provides a simpler implementation for the batched execution of compositional falsification since we initialize a new sampler for each batch. One can use active sampling strategies like cross-entropy, simulated annealing, Bayesian optimization, etc. by saving the sampler state so that the sampler state would be preserved between the interleavings of different falsification processes. Another way to use active samplers is to run the falsification process of each sub-scenario either concurrently or in parallel instead of running them in batched mode. However, these implementations are outside the scope of this work as they require diligent engineering efforts.

Baseline. The baseline for our evaluation is the *monolithic* simulation-based analysis approach that is currently supported by SCENIC and VerifAI. Specifically, this approach treats the SCENIC program as a black-box sampler and does not leverage the compositional structure of the program. It samples initial conditions for the entire scenario and rolls out the entire trajectory until the end. The termination condition for the baseline is defined in a similar way to our method, i.e., for statistical falsification, the search ends either when a counter-example is found or when the output distribution of the entire SCENIC program stabilizes, and for statistical verification, we run simulations, again, until the output distribution stabilizes.

Metrics for Evaluation. To demonstrate the efficacy of our method compared to the monolithic baseline, we focus on the total number of simulator steps and the estimated specification satisfaction probability. For falsification, we analyze the number of simulator steps taken until the falsification process ends. Due to the inherent randomness of both statistical methods, we run the falsification process with 10 different random seeds and analyze the mean and the standard deviation of the number of simulator steps. For verification, we again focus on the number of simulator steps taken until convergence, and, we compare the estimated specification satisfaction probability of both methods.

6.3   Case Study 1

We use the compositional SCENIC program from Fig. 1 to test this system against the system-level specification. The program defines four sub-scenarios: subScenario1, subScenario2L, subScenario2S, and subScenario2R. subScenario1 is a sub-scenario starting at the straight road segment and ending at the intersection (see Fig. 2a). This sub-scenario defines possible initial positions and orientations for both cars. Once subScenario1 is over, the next sub-scenario is sampled uniformly at random from the other three. subScenario2L defines the sub-scenario where Leader turns left (see Fig. 2b), subScenario2S is the sub-scenario for going straight at the intersection (see Fig. 2c), and subScenario2R is the case for turning right (see Fig. 2d). All sub-scenarios at the intersection have an adversarial obstacle to trick the image processing and segmentation performed by Follower. Specifically, they all sample positions and colors for a box that can potentially cause Follower to violate the safety specification by mixing Leader with the obstacle. The space of possible positions for the obstacle, in each sub-scenario, is defined to be either on the right-most or the left-most lanes so that the yellow line and the inner lanes are not blocked for Leader. However, if the Leader takes the turn too wide, it could still collide with the obstacle, which would cause a specification violation. The color space for the obstacle consists of nine different colors, only one of which can fool Follower. If the obstacle is black and visible from Follower, it could corrupt the angle and the distance estimates and therefore potentially cause a specification violation. Notice that in our implementation, we manually decomposed sub-scenario definitions of the monolithic Scenic program since Scenic's current Webots interface does not allow the usage of sub-scenarios.

Falsification. To understand the performance gains of our method compared to the monolithic baseline, we run both our method and the monolithic baseline with 10 different random seeds. We run our method in batched mode with a batch size of 5. Figure 3a presents the results of the experiments for both uniform and Halton sampling strategies. Both methods find counter-examples before converging to a stable distribution. However, the compositional method finds counter-examples by taking fewer simulator steps on average. Moreover, the standard deviation of the total number of simulator steps is much smaller compared to the monolithic baseline. An important detail to note here is that when we compare the sampling strategies, we see that Halton finds counter-examples earlier compared to the uniform sampling strategy. This result is aligned with the intuition that Halton sampling provides a more uniform coverage compared to uniform sampling which uses pseudorandom number generators.

Statistical Verification. For comparing the performances of both methods for statistical verification, we run both until convergence, i.e., until their output distributions stabilize w.r.t. to the stabilization metric given in Sect. 6.2. For this experiment, we set the threshold for convergence to $\Delta = 0.001$ and run both methods until the change in their SEM values drops down to this threshold. Figure 3b presents a comparison between the total number of simulator steps taken by each method before converging to a stable output distribution. With uniform sampling, the compositional method provides a 3.85× speed up, and with Halton sampling, our method is 4.18× faster. Notice that with Halton sampling, both methods take slightly more simulator steps compared to the uniform sampling strategy. This is due to the fact that the coverage provided by Halton sampling makes the convergence of the output distributions harder.

We also compare the estimated probabilities output by the methods. Table 1 presents these results for both sampling strategies. The probability for the compositional method is calculated by combining the results from sub-scenarios. Since we sample among subScenario2L, subScenario2S, and subScenario2R uniformly at random, their probabilities are averaged, and since subScenario1 precedes the other three, its estimated probability is multiplied by the calculated average. Table 1 shows that both methods converge to similar specification satisfaction probabilities with minor differences. However, the compositional approach uses fewer simulations to converge to this value. Moreover, the average simulation length (i.e., the average number of simulator steps) taken by our method is significantly less than the monolithic approach. For the compositional method, the average simulation length is calculated by summing the number of simulation steps of all sub-scenarios and dividing it by the total number of simulation runs, i.e., 383. Notice that compared to the monolithic approach, our compositional method provides more information about the safety of the system in different sub-scenarios. For example, we see that the system does not violate the system-level specification in subScenario1, along with the individual specification satisfaction probabilities for each sub-scenario, whereas the monolithic approach does not provide any insight into the system behavior across different sub-scenarios. We conclude by noting that on a Quad-Core Intel i7 processor clocked at 2.3 GHz and a 32 GB main memory, our compositional statistical verification method took a little over 2 h to converge for both uniform and Halton sampling, whereas the monolithic baseline took 6 h for uniform sampling and a little over 8 h for Halton sampling to converge.

6.4   Case Study 2

We build on top of the first case study by adding two uniformly sampled sub-scenarios before the first sub-scenario: subScenario0W and subScenario0B. Both of these sub-scenarios start at the straight road segment connecting to

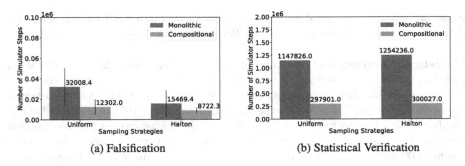

(a) Falsification   (b) Statistical Verification

Fig. 3. Experiment results for falsification and statistical verification of Case Study 1.

Table 1. Estimated specification satisfaction probabilities.

	Uniform Sampling			Halton Sampling		
	Estimated Probability	Number of Sim	Mean Sim Length	Estimated Probability	Number of Sim	Mean Sim Length
subScenario1	1.00	76	1100.07	1.00	72	1100.08
subScenario2L	0.91	187	657.04	0.90	188	657.23
subScenario2S	0.90	70	685.97	0.93	68	688.71
subScenario2R	0.88	50	868.22	0.90	58	869.48
Compositional	**0.90**	**383**	**777.81**	**0.91**	**386**	**777.27**
Monolithic	**0.88**	**639**	**1796.28**	**0.89**	**698**	**1796.90**

the road segment of subScenario1. subScenario0W samples a position for a wall that blocks half of the road (Fig. 2e), and subScenario0B (Fig. 2f) samples positions for three oil barrels. Both of these sub-scenarios can potentially cause a specification violation if either Leader or Follower cannot perform the necessary maneuver on time to avoid a collision with these obstacles. Specifically, Leader's controller uses its LiDAR sensor to sense surrounding obstacles and attempts to avoid them while still following the yellow line whereas Follower does not implement any obstacle avoidance procedure, so to avoid obstacles, its needs to follow the maneuvers of Leader precisely.

Falsification. Similar to the previous case study, we run both methods with 10 different random seeds, and our method is, again, run in the batched mode with a batch size of 5. Figure 4a presents the results for falsification. Similar to the previous case study, both methods find counter-examples before their output distributions stabilize. Figure 4a shows that our method finds counter-examples significantly faster than the baseline, and its standard deviation is more stable. Between uniform and Halton sampling strategies, we observe a similar pattern to that observed in 6.3, i.e., due to its uniform coverage property, Halton sampling finds counter-examples slightly faster. Notice that the simulator steps in these experiments are smaller than the previous one since the new initial sub-scenarios can also potentially cause a specification violation, whereas in the previous case study, we have not observed any specification violation in the first sub-scenario; therefore, we find counter-examples earlier in this case study.

Statistical Verification. To compare the compositional statistical verification with the monolithic baseline, we run both until their output distributions stabilize. However, for this experiment, we set the convergence threshold to a larger value, i.e., $\Delta = 0.005$, and we also set an upper bound of 100 simulations for the number of simulations performed. Specifically, the statistical verification process terminates either when the output distributions converge or when the process reaches 100 simulations. The motivation for this decision is to understand how the proposed method compares when fewer simulations are performed, which causes output distributions to be less accurate for each sub-scenario. With the given threshold value, i.e., $\Delta = 0.005$, the compositional approach stabilizes before reaching 100 simulation runs whereas the monolithic baseline reaches the upper bound of 100 simulations before its output distribution converges. Figure 4b presents the results for this experiment. We observe that the proposed approach performs better than the baseline, and we also see a slight increase in the total number of simulator steps due to Halton sampling. Since the baseline cannot converge to a stable output distribution before 100 simulations, its results are statistically less reliable than the results for the compositional method, and its total number of simulator steps is upper-bounded by 100 simulations, not the reliability of its output distribution.

Table 2 presents the comparison between the specification satisfaction probabilities output by both methods. The estimated probability for the compositional method is calculated by combining the results for each sub-scenario. Table 2 shows that even with a less accurate output distribution approximation, probabilities estimated by both methods are close to each other. Moreover, even though the number of simulations performed by the compositional method is more than the monolithic baseline (which is due to the fact that the baseline reaches the upper bound for the number of simulations), the average simulation length (i.e., the average number of simulator steps) is much smaller than the baseline since the compositional approach performs shorter simulations at the sub-scenario level. The average simulation length for the compositional method is calculated by combining the results from all sub-scenarios. Note that our method also provides more insight into the system behavior. For example, in Table 2, we observe that `subScenario0W` has the smallest specification satisfaction probability, which implies that the system does not perform well in the presence of large obstacles blocking half of the road. We conclude by noting that on the same hardware as the previous case study, our compositional statistical verification method took a little over 1 h to converge for both uniform and Halton sampling, whereas the monolithic baseline took 1.5 h to reach the simulation limit for both sampling strategies.

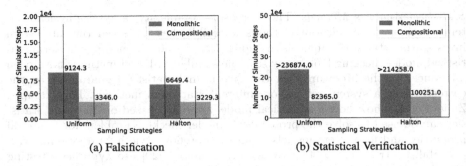

(a) Falsification   (b) Statistical Verification

Fig. 4. Experiment results for falsification and statistical verification of Case Study 2.

Table 2. Estimated Specification Satisfaction Probabilities for Case Study 2.

	Uniform Sampling			Halton Sampling		
	Estimated Probability	Number of Sim	Mean Sim Length	Estimated Probability	Number of Sim	Mean Sim Length
subScenario0W	0.63	41	924.49	0.55	53	861.08
subScenario0B	0.94	31	1235.32	0.90	30	1159.70
subScenario1	1.00	8	1122.75	1.00	25	1122.92
subScenario2L	0.92	63	656.05	0.94	62	660.84
subScenario2S	0.92	26	687.88	0.88	26	683.46
subScenario2R	0.94	16	885.44	0.93	15	895.73
Compositional	**0.73**	**185**	**857.10**	**0.66**	**211**	**856.30**
Monolithic	**0.69**	**Timeout**	**Timeout**	**0.61**	**Timeout**	**Timeout**

7   Related Work

Compositional Analysis Methods. Formal compositional analysis techniques have
a long history in the design and verification of systems [3–6,8,10,15,18]. Many of
these methods are based on assume-guarantee reasoning. These include methods
concerned with compositional reasoning for properties expressed in temporal
logics [3,5], approaches with a focus on compositional verification for models
such as interface and I/O automata [10,15], and those for the contract-based
design of systems [2,18]. With the rise of ML-based components, approaches
for the compositional verification of systems with black-box components have
been investigated. For example, an approach for the compositional falsification
of systems with DNN components was introduced in [8]. An initial investigation
of compositional verification for these types of systems was introduced in [19]. In
contrast to these approaches, our introduced framework provides a compositional
approach from a simulation-based, not model-based, analysis perspective, with
the goal of increasing the scalability of simulation-based methods.

Statistical Analysis Methods. The increasing complexity of cyber-physical systems, making combinatorial methods infeasible, has increased the interest in investigating statistical analysis methods [1,21,27–30]. Coined by the term statistical model checking [16], many scalable simulation-based methods have been introduced in the literature that can give formal statistical guarantees on the correctness of a system relying on different statistical methods. For example, Zuliani et al. show how a statistical model approach based on Bayesian statistics can be used to solve the probabilistic model checking problem for temporal properties and for system models given by Stateflow-style hybrid systems with probabilistic transitions [30]. Younes and Simmons [29] use hypothesis testing and discrete-event simulation to perform probabilistic verification of continuous-time stochastic processes. David et al. [7] present an approach based on statistical model checking to check the correctness of timed systems. In addition to handling systems with large state spaces, a significant benefit of using statistical model checking is that it can handle systems whose implementation models are unknown. For example, Sen et al. [22] present a statistical approach for the verification of stochastic systems based on Monte Carlo simulation and statistical hypothesis testing, with no knowledge of a formal model for the system. An improved algorithm is provided by Younes [26]. Our framework can be instantiated with all the methods mentioned above, allowing for a compositional approach to applying these statistical model-checking methods.

8   Conclusion

We presented a framework for the compositional simulation-based analysis of AI-based autonomous systems. Given a simulation-based analysis task, our approach decomposes the task into several smaller simulation-based analysis tasks avoiding the execution of expensive long-running simulations. Results for the overall tasks are computed by stitching together the results obtained from the smaller analysis tasks. We show how our framework can be used to generate compositional algorithms for falsification and statistical verification. Our experimental results show the scalability and efficacy of our approach in comparison to monolithic simulation-based analysis methods.

References

1. Agha, G., Palmskog, K.: A survey of statistical model checking. ACM Trans. Model. Comput. Simul. **28**(1), 1–39 (2018)
2. Benveniste, A., Caillaud, B., Ferrari, A., Mangeruca, L., Passerone, R., Sofronis, C.: Multiple viewpoint contract-based specification and design. In: de Boer, F.S., Bonsangue, M.M., Graf, S., de Roever, W.-P. (eds.) FMCO 2007. LNCS, vol. 5382, pp. 200–225. Springer, Heidelberg (2008). https://doi.org/10.1007/978-3-540-92188-2_9
3. Bhaduri, P., Ramesh, S.: Interface synthesis and protocol conversion. Form. Asp. Comput. **20**(2), 205–224 (2008)

4. Chilton, C., Jonsson, B., Kwiatkowska, M.Z.: Compositional assume-guarantee reasoning for input/output component theories. Sci. Comput. Program. **91**, 115–137 (2014)
5. Clarke, E.M., Long, D.E., McMillan, K.L.: Compositional model checking. In: Proceedings of the Fourth Annual Symposium on Logic in Computer Science (LICS 1989), Pacific Grove, California, USA, 5–8 June 1989, pp. 353–362. IEEE Computer Society (1989)
6. Cobleigh, J.M., Giannakopoulou, D., PǍsǍreanu, C.S.: Learning assumptions for compositional verification. In: Garavel, H., Hatcliff, J. (eds.) TACAS 2003. LNCS, vol. 2619, pp. 331–346. Springer, Heidelberg (2003). https://doi.org/10.1007/3-540-36577-X_24
7. David, A., Larsen, K.G., Legay, A., Mikučionis, M., Wang, Z.: Time for statistical model checking of real-time systems. In: Gopalakrishnan, G., Qadeer, S. (eds.) CAV 2011. LNCS, vol. 6806, pp. 349–355. Springer, Heidelberg (2011). https://doi.org/10.1007/978-3-642-22110-1_27
8. Dreossi, T., Donzé, A., Seshia, S.A.: Compositional falsification of cyber-physical systems with machine learning components. J. Autom. Reason. **63**(4), 1031–1053 (2019)
9. Dreossi, T., et al.: VERIFAI: a toolkit for the formal design and analysis of artificial intelligence-based systems. In: Dillig, I., Tasiran, S. (eds.) CAV 2019. LNCS, vol. 11561, pp. 432–442. Springer, Cham (2019). https://doi.org/10.1007/978-3-030-25540-4_25
10. Emmi, M., Giannakopoulou, D., Pǎsǎreanu, C.S.: Assume-guarantee verification for interface automata. In: Cuellar, J., Maibaum, T., Sere, K. (eds.) FM 2008. LNCS, vol. 5014, pp. 116–131. Springer, Heidelberg (2008). https://doi.org/10.1007/978-3-540-68237-0_10
11. Fremont, D.J., et al.: Scenic: a language for scenario specification and data generation. Mach. Learn. **112**, 3805–3849 (2023)
12. Halton, J.H.: On the efficiency of certain quasi-random sequences of points in evaluating multi-dimensional integrals. Numer. Math. **2**, 84–90 (1960)
13. Hastie, T., Tibshirani, R., Friedman, J.H., Friedman, J.H.: The Elements of Statistical Learning: Data Mining, Inference, and Prediction, vol. 2. Springer, New York (2009). https://doi.org/10.1007/978-0-387-21606-5
14. Koymans, R.: Specifying real-time properties with metric temporal logic. Real-Time Syst. **2**(4), 255–299 (1990)
15. Larsen, K.G., Nyman, U., Wąsowski, A.: Interface input/output automata. In: Misra, J., Nipkow, T., Sekerinski, E. (eds.) FM 2006. LNCS, vol. 4085, pp. 82–97. Springer, Heidelberg (2006). https://doi.org/10.1007/11813040_7
16. Legay, A., Lukina, A., Traonouez, L.M., Yang, J., Smolka, S.A., Grosu, R.: Statistical model checking. In: Steffen, B., Woeginger, G. (eds.) Computing and Software Science. LNCS, vol. 10000, pp. 478–504. Springer, Cham (2019). https://doi.org/10.1007/978-3-319-91908-9_23
17. Michel, O.: Webots: professional mobile robot simulation. J. Adv. Robot. Syst. **1**(1), 39–42 (2004)
18. Nuzzo, P., Li, J., Sangiovanni-Vincentelli, A.L., Xi, Y., Li, D.: Stochastic assume-guarantee contracts for cyber-physical system design. ACM Trans. Embed. Comput. Syst., **18**(1), 2:1–2:26 (2019)
19. Pasareanu, C.S., Gopinath, D., Yu, H.: Compositional verification for autonomous systems with deep learning components. CoRR, abs/1810.08303 (2018)

20. Saikrishna, V., Ray, S.: MML inference of hierarchical probabilistic finite state machine. In: 2019 Cybersecurity and Cyberforensics Conference (CCC), pp. 78–84 (2019)
21. Sen, K., Viswanathan, M., Agha, G.: VESTA: a statistical model-checker and analyzer for probabilistic systems. In: Second International Conference on the Quantitative Evaluation of Systems (QEST 2005), pp. 251–252 (2005)
22. Sen, K., Viswanathan, M., Agha, G.: Statistical model checking of black-box probabilistic systems. In: Alur, R., Peled, D.A. (eds.) CAV 2004. LNCS, vol. 3114, pp. 202–215. Springer, Heidelberg (2004). https://doi.org/10.1007/978-3-540-27813-9_16
23. Seshia, S.A., Sadigh, D., Sastry, S.S.: Toward verified artificial intelligence. Commun. ACM **65**(7), 46–55 (2022)
24. Webots. http://www.cyberbotics.com Open-source Mobile Robot Simulation Software
25. Yannakakis, M.: Hierarchical state machines. In: van Leeuwen, J., Watanabe, O., Hagiya, M., Mosses, P.D., Ito, T. (eds.) TCS 2000. LNCS, vol. 1872, pp. 315–330. Springer, Heidelberg (2000). https://doi.org/10.1007/3-540-44929-9_24
26. Younes, H.L.S.: Probabilistic verification for "black-box" systems. In: Etessami, K., Rajamani, S.K. (eds.) CAV 2005. LNCS, vol. 3576, pp. 253–265. Springer, Heidelberg (2005). https://doi.org/10.1007/11513988_25
27. Younes, H.L.S.: Ymer: a statistical model checker. In: Etessami, K., Rajamani, S.K. (eds.) CAV 2005. LNCS, vol. 3576, pp. 429–433. Springer, Heidelberg (2005). https://doi.org/10.1007/11513988_43
28. Younes, H.L., Kwiatkowska, M., Norman, G., Parker, D.: Numerical vs. statistical probabilistic model checking. Int. J. Softw. Tools Technol. Transf. **8**(3), 216–228 (2006)
29. Younes, H.L.S., Simmons, R.G.: Statistical probabilistic model checking with a focus on time-bounded properties. Inf. Comput. **204**(9), 1368–1409 (2006)
30. Zuliani, P., Platzer, A., Clarke, E.M.: Bayesian statistical model checking with application to Stateflow/simulink verification. Formal Meth. Syst. Des. **43**(2), 338–367 (2013)

Decentralized Predicate Detection Over Partially Synchronous Continuous-Time Signals

Charles Koll[1], Anik Momtaz[2], Borzoo Bonakdarpour[2],
and Houssam Abbas[1(✉)]

[1] Oregon State University, Corvallis, USA
{kollch,houssam.abbas}@oregonstate.edu
[2] Michigan State University, East Lansing, USA
{momtazan,borzoo}@msu.edu

Abstract. We present the first decentralized algorithm for detecting predicates over continuous-time signals under partial synchrony. A distributed cyber-physical system (CPS) consists of a network of agents, each of which measures (or computes) a continuous-time signal. Examples include distributed industrial controllers connected over wireless networks and connected vehicles in traffic. The safety requirements of such CPS, expressed as logical predicates, must be monitored at runtime. This monitoring faces three challenges: first, every agent only knows its own signal, whereas the safety requirement is global and carries over multiple signals. Second, the agents' local clocks drift from each other, so they do not even agree on the time. Thus, it is not clear which signal values are actually synchronous to evaluate the safety predicate. Third, CPS signals are continuous-time so there are potentially uncountably many safety violations to be reported. In this paper, we present the first decentralized algorithm for detecting conjunctive predicates in this setup. Our algorithm returns all possible violations of the predicate, which is important for eliminating bugs from distributed systems regardless of actual clock drift. We prove that this detection algorithm is in the same complexity class as the detector for discrete systems. We implement our detector and validate it experimentally.

Keywords: Predicate detection · Distributed systems · Partial synchrony · Cyber-physical systems

1 Introduction: Detecting All Errors in Distributed CPS

This paper studies the problem of detecting all property violations in a distributed cyber-physical systems (CPS). A *distributed CPS* consists of a network of communicating agents. Together, the agents must accomplish a common task and preserve certain properties. For example, a network of actuators

---

Supported by NSF SHF awards 2118179 and 2118356.

in an industrial control system must maintain a set point, or a swarm of drones must maintain a certain geometric formation. In these examples, we have N agents generating N continuous-time and real-valued signals $x_n, 1 \leq n \leq N$, and a *global property* of all these signals must be maintained, such as the property $(x_1 > 0) \wedge \ldots (x_N > 0)$. At runtime, an algorithm continuously monitors whether the property holds.

These systems share the following characteristics: first, CPS signals are *analog* (continuous-time, real-valued), and the global properties are continuous-time properties. From a distributed computing perspective, this means that every moment in continuous-time is an event, yielding uncountably many events. Existing reasoning techniques from the discrete time settings, by contrast, depend on there being at the most countably many events.

Second, each agent in these CPS has a *local clock* that drifts from other agents' clocks: so if agent 1 reports $x_1(3) = 5$ and agent 2 reports that $x_2(3) = -10$, these are actually not necessarily synchronous measurements. So we must redefine property satisfaction to account for unknown drift between clocks. For example, if the local clocks drift by at most 1 s, then the monitor must actually check whether any value combination of $x_1(t), x_2(s)$ violates the global property, with $|t - s| \leq 1$. We want to identify any scenario where the system execution *possibly* [5] violates the global property; the actual unknown execution may or may not do so.

Clock drift raises a third issue: the designers of distributed systems want to know *all the ways* in which an error state could occur. E.g., suppose again that the clock drift is at most 1, and the designer observes that the values $(x_1(1), x_2(1.1))$ violate the specification, and eliminates this bug. But when she reruns the system, the actual drift is 0.15 and the values $(x_1(1), x_2(1.15))$ also violate the spec. Therefore all errors, resulting from all possible clock drifts within the bound, must be returned to the designers. This way the designers can guarantee the absence of failures regardless of the actual drift amount. When the error state is captured in a predicate, this means that all possible satisfactions of the predicate must be returned. This is known as the *predicate detection* problem. We distinguish it from predicate monitoring, which requires finding only one such satisfaction, not all.

Finally, in a distributed system, a central monitor which receives all signals is a single point of failure: if the monitor fails, predicate detection fails. Therefore, ideally, the detection would happen in decentralized fashion.

In this work, we solve the problem of decentralized predicate detection for distributed CPS with drifting clocks under partial synchrony.

Related Work. There is a rich literature dealing with decentralized predicate detection in *the discrete-time setting*: e.g. [4] detects regular discrete-time predicates, while [7] detects lattice-linear predicates over discrete states, and [18] performs detection on a regular subset of Computation Tree Logic (CTL). We refer the reader to the books by Garg [6] and Singhal [10] for more references. By contrast, we are concerned with *continuous-time* signals, which have uncountably many events and necessitate new techniques. For instance, one cannot directly iterate through events as done in the discrete setting.

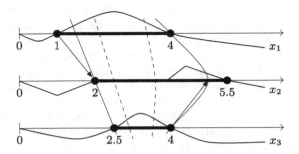

Fig. 1. An example of a continuous-time distributed signal with 3 agents. Three time-lines are shown, one per agent. The signals x_n are also shown, and the local time intervals over which they are non-negative are solid black. The skew ϵ is 1. The Happened-before relation is illustrated with solid arrows, e.g. between $e_1^1 \rightarrow e_2^2$, and $e_3^4 \rightarrow e_2^5$. These are not message transmission events, rather they follow from Definition 3. Some satisfying cuts for the predicate $\phi = (x_1 \geq 0) \wedge (x_2 \geq 0) \wedge (x_3 \geq 0)$ are shown as dashed arcs, and the extremal cuts as solid arcs. All extremal cuts contain root events, and leftmost cut A also contains non-root events.

The recent works [14,15] do *monitoring* of temporal formulas over partially synchronous analog distributed systems - i.e., they only find one satisfaction, not all. Moreover, their solution is centralized.

More generally, one finds much work on monitoring temporal logic properties, especially Linear Temporal Logic (LTL) and Metric Temporal Logic (MTL), but they either do monitoring or work in discrete-time. Notably, [1] used a three-valued MTL for monitoring in the presence of failures and non-FIFO communication channels. [3] monitors satisfaction of an LTL formula. [16] considered a three-valued LTL for distributed systems with asynchronous properties. [2] addressed the problem with a tableau technique for three-valued LTL. Finally, [19] considered a past-time distributed temporal logic which emphasizes distributed properties over time.

Illustrative Example. It is helpful to overview our algorithm and key notions via an example before delving into the technical details. An example is shown in Fig. 1. Three agents produce three signals x_1, x_2, x_3. The decentralized detector consists of three local detectors D_1, D_2, D_3, one on each agent. Each x_n is observed by the corresponding D_n. The predicate $\phi = (x_1 \geq 0) \wedge (x_2 \geq 0) \wedge (x_3 \geq 0)$ is being detected. It is possibly true over the intervals shown with solid black bars; their endpoints are measured on the local clocks. The detector only knows that the maximal clock skew is $\epsilon = 1$, but not the actual value, which might be time-varying.

Because of clock skew, any two local times within ϵ of each other must be considered as potentially concurrent, i.e. they might be measured at a truly synchronous moment. For example, the triple of local times $[4, 4.5, 3.6]$ might have been measured at the global time 4, in which case the true skews were 0, 0.5, and -0.4 respectively. Such a triple is (loosely speaking) called a *consistent cut* (Definition 4). The detector's task is to find all consistent cuts that satisfy the predicate. In continuous time, there can be uncountably many, as in Fig. 1; the dashed lines show two satisfying consistent cuts, or satcuts for short.

In this example, our detector outputs two satcuts, $[1.5, 2, 2.5]$ and $[4, 5, 4]$, shown as thin solid lines. These two have the special property (shown in this paper) that every satcut lies between them, and every cut between them is a satcut. For this reason we call them *extremal satcuts* (Definition 6). Thus these two satcuts are a finite representation of the uncountable set of satcuts, and encode all the ways in which the predicate might be satisfied.

We note three further things: the extremal satcuts are not just the endpoints of the intervals, and simply inflating each interval by ϵ and intersecting them does not yield the satcuts. Each local detector must somehow learn of the relevant events (and only those) on other agents, to determine whether they constitute extremal satcuts.

Contributions. In this paper, we present the first *decentralized predicate detector for distributed CPS*, thus enhancing the rigor of distributed CPS design.

- Our solution is fully decentralized: each agent only ever accesses its own signal, and exchanges a limited amount of information with the other agents.
- It is an online algorithm, running simultaneously with the agents' tasks.
- It applies to an important class of global properties that are conjunctions of local propositions.
- We introduce a new notion of clock, the *physical vector clock*, which might be of independent interest. A physical vector clock orders continuous-time events in a distributed computation without a shared clock.
- Our algorithm can be deployed on top of existing infrastructure. Specifically, our algorithm includes a modified version of the classical detector of [4], and so can be deployed on top of existing infrastructure which already supports that detector.

Organization. In Sect. 2, we give necessary definitions and define the problem. In Sect. 3 we establish fundamental properties of the uncountable set of events S_E satisfying the predicate. Our detector is made of two processes: a decentralized abstractor presented in Sect. 4, and a decentralized slicer presented in Sect. 5. Together, they compute a finite representation of the uncountable S_E. The complexity of the algorithm is also analyzed in Sect. 5. Section 6 demonstrates an implementation of the detector, and Sect. 7 concludes. All proofs are in the report [9].

2   Preliminaries and Problem Definition

We first set some notation. The set of reals is $\mathbb{R}$, the set of non-negative reals is $\mathbb{R}_{\geq 0}$. The integer set $\{1, \ldots, N\}$ is abbreviated as $[N]$. *Global* time values (kept by an *imaginary* global clock) are denoted by χ, χ', χ_1, χ_2, etc., while the symbols t, t', t_1, t_2, s, s', s_1, s_2, etc. denote *local* clock values specific to given agents which will always be clear from the context. A *lattice* is a set S equipped with a partial order relation $\sqsubseteq$ s.t. every 2 elements have a supremum, or *join*, and an infimum, or *meet*. An *increasing* function f is one s.t. $t < t' \implies f(t) < f(t')$. Notation $(x_n)_n$ indicates a sequence $(x_1, \ldots, x_N)$ where N is always clear from context.

2.1   The Continuous-Time Setup

This section defines the setup of this study. It generalizes the classical discrete-time setup, and follows closely the setup in [15]. We assume a loosely coupled system with asynchronous message passing between agent monitors. Specifically, the system consists of N reliable *agents* that do not fail, denoted by $\{A_1, A_2, \ldots, A_N\}$, without any shared memory or global clock. The output signal of agent A_n is denoted by x_n, for $1 \leq n \leq N$. Agents can communicate via FIFO lossless channels. There are no bounds on message transmission times.

In the discrete-time setting, an event is a value change in an agent's variables. The following definition generalizes this to the continuous-time setting.

Definition 1 (Output signal and events). *An output signal (of some agent) is a function $x : \mathbb{R}_{\geq 0} \to \mathbb{R}$, which is right-continuous (i.e., $\lim_{s \to t+} x(s) = x(t)$ at every t), and left-limited (i.e., $\lim_{s \to t-} |x(s)| < \infty$ for all t).*

In an agent A_n, an event is a pair $(t, x_n(t))$, where t is the local time kept by the agent's local clock. This will often be abbreviated as e_n^t to follow standard notation from the discrete-time literature.

Note that an output signal can contain discontinuities.

Definition 2 (Left and right roots). *A root is an event e_n^t where $x_n(t) = 0$ or a discontinuity at which the signal changes sign: $sgn(x_n(t)) \neq sgn(\lim_{s \to t-} x_n(s))$. A left root e_n^t is a root preceded by negative values: there exists a positive real δ s.t. $x_n(t - \alpha) < 0$ for all $0 < \alpha \leq \delta$. A right root e_n^t is a root followed by negative values: $x_n(t + \alpha) < 0$ for all $0 < \alpha \leq \delta$.*

In Fig. 1, the only left root of x_2 is $e_2^2 = (2, x_2(2)) = (2, 0)$. The single right root of x_2 is $e_2^{5.5}$. Notice that intervals where the signal is identically 0 are allowed, as in x_2.

We will need to refer to a global clock which acts as a 'real' time-keeper. This global clock is a theoretical object used in definitions and theorems, and is *not* available to the agents. We make these assumptions:

Assumption 1.(a) (Partial synchrony) The local clock of an agent A_n is an increasing function $c_n : \mathbb{R}_{\geq 0} \to \mathbb{R}_{\geq 0}$, where $c_n(\chi)$ is the value of the local clock at global time χ. For any two agents A_n and A_m, we have:

$$\forall \chi \in \mathbb{R}_{\geq 0} : |c_n(\chi) - c_m(\chi)| < \epsilon$$

with $\epsilon > 0$ being the maximum *clock skew*. The value ϵ is known by the detector in the rest of this paper. In the sequel, we make it explicit when we refer to 'local' or 'global' time.

(b) (Starvation-freedom and non-Zeno) Every signal x_n has infinitely many roots in $\mathbb{R}_{\geq 0}$, with a finite number of them occurring in any bounded interval.

Remark 1. Our detection algorithm can trivially handle multi-dimensional output signals x_n. We skip this generalization for clarity of exposition.

Remark 2. In distributed systems, agents typically exchange messages as part of normal operation. These messages help establish an ordering between events (a Send occurs before the corresponding Receive). This extra order information can be incorporated in our detection algorithm with extra bookkeeping.
We do *not* assume that the clock drift is constant - it can vary with time. It is assumed to be uniformly bounded by ϵ, which can be achieved by using a clock synchronization algorithm, like NTP [13].

A distributed signal is modeled as a set of events partially ordered by Lamport's *happened-before* relation [11], adapted to the continuous-time setting.

Definition 3 (Analog Distributed signal). *A distributed signal on N agents is a tuple $(E, \rightarrow)$, in which E is a set of events*

$$E = \{e_n^t \mid n \in [N], \ t \in \mathbb{R}_{\geq 0}\}$$

such that for all $t \in \mathbb{R}_{\geq 0}, n \in [N]$, there exists an event e_n^t in E, and t is local time in agent A_n. The happened-before *relation* $\rightarrow \subseteq E \times E$ *between events is such that:*

(a) In every agent A_n, all events are totally ordered, that is,

$$\forall t, t' \in \mathbb{R}_{\geq 0} : (t < t') \implies (e_n^t \rightarrow e_n^{t'}).$$

(b) For any two events $e_n^t, e_m^{t'} \in E$, if $t + \epsilon \leq t'$, then $e_n^t \rightarrow e_m^{t'}$.
(c) If $e \rightarrow f$ and $f \rightarrow g$, then $e \rightarrow g$.

We denote $E[n]$ the subset of events that occur on A_n, i.e. $E[n] := \{e_n^t \in E\}$

The happened-before relation, $\rightarrow$, captures what can be known about event ordering in the absence of perfect synchrony. Namely, events on the same agent can be linearly ordered, and at least an ϵ of time must elapse between events on different agents for us to say that one happened before the other. Events from different agents closer than an ϵ apart are said to be *concurrent*.

Conjunctive Predicates. This paper focuses on specifications expressible as *conjunctive predicates* ϕ, which are conjunctions of N linear inequalities.

$$\phi := (x_1 \geq 0) \wedge (x_2 \geq 0) \wedge \ldots \wedge (x_N \geq 0). \tag{1}$$

These predicates model the simultaneous co-occurrence, in global time, of events of interest, like 'all drones are dangerously close to each other'. Equation (1) also captures the cases where some conjuncts are of the form $x_n \leq 0$ and $x_n = 0$. If

N numbers (a_n) satisfy predicate ϕ (i.e., are all non-negative), we write this as $(a_1, \ldots, a_N) \models \phi$. Henceforth, we say 'predicate' to mean a conjunctive predicate. Note that the restriction to linear inequalities does not significantly limit our ability to model specifications. If an agent n has some signal x_n with which we want to check $f(x_n) \geq 0$ for some arbitrary function f, then the agent can generate an auxiliary signal $y_n := f(x_n)$ so that we can consider the linear inequality $y_n \geq 0$.

What does it mean to say that a distributed signal satisfies ϕ? And at what moment in time? In the ideal case of perfect synchrony ($\epsilon = 0$) we'd simply say that E satisfies ϕ at χ whenever $(x_1(\chi), \ldots, x_N(\chi)) \models \phi$. We call such a synchronous tuple $(x_n(\chi))_n$ a *global state*. But because the agents are only synchronized to within an $\epsilon > 0$, it is not possible to guarantee evaluation of the predicate at true global states. The conservative thing is to treat concurrent events, whose local times differ by less than ϵ, as being simultaneous on the global clock. E.g., if $N = 2$ and $\epsilon = 1$ then $(x_1(1), x_2(1.5))$ is treated as a possible global state. The notion of consistent cut, adopted from discrete-time distributed systems [8], formalizes this intuition.

Definition 4 (Consistent Cut). *Given a distributed signal $(E, \rightarrow)$, a subset of events $C \subset E$ is said to form a* consistent cut *if and only if when C contains an event e, then it contains all events that happened-before e. Formally,*

$$\forall e \in E : (e \in C) \wedge (f \rightarrow e) \implies f \in C. \tag{2}$$

We write $C[n]$ for the cut's local events produced on A_n, and $C^\tau[n] := \{t \mid e_n^t \in C[n]\}$ for the timestamps of a cut's local events.

From this and Definition 3 (c) it follows that if $e_m^{t'}$ is in C, then C also contains every event e_n^t such that $t + \epsilon \leq t'$. Thus to avoid trivialities, we may assume that C contains at least one event from every agent.

A consistent cut C is represented by its *frontier* $\mathsf{front}(C) = \left(e_1^{t_1}, \ldots, e_N^{t_N}\right)$, in which each $e_n^{t_n}$ is the last event of agent A_n appearing in C. Formally:

$$\forall n \in [N], \ t_n := \sup C^\tau[n] = \sup\{t \in \mathbb{R}_{\geq 0} \mid e_n^t \in C[n]\}.$$

Henceforth, we simply say 'cut' to mean a consistent cut, and we denote a frontier by $(e_n^{t_n})_n$. We highlight some easy yet important consequences of the definition: on a given agent A_n, $e_n^t \in C$ for all $t < t_n$, so the timestamps of the cut's local events, $C^\tau[n]$, form a left-closed interval of the form $[0, a]$, $[0, a)$ or $[0, \infty)$. Moreover, either $C^\tau[n] = [0, \infty)$ for all n, in which case $C = E$, or every $C^\tau[n]$ is bounded, in which case every t_n is finite and $|t_n - t_m| \leq \epsilon$ for all n, m. *Thus the frontier of a cut is a possible global state.* This then justifies the following definition of distributed satisfaction.

Definition 5. (*Distributed Satisfaction; S_E*) *Given a predicate ϕ, a distributed signal $(E, \rightarrow)$ over N agents, and a consistent cut C of E with frontier*

$$\mathsf{front}(C) = \Big((t_1, x_1(t_1)), \ldots, (t_N, x_N(t_N)) \Big)$$

we say that C satisfies ϕ iff $(x_1(t_1), x_2(t_2), \ldots, x_N(t_N)) \models \phi$. We write this as $C \models \phi$, and say that C is a satcut. *The set of all satcuts in E is written S_E.*

2.2 Problem Definition: Decentralized Predicate Detection

The detector seeks to find *all* possible global states that satisfy a given predicate, i.e. all satcuts in S_E. In general, S_E is uncountable.

Architecture. The system consists of N agents with partially synchronous clocks with drift bounded by a known ϵ, generating a continuous-time distributed signal $(E, \rightarrow)$. Agents communicate in a FIFO manner, where messages sent from an agent A_1 to an agent A_2 are received in the order that they were sent.

Problem Statement. Given $(E, \rightarrow)$ and a conjunctive predicate ϕ, find a decentralized detection algorithm that computes a finite representation of S_E. The detector is decentralized, meaning that it consists of N local detectors, one on each agent, with access only to the local signal x_n (measured against the local clock), and to messages received from other agents' detectors.

By computing a representation of all of S_E (and not some subset), we account for asynchrony and the unknown orderings of events within ϵ of each other. One might be tempted to propose something like the following algorithm: detect all roots on all agents, then see if any N of them are within ϵ of each other. This quickly runs into difficulties: first, a satisfying cut is not necessarily made up of roots; some or all of its events can be interior to the intervals where x_n's are positive (see Fig. 2). Second, the relation between roots and satcuts must be established: it is not clear, for example, whether even satcuts made of only roots are enough to characterize all satcuts (it turns out, they're not). Third, we must carefully control how much information is shared between agents, to avoid the detector degenerating into a centralized solution where everyone shares everything with everyone else.

3 The Structure of Satisfying Cuts

We establish fundamental properties of satcuts. In the rest of this paper we exclude the trivial case $C = E$. Proposition 1 mirrors a discrete-time result [4].

Proposition 1. *The set of satcuts for a conjunctive predicate is a lattice where the join and meet are the union and intersection operations, respectively.*

We show that the set of satcuts is characterized by special elements, which we call the leftmost and rightmost cuts.

Definition 6 (Extremal cuts). *Let S_E be the set of all satcuts in a given distributed signal $(E, \rightarrow)$. For an arbitrary $C \in S_E$ with frontier $(e_n^{t_n})_n$ and positive real α, define $C - \alpha$ to be the set of cuts whose frontiers are given by*

$$(e_1^{t_1-\delta_1}, e_2^{t_2-\delta_2}, \ldots, e_N^{t_N-\delta_N}) \text{ s.t. for all } n: 0 \leq \delta_n \leq \alpha \text{ and for some } n. \ \delta_n > 0$$

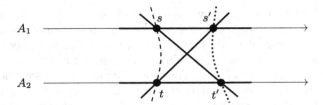

Fig. 2. Two satcuts for a pair of agents A_1 and A_2, shown by the solid lines (s, t') and (s', t). Their intersection is (s, t), shown by a dashed arc, and their union is (s', t'), shown by a dotted arc. For a conjunctive predicate ϕ, the intersection and union are also satcuts, forming a lattice of satcuts.

A leftmost satcut *is a satcut $C \in S_E$ for which there exists a positive real α s.t. $C - \alpha$ and S_E do not intersect. The set $C + \alpha$ is similarly defined. A* rightmost cut C *(not necessarily sat) is one for which there exists a positive real α s.t. $C + \alpha$ and S_E do not intersect, and $C - \alpha \subset S_E$. We refer to leftmost and rightmost (sat)cuts as* extremal cuts.

Intuitively, $C - \alpha$ $(C + \alpha)$ is the set of all cuts one obtains by slightly moving the frontier of C to the left (right) by amounts less than α. If doing so always yields non-satisfying cuts, then C is a leftmost satcut. If moving C slightly to the right always yields unsatisfying cuts, but moving it slightly left yields satcuts, then C is a rightmost cut. The reason we don't speak of rightmost *satcuts* is that we only require signals to be left-limited, not continuous. If signals x_n are all continuous, then rightmost cuts are all satisfying as well.

In a signal, there are multiple extremal cuts. Figure 2 suggests, and Lemma 1 proves, that all satcuts live between a leftmost satcut and rightmost cut.

Lemma 1 (Satcut intervals). *Every satcut of a conjunctive predicate lies in-between a leftmost satcut and rightmost cut, and there are no non-satisfying cuts between a leftmost satcut and the first rightmost cut that is greater than it in the lattice order.*

Thus we may visualize satcuts as forming N-dimensional intervals with endpoints given by the extremal cuts. The main result of this section states that there are finitely many extremal satcuts in any bounded time interval, so the extremal satcuts are the finite representation we seek for S_E.

Theorem 1. *A distributed signal has finitely many extremal satcuts in any bounded time interval.*

Therefore, it is conceivably possible to recover algorithmically the extremal cuts, and therefore all satcuts by Lemma 1. The rest of this paper shows how.

4   The Abstractor Process

Having captured the structure of satcuts, we now define the distributed *abstractor process* that will turn our continuous-time problem into a discrete-time one, amenable to further processing by our modified version of the slicer algorithm of [4]. This abstractor also has the task of creating a happened-before relation. We first note a few complicating factors. First, this will not simply be a matter of sampling the roots of each signal. That is because extremal cuts can contain non-root events, as shown in Fig. 1. Thus the abstractor must somehow find and sample these non-root events as part of its operation. Second, as in the discrete case, we need a kind of clock that allows the local detector to know the happened-before relation between events. The local timestamp of an event, and existing clock notions, are not adequate for this. Third, to establish the happened-before relation, there is a need to exchange event information between the processes, without degenerating everything into a centralized process (by sharing everything with everyone). This complicates the operation of the local abstractors, but allows us to cut the number of messages in half.

4.1 Physical Vector Clocks

We first define Physical Vector Clocks (PVCs), which generalize vector clocks [12] from countable to uncountable sets of events. They are used by the abstractor process (next section) to track the happened-before relation. A PVC captures one agent's knowledge, at appropriate local times, of events at other agents.

Definition 7 (Physical Vector Clock). *Given a distributed signal $(E, \rightarrow)$ on N agents, a Physical Vector Clock, or PVC, is a set of N-dimensional timestamp vectors $\mathbf{v}_n^t \in \mathbb{R}_{\geq 0}^N$, where vector $\mathbf{v}_n^t$ is defined by the following:*

(1) Initialization: $\mathbf{v}_n^0[i] = 0, \quad \forall i \in \{1, \ldots, N\}$
(2) Timestamps store the local time of their agent: $\mathbf{v}_n^t[n] = t$ for all $t > 0$.
(3) Timestamps keep a consistent view of time: Let V_n^t be the set of all timestamps $\mathbf{v}_m^s$ s.t. e_m^s happened-before e_n^t in E. Then:

$$\mathbf{v}_n^t[i] = \max_{\mathbf{v}_m^s \in V_n^t}(\mathbf{v}_m^s[i]), \quad \forall i \in [N] \setminus \{n\}, t > 0$$

PVCs are partially ordered: $\mathbf{v}_n^t < \mathbf{v}_m^{t'}$ iff $\mathbf{v}_n^t \neq \mathbf{v}_m^{t'}$ and $\mathbf{v}_n^t[i] \leq \mathbf{v}_m^{t'}[i] \ \forall i \in [N]$.

We say $\mathbf{v}_n^t$ is *assigned* to e_n^t. The detection algorithm can now know the happened-before relation by comparing PVCs.

Theorem 2. *Given a distributed signal $(E, \rightarrow)$, let V be the corresponding set of PVC timestamps. Then $(V, <)$ and $(E, \rightarrow)$ are order isomorphic, i.e., there is a bijective mapping between V and E s.t. $e_n^t \rightarrow e_m^{t'}$ iff $\mathbf{v}_n^t < \mathbf{v}_m^{t'}$.*

Definition 7 is not quite a constructive definition. We need a way to actually compute PVCs. This is enabled by the next theorem.

Theorem 3. *The assignment*

$$\mathbf{v}_n^t = \begin{cases} [0, \ldots, 0, t, 0, \ldots, 0], & t < \epsilon \\ [t - \epsilon, \ldots, t - \epsilon, t, t - \epsilon, \ldots, t - \epsilon], & t \geq \epsilon \end{cases}$$

where the t is in the nth position in both cases, satisfies the conditions of PVC in Definition 7.

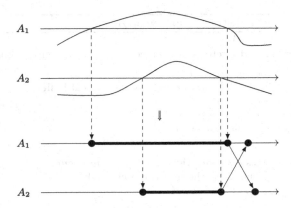

A_1

A_2

A_1

A_2

Fig. 3. A distributed signal of two agents (top) and the output of the abstractor (bottom). The abstractor marks zero-crossings as discrete root events and creates new events (dark circles) to maintain consistency.

4.2   Abstractor Description

The abstractor is described in Algorithm 1 on page 224. Its output is a stream of discrete-time events, their correct PVC values, and the relation $\rightarrow$ between them - i.e., a discrete-time distributed signal. This signal is processed by the local slicer processes as it is being produced by the abstractor.

The abstractor runs as follows. It is decentralized, meaning that there is a *local* abstractor running on each agent. Agent A_n's local abstractor maintains a buffer of discrete events, and consists of two trigger processes. The first is triggered when a root is detected (by a local zero-finding algorithm; line 1). It stores the root's information in a local buffer (for future processing). *If it is a right root*, it also sends it to the other agents. The second trigger process (line 6) is triggered when the agent *receives* a right root information from some other process, at which point it does three things: it creates a local discrete event and a corresponding relation $\rightsquigarrow$ between events (Lines 8-9), it updates events in its local buffer to see which ones can be sent to the local slicer process (described in Sect. 5), and then it sends them. It is clear, by construction, that $\rightsquigarrow$ is a happened-before relation: it is the subset of $\rightarrow$ needed for detection purposes.

Before an event e_n^t is sent to the slicer, it must have a PVC that correctly reflects the happened-before relation. This means that all events that happened-before e_n^t must be known to agent n, which uses them to update the PVC timestamps. This happens when events have reached agent A_n from every other agent, with timestamps that place them after e_n^t (line 11). This is guaranteed to happen by the starvation-free assumption 1.(b).

The output of a local abstractor is a stream of discrete events, so that *the output of the decentralized abstractor as a whole is a distributed discrete-time signal*. See Fig. 3.

Algorithm 1: Local abstractor for agent A_n

Data: Signal of agent A_n
Result: A stream of discrete events which are roots or ϵ-offset from roots

1   **trigger** *found a root e_n^t at local time t*:
2   **add** e_n^t *info* $(n, t,$ PVC, left or right root$)$ to local buffer
3   **if** e_n^t *is right root*:
4   **for each** *agent $m \neq n$*:
5   **send** e_n^t *info* to agent m

6   **trigger** *received message about* right root e_m^t *from agent A_m*:
7   Set $t' := t + \epsilon$, where ϵ is the maximum clock skew
8   **create** *local event $e_n^{t'}$*
9   **create** *relation $e_m^t \rightsquigarrow e_n^{t'}$* (setting the PVC for $e_n^{t'}$ appropriately)
       `/* Info for created event includes that it` *came* `from a right`
       `root` e_m^t`, not necessarily that it` *is* `a root`   `*/`
10   **add** $e_n^{t'}$ *info* $(n, t',$ PVC, from right root$)$ to local buffer
       `/* Ready events are those whose PVCs will not be updated`
       `anymore. See text for details.`   `*/`
11   **if** *A_n received at least one message about a* right root $e_k^{t_k}$ *from every other*
       agent A_k such that $t_k \geq t$:
         `/* Visit events in the buffer, forwarding ones that are`
         `ready to the slicer.`   `*/`
12   **for each** *event e_n^s in the local buffer*:
13   Set $\mathbf{v}_n^s[n] = s$ and $\mathbf{v}_n^s[k] = s - \epsilon$ for all $k \neq n$
14   Remove e_n^s from buffer and **send** it to local slicer

---

Given that all right roots are assigned discrete events by the first trigger, and given that ϵ-offset events are also created from them by the second trigger (line 8), we have the following.

Theorem 4. *All events in rightmost cuts are generated by the abstractor. Moreover, a rightmost cut of E is also a cut of the discrete signal returned by the abstractor.*

Thus the slicer process, described in the following section, can find the rightmost cuts when it processes the discrete signal. What about the leftmost satcuts? These will be handled by the slicer using the PVCs, as will be shown in the next section. Doing it this way relieves the abstractor from having to communicate the left roots between processes, thus saving on messages and their wait times.

5   The Slicer Process for Detecting Predicates

The second process in our detector is a decentralized *slicer process*, so-called to keep with the common terminology in discrete distributed systems [6]. The slicer is decentralized: it consists of N local slicers $\mathcal{S}_n$, one per agent. The slicer runs in parallel with the abstractor and processes the abstractor's output as it is produced. Recall that the abstractor's output consists of a stream of discrete events, coming from the N agents. These events are either roots or ϵ-offset from roots. If an event is a left root or ϵ-offset from a left root, we will call it a left event. We define right events similarly. We will write F_n for those events, output by the abstractor, that occurred on A_n.

Every slicer $\mathcal{S}_n$ maintains a *token* T_n, which is a constant-size data structure to keep track of satcuts that contain A_n events. Specifically, for every event e_n^t in F_n, the token T_n is forwarded between the agents, collecting information to determine whether there exists a satcut that contains e_n^t. We say the slicer is trying to *complete* e_n^t. The token's updates are such that it will find that satcut if it exists, or determines that none exists; either way, it is then reset and sent back to its parent process A_n to handle the next event in F_n.

Let e_n^t be an event that the slicer is currently trying to complete. The token's updates vary, depending on whether it is currently completing a left event, or a right event. *If T_n is completing a right event*, the token is updated as follows. The token currently has a cut whose frontier contains e_n^t, which is either a satcut or not. If it is, the token has successfully completed the event and is returned to A_n to handle the next event in F_n. If not, then by the property of *regular* predicates [4], there exists a *forbidden event* e_m^s on the frontier of the cut which either prevents the cut from being consistent or from satisfying the predicate. T_n is sent to the process A_m containing this forbidden event. T_n's so-called target event, whose inclusion may give T_n a satcut, is the event on A_m following the forbidden e_m^s. If the token does not find a next event following e_m^s, then the token is kept by $\mathcal{S}_m$ until it receives the next event from the abstractor (which is guaranteed to happen under the starvation-free assumption). After the token retrieves the next event, the updates to the token and progression of $\mathcal{S}_n$ then follow the CGNM slicer [4]. Space limitations make it impossible to describe the CGNM slicer here, and we refer the reader to the detailed description in [4].

If handling a left event, the token is updated as follows. First, as before, T_n is sent to the process A_m which generates the forbidden e_m^s – i.e., which prevents T_n from completing e_n^t. T_n's target event may not be the next event on that process following e_m^s: that's because if e_n^t is a left root, there may exist a left event $e_m^{t-\epsilon}$ on A_m which is part of a continuous-time leftmost satcut (by Definition 3), but which was not created by the abstractor. In this case, if the token were to follow the updates for a right event, it would skip a potential satcut. Instead, the slicer $\mathcal{S}_m$ will create this event: namely, if $\mathcal{S}_m$ sees a new event $e_m^{s'}$ where $s' > t - \epsilon$, it knows that $e_m^{t-\epsilon}$ has not and will not show up (will not be produced by the abstractor) because messages are FIFO. The slicer at this point creates the new event $e_m^{t-\epsilon}$. This is valid since in continuous-time, by definition, every moment has a corresponding event on every agent. Once the token retrieves this created $e_m^{t-\epsilon}$ as its new target, the updates to the token and progression of $\mathcal{S}_n$ follow the CGNM slicer [4], similarly to the right event scenario.

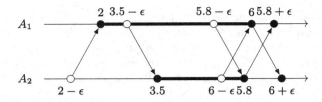

Fig. 4. Example of Subsect. 5.1. Bold intervals are where the local signals are non-negative. The happened-before relation is illustrated with solid arrows. The predicate is $\phi = (x_1 \geq 0) \wedge (x_2 \geq 0)$. Solid circles represent discrete events returned by the abstractor; hollow circles are those created by the slicers. The leftmost satcut of this example is $[3.5 - \epsilon, 3.5]$ and the rightmost is $[6, 5.8]$.

<u>Correctness of $\mathcal{S}$.</u> We will show that all extremal cuts of the continuous-time signal are included in the discrete lattice of satcuts of the discrete signal. Since the CGNM slicer computes the discrete lattice, this means in particular that it computes the extremal cuts that are in it. From these extremal cuts, we can then recover the continuous-time satcuts by Lemma 1.

Theorem 5. *Our slicer returns all extremal cuts.*

We give the space and time complexity of the overall detector. Since this is an online detector which runs forever (as long as the system is alive), we must fix a time interval for the analysis.

Theorem 6. *The time complexity for each agent is $O(2RN)$, where R is the number of right roots in the given analysis interval. The detector consumes $O(N^3)$ memory to store the tokens. If roots are uniformly distributed, then the local buffers of the abstractor and slicer grow at the most to size $O(N^2)$.*

Finally, there is no bound on detection delay, since we don't assume any bounds on message transmission time. Assuming some bound on transmission delay yields a corresponding bound on detection delay.

5.1 Worked-Out Example

We now work through an example execution of the detector on Fig. 4. We focus on agent A_2, its abstractor $\mathcal{A}_2$, slicer $\mathcal{S}_2$ and its token T_2.

1. Agent A_2 encounters a left root in the signal at local time 3.5. This information is forwarded to the abstractor.
2. The abstractor $\mathcal{A}_2$ adds the new root to its buffer with a PVC $=[3.5 - \epsilon, 3.5]$.
3. A_2 finds a right root in the signal at local time 5.8 and forwards it to $\mathcal{A}_2$.
4. The abstractor sends the root information to agent A_1. It then adds this root to its buffer with a PVC timestamp of $[5.8 - \epsilon, 5.8]$.
5. Abstractor $\mathcal{A}_2$ receives a message from A_1 about a right root at A_1's local time 6. Note that this is the first knowledge A_2 has about anything that is occurring on A_1, even though A_1 has already found a left root.

6. A_2 uses A_1's message to create a new local event at $6 + \epsilon$ with PVC $[6, 6 + \epsilon]$.
7. A_2 also adds this new local event to its buffer. Since all messages are FIFO, A_2 knows that there will be no new messages which will create events before $6 + \epsilon$. Thus, it can remove both of the events 3.5 and 5.8 from the buffer and forward them to its local slicer S_2. At this point both of A_1's events have been forwarded to *its* slicer, although A_2 has no knowledge of this.
8. The slicer S_2 receives an event with a PVC $[3.5 - \epsilon, 3.5]$. Token T_2 is waiting for the next event, so it adds this event to its potential cut.
9. The token is processed with its new potential cut. The cut is found to be inconsistent since T_2 has no information about any A_1 events.
10. The token's target is set to be $3.5 - \epsilon$ on A_1 and the token is sent to A_1.
11. A_1 receives T_2. It walks through its local events 2 and 6 and determines that T_2's target event is between the two.
12. S_1 creates a new event $e_1^{3.5-\epsilon}$ and notes that $x_1(3.5 - \epsilon) \geq 0$.
13. Token T_2 incorporates the new event to its potential cut. The new potential cut is consistent and satisfies the predicate. It is then sent back to A_2.
14. A_2 receives T_2. T_2 indicates a satisfying cut, which the agent outputs as a result. It then advances T_2 to its next event at time 5.8.
15. T_2 has the current cut of $[3.5 - \epsilon, 5.8]$. This is not consistent, so it is given the target $5.8 - \epsilon$ on A_1. It is then sent to A_1.
16. A_1 receives the token. S_1 walks through its local events and finds that the token's target is between the left root and the right root.
17. S_1 creates a new event at $5.8 - \epsilon$ and notes that $x_1(5.8 - \epsilon) \geq 0$.
18. The token adds the event to its potential cut. It finds that its new potential cut is consistent and satisfies the predicate. It is then sent back to A_2.
19. A_2 receives T_2 and outputs the satcut. The algorithm then continues with new events as they occur.

Through this example, agent A_2 discovered the satcuts $[3.5 - \epsilon, 3.5]$ and $[5.8 - \epsilon, 5.8]$. The first is the leftmost satcut of the interval of satcuts. A_1 discovered an additional satcut $[6, 6 - \epsilon]$. Joining this satcut with A_2's second satcut returns a result of $[6, 5.8]$, which is the rightmost satcut of the interval of satcuts.

6   Case Studies and Evaluation

We implemented our detection algorithm and ran experiments to 1) illustrate its operation, and 2) observe runtime scaling with number of agents and with average rate of events. The detector was implemented in Julia for ease of prototyping, but future versions will be in C for speed. All experiments are replicated to exhibit 95% confidence interval. Experiments were run on a single thread of an Ubuntu machine powered by an AMD Ryzen 7 5800X CPU @ 3.80GHz. Code can be found at https://github.com/sabotagelab/phryctoria.

We consider two sources of data: the first is a set of N synthetically generated signals, $N = 1...6$. Each signal has a 5s duration, and is generated randomly while ensuring an average root rate of μ_n. That is, on average, μ_n roots exist in every second of signal x_n. For the second source of data, we use the Fly-by-Logic toolbox [17] to control up to 6 simulated UAVs (i.e., drones) performing various reach-avoid missions. Their 3-dimensional trajectories are recorded over 6 s. We monitor the predicate "All UAVs are at a height of at least $10m$ simultaneously". Maximum clock skew ϵ is set to 0.05 s.

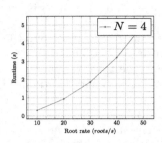

(a) Runtime vs root rate on 4 synthetic signals.

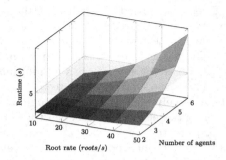

(b) Online monitoring. The red horizontal plane indicates the runtime threshold (namely, 5s) below which it is possible to do online detection.

Fig. 5. Runtime vs root rate and N on synthetic data.

Effect of root rate (μ_n) on runtime. We use 4 synthetic signals of $5s$ duration, and measure the detection runtime as the root rate for all signals is varied between $10roots/s$ and $50roots/s$. Figure 5a shows the results. Naturally, as μ_n increases, so does the runtime due to having to process more tokens.

Online detection. We want to identify when it is possible for us to perform online detection with the Julia implementation, i.e. such that the detector finishes before the end of the signal being processed. To this end, we use the synthetic signals of duration 5 s and vary both root rate and number of agents. Figure 5b shows the results: all combinations of root rates and number of agents with runtimes under the threshold of 5 s can be performed online with the hardware setup used for these experiments.

Effect of number of agents on runtime. Fig. 6 shows the effect of number of agents N on runtime. As expected, the runtime increases with N.

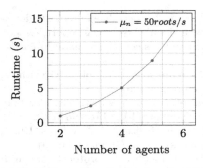

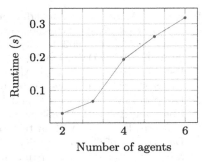

(a) Detection of synthetic signals at 50 roots/s

(b) Detection of UAV signals

Fig. 6. Runtime vs number of agents.

7 Conclusion

We have defined the first decentralized algorithm for continuous-time predicate detection in partially synchronous distributed CPS. To do so we analyzed the structure of satisfying consistent cuts for conjunctive predicates, introduced a new notion of clock, and modified a classical discrete-time predicate detector.

References

1. Basin, D., Klaedtke, F., Zălinescu, E.: Failure-aware runtime verification of distributed systems. In: 35th IARCS Annual Conference on Foundations of Software Technology and Theoretical Computer Science (FSTTCS 2015), vol. 45, pp. 590–603. Schloss Dagstuhl-Leibniz-Zentrum für Informatik (2015)
2. Bataineh, O., Rosenblum, D.S., Reynolds, M.: Efficient decentralized LTL monitoring framework using tableau technique. ACM Trans. Embed. Comput. Syst. (TECS) **18**(5s), 1–21 (2019)
3. Bauer, A., Falcone, Y.: Decentralised LTL monitoring. Formal Meth. Syst. Des. **48**, 46–93 (2016)
4. Chauhan, H., Garg, V.K., Natarajan, A., Mittal, N.: A distributed abstraction algorithm for online predicate detection. In: 2013 IEEE 32nd International Symposium on Reliable Distributed Systems, pp. 101–110. IEEE, Braga, Portugal (2013)
5. Cooper, R., Marzullo, K.: Consistent detection of global predicates. ACM SIGPLAN Not. **26**(12), 167–174 (1991)
6. Garg, V.: Elements of Distributed Computing. Wiley, Hoboken (2002)
7. Garg, V.K.: Predicate detection to solve combinatorial optimization problems. In: Proceedings of the 32nd ACM Symposium on Parallelism in Algorithms and Architectures, pp. 235–245 (2020)
8. Garg, V.K., Mittal, N.: On slicing a distributed computation. In: Proceedings of the 21st International Conference on Distributed Computing Systems (ICDCS 2001), Phoenix, Arizona, USA, 16–19 April 2001, pp. 322–329. IEEE Computer Society (2001). https://doi.org/10.1109/ICDSC.2001.918962

9. Koll, C., Momtaz, A., Bonakdarpour, B., Abbas, H.: Decentralized predicate detection over partially synchronous continuous-time signals. Technical report, Oregon State University (2023). https://www.houssamabbas.com/wp-content/uploads/2023/08/RV_23_DMon-1.pdf
10. Kshemkalyani, A., Singhal, M.: Distributed Computing: Principles, Algorithms, and Systems. Cambridge University Press, Cambridge (2011)
11. Lamport, L.: Time, clocks, and the ordering of events in a distributed system. Commun. ACM **21**(7), 558–565 (1978). https://doi.org/10.1145/359545.359563
12. Mattern, F., et al.: Virtual time and global states of distributed systems. Univ., Department of Computer Science, D 6750 Kaiserslautern, Germany (1989)
13. Mills, D., Martin, J., Burbank, J., Kasch, W.: Network time protocol version 4: Protocol and algorithms specification. Technical report, Internet Engineering Task Force (2010)
14. Momtaz, A., Abbas, H., Bonakdarpour, B.: Monitoring signal temporal logic in distributed cyber-physical systems. In: Proceedings of the ACM/IEEE 14th International Conference on Cyber-Physical Systems (with CPS-IoT Week 2023), pp. 154–165. ICCPS 2023, Association for Computing Machinery, New York, NY, USA (2023). https://doi.org/10.1145/3576841.3585937
15. Momtaz, A., Basnet, N., Abbas, H., Bonakdarpour, B.: Predicate monitoring in distributed cyber-physical systems. In: Feng, L., Fisman, D. (eds.) RV 2021. LNCS, vol. 12974, pp. 3–22. Springer, Cham (2021). https://doi.org/10.1007/978-3-030-88494-9_1
16. Mostafa, M., Bonakdarpour, B.: Decentralized runtime verification of LTL specifications in distributed systems. In: 2015 IEEE International Parallel and Distributed Processing Symposium, pp. 494–503. IEEE (2015)
17. Pant, Y.V., Abbas, H., Mangharam, R.: Smooth operator: control using the smooth robustness of temporal logic. In: 2017 IEEE Conference on Control Technology and Applications (CCTA), pp. 1235–1240. IEEE (2017)
18. Sen, A., Garg, V.K.: Detecting temporal logic predicates in distributed programs using computation slicing. In: Papatriantafilou, M., Hunel, P. (eds.) OPODIS 2003. LNCS, vol. 3144, pp. 171–183. Springer, Heidelberg (2004). https://doi.org/10.1007/978-3-540-27860-3_17
19. Sen, K., Vardhan, A., Agha, G., Rosu, G.: Efficient decentralized monitoring of safety in distributed systems. In: Proceedings. 26th International Conference on Software Engineering, pp. 418–427. IEEE (2004)

Flexible Runtime Security Enforcement with Tagged C

Sean Anderson$^{(\boxtimes)}$ ⓘ, Allison Naaktgeboren ⓘ, and Andrew Tolmach ⓘ

Portland State University, Portland, OR, USA
{ander28,naak,tolmach}@pdx.edu

Abstract. We introduce Tagged C, a novel C variant with built-in tag-based reference monitoring that can be enforced by hardware mechanisms such as the PIPE (Processor Interlocks for Policy Enforcement) processor extension. Tagged C expresses security policies at the level of C source code. It is designed to express a variety of dynamic security policies, individually or in combination, and enforce them with compiler and hardware support. Tagged C supports multiple approaches to security and varying levels of strictness. We demonstrate this range by providing examples of memory safety, compartmentalization, and secure information flow policies. We also give a full formalized semantics and a reference interpreter for Tagged C.

1 Introduction

Many essential technologies rely on new and old C code. Operating systems (Linux, Windows, OSX, BSD), databases (Oracle, sqlite3), the internet (Apache, NGNIX, NetBSD, Cisco IOS), and the embedded devices that run our homes and hospitals are built in and on C. The safety of these technologies depends on the security of their underlying C codebases. Insecurity can arise from C undefined behavior (UB) such as memory errors (e.g. buffer overflows, use-after-free, double-free), logic errors (e.g. SQL injection, input-sanitization flaws), or larger-scale architectural flaws (e.g. over-provisioning access rights).

Although static analyses can detect and mitigate many C insecurities, a last line of defense against undetected or unfixable vulnerabilities is runtime enforcement of *security policies* using a reference monitor [1]. In particular, many useful policies can be specified in terms of flow constraints on *metadata tags*, which augment the underlying data with information like type, provenance, ownership, or security classification. A tag-based policy takes the form of a set of rules that check and update the metadata tags at key points during execution; if a rule violation is encountered, the program *failstops*. Although monitoring based on metadata tags is less flexible and powerful than monitoring based on the underlying data values, it can still enforce many useful security properties, including both low-level concerns such as memory safety and high-level properties such as secure information flow [13] or mandatory access control [20].

Tag-based policies are especially well-suited for efficient hardware enforcement, using processor extensions such as ARM MTE [2], STAR [17], and PIPE.

P. Katsaros and L. Nenzi (Eds.): RV 2023, LNCS 14245, pp. 231–250, 2023.
https://doi.org/10.1007/978-3-031-44267-4_12

PIPE[1] (Processor Interlocks for Policy Enforcement) [4,5], the specific motivator for our work, is a programmable hardware mechanism that supports monitoring at the granularity of individual instructions. Each value in memory and registers is extended with a metadata tag. Before executing each instruction, PIPE checks the opcode and the tags on its operands to see if the operation should be permitted according to a tag rule, and if so, what tags should be assigned to the result. PIPE is highly flexible: it supports arbitrary software-defined tag rules over large (word-sized) tags with arbitrary structure, which enables fine-grained policies and composition of multiple policies. This flexibility is useful because security needs may differ among codebases, and even within a codebase. A conservative, one-size-fits-all policy might be too strong, causing failstops during normal execution. Sensitive code might call for specialized protection.

But PIPE policies can be difficult for a C engineer to write: their tags and rules are defined in terms of individual machine instructions and ISA-level concepts, and in practice they depend on reverse engineering the behavior of specific compilers. Moreover, some security policies can only be expressed in terms of high-level code features that are not preserved at machine level, such as function arguments, structured types, and structured control flow.

To address these problems, we introduce a *source-level* specification framework, *Tagged C*, which allows engineers to describe policies in terms of familiar C-level concepts, with tags attached to C functions, variables and data values, and rules triggered at *control points* that correspond to significant execution events, such as function calls, expression evaluation, and pointer-based memory accesses. Control points resemble "join points" in aspect-oriented programming, but the "advice" in this case can only take the form of manipulating tags, not data. In previous work on the Tagine project [10], we outlined such a framework for a toy source language and showed how high-level policies could be compiled to ISA-level policies and enforced using PIPE-like hardware. Here we extend this approach to handle the full, real C language, by giving a detailed design for the necessary control points and showing how they are integrated into C's dynamic semantics. Although motivated by PIPE, Tagged C is not tied to any particular enforcement mechanism. We currently implement it using a modified C interpreter rather than a compiler. We validate the design of Tagged C by using it to specify a range of interesting security policies, including compartmentalization, memory protection, and secure information flow.

Formally, Tagged C is defined as a variant C semantics that instruments ordinary execution with control points. At each control point, a user-defined set of tag rules is consulted to propagate tags and potentially halt execution. In the limiting case where no tag rules are defined, the semantics is similar to that of ordinary C, except that the memory model is very concrete; data pointers are just integers, and all globals, dynamically-allocated objects, and address-taken objects are allocated in the same integer-addressed memory space. Memory behaviors that would be undefined in standard C are given a definition consistent

---

[1] Variants of PIPE have been called PUMP [15] or SDMP [27] and marketed commercially under the names Dover CoreGuard and Draper Inherently Secure Processor.

with the behavior of a typical compiler. We build the Tagged C semantics on top of the CompCert C semantics, which is formalized as part of the CompCert verified compiler [22,23]. For prototyping and executing example policies, we provide a reference interpreter[2], also based on that of CompCert, written in the Gallina functional language of the Coq Proof Assistant [12]. Tag types and rules are also written directly in Gallina.

The choice of control points and their associations with tag rules, as well as the tag rules' signatures, form the essence of Tagged C's design. We have validated this design on the three classes of policies explored in this paper, and, outside of a few known limitations related to `malloc` (Sect. 4.2), we believe it is sufficiently expressive to describe most other flow-based policies, although further experience is needed to confirm this.

Contributions. In summary, we offer the following contributions:

- The design of a comprehensive set of *control points* at which the C language interfaces with a tag-based policy. These expand on prior work by encompassing the full C language while being powerful enough to enable a range of policies even in the presence of C's more challenging constructs (e.g., `goto`, conditional expressions, etc.).
- Tagged C policies enforcing: (1) compartmentalization, including a novel compartmentalization policy with separate public and private memory; (2) memory safety, with realistic memory models that support varying kinds of low-level idioms; and (3) secure information flow.
- A full formal semantic definition for Tagged C, formalized in Coq, describing how the control points interact with programs, and an interpreter, implemented and verified against the semantics in Coq and extracted to OCaml.

The paper is organized as follows. Section 2 gives a high-level introduction of metadata tagging by example. Section 3 summarizes the Tagged C language as a whole and its control points. Section 4 describes three example policies and how their needs inform our choices of control points. Section 5 describes the Coq-based implementation of Tagged C. Section 6 discusses related work, and Sect. 7 describes future work.

2   Metadata Tags and Policies, by Example

Consider a straightforward security requirement for a program that handles sensitive passkeys: "do not leak passkeys on insecure channels." This is an instance of a broad class of *secure information flow* (SIF) policies. Suppose the code on the left in Fig. 1a is part of such a system, where `psk` is expected to be a passkey and `printi` prints an integer to an insecure channel, so `f` indirectly performs a leak via the local variable `x`. We now explain how a monitor specified in Tagged C could detect such a leak. (Of course, this particular leak could also be easily found using static analysis.)

---

[2] Available at https://github.com/SNoAnd/Tagged-C.

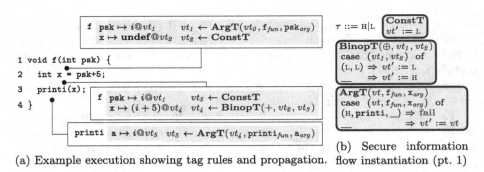

(a) Example execution showing tag rules and propagation.

(b) Secure information flow instantiation (pt. 1)

Fig. 1. Tag Rules and Instantiation (Color figure online)

In Tagged C, all values carry a metadata tag. Whenever execution reaches a control point, it consults an associated tag rule, to check whether the next execution step should be allowed to continue and if so, to update the tags. A policy consists of a tag type definition and instantiations of the tag rules for every control point. For a simple SIF policy like this one, the tag type is an enumeration containing H (high security) and L (low security). In this case, the input psk arrives in f with the tag H. This tag will be propagated along with the value through variable accesses, assignments, and arithmetic, according to generic rules that are not specific to this program. Finally, a program-specific argument-handling rule for printi will check that the tag is L; since it is not, the rule will cause a failstop.

To explain the mechanics of Tagged C, we first show in Fig. 1a the policy-independent framework under which tag rules are triggered in this program: the initial tag on psk (vt_0) passes through the **ArgT** tag rule, is combined with the tag on the constant 5 via the **BinopT** tag rule, and then is passed to **ArgT** again on the call to obtain the tag on the parameter inside printi (here called a). Figure 1a maps three points in the execution of f to descriptions of the corresponding program states, with the input value and all tags treated symbolically. In each state, the first column (white) shows the active function, the second (gray) gives the symbolic values and tags of variables in the local environment, and the third (blue) shows the rules that produce those tags. Throughout the paper, we highlight tag-related metavariables, rules, etc. in blue. We write $v@vt$ for value v tagged with vt. Tags that are derived from identifiers are subscripted with the identifier namespace, e.g. f_{fun} is the tag associated with the function name f. **undef** denotes an uninitialized value.

The SIF policy described informally above is implemented by instantiating the tag rules as shown in Fig. 1b. The resulting behavior is best understood by mentally "weaving" together the two figures. Suppose f is called with an argument value $i@H$. This first invocation of **ArgT** simply passes the H tag on to the output vt_1, because the name of the function being called does not match printi. In tag rules, the assignment operator := denotes an assignment to the

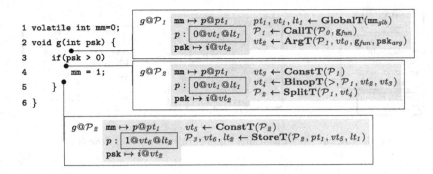

Fig. 2. Second example showing tag rules and tag propagation.

named tag-rule output, by convention written as primed metavariables t'. The initial tag vt_2 on local variable x and the tag vt_3 on the constant 5 come from **ConstT**, which tags all constants as L. The result of the addition on line 2 is tagged by **BinopT** as the higher of the two inputs, so vt_4 is H. Finally, upon entry into printi, **ArgT** is invoked again; this time it failstops. Note that in this policy, **ArgT** is code-specific (it checks for a particular function name printi) whereas the other rules are generic.[3]

As a second example, Fig. 2 steps through the execution of a function g that adds two new wrinkles: we need to keep track of metadata associated with addresses and with the program's control-flow state. We suppose mm is a memory-mapped device register that can be read from outside the program, so we want to avoid storing the passkey there; therefore we need a way to monitor stores to memory. Furthermore, although this code does not leak the passkey directly, it does so indirectly: since the store to mm is conditional on testing psk, an outside observer of mm can deduce one bit of the key (an *implicit flow* [13]).

In addition to tags on values, Tagged C attaches tags to memory locations (*location tags*, ranged over by lt) and tracks a special global tag called the PC tag (ranged over by $\mathcal{P}$, and attached to the function name in our diagrams). Tagged C initializes the tags on mm with the **GlobalT** rule. The PC tag at the point of call, $\mathcal{P}_0$, is fed to **CallT** to determine a new PC tag inside of g. And the if-statement consults the **SplitT** rule to update the PC tag inside of its branch based on the value-tag of the expression psk < 0. Once inside the conditional, when the program assigns to mm, it must consult the **StoreT** rule.

Figure 3 shows an instantiation of these rules that extend our previous SIF policy. The rule for globals initializes the location tag of mm to L, as a low-security output channel, and marks all other addresses H. **CallT** sets the PC tag to L on entry to each function. Whenever execution branches on a high-tagged value, the PC tag will be set to H. We modify the previous rules so that all expressions

---

[3] For simplicity, we omit showing tag rules that play no interesting role in this example: **AccessT** and **AssignT**, which are triggered each time a variable is read and assigned, respectively, and **CallT**, which is triggered by the call itself.

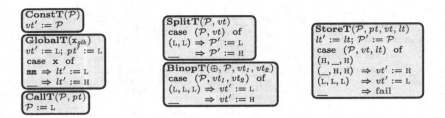

Fig. 3. Tag rule instantiations for secure information flow (pt. 2)

propagate the higher of the PC tag and the relevant value tag(s). This is shown for the updated **BinopT** in Fig. 3; the **ArgT** rule needs a similar adjustment. When an assignment is to a memory location, the store rule will check the tag on that location against the value being written, and failstop if a high value would be written to a low location. For this program, **SplitT** will set the PC tag to H, as it branches on a value derived from psk; then, at the write to mm, **StoreT** will fail rather than write to a low address in a high context.

3   The Tagged C Language: Syntax and Semantics

Tagged C contains almost all features of full ISO C 99.[4] Its semantics is based on that of CompCert C [22], a formalization of the C standard into a small-step reduction semantics. Tagged C's semantics differs from CompCert C's in two key respects: tag support and memory model.

Tags. Tagged C's values and states are annotated with metadata tags, and its reductions contain control points, which are hooks within the operational semantics at which the tag policy is consulted and either tags are updated, or the system failstops. Tagged C relies on a fixed number of predefined control points, which we keep small in order to simplify and organize the task of the policy designer. A control point consists of the name of a *tag rule* and the bindings of its inputs and outputs. For example, consider the expression step reduction for binary operations:

$$\frac{v_1 \langle \oplus \rangle v_2 = v'}{e = Ebinop \ \oplus \ v_1 \ v_2} \qquad \frac{v_1 \langle \oplus \rangle v_2 = v' \quad vt' \leftarrow \mathbf{BinopT}(\oplus, \mathcal{P}, vt_1, vt_2)}{e = Ebinop \ \oplus \ v_1@vt_1 \ v_2@vt_2}$$
$$\frac{}{m, e \Rightarrow_{\mathrm{RH}} m, v'} \qquad \qquad \frac{}{\mathcal{P}, m, te, e \Rightarrow_{\mathrm{RH}} \mathcal{P}, m, te, v'@vt'}$$

On the left, the ordinary "tagless" version of the rule reduces a binary operation on two inputs to a single value. On the right, the Tagged C version adds tags to the operands and tags the result based on the **BinopT** rule.

---

[4] It inherits the limitations of CompCert C, primarily that setjump and longjump may not work, and variable-length arrays are not supported.

Table 1. Full list of tag-rule signatures and control points.

Rule Name	Inputs	Outputs	Control Points
CallT	$\mathcal{P}, pt$	$\mathcal{P}'$	Update PC tag at call
ArgT	$\mathcal{P}, vt, \mathtt{f}_{fun}, \mathtt{x}_{arg}$	$\mathcal{P}', vt'$	Per argument at call
RetT	$\mathcal{P}_{CLE}, \mathcal{P}_{CLR}, vt$	$\mathcal{P}', vt'$	Handle PC tag, return value
LoadT	$\mathcal{P}, pt, vt, lt$	vt'	Memory
StoreT	$\mathcal{P}, pt, vt, lt$	$\mathcal{P}', vt', lt'$	Memory stores
AccessT	$\mathcal{P}, vt$	vt'	Variable accesses
AssignT	$\mathcal{P}, vt_1, vt_2$	$\mathcal{P}', vt'$	Variable assignments
UnopT	$\odot, \mathcal{P}, vt$	vt'	Unary operation
BinopT	$\oplus, \mathcal{P}, vt_1, vt_2$	vt'	Binary operation
ConstT	$\mathcal{P}$	vt'	Applied to constants/literals
InitT	$\mathcal{P}$	vt'	Applied to fresh variables
SplitT	$\mathcal{P}, vt, \mathrm{L}_{lbl}$	$\mathcal{P}'$	Statement control split points
LabelT	$\mathcal{P}, \mathrm{L}_{lbl}$	$\mathcal{P}'$	Labels/arbitrary code points
ExprSplitT	$\mathcal{P}, vt$	$\mathcal{P}'$	Expression control split points
ExprJoinT	$\mathcal{P}, vt$	$\mathcal{P}', vt'$	Join points in expressions
GlobalT	$\mathtt{x}_{glb}, \mathtt{ty}_{typ}$	pt', vt', lt'	Program initialization
LocalT	$\mathcal{P}, \mathtt{ty}_{typ}$	$\mathcal{P}', pt', lt'$	Stack allocation (per local)
DeallocT	$\mathcal{P}, \mathtt{ty}_{typ}$	$\mathcal{P}', vt', lt'$	Stack deallocation (per local)
ExtCallT	$\mathcal{P}, pt, \overline{vt}$	$\mathcal{P}'$	Call to linked code
MallocT	$\mathcal{P}, pt, vt$	$\mathcal{P}', pt', vt', lt'$	Call to `malloc`
FreeT	$\mathcal{P}, pt, vt$	$\mathcal{P}', vt', lt'$	Call to `free`
FieldT	$\mathcal{P}, pt, \mathtt{ty}_{typ}, \mathtt{x}_{glb}$	pt'	Structure/union field access
PICastT	$\mathcal{P}, pt, lt, \mathtt{ty}_{typ}$	vt'	Cast from pointer to scalar
IPCastT	$\mathcal{P}, vt, lt, \mathtt{ty}_{typ}$	pt'	Cast from scalar to pointer
PPCastT	$\mathcal{P}, pt_1, pt_2, lt_1, lt_2, \mathtt{ty}_{typ}$	pt'	Cast between pointers
IICastT	$\mathcal{P}, vt_1, \mathtt{ty}_{typ}$	pt'	Cast between scalars

The tag rule itself is instantiated as a partial function; if a policy leaves a tag rule undefined on some inputs, then those inputs violate the policy, sending execution into a special failstop state. The names and signatures of all the tag rules, and their corresponding control points, are listed in Table 1. In these signatures, we use the metavariable $\mathcal{P}$ to denote the PC tag, pt for tags that will be attached to pointer values, vt for tags that will be attached to values in general, and lt for tags that are associated with specific addresses in memory. We also range over different classes of identifiers with the metavariables: $\mathtt{f}_{fun}$, function identifiers; $\mathtt{x}_{arg}$, function arguments; $\mathtt{x}_{glb}$, global variable names; L_{lbl}, labels; and $\mathtt{ty}_{typ}$, types. We briefly summarize the rules below, and give motivating examples of their use in Sect. 4.

Memory. Unlike CompCert C, Tagged C has no memory-related UB. Comp-Cert C models memory as a collection of disjoint blocks, and treats each variable as having its own block. Pointers are described by a (block, offset) pair, and invalid pointer accesses (out-of-bounds, use after free, etc.) produce UB. Tagged C instead separates variables into public and private data. Public data (all heap data, globals, arrays, structs, and address-taken locals) share a single flat address space (possibly with holes), and pointers are offsets into this space. Pointer accesses outside of this space cause an explicit failstop, rather than UB. Private data (non-address-taken locals, parameters) live in a separate, abstract environment. Program-specified stores, e.g. writes through pointers, can cause arbitrary damage to public data, but do not affect private data. This model is strong enough to support a reasonable notion of semantics-preserving compilation, without making any commitment about fine-grained memory safety, which is intentionally left for explicit tag policies to specify (see Sect. 4.1). In an implementation that compiles to PIPE, the private data can be protected by a small number of "built-in" tags.

Control Points. In our scheme, pure expressions take as arguments the PC tag $\mathcal{P}$ and any operand tags, and produce a tag for the result of the expression (**ConstT** for constants, **UnopT** and **BinopT** for operations, **FieldT** for struct and union fields, and **AccessT** and **LoadT** as described below). Impure expressions additionally produce a new PC tag (**AssignT**, **StoreT**, and **ExprSplitT**).

The distinction between **AccessT** and **LoadT**, and between **AssignT** and **StoreT**, corresponds to private (non-address-taken) and public (allocated in public memory) variables. All reads of variables invoke **AccessT**, and all assignments invoke **AssignT**, so that the behavior of the variable itself is independent of where it is stored. Public variables additionally use the **LoadT** and **StoreT** rules to add restrictions to how variables in memory are accessed.

The **ExprSplitT** tag rule updates the PC tag when an expression branches based on a value; it is paired with **ExprJoinT**, which updates the PC tag again when the branches have rejoined. Similarly, **SplitT** updates the PC during branching statements. The **LabelT** rule can changes the PC tag at any labeled point in execution, and handles join points following branch statements.

CallT and **RetT** update the PC tag on entry and exit from a function. **CallT** is parameterized by the function pointer being called and the PC tag. **RetT** is parameterized by both the caller's PC tag ($\mathcal{P}_{CLR}$) and the callee's ($\mathcal{P}_{CLE}$); it can also update the return value's tag. **ArgT** updates tags on any arguments, based on the function and argument names.

Newly initialized variables are tagged according to the **InitT** rule, as well as **LocalT** if they are public locals; the lt' tag returned by the latter is used to tag the memory occupied by the variable. Similarly, global variables are initialized before runtime based on the **GlobalT** rule. **DeallocT** returns an lt' tag used to re-tags the memory of deallocated locals.

The heap equivalents of **LocalT** and **DeallocT** are **MallocT** and **FreeT**. Again, the lt' tags returned by these functions are used to tag and re-tag the allocated memory. Other library functions have the tags of their results tagged by the **ExtCallT** tag rule.

The cast rules are specialized based on whether the original type or the new type is a pointer, or both, because casts to and from pointers can make use of the location tags at their targets. This enables our PNVI memory safety policy (Sect. 4.1), and more generally policies that keep track of the correspondence between pointers and their targets.

There is always the chance that new policies might arise for which our current set of control points proves to be inadequate. There is no conceptual reason why control points cannot be added or given modified signatures as needed, but extending the interpreter and (eventually) the compiler would be non-trivial. Care needs to be taken in designing control points that are amenable to compilation for PIPE: tag rule evaluation has a complicated interaction with compiler optimization [10], and some potentially useful tag rule signatures (such as updating tags on operation inputs to enforce non-aliasing of pointers) would require the compiler to generate extra instructions to work around limitations of the PIPE hardware.

Combining Policies. Multiple policies can be enforced in parallel. If policy A has tag type τ_A and policy B has τ_B, then policy $A \times B$ should have tag type $\tau = \tau_A \times \tau_B$. Its tag rules should apply the rules of A to the left projection of all inputs and the rules of B to the right projection to generate the components of the new tag. If either side failstops, the entire rule should failstop.

This process can be applied to any number of different policies, allowing, for instance, a combination of a baseline memory safety policy with several more targeted information-flow policies. Alternatively, a policy can delegate to tag rules from other, related policies, as illustrated in Sect. 4.2, below.

4 Example Policies

In this section, we discuss concrete policy implementations and how they motivate Tagged C's control point design. Memory safety policies inform our requirements for memory tags and type casts. Compartmentalization policies depend on the call- and return-related control points, to keep track of the active compartment. Secure information flow policies expose the many places where the user may need to reference identifiers from their program in the policy itself. Taken together, these example policies illustrate Tagged C's breadth of application.

4.1 Memory Safety

Tagged C can be used to enforce memory safety with respect to different *memory models*—formal or informal descriptions of how C should handle memory. Here we discuss the CompCert C memory model and two models proposed by Memarian et al. [24] for the purposes of supporting low-level idioms in the presence of compiler optimization, focusing in particular on how they handle casts from pointers to integers and back.

While the idea of a valid pointer may seem obvious, the precise definition can vary. The C standard does not support arbitrary arithmetic on pointers or their integer casts. In practice, it is common for programs to violate the C standard to various degrees; see Fig. 4. For example, if objects are known to be aligned to 2^n-byte boundaries, the low-order n bits of pointers can be "borrowed" to store other data [25]. The possible presence of these low-level idioms means that there is no one-size-fits all memory safety policy. CompCert C's definition of a valid pointer allows the pointer to be cast into an integer and back, but only if its value does not change in the interim. This is very strict! Programs that use low-level idioms would failstop if run under a policy that enforces this.

Memarian et al.'s first memory model, *provenance via integer* (PVI), treats memory as a flat address space, and pointers as integers with additional provenance information associating them to their objects. Pointers maintain this provenance even through casts to integers and the application of arithmetic operations. When cast back, the pointers will still be associated with the same object. This enables many low-level idioms, while still forbidding memory-safety violations like buffer overflows.

On the other hand, their second model, *provenance not via integer* (PNVI), clears the provenance of a pointer when it is cast to an integer. When an integer is cast to a pointer (whether or not it was previously derived from a pointer), it takes on the provenance of whatever it points to at that time. The security properties of this memory model are questionable, but it is a realistic option for a compiler to choose and can support idioms that PVI cannot.

Implementation. The basic idea for enforcing any of the above memory safety variants is a "lock and key" approach [5,11]. When an object is allocated, it is assigned a unique "color," and its memory locations as well as its pointer are tagged with that color, written CLR(c). The default tag N indicates a non-pointer or non-allocated location. The PC tag will also be CLR(c), tracking the next available color for new allocations. These rules are given in Figs. 5 and 6. Operations that are valid on pointers in a given memory model maintain the pointer's color, and loads and stores are legal if it matches the target memory location tag. (The **assert** command failstops if its argument does not hold.)

The specific memory models (Fig. 6) behave differently when pointers are cast to integers and back. The CompCert C variant marks that the integer has been cast from a valid pointer, and restores that provenance when cast back. But **BinopT** will failstop if the integer is actually modified between the casts. PVI simply keeps the provenance and allows all operations between casts. PNVI accesses the memory pointed to by the cast pointer and takes its location tag.

Memory safety considerations also inform the design of control points related to allocating, deallocating, and accessing memory. Drawing from CompCert C, Tagged C abstracts over "external" functions like **malloc** and **free**, rather than treat their implementation as ordinary code. In a concrete system, these would be replaced by their library equivalents. **ExtCallT** models the desired tag behavior of general external functions in the Tagged C semantics, but **MallocT**($\mathcal{P}, pt, vt$) and **FreeT**($\mathcal{P}, pt, vt$) are special cases because they also need to retag memory; the location tag lt returned by each of them is copied across the allocated region.

```
1 int x[1],y[1];
2 int p = (int) x;
3 int q = (int) y;
4 int r = q | 0x1;
5 *(int *) p = 0;
6 *(int *) (r & 0xfffffffe) = 0;
7 *(int *) (p + (q - p)) = 0;
8 x[1] = 0;
```

$y \mapsto a@pt_1$

$q \mapsto a@vt_1$

$r \mapsto a@vt_3$

$a : \boxed{0@vt_5@lt_2}$

$\mathcal{P}_1, pt_1, lt_1 \leftarrow \mathbf{LocalT}(\mathcal{P}_0, \text{int}_{typ})$

$vt_1 \leftarrow \mathbf{PICastT}(\mathcal{P}_1, pt_1, lt_1, \text{int}_{typ})$

$vt_2 \leftarrow \mathbf{ConstT}(\mathcal{P}_1)$

$vt_3 \leftarrow \mathbf{BinopT}(|, \mathcal{P}_1, vt_1, vt_2)$

$vt_4 \leftarrow \mathbf{BinopT}(\&, \mathcal{P}_1, vt_3, vt_2)$

$pt_2 \leftarrow \mathbf{IPCastT}(\mathcal{P}_1, vt_4, lt_1, \text{int}*_{typ})$

$\mathcal{P}_2, vt_5, lt_2 \leftarrow \mathbf{StoreT}(\mathcal{P}_1, pt_2, vt_2, lt_1)$

Fig. 4. Memory safety and pointer casts, tracing y, q, and r. (Assume **int** and pointers are 32 bits.) Line (5) is always legal, (6) is illegal in CompCert C due to bitwise arithmetic not preserving provenance, (7) is also illegal in PVI due to combining provenance of multiple objects, and (8) is illegal in all models.

$$\tau ::= \text{CLR}(c) \ c \in \mathbb{N}$$
$$| \quad \text{N}$$

LocalT$(\mathcal{P}, ty_{typ})$
let CLR$(c) := \mathcal{P}$ in
$\mathcal{P}' := \text{CLR}(c+1)$
$pt' := \mathcal{P}$
$vt' := \text{N}; \ lt' := \mathcal{P}$

MallocT$(\mathcal{P}, pt, vt)$
let CLR$(c) := \mathcal{P}$ in
$\mathcal{P}' := \text{CLR}(c+1)$
$pt' := \mathcal{P}$
$vt' := \text{N}; \ lt' := \mathcal{P}$

LoadT$(\mathcal{P}, pt, vt, lt)$
assert $pt = lt$
$vt' := vt$

StoreT$(\mathcal{P}, pt, vt, lt)$
assert $pt = lt$
$\mathcal{P}' := \mathcal{P}; \ vt' := vt; \ lt' := lt$

Fig. 5. Generic Memory Safety Rules

Temporal Memory Safety. The tag rules described so far only enforce spatial memory safety, but Tagged C can also enforce temporal safety. A full memory safety policy prevents use-after-free and double-free errors by either retagging a deallocated region, or using the PC tag to track the set of live objects and revoking permissions on an object as soon as it is freed.

4.2 Compartmentalization

In principle, the monitoring techniques in the previous section could be used to detect all unintended memory safety violations (albeit only at run time) and ultimately to fix them. But in reality, the cost and risk of regressions may make it undesirable to fix bugs in older code [7]. A compartmentalization policy can isolate potentially risky code, such as code with unfixed (or intentional) UB, from safety-critical code, and enforce the *principle of least privilege*. Even in the absence of language-level errors, compartmentalization can usefully restrict how code in one compartment may interact with another. External libraries are effectively required for most software to function yet represent a supply-chain threat; isolating them prevents vulnerabilities in the library from compromising critical code, and limits the tools available to attackers in the event of a compromise.

Assume we have been given a compartmentalization policy, with at least two compartments, to add to the system after development. The compartments and what belongs in them are represented in the policy by a set of compartment identifiers, ranged over by C, and a map from function and global identifiers to compartments, written as $comp(id)$.

PICastT($\mathcal{P}, pt, lt, \text{ty}_{typ}$)
case pt of
CLR(c) $\Rightarrow$ $vt' := CAST(\text{CLR}(c))$
___ $\Rightarrow$ $vt' := pt$

IPCastT($\mathcal{P}, vt, lt, \text{ty}_{typ}$)
case vt of
$CAST(\text{CLR}(c)) \Rightarrow pt' := \text{CLR}(c)$
___ $\Rightarrow vt' := pt$

$\tau ::= \ldots \mid CAST(\text{CLR}(c))$

BinopT($\oplus, \mathcal{P}, vt_1, vt_2$)
case $(\oplus, vt_1, vt_2)$ of
$(+, \text{CLR}(c), \text{N})$
$(+, \text{N}, \text{CLR}(c))$ $\Rightarrow vt' := \text{CLR}(c)$
$(\_, \text{N}, \text{N})$
$(-, \text{CLR}(c), \text{CLR}(c)) \Rightarrow vt' := \text{N}$
___ $\Rightarrow$ fail

(a) CompCert C Rules

IPCastT($\mathcal{P}, vt, lt, \text{ty}_{typ}$)
$pt' := vt$

PICastT($\mathcal{P}, pt, lt, \text{ty}_{typ}$)
$vt' := pt$

BinopT($\oplus, \mathcal{P}, vt_1, vt_2$)
case (vt_1, vt_2) of
$(\text{CLR}(c), \text{N})$
$(\text{N}, \text{CLR}(c))$ $\Rightarrow vt' := \text{CLR}(c)$
(N, N)
$(\text{CLR}(c_1), \text{CLR}(c_2)) \Rightarrow vt' := \text{N}$

(b) PVI Rules

IPCastT($\mathcal{P}, vt, lt, \text{ty}_{typ}$)
$pt' := lt$

PICastT($\mathcal{P}, pt, lt, \text{ty}_{typ}$)
$vt' := \text{N}$

BinopT($\oplus, \mathcal{P}, vt_1, vt_2$)
case $(\oplus, vt_1, vt_2)$ of
$(+, \text{CLR}(c), \text{N})$
$(+, \text{N}, \text{CLR}(c))$ $\Rightarrow vt' := \text{CLR}(c)$
$(\_, \text{N}, \text{N})$
$(-, \text{CLR}(c), \text{CLR}(c)) \Rightarrow vt' := \text{N}$
___ $\Rightarrow$ fail

(c) PNVI Rules

Fig. 6. Specialized Memory Safety Rules

$\tau ::= C \mid \text{N}$

CallT($\mathcal{P}, pt$)
$\mathcal{P}' := comp(pt)$

RetT($\mathcal{P}_{CLE}, \mathcal{P}_{CLR}, vt$)
$\mathcal{P}' := \mathcal{P}_{CLR}; vt' := vt$

MallocT($\mathcal{P}, pt, vt$)
$\mathcal{P}' := \mathcal{P}; pt' := \text{N};$
$vt' := \text{N}; lt' := \mathcal{P}$

LocalT($\mathcal{P}, \text{ty}_{typ}$)
$\mathcal{P}' := \mathcal{P}; pt' := \text{N};$
$vt' := \text{N}; lt' := \mathcal{P}$

LoadT($\mathcal{P}, pt, vt, lt$)
assert $\mathcal{P} = lt$
$vt' := vt$

StoreT($\mathcal{P}, pt, vt, lt$)
assert $\mathcal{P} = lt$
$\mathcal{P}' := \mathcal{P}; vt' := \text{N}; lt' := lt$

Fig. 7. Simple Compartmentalization Policy

Implementation. Compartmentalization requires the policy to keep track of the active compartment, which means keeping track of function pointers. In Tagged C, function pointers are the exception to the concrete memory model. They carry symbolic values that refer uniquely to their target functions. If f is located at the symbolic address α, then the expression &f evaluates to $\alpha@\text{f}_{fun}$. When the function pointer is called, Tagged C invokes **CallT**($\mathcal{P}, pt$), where pt is the function pointer's tag, to update the PC tag. On return, in addition to handling the return value (if any), **RetT**($\mathcal{P}_{CLE}, \mathcal{P}_{CLR}, vt$) determines a new PC tag based on the one before the call ($\mathcal{P}_{CLR}$) and the one at the time of return ($\mathcal{P}_{CLE}$). In our compartmentalization policy (Fig. 7), we define a tag to be a compartment identifier or the default N tag. The PC tag always carries the compartment of the active function, kept up to date by the **CallT** and **RetT** rules.

Once the policy knows which compartment is active, it must ensure that compartments do not interfere with one another's memory. A simple means of doing so is given in Fig. 7: any object allocated by a given compartment, whether on the stack or via malloc, is tagged with that compartment's identity, and can only be accessed while that compartment is active. This is very limiting,

$$\tau ::= \text{N} \mid C \mid \text{CLR}(c) \mid (C, \text{CLR}(c))$$

StoreT$(\mathcal{P}, pt, vt, lt)$
let $(C, \text{CLR}(c)) := \mathcal{P}$ in
case lt of
$C' \Rightarrow$ **StoreT**$_C(C, \text{N}, vt, C')$
$\_\_ \Rightarrow$ **StoreT**$_{MS}(\text{CLR}(c), pt, vt, lt)$

MallocT$(\mathcal{P}, pt, vt)$
let $(C, \text{CLR}(c)) := \mathcal{P}$ in
case pt of
malloc_{fun} $\Rightarrow$ **MallocT**$_C(C, pt, vt)$
$\text{malloc\_share}_{fun} \Rightarrow$
   $\text{CLR}(c'), pt', vt', lt' \leftarrow$ **MallocT**$_{MS}(\text{CLR}(c), pt, vt)$
   $\mathcal{P}' := (C, \text{CLR}(c')); pt' := pt'$
   $vt' := vt'; lt' := lt'$

Fig. 8. Selected rules for Compartmentalization with Shared Capabilities, combining Compartmentalization rules (subscript C, Fig. 7) with Memory Safety rules (subscript MS, Fig. 5)

however! In practice, compartments need to be able to share memory, such as in the common case where libraries have separate compartments from application code. One solution is to allow compartments to share selected objects by passing their pointers, treating them as *capabilities*—unforgeable tokens of privilege.

Distinguishing shareable memory from memory that is local to a compartment is difficult without modifying source code. In order to be minimally intrusive, we create a variant identifier for `malloc`, `malloc_share`, which maps to the same address (i.e., it still calls the same function) but has a different name tag and can therefore be used to specialize the tag rule. An engineer might manually select which allocations are shareable, or perhaps rely on some form of escape analysis to detect shareable allocations automatically.

The policy in Fig. 8 essentially combines the simple compartmentalization policy and a memory safety policy. The PC tag carries both the current compartment color, for tagging unshared allocations, and the next free color, for tagging shared allocations. **MallocT** applies a color tag to shareable allocations, and N to local ones. During loads and stores, the location tag of the target address determines which parent property applies.

Compartmentalization Variants. Using program-specific tags for globals and functions, a policy like the one above can be extended with a Mandatory Access Control (MAC) policy [20]. Here, a table explicitly identifies which compartments may call one another's functions, which global variables they can access, and with which other compartments they can share memory.

Malloc Limitations. The way Tagged C currently handles `malloc` is unsatisfactory. First, as noted above, there is no easy way to distinguish different static `malloc` call locations; our use of variant names is something of a hack. A more principled solution might draw on pointcuts to identify specific calls to `malloc`. Further, `malloc` does not get access to type information; it takes just a size and returns a `void *`, which the caller must cast to a pointer of the desired type (at an arbitrary future point). Therefore, Tagged C cannot easily enforce substructural memory safety (i.e. protecting fields within a single struct from overflowing into each other) or other properties that call for allocated regions to be tagged

```
1 void h(int id, int psk) {
2    int fmt = check_format(psk);
3    switch(fmt) {
4      case OLD:
5        psk = update(id, psk); break;
6      case INVALID:
7        psk = 0; break;
8      case DEFAULT:
9    }
10 J: printf("Updating user %d", id); // join point
11   update(id, psk);
12 }
```

$$\text{h@}\mathcal{P}_1 \quad \text{fmt@}vt_1$$

$$\text{h@}\mathcal{P}_2 \quad \mathcal{P}_2 \leftarrow \text{SplitT}(\mathcal{P}_1, vt_1)$$

$$\text{h@}\mathcal{P}_3 \quad \mathcal{P}_3 \leftarrow \text{LabelT}(\mathcal{P}_2, J_{lbl})$$

Fig. 9. Not an Implicit Flow

according to their types. This is a well-known impediment to improving C memory safety; previous work (e.g. [26]) has often adopted non-standard versions of malloc that take more informative parameters. This is not satisfactory for protecting legacy code, but we do not yet see a good alternative.

4.3   Secure Information Flow

Finally, we return to the family of *secure information flow* (SIF) [14] policies introduced in Sect. 2. SIF deals with enforcing higher-level security concerns, so it useful even in code with no language-level errors.

In Fig. 9, the program checks the format of the passkey psk, which is tagged H, and uses a switch statement to perform operations on it based on the result. As in Fig. 2, this means that the policy should "raise" the PC tag to H to indicated that the program's control-flow depends on psk. But after control reaches label J, the PC tag can be lowered again, because code execution from this point on no longer depends on psk. J is a *join point*: the point in a control-flow graph where all possible routes from the split to a return have re-converged, which can be identified statically as the immediate post-dominator of the split point [14].

In order to support policies that reason about splits and joins, we introduce the **SplitT** and **LabelT** tag rules. Every transition that tests a value as part of a conditional or loop contains a control point that invokes **SplitT**, passing the label for the corresponding joint point. (This label argument is optional, both because some policies may not care about join points.) This way, the policy can react when execution reaches that label via the **LabelT** rule.

In the full SIF policy, we keep track of the pending join points within the PC tag, and lower the PC tag when execution reaches the join point. (A similar approach applies to conditional expressions, but we omit the details here.) In addition to L and H, the SIF policy tracks a PC tag written using the constructor

$$\tau ::= \text{H} \mid \text{L} \mid \text{PC } lbls$$

$$|t| \triangleq \begin{cases} \text{L} & \text{if } t = \text{L or } t = \text{PC } \mathtt{f}_{fun}\emptyset \\ \text{H} & \text{otherwise} \end{cases}$$

$$t_1 \sqcup t_2 \triangleq \begin{cases} \text{L} & \text{if } |t_1| = |t_2| = \text{L} \\ \text{H} & \text{otherwise} \end{cases}$$

$$\mathbf{SplitT}(\mathcal{P}, vt, L_{lbl})$$
$$\text{case } \mathcal{P}, vt \text{ of}$$
$$\text{PC } \mathtt{f}_{fun}\, lbls, \text{H} \Rightarrow$$
$$\quad \mathcal{P}' := \text{PC } \mathtt{f}_{fun}(lbls \cup \mathrm{L}_{lbl})$$
$$\quad \_, \text{L} \qquad \Rightarrow \mathcal{P}' := \mathcal{P}$$

$$\mathbf{LabelT}(\mathcal{P}, \mathrm{L}_{lbl})$$
$$\text{let PC } \mathtt{f}_{fun}\, lbls := \mathcal{P} \text{ in}$$
$$\mathcal{P}' := \text{PC } \mathtt{f}_{fun}(lbls - \mathrm{L}_{lbl})$$

Fig. 10. SIF Conditionals

PC, which carries a set of label identifiers to record the join points of tainted statement scopes. Initially, the PC tag is PC $\mathtt{f}_{fun}\emptyset$, which corresponds to "low" security. The join operator, $\cdot \sqcup \cdot$, takes the higher of its arguments after reducing a PC tag into either H or L (Fig. 10).

In order to use this version of SIF, the program must undergo a minor automatic transformation by the compiler or interpreter, introducing explicit labels at all join points that don't already have one. In the example, J becomes an explicit label in the code. The internal syntactic form of each conditional statement (if, switch, while, do-while, and for) carries this label (optionally, since there might not be a join point if all arms of the conditional execute an explicit return). If the conditional branches on a high value, **SplitT** adds the label to the set in the PC tag. Later, when execution reaches a label, **LabelT** deletes it from the set. If the set is non-empty, there is at least one high split point that has not yet reached its join point, so we treat the PC tag as high. When execution reaches the last join point and the set is empty, the PC tag is treated as low, because it is no longer possible to deduce which path was taken.

SIF Variants. SIF can cover many different policies. We have shown an instance of a confidentiality policy, but SIF can also support integrity ("insecure inputs do not affect secure data"), intransive policies ("data can flow from A to B and B to C, but not from A to C"), and policies with more than two security levels.

To give a couple of more realistic examples, an intransitive integrity policy can be used to protect against SQL injections by requiring unsafe inputs to pass through a sanitizer before they can be appended to a query. Similarly, a more complex SIF policy could ensure that data at rest is always encrypted, by setting a low security level to the outputs of an encryption routine and a high level to the outputs of its corresponding decryption routine.

5 Implementation

Our current Coq-based implementation of Tagged C consists of a formal semantics and a matching interpreter written in Coq's Gallina language (similar to functional languages such as OCaml or Haskell). These are based on the Csem and Cexec modules from the CompCert compiler (version 3.10) [21]. The interpreter can be extracted to a stand-alone OCaml program that can then be further compiled to machine code.

To adapt CompCert, we replace the standard block-offset memory with a concrete one, leaving the block-based system to handle only function pointers. We rework global environments to separate (symbolic) function pointers from other (concrete) pointers. We also add a temporary environment to contain non-memory variables, and semantic rules to deal with them. Most importantly, we thread the PC tag into the state, and add control points to the relevant semantic rules. These changes appear in both the semantics and the corresponding interpreter code. To extend the existing CompCert proof that the interpreter is correct with respect to the semantics requires updating the proof automation to handle concrete memory and tags.

The semantics and interpreter are parameterized by a Coq module type `Policy`, which specifies the type signatures of the tag rules. A policy is written directly in Gallina as a module that instantiates `Policy` by defining the type of tags and the body of each tag rule. A full policy fits into 70 lines of Gallina. To illustrate, Fig. 11 shows fragments of the `Policy` signature, its instantiation in the PVI memory safety policy, and its use in the Coq semantics.

PIPE, Tag Sizes, and Policy States. Ultimately, we wish to compile Tagged C to run efficiently on PIPE-equipped hardware, which raises some issues that are not currently visible at the level of the Coq interpreter. For example, the Coq model of Tagged C allows unbounded tags. In reality, PIPE tags are large, but bounded. This means that, for instance, the naïve implementation of PVI memory safety described here runs the risk of overflowing the number of possible colors. Enforcement of temporal safety will not be feasible in long-running programs that regularly allocate memory, even if their total memory footprint is bounded, unless the policy can reclaim the tags on previously freed objects.

Also, the Coq model assumes that all tag rules are pure functions of the tag inputs; any state carried by the policy must be encoded in the PC tag. In practice, PIPE allows tag rules to be implemented by arbitrary code, which can persist private state (separate from the application being monitored) over multiple rule invocations; this approach may support more efficient policy designs.

6   Related Work

Like many monitoring systems, Tagged C can be seen as a species of aspect-oriented programming (AOP) [19]. An AOP language distributes *join points*[5] throughout its semantics, and the programmer separately writes *advice* in the form of additional code that should execute before or after various join points according to a *pointcut* specification. The compiler or runtime *weaves* the advice together with the main code. Our control points are a kind of join point, and our tag rules combine the roles of pointcuts and advice; weaving is done at runtime according to the tagged semantics. Unlike advice in most AOP systems, our tag rules are constrained to inspect only tags, not arbitrary parts of program state, which limits their expressiveness. Also, tag rules are evaluated separately from

---

[5] Not to be confused with the control-flow graph join points discussed in Sect. 4.3.

```
Module Type Policy.
    Parameter tag : Type.                    Inductive PolResult (A: Type) :=
    Parameter def_tag : tag.                 | PolSuccess (res: A)
    Parameter InitPCT : tag.                 | PolFail (r: string)
    Parameter BinopT : binary_operation -> tag -> tag -> tag -> PolResult (tag * tag).
    Parameter LoadT : tag -> tag -> tag -> list tag -> PolResult tag.
    ...
Module PVI:Policy.
    Inductive tag :=                         Definition def_tag := N.
    | N.                                     Definition InitPCT := Dyn 0.
    | Dyn (c:nat).

    Definition BinopT op pct vt1 vt2 :=      Definition LoadT pct pt vt lts :=
      match vt1, vt2 with                      match pt with
      | Dyn c, N => PolSuccess (pct, Dyn c)    | N => PolFail "PVI::LoadT N"
      | N, Dyn c => PolSuccess (pct, Dyn c)    | _ => if forallb (=? pt) lts
      | N, N => PolSuccess (pct, N)                 then PolSuccess vt
      | Dyn c1, Dyn c2 => PolSuccess (pct, N)       else PolFail "PVI::LoadT Ptr"
      end.                                     end.
    ...
Module Csem (Import P: Policy).

    Inductive rred (PCT:tag) : expr -> mem -> trace -> tag -> expr -> mem -> Prop :=
    | red_binop: forall op v1 vt1 ty1 v2 vt2 ty2 ty m v vt' PCT',
      sem_binary_operation (snd ge) op v1 ty1 v2 ty2 m = Some v ->
      PolSuccess (PCT', vt') = BinopT op PCT vt1 vt2 ->
      rred PCT (Ebinop op (Eval (v1,vt1) ty1) (Eval (v2,vt2) ty2) ty) m E0
      PCT' (Eval (v,vt') ty) m
    | red_rvalof: forall ofs pt lts bf ty m tr v vt vt',
      deref_loc ty m ofs pt bf tr (v,vt) lts ->
      PolSuccess vt' = LoadT PCT pt vt lts -> PolSuccess vt'' = AccessT PCT vt'
      rred PCT (Evalof (Eloc ofs pt bf ty) ty) m tr PCT (Eval (v,vt'') ty) m
    | ...
    ...
```

Fig. 11. Fragments of Coq implementation.

the system being monitored and so cannot be used to "correct" bad behavior; all they can do is cause a failstop. These limitations follow from our goal of implementing Tagged C using efficient PIPE hardware.

Many AOP-like systems for C runtime verification treat join points as events in a trace, and specify valid traces using a formalism such as state machines (e.g. RMOR [18] and SLIC [6]) or temporal logics (e.g. [9]). Trace checking of this kind can be implemented on top of Tagged C, as long as events do not rely on values. Events are typically coarse-grained (e.g. function entries and exits), although some systems (e.g. [16]) support very general forms of event definition based on matching syntactic patterns in code. Tagged C is unusual in that it supports very low-level and fine-grained events (e.g. individual arithmetic operations and casts) and because a monitoring action (perhaps a no-op) is specified for every potential event point.

Numerous systems have targeted information flow, memory safety, and compartmentalization in C; we can discuss just a few here. Cassel et al.'s FlowNotations [8] use type annotations to specify "tainted" and "trusted" data, and statically check a program's information flow using the C type system. Their annotation system elegantly connects the C syntax to their enforcement mechanism, and would make a good annotation scheme for a Tagged-C SIF policy, with "tainted" and "trusted" types being transformed into variable-specific tags. Unlike their static approach, our enforcement is dynamic, meaning that it sacrifices flow-sensitivity for permissiveness [28]. Dynamic systems also exist, such as Faceted Information Flow [3], which takes advantage of concurrency to simulate multiple simultaneous runs and check directly for leaked data. Faceted IFC has not been applied at the C level, and for our use cases, would suffer from the overhead of running multiple executions simultaneously.

The CHERI hardware capability system has been used by Tsampas et al. for compartmentalization [29], and by Filardo et al. for temporal memory safety [30]. Like PIPE, CHERI can support a range of security policies, although it is ill-suited for information-flow-style policies. Despite this, it would be worth exploring whether a useful subset of Tagged C's control points could be implemented by a CHERI backend.

7   Conclusion and Future Work

We have introduced a C variant that provides a general mechanism to describe security policies, exemplified by memory safety, compartmentalization, and secure-information-flow policies. Each category of policy can be applied flexibly to meet the security needs of a particular program. From this proof of concept, we can see several natural extensions to make Tagged C more practical to use.

An interpreter is useful for testing policies, but our main goal has always been to produce a compiler from Tagged C to machine code for a PIPE-equipped processor. The basic strategy for compilation was outlined in the Tagine project [10]. We are currently working to extend the CompCert compiler to handle Tagged C, with the ultimate goal of also extending CompCert's semantics preservation guarantees to cover tagged semantics. Policies are also written in Gallina, the language embedded in Coq [12]. This is fine for a proof-of-concept, but not satisfactory for real use by software engineers. We plan to develop a domain-specific policy language to make it easier to write Tagged C policies.

One reason for prototyping Tagged C in the Coq Proof Assistant is to lay the groundwork for formal proofs of its properties. We have not yet proven the correctness of our example policies. For each family of policies that we discuss, we aim to give a higher-level formal specification (e.g., a non-interference property for SIF) and prove that it holds on all programs run under that property.

Acknowledgements. We thank the reviewers for their valuable feedback, and Roberto Blanco for his advice during the writing process. This work was supported by the National Science Foundation under Grant No. 2048499, Specifying and Verifying Secure Compilation of C Code to Tagged Hardware.

References

1. Anderson, J.P.: Computer security technology planning study. Technical report ESD-TR-73-51, U.S. Air Force Electronic Systems Division (1972). http://csrc.nist.gov/publications/history/ande72.pdf

2. Armv8.5-a memory tagging extension white paper. https://developer.arm.com/-/media/Arm%20Developer%20Community/PDF/Arm_Memory_Tagging_Extension_Whitepaper.pdf

3. Austin, T.H., Flanagan, C.: Multiple facets for dynamic information flow. In: Proceedings of the 39th Annual ACM SIGPLAN-SIGACT Symposium on Principles of Programming Languages, POPL 2012, pp. 165–178. Association for Computing Machinery (2012). https://doi.org/10.1145/2103656.2103677

4. Azevedo de Amorim, A., et al.: A verified information-flow architecture. J. Comput. Secur. **24**(6), 689–734 (2016). https://doi.org/10.3233/JCS-15784

5. Azevedo de Amorim, A., et al.: Micro-policies: formally verified, tag-based security monitors. In: 2015 IEEE Symposium on Security and Privacy, pp. 813–830 (2015). https://doi.org/10.1109/SP.2015.55

6. Ball, T., Rajamani, S.: SLIC: a specification language for interface checking (of C). Technical report MSR-TR-2001-21 (2002). https://www.microsoft.com/en-us/research/publication/slic-a-specification-language-for-interface-checking-of-c/

7. Bessey, A., et al.: A few billion lines of code later: using static analysis to find bugs in the real world. Commun. ACM **53**(2), 66–75 (2010). https://doi.org/10.1145/1646353.1646374

8. Cassel, D., Huang, Y., Jia, L.: Uncovering information flow policy violations in C programs (extended abstract). In: Sako, K., Schneider, S., Ryan, P.Y.A. (eds.) ESORICS 2019. LNCS, vol. 11736, pp. 26–46. Springer, Cham (2019). https://doi.org/10.1007/978-3-030-29962-0_2

9. Chabot, M., Mazet, K., Pierre, L.: Automatic and configurable instrumentation of C programs with temporal assertion checkers. In: 2015 ACM/IEEE International Conference on Formal Methods and Models for Codesign (MEMOCODE), pp. 208–217 (2015). https://doi.org/10.1109/MEMCOD.2015.7340488

10. Chhak, C., Tolmach, A., Anderson, S.: Towards formally verified compilation of tag-based policy enforcement. In: Proceedings of the 10th ACM SIGPLAN International Conference on Certified Programs and Proofs, pp. 137–151 (2021). https://doi.org/10.1145/3437992.3439929

11. Clause, J., Doudalis, I., Orso, A., Prvulovic, M.: Effective memory protection using dynamic tainting. In: Proceedings of the 22nd IEEE/ACM International Conference on Automated Software Engineering, pp. 284–292 (2007). https://doi.org/10.1145/1321631.1321673

12. Coq Team: The Coq proof assistant. https://coq.inria.fr

13. Denning, D.E.: A lattice model of secure information flow. Commun. ACM **19**(5), 236–243 (1976). https://doi.org/10.1145/360051.360056

14. Denning, D.E., Denning, P.J.: Certification of programs for secure information flow. Commun. ACM **20**(7), 504–513 (1977). https://doi.org/10.1145/359636.359712

15. Dhawan, U., et al.: Architectural support for software-defined metadata processing. In: Proceedings of the Twentieth International Conference on Architectural Support for Programming Languages and Operating Systems, pp. 487–502 (2015). https://doi.org/10.1145/2694344.2694383

16. Engler, D.R., Chelf, B., Chou, A., Hallem, S.: Checking system rules using system-specific, programmer-written compiler extensions. In: OSDI, pp. 1–16 (2000)

17. Gollapudi, R., et al.: Control flow and pointer integrity enforcement in a secure tagged architecture. In: 2023 IEEE Symposium on Security and Privacy (SP), pp. 2974–2989 (2023). https://doi.ieeecomputersociety.org/10.1109/SP46215.2023.00102

18. Havelund, K.: Runtime verification of C programs. In: Suzuki, K., Higashino, T., Ulrich, A., Hasegawa, T. (eds.) FATES/TestCom -2008. LNCS, vol. 5047, pp. 7–22. Springer, Heidelberg (2008). https://doi.org/10.1007/978-3-540-68524-1_3
19. Kiczales, G., et al.: Aspect-oriented programming. In: Akşit, M., Matsuoka, S. (eds.) ECOOP 1997. LNCS, vol. 1241, pp. 220–242. Springer, Heidelberg (1997). https://doi.org/10.1007/BFb0053381
20. Lampson, B.W.: Protection. SIGOPS Oper. Syst. Rev. 8(1), 18–24 (1974). https://doi.org/10.1145/775265.775268
21. Leroy, X.: Compcert 3.10. https://github.com/AbsInt/CompCert/releases/tag/v3.10
22. Leroy, X.: Formal verification of a realistic compiler. Commun. ACM 52(7), 107–115 (2009). https://doi.org/10.1145/1538788.1538814
23. Leroy, X.: A formally verified compiler back-end. J. Autom. Reason. 43(4), 363–446 (2009). https://doi.org/10.1007/s10817-009-9155-4
24. Memarian, K., et al.: Exploring C semantics and pointer provenance. Proc. ACM Program. Lang. 3(POPL), 1–32 (2019). https://doi.org/10.1145/3290380
25. Memarian, K., et al.: Into the depths of C: elaborating the de facto standards. SIGPLAN Not. 51(6), 1–15 (2016). https://doi.org/10.1145/2980983.2908081
26. Michael, A.E., et al.: MSWasm: soundly enforcing memory-safe execution of unsafe code. Proc. ACM Program. Lang. 7(POPL), 425–454 (2023). https://doi.org/10.1145/3571208
27. Roessler, N., DeHon, A.: Protecting the stack with metadata policies and tagged hardware. In: Proceedings of the 2018 IEEE Symposium on Security and Privacy, SP 2018, pp. 478–495 (2018). https://doi.org/10.1109/SP.2018.00066
28. Russo, A., Sabelfeld, A.: Dynamic vs. static flow-sensitive security analysis. In: 2010 23rd IEEE Computer Security Foundations Symposium, pp. 186–199 (2010). https://doi.org/10.1109/CSF.2010.20
29. Tsampas, S., El-Korashy, A., Patrignani, M., Devriese, D., Garg, D., Piessens, F.: Towards automatic compartmentalization of C programs on capability machines (2017). https://api.semanticscholar.org/CorpusID:32838507
30. Filardo, N.W., et al.: Cornucopia: temporal safety for CHERI heaps. In: 2020 IEEE Symposium on Security and Privacy (SP), pp. 608–625 (2020). https://doi.org/10.1109/SP40000.2020.00098

Pattern Matching for Perception Streams

Jacob Anderson$^{(\boxtimes)}$ ⓘ, Georgios Fainekos ⓘ, Bardh Hoxha ⓘ,
Hideki Okamoto ⓘ, and Danil Prokhorov ⓘ

Toyota Motor North America, Research and Development, Ann Arbor, MI, USA
{jacob.anderson,georgios.fainekos,bardh.hoxha,hideki.okamoto,
danil.prokhorov}@toyota.com

Abstract. We introduce Spatial Regular Expressions (SpREs) as a novel querying language for pattern matching over perception streams containing spatial and temporal data. To highlight the capabilities of SpREs, we developed the STREM tool as a matching framework that works in both the offline and online domain. We demonstrate the tool through an offline example with an AV dataset, an online example through an integration with the ROS and CARLA simulators, and an initial set of performance benchmarks on various SpRE queries. From our designed matching framework, we are able to find over 20,000 matches within 296 ms making it highly usable in runtime monitoring applications.

Keywords: Pattern matching · Regular expressions · Spatial logic · Computer vision · Runtime monitoring

1 Introduction

Perception systems are utilized across a wide range of applications—from Autonomous Vehicles (AVs) [20, 29, 43], to sports media analysis [35, 40], to Closed-Circuit Televisions (CCTVs) [36], and more [14, 21, 27, 37]. These systems may be composed of various sensor and sensor fusion technologies such as Light Detecting and Radar (LiDAR), radar, cameras, etc. to support complex Computer Vision (CV) tasks in both the *offline* and *online* domain that generate and require a significant amount of data to effectively operate [5]. To improve upon these perception systems and further Machine Learning (ML) activities, large datasets are released for CV tasks in hopes of providing more exposure to these systems before deployment [13, 26]. These perception-based datasets are further extended to Autonomous Driving System (ADS) applications where the perception system consists of a suite of sensors. Examples of such datasets include the popular Waymo Open [34], Woven Planet ("L5") Perception [22], and NuScenes [9] along with several others [30, 39, 42]. Therefore, as these perception systems become more comprehensive, methods and tools that enable querying of such stream data for specific scenarios in *testing*, *training*, and *monitoring* become increasingly important.

For a given perception stream, however, filtering and searching for scenarios of interest is not well-supported nor a ubiquitous process as the size of

P. Katsaros and L. Nenzi (Eds.): RV 2023, LNCS 14245, pp. 251–270, 2023.
https://doi.org/10.1007/978-3-031-44267-4_13

data, selected schema, and present sensor suite varies. Within the offline setting, perception streams produced by AV companies provide minimal frameworks to interface and filter data according to a pre-defined schema. As for the online setting, perception systems streaming data in real-time are not traditionally responsible for identifying scenarios. Therefore, this work aims to address the problem of querying complex and dynamic perception streams comprised of spatially- and temporally-aligned data offline and online.

In the work presented in this paper, we introduce Spatial Regular Expressions (SpREs): a novel querying language for efficient and flexible matching of perception streams. SpREs combine Regular Expressions (REs) [1] with the modal logic of topology $\mathcal{S}4_u$ [25]. The language is designed with ease-of-use in mind by following syntactic similarities of classic RE tools such as *grep* and *egrep* [16] while enabling reasoning over topological relations. The querying language has been implemented in the Spatio-Temporal Regular Expression Matcher (STREM) tool to support offline and online searching capabilities. The SpRE queries can be efficiently solved due to the reduction of the pattern matching problem to the one for REs, which in turn allows us to utilize well-established libraries [18] for fast processing. Furthermore, its modular design and compatibility with Linux, Bash, and any Command Line Interface (CLI) tools make the system more versatile and extendable for use in *verification* and *validation* process pipelines. Our formulation of the SpRE language (Sect. 3) is also general enough to utilize other branches of logic without major restructuring.

Contributions. From this work, the set of contributions are as follows:

- The RE $\times \mathcal{S}4_u$ querying language (and associated semantics) for pattern matching spatio-temporal sequences of events in perception streams.
- The STREM tool for offline and online pattern matching of perception streams with the novel querying language.
- An offline demonstration of the STREM tool using the Woven Planet ("L5") Perception AV dataset.
- An online demonstration of STREM through integration with the Robot Operating System (ROS) and Car Learning to Act (CARLA) simulator stack.

2   Preliminaries

We let $\mathbb{Z}$ be the set of all integers, $\mathbb{N}$, $\mathbb{N}_0$ be the set of natural numbers with and without 0, and $\mathbb{R}$ be the set of real numbers. Furthermore, $\mathbb{B}$ represents the set of booleans $\{\top, \bot\}$ where true and false are the boolean constants true and false, respectively. Furthermore, given a set A, $\mathcal{P}(A)$ denotes the powerset of A, and $|A|$ represents the cardinality of A.

2.1   Perception Stream

We consider a perception stream $\mathcal{S} = \mathcal{F}_0, \mathcal{F}_1, \mathcal{F}_2, \mathcal{F}_3, \ldots$ to be a discrete sequence of frames $\mathcal{F}_i$ where $i \in \mathcal{N}_0$ represents the ith frame of the stream. We use $\preceq$

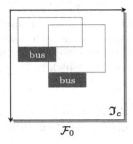 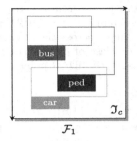 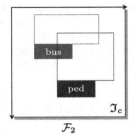

Fig. 1. An example perception stream S containing the frames $\mathcal{F}_0, \mathcal{F}_1, \mathcal{F}_2$ of a camera sensor channel c with pixel space $\mathfrak{I}_c$. For each object in a given frame, a classification and bounding box is minimally assumed to be annotated. In addition, each frame may be augmented with other sensor data relevant to the system to provide further context such as GPS, IMU, etc.

to denote the subsequence relation, i.e., $S' \preceq S$ where $S' = (\mathcal{F}_i, \ldots, \mathcal{F}_j)$ is a subsequence of S. For readability, we henceforth refer to a subsequence S' of S as a range of frames using the shorthand notation $\mathcal{F}_{i,j}$ where $i \leq j$. For example, an instance of the subsequence of frames $\mathcal{F}_{0,2}$ from some perception stream S is provided in Fig. 1.

Each frame $\mathcal{F}_i$ in the perception stream is considered a *key frame* that contains data generated from one or more sensor channels channels. A key frame is a frame where the timestamp difference between each sample from a sensor in $\mathcal{C}$ is within some threshold $\epsilon_t \in \mathbb{R}$. For example, a frame of an AV affixed with a front, front-left, front-right, and rear camera sensor channels is a key frame if and only if the timestamp difference between all samples occur within a period of 0.001 s. Furthermore, each frame contains a finite set of object annotations (henceforth, "objects") O from the entire stream S of objects $\mathcal{O}$ consisting of query-able information. That is, each object $o \in \mathcal{O}$ may be annotated with a label (e.g., *car, pedestrian, sign, bus, animal*, etc.), a unique identifier ("ID"), 2D/3D bounding box, confidence score, segmentation map, LiDAR points, etc.

In the following, we assume that given an object $o \in \mathcal{O}$, we have defined functions that return the required annotation and/or auxiliary data. For example, for retrieving qualitative attributes, we define the function $\mathfrak{A} : \mathcal{O} \times \mathcal{K} \to \mathcal{A}$ where $\mathcal{K}$ is a set of keys and $\mathcal{A}$ is a set of attributes. We will not formally define the sets $\mathcal{K}$ and $\mathcal{A}$ since they are dataset dependent, but as an example, we could have `class` and `color` as keys, and `bus` and `green` as the corresponding attributes. When formulating a query, we are searching to find in a frame an object that satisfies certain attributes, e.g., a *green bus*. In addition, for retrieving the 2D (axis-aligned) bounding box information of objects, we define the function $\mathfrak{B}_c : \mathcal{O} \to \mathcal{P}(\mathfrak{I}_c)$ where $\mathfrak{I}_c \subseteq \mathbb{N}^2$ is the set of pixels for a camera sensor channel $c \in \mathcal{C}$; and the function $\mathfrak{B} :\to \mathcal{P}(\mathcal{E})$ returns the 3D rectangular bounding box of any object $o \in \mathcal{O}$ in the working environment $\mathcal{E} \subseteq \mathbb{R}^3$ of a perception system. Table 1 presents a detailed layout of Fig. 1 with annotated information for each object.

Table 1. An example of annotated data from a perception stream. Each object has some attributes along with some bounding box ("BB") data. Depending on the application, the object IDs may be unique across the stream, unique only in each frame, or unique to each frame for each class of objects. In addition, each object may be annotated with additional data such as LiDAR points, color (if applicable), etc.

$\mathcal{F}_0$	$\mathcal{F}_1$	$\mathcal{F}_2$
(bus, red, ID: 1, BB)	(bus, red, ID: 1, BB)	(bus, red, ID: 1, BB)
(bus, yellow, ID: 2, BB)	(pedestrian, child, ID: 2, BB)	(pedestrian, child, ID: 2, BB)
	(car, sedan, ID: 3, BB)	

3 Spatial Regular Expressions

SpRE (pronounced /spriː/) is a querying language designed to capture scenarios of perception streams. The RE $\times \mathcal{S}4_u$ language leverages the power of pattern matching from REs [1] with the topological reasoning of $\mathcal{S}4_u$ logic [25]. The practice of merging a formal logic with an RE-based language to produce an extended, more expressive version has previously been studied in [7,38]. However, these efforts primarily focus on extending temporal-based logics such as Linear Temporal Logic (LTL) [31] with REs, whereas current extensions to spatial-based logics with REs is unheard of to the best of our knowledge—particularly, the $\mathcal{S}4_u$ branch of logic. Thus, the SpRE language aims to provide a formal approach in extending pattern-based constructs with spatial-based formulas.

Within this section, we first introduce the formal syntax of the SpRE language followed by its semantics interpreted over perception streams.

Syntax. The SpRE syntax consists of three interdependent grammars joined to form the complete querying language. The first two grammars (Definitions 1 and 2) are inspired by the $\mathcal{S}4$ and $\mathcal{S}4_u$ modal logics for topological spaces, respectively; and the last grammar (Definition 3) is inspired by classic REs traditionally used in *string matching* problems.

Spatial Formulas. The syntactic makeup of the spatial logic component of a SpRE is divided into two grammars: (1) $\mathcal{S}4_u^+$ ("spatial terms") inspired by $\mathcal{S}4$ [25], and (2) $\mathcal{S}4_u^+$ ("spatial formulas") inspired by $\mathcal{S}4_u$ [25]. Although the two logics ($\mathcal{S}4^+$, $\mathcal{S}4_u^+$) use an identical syntax to their counterparts ($\mathcal{S}4$, $\mathcal{S}4_u$), we re-introduce them here as new semantics for these logics will be defined later.

The spatial terms enable set operations over set based attributes of objects such as bounding boxes. The motivation behind spatial terms is to enable representation of the topological relations between different objects, e.g., the intersection of the bounding boxes of a *green bus* and a *yellow car*.

Definition 1 ($\mathcal{S}4^+$ Syntax). *The structure of an $\mathcal{S}4^+$ formula τ is inductively defined by the following grammar:*

$$\tau ::= \alpha \mid \bar{\tau} \mid \tau_1 \sqcap \tau_2 \mid \tau_1 \sqcup \tau_2 \mid \mathbf{I}\,\tau \mid \mathbf{C}\,\tau$$

where α is an atomic proposition ranging over sets of attributes $\mathcal{P}(\mathcal{A})$; $^-$ is the unary operator for complement; $\sqcap$ and $\sqcup$ are the binary operators for intersection and union; and $\mathbf{I}$ and $\boldsymbol{C}$ are the interior and closure operators.

Spatial formulas extend spatial terms by enabling emptiness checks and subset relations. For example, we will be able to answer a query which requires an non-empty intersection between the *green bus* and the *yellow car*.

Definition 2 ($\mathcal{S}4_u^+$ Syntax). *Given the spatial terms τ, τ_1, and τ_2, the structure of an $\mathcal{S}4_u^+$ formula ϕ is inductively defined by the following grammar:*

$$\phi ::= \alpha \mid \boxdot \tau \mid \tau_1 \sqsubseteq \tau_2 \mid \neg \phi \mid \phi \wedge \phi \mid \phi \vee \phi$$

where α is an atomic proposition ranging over sets of attributes $\mathcal{P}(\mathcal{A})$; $\boxdot$ and $\sqsubseteq$ are the boolean operators for set emptiness and set inclusion; and $\neg$, $\wedge$, and $\vee$ are the standard propositional logic operators.

Pattern Constructs. The syntax of a SpRE combines the RE elements with the previously defined $\mathcal{S}4_u^+$ elements to form a spatial-capable RE. Apart from the classic RE operators, SpRE patterns operate over symbols from the alphabet Σ that are resolved through spatial formulas.

Remark 1 (Alphabet). We consider the alphabet $\Sigma = \{\sigma_1, \sigma_2, ..., \sigma_n\} = \mathcal{P}(\mathcal{O})$ where each symbol represents a possible combination of the objects from the perception stream $\mathcal{S}$. The main intuition is that for every frame of the stream of perception data, we would like to match a symbol with only the relevant objects for the given SpRE query—see Example 1 below.

Example 1. Consider the data presented in Table 1. The alphabet Σ will contain 64 symbols in total. Some examples of symbols from Σ could be:

$$\sigma_1 = \{(\text{bus, red, ID: 1, BB})\}$$
$$\sigma_2 = \{(\text{pedestrian, child, ID: 2, BB}), (\text{bus, yellow, ID: 2, BB})\}$$
$$\sigma_3 = \{(\text{bus, red, ID: 1, BB}), (\text{car, sedan, ID: 3, BB})\}$$

When we query for *bus*, we would like our pattern matching algorithm to return σ_1 in the matching strings, but not σ_2 or σ_3.

Definition 3 (SpRE Syntax). *Given the spatial formula ϕ, the structure of a SpRE query is inductively defined by the following grammar:*

$$Q ::= \phi \mid Q_1 \mid Q_2 \mid Q_1 \cdot Q_2 \mid Q*$$

where the operators $\mid$, $\cdot$, and * are the standard RE operations alternation, concatenation, and Kleene-star, respectively.

Semantics. Pattern matching on perception streams differs from the standard string pattern matching. When querying perception data, the goal is to identify annotations represented as abstract objects affixed with some attributes. For example, a query could be *"Find all sequences where a car appears in at least three consecutive frames"*. In such a query, we do not ask for a specific car with a unique identity (which is not known in advance), but rather for any car. In addition, there may be multiple cars in a frame which implies that all of them should be candidates for a pattern match. In other words, even though our patterns in SpREs are over object attributes, our queries should return strings where each symbol is a set of corresponding specific objects.

We define the semantics of $\mathcal{S}4^+$ expressions through a valuation function $[\![\ ]\!] : \mathcal{P}(\mathcal{O}) \rightarrow \mathcal{P}(\mathcal{P}(W))$ where W is the spatial reasoning space that resolves to either the camera sensor's image space $\mathfrak{I}_c$ (i.e., pixels) or the working environment $\mathcal{E}$, $\mathcal{P}(W)$ is all possible bounding boxes from the reasoning space, and $\mathcal{P}(\mathcal{P}(W))$ is the set of all possible sets of all bounding boxes. The spatial terms of $\mathcal{S}4^+$ specify set-theoretic operations over bounding boxes of objects from the perception stream $\mathcal{S}$. We define the semantics of $\mathcal{S}4_u^+$ using a boolean satisfaction relation since our goal is to determine whether certain relations are true or not over bounding boxes and other object annotations.

Definition 4 ($\mathcal{S}4^+$ Semantics). *Given a set of objects $O \subseteq \mathcal{O}$, the semantics of an $\mathcal{S}4^+$ formula is inductively defined as follows:*

$$[\![\alpha]\!](O) = \{\mathfrak{B}(o) \mid o \in O . \forall a \in \alpha . \exists k \in \mathcal{K} . \mathfrak{A}(o,k) = a\}$$
$$[\![\bar{\tau}]\!](O) = \{\bar{S} \mid S \in [\![\tau]\!](O)\}$$
$$[\![\tau_1 \sqcap \tau_2]\!](O) = \{S_1 \cap S_2 \mid S_i \in [\![\tau_i]\!](O)\}$$

Informally, given a set of objects O from a frame, the valuation of the spatial term α is the set of bounding boxes of all the objects which satisfy all the attributes in α.

Definition 5 ($\mathcal{S}4^+$ Semantics). *Given a set of objects $O \subseteq \mathcal{O}$, the semantics of an $\mathcal{S}4_u^+$ formula is inductively defined as follows:*

$O \vDash \alpha$	iff	$\exists o \in O . \forall a \in \alpha . \exists k \in \mathcal{K} . \mathfrak{A}(o,k) = a$
$O \vDash \neg \phi$	iff	$O \nvDash \phi$
$O \vDash \phi_1 \wedge \phi_2$	iff	$O \vDash \phi_1$ and $O \vDash \phi_2$
$O \vDash \boxed{\exists} \tau$	iff	$\exists A \in [\![\tau]\!](O). A \neq \emptyset$
$O \vDash \tau_1 \sqsubseteq \tau_2$	iff	$\exists A_1 \in [\![\tau_1]\!](O). \exists A_2 \in [\![\tau_2]\!](O). A_1 \subseteq A_2$

Notice that the models (i.e., sets of objects) that satisfy a spatial formula ϕ are not minimal. For instance, using the symbols from Example 1, we have $\sigma_1 \vDash bus$, but also $\sigma_2 \vDash bus$ and $\sigma_3 \vDash bus$. In the *pattern matching* problem, we typically care more so about the sequence of frames $\mathcal{F}_{i,j}$ that satisfy the pattern Q rather than which exact objects are part of the pattern.

Definition 6 (SpRE Semantics). *Given the alphabet Σ, the language described by a SpRE query Q is inductively defined as follows:*

$$\mathcal{L}(\phi) = \{\sigma \in \Sigma \mid \sigma \vDash \phi\}$$
$$\mathcal{L}(Q_1 | Q_2) = \mathcal{L}(Q_1) \cup \mathcal{L}(Q_2)$$
$$\mathcal{L}(Q_1 \cdot Q_2) = \mathcal{L}(Q_1)\mathcal{L}(Q_2)$$
$$\mathcal{L}(Q*) = \bigcup_{i=0}^{\infty} \mathcal{L}(Q^i)$$

where Q^i denotes the concatenation of pattern Q a total of i times.

One notable difference from the standard language definition for a RE is that now our base case, i.e., the spatial formulas ϕ evaluate to sets of symbols as demonstrated in Example 1. This reflects the observation that at each frame we may have several matching objects for our query.

4   Perception Stream Matching

In this section, we provide a formulation of the problem of pattern matching against perception streams in both the offline and online domain. Furthermore, we introduce the STREM tool as our matching framework that implements the semantics of SpREs introduced in Sect. 3 to search over perception streams.

4.1   Problem Formulation

Informally, the traditional problem of pattern matching considers a finite word w and a pattern p from some finite alphabet Σ such that the goal is to find all non-overlapping subsets of w that contain an exact match of p. From Boyer-Moore (BM) [8] to Knuth-Morris-Pratt (KMP) [24], many algorithms have been developed to solve this problem of searching through strings [3]. In this work, we extend upon this idea with the modification that our search pattern p is symbolically a SpRE query Q, and our word w is a perception stream $\mathcal{S}$. We consider this problem in the both offline and online domain.

Offline Matching. We consider pattern matching in the offline domain primarily motivated by the presence of publicly available AV-based perception datasets [9,22,30,34,42]. These datasets provide a large suite of perception data collected for and used by ADS applications. However, to our knowledge, the capabilities and frameworks to search through these datasets for said applications are not well-supported or require a significant effort to do so. The offline pattern matching problem for perception streams is formalized below in Problem 1.

Problem 1 (Offline Perception Stream Matching). Given a *finite* perception stream $\mathcal{S}$ and a SpRE query Q, then starting from frame 0, find the set of all non-overlapping leftmost longest frame subsequences $\{\mathcal{F}_{i_1,j_1}, \ldots, \mathcal{F}_{i_n,j_n}\}$ in $\mathcal{S}$ such that $i_k \leq j_k$, $j_k \leq i_{k+1}$ and $j_n \leq |\mathcal{S}|$ and $\mathcal{F}_{i_k,j_k} \in \mathcal{L}(Q)$ for all $k \leq n$.

Online Matching. We also consider pattern matching in the online domain to perform filtering and querying of perception streams generated in realtime. Applications of such use cases include monitoring of AVs deployed, CCTV camera alerts, and any perception-based systems generating data where detection of scenarios in realtime are of importance.

Regarding the procedure of matching online, the framework is re-run at every time instance l when a new frame $\mathcal{F}_l$ is received and returns the maximal query matched up to that point $\mathcal{F}_{i_k,j_k}$ with $j_k = l$ (or none if no match). The online pattern matching problem for perception streams is formalized below in Problem 2.

Problem 2 (Online Perception Stream Matching). Given a perception stream $\mathcal{S}$ and a SpRE query Q, then at every incoming frame $\mathcal{F}_j$ of $\mathcal{S}$, find the longest subsequence of frames $\mathcal{F}_{i,j}$ such that $0 \leq i \leq j$ and $\mathcal{F}_{i,j} \in \mathcal{L}(Q)$.

4.2   Spatio-Temporal Regular Expression Matcher

Our SpRE matching framework follows the same principles as the classic RE matching frameworks [2]. Standard string matching approaches translate an RE to a Deterministic Finite Automata (DFA) D which is then used to process the strings. Our framework deviates from the established approaches using DFAs since each frame contains multiple objects which may satisfy different $\mathcal{S}4_u^+$ formulas and all potential matches need to be tracked simultaneously.

Example 2. Consider the data stream in Table 1 and assume that we only care about the classes and properties, e.g., we want to find two frames where a *red bus* appears. If we treat each object in each frame as a symbol of the form (`class`, `property`), then the data stream represents $2 \times 3 \times 2 = 12$ strings. Two example strings from Table 1 are (`bus`,`red`)(`bus`,`red`)(`bus`,`red`) and (`bus`,`red`)(`car`, `sedan`)(`bus`,`red`). As the length of the data stream increases, the number of strings that we need to consider increases exponentially in the worst case.

Especially in the case of online query matching, an approach that extracts strings from a perception stream to match against a DFA quickly becomes unmanageable. In this work, we take a more pragmatic approach which in practice works well. We treat each syntactically equivalent $\mathcal{S}4_u^+$ formula as a unique symbol and translate the SpRE into an RE. Even though we can now use the standard RE to DFA algorithms, the resulting automaton in execution becomes nondeterministic. This process can be easily visualized through Example 3 below.

Example 3. In the following, we use the convention that an atomic proposition (i.e., a set of attributes) is represented as an augmented *character class* familiar to `grep`. For readability, $\mathcal{S}4_u^+$ formulas are also surrounded by brackets. Using this notation, the formula [`<nonempty>`(`[:car:]`&`[:ped:]`)] is an $\mathcal{S}4_u^+$ formula that is only true when a frame contains a *car* and a *pedestrian* with interesecting bounding boxes. Since the operator `<nonempty>` applies only to spatial terms,

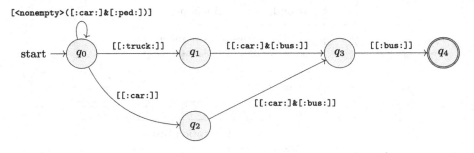

Fig. 2. SpRE to DFA.

we know that [:car:]&[:ped:] is an $S4^+$ subformula where & is the operator for set intersection.

From the previously introduced notation, we provide the following SpRE pattern written below

$$[\texttt{<nonempty>}(\texttt{[:car:]}\&\texttt{[:ped:]})]*(\texttt{[[:truck:]]}|\texttt{[[:car:]]})$$
$$\texttt{[[:car:]}\&\texttt{[:bus:]]}\,\texttt{[[:bus:]]}$$

that matches zero or more (*) frames where a *car* and *pedestrian* overlap, followed by ($\cdot$) a frame with either (|) a *truck* or a *car*, followed by ($\cdot$) one frame that contains a *car* and a *bus*, and ending with ($\cdot$) a frame with a *bus*.

The resulting automaton that accepts perception streams that match the SpRE above is presented in Fig. 2. Notice that in the resulting automaton, the transitions between states are labeled by $S4_u^+$ formulas and, hence, the execution semantics is that of a Nondeterministic Finite Automata (NFA). That is, in each state, multiple transitions may be activated. For example, in state q_0 if the current frame contains a *truck* and a *car*, then both transitions to q_1 and to q_2 are activated. In principle, tracking multiple states for an NFA execution scales better than constructing single-symbol strings from a stream for tracking with a DFA. In the worst case, the total number of states of the DFA that we need to keep track off is order of magnitudes smaller than the number of all possible single symbol strings that we need to consider.

Software Tool. STREM is a CLI tool[1] developed with *Rust* [28] to find scenarios of interest in perception streams that match a given SpRE query. It functions in both the offline and online domain to search over perception-based datasets or realtime streams, respectively. An illustration of its core components is provided in Fig. 3. As input, the tool accepts a SpRE query and a perception stream. As output, it incrementally returns the set of matches where each match is a range of frames from the provided perception stream that matched the pattern. The five constituent components of the tool are grouped into two functionalities: the frontend and the backend. The frontend handles all input-/output-related

---

[1] https://crates.io/crates/strem.

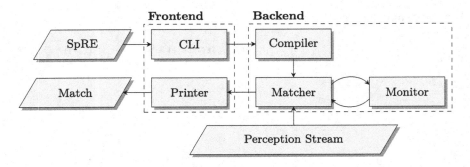

Fig. 3. The architectural design of STREM.

activities pertinent to the usability of the tool; and the backend is concerned only with the core matching framework and procedures. Henceforth, we focus on the backend components that support the main contributions of this work: the *Compiler*, *Matcher*, and *Monitor* modules.

The *Compiler* is responsible for translating a SpRE into a symbolic-Abstract Syntax Tree (s-AST)—an Intermediate Representation (IR) form interpretable by the *Monitor* and *Matcher* modules. The *Monitor* is responsible for evaluating $\mathcal{S}4_u^+$ formulas against perception stream frames. The *Matcher* is responsible for constructing DFAs from s-ASTs and running the matching algorithms.

Spatial Matching Algorithms. The pattern matching procedure involves both the *Matcher* and the *Monitor*—as depicted in Fig. 3. The *Matcher* receives from the *Monitor* which $\mathcal{S}4_u^+$ formulas were satisfied and, then, it takes the appropriate transitions to the next states. Recall that in our framework multiple transitions on the DFA may become active. Therefore, the execution semantics of the DFA in the *Matcher* are effectively the execution semantics of an NFA. Nevertheless, our constructions are syntactically DFA and, in the following, we will still refer to them as DFA.

The algorithm to match against a perception stream given some DFA that recognizes a valid SpRE query is shown in Algorithm 1. This algorithm is generalized for both offline and online applications and any differences in the assumptions and procedures are highlighted in the sections that follow.

Offline Algorithm. The offline matching procedure matches over a finite perception stream from frame $\mathcal{F}_0$ up to frame $\mathcal{F}_l$ by utilizing a *forward* DFA. Notably, the offline variant assumes that all frames within $\mathcal{S}$ are present at the beginning of the execution of the matching algorithm.

Online Algorithm. The online matching procedure matches over a perception stream by utilizing a *reverse* DFA. For each new frame received, the online algorithm variant is ran. We use a reverse DFA in the online problem as matching backwards (i.e., from frame $\mathcal{F}_l$ down to frame $\mathcal{F}_0$) ensures that the matching procedure terminates (in the worst case at frame $\mathcal{F}_0$). However, in practice, it is recommended that the termination of the match be triggered by some finite horizon (i.e., maximum length) for which the SpRE query will match up to. For certain queries, we can compute the finite length needed to determine if a match is possible. The length of an online SpRE query can be computed as follows:

Definition 7 (SpRE Horizon). *The horizon $\mathcal{H}$ of a SpRE query Q is inductively defined as follows:*

$$\mathcal{H}(\phi) = 1 \qquad \mathcal{H}(Q_1 | Q_2) = \max(\mathcal{H}(Q_2), \mathcal{H}(Q_2))$$
$$\mathcal{H}(Q*) = \infty \quad \mathcal{H}(Q_1 \cdot Q_2) = \mathcal{H}(Q_1) + \mathcal{H}(Q_2)$$

where ϕ is a spatial formula.

When $\mathcal{H}(Q)$ is finite, i.e., there is no Kleene-star operator, then we know that the online algorithm will only need to use up to $\mathcal{H}(Q)$ frames in the past. As an alternative to the Kleene-star operator, in our implementation, we provide the *range* operator to capture bounded-ness (see Sect. 5). If a Kleene-star operator must be used, then a hard bound on the maximum length should be used to keep the monitoring time predictable, in the worst case.

Algorithm 1: SPATIALMATCHING

This algorithm represents the offline variant. For the online variant, replace each line with its corresponding comment to the right.

Input: A perception stream $\mathcal{S}$, an initial frame index $i \in \mathcal{S}$.
Output: A range $[start, end)$ corresponding to the indices from $\mathcal{S}$.
Data: A set A of distinct active states from the DFA.

1	$start \leftarrow i$;	// $end \leftarrow |\mathcal{S}|$
2	$end \leftarrow start$;	// $start \leftarrow end - 1$
3	**foreach** $\mathcal{F} \in \mathcal{S}$ **do**	// $\mathcal{S} = (\mathcal{S})$
4	**foreach** $(\sigma_s,\ \sigma)$ **do**	
5	**if** $\mathcal{F} \vDash \sigma$ **then**	
6	$symbols.\text{push}(\sigma_s)$	
7	**end**	
8	**end**	
9	**foreach** $\sigma_s \in symbols$ **do**	
10	$A.\text{insert}(\delta(\sigma_s))$	
11	**end**	
12	**if** A **contains** *accepting* **then**	
13	$end \leftarrow \mathcal{F}.index$;	// $start \leftarrow \mathcal{F}.index$
14	**else if** A **all** *dead* **then**	
15	break	
16	**end**	
17	**end**	
18	**return** $(start, end)$	

Complexity. The time complexity depends on the data stream $\mathcal{S}$ and the query Q. Let $|\mathcal{S}|$ be the total number of frames in the perception stream, and $|O_i|$ be the number of objects in the ith frame where O_i is the set of objects in the frame $\mathcal{F}_i \in \mathcal{S}$. The query Q is translated into a DFA D with set of states D_S and transition relation D_Δ with $|D_S|$ denoting the number of states, and $|D_\Delta|$ denoting the total number of transitions, respectively. Recall that the transitions in D are labeled by spatial formulas from Q. That is, the transitions have the form $(s, \phi_k, s') \in D_\Delta$. We denote by $|\phi_k|$ the size of the parse tree (number of nodes) of ϕ_k since evaluating ϕ_k will require traversing its parse tree.

We first evaluate the time complexity of the *Monitor*, followed by the *Matcher*, followed by the combination of the two. For the *Monitor* to evaluate a spatial formula ϕ_k against a frame, if the $\mathcal{S}4_u^+$ formula ϕ_k contains no spatial operations, then its evaluation takes linear time in the tree traversal of ϕ_k (number of internal nodes $(|\phi_k| - 1)/2$) and linear time in the number of objects $|O_i|$ in a frame for each leaf (number of leaves $(|\phi_k| + 1)/2$) in order to find objects with specific attributes. Thus, the complexity of running the monitor is $\mathcal{O}(|\phi_k| \times |O_i|)$. As a special case, if Q only contains queries about class labels, then we can use a hash table storing whether an object of some class appears in a frame or not, giving us $\mathcal{O}(1)$ evaluation of the leaves of ϕ_k.

The *Matcher* keeps track of the active states in the DFA and, for each state, checks all the formulas in the outgoing transitions by calling the *Monitor*. In the worst case, $|D_S|$ states will be active, which implies that all the transitions in D_Δ must be checked. Thus, there will be $\mathcal{O}(|D_\Delta|)$ calls to the *Monitor*. Since the *Matcher* will be called $|\mathcal{S}|$ times, the complexity of the offline algorithm is

$$\mathcal{O}\big(|\mathcal{S}| \times |D_\Delta| \times \max_k(|\phi_k|) \times \max_i(|O_i|)\big)$$

whereas the online algorithm pays this cost for every new frame that appears within the perception stream.

If spatial operations are present in the spatial formulas, then the worst-case time complexity increases. Spatial terms in Definition 4 evaluate to collections of bounding sets in 2D or 3D. Therefore, the leaf nodes of ϕ_k represent collections of sets, and the internal nodes apply set operations such as union, intersection, complementation, and set difference. The computational cost of the set operations depends on the set representation (e.g., orthogonal polyhedra, vertex representation, polytopes, zonotopes, etc.). Here, we will not consider the representation of the sets explicitly, and refer the reader to [19].

Remark 2 (Best-Case Scenario). Our querying problem can be reduced to standard regular expression matching when: (1) all $\mathcal{S}4_u^+$ formulas are strictly atomic propositions, (2) the number of object attributes to search over are few in numbers, and (3) the attributes are not quantitative (e.g., no bounding box).

5   Examples and Benchmarks

To demonstrate the application of STREM, we provide two use cases of the tool: (A) an offline example of searching through the Woven Planet ("L5") Perception dataset [22] and (B) an online example of monitoring an AV's perception system through the CARLA simulator [12] with ROS [32]. Furthermore, we provide an initial set of performance benchmarks of the tool. For all queries, we use the STREM implementation-level syntax equivalents in Table 2.

Table 2. SpRE implementation equivalencies

Notation	I	·	*	$\exists$		¬	∧	∨	⊓	⊔
Symbol	I		*	`<nonempty>`		~	&	I	&	I

Furthermore, the range meta-operator ($\{m, n\}$) is used to support constraint concatenations. The operational equivalence is shown below:

$$Q\{m,n\} \equiv \overbrace{Q \cdot \ldots \cdot Q}^{m \text{ concatenations}} \mid \overbrace{Q \cdot \ldots \cdot Q}^{m+1 \text{ concatenations}} \mid \ldots \mid \overbrace{Q \cdot \ldots \cdot Q}^{n \text{ concatenations}}$$

where $0 \leq m \leq n$. In addition, the range operator support two other functions: (1) $Q\{m\}$ matches Q exactly m times; and (2) $Q\{m,\} = Q\{m,\infty\}$ matches Q m or more times.

5.1 Example A: Offline Matching Examples

We demonstrate the offline searching capabilities of the STREM tool on the Woven Planet ("L5") Perception dataset: a collection of sensor and ground-truth labels used in training and evaluation of AV perception systems. The dataset is comprised of 10 sensor channels, 360 scenes, 9 object classifications, over 300K frames, and over 1.2M object annotations yielding slightly over 186 GBs of data to search from.

Example A.1. In ADS applications, it is important to distinguish between cyclists and pedestrians as the intent and behavior of both differ. Therefore, to improve the resilience of a perception system against mis-identification, filtering for scenarios where the two classifications overlap (i.e., potential cases of ambiguity) strengthens Deep Neural Networks (DNNs) on such edge cases (Fig. 4).

Query 1. Find all longest sequences of frames where a detected *pedestrian* overlaps with a detected *cyclist*.

```
[<nonempty>([:pedestrian:]&[:bicycle:])]*
```

where the SpRE matches zero or more frames (*) where the intersection of a *pedestrian* and *bicycle* bounding box is non-empty.

From the results, a total of 62 unique matches were found where each match contains a sequence of frames with a pedestrian and cyclist overlapping.

Fig. 4. A selection of three separately matching frames from the Woven Planet ("L5") Perception dataset where a *pedestrian* (blue) overlaps with a *cyclist* (green).

Example A.2. While queries targeting individual scenarios are useful for simple matching, more complex queries are needed to capture scenarios that can not be consolidated to a single frame and represent an evolution of events. For instance, consider the scenario where a pedestrian is initially occluded by a vehicle, unobstructed, and then occluded again by a vehicle (Fig. 5).

Query 2. Find a sequence of frames where a *pedestrian* and *car* occlusion occurs for one or more frames, followed by an unobstructed *pedestrian* for one or more frames, followed by an occlusion of a *pedestrian* and a *car* for one or more frames.

```
[<nonempty>([:pedestrian:]&[:car:])]{1,}
[[:pedestrian:]&~<nonempty>([:pedestrian:]&[:car:])]{1,}
[<nonempty>([:pedestrian:]&[:car:])]{1,}
```

where the SpRE matches a sequence of scenarios (i.e., sub-scenario) where each sub-scenario must be at least one frame ({1, }) long. The first sub-scenario matches the intersection of a *pedestrian* and *car* bounding box is non-empty. The second sub-scenario matches the case where a *pedestrian* exists and the intersection of a *pedestrian* with a *car* is empty. The last sub-scenario matches the same as the first sub-scenario.

F: 009   F: 013   F: 034

Fig. 5. The results of running Query 2 through STREM on the Woven Planet ("L5") Perception dataset. From left to right, the matching frames include an instance of a *car* (red) occluding a *pedestrian* (blue), a *pedestrian*, and a *car* occluding a *pedestrian*.

From the results, a total of 336 uniques matches of three or more frames were found that matched the evolution of scenarios as described in the SpRE query.

5.2   Example B: Online Matching

To demonstrate the online searching capabilities of STREM, we developed a ROS package that bridges the CARLA simulator with the STREM tool by using the standard *topics* infrastructure provided by ROS. This design allows additional ROS applications (e.g., robots, AVs, etc.) to easily integrate and subscribe to the match results published by the STREM tool.

Simulator Setup. For each example, the CARLA server was populated with 50 vehicles (e.g., trucks, sedans, etc.), 20 walkers (i.e., pedestrians), and a single *ego* vehicle affixed with a one front-facing camera sensor. From the set of labels provided by CARLA, we capture bounding box information for the following actor types: (1) traffic signs, (2) traffic lights, (3) vehicles, and (4) walkers.

For all examples, the experiments were run on a Linux workstation running Ubuntu 20.04.6 with an AMD Ryzen 7 5800X, an NVIDIA GeForce RTX 3070, and 16 GBs of RAM with CARLA v0.9.13 at 60 Hz and ROS Noetic (Focal).

Example B.1. Within the deployment of AVs, monitoring the perception stream for critical scenarios is a runtime-centric activity that requires a continuous analysis of the results of the perception system in order to take decisive actions quickly. An example of such a critical scenario common to AVs is in the occlusion of people by other vehicles in the scene. Within this situation, limited information is available to the system and naturally additional caution should be taken. However, reporting this information is not an inherent responsibility of the perception system. As such, the STREM tool provides the capability to instantaneously report frames in realtime where a pedestrian is occluded by some other object detected within a scene to allow the ADS to take action.

In this example, we consider the scenario in CARLA where a bounding box of a pedestrian and a vehicle annotation overlap one another. The formalization of this pattern is presented in Query 3 below.

Query 3. Report every frame where a *pedestrian* and *vehicle* overlap.

```
[<nonempty>([:pedestrian:]&[:vehicle])]
```

where the SpRE matches a single frame such that the intersection of the bounding boxes of a *pedestrian* and a *vehicle* classification is non-empty.

A illustrative example of some frames reported by STREM during the simulation are showcased in Fig. 6.

Example B.2. Another critical scenario that a perception system may experience is in an eventual case that information becomes missing (i.e., the presence of an object disappears from sight).

In this example, we consider the scenario in CARLA where perceived traffic signs are detected followed by an occlusion of some sign within the frame.

F: 9354   F: 15407   F: 16869

Fig. 6. A series of matching frames with object detections within the CARLA simulator where a *pedestrian* and *vehicle* intersect as expressed in Query 3.

Query 4. Find a traffic *sign* within the last 200 frames that is eventually occluded by a *vehicle* or *pedestrian*.

$$[[:sign:]]\{1,200\}$$
$$[<nonempty>(([:vehicle:]|[:pedestrian:])\&[:sign:])]$$

where the SpRE matches at least 1 and at most 200 frames ($\{1, 200\}$) initially that contain a *sign* annotation, and ends with one frame where the resulting intersection of the bounding box of a *sign* with the bounding box of either a *vehicle* or *pedestrian* is non-empty.

A illustrative example of some frames reported by STREM during the simulation are showcased in Fig. 7.

F: 22215   F: 22341   F: 22358

Fig. 7. A series of matching frames with object detections within the CARLA simulator where a vehicle (red) eventually occludes a traffic sign (pink) in the green circle. (Color figure online)

5.3 Benchmarks

To evaluate the performance of the STREM tool, we ran several different queries against the Woven Planet ("L5") Perception dataset. For each query, the average running time of 10 samples of the matching algorithm was evaluated against 0 to 150K frames. The results are summarized in Fig. 8. The benchmarks were ran on a Linux workstation running Fedora 37 (6.2.14-200.fc37.x86_64) with an AMD Ryzen 7 Pro 4750U processor with Radeon Graphics, 32 GBs of RAM, and a *wall clock* time of 30 s.

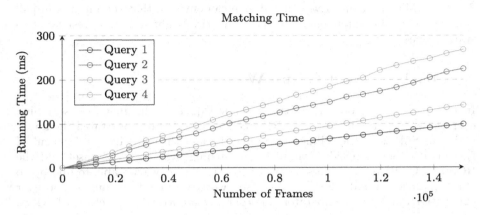

Fig. 8. Running time performance of STREM.

6   Related Work

The problem of querying video/multimedia datasets has a long history. Among the earliest works, [10] presents a spatio-temporal logic that can encode relationships among objects within image sequences. More recently, the Video Event Query Language (VEQL) was proposed in [41] (the paper also contains an exhaustive review of other video query languages). VEQL is a declarative language similar to SQL and it is used for monitoring of video data streams. It supports some ad hoc spatial and topological operators and some basic temporal relations through the Allen Interval Algebra (AIA) [4]. Besides the obvious differences of monitoring AIA (AIA can be encoded in LTL [33]) versus RE pattern matching, SpRE fully incorporates $S4_u$ and it can foundationally support other modal logics of space (and time). Beyond queries, Timed Quality Temporal Logic (TQTL) was proposed in [11] to enable basic sanity checks over video feeds of automotive systems using object annotations. Furthermore, an online monitoring algorithm for TQTL was presented in [6].

Typically, perception data streams from automotive applications contain not only image sequences, but also data from a range of other sensing modalities, e.g., radar, lidar, infrared, etc. In [19], Spatio-Temporal Perception Logic (STPL) was introduced which combines TQTL [11] with an extension of the spatial-temporal logic PTL $\times S4_u$ [17] to support reasoning over spatial conditions such as intersection and distances between bounding boxes. In principle, temporal logics could be used for pattern matching after some modifications to their monitoring algorithms, but in practice, their syntax is not well suited for describing

268 J. Anderson et al.

patterns. In another line of work, a querying method for sim-to-real applications is presented in [23] which uses the Scenic probabilistic programming language [15]. Abstract static scenarios of interest are expressed in Scenic which are then queried over labeled datasets through a conversion into a Satisfiability Modulo Theory (SMT) problem. Even though one can envision that the method in [23] can eventually be extended to temporal queries, right now it is restricted to static scenes.

7 Conclusion and Future Work

In this paper, we proposed SpRE as a novel querying language for searching over perception streams using an RE $\times S4_u$ design. We demonstrated the application of SpREs in the offline and online domain through the development of the STREM tool alongside examples of matching over an AV dataset and the ROS and CARLA simulators, respectively. From this, we are able to find up to 20K+ matches in under 296 ms. As future work, we plan to include support for existential and universal operators in order to support a richer set of behaviors.

References

1. Aho, A.V.: Pattern matching in strings. In: Formal Language Theory, pp. 325–347. Elsevier (1980)
2. Aho, A.V., Lam, M.S., Sethi, R., Ullman, J.D.: Compilers: Principles, Techniques and Tools. Addison-Wesley, Pearson (2020)
3. Alfred, V.: Algorithms for finding patterns in strings. In: Algorithms and Complexity, vol. 1, p. 255 (2014)
4. Allen, J.F.: Maintaining knowledge about temporal intervals. Commun. ACM **26**(11), 832–843 (1983)
5. Bai, Z., et al.: Cyber mobility mirror: a deep learning-based real-world object perception platform using roadside LiDAR. IEEE Trans. Intell. Transp. Syst. **24**, 9476–9489 (2023)
6. Balakrishnan, A., Deshmukh, J., Hoxha, B., Yamaguchi, T., Fainekos, G.: PerceMon: online monitoring for perception systems. In: Feng, L., Fisman, D. (eds.) RV 2021. LNCS, vol. 12974, pp. 297–308. Springer, Cham (2021). https://doi.org/10.1007/978-3-030-88494-9_18
7. Beer, I., Ben-David, S., Eisner, C., Fisman, D., Gringauze, A., Rodeh, Y.: The temporal logic sugar. In: Berry, G., Comon, H., Finkel, A. (eds.) CAV 2001. LNCS, vol. 2102, pp. 363–367. Springer, Heidelberg (2001). https://doi.org/10.1007/3-540-44585-4_33
8. Boyer, R.S., Moore, J.S.: A fast string searching algorithm. Commun. ACM **20**(10), 762–772 (1977)
9. Caesar, H., et al.: nuScenes: a multimodal dataset for autonomous driving. In: Proceedings of the IEEE/CVF Conference on Computer Vision and Pattern Recognition, pp. 11621–11631 (2020)
10. Del Bimbo, A., Vicario, E., Zingoni, D.: Symbolic description and visual querying of image sequences using spatio-temporal logic. IEEE Trans. Knowl. Data Eng. **7**(4), 609–622 (1995)

11. Dokhanchi, A., Amor, H.B., Deshmukh, J.V., Fainekos, G.: Evaluating perception systems for autonomous vehicles using quality temporal logic. In: Colombo, C., Leucker, M. (eds.) RV 2018. LNCS, vol. 11237, pp. 409–416. Springer, Cham (2018). https://doi.org/10.1007/978-3-030-03769-7_23

12. Dosovitskiy, A., Ros, G., Codevilla, F., Lopez, A., Koltun, V.: CARLA: an open urban driving simulator. In: Conference on Robot Learning, pp. 1–16. PMLR (2017)

13. Everingham, M., Van Gool, L., Williams, C.K., Winn, J., Zisserman, A.: The pascal visual object classes (VOC) challenge. Int. J. Comput. Vis. **88**, 303–338 (2010)

14. Fang, W., et al.: Computer vision applications in construction safety assurance. Autom. Constr. **110**, 103013 (2020)

15. Fremont, D.J., Dreossi, T., Ghosh, S., Yue, X., Sangiovanni-Vincentelli, A.L., Seshia, S.A.: Scenic: a language for scenario specification and scene generation. In: Proceedings of the 40th ACM SIGPLAN Conference on Programming Language Design and Implementation, pp. 63–78 (2019)

16. Friedl, J.E.: Mastering Regular Expressions. O'Reilly Media Inc., Sebastopol (2006)

17. Gabelaia, D., Kontchakov, R., Kurucz, A., Wolter, F., Zakharyaschev, M.: Combining spatial and temporal logics: expressiveness vs. complexity. J. Artif. Intell. Res. **23**, 167–243 (2005)

18. Gallant, A.: regex-automata (2023). https://github.com/rust-lang/regex

19. Hekmatnejad, M., Hoxha, B., Deshmukh, J.V., Yang, Y., Fainekos, G.: Formalizing and evaluating requirements of perception systems for automated vehicles using spatio-temporal perception logic. arXiv preprint arXiv:2206.14372 (2022)

20. Janai, J., Güney, F., Behl, A., Geiger, A., et al.: Computer vision for autonomous vehicles: problems, datasets and state of the art. Found. Trends® Comput. Graph. Vis. **12**(1–3), 1–308 (2020)

21. Kapach, K., Barnea, E., Mairon, R., Edan, Y., Ben-Shahar, O.: Computer vision for fruit harvesting robots-state of the art and challenges ahead. Int. J. Comput. Vis. Robot. **3**(1–2), 4–34 (2012)

22. Kesten, R., et al.: Woven planet perception dataset 2020 (2019). https://woven.toyota/en/perception-dataset

23. Kim, E., et al.: Querying labelled data with scenario programs for sim-to-real validation. In: 2022 ACM/IEEE 13th International Conference on Cyber-Physical Systems (ICCPS), pp. 34–45. IEEE (2022)

24. Knuth, D.E., Morris, J.H., Jr., Pratt, V.R.: Fast pattern matching in strings. SIAM J. Comput. **6**(2), 323–350 (1977)

25. Kontchakov, R., Kurucz, A., Wolter, F., Zakharyaschev, M.: Spatial logic+ temporal logic=?. In: Handbook of Spatial Logics, pp. 497–564 (2007)

26. Lin, T.-Y., et al.: Microsoft COCO: common objects in context. In: Fleet, D., Pajdla, T., Schiele, B., Tuytelaars, T. (eds.) ECCV 2014. LNCS, vol. 8693, pp. 740–755. Springer, Cham (2014). https://doi.org/10.1007/978-3-319-10602-1_48

27. Lu, D., et al.: CAROM air-vehicle localization and traffic scene reconstruction from aerial videos. arXiv preprint arXiv:2306.00075 (2023)

28. Matsakis, N.D., Klock, F.S.: The rust language. ACM SIGAda Ada Lett. **34**(3), 103–104 (2014)

29. Meng, T., Huang, J., Chew, C.M., Yang, D., Zhong, Z.: Configuration and design schemes of environmental sensing and vehicle computing systems for automated driving: a review. IEEE Sens. J. **23**, 15305–15320 (2023)

30. Pitropov, M., et al.: Canadian adverse driving conditions dataset. Int. J. Robot. Res. **40**(4–5), 681–690 (2021)

31. Pnueli, A.: The temporal logic of programs. In: 18th Annual Symposium on Foundations of Computer Science (SFCS 1977), pp. 46–57. IEEE (1977)
32. Quigley, M., et al.: ROS: an open-source robot operating system. In: ICRA Workshop on Open Source Software, p. 5. No. 3.2 in 3, Kobe, Japan (2009)
33. Roşu, G., Bensalem, S.: Allen linear (interval) temporal logic – translation to LTL and monitor synthesis. In: Ball, T., Jones, R.B. (eds.) CAV 2006. LNCS, vol. 4144, pp. 263–277. Springer, Heidelberg (2006). https://doi.org/10.1007/11817963_25
34. Sun, P., et al.: Scalability in perception for autonomous driving: Waymo open dataset. In: Proceedings of the IEEE/CVF Conference on Computer Vision and Pattern Recognition, pp. 2446–2454 (2020)
35. Thomas, G., Gade, R., Moeslund, T.B., Carr, P., Hilton, A.: Computer vision for sports: current applications and research topics. Comput. Vis. Image Underst. **159**, 3–18 (2017)
36. Turtiainen, H., Costin, A., Lahtinen, T., Sintonen, L., Hamalainen, T.: Towards large-scale, automated, accurate detection of CCTV camera objects using computer vision. applications and implications for privacy, safety, and cybersecurity. arXiv preprint arXiv:2006.03870 (2020)
37. Ward, T.M., et al.: Computer vision in surgery. Surgery **169**(5), 1253–1256 (2021)
38. Wolper, P.: Temporal logic can be more expressive. Inf. Control **56**(1–2), 72–99 (1983)
39. Xiao, P., et al.: PandaSet: advanced sensor suite dataset for autonomous driving. In: 2021 IEEE International Intelligent Transportation Systems Conference (ITSC), pp. 3095–3101. IEEE (2021)
40. Xu, Z., Julius, A.A.: Census signal temporal logic inference for multiagent group behavior analysis. IEEE Trans. Autom. Sci. Eng. **15**(1), 264–277 (2016)
41. Yadav, P., Curry, E.: VidCEP: complex event processing framework to detect spatiotemporal patterns in video streams. In: 2019 IEEE International conference on big data (big data), pp. 2513–2522. IEEE (2019)
42. Yu, F., et al.: Bdd100k: a diverse driving dataset for heterogeneous multitask learning. In: Proceedings of the IEEE/CVF Conference on Computer Vision and Pattern Recognition, pp. 2636–2645 (2020)
43. Zhang, Y., Carballo, A., Yang, H., Takeda, K.: Perception and sensing for autonomous vehicles under adverse weather conditions: a survey. ISPRS J. Photogrammetry Remote Sens. **196**, 146–177 (2023)

Learning Monitor Ensembles
for Operational Design Domains

Hazem Torfah[1]([⊠]), Aniruddha Joshi[1,2], Shetal Shah[2], S. Akshay[2],
Supratik Chakraborty[2], and Sanjit A. Seshia[1]

[1] University of California, Berkeley, USA
torfah@berkeley.edu
[2] Indian Institute of Technology Bombay, Mumbai, India

Abstract. We investigate the role of ensemble methods in learning run-time monitors for operational design domains of autonomous systems. An operational design domain (ODD) of a system captures the conditions under which we can trust the components of the system to maintain its safety. A runtime monitor of an ODD predicts, based on a sequence of monitorable observations, whether the system is about to exit the ODD. For black-box systems, a key challenge in learning an ODD monitor is obtaining a monitor with a high degree of accuracy. While statistical theories such as that of probably approximate learning (PAC) allow us to provide guarantees on the accuracy of a learned ODD monitor up to a certain confidence probability (by bounding the number of needed training examples), practically, there will always remain a chance, that using such a one-shot approach will result in monitors with a high misclassification rate. To address this challenge we consider well-known ensemble learning algorithms and utilize them for learning ODD ensembles. We derive theoretical bounds on the estimated misclassification risk of ensembles, showing that it reduces exponentially with the number of monitors and linearly with the risk of individual monitors. An empirical evaluation of the impact of different ensemble learning methods on a case study from autonomous driving demonstrates the advantage of this approach.

Keywords: Autonomous systems · Operational design domains · Ensemble methods

1 Introduction

Autonomous cyber-physical systems increasingly rely on artificial intelligence (AI) to perform a variety of challenging decision making tasks. Machine learning (ML) has been the driving force in addressing many of these challenges, especially in complex tasks such as perception. While indispensable for autonomy, ML models, such as deep neural networks, are unpredictable and could, under unanticipated changes in the environment, produce faulty outcomes that endanger the safety of a system. It is, therefore, crucial to capture the conditions

P. Katsaros and L. Nenzi (Eds.): RV 2023, LNCS 14245, pp. 271–290, 2023.
https://doi.org/10.1007/978-3-031-44267-4_14

under which an ML-based system is designed to behave correctly, also known as its *operational design domain* (ODD) [20], and construct a runtime monitor that implements the boundaries defined by an ODD and triggers the right contingency mechanisms when these boundaries are not met.

In this paper, we study the problem of learning runtime monitors for ODDs. Specifically, we investigate the role of ensemble methods, such as selection algorithms (e.g., expert-selection or multi-armed bandit techniques) or fusion algorithms (e.g., majority voting methods) in learning monitors for ODDs of blackbox systems. Learning a monitor for an ODD requires capturing the relation between the safety specification and the observable input space of the monitor. While a system-level safety specification might be defined over any system variables, some that may not be (immediately) observable at runtime, a monitor of the ODD is necessarily defined over an observable space of inputs, usually determined by the sensor interface of the system. This, especially, means that a direct translation of the system-level specification into an ODD monitor is not possible, and we, therefore, have to learn the monitor by relating sequences of the observable input to the corresponding valuation of the system-level specification. We show that capturing this relation can be done more accurately by applying ensemble methods to learn the ODD monitors.

Consider, for example, the autonomous vehicle system depicted in Fig. 1. The autonomous vehicle is equipped with a controller that uses an image-based convolutional neural network (CNN) to compute the steering angle of the vehicle. In this setting, a safety specification of interest might be a specification that requires the vehicle to never deviate by more than half a meter from the center of the lane. The true distance to the centerline of the lane is, however, not observable at runtime, and, therefore, we cannot synthesize a monitor that validates the system-level property directly at runtime. We can, however, create a monitor, the ODD monitor, that determines, based on other observable features, whether the CNN-based controller can be trusted to produce the right steering angles, or at least values that do not lead to violation of the system-level property. The behavior of the CNN may be influenced by many factors. For example, it may depend on certain weather conditions, lighting conditions, the objects on the road, certain traffic situations, some road features such as turns, circles, or intersections, as well as information about the state of the system. An ODD can then be defined in terms of any subset of the latter factors, which we denote by the observable features. An ODD monitor receives valuations of these features, predicts the validity of the system-level specification, and, if necessary, triggers a switch to a (verified) safe controller.

In general, while statistical learning theories such as probably approximately correct (PAC) learning [21] allow us to apply a one-shot learning approach with high confidence in the accuracy of a learned ODD monitor, it comes with two main drawbacks. First, as we can see from our example in Fig. 1, ODD monitors are defined over a high-dimensional space of monitoring inputs. To obtain monitors with high confidence in their accuracy, PAC approaches require the creation of a large training set that makes learning less scalable. Second, even if we can match the PAC confidence expectations, the accuracy of a monitor depends on

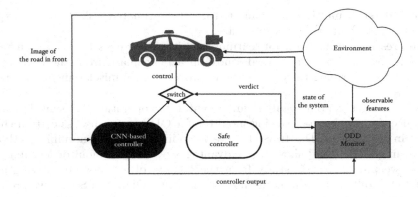

Fig. 1. An autonomous vehicle system with a CNN-based controller integrated into a ODD monitoring architecture.

the chosen sample set and there is still a risk of obtaining a monitor with a high misclassification rate. Using ensemble methods we show that we can reduce this risk. We prove that with every monitor added to the ensemble, the estimated risk of misclassification decreases exponentially. Furthermore, the individual monitors of the ensemble need not be learned using large training data sets. For a large enough ensemble of weakly learned monitors (i.e. those learned with lower confidence, using a lower number of training data), an ensemble method compensates for the weakness of any individual monitor by making use of the results of multiple monitors.

We present a systematic approach for learning ensembles of ODD monitors that builds on VERIFAI, an open-source toolkit for the formal design and analysis of systems that include AI or ML components [5]. A good monitor for the ODD requires choosing the right observable feature space over which the monitor is defined and creating a diverse set of samples. For the latter, coverage is key, i.e., when simulating the system, we need to sample from a diverse set of scenarios in which we simulate the system, and collect data. To tackle this problem we rely on a model of the environment given by a probabilistic program. More specifically, we use SCENIC, a probabilistic programming language for modeling environments [6], where scenarios are defined as distributions over spatial and temporal configurations of objects and agents. We show the advantage of our approach using a case study from the domain of autonomous driving. Particularly, we show how ensembles of increasing size allow us to converge to monitors with improved misclassification rates.

We summarize our contributions as follows:

- We investigate the role of ensemble methods in learning monitors for the operational design domain of black-box autonomous systems.
- We prove that in comparison to using one-shot PAC-learning methods, ensemble methods provide a tighter bound on the risk of misclassification. Particularly, we show for fusion methods such as majority voting, and selection

274 H. Torfah et al.

methods such multi-armed bandit, that the estimated risk decreases exponentially with growing ensemble size.
– We present a framework for learning monitor ensembles for ODDs and use the framework in an empirical study on a benchmark from the domain of autonomous driving that shows the improvements in misclassification rates.

Outline. In Sect. 2 we formally define monitorable operational design domains, introduce the problem of learning monitors for ODDs, and discuss certain challenges in learning ODDs. In Sect. 3 we introduce different ensemble methods for learning ODDs, and show their advantages over single monitor learning. In Sect. 4, we present a case study from the domain of autonomous driving and evaluate the different learning methods for learning ODDs. In Sect. 5 we present related work, and conclude in Sect. 6.

2 Monitorable Operational Design Domains

In this section, we recap the formal definition of monitorable ODDs, and restate the problem of learning optimal ODD monitor [26]. We also discuss some the challenges in learning monitors for ODDs, specifically, why methods based on PAC-learning might not suitable for learning such monitors. In a Sect. 3, we show how to use ensemble methods in learning ODD monitors and how these methods help in overcoming the challenges we discuss in this section.

2.1 Monitorable Operational Design Domains

Let $S, \varphi \subseteq V_{sys}^*$ be a system and a safety specification over the system-level alphabet V_{sys}. The operational design domain O of S and φ is defined by the tuple $O_{S,\varphi} = (V_{obs}, obs, d)$, where V_{obs} defines a set of observable inputs, $obs: V_{sys}^* \rightarrow V_{obs}^*$ defines the relation between sequences of system-level and observable inputs, and $d \in \mathbb{N}$ is a prediction horizon. In its most conservative definition, an operational design domain $O_{S,\varphi}$ defines a set

$$\llbracket O_{S,\varphi} \rrbracket = \{\sigma \in V_{obs}^* \mid \forall \tau \in V_{sys}^*.\ obs(\tau) = \sigma \implies \forall \tau' \in V_{sys}^d.\ \tau \cdot \tau' \notin \overline{\varphi}\}.$$

Here V_{sys}^d refers to words of length d over V_{sys}, while $\overline{\varphi}$ is the complement of φ. The ODD $O_{S,\varphi}$ defines a set of traces, σ, over the observable input V_{obs}, that for any system-level trace τ over V_{sys} which induces σ, i.e., $obs(\tau) = \sigma$, a continuation of τ for another d steps, i.e., extending τ with any τ' of length d, will not result in an execution $\tau \cdot \tau'$ that violates the system-level specification φ. A runtime monitor M for an ODD O over observations V_{obs} is a program that implements a function $f_M: V_{obs}^* \rightarrow \mathbb{B}$, such that, for every trace $\sigma \in V_{obs}^*$, $f_M(\sigma)$ if and only if $\sigma \in \llbracket O \rrbracket$.

The definition of ODDs as given above is, however, in general too strong to be used in practice. Learning monitors that exactly capture the set of observations defined by the ODD will result in very conservative monitors. Ambiguities resulting from mapping several system-level traces to the same observational trace, may render that trace as violating simply because it can be mapped to a single violating trace on the system-level. The probability of that system-level trace happening may be very low. Furthermore, the class of monitors may not always include a monitor for the exact ODD. Semantically speaking, the monitors within a class typically cover only a subset of monitors over V_{obs}. To this end, a more suitable formulation of the problem of learning monitors for ODDs is a quantitative one where we search for a monitor that is optimal with respect to a measure over the set of misclassified system-level traces. Particularly, the measure is applied over two distinct sets of misclassified traces, the set of false positives and that of false negatives.

For an ODD $O_{S,\varphi} = (V_{obs}, obs, d)$, the set of false positives describes system-level traces τ that cannot be extended with a trace τ' of length d such that $\tau \cdot \tau'$ violates φ, yet the induced observation $\sigma = obs(\tau)$ is rejected by the monitor. This set can be formally defined as follows. For a language L, let L^{-d}, for $d \in \mathbb{N}$, define the set of trimmed words $L^{-d} = \{\alpha_0 \alpha_1 \ldots \alpha_{k-d} \mid \alpha_0 \alpha_1 \ldots \alpha_k \in L, k \in \mathbb{N} \text{ s.t. } k - d \geq 0\}$. Let then $T_p = (S \cap \varphi)^{-d}$ be the set of traces resulting from computing the d-trimmings of all traces of S that satisfy φ. For a monitor M, the set of false positives can then be defined by the set $FP = T_p \setminus obs^{-1}(f_M)$, where obs^{-1} is the inverse function of obs. The set of false negatives defines all system-level traces τ that can be extended by a trace τ' of length d such that $\tau \cdot \tau'$ violates φ, yet the induced observation $\sigma = obs(\tau)$ is accepted by the monitor. For a monitor M, the set of false negatives can be defined by the set $FN = T_n \cap obs^{-1}(f_M)$, where $T_n = (S \cap \overline{\varphi})^{-d}$. Following these definitions of false positives and false negatives, the ODD monitor learning problem can then be defined as the following quantitative optimization problem.

Problem 1 (Optimal Monitor Synthesis for ODDs [26])
For an operational design domain $O_{S,\varphi} = (V_{obs}, obs, d)$ of a system S and a specification φ over V_{sys}^*, a class of monitors $\mathcal{M}$ over V_{obs}, a measure $\mu \colon \mathcal{P}(V_{sys}^*) \to \mathbb{R}^+$, and a bias $w_{fn} \in \mathbb{R}^+$, find a monitor $M \in \mathcal{M}$, such that,

$$M \in \arg\min_{M' \in \mathcal{M}} \ \mu(T_p \setminus obs^{-1}(f_{M'})) + w_{fn} \cdot \mu(T_n \cap obs^{-1}(f_{M'})).$$

The measure μ over the sets of false positives and negatives resembles a loss function with respect to system-level traces. An example of such measure is the rate of false positives and false negatives with respect to entire set (or a sampled portion) of the set of system traces.

Remark 1. Notice that an ODD is always defined with respect to a system and the ODD monitor will predict whether that system is about to violate the specification. This particularly means that responsibility for failure could be any of the components of the system influencing the validity of the system-level specification. Implementing a safe contingency component and integrating it into the system requires careful analysis and is beyond the scope of this paper.

2.2   Challenges in Learning Optimal ODDs

In our ODD monitor learning setting, probably approximate correct learning methods come with the big advantage of allowing us to learning ODDs with statistical guarantees on their optimality. For a given confidence parameter δ and an error margin ϵ, assuming a class of monitors with a finite VC dimension (e.g., decision trees, decision diagram, automata), PAC methods determine the number of i.i.d. samples needed to obtain a monitor close to the optimal monitor with high confidence [21]. Formally, PAC methods allow for the construction of a monitor M with $Pr(L_M - L_{opt} \leq \epsilon) \geq 1 - \delta$, where L_{opt} and L_M are the losses of the optimal monitor within the class of monitors and the loss of the learned monitor, respectively.

While, statistically speaking, for very low values of δ and ϵ we obtain a close-to optimal monitor with high confidence, practically we are still confronted with two challenges:

– In a high-dimensional space, such as in the case of the ODD in our autonomous vehicle example, strong PAC guarantees, i.e., for low values of δ and ϵ, require the generation of a very large set of training data, which causes a scalability problem (especially in the case of symbolic learning algorithms [25]), in learning the ODD monitor.
– Even if we manage to overcome the scalability problem by learning over large data sets, the fact that PAC only provides statistical guarantees on the accuracy of a learned monitor implies there will always be a chance (of probability δ) of obtaining a monitor with a high misclassification rate. Indeed, one needs to apply a PAC learning algorithm several times in order to reduce the risk of obtaining of a "bad" monitor. Which brings us to the role of ensemble methods in overcoming this challenge.

In the next section, we show that using the ensemble method we can reduce the risk of obtaining a bad monitor. In fact we show that with growing ensembles, we can reduce the bounds on this risk exponentially. Furthermore, using ensembles we can also overcome the problem of having to learn individual monitors with strong PAC guarantees. We show that the change in the confidence and error margin values of the individual monitors influences the bound on the risk of the ensemble monitor only linearly. This allows us to learn individual monitors using weaker PAC guarantees without sacrificing the overall accuracy of a monitor learned by an ensemble method.

3   Learning Monitor Ensembles for Operational Design Domains

We now show that an upper bound of the overall risk of an ensemble monitor reduces exponentially with the count of monitors, and linearly with the risk of individual monitors. In the following discussion, the input to every (individual or ensemble) monitor M is assumed to be sampled from a distribution D over the input space. The risk of M, denoted $R(M)$, is the probability of M returning an incorrect classification result. If M is PAC-learned, the loss function used for PAC learning is assumed to be $\mathbb{E}_{(x,y)\sim D}\ \ell_M(x,y)$, where x is an input sampled from the input space, y is the corresponding correct output label, and $\ell_M(x,y)$ is the 0-1 loss, i.e. $\ell_M(x,y) = 0$ if $M(x) \neq y$ and 1 if $M(x) = y$. It is easy to see that $R(M) = \mathbb{E}_{z\sim D}\ \ell_M(z)$. Given an arbitrary ensemble of monitors $\Gamma = \{M_1,\ldots M_n\}$ and a distribution Q over Γ, the *Gibbs monitor* $M_{G,\Gamma,Q}$ is a special ensemble monitor that randomly chooses an M_i according to distribution Q and outputs the result of the chosen M_i. For our purposes, the distribution Q is always the uniform distribution over Γ, and hence we omit mentioning it in the subscript of $M_{G,\Gamma,Q}$. Furthermore, we always choose the ensemble Γ by independently generating each M_i from a given (PAC-learnable) class $\mathcal{M}$ of monitors using (ε, δ)-PAC learning. Notice that the above way of choosing Γ implicitly induces a distribution, say D', on all n-monitor ensembles.

3.1   Using Majority Voting

Our first ensemble monitor outputs a decision based on a majority vote (MV). Theorem 1 bounds the risk of the majority-vote monitor, making use of the following well-known result from learning theory.

Lemma 1 (PAC-Bayes Theorem [8,15]). *For every ensemble Γ of monitors, let $M_{MV,\Gamma}$ denote the majority-vote monitor and $M_{G,\Gamma}$ denote the Gibbs monitor. Then $R(M_{MV,\Gamma}) \leq 2 \cdot R(M_{G,\Gamma})$.*

Theorem 1. *Let $\Gamma = \{M_1,\ldots,M_n\}$ be an ensemble of monitors obtained by independently generating each M_i from a class $\mathcal{M}$ of monitors using (δ,ϵ)-PAC learning. Then the following holds for the majority-vote monitor $M_{MV,\Gamma}$:*

$$\mathbb{E}_{\Gamma\sim D'}[R(M_{MV,\Gamma})] \leq \min_{\gamma\in[0,1-\delta]} 2 \cdot \left[(L_{opt}+\epsilon+\delta+\gamma) + e^{-\gamma^2 n}((1-\gamma)(L_{opt}+\epsilon)+1)\right]$$

where L_{opt} is the loss of the optimal monitor in the class $\mathcal{M}$.

Proof. From Lemma 1, we know that $R(M_{MV,\Gamma}) \leq 2 \cdot R(M_{G,\Gamma})$. We prove below an upper bound of $R(M_{G,\Gamma})$, thus bounding $R(M_{MV,\Gamma})$.

We can characterize each sampled ensemble Γ of size n by the number of monitors M with $L(M) - L_{opt} \leq \epsilon$. We will call such monitors as "strong" monitors. We denote the set of ensembles with $k \leq n$ strong monitors by Ω_k. Using this characterization, the estimated risk of a Gibbs monitor over an ensemble of monitors can be defined as:

$$\mathbb{E}_{\Gamma\sim D'}[R(M_{G,\Gamma})] = \sum_{k=0}^{n}\sum_{\Gamma\in\Omega_k} \Pr(\Gamma) \cdot \frac{1}{n}\sum_{M_i\in\Gamma}\mathbb{E}_{(x,y)\sim D}[\mathbb{1}(M_i(x)\neq y)] \quad (1)$$

where $Pr(\Gamma)$ is the probability of choosing the ensemble Γ, and the risk $R(M_{G,\Gamma})$ of a Gibbs monitor for a specific ensemble Γ (assuming each $M_i \in \Gamma$ is chosen uniformly randomly) is $\frac{1}{n}\sum_{M_i\in\Gamma}\mathbb{E}_{(x,y)\sim D}[\mathbb{1}(M_i(x)\neq y)]$, with $\mathbb{1}$ being the indicator function.

The expression $\mathbb{E}_{(x,y)\sim D}[\mathbb{1}(M_i(x)\neq y)]$ define the loss $L(M_i)$ of an individual monitor M_i, and therefore, the estimated risk can be rewritten as:

$$\mathbb{E}_{\Gamma\sim D'}[R(M_{G,\Gamma})] = \sum_{k=0}^{n}\sum_{\Gamma\in\Omega_k}\Pr(\Gamma)\cdot\frac{1}{n}\sum_{M_i\in\Gamma}L(M_i) \qquad (2)$$

The loss $L(M_i)$ depends on the strength of monitor M_i. Recall that Γ has k strong monitors. If M_i is a strong monitor, then $L(M_i)$ is subject to the guarantee $|L(M_i) - L_{opt}| \leq \epsilon$. Otherwise, $L(M_i)$ is subject to $|L(M_i) - L_{opt}| > \epsilon$. In the former case, $L(M_i)$ can be bounded from above by $L_{opt} + \epsilon$. In the latter case, we simply bound $L(M_i)$ by 1. The estimated risk can thus be bounded by:

$$\mathbb{E}_{\Gamma\sim D'}[R(M_{G,\Gamma})] \leq \sum_{k=0}^{n}\sum_{\Gamma\in\Omega_k}\Pr(\Gamma)\cdot\frac{1}{n}(k\cdot(L_{opt}+\epsilon)+(n-k)) \qquad (3)$$

In remains to show that $\Pr(\Gamma)$ can be bounded in terms of δ,ϵ and n. To this end, we use Hoefdding's Theorem [9] to make the following distinction on the values of k.

Let $Z_1,\ldots,Z_n$ be independent Bernoulli random variables, such that $Z_i = \mathbb{1}(L(M_i) - L_{opt} \leq \epsilon)$. Let $p = \Pr(Z_i = 1)$; notice that using PAC-learning to choose the M_i's guarantees that $p \geq 1 - \delta$. Using Hoefdding's Theorem, it now follows that $\Pr(n\cdot p - \sum_{i\leq n}Z_i \geq t) \leq e^{-2\frac{t^2}{n}}$ for any $t > 0$. We replace t with $t = \gamma\cdot n$ for $\gamma\in[0, 1-\delta]$, thus obtaining the inequality $\Pr(n\cdot p - \sum_{i\leq n}Z_i \geq \gamma\cdot n) \leq e^{-2\gamma^2\cdot n}$. Given that $\sum_{i\leq n}Z_i = k$ for a specific Γ, we rewrite the summation over k in Eq. 3 by making the following distinction over the values of k. We distinguish the cases for $k < n\cdot p - \gamma\cdot n$ and $k \geq n\cdot p - \gamma\cdot n$.

For the case of $k < n\cdot p - \gamma\cdot n$, we can derive the following bound. We can trivially follow that $k\cdot(L_{opt}+\epsilon) < n\cdot(p-\gamma)(L_{opt}+\epsilon)$. We can also follow that $n > n - k > n - n\cdot(p-\gamma)$. As a consequence we can infer that $\frac{1}{n}\cdot(k\cdot(L_{opt}+\epsilon)+(n-k)) < (p-\gamma)\cdot(L_{opt}+\epsilon)+1$. Lastly, this implies that

$$\sum_{k=0}^{n\cdot p-\gamma\cdot n-1}\sum_{\Gamma\in\Omega_k}\Pr(\Gamma)\cdot\frac{1}{n}(k\cdot(L_{opt}+\epsilon)+(n-k)) \leq e^{-2\gamma^2\cdot n}((p-\gamma)\cdot(L_{opt}+\epsilon)+1)$$

$$(4)$$

For the case of $k \geq n\cdot p - \gamma\cdot n$, we do a similar analysis. It follows that $\frac{1}{n}\cdot(k\cdot(L_{opt}+\epsilon)+n-k) \leq L_{opt}+\epsilon+1-p+\gamma$, and in turn

$$\sum_{k=n\cdot p-\gamma\cdot n}^{n}\sum_{\Gamma\in\Omega_k}\Pr(\Gamma)\cdot\frac{1}{n}(k\cdot(L_{opt}+\epsilon)+(n-k)) \leq L_{opt}+\epsilon+1-p+\gamma \quad (5)$$

Combining Eqs. (4) and (5), and because both hold for any value of $\gamma\in[0, 1-\delta]$, our main result follows:

$$\mathbb{E}_{\Gamma \sim D'}[R(M_{MV,\Gamma})] \leq \min_{\gamma \in [0,1-\delta]} 2 \cdot \left[(L_{opt} + \epsilon + \delta + \gamma) + e^{-\gamma^2 n}((1-\gamma)(L_{opt} + \epsilon) + 1) \right]$$

$\square$

Corollary 1. *For sufficiently large n, the bound on the estimated risk of the majority voting monitor is monotonically decreasing.*

3.2 Using Multi-armed Bandits

Multi-armed bandits are a class of reinforcement learning problems where one has n actions and at any given time step, an agent has to choose between these actions to maximize rewards. This is a classic example of trading off exploration vs exploitation, which is exactly what we want to do when selecting the output of one monitor from within an ensemble.

In our context, each action amounts to seeking the output of a (potentially weak) monitor. At any given time step, the ensemble monitor can choose one of the monitors, say M_i, and uses the output of M_i as its output for that time step. The literature on multi-armed bandits indicates that Thompson sampling [19] is a highly effective strategy for choosing the actions in each time step, and we follow this approach. Thompson sampling dynamically biases the probabilities of choosing different monitors in favour of the one with the least risk, based on the outcomes seen so far. This allows us to dynamically select a monitor as time evolves. Note that this approach requires us to keep all monitors available when running the ensemble monitor.

We also used an alternative approach where we used an offline phase to select the most promising monitor in the ensemble, and used only this monitor subsequently. The offline phase itself uses Thompson sampling to identify with high probability the monitor with the least risk.

Theorem 2. *Let $\Gamma = \{M_1, \ldots, M_n\}$ be as in Theorem 1, and let $M_{mab,\Gamma}$ be the monitor with lowest estimated $L(M_i)$ chosen using Thompson sampling in an offline phase. Then the following holds:*

$$\mathbb{E}_{\Gamma \sim D'}[R(M_{mab,\Gamma})] \leq \min_{\gamma \in [0,1-\delta]} e^{-2n\gamma^2} \cdot ((L_{opt} + \varepsilon)(1-\delta-\gamma) + 1) + (L_{opt} + \varepsilon + \delta - \gamma)$$

Proof. Let T_k denote the event that k out of n monitors in Γ are "strong" (using terminology from the proof of Theorem 1). Then

$$\mathbb{E}_{\Gamma \sim D'}[R(M_{mab,\Gamma})] = \sum_{k=0}^{n} \mathbb{E}[R(M_{mab,\Gamma}) \mid T_k] \cdot Pr[T_k] \tag{6}$$

Let H_k^{TS} denote the probability of choosing a strong monitor from among k strong monitors in Γ, when using Thompson sampling (TS) in the offline phase.

Let $H_k^{Unif} = \frac{k}{n}$ denote the same probability when using uniform random sampling in the offline phase. Clearly, $H_k^{TS} \geq H_k^{Unif} = \frac{k}{n}$. Since $L(M_i) \leq L_{opt} + \epsilon$ for each strong monitor M_i, it follows that $\mathbb{E}[R(M_{mab,\Gamma}) \mid T_k] < \frac{k}{n}(L_{opt} + \epsilon) + \frac{n-k}{n}$.

Using the same reasoning as in the proof of Theorem 1, we now choose a parameter $\gamma \in [0, 1-\delta)$ and split the summation in Eq. 6 into two parts: (a) $k \leq n \cdot (1-\delta-\gamma)$ and (b) $k > n \cdot (1-\delta-\gamma)$. In case (a), we use $Pr[T_k] \leq e^{-2\gamma^2 n}$ using Hoeffding's Theorem, and $\mathbb{E}[R(M_{mab,\Gamma})] < (L_{opt} + \varepsilon) \cdot \frac{k}{n} + \frac{n-k}{n}) < (L_{opt} + \varepsilon)(1 - \delta - \gamma) + 1$. In case (b), we use $Pr[T_k] \leq 1$ and $\mathbb{E}[R(M_{mab,\Gamma})] < (L_{opt} + \varepsilon) + (\delta - \gamma)$. Combining parts (a) and (b) gives us the required bound. $\qquad\square$

Corollary 2. *For sufficiently large n, the bound on the estimated risk of the multi-armed bandit monitor is monotonically decreasing.*

4 Empirical Study

In this section, we use an instance of our motivating example in Fig. 1 to demonstrate the impact of using ensembles of ODD monitors in comparison to single-learned ODD monitors. We particularly use the methods of majority voting and a multi-armed bandit method that incorporates Thompson sampling during the offline testing phase. Our evaluation is performed over ensembles of growing size, comparing the rates of false negatives and false positives, especially to the average of the same rates over the individual monitors of an ensemble. We start with a description of the experimental setup and framework in Sects. 4.1 and 4.2, and present our results in Sect. 4.4 and 4.5.

4.1 Case Study

We use the example presented in Fig. 1 providing implementations for the CNN-based controller and safe controller. The goal is to use ensemble methods to learn an ODD monitor that implements the switching logic between the two controllers. The CNN-based controller is composed of a CNN that for a given image of the road in front of the vehicle returns the cross-track error (CTE), i.e., the distance of the vehicle to the center of the lane. The architecture and training of the CNN are irrelevant to the ODD monitor learning process, and throughout our entire evaluation process, we assume the entire CNN-based controller is a black box[1]. The CTE computed by the CNN is forwarded to a PID controller that uses this information to compute the steering angle of the car. The safe controller uses the same PID controller, but the latter is fed with ground truth values for the CTE.

---

[1] For the interested reader, the CNN had three convolutional layers with 24, 48, 96 filters, respectively, with a 5×5 kernel size, composed with an inner dense layer with 512 units using ReLU activation. The CNN was trained on 99k images collected at restricted weather and time of the day conditions, and labeled with the correct CTE.

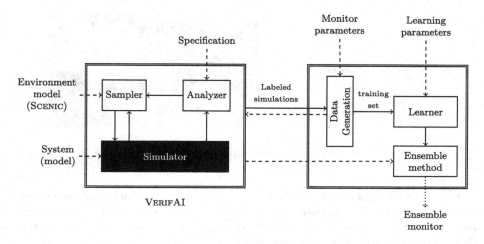

Fig. 2. Extension of VERIFAI with ODD ensemble learning

Our monitors are learned for fixed length input windows (fixed length history of data) of length 15 and a prediction horizon of 10 steps. The training data used in learning the monitors comprises sequence of values of a number of features, such as precipitation, cloudiness, sun angle, averaged radar points (left, front, right), road information (approaching a turn or junction), and the controls produced by the controllers. The labels of the training data are boolean labels based on whether a lane invasion or a collision occurred.

4.2 Framework and Implementation

The implementation of our framework builds on VERIFAI, a toolkit for the formal design and analysis of AI/ML-based systems [5]. The general workflow of VERIFAI is depicted in the left part of Fig. 2. Given an executable model of the system with the black-box (ML) component, a model of the environment in which the system is to be executed, given as a probabilistic program written in SCENIC [7], from which different simulation can be sampled, we use VERIFAI to run simulations and evaluate them according to a provided system-level specification i.e., one defining a property of the system (for example, the vehicle should never exit its lane nor collide with any object).

Each monitor of the ensemble is then generated in the following manner. A predefined number of simulations are sampled from the SCENIC program and each executed for a given number of simulation steps. The SCENIC program used in our experiments is depicted in Fig. 3. It defines a uniform distribution over different features such as weather conditions, times of the day, and different lanes of the world, as well as a point in the center of these lanes. For each simulation, VERIFAI samples an initial value to the various features, as shown by the snapshots on the right of Fig. 3, and subsequently simulates a run of the vehicle on the road for the pre-determined number of time-steps, and according

```
param weather =
        Uniform('ClearNoon', 'CloudyNoon',
                'WetNoon', 'MidRainyNoon',
                'ClearSunSet')

lane = Uniform(*network.lanes)
start = OrientedPoint on lane.centerline

ego = Car at start,
        with visibleDistance 60,
        with behavior EgoBehavior(10)
```

Fig. 3. Scenic program and corresponding sampled scenes

to the behavior `EgoBehavior`, which defines the implementation of the system as described in the last section. In our experiments, we particularly use SCENIC's interface to the open-source Carla driving simulator [4]. Each simulation step is then evaluated according to the specification.

The evaluated simulations are then forwarded to another component for data generation. The data generation component performs several operations on top of the simulation traces, creating the training data by applying certain filters, transformations, and slicing (see, e.g., [23,26]). Each row in the training data represents the input to a monitor and is of size equal to the number of features times the length of the input window and the label is an occurrence of a lane invasion or collision p time steps in the future, where p is the prediction horizon.

Once the training data is obtained, we can use any model-building algorithm to build one ODD monitor. In our experiments, we use the Decision Tree Classifiers from the `sklearn` Python package. Every monitor learned is forwarded to the ensemble method to create the ensemble monitor. We learned 100 ODD monitors and applied the methods of majority voting and multi-armed bandit varying the number of monitors in an ensemble from 10 to 100 with steps of size 10. For each monitor, we collected data from 50 SCENIC simulations, each run for 500 time steps.

4.3   Evaluation

After computing an ensemble monitor, using one of the ensemble methods, we evaluate the monitor using the following metrics: percentage of false positives and percentage of false negatives. An output of the ensemble is a false positive if the ensemble monitor determines that the safe controller should be used but instead, if the CNN Controller was used, there would still be no collision or lane invasion. Similarly, a false negative is one where the ensemble monitor determines that a CNN Controller should be used but using that results in collision prediction-horizon many time steps in the future.

The implementation of our tool is in Python and all experiments were conducted on a machine with a 3.5 GHz 10-Core CPU, 64 GB of RAM, and a GPU with 6 GPCs and a total 3072 cores.

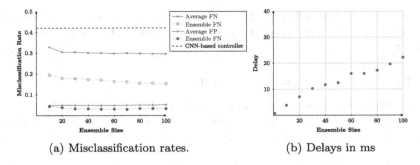

(a) Misclassification rates.   (b) Delays in ms

Fig. 4. Results for ODD monitors learned using Majority Voting for growing ensemble sizes. The majority vote threshold is 0.5. In the plot for misclassification rates, the black dashed line represents the misclassification of the CNN-based controller. The red plot with 'x' symbol and the teal plot with '+' symbol represents the average rate of false negatives and false positives, respectively, over the monitors of the ensemble for growing ensemble sizes. The dotted red plot with hollow circles and dotted teal plot with filled circles represent the false negative and false positive rates, respectively, of the majority vote for growing ensembles. The delay plot shows the time needed to compute a prediction for growing ensembles. (Color figure online)

4.4 Experiment: Majority Voting

Figure 4 shows the performance of the ODD ensemble when Majority Voting was used to determine the output of the ensemble. The performance is determined by evaluating a monitor over 500 simulation runs, each of length 500 steps. The number of ODD monitors used in the ensemble is plotted along the X-axis. In Fig. 4a, the Y-axis gives the misclassification rate. The black dashed line represents the misclassification of the CNN-based controller, in terms of violating the system-level specification. The red plot with 'x' symbol and the teal plot with '+' symbol represents the average rate of false negatives and false positives, respectively, over the monitors of the ensemble for growing ensemble sizes. The dotted red plot with hollow circles and dotted teal plot with filled circles represent the false negative and false positive rates, respectively, of the majority vote for growing ensembles. From Fig. 4a, it is clear that using an ensemble improves the error classification than using only a single monitor to govern the use of the CNN controller. Moreover, we can see that as we increase the number of monitors in the ensemble, both the percentage of false positives and the percentage of false negatives decrease, reducing the misclassification rate of the ensemble of ODD monitors, highlighting the need and usefulness of using an ensemble of ODD monitors.

One aspect of Majority Voting is that each monitor of the ensemble has to be evaluated to obtain the output of the ensemble. This could be of concern as an increase in the number of monitors could increase the time taken to determine the output of the ensemble. Figure 4b shows the time (in milliseconds) needed to compute a prediction for growing ensembles. As can be seen from the figure, the time taken to evaluate a monitor is linearly increasing but for 100 monitors is still small, and does not really result in a significant delay in determining the output/prediction of the ensemble.

4.5 Experiment: Multi-armed Bandit

In this section, we present our findings from applying a version of the multi-armed bandit method that uses Thompson sampling. We describe both the selection procedure and how we evaluated the selected monitors.

Selecting the Best Monitor in Multi-arm Bandit. After the 100 monitors are learned, we select the best monitor using the well-known Thompson sampling algorithm [19]. It efficiently balances the exploration and exploitation of monitors (i.e., arms) to converge at the arm which gives the maximum reward.

For this, we first used the same SCENIC program used earlier to generate data for the selection of the best monitor. For this, the SCENIC program with Carla was run for 100 simulations, each simulation for 500 time-steps to get a data set, D, containing 46,900 data points (resulting from slicing each simulation according to a window length 15 and prediction horizon 10 and after removing a few initialization steps).

We use this data set to determine the best monitor in the following manner. For each monitor, m_i, a Beta distribution with parameters $\alpha_i > 0$, $\beta_i > 0$ is maintained. Here α_i and β_i indicate the success and failure of the monitor. Initially, both α_i and β_i are assigned 1, and the values are updated whenever the arm corresponding to the monitor is pulled, i,e, the monitor is tested. An arm pull is called a round and the selection of the best monitor is done over many rounds. In each arm pull (round), the following is done:

- We sample from the Beta distribution of each monitor and choose the monitor, m_j (expert for this round) corresponding to the highest sample.
- We then uniformly randomly sample a data point from the data set D and test the chosen arm on this data point.
- if the prediction of the chosen monitor, m_j matches with the label of the data point, we update the α_j else we update β_j thus updating the Beta distribution of m_j.

We keep repeating these rounds of arm pulls until convergence. We define a convergence criterion over a fixed stabilization window (not to be confused with the input window of the monitor), where, by a window, we mean a number of consecutive rounds. The convergence criterion is as follows:

- There should be only one monitor with the highest mean in the window.
- This monitor should have a small dispersion index in the window.

The dispersion index for the beta distribution $\mathcal{B}(\alpha, \beta)$ with parameters α and β is the variance of the distribution divided by its mean, and is given by

$$\text{Dispersion Index}(\mathcal{B}(\alpha, \beta)) = \frac{Var(\mathcal{B}(\alpha, \beta))}{Mean(\mathcal{B}(\alpha, \beta))} := \frac{\beta}{(\alpha + \beta)(\alpha + \beta + 1)}$$

Let the bound on the dispersion index be C, and the stabilization window W. Let α and β be the parameters corresponding to the beta distribution of M. Then, the convergence criteria is as follows:

- there should be only one monitor M with the highest mean in W.
- Then the dispersion index of M must be at most C for each round in the window W

Once the convergence criterion is satisfied, the monitor with the highest mean is chosen as the expert, and we terminate this phase. We show the results for two different bounds on dispersion index, namely $C := 10^{-4}$ and $C := 10^{-3}$ in Figs. 5b and 5d, respectively. We plot the number of rounds until convergence on the Y-axis and the number of monitors in the ensemble on the X-axis. The window length for both the plots is $|W| = 10^3$. As expected, we take more rounds to converge when $C := 10^{-4}$ than $C := 10^{-3}$. For example, for 40 monitors, we take 10087 rounds to converge when $C := 10^{-4}$ whereas we take 2221 rounds when $C := 10^{-3}$.

Results. After selecting the best monitor for the Multi-Armed Bandit strategy, we next generate the test data to evaluate our ensemble. The test data generated used a SCENIC program which was similar to the program used to generate training data with small modifications in the parameters of the environment. The SCENIC program for testing was executed 500 times, each simulation 500 time steps long. This data set contains 234,500 rows. As mentioned earlier, we computed the percentage of false positives and the percentage of false negatives.

We tested the best monitor chosen using Thompson sampling on the generated data set. The prediction of the best monitor chosen in the selection phase is considered to be the prediction/output of the ensemble. We present the misclassification plots in Figs. 5a and 5c. As before, the black dashed line represents the misclassification of the CNN-based controller. The red plot with 'x' symbols and the teal plot with '+' symbols represent the average rate of false negatives and false positives, respectively, over the monitors in the ensemble for growing ensemble sizes. That is, for each ensemble, it contains the average rate of false negatives and false positives, respectively, over the ensemble. The dashed red plot with hollow circles and the dotted teal plot with filled circles represent the false negative and false positive rates of the best selected monitor for growing ensembles.

As seen from Figs. 5a and 5c, the misclassification rate using the ensemble monitor is lower than that of solely using the CNN-based controller. The misclassification rate of best expert is less than the average misclassification rate over monitors in the ensemble, and hence using the best expert helps us reduce the overall misclassification rate. Note again that, the misclassification rate is the sum of false negative and false positive rates. In few rounds, the misclassification rates were close to the average rates (for monitor 43). Such anomalies may occur because a non-optimal monitor may get chosen as an expert in the evaluation phase, due to the probabilistic nature (of the sampling) in the evaluation phase.

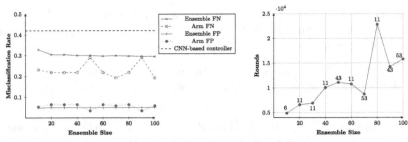

(a) Misclassification rates for a bound of 10^{-4} on the dispersion index.

(b) Rounds until convergence for a bound of 10^{-4} on the dispersion index.

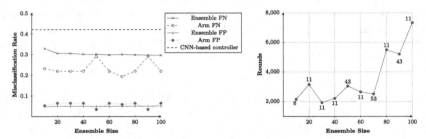

(c) Misclassification rates for a bound of 10^{-3} on the dispersion index.

(d) Rounds until convergence for a bound of 10^{-3} on the dispersion index.

Fig. 5. Results for using multi-armed bandit for growing sizes of ensembles up to 100 monitors. Figures a and b represent the results for a bound of 10^{-4} on the dispersion index, and a stabilization window of length 10^3. Figures c and d represent the results for a bound of 10^{-3} on the dispersion index, and a stabilization window of length 10^3. In the plots for misclassification rates, the black dashed line represents the misclassification of the CNN-based controller. The red plot with 'x' symbols and teal plot with '+' symbols represent the average rate of false negatives and false positives respectively, over the monitors in the ensemble for growing ensemble sizes. The dashed red plot with hollow circles and the dotted teal plot with filled circles represent the false negatives and false positives of the best selected monitor for growing ensemble sizes. The convergence plots show the number of rounds needed for converging in selection phase. Each point is labeled with the id of the best selected monitor. (Color figure online)

Also, since the convergence criteria does not consider other monitors, some good monitors may not get enough iterations for their mean to converge to a high value. Therefore their mean may remain low with a relatively high variance. To reduce the chances of such anomalies we have to increase the window length or decrease the dispersion index bound.

In summary, our experimental results demonstrate that the use of ensembles helps reduce the overall misclassificationrates and improve the performance of ODD monitors. We remark that the theoretical analysis in Sect. 3 is a conservative treatment of an upper bound of the misclassification rate under idealized assumptions. Our experiments however show that the actual misclassification rates are already lower than the ensemble average even with 10 or 20 monitors. In the experiments using Thompson sampling, since we pre-select a monitor using an extensive offline selection phase, the probability that we miss a strong monitor is low even for small ensemble sizes like 10 or 20. We see the effect of this by noticing that monitor 11, which was chosen as a strong monitor with only 20 monitors in the ensemble, reappears as a strong monitor with larger number of monitors in the ensemble as well (see Figs. 5b and 5d). This explains why we do not see a decline in the misclassification rate for increasing ensemble sizes. In contrast, in the Majority Voting case there is no pre-selection, and therefore the reduction in misclassification rate with ensemble size shows more clearly.

5   Related Work

Operational Design Domains. A key aspect in assuring the safety of AI-based autonomous systems is to clearly understand their capabilities and limitations and therefore establish the operational design domains of the system [2,13,14]. Several works have been dedicated to investigating ways of describing ODDs. Some of them are textual and follow a structured natural language format for describing ODDs [20,27]. Others include a tabular description defining a checklist of rules and functional requirements that need to be checked to guarantee a safe operation of the system [22]. A generic taxonomy of the different ODD representation formats is presented in BSI PAS 1883 standard [10]. While the approaches above concentrate on the design of languages for describing ODDs, many works have concluded that there also is a necessity for ODDs to be executable, e.g., to enable the construction of monitors that can be used at runtime [3]. To this end, there has been a focus on developing machine-readable domain-specific languages for specifying ODDs [11]. Our work builds upon previous work [24,26] which presents a framework for the automated construction of monitorable ODDs via a counterexample-guided learning approach.

PAC-Based Learning. There has been considerable work in finding interpretations of machine learning models which are used as black boxes. These include [1,12,16–18], to name a few. In [25], an algorithm to construct interpretations of black boxes with PAC guarantees is presented. In [26], the authors show how run time monitors can be build from black box machine learning models. In this paper, we draw from the work in [25] and [26] to learn an ensemble of run-time monitors from black box machine learning models. To the best of our knowledge, our work is the first to investigate the PAC-learnability of ODD monitors and how ensemble methods can be used to improve the accuracy of these monitors.

6   Conclusion

In this paper, we developed a new framework for learning monitor ensembles for ODDs, which allows us to go beyond the PAC guarantees for obtaining a single ODD monitor. We examine two ensemble approaches in detail, Majority Voting and Multi-armed Bandit methods, and show theoretical results on how using these methods reduced the bound on the risk of misclassification. Further, we perform a detailed empirical study on a benchmark from the domain of autonomous driving which show that with larger ensembles we converge to monitors with improved misclassification rates. As future work, we would like to explore other ensemble approaches, tighter bounds on the risks of ensembles, as well as enrich the feature space to obtain even better monitors for the case-study. Another interesting line of future work is the exploration and study of an ensemble of PAC monitors with a special focus to investigate the extent to which the individual PAC monitors can be relaxed such that the ensemble achieves similar misclassification rates as those given by a strong PAC monitor.

Acknowledgments. This work is partially supported by NSF grants 1545126 (VeHI-CaL, including an NSF-TiH grant) and 1837132, by the DARPA contracts FA8750-18-C-0101 (AA) and FA8750-20-C-0156 (SDCPS), by Berkeley Deep Drive, by C3DTI, and by Toyota under the iCyPhy center. Financial support from TiH-IoT, IIT Bombay vide grant TIH-IOT/06-2022/IC/NSF/SL/NIUC-2022-05/001 under TiH-IoT US-India Collaborative Research Program 2022 is gratefully acknowledged. Funds from the latter grant were used to partially support Shetal Shah, Aniruddha Joshi, S. Akshay and Supratik Chakraborty for work reported in the current paper.

References

1. Avellaneda, F.: Efficient inference of optimal decision trees. In: AAAI 2020, pp. 3195–3202. AAAI Press (2020)
2. Blumenthal, M.S., Fraade-Blanar, L., Best, R., Irwin, J.L.: Safe Enough: Approaches to Assessing Acceptable Safety for Automated Vehicles. RAND Corporation, Santa Monica (2020). https://doi.org/10.7249/RRA569-1
3. Colwell, I., Phan, B., Saleem, S., Salay, R., Czarnecki, K.: An automated vehicle safety concept based on runtime restriction of the operational design domain. In: 2018 IEEE Intelligent Vehicles Symposium (IV), pp. 1910–1917 (2018). https://doi.org/10.1109/IVS.2018.8500530
4. Dosovitskiy, A., Ros, G., Codevilla, F., Lopez, A., Koltun, V.: CARLA: an open urban driving simulator. In: Proceedings of the 1st Annual Conference on Robot Learning, pp. 1–16 (2017)
5. Dreossi, T., et al.: VERIFAI: a toolkit for the formal design and analysis of artificial intelligence-based systems. In: Dillig, I., Tasiran, S. (eds.) CAV 2019. LNCS, vol. 11561, pp. 432–442. Springer, Cham (2019). https://doi.org/10.1007/978-3-030-25540-4_25
6. Fremont, D.J., Dreossi, T., Ghosh, S., Yue, X., Sangiovanni-Vincentelli, A.L., Seshia, S.A.: Scenic: a language for scenario specification and scene generation. In: PLDI, pp. 63–78. ACM (2019)
7. Fremont, D.J., et al.: Scenic: a language for scenario specification and data generation (2020). https://arxiv.org/abs/1809.09310
8. Germain, P., Lacasse, A., Laviolette, F., Marchand, M., Roy, J.: Risk bounds for the majority vote: from a PAC-Bayesian analysis to a learning algorithm. CoRR abs/1503.08329 (2015). http://arxiv.org/abs/1503.08329

9. Hoeffding, W.: Probability inequalities for sums of bounded random variables. J. Am. Stat. Assoc. **58**(301), 13–30 (1963). https://doi.org/10.1080/01621459. 1963.10500830. https://www.tandfonline.com/doi/abs/10.1080/01621459.1963. 10500830

10. The British Standards Institution: Operational design domain (ODD) taxonomy for an automated driving system (ADS) - specification. BSI PAS 1883 (2020)

11. Irvine, P., Zhang, X., Khastgir, S., Schwalb, E., Jennings, P.: A two-level abstraction ODDdefinition language: Part i*. In: 2021 IEEE International Conference on Systems, Man, and Cybernetics (SMC), pp. 2614–2621. IEEE Press (2021). https://doi.org/10.1109/SMC52423.2021.9658751

12. Jha, S., Sahai, T., Raman, V., Pinto, A., Francis, M.: Explaining AI decisions using efficient methods for learning sparse boolean formulae. J. Autom. Reason. **63**(4), 1055–1075 (2019)

13. Khastgir, S., Birrell, S.A., Dhadyalla, G., Jennings, P.A.: Calibrating trust through knowledge: introducing the concept of informed safety for automation in vehicles. Transp. Res. Part C Emerg. Technol. **96**, 290–303 (2018)

14. Khastgir, S., Brewerton, S., Thomas, J., Jennings, P.: Systems approach to creating test scenarios for automated driving systems. Reliab. Eng. Syst. Saf. **215**, 107610 (2021). https://doi.org/10.1016/j.ress.2021.107610. https://www. sciencedirect.com/science/article/pii/S0951832021001551

15. McAllester, D.: Simplified PAC-Bayesian margin bounds. In: Schölkopf, B., Warmuth, M.K. (eds.) COLT-Kernel 2003. LNCS (LNAI), vol. 2777, pp. 203–215. Springer, Heidelberg (2003). https://doi.org/10.1007/978-3-540-45167-9_16

16. Narodytska, N., Ignatiev, A., Pereira, F., Marques-Silva, J.: Learning optimal decision trees with SAT. In: Lang, J. (ed.) International Joint Conference on Artificial Intelligence, IJCAI 2018. ijcai.org (2018)

17. Pedreschi, D., Giannotti, F., Guidotti, R., Monreale, A., Ruggieri, S., Turini, F.: Meaningful explanations of black box AI decision systems. In: AAAI (2019)

18. Ribeiro, M.T., Singh, S., Guestrin, C.: "why should i trust you?": explaining the predictions of any classifier. In: Knowledge Discovery and Data Mining, KDD 2016. Association for Computing Machinery (2016)

19. Russo, D.J., Van Roy, B., Kazerouni, A., Osband, I., Wen, Z.: A tutorial on thompson sampling. Found. Trends Mach. Learn. **11**(1), 1–96 (2018). https://doi.org/10. 1561/2200000070

20. SAE on-Road Automated Driving Committee and others: SAE J3016. Taxonomy and definitions for terms related to driving automation systems for on-road motor vehicles. Technical report

21. Shalev-Shwartz, S., Ben-David, S.: Understanding Machine Learning: From Theory to Algorithms. Cambridge University Press, Cambridge (2014)

22. Thorn, E., Kimmel, S.C., Chaka, M.: A framework for automated driving system testable cases and scenarios (2018)

23. Torfah, H., Junges, S., Fremont, D.J., Seshia, S.A.: Formal analysis of AI-based autonomy: from modeling to runtime assurance. In: Feng, L., Fisman, D. (eds.) RV 2021. LNCS, vol. 12974, pp. 311–330. Springer, Cham (2021). https://doi.org/ 10.1007/978-3-030-88494-9_19

24. Torfah, H., Seshia, S.A.: Runtime monitors for operational design domains of black-box ML-models. In: NeurIPS ML Safety Workshop (2022). https://openreview. net/forum?id=6_AtjSBhqx

25. Torfah, H., Shah, S., Chakraborty, S., Akshay, S., Seshia, S.A.: Synthesizing pareto-optimal interpretations for black-box models. In: Proceedings of the IEEE Interna-

tional Conference on Formal Methods in Computer-Aided Design (FMCAD), pp. 153–162. IEEE (2021)

26. Torfah, H., Xie, C., Junges, S., Vazquez-Chanlatte, M., Seshia, S.A.: Learning monitorable operational design domains for assured autonomy. In: Bouajjani, A., Holík, L., Wu, Z. (eds.) ATVA 2022. LNCS, vol. 13505, pp. 3–22. Springer, Cham (2022). https://doi.org/10.1007/978-3-031-19992-9_1

27. Zhang, X., Khastgir, S., Jennings, P.: Scenario description language for automated driving systems: a two level abstraction approach. In: 2020 IEEE International Conference on Systems, Man, and Cybernetics (SMC), pp. 973–980 (2020). https://doi.org/10.1109/SMC42975.2020.9283417

Monitoring Algorithmic Fairness Under Partial Observations

Thomas A. Henzinger, Konstantin Kueffner, and Kaushik Mallik$^{(\boxtimes)}$

Institute of Science and Technology Austria (ISTA), Klosterneuburg, Austria
kaushik.mallik@ist.ac.at

Abstract. As AI and machine-learned software are used increasingly for making decisions that affect humans, it is imperative that they remain fair and unbiased in their decisions. To complement design-time bias mitigation measures, runtime verification techniques have been introduced recently to monitor the algorithmic fairness of deployed systems. Previous monitoring techniques assume full observability of the states of the (unknown) monitored system. Moreover, they can monitor only fairness properties that are specified as arithmetic expressions over the probabilities of different events. In this work, we extend fairness monitoring to systems modeled as partially observed Markov chains (POMC), and to specifications containing arithmetic expressions over the expected values of numerical functions on event sequences. The only assumptions we make are that the underlying POMC is aperiodic and starts in the stationary distribution, with a bound on its mixing time being known. These assumptions enable us to estimate a given property for the entire distribution of possible executions of the monitored POMC, by observing only a single execution. Our monitors observe a long run of the system and, after each new observation, output updated PAC-estimates of how fair or biased the system is. The monitors are computationally lightweight and, using a prototype implementation, we demonstrate their effectiveness on several real-world examples.

1 Introduction

Runtime verification complements traditional static verification techniques, by offering lightweight approaches for verifying properties of systems from a single long observed execution trace [8]. Recently, runtime verification was used to monitor biases in machine-learned decision-making softwares [3,28,29]. Decision-making softwares are being increasingly used for making critical decisions affecting humans; example areas include judiciary [12,17], policing [19,39], and banking [38]. It is important that these softwares are unbiased towards the protected attributes of humans, like gender and ethnicity. However, they were shown to be biased on many occasions in the past [17,36,42,46]. While many offline approaches were proposed for mitigating such biases [10,11,51,53] runtime verification introduces a new complementary tool to oversee *algorithmic fairness*

P. Katsaros and L. Nenzi (Eds.): RV 2023, LNCS 14245, pp. 291–311, 2023.
https://doi.org/10.1007/978-3-031-44267-4_15

of deployed decision-making systems [3,28,29]. In this work, we extend runtime verification to monitor algorithmic fairness for a broader class of system models and a more expressive specification language.

Prior works on monitoring algorithmic fairness assumed that the given system is modeled as a Markov chain with unknown transition probabilities but with fully observable states [3,29]. A sequence of states visited by the Markov chain represents a (randomized) sequence of events generated from the interaction of the decision-making agent and its environment. The goal is to design a monitor that will observe one such long sequence of states, and, after observing every new state in the sequence, will compute an updated PAC-estimate of how fair or biased the system is.

In the prior works, the PAC guarantee on the output hinges on the full observability and the Markovian structure of the system [3,28,29]. While this setup is foundational, it is also very basic, and is not fulfilled by many real-world examples. Consider a lending scenario where at every step a bank (the decision-maker) receives the features (e.g., the age, gender, and ethnicity) of a loan applicant, and decides whether to grant or reject the loan. To model this system using the existing setup, we would need to assume that the monitor can observe the full state of the system which includes all the features of every applicant. In reality, the monitor will often be a third-party system, having only partial view of the system's states.

We address the problem of designing monitors when the systems are modeled using partially observed Markov chains (POMC) with unknown transition probabilities. The difficulty comes from the fact that a random observation sequence that is visible to the monitor may not follow a Markovian pattern, even though the underlying state sequence is Markovian. We overcome this by making the assumption that the POMC starts in the stationary distribution, which in turn guarantees a certain uniformity in how the observations follow each other. We argue that the stationarity assumption is fulfilled whenever the system has been running for a long time, which is suitable for long term monitoring of fairness properties. With the help of a few additional standard assumptions on the POMC, like aperiodicity and the knowledge of a bound on the mixing time, we can compute PAC estimates on the degree of algorithmic fairness over the distribution of all runs of the system from a single monitored observation sequence.

Besides the new system model, we also introduce a richer specification language—called bounded specification expressions (BSE). BSE-s can express many common algorithmic fairness properties from the literature, such as demographic parity [18], equal opportunity [27], and disparate impact [21]. Furthermore, BSE-s can express new fairness properties which were not expressible using the previous formalism [3,29]. In particular, BSE-s can express quantitative fairness properties, including fair distribution of expected credit scores and fair distribution of expected wages across different demographic groups of the population; details can be found, respectively, in Example 5 and 6 in Sect. 3.2.

The building block of a BSE is an atomic function, which is a function that assigns bounded numerical values to observation sequences of a particular length.

Using an atomic function, we can express weighted star-free regular expressions (every word satisfying the given regular expression has a numerical weight), average response time-like properties, etc. A BSE can contain many different atomic functions combined together through a restricted set of arithmetic, relational, and logical operations. We define two fragments of BSE-s: The first one is called QuantBSE, which contains only arithmetic expressions over atomic functions, and whose semantic value is the expected value of the given expression over the distribution of runs of the POMC. The second one is called QualBSE, which turns the QuantBSE expressions into boolean expressions through relational (e.g., whether a QuantBSE expression is greater than zero) and logical operators (e.g., conjunction of two relational sentences), and whose semantic value is the expected truth or falsehood of the given expression over the distribution of runs of the POMC.

For any given BSE, we show how to construct a monitor that observes a single long observation sequence generated by the given POMC with unknown transition probabilities, and after each observation outputs an updated numerical estimate of the actual semantic value of the BSE for the observed system. The heart of our approach is a PAC estimation algorithm for the semantic values of the atomic functions. The main difficulty stems from the statistical dependence between any two consecutive observations, which is a side-effect of the partial observability of the states of the Markov chain, and prevents us from using the common PAC bounds that were used in the prior works that assumed full observability of the POMC states [3,29]. We show how the problem can be cast as the statistical estimation problem of estimating the expected value of a function over the states of a POMC which satisfies a certain bounded difference property. This estimation problem can be solved using a version of McDiarmid's concentration inequality [44], for which we need the additional assumptions that the given POMC is aperiodic and that a bound on its mixing time is known. We use McDiarmid's inequality to find the PAC estimate of every individual atomic function of the given BSE. The individual PAC estimates can then be combined using known methods to obtain the overall PAC estimate of the given BSE [3].

Our monitors are computationally lightweight, and produce reasonably tight PAC bounds of the monitored properties. Using a prototype implementation, we present the effectiveness of our monitors on two different examples. On a real-world example, we showed how our monitors can check if a bank has been fair in giving loans to individuals from two different demographic groups in the population, and on an academic example, we showed how our monitors' outputs improve as the known bound on the mixing time gets tighter.

The proofs of the technical claims are omitted due to limitation of space, and can be found in the longer version of the paper [30].

1.1   Related Work

There are many works in AI and machine-learning which address how to eliminate or minimize decision biases in learned models through improved design principles [10,11,18,27,47,51,53]. In formal methods, too, there are some works which statically verify absence of biases of learned models [2,6,25,26,34,41,49]. All of these works are static interventions and rely on the availability of the system model, which may not be always true.

Runtime verification of algorithmic fairness, through continuous monitoring of decision events, is a relatively new area pioneered by the work of Albarghouthi et al. [3]. We further advanced their idea in our other works which appeared recently [28,29]. In those works, on one hand, we generalized the class of supported system models to Markov chains and presented the new Bayesian statistical view of the problem [29]. On the other hand, we relaxed the time-invariance assumption on the system [28]. In this current paper, we limit ourselves to time-invariant systems but extend the system models to partially observed Markov chains and consider the broader class of BSE properties, which enables us to additionally express properties whose values depend on observation sequences.

Traditional runtime verification techniques support mainly temporal properties and employ finite automata-based monitors [4,7,16,40]. In contrast, runtime verification of algorithmic fairness requires checking statistical properties, which is beyond the limit of what automata-based monitors can accomplish. Although there are some works on quantitative runtime verification using richer types of monitors (with counters/registers like us) [24,31,32,43], the considered specifications usually do not extend to statistical properties such as algorithmic fairness.

Among the few works on monitoring statistical properties of systems, a majority of them only provides asymptotic correctness guarantees [22,50], whereas we provide anytime guarantees. On the other hand, works on monitoring statistical properties with finite-sample (nonasymptotic) guarantees are rare and are restricted to simple properties, such as probabilities of occurrences of certain events [9] and properties specified using certain fragments of LTL [45]. Monitoring POMCs (the same modeling formalism as us) were studied before by Stoller et al. [48], though the setting was a bit different from ours. Firstly, they only consider LTL properties, and, secondly, they assume the system model to be known by the monitor. This way the task of the monitor effectively reduces to a state estimation problem from a given observation sequence.

Technique-wise, there are some similarities between our work and the works on statistical model-checking [1,13,15,52] in that both compute PAC-guarantees on satisfaction or violation of a given specification. However, to the best of our knowledge, the existing statistical model-checking approaches do not consider algorithmic fairness properties.

2   Preliminaries

2.1   Notation

We write $\mathbb{R}$, $\mathbb{R}^+$, $\mathbb{N}$, and $\mathbb{N}^+$ to denote the sets of real numbers, positive real numbers, natural numbers (including zero), and positive integers, respectively.

Let Σ be a countable alphabet. We write Σ^* and Σ^ω to denote, respectively, the set of every finite and infinite word over Σ. Moreover, Σ^∞ denotes the set of finite and infinite words, i.e., $\Sigma^\infty := \Sigma^* \cup \Sigma^\omega$. We use the convention that symbols with arrow on top will denote words, whereas symbols without arrow will denote alphabet elements. Let $\overrightarrow{s} = s_1 s_2 \ldots$ be a word. We write $\overrightarrow{s}_i$ to denote the i-th symbol s_i, and write $\overrightarrow{s}_{i..j}$ to denote the subword $s_i \ldots s_j$, for $i < j$. We use the convention that the indices of a word begin at 1, so that the length of a word matches the index of the last symbol.

Let $\overrightarrow{s} \in \Sigma^*$ and any $\overrightarrow{t} \in \Sigma^\infty$ be two words. We denote the concatenation of $\overrightarrow{s}$ and $\overrightarrow{t}$ as $\overrightarrow{s}\,\overrightarrow{t}$. We generalize this to sets of words: For $S \subseteq \Sigma^*$ and $T \subseteq \Sigma^\infty$, we define the concatenation $ST := \{\overrightarrow{s}\,\overrightarrow{t} \mid \overrightarrow{s} \in S, \overrightarrow{t} \in T\}$. We say $\overrightarrow{s}$ is a prefix of $\overrightarrow{r}$, written $\overrightarrow{s} \prec \overrightarrow{r}$, if there exists a word $\overrightarrow{t} \in \Sigma^\infty$ such that $\overrightarrow{s}\,\overrightarrow{t} = \overrightarrow{r}$.

Suppose $\mathbb{T} \subseteq \mathbb{R}$ is a subset of real numbers, $v \in \mathbb{T}^n$ is a vector of length n over $\mathbb{T}$, and $M \in \mathbb{T}^{n \times m}$ is a matrix of dimension $n \times m$ over $\mathbb{T}$; here m, n can be infinity. We use v_i to denote the i-th element of v, and M_{ij} to denote the element at the intersection of the i-th row and the j-th column of M. A probability distribution over a set S is a vector $v \in [0,1]^{|S|}$, such that $\sum_{i \in [1;|S|]} v_i = 1$.

2.2 Randomized Event Generators: Partially Observed Markov Chains

We use partially observed Markov chains (POMC) as sequential randomized generators of events. A POMC is a tuple $(Q, M, \lambda, \Sigma, \ell)$, where $Q = \mathbb{N}^+$ is a countable set of states, M is a stochastic matrix of dimension $|Q| \times |Q|$, called the *transition probability matrix*, λ is a probability distribution over Q representing the *initial state distribution*, Σ is a countable set of *observations*, and $\ell \colon Q \to \Sigma$ is a function mapping every state to an *observation*. All POMCs in this paper are time-homogeneous, i.e., their transition probabilities do not vary over time.

Semantically, every POMC $\mathcal{M}$ induces a probability measure $\mathbb{P}_{\mathcal{M}}(\cdot)$ over the generated state and observation sequences. For every finite state sequence $\overrightarrow{q} = q_1 q_2 \ldots q_t \in Q^*$, the probability that $\overrightarrow{q}$ is generated by $\mathcal{M}$ is given by $\mathbb{P}_{\mathcal{M}}(\overrightarrow{q}) = \lambda_{q_1} \cdot \prod_{i=1}^{t-1} M_{q_i q_{i+1}}$. Every finite state sequence $\overrightarrow{q} \in Q^*$ for which $\mathbb{P}_{\mathcal{M}}(\overrightarrow{q}) > 0$ is called a finite *internal path* of $\mathcal{M}$; we omit $\mathcal{M}$ if it is clear from the context. The set of every internal path of length n is denoted as $Q^n(\mathcal{M})$, and the set of every finite internal path is denoted as $Q^*(\mathcal{M})$.

Every finite internal path $\overrightarrow{q}$ can be extended to a set of infinite internal paths, which is called the cylinder set induced by $\overrightarrow{q}$, and is defined as $Cyl(\overrightarrow{q}) := \{\overrightarrow{r} \in Q^\omega \mid \overrightarrow{q} \prec \overrightarrow{r}\}$. The probability measure $\mathbb{P}_{\mathcal{M}}(\cdot)$ on finite internal paths induces a pre-measure on the respective cylinder sets, which can be extended to a unique measure on the infinite internal paths by means of the Carathéodory's extension theorem [5, pp. 757]. The probability measure on the set of infinite internal paths is also denoted using $\mathbb{P}_{\mathcal{M}}(\cdot)$.

An external observer can only observe the observable part of an internal path of a POMC. Given an internal path $\overrightarrow{q} = q_1 q_2 \ldots \in Q^\infty$, we write $\ell(\overrightarrow{q})$ to denote the observation sequence $\ell(q_1)\ell(q_2) \ldots \in \Sigma^\infty$. For a set of internal paths $S \subseteq Q^\infty$, we write $\ell(S)$ to denote the respective set of observation sequences $\{\overrightarrow{w} \in \Sigma^\infty \mid \exists \overrightarrow{q}\,.\,\overrightarrow{w} = \ell(\overrightarrow{q})\}$. An observation sequence $\overrightarrow{w} \in \Sigma^\infty$ is called an *observed* path (of $\mathcal{M}$) if there exists an internal path $\overrightarrow{q}$ for which $\ell(\overrightarrow{q}) = \overrightarrow{w}$.

As before, we write $\Sigma^n(\mathcal{M})$ for the set of every observed path of length n, and $\Sigma^*(\mathcal{M})$ for the set of every finite observed path.

We also use the inverse operator of ℓ to map every observed path $\overrightarrow{w}$ to the set of possible internal paths: $\ell^{-1}(\overrightarrow{w}) := \{\overrightarrow{q} \in Q^\infty \mid \ell(\overrightarrow{q}) = \overrightarrow{w}\}$. Furthermore, we extend $\ell^{-1}(\cdot)$ to operate over sets of observation sequences in the following way: For any given $S \subseteq \Sigma^\infty$, define $\ell^{-1}(S) := \{\overrightarrow{q} \mid \exists \overrightarrow{w} \in S . \ell(\overrightarrow{q}) = \overrightarrow{w}\}$.

We abuse the notation and use $\mathbb{P}_{\mathcal{M}}(\cdot)$ to denote the induced probability measure on the set of observed paths, defined in the following way. Given every set of finite observed paths $S \subseteq \Sigma^*$, we define $\mathbb{P}_{\mathcal{M}}(S) := \sum_{\overrightarrow{q} \in \ell^{-1}(S)} \mathbb{P}_{\mathcal{M}}(\overrightarrow{q})$. When the paths in a given set are infinite, the sum is replaced by integral. We write $\overrightarrow{W} \sim \mathcal{M}$ to denote the random variable that represents the distribution over finite sample observed paths generated by the POMC $\mathcal{M}$.

Example 1. As a running example, we introduce a POMC that models the sequential interaction between a bank and loan applicants. Suppose there is a population of loan applicants, where each applicant has a credit score between 1 and 4, and belongs to either an advantaged group A or a disadvantaged group B. At every step, the bank receives loan application from one applicant, and, based on some unknown (but non-time-varying) criteria, decides whether to grant loan or reject the application. We want to monitor, for example, the difference between loan acceptance probabilities for people belonging to the two groups.

The underlying POMC $\mathcal{M}$ that models the sequence of loan application events is shown in Fig. 1. A possible internal path is $S(A,1)NS(A,4)YSB$

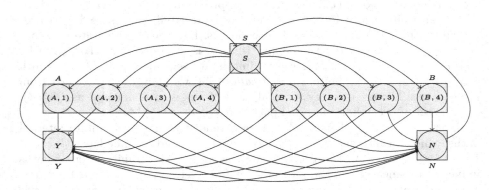

Fig. 1. The POMC modeling the sequential interaction between the bank and the loan applicants. The states S, Y, and N respectively denote the start state, the event that the loan was granted ("Y" stands for "Yes"), and the event that the loan was rejected ("N" stands for "No"). Every middle state (X,i), for $X \in \{A,B\}$ and $i \in \{1,2,3,4\}$, represents the group (A or B) and the credit score i of the current applicant. The states S,Y,N are fully observable, i.e., their observation symbols coincide with their state symbols. The middle states are partially observable, with every (A,i) being assigned the observation A and every (B,i) being assigned the observation B. The states with the same observation belong to the same shaded box.

$(A, 3)N \ldots$, whose corresponding observed path is $SANSAYSBN\ldots$. In our experiments, we use a more realistic model of the POMC with way more richer set of features for the individuals.

2.3 Register Monitors

Our register monitors are adapted from the polynomial monitors of Ferrère et al. [23], and were also used in our previous work (in a more general randomized form) [29]. Let R be a finite set of integer variables called registers. A function $v \colon R \to \mathbb{N}$ assigning concrete value to every register in R is called a valuation of R. Let $\mathbb{N}^R$ denote the set of all valuations of R. Registers can be read and written according to relations in the signature $S = \langle 0, 1, +, -, \times, \div, \leq \rangle$. We consider two basic operations on registers:

- A *test* is a conjunction of atomic formulas over S and their negation;
- An *update* is a mapping from variables to terms over S.

We use $\Phi(R)$ and $\Gamma(R)$ to respectively denote the set of tests and updates over R. *Counters* are special registers with a restricted signature $S = \langle 0, 1, +, -, \leq \rangle$.

Definition 1 (Register monitor). *A register monitor is a tuple $(\Sigma, \Lambda, R, v_{\text{in}}, f, T)$ where Σ is a finite input alphabet, Λ is an output alphabet, R is a finite set of registers, $v_{\text{in}} \in \mathbb{N}^R$ is the initial valuation of the registers, $f \colon \mathbb{N}^R \to \Lambda$ is an output function, and $T \colon \Sigma \times \Phi(R) \to \Gamma(R)$ is the transition function such that for every $\sigma \in \Sigma$ and for every valuation $v \in \mathbb{N}^R$, there exists a unique $\phi \in \Phi(R)$ with $v \models \phi$ and $T(\sigma, \phi) \in \Gamma(R)$.*

We refer to register monitors simply as monitors, and we fix the output alphabet Γ as the set of every real interval.

A *state* of a monitor $\mathcal{A}$ is a valuation of its registers $v \in \mathbb{N}^R$; the initial valuation v_{in} is the initial state. The monitor $\mathcal{A}$ *transitions* from state v to another state v' on input $\sigma \in \Sigma$ if there exists ϕ such that $v \models \phi$, there exists an update $\gamma = T(\sigma, \phi)$, and if v' maps every register x to $v'(x) = v(\gamma(x))$. The transition from v to v' on input σ is written as $v \xrightarrow{\sigma} v'$. A *run* of $\mathcal{A}$ on a word $w_1 \ldots w_t \in \Sigma^*$ is a sequence of transitions $v_1 = v_{\text{in}} \xrightarrow{w_1} v_2 \xrightarrow{w_2} \ldots \xrightarrow{w_t} v_{t+1}$. The *semantics* of the monitor is the function $[\![\mathcal{A}]\!] \colon \Sigma^* \to \Lambda$ that maps every finite input word to the last output of the monitor on the respective run. For instance, the semantics of $\mathcal{A}$ on the word $\vec{w}$ is $[\![\mathcal{A}]\!](\vec{w}) = f(v_{t+1})$. An illustrative example of register monitors can be found in our earlier work [29, Sec. 2.2].

3 Monitoring Quantitative Algorithmic Fairness Properties

In our prior work on monitoring algorithmic fairness for *fully* observable Markov chains [29], we formalized (quantitative) algorithmic fairness properties using the so-called Probabilistic Specification Expressions (PSE). A PSE φ is an arithmetic expression over the variables of the form v_{ij}, for $i, j \in Q$ for a finite set Q. The semantics of φ is interpreted statically over a given Markov chain M with state space Q, by replacing every v_{ij} with the transition probability from the state i to the state j in M. The algorithmic question we considered is that given a PSE φ, how to construct a monitor that will observe one long path of an unknown Markov chain, and after each observation will output a PAC estimate of the value of φ with a pre-specified confidence level.

An exact representation of the above problem formulation is not obvious for POMCs. In particular, while it is reasonable to generalize the semantics of PSEs to be over the probabilities between *observations* instead of probabilities between states, it is unclear how these probabilities will be defined. In the following, we use simple examples to illustrate several cruxes of formalizing algorithmic fairness on POMCs, and motivate the use of the assumptions of stationary distribution, irreducibility, and positive recurrence (formally stated in Assumption 1) to mitigate the difficulties. These assumptions will later be used to formalize the algorithmic fairness properties in Sect. 3.2.

In the following, we will write π to denote the *stationary distribution* of Markov chains with transition matrix M, i.e., $\pi = M\pi$.

3.1 Role of the Stationary Distribution

First, we demonstrate in the following example that POMCs made up of unfair sub-components may have overall fair behavior in the stationary distribution, which does not happen for fully observable Markov chains.

Example 2. Suppose there are two coins A and B, where A comes up with heads with probability 0.9 and B comes up with tails with probability 0.9. We observe a sequence of coin tosses (i.e., the observations are heads and tails), without knowing which of the two coins (the state) was tossed. If the choice of the coin at each step is made uniformly at random, then, intuitively, the system will produce fair outcomes in the long run, with equal proportions of heads and tails being observed in expectation. Thus, although each coin was unfair, we can still observe overall fair outcome, provided the fraction of times each coin was chosen in the stationary distribution balances out the unfairness in the coins themselves.

To make the above situation more concrete, imagine that the underlying POMC has two states a, b (e.g., a, b represent the states when A, B are selected for tossing, respectively) with the same observation (which coin is selected is unknown to the observer), where the measures of the given fairness condition (e.g., the biases of the coins A, B) are given by f_a, f_b. We argue that, intuitively, the overall fairness of the POMC is given by $\pi_a f_a + \pi_b f_b$. This type of analysis is unique to POMCs, whereas for fully observable Markov chains, computation of fairness is simpler and can be done without involving the stationary distribution.

In the next example, we demonstrate some challenges of monitoring fairness when we express fairness by weighing in the stationary distribution as above.

Example 3. Consider the setting of Example 2, and suppose now only the initial selection of the coin happens uniformly at random but subsequently the same coin is used forever. If we consider the underlying POMC, both π_a, π_b will be 0.5, because the initial selection of the coin happens uniformly at random. However, the monitor will observe the toss outcomes of only one of the two coins on a given trace. It is unclear how the monitor can extrapolate its estimate to the overall fairness property $\pi_a f_a + \pi_b f_b$ in this case.

To deal with the situations described in Example 2 and Example 3, we will make the following assumption.

Assumption 1. *We assume that the POMCs are irreducible, positively recurrent, and are initialized in their stationary distributions.*

The irreducibility and positive recurrence guarantees existence of the stationary distribution. Assumption 1 ensures that, firstly, we will see every state infinitely many times (ruling out the above corner-case), and, secondly, the proportion of times the POMC will spend in all the states will be the same (given by the stationary distribution) all the time. While Assumption 1 makes it easier to formulate and analyze the algorithmic fairness properties over POMCs, monitoring these properties over POMCs still remains a challenging problem due to the non-Markovian nature of the observed path.

3.2 Bounded Specification Expressions

We introduce bounded specification expressions (BSE) to formalize the fairness properties that we want to monitor. A BSE assigns values to finite word patterns of a given alphabet. The main components of a BSE are *atomic functions*, where an atomic function f_n assigns bounded real values to observation sequences of length n, for a given $n \in \mathbb{N}^+$. An atomic function f_n can express quantitative star-free regular expressions, assigning real values to words of length n.

Following are some examples. Let $\Sigma = \{r, g\}$ be an observation alphabet, where r stands for "request" and g stands for "grant." A boolean atomic function f_2, with $f_2(rr) = 0$ and $f_2(\overrightarrow{w}) = 1$ for every $\overrightarrow{w} \in \Sigma^2 \setminus \{rr\}$, can express the property that two requests should not appear consecutively. An integer-valued atomic function f_{10}, with $f_{10}(rr^i g \overrightarrow{w}) = i$ when $i \in [0; 8]$ and $\overrightarrow{w} \in \Sigma^{8-i}$, and with $f_{10}(\overrightarrow{z}) = 8$ when $\overrightarrow{z} \in \Sigma^{10} \setminus rr^i g \Sigma^{8-i}$, assigns to any sub-sequence the total waiting time between a request and the subsequent grant, while saturating the waiting time to 8 when it is above 8. The specified word-length n for any atomic function f_n is called the *arity* of f_n. Let P be the set of all atomic functions over a given observation alphabet.

A BSE may also contain arithmetic and/or logical connectives and relational operators to express complex value-based properties of an underlying probabilistic generator, like the POMCs. We consider two fragments of BSE-s, expressing qualitative and quantitative properties, and called, respectively, QualBSE and QuantBSE in short. The syntaxes of the two types of BSE-s are given as:

(QuantBSE) $\varphi ::= \kappa \in \mathbb{R} \mid f \in P \mid \varphi + \varphi \mid \varphi \cdot \varphi \mid 1 \div \varphi \mid (\varphi),$ (1a)

(QualBSE) $\psi ::= true \mid \varphi \geq 0 \mid \neg\psi \mid \psi \wedge \psi.$ (1b)

The semantics of a QuantBSE φ over the alphabet Σ is interpreted over POMCs satisfying Assumption 1 and with observations Σ. When φ is an atomic function $f\colon \Sigma^n \to [a, b]$ for some $n \in \mathbb{N}^+$, $a, b \in \mathbb{R}$, then, for a given POMC $\mathcal{M}$, the semantics of φ is defined as follows. For every time $t \in \mathbb{N}^+$,

$$\varphi(\mathcal{M}) = f(\mathcal{M}) := \int_{\Sigma^\omega} f(\overrightarrow{w}_{t:t+n-1}) d\mathbb{P}_{\mathcal{M}}(\overrightarrow{w}). \quad (2)$$

The definition of $f(\mathcal{M})$ is well-defined, because $f(\mathcal{M})$ will be the same for every t, since the POMC will remain in the stationary distribution forever (by Assumption 1 and by the property of stationary distributions). Intuitively, the semantics $f(\mathcal{M})$ represents the expected value of the function f on any sub-word of length n on any observed path of the POMC, when it is known that the POMC is in the stationary distribution (Assumption 1).

The arithmetic operators in QuantBSE-s have the usual semantics ("+" for addition, "−" for difference, "·" for multiplication, and "÷" for division).

On the other hand, the semantics of a QualBSE ψ is boolean, which inductively uses the semantics of the constituent φ expressions. For a QualBSE $\psi = \varphi \geq 0$, the semantics of ψ is given by:

$$\psi(\mathcal{M}) := \begin{cases} true & \text{if } \varphi(\mathcal{M}) \geq 0, \\ false & \text{otherwise.} \end{cases}$$

The semantics of the boolean operators in ψ is the usual semantics of boolean operators in propositional logic. The following can be added as syntactic sugar: "$\varphi \geq c$" for a constant c denotes "$\varphi' \geq 0$" with $\varphi' := \varphi - c$, "$\varphi \leq c$" denotes "$-\varphi \geq -c$," "$\varphi = c$" denotes "$(\varphi \geq c) \wedge (\varphi \leq c)$," "$\varphi > c$" denotes "$\neg(\varphi \leq c)$," "$\varphi < c$" denotes "$\neg(\varphi \geq c)$," and "$\psi \vee \psi$" denotes "$\neg(\neg\psi \wedge \neg\psi)$."

Fragment of BSE: Probabilistic Specification Expressions (PSEs): In our prior work [29], we introduced PSEs to model algorithmic fairness properties of Markov chains with fully observable state space. PSEs are arithmetic expressions over atomic variables of the form v_{ij}, where i, j are the states of the given Markov chain, and whose semantic value equals the transition probability from i to j. The semantics of a PSE is then the valuation of the expression obtained by plugging in the respective transition probabilities. We can express PSEs using QuantBSE-s as below. For every variable v_{ij} appearing in a given PSE, we use the atomic function f that assigns to every finite word $\overrightarrow{w} \in \Sigma^*$ the ratio of the number of (i, j) transitions to the number of occurrences of i in $\overrightarrow{w}$. We will denote the function f as $P(j \mid i)$ in this case, and, in general, i, j can be observation labels for the case of QuantBSE-s. It is straightforward to show that semantically the two expressions will be the same. On the other hand, QuantBSE-s are strictly more expressive than PSEs. For instance, unlike PSEs, QuantBSE-s can specify probability of transitioning from one observation label to another, the average number of times a given state is visited on any finite path of a Markov chain, etc.

Fragment of BSE: Probabilities of Sequences: We consider a useful fragment that expresses the probability that a sequence from a given set $S \subseteq \Sigma^*$ of finite observation sequences will be observed at any point in time on any observed path. We assume that the length of every sequence in S is uniformly bounded by some integer n. Let $\overline{S} \subseteq \Sigma^n$ denote the set of extensions of sequences in S up to length n, i.e., $\overline{S} := \{\overrightarrow{w} \in \Sigma^n \mid \exists \overrightarrow{u} \in S . \overrightarrow{u} \prec \overrightarrow{w}\}$. Then the desired property will be expressed simply using an atomic function with $f \colon \Sigma^n \to \{0, 1\}$ being the indicator function of the set $\overline{S}$, i.e., $f(\overrightarrow{w}) = 1$ iff $\overrightarrow{w} \in \overline{S}$. It is straightforward to show that, for a given POMC $\mathcal{M}$, the semantics $f(\mathcal{M})$ expresses the desired property. For a set of finite words $S \subseteq \Sigma^*$, we introduce the shorthand notation $P(S)$ to denote the probability of seeing an observation from the set S at any given point in time. Furthermore, for a pair of sets of finite words $S, T \subseteq \Sigma^*$, we use the shorthand notation $P(S \mid T)$ to denote $P(TS)/P(T)$, which represents the conditional probability of seeing a word in S after we have seen a word in T.

Example 4 (Group fairness). Consider the setting in Example 1. We show how we can represent various group fairness properties using QuantBSE-s. Demographic parity [18] quantifies bias as the difference between the probabilities of individuals from the two demographic groups getting the loan, which can be expressed as $P(Y \mid A) - P(Y \mid B)$. Disparate impact [21] quantifies bias as the ratio between the probabilities of getting the loan across the two demographic groups, which can be expressed as $P(Y \mid A) \div P(Y \mid B)$.

In prior works [3, 29], group fairness properties could be expressed on strictly less richer class of fully observed Markov chain models, where the features of each individual were required to contain only their group information. An extension to the model of Example 1 is not straightforward as the confidence interval used in these works would not be applicable.

Example 5 (Social fairness). Consider the setting in Example 1, except that now the credit score of each individual will be observable along with their group memberships, i.e., each observation is a pair of the form (X, i) with $X \in \{A, B\}$ and $i \in \{1, 2, 3, 4\}$. There may be other non-sensitive features, such as age, which may be hidden. We use the social fairness property [28] quantified as the difference between the expected credit scores of the groups A and B. To express this property, we use the unary atomic functions $f_1^X \colon \Sigma \to \mathbb{N}$, for $X \in \{A, B\}$, such that $f_1^X \colon (Y, i) \mapsto i$ if $Y = X$ and is 0 otherwise. The semantics of f_1^X is the expected credit score of group X scaled by the probability of seeing an individual from group X. Then social fairness is given by the QuantBSE $\varphi = \frac{f_1^A}{P(A)} - \frac{f_1^B}{P(B)}$.

Example 6 (Quantitative group fairness). Consider a sequential hiring scenario where at each step the salary and a sensitive feature (like gender) of a new recruit are observed. We denote the pair of observations as (X, i), where $X \in \{A, B\}$ represents the group information based on the sensitive feature and i represents the salary. We can express the disparity in expected salary of the two groups in a similar manner as in Example 5. Define the unary functions $f_1^X \colon \Sigma \to \mathbb{N}$, for $X \in \{A, B\}$, such that $f_1^X \colon (Y, i) \mapsto i$ if $Y = X$ and is 0 otherwise. The semantics of f_1^X is the expected salary of group X scaled by the probability of seeing an individual from group X. Then the group fairness property is given by the QuantBSE $\varphi = \frac{f_1^A}{P(A)} - \frac{f_1^B}{P(B)}$.

3.3 Problem Statement

Informally, our goal is to build monitors that will observe randomly generated observed paths of increasing length from a given unknown POMC, and, after each observation, will generate an updated estimate of how fair or biased the system was until the current time. Since the monitor's estimate is based on statistics collected from a finite path, the output may be incorrect with some probability. That is, the source of randomness is from the fact that the prefix is a finite sample of the fixed but unknown POMC.

For a given $\delta \in (0, 1)$, and a given BSE φ, we define a *problem instance* as the tuple (φ, δ).

Problem 1 (Monitoring QuantBSE-s). *Suppose (φ, δ) is a problem instance where φ is a QuantBSE. Design a monitor $\mathcal{A}$, with output alphabet $\{[l, u] \mid l, u \in \mathbb{R} . l < u\}$, such that for every POMC $\mathcal{M}$ satisfying Assumption 1, we have:*

$$\mathbb{P}_{\overrightarrow{W} \sim \mathcal{M}} \left(\varphi(\mathcal{M}) \in [\![\mathcal{A}]\!](\overrightarrow{W}) \right) \geq 1 - \delta. \tag{3}$$

The estimate $[l, u] = [\![\mathcal{A}]\!](\overrightarrow{w})$ is called the $(1 - \delta) \cdot 100\%$ *confidence interval* for $\varphi(M)$. The radius, given by $\varepsilon = 0.5 \cdot (u - l)$, is called the *estimation error*, the quantity δ is called the *failure probability*, and the quantity $1 - \delta$ is called the *confidence*. Intuitively, the monitor outputs the estimated confidence interval that contains the range of values within which the true semantic value of φ falls with $(1 - \delta) \cdot 100\%$ probability. The estimate gets more precise as the error gets smaller, and the confidence gets higher. We will prefer the monitor with the maximum possible precision, i.e., having the least estimation error for a given δ.

Problem 2 (Monitoring QualBSE-s). *Suppose (φ, δ) is a problem instance where φ is a QualBSE. Design a monitor $\mathcal{A}$, with output alphabet $\{true, false\}$, such that for every POMC $\mathcal{M}$ satisfying Assumption 1, we have:*

$$\mathbb{P}_{\overrightarrow{W} \sim \mathcal{M}} \left(\psi(\mathcal{M}) \mid [\![\mathcal{A}]\!](\overrightarrow{W}) = true \right) \geq 1 - \delta, \tag{4}$$

$$\mathbb{P}_{\overrightarrow{W} \sim \mathcal{M}} \left(\neg\psi(\mathcal{M}) \mid [\![\mathcal{A}]\!](\overrightarrow{W}) = false \right) \geq 1 - \delta. \tag{5}$$

Unlike Problem 1, the monitors addressing Problem 2 do not output an interval but output a boolean verdict. Intuitively, the output of the monitor for Problem 2 is either *true* or *false*, and it is required that the semantic value of the property ψ is, respectively, *true* or *false* with $(1 - \delta) \cdot 100\%$ probability.

4   Construction of the Monitor

Our overall approach in this work is similar to the prior works [3,28,29]: We first compute a point estimate of the given BSE from the finite observation sequence of the POMC, and then compute an interval estimate through known concentration inequalities. However, the same concentration inequalities as the prior works cannot be applied, because they required two successive observed events be independent, which is not true for POMCs. For instance, in Example 3, if we start the sequence of tosses by first tossing coin A, then we know that the subsequent tosses are going to be done using A only, thereby implying that the outcomes of the future tosses will be statistically dependent on the initial random process that chooses between the two coins at the first step.

We present a novel theory of monitors for BSE-s on POMCs satisfying Assumption 1, using McDiarmid-style concentration inequalities for hidden Markov chains. In Sect. 4.1 and 4.2, we first present, respectively, the point estimator and the monitor for an individual atom. In Sect. 4.3, we build the overall monitor by combining the interval estimates of the individual atoms through interval arithmetic and union bound.

4.1   A Point Estimator for the Atoms

Consider a BSE atom f. We present a point estimator for f, which computes an estimated value of $f(\mathcal{M})$ from a finite observed path $\overrightarrow{w} \in \Sigma^t$, of an arbitrary length t, of the unknown POMC $\mathcal{M}$. The point estimator $\hat{f}(\cdot)$ is given as:

$$\hat{f}(\overrightarrow{w}) := \frac{1}{t-n+1} \sum_{i=1}^{t-n+1} f(\overrightarrow{w}_{i..i+n-1}). \tag{6}$$

In the following proposition, we establish the unbiasedness of the estimator $\hat{f}(\cdot)$, a desirable property that says that the expected value of the estimator's output will coincide with the true value of the property that is being estimated.

Proposition 1. *Let $\mathcal{M}$ be a POMC satisfying Assumption 1, $f\colon \Sigma^n \to [a,b]$ be a function for fixed n, a, and b, and $\overrightarrow{W} \sim \mathcal{M}$ be a random observed path of an arbitrary length $|\overrightarrow{W}| = t > n$. Then $\mathbb{E}(\hat{f}(\overrightarrow{W})) = f(\mathcal{M})$.*

The following corollary establishes the counterpart of Proposition 1 for the fragment of BSE with probabilities of sequences.

Corollary 1. *Let $\mathcal{M}$ be a POMC satisfying Assumption 1, $\Lambda \subset \Sigma^*$ be a set of bounded length observation sequences with bound n, $f : \Sigma^n \to \{0,1\}$ be the indicator function of the set $\overline{\Lambda}$, and $\overrightarrow{W} \sim \mathcal{M}$ be a random observed path of an arbitrary length $|\overrightarrow{W}| > n$. Then $\mathbb{E}(\hat{f}(\overrightarrow{W})) = P(\Lambda)$.*

4.2 The Atomic Monitor

A monitor for each individual atom is called an atomic monitor, which serves as the building block for the overall monitor. Each atomic monitor is constructed by computing an interval estimate of the semantic value $f(\mathcal{M})$ for the respective atom f on the unknown POMC $\mathcal{M}$. For computing the interval estimate, we use the McDiarmid-style inequality (details are in the longer version [30]) to find a bound on the width of the interval around the point estimate $\hat{f}(\cdot)$.

Algorithm 1. $Monitor_{(f,\delta)}$: Monitor for (f, δ) where $f: \Sigma^n \to [a, b]$ is an atomic function of a BSE

1: **function** $Next(\sigma)$
2:     $t \leftarrow t + 1$ ▷progress time
3:     **if** $t < n$ **then**   ▷too short observation sequence
4:         $\overrightarrow{w}_t \leftarrow \sigma$
5:         **return** $\bot$ ▷inconclusive
6:     **else**
7:         $\overrightarrow{w}_{1..n-1} \leftarrow \overrightarrow{w}_{2..n}$ ▷shift window
8:         $\overrightarrow{w}_n \leftarrow \sigma$ ▷add the new observation
9:         $x \leftarrow f(\overrightarrow{w})$ ▷latest evaluation of f
10:         $y \leftarrow (y * (t - n) + x) / (t - n + 1)$ ▷running av. impl. of Eq. 6
11:         $\varepsilon \leftarrow \sqrt{-\ln(\delta/2) \cdot \frac{t \cdot \min(t - n + 1, n) \cdot \tau_{mix}}{2(t - n + 1)^2}}$ ▷ PAC bound, see [30]
12:             **return** $[y - \varepsilon, y + \varepsilon]$ ▷confidence interval
13:         **end if**
14: **end function**

1: **function** $Init()$
2:     $t \leftarrow 0$ ▷current time
3:     $y \leftarrow 0$ ▷current point estimate
4:     $\overrightarrow{w} \leftarrow \underbrace{\bot \ldots \bot}_{n \text{ times}}$ ▷a dummy word of length n, where $\bot$ is the dummy symbol
5: **end function**

McDiarmid's inequality is a concentration inequality bounding the distance between the sample value and the expected value of a function satisfying the bounded difference property when evaluated on independent random variables. There are several works extending this result to functions evaluated over a sequence of dependent random variables, including Markov chains [20,35,44]. In order to use McDiarmid's inequality, we will need the following standard [37] additional assumption on the underlying POMC.

Assumption 2. *We assume that the POMCs are aperiodic, and that the mixing time of the POMC is bounded by a known constant τ_{mix}.*

We summarize the algorithmic computation of the atomic monitor in Algorithm 1, and establish its correctness in the following theorem.

Theorem 1 (Solution of Problem 1 for atomic formulas). *Let (f, δ) be a problem instance where $f: \Sigma^n \to [a, b]$ is an atomic formula for some fixed n, a, and b. Moreover, suppose the given unknown POMC satisfies Assumption 2. Then Algorithm 1 implements a monitor solving Problem 1 for the given problem instance. The monitor requires $\mathcal{O}(n)$-space, and, after arrival of each new observation, computes the updated output in $\mathcal{O}(n)$-time.*

The confidence intervals generated by McDiarmid-style inequalities for Markov chains tighten in relation to the mixing time of the Markov chain. This means the slower a POMC mixes, the longer the monitor needs to watch to be able to obtain an output interval of the same quality.

4.3   The Complete Monitor

The final monitors for QuantBSE-s and QualBSE-s are presented in Algorithm 3 and Algorithm 2, respectively, where we recursively combine the interval estimates of the constituent sub-expressions using interval arithmetic and the union bound. Similar idea was used by Albarghouthi et al. [3]. The correctness and computational complexities of the monitors are formally stated below.

Theorem 2 (Solution of Problem 1). *Let $(\varphi_1 \odot \varphi_2, \delta_1 + \delta_2)$ be a problem instance where φ_1, φ_2 are a pair of QuantBSE-s and $\odot \in \{+, \cdot, \div\}$. Moreover, suppose the given unknown POMC satisfies Assumption 2. Then Algorithm 3 implements the monitor $\mathcal{A}$ solving Problem 1 for the given problem instance. If the total number of atoms in $\varphi_1 \odot \varphi_2$ is k and if the arity of the largest atom in $\varphi_1 \odot \varphi_2$ is n, then $\mathcal{A}$ requires $\mathcal{O}(k + n)$-space, and, after arrival of each new observation, computes the updated output in $\mathcal{O}(k \cdot n)$-time.*

Theorem 3 (Solution of Problem 2). *Let (ψ, δ) be a problem instance where ψ is a QualBSE. Moreover, suppose the given unknown POMC satisfies Assumption 2. Then Algorithm 2 implements the monitor $\mathcal{A}$ solving Problem 2 for the given problem instance. If the total number of atoms in ψ is k and if the arity of the largest atom in ψ is n, then $\mathcal{A}$ requires $\mathcal{O}(k + n)$-space, and, after arrival of each new observation, computes the updated output in $\mathcal{O}(k \cdot n)$-time.*

Algorithm 2. $Monitor_{(\psi,\delta)}$

1: **function** *Init*()
2:     **if** $\psi \equiv \varphi \geq 0$ **then**
3:         $\mathcal{A} \leftarrow Monitor_{(\varphi,\delta)}$
4:         $\mathcal{A}.Init()$
5:     **else if** $\psi \equiv \neg\psi_1$ **then**
6:         $\mathcal{A} \leftarrow Monitor_{(\psi_1,\delta)}$
7:         $\mathcal{A}.Init()$
8:     **else if** $\psi \equiv \psi_1 \wedge \psi_2$ **then**
9:         Choose δ_1, δ_2 s.t. $\delta = \delta_1 + \delta_2$
10:         $\mathcal{A}_1 \leftarrow Monitor_{(\psi_1,\delta_1)}$
11:         $\mathcal{A}_2 \leftarrow Monitor_{(\psi_2,\delta_2)}$
12:         $\mathcal{A}_1.Init()$
13:         $\mathcal{A}_2.Init()$
14:     **end if**
15: **end function**

1: **function** *Next*(σ)
2:     **if** $\psi \equiv \varphi \geq 0$ **then**
3:         $[l, u] \leftarrow \mathcal{A}.Next(\sigma)$
4:         **if** $l \geq 0$ **then return** *true*
5:         **else if** $u \leq 0$ **then return** *false*
6:         **else return** $\bot$ ▷don't know, we
          assume $\neg\bot = \bot \wedge true = \bot \wedge false = \bot$.
7:         **end if**
8:     **else if** $\psi \equiv \neg\psi_1$ **then**
9:         **return** $\neg (\mathcal{A}.Next(\sigma))$
10:     **else if** $\psi \equiv \psi_1 \wedge \psi_2$ **then**
11:         **return** $\mathcal{A}_1.Next(\sigma) \wedge \mathcal{A}_2.Next(\sigma)$
12:     **end if**
13: **end function**

---

5   Experiments

We implemented our monitoring algorithm in Python, and applied it to the real-world lending example [14] described in Example 1 and to an academic example called hypercube. We ran the experiments on a MacBook Pro (2023) with Apple M2 Pro processor and 16 GB of RAM.

The Lending Example. The underlying POMC model (unknown to the monitor) of the system is approximately as shown in Fig. 1 with a few differences. Firstly, we added a low-probability self-loop on the state S to ensure aperiodicity. Secondly, we considered only two credit score levels.

Thirdly, there are more hidden states (in total 171 states) in the system, like the action of the individual (repaying the loan or defaulting), etc. We monitor demographic parity, defined as $\varphi_{\mathsf{DP}} := P(Y \mid A) - P(Y \mid B)$, and an absolute version of it, defined as $\varphi_{\mathsf{TDP}} := P(AY) - P(BY)$. While φ_{DP} represents the difference in probabilities of giving loans to individuals from the two groups (A and B), φ_{TDP} represents the difference in joint probabilities of selecting and then giving loans to individuals from the two groups.

Algorithm 3. $Monitor_{(\varphi_1 \odot \varphi_2, \delta_1 + \delta_2)}$

1: **function** $Init()$
2:    $\mathcal{A}_1 \leftarrow Monitor_{(\varphi_1, \delta_1)}$
3:    $\mathcal{A}_2 \leftarrow Monitor_{(\varphi_2, \delta_2)}$
4:    $\mathcal{A}_1.Init()$
5:    $\mathcal{A}_2.Init()$
6: **end function**
1: **function** $Next(\sigma)$
2:    $[l_1, u_1] \leftarrow \mathcal{A}_1.Next(\sigma)$
3:    $[l_2, u_2] \leftarrow \mathcal{A}_2.Next(\sigma)$
4:    **return** $[l_1, u_1] \odot [l_2, u_2]$ ▷interval arithmetic
5: **end function**

None of the two properties can be expressed using the previous formalism [3,29], because φ_{DP} requires conditioning on observations, and φ_{TDP} requires expressing absolute probabilities, which were not considered before.

After receiving new observations, the monitors for φ_{DP} and φ_{TDP} took, respectively, 47 µs and 18 µs on an average (overall 43 µs–0.2 s and 12 µs–3.2 s) to update their outputs, showing that our monitors are fast in practice.

Figure 2 shows the outputs of the monitors for $\delta = 0.05$ (i.e., 95% confidence interval). For the POMC of the lending example, we used a pessimistic bound $\tau_{\mathsf{mix}} = 170589.78$ steps on the mixing time (computation as in [33]), with which the estimation error ε shrinks rather slowly in both cases. For example, for φ_{TDP}, in order to get from the trivial value $\varepsilon = 1$ (the confidence interval spans the entire range of possible values) down to $\varepsilon = 0.1$, the monitor requires about $4 \cdot 10^9$ observations. For φ_{DP}, the monitor requires even more number of observations ($\sim 10^{12}$) to reach the same error level. This is because φ_{DP} involves conditional probabilities requiring divisions, which amplify the error when composed using interval arithmetics. We conclude that a direct division-free estimation of the conditional probabilities, together with tighter bounds on the mixing time will significantly improve the long-run accuracy of the monitor.

The Hypercube Example. We considered a second example [37, pp. 63], whose purpose is to demonstrate that the tightness of our monitors' outputs is sensitive to the choice of the bound on the mixing time. The POMC models

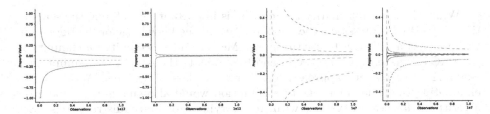

Fig. 2. Monitoring φ_{DP} (first, third) and φ_{TDP} (second, fourth) on the lending (first, second) and the hypercube (third, fourth) examples. The <u>first and second</u> plots show the computed 95%-confidence interval (solid) and the true value of the property (dashed) for the lending POMC. In reality, the monitor was run for about 7×10^8 steps until the point estimate nearly converged, though the confidence interval was trivial at this point (the whole interval $[-1,1]$), owing to the pessimistic bound τ_{mix}. In the figure, we have plotted a projection of how the confidence interval would taper over time, had we kept the monitor running. The <u>third and fourth</u> plots summarize the monitors' outputs over 100 executions of the hypercube POMC. The solid lines are the max and min values of the point estimates, the dashed lines are the boundaries of all the 95%-confidence intervals (among the 100 executions) with the conservative bound τ_{mix} (green) and the sharper bound $\tau_{true\,mix}$ (orange) on the mixing time.

a random walk along the edges of a hypercube $\{0,1\}^n$, where each vertex of the hypercube represents a state in the POMC and states starting with 0 and 1 are mapped to the observations a and b, respectively. We fix n to 3 in our experiments. At every step, the current vertex is chosen with probability $1/2$, and every neighbor is chosen with probability $1/2n$. A tight bound on the mixing time of this POMC is given by $\tau_{true\,mix} = n(\log n + \log 4)$ steps [37, pp. 63]. We consider the properties $\psi_{DP} := P(a \mid a) - P(b \mid b)$ and $\psi_{TDP} := P(aa) - P(bb)$.

We empirically evaluated the quality of the confidence intervals computed by our monitor (for ψ_{DP} and ψ_{TDP}) over a set of 100 sample runs, and summarize the findings in the third and fourth plots of Fig. 2. We used $\tau_{mix} = 204.94$ steps and $\tau_{true\,mix} = 7.45$ steps, and we can observe that in both cases, the output with $\tau_{true\,mix}$ is significantly tighter than with τ_{mix}. Compared to the lending example, we obtain reasonably tight estimate with significantly smaller number of observations, which is due to the smaller bounds on the mixing time.

6   Conclusion

We generalized runtime verification of algorithmic fairness to systems modeled using POMCs and a specification language (BSE) with arithmetic expressions over numerical functions assigning values to observation sequences. Under the assumptions of stationary initial distribution, aperiodicity, and the knowledge of a bound on the mixing time, we presented a runtime monitor, which monitors a long sequence of observations generated by the POMC, and after each observation outputs an updated PAC estimate of the value of the given BSE.

While the new stationarity assumption is important for defining the semantics of the BSE expressions, the aperiodicity and the knowledge of the bound on the mixing time allow us to use the known McDiarmid's inequality for computing the PAC estimate. In future, we intend to eliminate the latter two assumptions, enabling us to use our approach for a broader class of systems. Additionally, eliminating the time-homogeneity assumption would also enable us to monitor algorithmic fairness of systems with time-varying probability distributions [28].

Acknowledgments. This work is supported by the European Research Council under Grant No.: ERC-2020-AdG 101020093.

References

1. Agha, G., Palmskog, K.: A survey of statistical model checking. ACM Trans. Model. Comput. Simul. (TOMACS) **28**(1), 1–39 (2018)
2. Albarghouthi, A., D'Antoni, L., Drews, S., Nori, A.V.: FairSquare: probabilistic verification of program fairness. Proc. ACM Program. Lang. **1**(OOPSLA), 1–30 (2017)
3. Albarghouthi, A., Vinitsky, S.: Fairness-aware programming. In: Proceedings of the Conference on Fairness, Accountability, and Transparency, pp. 211–219 (2019)
4. Baier, C., Haverkort, B., Hermanns, H., Katoen, J.P.: Model-checking algorithms for continuous-time Markov chains. IEEE Trans. Softw. Eng. **29**(6), 524–541 (2003). https://doi.org/10.1109/TSE.2003.1205180
5. Baier, C., Katoen, J.P.: Principles of Model Checking. MIT Press, Cambridge (2008)
6. Balunovic, M., Ruoss, A., Vechev, M.: Fair normalizing flows. In: International Conference on Learning Representations (2021)
7. Bartocci, E., et al.: Specification-based monitoring of cyber-physical systems: a survey on theory, tools and applications. In: Bartocci, E., Falcone, Y. (eds.) Lectures on Runtime Verification. LNCS, vol. 10457, pp. 135–175. Springer, Cham (2018). https://doi.org/10.1007/978-3-319-75632-5_5
8. Bartocci, E., Falcone, Y.: Lectures on Runtime Verification. Springer, Cham (2018). https://doi.org/10.1007/978-3-319-75632-5
9. Bartolo Burlò, C., Francalanza, A., Scalas, A., Trubiani, C., Tuosto, E.: Towards probabilistic session-type monitoring. In: Damiani, F., Dardha, O. (eds.) COORDINATION 2021. LNCS, vol. 12717, pp. 106–120. Springer, Cham (2021). https://doi.org/10.1007/978-3-030-78142-2_7
10. Bellamy, R.K., et al.: AI fairness 360: an extensible toolkit for detecting and mitigating algorithmic bias. IBM J. Res. Dev. **63**(4/5), 4–1 (2019)
11. Bird, S., et al.: Fairlearn: a toolkit for assessing and improving fairness in AI. Microsoft, Technical report. MSR-TR-2020-32 (2020)
12. Chouldechova, A.: Fair prediction with disparate impact: a study of bias in recidivism prediction instruments. Big Data **5**(2), 153–163 (2017)
13. Clarke, E.M., Zuliani, P.: Statistical model checking for cyber-physical systems. In: Bultan, T., Hsiung, P.-A. (eds.) ATVA 2011. LNCS, vol. 6996, pp. 1–12. Springer, Heidelberg (2011). https://doi.org/10.1007/978-3-642-24372-1_1
14. D'Amour, A., Srinivasan, H., Atwood, J., Baljekar, P., Sculley, D., Halpern, Y.: Fairness is not static: deeper understanding of long term fairness via simulation studies. In: Proceedings of the 2020 Conference on Fairness, Accountability, and Transparency, FAT* 2020, pp. 525–534 (2020)

15. David, A., Du, D., Guldstrand Larsen, K., Legay, A., Mikučionis, M.: Optimizing control strategy using statistical model checking. In: Brat, G., Rungta, N., Venet, A. (eds.) NFM 2013. LNCS, vol. 7871, pp. 352–367. Springer, Heidelberg (2013). https://doi.org/10.1007/978-3-642-38088-4_24

16. Donzé, A., Maler, O.: Robust satisfaction of temporal logic over real-valued signals. In: Chatterjee, K., Henzinger, T.A. (eds.) FORMATS 2010. LNCS, vol. 6246, pp. 92–106. Springer, Heidelberg (2010). https://doi.org/10.1007/978-3-642-15297-9_9

17. Dressel, J., Farid, H.: The accuracy, fairness, and limits of predicting recidivism. Sci. Adv. **4**(1), eaao5580 (2018)

18. Dwork, C., Hardt, M., Pitassi, T., Reingold, O., Zemel, R.: Fairness through awareness. In: Proceedings of the 3rd Innovations in Theoretical Computer Science Conference, pp. 214–226 (2012)

19. Ensign, D., Friedler, S.A., Neville, S., Scheidegger, C., Venkatasubramanian, S.: Runaway feedback loops in predictive policing. In: Conference on Fairness, Accountability and Transparency, pp. 160–171. PMLR (2018)

20. Esposito, A.R., Mondelli, M.: Concentration without independence via information measures. arXiv preprint arXiv:2303.07245 (2023)

21. Feldman, M., Friedler, S.A., Moeller, J., Scheidegger, C., Venkatasubramanian, S.: Certifying and removing disparate impact. In: proceedings of the 21th ACM SIGKDD International Conference on Knowledge Discovery and Data Mining, pp. 259–268 (2015)

22. Ferrere, T., Henzinger, T.A., Kragl, B.: Monitoring event frequencies. In: 28th EACSL Annual Conference on Computer Science Logic, vol. 152 (2020)

23. Ferrère, T., Henzinger, T.A., Saraç, N.E.: A theory of register monitors. In: Proceedings of the 33rd Annual ACM/IEEE Symposium on Logic in Computer Science, pp. 394–403 (2018)

24. Finkbeiner, B., Sankaranarayanan, S., Sipma, H.: Collecting statistics over runtime executions. Electron. Notes Theor. Comput. Sci. **70**(4), 36–54 (2002)

25. Ghosh, B., Basu, D., Meel, K.S.: Justicia: a stochastic sat approach to formally verify fairness. arXiv preprint arXiv:2009.06516 (2020)

26. Ghosh, B., Basu, D., Meel, K.S.: Algorithmic fairness verification with graphical models. arXiv preprint arXiv:2109.09447 (2021)

27. Hardt, M., Price, E., Srebro, N.: Equality of opportunity in supervised learning. In: Advances in Neural Information Processing Systems, vol. 29 (2016)

28. Henzinger, T., Karimi, M., Kueffner, K., Mallik, K.: Runtime monitoring of dynamic fairness properties. In: Proceedings of the 2023 ACM Conference on Fairness, Accountability, and Transparency, pp. 604–614 (2023)

29. Henzinger, T.A., Karimi, M., Kueffner, K., Mallik, K.: Monitoring algorithmic fairness. In: Enea, C., Lal, A. (eds.) Computer Aided Verification, pp. 358–382. Springer, Cham (2023). https://doi.org/10.1007/978-3-031-37703-7_17

30. Henzinger, T.A., Kueffner, K., Mallik, K.: Monitoring algorithmic fairness under partial observations. arXiv preprint arXiv:2308.00341 (2023)

31. Henzinger, T.A., Saraç, N.E.: Monitorability under assumptions. In: Deshmukh, J., Ničković, D. (eds.) RV 2020. LNCS, vol. 12399, pp. 3–18. Springer, Cham (2020). https://doi.org/10.1007/978-3-030-60508-7_1

32. Henzinger, T.A., Saraç, N.E.: Quantitative and approximate monitoring. In: 2021 36th Annual ACM/IEEE Symposium on Logic in Computer Science (LICS), pp. 1–14. IEEE (2021)

33. Jerison, D.: General mixing time bounds for finite Markov chains via the absolute spectral gap. arXiv preprint arXiv:1310.8021 (2013)

34. John, P.G., Vijaykeerthy, D., Saha, D.: Verifying individual fairness in machine learning models. In: Conference on Uncertainty in Artificial Intelligence, pp. 749–758. PMLR (2020)
35. Kontorovich, A., Raginsky, M.: Concentration of measure without independence: a unified approach via the martingale method. In: Carlen, E., Madiman, M., Werner, E.M. (eds.) Convexity and Concentration. TIVMA, vol. 161, pp. 183–210. Springer, New York (2017). https://doi.org/10.1007/978-1-4939-7005-6_6
36. Lahoti, P., Gummadi, K.P., Weikum, G.: iFair: learning individually fair data representations for algorithmic decision making. In: 2019 IEEE 35th International Conference on Data Engineering (ICDE), pp. 1334–1345. IEEE (2019)
37. Levin, D.A., Peres, Y.: Markov Chains and Mixing Times, vol. 107. American Mathematical Society (2017)
38. Liu, L.T., Dean, S., Rolf, E., Simchowitz, M., Hardt, M.: Delayed impact of fair machine learning. In: International Conference on Machine Learning, pp. 3150–3158. PMLR (2018)
39. Lum, K., Isaac, W.: To predict and serve? Significance **13**(5), 14–19 (2016)
40. Maler, O., Nickovic, D.: Monitoring temporal properties of continuous signals. In: Lakhnech, Y., Yovine, S. (eds.) FORMATS/FTRTFT -2004. LNCS, vol. 3253, pp. 152–166. Springer, Heidelberg (2004). https://doi.org/10.1007/978-3-540-30206-3_12
41. Meyer, A., Albarghouthi, A., D'Antoni, L.: Certifying robustness to programmable data bias in decision trees. In: Advances in Neural Information Processing Systems, vol. 34, 26276–26288 (2021)
42. Obermeyer, Z., Powers, B., Vogeli, C., Mullainathan, S.: Dissecting racial bias in an algorithm used to manage the health of populations. Science **366**(6464), 447–453 (2019)
43. Otop, J., Henzinger, T.A., Chatterjee, K.: Quantitative automata under probabilistic semantics. Logical Methods Comput. Sci. **15** (2019)
44. Paulin, D.: Concentration inequalities for Markov chains by Marton couplings and spectral methods (2015)
45. Ruchkin, I., Sokolsky, O., Weimer, J., Hedaoo, T., Lee, I.: Compositional probabilistic analysis of temporal properties over stochastic detectors. IEEE Trans. Comput. Aided Des. Integr. Circuits Syst. **39**(11), 3288–3299 (2020)
46. Scheuerman, M.K., Paul, J.M., Brubaker, J.R.: How computers see gender: an evaluation of gender classification in commercial facial analysis services. Proc. ACM Hum.-Comput. Interact. **3**(CSCW), 1–33 (2019)
47. Sharifi-Malvajerdi, S., Kearns, M., Roth, A.: Average individual fairness: algorithms, generalization and experiments. In: Advances in Neural Information Processing Systems, vol. 32 (2019)
48. Stoller, S.D., et al.: Runtime verification with state estimation. In: Khurshid, S., Sen, K. (eds.) RV 2011. LNCS, vol. 7186, pp. 193–207. Springer, Heidelberg (2012). https://doi.org/10.1007/978-3-642-29860-8_15
49. Sun, B., Sun, J., Dai, T., Zhang, L.: Probabilistic verification of neural networks against group fairness. In: Huisman, M., Păsăreanu, C., Zhan, N. (eds.) FM 2021. LNCS, vol. 13047, pp. 83–102. Springer, Cham (2021). https://doi.org/10.1007/978-3-030-90870-6_5
50. Waudby-Smith, I., Arbour, D., Sinha, R., Kennedy, E.H., Ramdas, A.: Time-uniform central limit theory, asymptotic confidence sequences, and anytime-valid causal inference. arXiv preprint arXiv:2103.06476 (2021)

51. Wexler, J., Pushkarna, M., Bolukbasi, T., Wattenberg, M., Viégas, F., Wilson, J.: The what-if tool: interactive probing of machine learning models. IEEE Trans. Vis. Comput. Graph. **26**(1), 56–65 (2019)
52. Younes, H.L.S., Simmons, R.G.: Probabilistic verification of discrete event systems using acceptance sampling. In: Brinksma, E., Larsen, K.G. (eds.) CAV 2002. LNCS, vol. 2404, pp. 223–235. Springer, Heidelberg (2002). https://doi.org/10.1007/3-540-45657-0_17
53. Zemel, R., Wu, Y., Swersky, K., Pitassi, T., Dwork, C.: Learning fair representations. In: International Conference on Machine Learning, pp. 325–333. PMLR (2013)

Short and Tool Papers

Short and Long Paper

AMT: A Runtime Verification Tool
of Video Streams

Valentin Besnard[1]([✉])[iD], Mathieu Huet[1], Stoyan Bivolarov[2],
Nourredine Saadi[1], and Guillaume Cornard[2]

[1] ATEME, Vélizy, France
{v.besnard,m.huet,n.saadi}@ateme.com
[2] ATEME, Rennes, France
{s.bivolarov,g.cornard}@ateme.com

Abstract. In the domain of video delivery, industrial software systems
that produce multimedia streams are increasingly more complex. To
ensure correctness of their behaviors, there is a strong need for verification and validation activities. In particular, formal verification seems
a promising approach for that. However, applying formal verification on
industrial legacy systems is challenging. Their intrinsic complexity, their
interactions, and the complexity of video standards that are constantly
evolving make the task difficult. To face these issues, this paper presents
the ATEME Monitoring Tool (AMT), a runtime verification tool used to
monitor formal properties on output streams of video delivery systems.
This tool can be used all along the product life cycle to make syntactic and semantic verification when analyzing bugs (on live streams or
on captures), developing new features, and doing non-regression checks.
Using the tool, we have successfully found and/or reproduce real issues
violating requirements of systems delivering over-the-top (OTT) streams.

Keywords: Runtime Verification · Monitoring · Linear Temporal
Logic · Video Streaming · Industrial Application

1 Introduction

In video streaming industry, software solutions are made of multiple products
chained together to distribute multimedia streams from television studios to
end-user devices. Each product is a software system with millions of lines of
code that need to evolve according to new standards and client needs. This
increasing complexity makes these software equipment sensible to design issues
and bugs. Therefore, they require verification and validation (V&V) to ensure the
correctness of their output streams. In particular, we are interested in verifying
over-the-top (OTT) streams such as HLS [25] and MPEG-DASH [3] used by
on-demand video platforms and TV channels over internet.

   All along the product life cycle, different analysis activities need to be applied:
verifying live streams when developing new features, analyzing issues occurring in

© The Author(s), under exclusive license to Springer Nature Switzerland AG 2023
P. Katsaros and L. Nenzi (Eds.): RV 2023, LNCS 14245, pp. 315–326, 2023.
https://doi.org/10.1007/978-3-031-44267-4_16

client ecosystems, and conducting non-regression checks. For all these activities, runtime verification seems a promising approach to get more confidence in the correctness of these software systems.

However, at least three main issues remain. *(1)* Application of formal verification techniques to industrial software products is a challenging task. Designing a formal model of the behavior of each product, that can be used by formal verification tools (e.g., model-checkers), is too complex and time-consuming. *(2)* In the video delivery domain, V&V tools quickly become outdated as new versions of norms and protocols are constantly released. Adapting to these new standards with few efforts is the second challenge. *(3)* The last one is that usually different tools are used to verify video streams (live or *a posteriori* on captures) with new features or bugs and carry out non-regression checks. Using the same tool to perform all these analysis activities would be helpful to mutualize V&V efforts.

To face these issues, we design the ATEME Monitoring Tool (AMT), a runtime verification tool that can be used to express and monitor formal properties on video streams. This work is (at least partially) an industrial application of the research work done in [9,10] by one of the author. To perform the verification task, AMT extracts metadata of video streams using parsers. A modular verification core, agnostic of the business domain, is then used to define the monitoring status of each property based on these metadata. The tool is based on the Semantic Transition Relation (STR) interface defined in [9], a generic interface allowing to link the verification core to the business knowledge provided by the parser (through the domain-specific metadata that have been parsed). To perform runtime verification, AMT neither uses a formal model of the system nor code instrumentation. Our approach relies on monitoring (input(s) and) output(s) of the product. Verifying the correctness of its output stream bolsters confidence in the product behavior itself.

Based on this approach, a working prototype of the tool has been implemented in Python. Due to its novelty, its access is currently limited to engineers of the ATEME company. It can be used to express monitorable properties as Linear Temporal Logic (LTL) formulas that are formally verified at runtime on output streams (e.g., OTT streams) of products. We applied AMT to different case studies by verifying properties corresponding to real requirements checked by Quality Assurance (QA) engineers. We show in this paper that we successfully detect and/or reproduce issues found in systems used by clients in production.

The remainder of this paper is organized as follows. Section 2 gives an overview of the approach. In Sect. 3, we present the language used for property specification while in Sect. 4 we detail the software architecture of AMT. In Sect. 5, we describe some experiments and their corresponding results. Section 6 reviews the state of the art and Sect. 7 finally concludes the paper.

2   Approach Overview

This section presents a theoretical overview of the approach as well as an overview of the tool architecture and a motivating example used to illustrate this paper.

Theoretical Overview: Similarly to model-checking, the approach used by AMT aims at proving that a system satisfies its specifications. Model-checkers perform an exhaustive state-space exploration of a formal model (defined as an abstraction of the system) in search of a counterexample that violates a property. While the formal model is a model of the system defined in *intension*, the explored state-space corresponds to a model of the system defined in *extension*.

In the domain of video delivery, the source code of software products is usually too complex such that it would require too much effort to define a formal model (i.e., the model in *intension*) to apply exhaustive verification techniques on it. Instead, AMT only relies on the model defined in *extension* by observing inputs and outputs of the system and their changes over time. With this "black-box approach", AMT has directly a point of view over the system behavior by relying on the observable part of the system state-space. Using this partial model in *extension*, AMT can verify properties at runtime but in counterpart, no exhaustive exploration can be performed.

Architecture Overview: Figure 1 gives an overview of the AMT architecture and of the setup in which it takes place. The *Product* (to be verified) processes one or multiple *InputStreams* to produce an *OutputStream*. In this project, we mainly target OTT media content using the HLS [25] or the MPEG-DASH [3] protocol. To perform formal verification with the AMT, some monitorable *Properties* first need to be specified based on the content of the *OutputStream* and all the settings, called *ServiceConfiguration*, used to configure a service (i.e., a TV channel) on the *Product*. To formally verify these properties at runtime, *AMT* is based on two main components *AMTParsing* and *AMTCore*. The former is in charge of parsing the multimedia *stream* and of storing the parsed metadata in a database, called *StreamStorage*. The latter is used to perform runtime verification by checking if the specified *Properties* hold on the given stream.

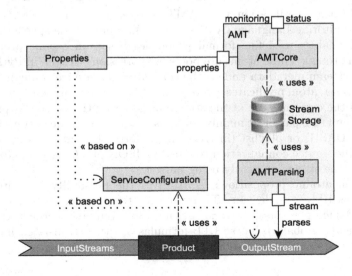

Fig. 1. Architecture overview of the AMT.

Motivating Example: To illustrate our approach, a bug named "Empty period in MPEG-DASH" will be used as a motivating example for the rest of this paper. This bug has been found in a MPEG-DASH manifest, also called MPD (for Manifest Presentation Description), produced by an OTT packager. It results in a period without any video segments. As shown in Fig. 2, the period does not contain a `SegmentTimeline` inside the `SegmentTemplate`. A `SegmentTimeline` is an XML attribute of the MPD used to list media segments (i.e., files containing the media content) when explicit addressing is used. This bug had remained undetected until now because it occurred only when a request was made within a span of a few milliseconds. For this motivating example, the requirement (R) that has to be checked is the following: "All periods of an MPD must contain a non-empty segment timeline for all streams".

```
<Period id="1" start="PT0S">
  [...]
  <AdaptationSet id="2" contentType="video" [...] >
    <SegmentTemplate initialization=[...] media=[...] />
    <!-- No SegmentTimeline in SegmentTemplate here -->
    <Representation id="avc1_800000=1" [...] />
  </AdaptationSet>
</Period>
```

Fig. 2. Excerpt from MPEG-DASH manifest with empty period bug.

3   Property Specification Using AML

To make runtime verification with AMT, properties need to be specified in ATEME Monitoring Language (AML). This is an home-made specification language that enables to define formal properties based on atomic propositions (also called atoms). These atoms are boolean expressions written in Python that depend on stream metadata and on the content of the service configuration. To access this data, atom predicates can rely on two keywords: `current` and `config`. `current` is the current state of the stream as given by the parser. Typically, in the case of an OTT parser, it mainly contains the content of the current manifest (in MPEG-DASH) or playlist (in HLS) in the form of an abstract syntax tree. `config` is the service configuration (defined in JSON or TOML) running on the product for the stream currently being parsed.

Based on atomic propositions, AML gives the possibility to write formal properties as LTL formulas. In LTL formulas, atoms are linked together using first order logic operators (e.g., **and**, **or**, **not**) and temporal modalities of LTL (e.g., [] means globally). These LTL formulas are then translated into Büchi automata with SPOT [18] to be used by the AMT. To be formally verified at runtime, properties defined in AML must belong to the class of monitorable properties, which includes all safety properties. To be monitorable, properties must satisfy two constraints: completeness and determinism. AMT checks these constraints at runtime by ensuring that it is always possible to execute one and only one step on the property automaton at each time.

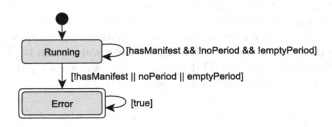

Fig. 3. Büchi automaton for empty period detection.

For our motivating example "Empty period in MPEG-DASH", three atoms are needed. The `hasManifest` atom is used to know if the manifest has been correctly fetched and parsed, `noPeriod` relays whether the parser found no periods in the manifest, and `emptyPeriod` checks that all periods have a non-empty segment timeline. These atoms are defined in AML as follows:

```
atom hasManifest = "current.manifest is not None"
atom noPeriod = "len(current.manifest.periods) == 0"
atom emptyPeriod = "for period in current.manifest.periods:
  for as in period.adaptation_sets:
    for st in as.segment_templates:
      if not st.segment_timelines or
        not st.segment_timelines[0].Ss:
        return True
  return False"
```

Based on these atoms, we can now express in AML the property corresponding to the requirement R of the motivating example:

```
property P1 = [] (hasManifest && !noPeriod && !emptyPeriod)
```

Figure 3 gives an illustration of this property as a Büchi automaton. The automaton stays in the *Running* state if no empty period have been encountered yet and goes into the *Error* state when either no manifest, no period, or an empty period is found. This last state is an acceptance state of the Büchi automaton, meaning that the property is violated when this state is reached.

4   Software Architecture

To perform the verification of properties written in AML, the software architecture of the AMT is based on two components: *AMTParsing* and *AMTCore*.
Both components rely on the Semantic Transition Relation (STR) interface to
control the execution of the property automaton and/or the execution of the
multimedia stream, which can also be seen as an automaton (e.g., one state for
each frame). The STR interface has been defined in [9,10]. As a reminder, the
STR interface has three functions: `initial` that gets the initial state of the
automaton, `actions` that gets the available execution steps from a given state,
and `execute` that executes a step from a given state and returns the target state.
With these three functions, the STR interface gives a semantic point of view on
the behavior of the product through its output stream.

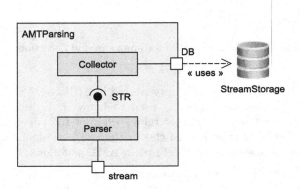

Fig. 4. Architecture of AMTParsing.

Figure 4 illustrates the first component of the architecture called *AMT-
Parsing*. It is responsible for parsing the streams and forwarding metadata to
the *StreamStorage* database. Currently, four parsers have been integrated into
AMT. For OTT, HLSParser based on https://pypi.org/project/m3u8/ parses
HLS playlists while DASHParser based on https://pypi.org/project/mpegdash/
parses Dynamic Adaptive Streaming over HTTP (MPEG-DASH) manifests.
Two parsers are also available for transport streams (TS): an home-made parser
called TSParser and FFMPEGParser based on FFMPEG [2]. When a stream
has been parsed, metadata of each parser configuration are sent to the *Collector*
via the STR interface and stored into the *StreamStorage* database.

The second component of the architecture is *AMTCore* illustrated on Fig. 5.
The *ParserProxy* fetches metadata in the *StreamStorage* database and exposes
it to its STR interface. Meanwhile, *LTL2Automata* transforms LTL formulas into Büchi automata using SPOT [18]. Based on STRs of *ParserProxy*
and *LTL2Automata*, the *SynchronousComposition* synchronously composes the
property automaton with the stream automaton. In other words, the property
automaton observe the execution of the stream automaton and will make one

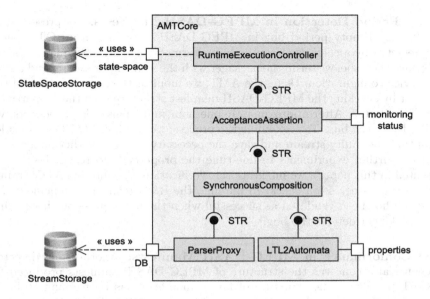

Fig. 5. Architecture of AMTCore for runtime verification.

step each time the stream automaton makes one step (for more details see [9,10]). For instance, the stream automaton makes one step each time a new playlist/-manifest is available for OTT parsers or each time a new video frame is available for FFMPEGParser. The result of the *SynchronousComposition* is forwarded to the *AcceptanceAssertion* component that outputs the *monitoring status* of each property. Finally, the *RuntimeExecutionController* controls the whole execution of the *AMTCore*. It also pushes the explored state-space into the *StateSpaceStorage* database in case a later offline analysis would be needed. For each step, AMT pushes in this database its whole execution state (i.e., all the stream metadata and the current state of Büchi automata) in JSON format.

With AMT, it is also possible to perform analysis on captures of client streams. To make the capture we have developed a tool called OTTDownloader that fetches and saves every media segment that composes the stream as well as a copy of the playlist/manifest at regular time intervals. AMT can then request files from the captured stream as if it were a live source using an HTTP origin server. This allows AMT to perform analysis on live sources or on captures.

5   Experiments and Results

In this section, we describe some of the most representative experiments of applying the AMT on different software products of the video streaming industry.

Empty Period Detection in MPEG-DASH Manifests: As presented in Sect. 2, the "Empty period bug in MPEG-DASH" is a bug in an OTT packager detected by a client that results in malformed MPEG-DASH manifests. To reproduce the issue, we setup the packager with the same input stream and a similar service configuration. Using the AMT, we monitor the output stream of the packager by checking the MPEG-DASH manifest structure with the property P1 defined in Sect. 3. After approximately one hour and thousands of requests, we finally detect the bug. To streamline the process, we employed OTTDownloader to capture the faulty stream and save the necessary files for further analysis.

After further experiments to fine-tune the property (and reach the version presented in this paper), we integrate this verification case into our V&V framework as a non-regression check. In parallel, the R&D team has implemented a fix, which has been validated as successful when the non-regression check using AMT no longer detects the bug.

XSD Conformance in MPEG-DASH Manifests: Another bug detected by clients also concerns the structure of MPEG-DASH manifests produced by an OTT packager. The structure of faulty manifests has been found to be in violation of the XML Schema Definition (XSD) for MPEG-DASH that dictates the structure and order of attributes in MPDs. We used AMT to detect the issue and validate the deployed fix as non-regression check. The property used for runtime verification is the following: `property P2 = []"validate_xml()"`. In this property, `"validate_xml()"` is an inlined atom that calls the helper function `validate_xml()`. This helper performs the validation of the manifest against the XSD using the Python library in [14]. For further investigations, we changed the input stream of the packager and its service configuration to increase the coverage and we found that the "UTCTiming" attribute was out of sequence.

Language Issues in HLS Playlists: Another experiment made with the AMT has been to check the correctness of HLS playlists delivered by an OTT packager. In [5], Apple defines a list of constraints to improve interoperability and compatibility of HLS streams with Apple devices. From this list, we select some constraints including the 8.10 requirement defined as "The LANGUAGE attribute MUST be included in every EXT-X-MEDIA tag that doesn't have TYPE=VIDEO". Based on this requirement, we write the following LTL formula based on two atoms `hasPlaylist` which checks we get an HLS playlist and `languageIncluded` which checks the "LANGUAGE" attribute in present for each non-video stream: `property P3 = [] (hasPlaylist -> languageIncluded)`. We verify this property at runtime with different set of parameters for the packager and we finally found a case where the "LANGUAGE" attribute was missing for an audio stream.

Feedbacks: Regarding performance, even if AMT is written in Python, its execution speed is mainly limited by the performance of the parser and by the physical time flow. Contrary to a model-checker that explores a state-space as fast as possible, AMT parses OTT manifest/playlist or video streams at runtime and is thus highly dependent on how these elements changes over the time (e.g., parsing an OTT manifest/playlist every 6 s is usually sufficient).

Through these experiments, we show that AMT can be applied on real use-cases to verify OTT streams. This demonstrates the effectiveness of AMT to help engineers analyzing software issues. However, we also notice some limitations of our approach that we provide here as additional results to these experiments. *(i)* Expression of atomic propositions and properties is challenging for users as it requires thorough understanding of the metadata returned by the parser and of the temporal modalities of LTL. *(ii)* AMT fetches the manifest/playlist of an OTT stream at regular time intervals and may miss faulty states if this manifest/playlist has changed more than once during this interval of time.

To mitigate these drawbacks, we improve the AMT with some new functionalities. For *(i)*, we add helper functions in AML that can be used in atomic propositions to simplify their expressions. For *(ii)*, we introduce a new parameter such that AMT can fetch OTT manifests/playlists as fast as possible (rather than at regular time intervals). This provides a better coverage of the changes over the OTT manifest/playlist.

6 Related Work

The work presented in this paper relies on runtime verification to check the correctness of software products by analyzing their output streams. Multiple other works provide facilities to apply V&V techniques to multimedia streams.

In the OTT industry, some validators have been developed to check the correctness of OTT streams such as the conformance tool of Dashif [17] for MPEG-DASH or the Media Stream Validator [6] for HLS. In the business domain of video delivery, engineers are also using tools like FFMPEG [2], TSDuck [4], or DVB Inspector [1] to parse, monitor, and display the content of MPEG transport streams. In comparison to these tools, AMT has a verification core agnostic of the business domain. Therefore, its usage is not restricted to a specific set of protocols or video standards.

Regarding formal verification, another interesting technique is model-checking. This technique has been applied in different studies for instance to check peer-to-peer streaming protocols with SPIN [26] and Simulink Design Verifier [23], and verify a lip-synchronization protocol [11] as well as other media constraints (e.g., latency) [12] with Uppaal. More recently, the work in [8] shows how to verify properties on processing pipelines, an implementation technique widely used in video transcoders. In comparison to AMT, all these works require a behavioral model of the system (i.e., a model defined in *intension*) to perform verification. In lack of such a model for industrial legacy systems, AMT relies on a black box approach which makes it applicable on these systems. Its efficiency is however limited to the failure coverage provided by monitorable properties contrary to model-checking which is exhaustive. Moreover, AMT has some similarities with model-checkers like the modularity of its verification core and the use of the STR interface, which are inspired from model-checkers including OBP2 [13], SPOT [18], and LTSmin [21].

More in relation with monitoring, different works provide the possibility to check some requirements at runtime. Similarly to our work, the technique used by [7,19] aims at synthesizing monitors from LTL formulas expressing safety properties. For Java programs, both the Monitoring-Oriented Programming (MOP) framework [15] and the Monitoring and Checking (MaC) architecture [22] can be used to check high-level requirements at runtime. In the UML [24] world, the work in [20] uses an embedded monitor to visualize the system behavior on UML diagrams in real-time while the work in [16] presents how to monitor extra functional properties on UML models. Compared to these tools, AMT is completely independent of the system to analyze (no instrumentation), not specific to a programming language (like Java or UML) and it can be easily extended (just by plugging in a new parser).

7   Conclusion

In this paper, AMT faces the challenge of applying formal verification to some industrial systems delivering multimedia streams. While formal verification tools usually require a formal model of the system to operate on, AMT directly monitors formal properties on the output stream of these systems.

Our tool is based on the STR interface that enables verifying formal properties using a generic verification core agnostic of the business domain. The architecture of AMT makes it easy to evolve as the required business knowledge is only used to implement the parser and write properties that need to be verified. Thanks to its architecture, the applicability of the tool can be extended to other standards and norms only by adding new parsers to it. In other words, if a protocol is not supported, we just need to add a parser for this protocol to be able to express and verify properties about it. In this paper, we also show that AMT can be used for different activities all along the product life cycle: to analyze bugs on clients streams, to validate the development of new features, and to avoid regressions. Using OTTDownloader, we can also easily capture streams in client ecosystems and make runtime verification *a posteriori* with AMT.

Through the performed experiments, we demonstrate the practical application of the tool on different examples. Using AMT, we detect some issues on MPEG-DASH manifests and on HLS playlists produced by different OTT packagers running in production. In some cases, AMT helps engineers to detect some known issues (seen by clients) on reproduction setup while in other cases, it has been used to find new bugs on software systems. This is in fact the most important: AMT has helped engineers to detect software issues and helped to bring more confidence in the correctness of product's behavior.

As future work, we plan to extend AMT with additional parsers to support more video streaming formats. We also aim to improve the verification capabilities of the tool for instance to be able to verify properties about the media content (e.g., MP4 content) of OTT streams.

References

1. DVB Inspector. https://www.digitalekabeltelevisie.nl/dvb_inspector/
2. FFMPEG. https://www.ffmpeg.org/
3. MPEG-DASH. https://www.mpeg.org/standards/MPEG-DASH/
4. TSDuck. https://www.tsduck.io/
5. Apple: HTTP Live Streaming (HLS) Authoring Specification for Apple Devices. https://www.developer.apple.com/documentation/http-live-streaming/hls-authoring-specification-for-apple-devices
6. Apple: Media Stream Validator. https://www.developer.apple.com/documentation/http_live_streaming/using_apple_s_http_live_streaming_hls_tools
7. Bauer, A., Leucker, M., Schallhart, C.: Runtime verification for LTL and TLTL. ACM Trans. Softw. Eng. Methodol. **20**(4), 1–64 (2011). https://doi.org/10.1145/2000799.2000800
8. Bédard, A., Hallé, S.: Model checking of stream processing pipelines. In: Combi, C., Eder, J., Reynolds, M. (eds.) 28th International Symposium on Temporal Representation and Reasoning (TIME 2021). Leibniz International Proceedings in Informatics (LIPIcs), Dagstuhl, Germany, vol. 206, pp. 5:1–5:17. Schloss Dagstuhl - Leibniz-Zentrum für Informatik (2021). https://doi.org/10.4230/LIPIcs.TIME.2021.5
9. Besnard, V.: EMI - Une approche pour unifier l'analyse et l'exécution embarquée à l'aide d'un interpréteur de modèles pilotable: application aux modèles UML des systèmes embarqués. Theses, ENSTA Bretagne - École nationale supérieure de techniques avancées Bretagne (2020)
10. Besnard, V., Teodorov, C., Jouault, F., Brun, M., Dhaussy, P.: Unified verification and monitoring of executable UML specifications: a transformation-free approach. Softw. Syst. Model. **20**(6), 1825–1855 (2021). https://doi.org/10.1007/s10270-021-00923-9
11. Bowman, H., Faconti, G., Katoen, J.P., Latella, D., Massink, M.: Automatic verification of a lip-synchronisation protocol using UPPAAL. Form. Asp. Comput. **10**(5), 550–575 (1998). https://doi.org/10.1007/s001650050032
12. Bowman, H., Faconti, G.P., Massink, M.: Specification and verification of media constraints using UPPAAL. In: Markopoulos, P., Johnson, P. (eds.) Design, Specification and Verification of Interactive Systems 1998, pp. 261–277. Springer, Vienna (1998). https://doi.org/10.1007/978-3-7091-3693-5_17
13. Brumbulli, M., Gaudin, E., Teodorov, C.: Automatic verification of BPMN models. In: 10th European Congress on Embedded Real Time Software and Systems (ERTS 2020), Toulouse, France (2020)
14. Brunato, D.: xmlschema. https://www.pypi.org/project/xmlschema/
15. Chen, F., D'Amorim, M., Roşu, G.: A formal monitoring-based framework for software development and analysis. In: Davies, J., Schulte, W., Barnett, M. (eds.) ICFEM 2004. LNCS, vol. 3308, pp. 357–372. Springer, Heidelberg (2004). https://doi.org/10.1007/978-3-540-30482-1_31
16. Ciccozzi, F.: From models to code and back: a round-trip approach for model-driven engineering of embedded systems. Ph.D. thesis, Mälardalen University, Embedded Systems (2014)
17. DASH Industry Forum: Dashif Conformance Tool. https://www.conformance.dashif.org/
18. Duret-Lutz, A., Poitrenaud, D.: SPOT: an extensible model checking library using transition-based generalized Büchi automata. In: Proceedings of the The IEEE

326   V. Besnard et al.

Computer Society's 12th Annual International Symposium on Modeling, Analysis, and Simulation of Computer and Telecommunications Systems, MASCOTS 2004, Washington, DC, USA, pp. 76–83. IEEE Computer Society (2004). https://doi.org/10.1109/MASCOT.2004.1348184

19. Havelund, K., Roşu, G.: Synthesizing monitors for safety properties. In: Katoen, J.-P., Stevens, P. (eds.) TACAS 2002. LNCS, vol. 2280, pp. 342–356. Springer, Heidelberg (2002). https://doi.org/10.1007/3-540-46002-0_24
20. Iyenghar, P., Pulvermueller, E., Westerkamp, C., Wuebbelmann, J., Uelschen, M.: Model-based debugging of embedded software systems. In: Lettnin, D., Winterholer, M. (eds.) Embedded Software Verification and Debugging. ES, pp. 107–132. Springer, New York (2017). https://doi.org/10.1007/978-1-4614-2266-2_5
21. Kant, G., Laarman, A., Meijer, J., van de Pol, J., Blom, S., van Dijk, T.: LTSmin: high-performance language-independent model checking. In: Baier, C., Tinelli, C. (eds.) TACAS 2015. LNCS, vol. 9035, pp. 692–707. Springer, Heidelberg (2015). https://doi.org/10.1007/978-3-662-46681-0_61
22. Kim, M., Viswanathan, M., Kannan, S., Lee, I., Sokolsky, O.: Java-MaC: a runtime assurance approach for Java programs. Formal Methods Syst. Des. **24**(2), 129–155 (2004). https://doi.org/10.1023/B:FORM.0000017719.43755.7c
23. Ojo, O.E., Oluwatope, A.O., Ajadi, S.O.: Formal verification of a peer-to-peer streaming protocol. J. King Saud Univ. Comput. Inf. Sci. **32**(6), 730–740 (2020). https://doi.org/10.1016/j.jksuci.2018.08.008
24. OMG: Unified Modeling Language (2017). https://www.omg.org/spec/UML/2.5.1/PDF
25. Pantos, R.: HTTP Live Streaming (2023). https://www.datatracker.ietf.org/doc/html/draft-pantos-hls-rfc8216bis
26. Velipasalar, S., Lin, C., Schlessman, J., Wolf, W.: Design and verification of communication protocols for peer-to-peer multimedia systems. In: 2006 IEEE International Conference on Multimedia and Expo, USA, pp. 1421–1424. IEEE Computer Society (2006). https://doi.org/10.1109/ICME.2006.262806

Bridging the Gap: A Focused DSL for RV-Oriented Instrumentation with BISM

Chukri Soueidi$^{(\boxtimes)}$ ⓘ and Yliès Falcone ⓘ

Univ. Grenoble Alpes, CNRS, Inria, Grenoble INP, LIG, 38000 Grenoble, France
{chukri.soueidi,ylies.falcone}@inria.fr

Abstract. We present a novel instrumentation language for BISM, a lightweight bytecode-level instrumentation tool for JVM languages. The new DSL aims to simplify the instrumentation process, making it more accessible to a wider user base. It employs an intuitive syntax, directly mapping to the key requirements of program instrumentation for runtime verification. It enhances productivity by eliminating boilerplate code and low-level details, while also supporting code generation and collaboration. The DSL balances expressiveness, and abstraction, bridging the gap between domain experts and the complexities of instrumentation specification.

1 Introduction

Instrumentation is a fundamental aspect of Runtime Verification (RV) [3,7,8]. It entails modifying the original code within a program to extract events or insert monitors that analyze its behavior. Instrumentation languages, as well as domain-specific languages (DSLs) in general, can be primarily classified into two categories: *external* and *internal* [9]. External DSLs are self-contained languages, complete with their own parsers or compilers, and are not necessarily dependent on any host language. They typically feature customized syntax designed specifically for the target domain. In contrast, internal DSLs are implemented as an application programming interface (API) within a host language. While internal languages offer seamless integration with the host language, external languages provide a focused syntax for domain-specific concerns, making them easier to understand and learn by domain experts. From here on, we will refer to internal languages as *APIs* and external languages as *DSLs*.

For runtime verification, a widely popular instrumentation language is AspectJ [10] which implements aspect-oriented programming (AOP) for Java. It provides both an API, which extends Java with AOP constructs, and a DSL, known as the AspectJ pointcut expression language, for defining pointcuts using a domain-specific syntax. Nonetheless, AspectJ exhibits certain limitations that hinder its effectiveness. One such limitation is the absence of bytecode coverage, which affects its applicability in multithreaded programs and low-level monitoring scenarios [15]. Another limitation is the inability to inline inserted instructions. Lastly, AspectJ is also known to introduce increased overhead to the base program after instrumentation. More recently, BISM (Bytecode-Level Instrumentation for Software Monitoring) [16,17] has been presented as an instrumentation tool for Java programs addressing these limitations. It is oriented more toward runtime verification and features an expressive and high-level instrumentation language inspired by AOP to facilitate its adoption. It has been used effectively in monitoring concurrent programs [12, 15] and for combining static analysis with runtime verification [13, 14].

At present, BISM employs an effective yet somewhat intricate API-based language for implementing transformers. This necessitates some degree of familiarity with Java and the BISM API, which could present challenges for the adoption of BISM as a tool. To make the process of instrumentation more approachable and user-friendly, we introduce a new DSL for BISM. Designed with user-friendliness in mind, the DSL has an intuitive syntax that maps directly to the core requirements of program instrumentation for runtime verification.

Balancing expressiveness and abstraction, our DSL offers comprehensive coverage of program aspects while reducing the complexity of instrumentation specifications. This abstraction, similar to fitting puzzle pieces together, streamlines transformer creation but comes with a moderate cost to performance and flexibility. The DSL eliminates boilerplate code and low-level implementation details, enhancing productivity and reducing the risk of errors. Its design also simplifies code maintenance, making it user-friendly for a broad range of expertise levels. The effectiveness of these enhancements is confirmed through our evaluation.

In our design, we incorporated both code generation and collaboration elements. The DSL can optionally generate equivalent API-based transformer code for more complex instrumentation tasks. It can also generate monitor interfaces from specifications, which promotes efficient collaboration between program developers and monitoring experts. These features not only simplify the instrumentation process but also ensure a clear separation of roles in runtime verification tasks. Notably, our proposed language is the only external specification language known to us that can target JVM bytecode instrumentation covering languages including Java, Scala, Kotlin, and Groovy. In summary, the new DSL for BISM aims to bridge the gap between domain experts and the complexities of implementing BISM transformers, streamlining the instrumentation process for a wide range of users.

2 DSL Design Considerations

In this section, we discuss the main design considerations for the new BISM DSL.

Intuitive Syntax: Instrumenting a program generally involves specifying three key requirements: (1) program points to capture (*joinpoints*), (2) the information needed from these joinpoints, and (3) the consumption of these events. Our DSL addresses these requirements by providing exactly these three main constructs: (1) *pointcuts*, (2) *events*, and (3) *monitors* to consume the captured events.

Expressiveness and Abstraction. BISM API offers remarkable expressiveness for covering all program aspects and extracting information from the executing program. We designed the DSL to retain this expressiveness while considerably simplifying the specification and providing a higher abstraction level. However, this abstraction comes with a moderate cost to flexibility in scenarios where fine-grained control over the instrumentation process is required. For instance, when some analysis is required within the instrumentation process which can be achieved with the BISM API.

Efficiency and Performance. Textual specifications for instrumentation often require parsing and compiling transformations. We optimized the DSL implementation with a focus on performance, striving to achieve reasonable execution times for parsing and applying instrumentation compared to using the native BISM API.

Usability Simplification. Crafting a BISM transformer requires implementing a Java class using the provided instrumentation API. The DSL is tailored to accommodate users with diverse expertise levels by eliminating boilerplate code and low-level implementation details, ultimately enhancing productivity, minimizing errors, and simplifying code maintenance.

Code Generation. Our DSL can create API-based transformer code from user-defined textual specifications, allowing further user customizations for complex instrumentation. It can also generate monitor interfaces, promoting collaboration between developers and monitoring experts.

3   BISM Background

BISM (Bytecode-Level Instrumentation for Software Monitoring) [16,17] is a lightweight instrumentation tool for Java that is designed to provide an expressive and high-level instrumentation language for runtime verification and enforcement. The tool is inspired by aspect-oriented programming (AOP) languages, utilizing separate classes called *transformers* to encapsulate joinpoint selection and advice inlining. BISM *selectors* facilitate the selection of joinpoints by associating each selector with a well-defined region in the bytecode, such as a single bytecode instruction, control-flow branch, or method call. Listing 1.1 shows the main available selectors.

```
Before/AfterInstruction          OnBasicBlockEnter/Exit
Before/AfterMethodCall           OnTrue/FalseBranchEnter
OnFieldSet/Get                   OnMethodEnter/Exit
```

Listing 1.1. BISM selectors

Static context objects allow users to extract at joinpoints information derived at compile time about instructions, basic blocks, methods, and classes. *Dynamic context objects* extract values that are only available at runtime, such as instance and static fields, local variables, method arguments, method results, executing class instances, and stack values. Additionally, BISM allows the creation of new local variables and arrays within the scope of a method to pass values required for instrumentation. *Advice methods* specify how to extract the desired information, such as invoking methods or printing. These advice methods enable the extraction of information at the identified joinpoints, based on the selected selectors and desired information extraction. A distinguishing feature of BISM is its ability to insert arbitrary bytecode instructions into the base program making it suitable for instrumenting inline monitors and enforcers.

```
public class IteratorTransformer extends Transformer {
 public void afterMethodCall(MethodCall mc, DynamicContext dc){
    // Filter to only method of interest
    if (mc.methodName.equals("iterator") &&
        mc.methodOwner.endsWith("List")) {

        // Access to dynamic data
        DynamicValue list = dc.getMethodTarget();
        DynamicValue iterator = dc.getMethodResult();

        // Create an ArrayList in the target method
        LocalArray la = dc.createLocalArray(mc.ins.basicBlock.method,
            Object.class);
        dc.addToLocalArray(la,list);
        dc.addToLocalArray(la,iterator);

        // Invoke the monitor after passing arguments
        StaticInvocation sti =
            new StaticInvocation("monitors.SafeListMonitor",
                "receive");
        sti.addParameter("create");
        sti.addParameter(la);
        invoke(sti);
    }
 }
}
```

Listing 1.2. A BISM transformer written in Java that intercepts the creation of an iterator

Users specify the instrumentation by extending a base `Transformer` type. Listing 1.2 presents a fragment of a transformer used in a parametric monitoring setup [1,5] where we monitor the **SafeIterator** property[1]. The BISM transformer, written in Java, uses the selector `afterMethodCall` to capture the return of an `Iterator` created from a `List.iterator()` method call. It uses the dynamic context object provided to retrieve the associated objects with the event. It also creates a local list to push the objects into it. Then, invokes a monitor passing an event name and the list as arguments.

4 The DSL for BISM

We here present the main abstractions and constructs provided by the DSL to address the user requirements of runtime verification and instrumentation.

4.1 Pointcuts

Pointcuts enable users to specify the joinpoints to capture from program execution. They can be denoted as follows: a pointcut *name*, a BISM selector along with a *pattern*, and an optional *guard*. Multiple selectors are chainable using the | | operator. The pattern restricts the scope of the selector to specific methods or fields (for field selectors), applying filters such as types, method signatures, or field names. Matching can be achieved with wildcards; for example, "`* .set*(..)`" matches any method that starts with "set". The optional guard allows the specification of a condition, essentially

---

[1] The property specifies that a `Collection` should not be updated when an iterator associated with it is created and being used.

a Boolean expression using static context objects from the joinpoint. The guard conditions may use comparisons of booleans, numerics, and strings, and can be chained with the conjunction operator (&&) to create complex conditions. In each DSL transformer, the definition of at least one pointcut is necessary.

```
pointcut pc1 after MethodCall(* BankAccount.*(..)) with (
    getNumberOfArgs = 3 && currentClassName = "Main")
        || after MethodCall(* *.*(..)) with (instruction.
            linenumber = 42)

pointcut pc2 before Instruction(* *.*(..))
                    with (isConditionalJump = true)
```

Listing 1.3. Example of pointcuts definition.

Listing 1.3 shows a composite pointcut pc1 that uses two selectors. The first selector captures calls to methods defined by the classBankAccount, but only captures calls that are invoked from the "Main" class and the called method has exactly three arguments. The second selector captures any method call occurring at line 42. This second guard showcases BISM's hierarchical context objects and how they can be accessed using dot notation. Pointcut pc2 captures any instruction that is a conditional jump.

4.2 Events

Events encapsulate the information that needs to be extracted from a pointcut. Each event must be associated with a single pointcut along with its arguments. Multiple events can be defined for each pointcut. An event includes a name and zero or more arguments. Arguments may comprise single values or lists of values, which can include BISM static or dynamic context objects, string literals, numbers, or lists. Lists are denoted as sequences of values, separated by commas, and enclosed in brackets.

```
event e1("call", [getMethodReceiver, getMethodResult]) on pc1

event e2([opcode,getStackValues]) on pc2 to console(List)
```

Listing 1.4. Example of events definition.

Listing 1.4 shows an event named e1, associated with the pointcut pc1, that is defined with the string literal "call" and a list of dynamic context objects which extract the called object and the result of the method. Event e2 is defined with a list of dynamic context objects (opcode, getStackValues) and is associated with the pointcut pc2. The DSL also provides a construct to print an event to the console, which is particularly useful during the debugging or profiling of a program. This event is associated with the output console(List) which prints the event information to the console.

4.3 Monitors

Monitors listen to the occurrence of one or several events, and they define the extraction points for these events during program execution. Each monitor is identified by a unique name, the class name and package locating its implementation, and the events it is set to listen to. Typically, the events are passed as parameters during the invocation of a monitor method. Events are mapped to the monitor method name with its argument types. Multiple monitors can be defined and each event can be listened to by more than one monitor.

```
monitor m1{
    class: com.MonitorX,
    events: [e1 to receive(String, List)]
}
```

Listing 1.5. Example of a monitor definition.

Listing 1.5 shows a monitor m1 corresponding to a class named com.MonitorX. Event e1 is mapped to the method receive with the argument types String and List. The specification can be simplified by directly associating the monitor with the event. However, this restricts the use of the event to only one monitor. Here is an equivalent specification without the explicit definition of a monitor.

```
event e1("create",[getMethodReceiver,getMethodResult])
                on pc1 to com.MonitorX.receive(String,List)
```

Listing 1.6. Simple monitor definition.

4.4   Code Generation

We here present the code generation facilities that bridge the gap between new and expert users of BISM, also the gap between monitoring experts and program developers.

Transformers for Complex Instrumentation Tasks. The Java-based API transformers allow users to write intricate analysis logic within transformers. Equipped with the full program context provided by BISM and the Java language, the user can write any piece of analysis code that can guide the instrumentation process. For example, in [14] such analysis was used to perform residual analysis which entails checking for safe instructions statically such that they can be ignored from the instrumentation. Starting with a simple text-based DSL specification where events of interest can be identified, users can gradually move to complex instrumentation logic using a full-fledged Java transformer. To facilitate this transition, we optionally generate and compile Java transformers equivalent to the provided textual specification files. Consequently, these specification files can act as bootstrappers for implementing more complex logic.

Monitor Interfaces. As discussed in Sect. 4.3, the process of creating an instrumentation specification often requires declaring a monitor to listen for events. In collaborative scenarios, a monitoring expert consults the developer to identify relevant events and their static and runtime context. Subsequently, the programmer creates a specification file capable of locating and extracting the necessary events, leaving the monitoring

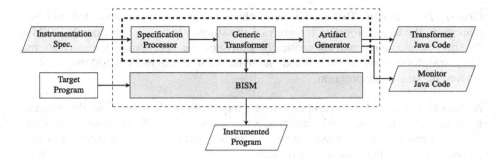

Fig. 1. Added modules on BISM (in blue) to support the external DSL. (Color figure online)

expert solely responsible for implementing the monitors. To optimize this collaboration, our DSL incorporates a feature to generate the monitor interfaces, that need to be implemented to listen to events. This capability substantially improves interoperability between different teams, fostering a more efficient and productive workflow when addressing complex instrumentation tasks.

```
package com;
import java.util.List;

public class MonitorX{
    public static void receive(String a1, List a2) {
    }
}
```

Listing 1.7. A generated monitor class.

Listing 1.7 shows the generated interface for the monitor in Listing 1.5. The user can then implement the `receive` method to perform the desired analysis logic.

5   Implementation

We implemented the DSL as an extension to BISM with 6 KLOC of Java code[2]. Figure 1 shows the three main modules we added to BISM which handle specification parsing, transformation application, and code generation. We provide more details on each module below.

Specification Processor. This module accepts the user's textual specification as input and parses it into a specification object. This object is an intermediate representation that embodies the desired transformations. The module also performs a series of checks to ensure the specification's validity, including the removal of duplicate rules and verification of well-formedness

---

[2] The tool is available at https://gitlab.inria.fr/bism/bism-dsl.

Generic Transformer. This module is in charge of applying user-specified transformations to the target program. It features a transformer template that extends BISM's `Transformer` type and automatically generates the appropriate transformations. These transformations are then turned into bytecode instructions by BISM that are then weaved into the target program.

Artifact Generator. Activated upon a user's request for code generation, this module generates an equivalent API-based transformer class utilizing BISM's API. Additionally, it generates a monitor class that can be implemented and used to monitor the instrumented program's behavior during runtime.

6   Evaluation

In this section, we provide an assessment of the DSL, specifically focusing on the overhead it introduces and the user experience[3].

6.1   Performance Evaluation

To evaluate the performance, we examine the overhead introduced by our DSL in comparison with both the BISM API and AspectJ. Our test case is the financial transaction system as described in [2]. We instrument this system to extract events from all method calls on `Iterator` objects, get field operations, and method executions. We test four distinct methodologies to write identical instrumentation specifications:

- **AspectJ DSL:** An aspect (`.aj`) is written using the DSL, requiring approximately 40 lines of code.
- **AspectJ API:** An API-based aspect (`.java`) is written, using annotations, requiring approximately 60 lines of code.
- **BISM DSL:** A transformer (`.spec`) is written with our proposed DSL for BISM, requiring approximately 20 lines of code.
- **BISM API:** An API-based BISM transformer (`.java`) is written using the API, requiring approximately 70 lines of code.

To ensure a fair comparison, we utilized features available across all four approaches[4]. Each benchmark was run 20 times, with each run producing 500K events, and the mean execution times are reported in Fig. 2a. The results showed that BISM API outperforms the other methods, running 1.14 times faster than BISM DSL, 1.7 times faster than AspectJ API, and 3.25 times faster than AspectJ DSL. This demonstrates that specifying instrumentation using the API generally leads to faster execution due to the extra delay incurred in DSL approaches from parsing the specification files. However, our proposed DSL outperforms AspectJ DSL and is even faster than AspectJ API, maintaining the effectiveness and efficiency of BISM in the context of software monitoring and instrumentation.

---

[3] The full details for the experiments can be found at https://gitlab.inria.fr/bism/bism-dsl-experiments.

[4] The experiment utilized AspectJ AJC 1.9.7 and JDK 11.

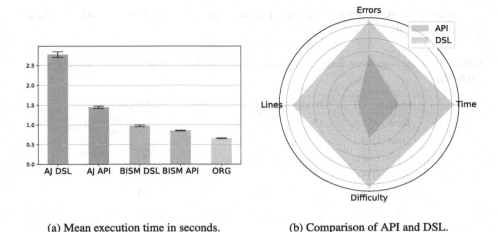

(a) Mean execution time in seconds.   (b) Comparison of API and DSL.

Fig. 2. Performance evaluation results.

6.2 User Experience Evaluation

Experiment Design. We conducted an experiment in which 10 participants, with various experience levels in Java and runtime verification, were instructed to write transformers for monitoring four different properties sourced from [2] using both methods. The experiment used a randomized block design. The participants were divided into two equal groups: Group A and Group B. Group A used the API for Properties 1 and 3 and the DSL for Properties 2 and 4. In contrast, Group B used the DSL for Properties 1 and 3 and the API for Properties 2 and 4. This design allowed each participant to gain experience with both methods, enabling a fair comparison between the two techniques across all properties.

Collected Metrics. For each property, the participants are asked to record the time they took to write the instrumentation, reported in minutes (**Time**). They also kept track of the number of mistakes they made during the process that necessitated recompilation and another run (**Errors**). In addition, the number of lines of code written for each transformer was noted, (**Lines**). Lastly, participants rated the difficulty of use on a scale of 1 to 5, where 1 signified very easy and 5 meant very hard, (**Difficulty**).

Results and Analysis. In Fig. 2b, we report each metric normalized to a 0–1 range based on their respective minimum and maximum values. Table 1 shows the average values for each metric. The results indicate a clear advantage of the DSL over the API for writing BISM transformers. Across all properties tested, the DSL not only needed significantly less time to implement but also resulted in fewer errors and less code. Furthermore, participants found the DSL easier to use. The good results of the DSL can be largely attributed to its concise syntax and straightforward usage. However, it is important to note that a considerable portion of errors in DSL mode were caused by improper referencing of the monitor and its package name, and the need for full specification of return types in patterns. Future iterations of the DSL will address these pattern specification issues.

Table 1. Average time taken, number of errors, number of lines, and difficulty for each property and mode.

Metric	Property 1	Property 2	Property 3	Property 4
Time (API)	15	13	5	7
Time (DSL)	8	7	2	2
Errors (API)	4	3	2	1
Errors (DSL)	3	3	0	0
Lines (API)	12	16	10	24
Lines (DSL)	7	5	5	9
Difficulty (API)	4	4	3	3
Difficulty (DSL)	3	3	1	1

7 Related Work and Conclusion

In this section, we review some of the relevant frameworks for Java program instrumentation and compare them to our proposed DSL for BISM. It is worth noting that our proposed language is the only *external* specification language we know of that can target bytecode instrumentation thereby covering JVM languages including Java, Scala, Kotlin, and Groovy. API-based frameworks such as ASM [4], BCEL [18], Soot [19], and Javassist [6] offer a wide range of low-level bytecode transformation capabilities. However, they demand a significant understanding of bytecode and can be verbose when implementing simple instrumentation specifications. ASM, in particular, was chosen over Soot for BISM due to its performance and compact size, while Javassist and BCEL provide better levels of abstraction from bytecode details. On the other end of the spectrum, aspect-oriented programming (AOP) frameworks like AspectJ [10] provide a high-level language for specifying instrumentation. However, AspectJ incurs considerable overhead, and cannot instrument at the bytecode level, limiting its usefulness in multithreaded programs and low-level monitoring scenarios. Balancing these approaches, DiSL [11] offers an extensible API-based instrumentation language with advanced features eliminating transformation interference. DiSL offers a complex set of features making it more suitable for dynamic analysis scenarios such as profiling. In comparison, BISM reduces execution overhead and allows for arbitrary code insertion, necessary for inlining monitors and enforcers.

Our proposed BISM DSL aims to simplify BISM usage by offering a focused syntax for instrumentation and runtime verification. However, it only supports a subset of the BISM features and lacks support for inserting arbitrary bytecode instructions. The potential for DSL and API full integration is currently under investigation. Moreover, we aim to add enforcement constructs to the DSL, allowing users to specify inlined enforcers.

References

1. Barringer, H., Falcone, Y., Havelund, K., Reger, G., Rydeheard, D.: Quantified event automata: towards expressive and efficient runtime monitors. In: Giannakopoulou, D., Méry, D. (eds.) FM 2012. LNCS, vol. 7436, pp. 68–84. Springer, Heidelberg (2012). https://doi.org/10.1007/978-3-642-32759-9_9

2. Bartocci, E., et al.: First international competition on runtime verification: rules, benchmarks, tools, and final results of CRV 2014. Int. J. Softw. Tools Technol. Transf. 21(1), 31–70 (2019). https://www.gitlab.inria.fr/crv14/benchmarks/

3. Bartocci, E., Falcone, Y., Francalanza, A., Reger, G.: Introduction to runtime verification. In: Bartocci, E., Falcone, Y. (eds.) Lectures on Runtime Verification. LNCS, vol. 10457, pp. 1–33. Springer, Cham (2018). https://doi.org/10.1007/978-3-319-75632-5_1

4. Bruneton, E., Lenglet, R., Coupaye, T.: ASM: a code manipulation tool to implement adaptable systems. In: Adaptable and Extensible Component Systems (2002). https://www.asm.ow2.io

5. Chen, F., Roşu, G.: Parametric trace slicing and monitoring. In: Kowalewski, S., Philippou, A. (eds.) TACAS 2009. LNCS, vol. 5505, pp. 246–261. Springer, Heidelberg (2009). https://doi.org/10.1007/978-3-642-00768-2_23

6. Chiba, S.: Load-time structural reflection in Java. In: Bertino, E. (ed.) ECOOP 2000. LNCS, vol. 1850, pp. 313–336. Springer, Heidelberg (2000). https://doi.org/10.1007/3-540-45102-1_16

7. Falcone, Y., Havelund, K., Reger, G.: A tutorial on runtime verification. In: Broy, M., Peled, D.A., Kalus, G. (eds.) Engineering Dependable Software Systems. NATO Science for Peace and Security Series, D: Information and Communication Security, vol. 34, pp. 141–175. IOS Press (2013). https://doi.org/10.3233/978-1-61499-207-3-141

8. Falcone, Y., Krstic, S., Reger, G., Traytel, D.: A taxonomy for classifying runtime verification tools. Int. J. Softw. Tools Technol. Transf. 23(2), 255–284 (2021). https://doi.org/10.1007/s10009-021-00609-z

9. Fowler, M., Parsons, R.: Domain-Specific Languages. Addison-Wesley, Upper Saddle River (2011)

10. Kiczales, G., Hilsdale, E., Hugunin, J., Kersten, M., Palm, J., Griswold, W.G.: Getting started with AspectJ. Commun. ACM 44(10), 59–65 (2001)

11. Marek, L., Villazón, A., Zheng, Y., Ansaloni, D., Binder, W., Qi, Z.: DiSL: a domain-specific language for bytecode instrumentation. In: Hirschfeld, R., Tanter, É., Sullivan, K.J., Gabriel, R.P. (eds.) Proceedings of the 11th International Conference on Aspect-Oriented Software Development, AOSD, Potsdam, Germany, pp. 239–250. ACM (2012)

12. Soueidi, C., El-Hokayem, A., Falcone, Y.: Opportunistic monitoring of multithreaded programs. In: Lambers, L., Uchitel, S. (eds.) FASE 2023. LNCS, vol. 13991, pp. 173–194. Springer, Cham (2023). https://doi.org/10.1007/978-3-031-30826-0_10

13. Soueidi, C., Falcone, Y.: Capturing program models with BISM. In: Hong, J., Bures, M., Park, J.W., Cerný, T. (eds.) SAC 2022: The 37th ACM/SIGAPP Symposium on Applied Computing, Virtual Event, 25–29 April 2022, pp. 1857–1861. ACM (2022). https://doi.org/10.1145/3477314.3507239

14. Soueidi, C., Falcone, Y.: Residual runtime verification via reachability analysis. In: Lal, A., Tonetta, S. (eds.) VSTTE 2022. LNCS, vol. 13800, pp. 148–1663. Springer, Cham (2023). https://doi.org/10.1007/978-3-031-25803-9_9

15. Soueidi, C., Falcone, Y.: Sound concurrent traces for online monitoring. In: Caltais, G., Schilling, C. (eds.) SPIN 2023. LNCS, vol. 13872, pp. 59–80. Springer, Cham (2023). https://doi.org/10.1007/978-3-031-32157-3_4

16. Soueidi, C., Kassem, A., Falcone, Y.: BISM: bytecode-level instrumentation for software monitoring. In: Deshmukh, J., Ničković, D. (eds.) RV 2020. LNCS, vol. 12399, pp. 323–335. Springer, Cham (2020). https://doi.org/10.1007/978-3-030-60508-7_18

17. Soueidi, C., Monnier, M., Falcone, Y.: Int. J. Softw. Tools Technol. Transfer 1–27 (2023). https://doi.org/10.1007/s10009-023-00708-z

18. The Apache Software Foundation: Apache commons. https://www.commons.apache.org. Accessed 18 June 2020

19. Vallée-Rai, R., Co, P., Gagnon, E., Hendren, L., Lam, P., Sundaresan, V.: Soot - a Java bytecode optimization framework. In: Proceedings of the 1999 Conference of the Centre for Advanced Studies on Collaborative Research, CASCON 1999, p. 13. IBM Press (1999)

CCMOP: A Runtime Verification Tool
for C/C++ Programs

Yongchao Xing[1,2], Zhenbang Chen[1,2]([✉]) (ID), Shibo Xu[1,2], and Yufeng Zhang[3] (ID)

[1] College of Computer, National University of Defense Technology, Changsha, China
{xingyc0979,zbchen}@nudt.edu.cn
[2] Key Laboratory of Software Engineering for Complex Systems, National University
of Defense Technology, Changsha, China
[3] College of Computer Science and Electronic Engineering, Hunan University,
Changsha, China
yufengzhang@hnu.edu.cn

Abstract. Runtime verification (RV) is an effective lightweight formal
method for improving software's reliability at runtime. There exist no
RV tools specially designed for C++ programs. This paper introduces
the first one, *i.e.*, CCMOP, which implements an AOP-based RV approach and supports the RV of general properties for C/C++ program.
CCMOP provides an AOP language specially designed for C++ program to define the events in RV. The instrumentation of RV monitor
is done at AST-level, which improves the efficiency of compilation and
the accuracy of RV. CCMOP is implemented based on JavaMOP and
an industrial-strength compiler. The results of extensive experiments on
100 real-world C/C++ programs (5584.3K LOCs in total) indicate that
CCMOP is robust and supports the RV of real-world C/C++ programs.

Keywords: Runtime Verification · C/C++ · Instrumentation · AOP

1 Introduction

Runtime verification (RV) [17] is a lightweight formal method for verifying program executions. Different from the traditional formal verification methods, such
as model checking [10] and theorem proving [12,19], which verify the whole
behavior of the program and often face state explosion problem [11] or need
labor-intensive manual efforts, runtime verification only verifies a trace (execution) of the program. When the program $\mathcal{P}$ is running, runtime verification
techniques collect $\mathcal{P}$'s running information and usually abstract the information
into events. A program *trace* t is an *event sequence*. Then, the verification is
carried out on the fly for the trace with respect to a formal property φ, *e.g.*, a
line-time temporal logic (LTL) property; If t does not satisfy φ [24], the runtime

CCMOP is available at https://rv-ccmop.github.io.

verification will take some efforts, *e.g.*, reporting a warning or error and terminating $\mathcal{P}$ in advance. In this way, runtime verification does not suffer from the scalability problem of traditional formal verification techniques.

Until now, there already exist many runtime verification tools [2] for different program languages, *e.g.*, RTC [21] and E-ACSL [29] for C programs, JavaMOP [4] and TraceMatches [1] for Java programs, to name a few. Usually, a runtime verification tool accepts a program $\mathcal{P}$ and a property φ. Then, the tool automatically generates a runtime monitor $\mathcal{M}$ for φ and instruments the monitor into $\mathcal{P}$. When the instrumented version of $\mathcal{P}$ is executed, $\mathcal{M}$ will online verify $\mathcal{P}$'s trace with respect to φ. Existing runtime verification tools differ in different aspects, including the target program's language, implementation mechanisms (*e.g.*, instrumentation and VM-based approaches), supported verification properties (*e.g.*, LTL, FSM, and CFG), *etc.* These tools are widely applied in different areas and backgrounds [17], which shows the effectiveness of runtime verification.

However, the RV tools for C++ programs are still in demand. Although there exist some sanitizer tools [14] of the LLVM platform [18] that instrument the monitor at the intermediate representation (IR) level, they can only monitor memory-specific properties. Besides, binary-level instrumentation-based RV tools, in principle, support C++ programs, but they also suffer the problems of overhead, across-platform, and inaccuracy [26,32]. As far as we know, there does not exist a runtime verification tool specially designed for C++ programs that supports general properties and instrument monitors at the source code level.

This paper presents CCMOP, *i.e.*, a runtime verification tool for C/C++ programs following the design of JavaMOP [4]. The runtime monitor of the property is first generated in an aspect-oriented programming (AOP) language. We have designed and implemented an AOP platform for C/C++ programs to support the automatic instrumentation of runtime monitors. Monitors can be transparently woven into the program during program compilation. The weaving is carried out at the source code level and on the program's abstract syntax tree (AST). We have implemented the AOP platform based on Clang [9], *i.e.*, an industrial-strength compiler. We have applied CCMOP for 100 real-world C/C++ programs to evaluate our tool. The results indicate that CCMOP can support the runtime verification of real-world C/C++ programs for general properties. The main contributions are as follows.

- We have implemented a runtime verification tool for C/C++ programs that supports the RV of general properties. As far as we know, CCMOP is the first source-level instrumentation-based RV tool for C++ programs.
- We have applied CCMOP for 100 real-world C/C++ programs (5584.3K LOCs in total) with standard C++ language features. The experimental results indicate that CCMOP supports the RV for large-scale C/C++ programs. The runtime overhead of CCMOP on C++ programs is 88% for the use-after-free property.

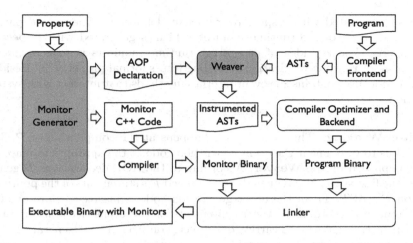

Fig. 1. CCMOP's framework.

2   Framework

Figure 1 shows the framework and basic workflow of CCMOP. The inputs are a property φ and a program $\mathcal{P}$, and the output is the executable binary of the program in which monitors are instrumented. The workflow can be divided into two stages: monitor generation and monitor weaving.

Monitor Generation. CCMOP adopts the RV framework of JavaMOP [4] that utilizes AOP for property specification and monitor instrumentation. The property syntax is a variant of JavaMOP's MOP syntax for C/C++ programs. A property φ is composed of the following two parts.

- The declarations of the events, defined by different AOP pointcuts [16], and the AOP language is explained in Sect. 3. Besides, we can also specify the C/C++ code that will be executed when the event is generated. For example, the following defines event **create** for each **new** statement in the C++ program, and the event **create** is generated after the execution of the **new** statement.

$$\texttt{event create after(void* key):expr(new *(...))\&\&result(key)\{\}} \quad (1)$$

- The formal property defined on the event level, which can be specified by different formalisms, including a logic (*e.g.*, LTL), an automaton (*e.g.*, FSM), and a regular expression, *etc.* The property gives the specification that the program should satisfy during program execution. If the execution satisfies or does not satisfy the property, some operations can be carried out. These operations can be C/C++ statements that are also given in the property.

Based on the property φ, CCMOP automatically generates two parts. The first part is the **AOP declarations** that are in charge of generating events, which are generated with respect to φ's event definitions. The second part is the C/C++ code of the runtime monitor, which is generated with respect to φ's property. The key idea of generating runtime monitors is to generate an automaton for runtime verification according to φ's formal property [3]. Besides, monitor code also contains the event interface methods that interact with system execution.

Monitor Weaving. The second stage happens at the compilation of $\mathcal{P}$. The main job is to instrument the event generation code at the appropriate places of $\mathcal{P}$, accomplished by the **Weaver**. According to the AOP declarations $\mathcal{D}$ generated at the first stage, **Weaver** finds the matched $\mathcal{P}$'s statements of the pointcuts in $\mathcal{D}$ on $\mathcal{P}$'s AST. Then, the event generation code is inserted before or after the statements according to the requirements of the event declarations in φ. Here, the instrumentation is carried out directly on AST. Event generation code invokes the event interface method in the monitor code to notify the monitor that an event is generated and the runtime checking needs to be carried out.

For example, the following code shows the source code after weaving the code for the event **create**. There exists a statement that the pointer **p** is assigned with the address returned by a **new** statement. After instrumentation, the pointer **p** will be passed as the parameter of the event **create**'s interface method invocation.

```
1  int main(){
2      int *p = new int;
3      int *key_1=p;
4      __RVC_UAF_create(key_1);
5      return 0;
6  }
```

After weaving, the instrumented AST will be used for compiler optimization and code generation in the later compilation stages. Finally, a binary that can generate events for RV is generated. After getting the binary that can generate events, we need to link the binary with the monitor binary that does the real verification job. The executable binary with runtime monitors (denoted by $\mathcal{P}_m$) is finally generated. Then, we can run $\mathcal{P}_m$ with different inputs, and the runtime monitors will carry out the operations defined in φ when φ is violated or satisfied.

In principle, our framework provides an online synchronous approach to runtime verification. The instrumentation for RV is carried out on AST, which enjoys the advantages including lower-overhead, across-platform, accuracy, *etc.*

3   Design and Implementation

AOP Language for C/C++. Figure 2 shows the critical parts of the AOP language for C/C++. The language is based on AspectJ [16], and the figure only shows the abbreviated version for the sake of brevity, where ϵ represents the empty string, $\langle \text{ID} \rangle$ represents an identity name, $\langle \text{IDs} \rangle$ represents a comma dotted $\langle \text{ID} \rangle$ sequence. The particular syntax elements for C/C++ are as follows.

⟨Advice⟩ ::= advice ⟨SPointCut⟩⟨VPointCuts⟩:(before | after | around)(⟨VarDecl⟩)
⟨SPointCut⟩ ::= call(⟨FuncDecl⟩) | expr(⟨CExprDecl⟩) | deref (⟨ScopedTypes⟩) |
     end() | ⟨SPointCut⟩ || ⟨SPointCut⟩
⟨VPointCuts⟩ ::= ε | && ⟨VPointCut⟩ | && ⟨VPointCut⟩ ⟨VPointCuts⟩
⟨VPointCut⟩ ::= args(⟨IDs⟩) | result(⟨ID⟩) | target(⟨ID⟩) | within(⟨SpaceDecl⟩)
⟨VarDecl⟩ ::= ε | ⟨ScopedType⟩ ⟨ID⟩ | ⟨ScopedType⟩ ⟨ID⟩,⟨VarDecl⟩
⟨FuncDecl⟩ ::= (% | ⟨ScopedType⟩) (⟨ScopedType⟩.⟨ID⟩ | ⟨ID⟩)(⟨ScopedTypes⟩ | ...)
⟨CExprDecl⟩ ::= new ⟨ExprDecl⟩ | delete ⟨ExprDecl⟩ | ⟨ExprDecl⟩
⟨ExprDecl⟩ ::= (⟨ScopedType⟩::* | ⟨ScopedType⟩ | *)(⟨ScopedTypes⟩ | ...)
⟨SpaceDecl⟩ ::= ⟨ScopedType⟩ | ⟨ScopedType⟩()
⟨ScopedTypes⟩ ::= ⟨ScopedType⟩ | ⟨ScopedType⟩,⟨ScopedTypes⟩
⟨ScopedType⟩ ::= ⟨BasicType⟩ | ⟨BasicType⟩::⟨ScopedType⟩ | ⟨ScopedType⟩*
⟨BasicType⟩ ::= ⟨ID⟩ | ⟨ID⟩<⟨ScopedTypes⟩> | ⟨PrimitiveTypes⟩

Fig. 2. The core syntax of the AOP language.

- We introduce deref to match the pointer dereferences in C/C++ programs. Here is an example of the pointcut for matching the dereferences of all string pointers: deref(std::basic_string<char> *).
- To support the namespace and template mechanisms in C++, we introduce ⟨ScopedType⟩, which is also compatible with matching the functions and types of C programs. Besides, we also introduce cexpr for matching the object management statements in C++ programs, including class constructors, new and delete statements. Furthermore, call(⟨FuncDecl⟩) also supports the matching of the operator functions in C++ program (*e.g.*, operator+(...)), and the details are omitted for the sake of brevity.

Similar to JavaMOP, ⟨Advice⟩ is used to capture the monitored objects. For example, the AOP declaration for the event create in (1) is as follows.

$$\text{advice expr(new *(...))\&\&result(key) : after(void* key)\{\}} \qquad (2)$$

Implementation. CCMOP's implementation is based on JavaMOP [4] and Clang [9]. We explain the two gray components in Fig. 1 as follows.

- **Monitor Generator.** We reused the MOP syntax of JavaMOP and modified it to enable the usage of our AOP language in Fig. 2 for defining events and the definitions of C/C++ code in event handlers. Besides, we have also developed the C++ runtime monitor code generator based on JavaMOP's RV-Monitor component. We support two specification languages: extended regular expression (ERE) and finite state machine (FSM). More specification languages in RV-Monitor are to be supported in the future.
- **Weaver.** We implemented the weaver for the AOP language in Fig. 2 based on Clang. We find the pointcut matched statements by Clang's AST matching framework [7]. Besides, the instrumentation defined in the AOP declarations is also carried out on AST, which is implemented by the AST transformation mechanism [8] of Clang. There are two advantages of AST-level instrumentation: First, compared with the source code text-based approach [6], it

is more precise for the advanced mechanisms in C/C++ programs, such as `#define` and `typedef`, which are widely used in real-world programs; Second, AST-level instrumentation is carried out just before the IR generation, which enables just one time of parsing instead of two times needed by the source code text-based instrumentation method [6].

Limitations. There are following limitations of CCMOP. First, due to the widespread use of `typedef` in C/C++, some types are translated to other types on the AST-level. However, the description of ⟨Advice⟩ needs to specify the types in ASTs. For example, `std::string` is translated to `std::basic_string<char>` in ASTs, and we need to use `std::basic_string<char>` in ⟨Advice⟩ specification to capture the objects of `std::string`. Second, CCMOP's event specification is limited and only supports specific types of events, e.g., method invocations, object constructions and memory operations. Third, CCMOP does not support multi-threaded C/C++ programs.

4   Evaluation

Basic Usage. CCMOP provides a script `wac` for compiling a single C/C++ file. The basic usage is demonstrated as follows, where we are compiling a single C++ file into the executable binary `demo`, and the RV with respect to the property will be carried out when running `demo`.

```
wac -cxx -mop <a property file> <a CPP file> -o demo
```

Besides, we also provide a meta-compiling [33] based script for real-world C/C++ projects with multiple files and employing standard build systems (e.g., `make` and `cmake`). More details are provided on our tool's website[1].

We evaluate CCMOP for answering the following three research questions.

- **Applicability.** Can CCMOP support the RV of real-world C/C++ programs (especially C++ programs) with different scales?
- **Overhead.** How about the overhead of CCMOP when doing the RV of real-world C/C++ programs? Here, we only care about time overhead.
- **Soundness and Precision.** How about the soundness and precision of CCMOP? Here, soundness means the ability to detect all bugs, and precision means no false alarms.

Benchmark Programs. To answer the first question, we applied CCMOP to different scaled benchmarks used in the literature of RV [6,34] and fuzzing [20]. Besides, we also get high-starred C++ projects from GitHub. Table 1 shows the benchmarks. In total, we have 100 real-world C/C++ programs. Our tool's website provides more details of our benchmark programs.

---

[1] https://rv-ccmop.github.io.

Table 1. C/C++ Benchmark Programs.

Type	Benchmark Name	Description
C	mini-benchmarks in MoveC [5,6]	126 mini-programs (2.6K LOCs in total)
	Ferry[34] and FuzzBench [20]	15 programs (2.5~228.5K LOCs)
	High-starred GitHub Projects	35 programs (0.1~239.5K LOCs)
C++	FuzzBench [20]	6 programs (10.5~538.6K LOCs)
	High-starred GitHub Projects	44 programs (1.0~675.2K LOCs)

Properties. Table 2 shows the properties used in the evaluation. The two properties, *i.e.*, use-after-free and memory leak, are used for both C and C++ programs. However, the event definitions are different. For C programs, we weave monitors when calling **malloc** and **free**; For C++ programs, we weave monitors to the **new** and **delete** statements.

Table 2. C/C++ Benchmark Properties.

Type	Property Name	Description
C	Use-after-free	Pointer is dereferenced after freed (`free`)
	Memory leak	Memory is allocated (`malloc`) but not freed
	Read-after-close	A `FILE` is read after close
C++	Use-after-free	Pointer is dereferenced after freed (`delete`)
	Memory leak	Memory is allocated (`new`) but not freed
	Safe Iterator	A collection should not be updated when it is being iterated

To answer the second question, we consider the C/C++ benchmarks that have many statements matching the property's pointcuts (*i.e.*, with non-negligible overhead) and provide test cases for demonstration and running. We compare CCMOP with LLVM's AddressSanitizer [26], which is widely used for memory checking of C/C++ programs, and the property is use-after-free[2].

To answer the third question, we applied CCMOP to SARD-100 [13] and Toyota ITC [28] benchmarks, in which source code is available. These two benchmarks focus on the detection of memory-related bugs (*e.g.*, memory leak and use-after-free). We evaluate CCMOP's soundness and precision for detecting memory leak and use-after-free bugs by running the programs with the test inputs provided by the benchmarks.

All the experiments were carried out on a laptop with a 2.60 GHz CPU and 32G memory, and the operating system is Ubuntu 20.04. The experimental result values of compilation time and runtime overhead are the averaged values of three runs' results.

---

[2] We disable the other checkers in AddressSanitizer with options mentioned in website.

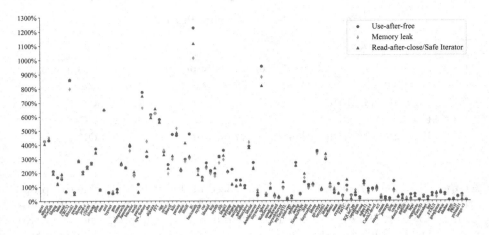

Fig. 3. Compilation time overhead.

Experimental Results. We applied CCMOP to do the RV for each benchmark program with respect to each property. Our tool can be successfully applied to 126 mini-benchmark programs from MoveC [6]. For the 100 real-world C/C++ programs, our tool can also support the weaving of RV monitors of all the properties during compilation. Figure 3 shows the result of compilation information.

The X-axis shows the program identities, where the first 50 programs are C programs, and the last 50 are C++ programs. The Y-axis shows the compilation time overhead compared with the original compilation time (denoted by C_O), *i.e.*, $(C_{RV} - C_O)/C_O$, where C_{RV} denotes the compilation time of RV. On average, the overheads of compilation time for use-after-free, memory leak, and read-after-close/safe-iterator are 2.01, 1.84, and 1.91, respectively. Due to the frequent usage of pointer operations, the overhead of use-after-free is usually the largest. For many programs (78%), the overhead is below 300%. There are nine small-scale programs whose overhead is over 500%. The reason is that the compilation of monitor code dominates the compilation procedure. For comparison, we applied LLVM's AddressSanitizer [26] to each benchmarks, and the average overhead of compilation time is 0.98.

Figure 4 shows the runtime overhead results for programs with notable changes.

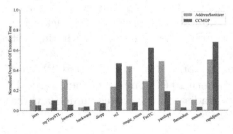

Fig. 4. Runtime overhead.

The X-axis displays the program name, and the Y-axis displays the overhead compared with the original program without RV. Each Y-axis value is calculated as follows: $log_{10}(T_{RV}/T_o)$, where T_o is the time of original program without RV, and T_{RV} is the time with RV. The figure shows that CCMOP's overhead is comparable with AddressSantinizer. The averaged overheads of AddressSantinizer and CCMOP are 81.9% and 88%, respectively. Furthermore, the results of the C benchmark programs (which have many memory operations) indicate that CCMOP's overhead is 961.6% on average. The detailed results are available on CCMOP's website.

Table 3 shows the results of soundness and precision on the two properties. For the property of memory leak, there are 5 and 18 test cases in SARD-100 [13] and Toyota ITC [28], respectively.

Table 3. Bug Detection Results of CCMOP.

Benchmark Name	Memory leak	Use-after-free
SARD-100 [13]	100%(5/5)	100%(9/9)
Toyota ITC [28]	100%(18/18)	80%(12/15)
Summary	100%(23/23)	87.5%(21/24)

CCMOP detected all bugs. For the property of use-after-free, there exist 9 and 15 test cases in SARD-100 and Toyota ITC, respectively. The majority of bugs (*i.e.*, 21 out of 24) can be detected. The reasons of missing bugs in three test cases are as follows: 1) in two test cases, there is no dereference of the freed pointer, but our property of use-after-free requires the dereference of the pointer; 2) in one case, there are nested pointer dereferences, on which CCMOP is limited and crashed. Besides, CCMOP does not produce any false alarms on these two benchmarks.

5   Related Work

There already exist many RV tools developed in different backgrounds. Therefore, we divide the existing tools according to the implementation level of instrumentation.

Source-Level. MoveC [6] is a RV tool for C programs and adopts source-code level instrumentation. MoveC supports the detection of segment, spatial and temporal memory errors, which is enabled by its monitoring data structure called smart status. Like MoveC, RTC [21] also implements the detection of memory errors and runtime type violations for C programs based on source-code instrumentation, and the implementation is based on the ROSE compiler platform [25]. E-ACSL [29] supports the checking of security properties for the C programs annotated with a formal specification language. Compared with these three tools, CCMOP supports the RV of C++ programs, and the instrumentation is carried out directly on ASTs. AspectC++ [31] is an AOP framework designed for C++ language and also instruments at the source-code level. However, AspectC++ does not support C programs well because the instrumented programs can only be compiled by a C++ compiler. Compared with AspectC++, our AOP framework has limited AOP features but supports both C and C++ programs.

IR-Level. There exist some RV tools that instrument monitors at IR-level, including Google's sanitizers [26,32], SoftBoundCETS [22,23], and Memsafe[30], *etc.* These tools enjoy the benefits of IR-level instrumentation and support multiple languages. However, all of the mentioned tools can only support detecting memory-related properties. Besides these tools for C-family languages, we also classify JavaMOP [4] and Tracematches [1] into this category. Both tools adopt AOP-based instrumentation for runtime monitors, and the weaving is carried out directly on Java class files. These two tools inspire our tool, and our implementation is based on JavaMOP.

Binary-Level. Some runtime monitoring tools adopt binary-level instrumentation of monitors. For example, MemCheck [27] is one of the most widely used tools for detecting memory errors and employs dynamic binary instrumentation (DBI) to implement memory runtime checks. Purify [15] is a commercial tool for detecting memory access-related errors for C/C++ programs and is also implemented based on DBI.

6   Conclusion and Future Work

This paper introduces CCMOP, a runtime verification tool for C/C++ programs. Inspired by JavaMOP [4], CCMOP adopts AOP-based monitor instrumentation and supports automatic monitor code generation and instrumentation. Moreover, CCMOP does instrumentation on the AST level. We have implemented CCMOP based on JavaMOP and Clang. To evaluate CCMOP, we have applied it to 100 real-world C/C++ programs, including 50 C++ programs. The experimental results indicate that CCMOP supports the RV of different scaled C/C++ programs and enables a transparent weaving of RV monitors.

The next step includes the following perspectives: 1) Improve the efficiency of RV by implementing more advanced RV optimization algorithms; 2) Support multi-threaded C/C++ programs; 3) Support more specification languages (*e.g.*, LTL and CFG).

Acknowledgments.. This research was supported by National Key R&D Program of China (No. 2022YFB4501903) and the NSFC Programs (No. 62172429 and 62002107).

References

1. Allan, C., Avgustinov, P., Christensen, A.S.: Adding trace matching with free variables to aspectJ. In: Proceedings of the 20th Annual ACM SIGPLAN Conference on Object-Oriented Programming, Systems, Languages, and Applications, OOPSLA 2005, pp. 345–364. ACM (2005)
2. Bartocci, E., et al.: Specification-based monitoring of cyber-physical systems: a survey on theory, tools and applications. In: Bartocci, E., Falcone, Y. (eds.) Lectures on Runtime Verification. LNCS, vol. 10457, pp. 135–175. Springer, Cham (2018). https://doi.org/10.1007/978-3-319-75632-5_5

3. Chen, F., Meredith, P.O., Jin, D., Rosu, G.: Efficient formalism-independent monitoring of parametric properties. In: ASE 2009, 24th IEEE/ACM International Conference on Automated Software Engineering, Auckland, pp. 383–394. IEEE Computer Society (2009)

4. Chen, F., Roşu, G.: Java-MOP: a monitoring oriented programming environment for java. In: Halbwachs, N., Zuck, L.D. (eds.) TACAS 2005. LNCS, vol. 3440, pp. 546–550. Springer, Heidelberg (2005). https://doi.org/10.1007/978-3-540-31980-1_36

5. Chen, Z., Wang, C., Yan, J.: Runtime detection of memory errors with smart status. In: ISSTA 2021: 30th ACM SIGSOFT International Symposium on Software Testing and Analysis, pp. 296–308. ACM (2021)

6. Chen, Z., Yan, J., Kan, S., Qian, J., Xue, J.: Detecting memory errors at runtime with source-level instrumentation. In: Proceedings of the 28th ACM SIGSOFT International Symposium on Software Testing and Analysis, ISSTA 2019, pp. 341–351. ACM (2019)

7. Clang: The AST Matcher Reference. www.clang.llvm.org/docs/LibASTMatchersReference.html

8. Clang: The Clang TreeTransform Class Template Reference. www.clang.llvm.org/doxygen/classclang_1_1TreeTransform.html

9. Clang-15.02: Clang - A C language family frontend for LLVM. www.clang.llvm.org/

10. Clarke, E.M., Grumberg, O., Long, D.E.: Model checking. In: Proceedings of the NATO Advanced Study Institute on Deductive Program Design, pp. 305–349 (1996)

11. Clarke, E.M., Klieber, W., Nováček, M., Zuliani, P.: Model checking and the state explosion problem. In: Meyer, B., Nordio, M. (eds.) LASER 2011. LNCS, vol. 7682, pp. 1–30. Springer, Heidelberg (2012). https://doi.org/10.1007/978-3-642-35746-6_1

12. Davis, M., Logemann, G., Loveland, D.W.: A machine program for theorem-proving. Commun. ACM 5(7), 394–397 (1962)

13. Delaitre, A.: Test Suite #100: C test suite for source code analyzer v2 - vulnerable (2015). www.samate.nist.gov/SRD/view.php?tsID=100

14. Google: sanitizers. www.github.com/google/sanitizers

15. IBM: The Purify Documentation. www.ibm.com/support/pages/tools-purify

16. Kiczales, G., Hilsdale, E., Hugunin, J., Kersten, M., Palm, J., Griswold, W.G.: An overview of AspectJ. In: Knudsen, J.L. (ed.) ECOOP 2001. LNCS, vol. 2072, pp. 327–354. Springer, Heidelberg (2001). https://doi.org/10.1007/3-540-45337-7_18

17. Leucker, M., Schallhart, C.: A brief account of runtime verification. J. Log. Algeb. Methods Program. 78(5), 293–303 (2009)

18. LLVM: The LLVM Compiler Infrastructure Project. www.llvm.org/

19. Loveland, D.W.: Automated theorem proving: a logical basis, Fundamental studies in computer science, vol. 6. North-Holland (1978)

20. Metzman, J., Szekeres, L., Simon, L.: Fuzzbench: an open fuzzer benchmarking platform and service. In: ESEC/FSE 2021: 29th ACM Joint European Software Engineering Conference and Symposium on the Foundations of Software Engineering, pp. 1393–1403. ACM (2021)

21. Milewicz, R., Vanka, R., Tuck, J.: Runtime checking C programs. In: Proceedings of the 30th Annual ACM Symposium on Applied Computing, pp. 2107–2114. ACM (2015)

22. Nagarakatte, S., Zhao, J., Martin, M.M.K.: CETS: compiler enforced temporal safety for C. In: Proceedings of the 9th International Symposium on Memory Management, ISMM 2010, pp. 31–40. ACM (2010)
23. Nagarakatte, S., Zhao, J., Martin, M.M.K., Zdancewic, S.: SoftBound: highly compatible and complete spatial memory safety for C. In: Proceedings of the 2009 ACM SIGPLAN Conference on Programming Language Design and Implementation, PLDI 2009, pp. 245–258. ACM (2009)
24. Pnueli, A.: The temporal logic of programs. In: 18th Annual Symposium on Foundations of Computer Science, Providence, pp. 46–57. IEEE Computer Society (1977)
25. ROSE: Main Page. www.rosecompiler.org/ROSE_HTML_Reference/index.html
26. Serebryany, K., Bruening, D., Potapenko, A., Vyukov, D.: AddressSanitizer: a fast address sanity checker. In: 2012 USENIX Annual Technical Conference, Boston, pp. 309–318. USENIX Association (2012)
27. Seward, J., Nethercote, N.: Using valgrind to detect undefined value errors with bit-precision. In: Proceedings of the 2005 USENIX Annual Technical Conference, pp. 17–30. USENIX (2005)
28. Shiraishi, S., Mohan, V., Marimuthu, H.: Test suites for benchmarks of static analysis tools. In: 2015 IEEE International Symposium on Software Reliability Engineering Workshops, ISSRE Workshops, pp. 12–15. IEEE Computer Society (2015)
29. Signoles, J., Kosmatov, N., Vorobyov, K.: E-ACSL, a runtime verification tool for safety and security of C programs (tool paper). In: RV-CuBES 2017. An International Workshop on Competitions, Usability, Benchmarks, Evaluation, and Standardisation for Runtime Verification Tools. Kalpa Publications in Computing, vol. 3, pp. 164–173. EasyChair (2017)
30. Simpson, M.S., Barua, R.: MemSafe: ensuring the spatial and temporal memory safety of C at runtime. Softw. Pract. Exp. **43**(1), 93–128 (2013)
31. Spinczyk, O., Lohmann, D., Urban, M.: AspectC++: an AOP extension for C++. Softw. Dev. J. **5**, 68–76 (2005)
32. Stepanov, E., Serebryany, K.: Memorysanitizer: fast detector of uninitialized memory use in C++. In: Proceedings of the 13th Annual IEEE/ACM International Symposium on Code Generation and Optimization, CGO 2015, pp. 46–55. IEEE Computer Society (2015)
33. WLLVM: The Whole Program LLVM Project. www.github.com/travitch/whole-program-llvm
34. Zhou, S., Yang, Z., Qiao, D.: Ferry: state-aware symbolic execution for exploring state-dependent program paths. In: 31st USENIX Security Symposium, USENIX Security 2022, pp. 4365–4382. USENIX Association (2022)

A Stream Runtime Verification Tool with Nested and Retroactive Parametrization

Paloma Pedregal[1,2(✉)] ⓘ, Felipe Gorostiaga[1,3(✉)] ⓘ, and César Sánchez[1] ⓘ

[1] IMDEA Software Institute, Madrid, Spain
{paloma.pedregal,felipe.gorostiaga}@imdea.org
[2] Universidad Politécnica de Madrid (UPM), Madrid, Spain
[3] CIFASIS, Rosario, Argentina

Abstract. In online monitoring, a monitor is synthesized from a formal specification, which later runs in tandem with the system under study. In offline monitoring the trace is logged as the system progresses to later do post-mortem analysis after the system has finished executing.

In this tool paper we demonstrate the use of *retroactive dynamic parametrization*, a technique that allows an online monitor to revisit the past log as it progresses. This feature enables new monitors to be incorporated into an already running system and to revisit the past for particular behaviors, based on new information discovered. Retroactive parametrization also allows a monitor to lazily ignore events and revisit and process them later, when the monitor discovers that it should have processed those events. We showcase the use of retroactive dynamic parametrization to perform network monitor denial of service attacks.

1 Introduction

Runtime verification (RV) [2,18] is a lightweight formal dynamic verification technique that analyzes a single trace of execution using a monitor derived from a specification. The initial specification languages to describe monitors in RV where borrowed from property languages for static verification, including linear temporal logic (LTL) [23], adapted to finite traces [3,8,19]. Most RV languages describe a monolithic monitor that later processes the events received. Dynamic parametrization (also known as parametric trace slicing) allows quantifying over objects and spawning new monitors that follow independently objects as they are discovered, like in Quantified Event Automata (QEA) [1].

Stream runtime verification [4,11,22] (SRV), pioneered by Lola [7] defines monitors by declaring the dependencies between output streams and input streams. The initial application domain of Lola was the testing of synchronous hardware. Temporal testers [24] were later proposed as a monitoring technique for LTL based on Boolean streams. Copilot [11,21,22] is a DSL similar to Lola, which declares dependencies between streams in a Haskell-based style, and then generates C monitors. Lola2.0 [9]

This work was funded in part by PRODIGY Project (TED2021-132464B-I00) funded by MCIN/AEI/10.13039/501100011033/ and the European Union NextGenerationEU/PRTR, and by a research grant from Nomadic Labs and the Tezos Foundation.

P. Katsaros and L. Nenzi (Eds.): RV 2023, LNCS 14245, pp. 351–362, 2023.
https://doi.org/10.1007/978-3-031-44267-4_19

extends Lola allowing dynamically parametrized streams, similarly to QEA. Stream runtime verification has also been extended recently to asynchronous and real-time systems [6,10,12,17]. HLola [5,13,15] is an implementation of Lola as an embedded DSL in Haskell, which allows borrowing datatypes from Haskell directly as Lola expressions, and using features like higher-order functions to ease the development of specifications and the runtime system. In this paper we use HLola and extend it with capabilities for retroactive dynamic parametrization.

In practice it is common to monitor properties that are defined after the system starts running, and we cannot or do not wish to stop the system. Therefore, the monitor will receive online new events after being installed. Then, one can (1) *ignore* that the monitor is started in the middle of the computation and pretend that the history starts after the monitor is installed, (2) *encode the lack of knowledge* of the monitor in the specification, or, (3) if the beginning of the trace was stored in an accessible *log*, allow the monitor to collaborate with the log to process the missing past events and then continue to process the future events online. The first option is the most natural and in many cases an acceptable solution, while the second option has been explored in [16], but these two options neglect the beginning of the trace which can sometimes affect the monitoring task. The third option requires a novel combination of *offline and online monitoring* offering the possibility of accessing the past of the trace. Moreover, enriching an SRV monitor with the ability of accessing the past allows the description of properties that revisit the past exploiting information discovered at a later time.

In this tool paper we demonstrate an extension of the tool HLola[1] which enables a novel dynamic instantiation of monitors called *retroactive dynamic parametrization*. The new tool offers dynamic parametrization and extends it with the ability to revisit the past of a live stream of events, effectively combining online and offline runtime verification. A longer version of this paper is available at [20].

2   Overview

Preliminaries. Stream Runtime Verification (SRV) generalizes monitoring algorithms to arbitrary data, by preserving the temporal dependencies and generalizing the datatypes using multi-sorted data theories. HLola is an extensible implementation of Lola [7] developed as an embedded DSL in Haskell, from which HLola borrows datatypes as data theories. HLola also allows the easy implementation of new powerful features as libraries with no changes to the core engine. The tool described in this paper incorporates retroactive parametrization to HLola.

A Lola specification $\langle I, O, E \rangle$ consists of (1) a set of typed input stream variables I, which correspond to the inputs observed by the monitor; (2) a set of typed output stream variables O which represent the outputs of the monitor as well as intermediate observations; and (3) defining equations, which associate every output $y \in O$ with a stream expression E_y that describes declaratively the intended values of y (in terms of the values of inputs and output streams).

The set of *stream expressions* of a given type is built from constants and function symbols as constructors (as usual), and also from *offset expressions* of the form $s\texttt{[now]}$,

---

[1] Available at https://github.com/imdea-software/hlola/.

or $s[k|d]$ where s is a stream variable, k is an integer number and d is a value of the type of s (used as default). For example, `altitude[now]` represents the value of stream `altitude` in the current instant, and `altitude[-1|0.0]` represents the value of stream `altitude` in the previous instant, with `0.0` as the value used at the first instant. HLola can be efficiently monitored, meaning that (most programs) can be monitored in constant space and in constant time per event (trace-length independent monitoring [5]).

As a byproduct of its design, HLola allows *static parametrization* in stream definitions, this is, streams that abstract away some concrete values, which are later instantiated by the compiler. Even though static parametrization is very useful to define libraries and clean specifications, parameters are expanded at static time before the monitor starts running, and parametric streams cannot be spawned with a value that is discovered at runtime. The keystone of the design of HLola is to use datatypes and functions from Haskell as the data theories of Lola. In turn, HLola also allows using Lola specifications as datatypes, via the function *runSpec* that executes a specification over the input trace and produces a value of the result type. This allows Lola specifications to be used as data theories within Lola, a feature called *nested monitoring* [14]. Nested monitors allow writing functions on streams as SRV specifications, creating and executing these specifications dynamically. In [14] nested monitors are created and destroyed within an instant and their final states are lost. Also, nested monitors cannot access the past of the trace before the beginning of the sub-trace they receive. In this tool paper we introduce novel features by relaxing these restrictions, gaining the ability to *combine offline and online runtime verification*. We allow nested monitors to be created dynamically and continue executing alongside their parent monitor. The states of the dynamically created nested monitors are carried on to the next instant, and they can inspect the full past of the system.

We introduce the following kinds of nested monitors:

1. Retroactive Nested Monitors, which can access events and trigger a finer analysis of the past of the trace when necessary. For example, consider monitoring network traffic, where the monitor receives (1) the source and destination of each IP packet, and (2) the packets per second in the last hundred instants.

We want to detect whether an address has received too many packets in the last hundred instants, which can be specified as follows: *if the packet flow is low, then there is no attack, but when the flow rate is above a predefined threshold (*`threshold_pps`*) we have to inspect the last hundred packets and check if a given address is under attack.* We can define a specification which only observes the packets per second in the last hundred instants, ignoring the source and destination of the IP packets. If the packets per second exceed `threshold_pps`, this triggers the creation of a *retroactive nested monitor*, which will retrieve the past of the trace using the new keyword `withTrace` and do the more expensive analysis of detecting if an address is in fact under attack. Note how this specification detects an attack at most one hundred instants after it happens. Also note that the nested monitors in this example are created, executed and destroyed at every instant.

2. (Forward) Dynamic Parametrization, which let us instantiate a parametric stream using dynamically discovered values, via the new keyword **over**. The over operator takes a parametric stream `strm` of type `S` with a parameter of type `P`, and a stream `params` of sets of values of type **P**, and creates an expression of type **Map P S**, whose keys at any given instant are the values in `params[now]`, and where the value associated to each key is the instantiation of s over the key. Using the over operator we can dynamically instantiate a parametric stream over a set of parameters that are discovered while processing the trace of input.

Consider a scenario where we are monitoring network traffic, and following every TCP 3-way handshake in which (1) the source sends a packet SYN, then (2) the destination sends SYN/ACK and then (3) the source sends ACK. We define a parametric stream which receives a pair of addresses and generates a value, which can be Valid or Error, depending on whether the handshake is correct or not. We cannot know statically for which pair of addresses we have to instantiate the parametrized stream, and therefore, the monitor has as parameter a pairs of addresses to follow. At every instant, the monitor can add a new pair of source and destination addresses. In this manner we can use a parametric stream over dynamic values using the over operator. Every time a new value is incorporated to the set of active parameters, we spawn a new monitor parametrized with the new value. Then, we preserve the state of this monitor between instants in an auxiliary stream, executing the nested monitor alongside the outer monitor until the auxiliary monitor is no longer needed, that is, until its associated parameter is removed from the set.

3. Retroactive Dynamic Parametrization, which allows revisiting the past of a trace every time the monitor discovers a new parameter to instantiate the parametric stream. The new parametrized stream continues to monitor in an online manner. The static parametrization already present in HLola is too limited to implement this feature because the monitor cannot know the state of a parametric stream over an arbitrary parameter in the middle of the trace unless the parameter was determined statically. Using static parametrization to implement dynamic parametrization is only feasible for small parameter sets, like Booleans or a small enumerated type, but it becomes unfeasible when the space of potential parameters is large.

To implement retroactive dynamic parametrization we add a new clause `withInit` to the over operator to describe an *initializer*, which indicates how the nested monitor can take its state up to the current instant. An initializer will typically call an external program with the corresponding arguments that indicate how to efficiently retrieve the elements in the past of the trace that are relevant to the parameter.

Consider the case of monitoring a file system assessing whether every time a file is read or written, it had been created previously. One way is to use *forward dynamic parametrization* following all the files as they are opened. With *retroactive* monitoring, we can start following a file id just when it is read or written, and only then (calling an external program) retrieve the past of the trace for that parameter. The external program can use an index to efficiently retrieve only the events relevant to a file id or even only the open events.

3   HLola with Dynamic Parametrization

We have implemented retroactive nested parametrization, forward dynamic parametrization and retroactive dynamic parametrization in HLola.

Dynamically mapping a parametric stream strm with a stream of set of parameters params of type **Set P** creates an auxiliary stream x_over_params of type **Map P MonitorState** that associates, at every instant, each parameter p in params with the state of the nested monitor corresponding to s<p>. The value of x 'over' params is simply the projection of the parametrized streams in the monitors of x_over_params[now]. There are three possibilities for the behavior of the auxiliary stream for given p:

(1) $p \in$ params[-1|∅] \ params[now]: the parameter was in the set in the previous instant, but it is no longer in the set in the current instant. In this case, p and its associated value are deleted from the map x_over_params[-1|∅].
(2) $p \in$ params[-1|∅] ∩ params[now]: the parameter was in the set and it is still in the set now. In this case, we feed the current event to the monitor associated with p and let it progress one step. Then, the value of the parametrized stream in the nested monitor is associated with p in the returned map.
(3) $p \in$ params[now] \ params[-1|∅]: the parameter was not in the set, but it is now. The monitor for p is installed, executing the initializer (possibly revisiting the past) to get the monitor up to date and ready to continue online. After installing the monitor, the new event is injected, and the value of s<p> is associated to p the returned map. Note that the past is only revisited when a new parameter is discovered. Once the stream is instantiated with the parameter, its corresponding nested monitor will continue executing over the future of the trace online.

Since we want HLola to support initialization from different sources (e.g. a DBMS, a blockchain node, or plain log files) the initializer of the internal monitors typically invokes an external program. This external program, called *adapter*, is in charge of recovering the trace and formatting it adequately for the monitor.

4   A Network Traffic Case Study and Empirical Evaluation

We report in this section an empirical evaluation of retroactive dynamic parametrization, implemented in our tool, that extends HLola [13]. We use our tool to implement monitors that describe several algorithms for the detection of distributed denial of service attacks (DDOS). All the experiments were executed on a Linux machine with 256 GB of RAM and 72 virtual cores (Xeon Gold 6154 @3 GHz) running Ubuntu 20.04. For conciseness we use RP to refer to retroactive parametrization, and non-RP to implementations that do not use retroactive parametrization (but use dynamic parametrization). We evaluate empirically the following hypotheses:

(**H1**) RP is functionally equivalent to non-RP.
(**H2**) RP and non-RP run at similar speeds, particularly when most dynamic instantiations turn out to be irrelevant.
(**H3**) RP consumes significantly less memory than non-RP, particularly when most instantiations are irrelevant.
(**H4**) Aggregated RP—where the monitor receives summaries of the trace that indicate if further processing is necessary—is functionally equivalent to RP.
(**H5**) Aggregated RP is much more efficient than RP and non-RP without aggregation.

The datasets for the experiments are (anonymized) samples of real network traffic collected by a Juniper MX408 router that routes the traffic of an academic network used by several tens of thousand of users (students and researchers) simultaneously, routing approximately 15 Gbps of traffic on average. The sampling ratio provided by the routers was 1 to 100 flows[2]. Each flow contains the metadata of the traffic sampled, with information such as source and destination ports and addresses, protocols and timestamps, but does not carry information about the contents of the packets. These flows are stored in aggregated batches of 5 minutes encoded in the **netflow** format.

Our monitors implement fourteen known DDOS network attacks detection algorithms. An attack is detected if the volume of connections to a destination address surpasses a fixed attack-specific threshold, and those connections come from a sufficiently large number of different attackers, identified by source IP address. The number of different source addresses communicating with a destination is known as the *entropy* of the destination. Each attack is concerned with a different port and protocol and considers a different entropy as potentially dangerous.

In order to process the network data needed by the monitors, we developed a Python adapter that uses `nfdump`, a toolset to collect and process netflow data. The tool `nfdump` can be used to obtain all the flows in a batch, optionally applying some simple filters, or to obtain summarized information about all the flows in the batch. For example, `nfdump` can provide all the flows received, filtered by a protocol or address, as well as the volume of traffic to the IP address that has received the most connections of a specific kind.

Our empirical evaluation consists of four datasets in which we knew whether each attack was present:

(D1) A batch of network flows with an attack based on malformed UDP packets (UDP packets with destination port 0). This batch contains 419938 flows, with less than 1% malformed UDP packets. The threshold for this attack is 2000 packets per second, which is surpassed in this batch for one single address, for which the entropy of 5 is exceeded.

(D2) A batch of network flows with no attack, containing 361867 flows, of which only 66 are malformed UDP packets (roughly, 0.001%).

(D3) A batch of network flows with no attack, but with many origin IP addresses and 100 destination addresses.

(D4) Intervals with several batches, where only one batch has an attack based on malformed UDP packets.

The monitors in our experiments follow the same attack description: *In a batch of 5 min of flow records, an address is under attack if it receives more than t_0 packets per second or bits per second from more than t_1 different source addresses (where t_0 and t_1 depend on the attack).*

We have implemented our monitors in three different ways[3]:

---

[2] Most detection systems use a much slower sampling of 1 to 1000 or even less.

[3] The specifications for **(S1)**, **(S2)** and **(S3)** as well as the instructions and dataset to execute them are available in a dedicated branch of the repository, at https://github.com/imdea-software/hlola/tree/RV2023.

(S1) Brute force: Using *(forward) dynamic parametrization*, the monitor calculates the number of packets and bits per second (which we call "volume") for all potential target IP addresses. It also computes the entropy for each potential target address and for each attack. For every flow, the monitor internally updates the information about the source address, destination and volume.

```
1  input String fileId
2  input Flow flow

3  define Int flowCounter = flowCounter[-1|0] + 1
4  define Bool firstFlow = fileId[now] /= fileId [-1|""]
5  define Bool lastFlow = fileId[now] /= fileId[1|""]

6  output [String] attacked_IPs = map detect attacks
7    where detect atk = (attack_detection atk)[now]

8  define String attack_detection <AttackData atk> =
9    if (markerRate atk)[now] > threshold atk then
10     if (ipEntropy atk)[now] > maxEntropy atk then
11       (maxDestAddress atk)[now]
12     else "Over threshold but not entropy"
13   else "No attack"

14 define Int markerRate <AttackData atk> = ...
21 define String maxDestAddress <AttackData atk> = ...

29 define AddrInfo addrInfo <AttackData atk> =
30   insertWith updt destAddr[now] (extractInfo atk flow[now]) prev
31   where
32     prev = if firstFlow[now] then empty else (addrInfo atk) [-1|empty]
33     updt (p,b,ts,te) (p',b',ts',te') = (p+p',b+b',min ts ts',max te te')

34 define Histogram attackHist <AttackData atk> = let
35   hist = if firstFlow[now] then empty else (attackHist atk) [-1|empty]
36   in insertWith (+) destAddr[now] 1 hist
```

The specification uses the `flowCounter` to perform retroactive dynamic parametrization. The stream `attacked_IPs` maps the parametric stream `attack_detection` over the list of attacks. The stream `attack_detection` checks that the marker (bits per seconds or packets per second) of the attack and the IP entropy of any address do not exceed the thresholds. If the thresholds are exceeded, the IP address most accessed (which is calculated in `maxDestAddress`) is considered to be under attack. The stream `markerRate` calculates the bits per seconds or packets per second of an attack, while the stream `maxDestAddress` calculates the most accessed address. The stream `addrInfo` keeps a map of the packets, bits, start time and endtime per destination address. Similarly, the stream `attackHist` keeps a map of the number of accesses per destination address. In this scenario, we calculate the `ipEntropy` (not shown in the monitor above) of every address at all times, and we simply return the size of the set of different origin IP addresses of the most accessed IP.

(S2) Retroactive: In this implementation, the monitor also analyzes all flows, calculating the volume of packets for each address, but in this case the monitor lazily avoids calculating the entropy, using *retroactive dynamic parametrization*. The monitor only calculates the entropy when the volume of traffic for an address surpasses the threshold. The monitor uses the over operator to revisit the past flows of the batch filtered by that attack, using the Python adapter which produces the subset of the flows required to compute the entropy. The monitoring then continues calculating the entropy until the end of the batch. The specification for this implementation is the same as in (S1), but with a different implementation of the IP entropy calculation:

```
37  define Int ipEntropy <AttackData atk> =
38    (maybe 0 size . listToMaybe . elems) mset
39    where
40      mset = setSrcForDestAddr atk 'over' maybeAddress atk
41            'withInit' initer atk fileId[now] flowCounter[now]
42  define (Set String) setSrcForDestAddr <AttackData atk> <String dst> = let
43    prevSet = if firstFlow[now] then empty
44              else (setSrcForDestAddr atk) [-1|empty]
45    in insert srcAddr[now] prevSet
46  define (Set String) maybeAddress <AttackData atk> =
47    if (attack_detection atk)[now] then singleton (maxDestAddress atk)[now]
48    else empty
```

In this case, we define a parametric stream setSrcForDestAddr that calculates the set of different origin IPs of a destination address. We define an auxiliary stream maybeAddress that contains the most accessed address, if it exceeds the threshold. The definition of ipEntropy will instantiate dynamically the stream setSrcForDestAddr with the most accessed address once it exceeds the threshold, with an initializer specific to the suspected attack and address. We compose different functions to retrieve the values of the map (which is at most one), and get the size of the corresponding set, if it exists, using 0 as the default value.

(S3) Aggregated: This specification uses *retroactive nested monitors with retroactive dynamic parametrization* to analyze summaries of batches of flows, executing a nested specification over the current batch and the suspected attack, when one of the markers is above a predefined threshold: the monitor receives a summary of a five minute batch of network data, as a single event containing fourteen attack markers. The monitor is based on the ability of the backend to pre-process batches using nfdump to obtain—for each attack and for the whole batch—the maximum volume of traffic for any IP address. If an attack marker is over the threshold, the monitor spawns a nested monitor which retrieves a subset of the flows for that batch and attack, and analyzes those flows in a more detailed way. This second nested monitor behaves like the retroactive parametrization in (S2). The aggregation of data provides a first, coarse overview serving as a necessary condition to spawn the expensive nested monitor. This is particularly useful because attacks are infrequent and the ratio of false positives of the summary detection is relatively low.

There are two great advantages to this implementation, in comparison to the implementation in (S2): the finer analysis of the flows will only be performed when the aggregated data indicates a possible attack, instead of all the time and for all flows; and when the nested monitor *is* triggered, it will be triggered with two parameters, a specific batch and attack, that will be used to filter the flows before processing them. Being able to filter the flows by the characteristics of a specific attack greatly reduces the amount of flows of the batch to a small percentage (for example, in the dataset (**D1**), which is a batch with an attack, less than 1% of the flows of the batch were part of the attack).

The nested specification `flowAnalyzer` is triggered by a marker which indicates a possible attack. This specification analyzes individual flows, and it is exactly the specification described in (**S2**), but it will be used to analyze all flows in a batch only if the aggregated marker is positive.

```
1 use innerspec flowAnalyzer
2 input String fileId
3 input Int marker <AttackData atk>

4 output [String] attacked_IPs = map detect attacks
5   where detect atk = (attack_detection atk)[now]

6 define String attack_detection <AttackData atk> =
7   if (marker atk)[now] > threshold atk then
8     runSpec (flowAnalyzer atk (flowRetriever atk fileId[now]))
9   else "No attack"
```

The constant `attacks` is a list of the attack data of the fourteen different attacks that the monitor can detect. The nested specification `flowAnalyzer` analyzes individual flows, and it can use **retroactive dynamic parametrization**, or (the less efficient) **non-retroactive dynamic parametrization**.

Results: In the first experiment we run the three implementations against dataset (**D4**). In this interval of multiple batches, only one of which contains an attack, all three implementations identify the batch with the attack and correctly detect the kind of attack and target address. This confirms empirically hypotheses (**H1**) and (**H4**).

In the second experiment we run specifications (**S1**) and (**S2**) against datasets (**D1**), (**D2**) and (**D3**). The results are reported in the following table:

	(D1) (Attack)	(D2) (No Attack)	(D3) (No Attack)
(S1) (Brute force)	18 m12.146 s	15 m51.599 s	16 m34.795 s
(S2) (Retroactive)	20 m43.921 s	17 m19.844 s	19 m30.518 s
(S3) (Aggregated)	0 m16.208 s	0 m2.109 s	0 m2.115 s

We can see that the running times for the brute force and retroactive implementations are similar, while the aggregated implementation is extremely fast in comparison, which empirically confirms (**H2**) and (**H5**). This is because (**S3**) exploits the summarized information, and does not find any marker over the threshold for the datasets (**D2**) and (**D3**) so the flows within the batch are never individually processed. For dataset (**D1**), a nested monitor will be executed because one of the markers (for the attack with malformed UDP packets) is over the threshold, but it will only try to detect the attack corresponding to that marker, and it will only receive a small subset of the flows (less than 1% of the flows of the batch are relevant for the attack). If all the markers for all the attacks were over their threshold and all the flows were implicated in the attacks, the time required would be closer to the retroactive implementation. The ad-hoc aggregation of data by the external tool is very efficient, as is the verification of this data by the monitor, so this implementation is especially advantageous when the positives (or false positives) are expected to be infrequent, and when most of the data can be filtered out before executing the nested monitor.

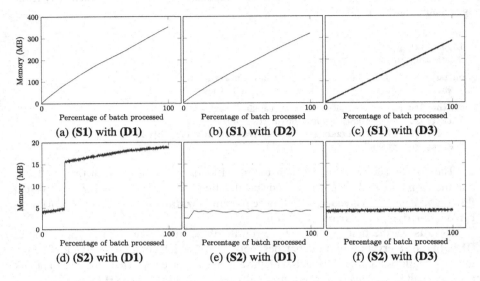

Fig. 1. Memory usage of the brute force (a), (b), (c) and retroactive (d), (e), (f).

In a third experiment we run a version of specifications **(S1)** and **(S2)**—instrumented with capabilities to measure memory consumption—on **(D1)**, **(D2)** and **(D3)**. The results, reported in Fig. 1, empirically confirm **(H3)**. For the three datasets, the memory used by the brute force approach increases linearly over time, as it has to keep track of the volume and IP entropy for every attack and every potential target address. On the other hand, the memory usage of the retroactive implementation remains close to constant, with a sudden increase when an attack is detected and the past flows have to be retrieved and processed.

5 Conclusions

In this paper we have introduced the concept of retroactive dynamic parametrization. In dynamic parametrization, proposed in QEA and Lola2.0, a new monitor (which is an instance of a generic monitor) is instantiated the first time a parameter is discovered. In retroactive dynamic parametrization the decision to instantiate a dynamic parametric monitor can be taken later in the future, for example when a given parameter is discovered to be interesting.

Effectively implementing retroactive parametrization requires the ability to revisit the history of the computation, a task that can be efficiently implemented with a logging system. Therefore, retroactive parametrization allows a fruitful combination of offline and online monitoring. Retroactive parametrization also allows monitors to be created in the middle of an execution without requiring to process the whole trace from the beginning.

We have implemented this technique in HLola and empirically evaluated its efficiency, illustrating that it can efficiently detect distributed denial of service attacks in realistic network traffic.

References

1. Barringer, H., Falcone, Y., Havelund, K., Reger, G., Rydeheard, D.: Quantified event automata: towards expressive and efficient runtime monitors. In: Giannakopoulou, D., Méry, D. (eds.) FM 2012. LNCS, vol. 7436, pp. 68–84. Springer, Heidelberg (2012). https://doi.org/10.1007/978-3-642-32759-9_9
2. Bartocci, E., Falcone, Y. (eds.): Lectures on Runtime Verification. LNCS, vol. 10457. Springer, Cham (2018). https://doi.org/10.1007/978-3-319-75632-5
3. Bauer, A., Leucker, M., Schallhart, C.: Monitoring of real-time properties. In: Arun-Kumar, S., Garg, N. (eds.) FSTTCS 2006. LNCS, vol. 4337, pp. 260–272. Springer, Heidelberg (2006). https://doi.org/10.1007/11944836_25
4. Bozzelli, L., Sánchez, C.: Foundations of Boolean stream runtime verification. Theor. Comput. Sci. **631**, 118–138 (2016)
5. Ceresa, M., Gorostiaga, F., Sánchez, C.: Declarative stream runtime verification (hLola). In: Oliveira, B.C.S. (ed.) APLAS 2020. LNCS, vol. 12470, pp. 25–43. Springer, Cham (2020). https://doi.org/10.1007/978-3-030-64437-6_2
6. Convent, L., Hungerecker, S., Leucker, M., Scheffel, T., Schmitz, M., Thoma, D.: TeSSLa: temporal stream-based specification language. In: Massoni, T., Mousavi, M.R. (eds.) SBMF 2018. LNCS, vol. 11254, pp. 144–162. Springer, Cham (2018). https://doi.org/10.1007/978-3-030-03044-5_10
7. D'Angelo, B., et al.: LOLA: runtime monitoring of synchronous systems. In: Proceedings of the 12th International Symposium of Temporal Representation and Reasoning (TIME 2005), pp. 166–174. IEEE CS Press (2005). https://doi.org/10.1109/TIME.2005.26
8. Eisner, C., Fisman, D., Havlicek, J., Lustig, Y., McIsaac, A., Van Campenhout, D.: Reasoning with temporal logic on truncated paths. In: Hunt, W.A., Somenzi, F. (eds.) CAV 2003. LNCS, vol. 2725, pp. 27–39. Springer, Heidelberg (2003). https://doi.org/10.1007/978-3-540-45069-6_3
9. Faymonville, P., Finkbeiner, B., Schirmer, S., Torfah, H.: A stream-based specification language for network monitoring. In: Falcone, Y., Sánchez, C. (eds.) RV 2016. LNCS, vol. 10012, pp. 152–168. Springer, Cham (2016). https://doi.org/10.1007/978-3-319-46982-9_10
10. Faymonville, P., Finkbeiner, B., Schwenger, M., Torfah, H.: Real-time stream-based monitoring. CoRR abs/1711.03829 (2017)
11. Goodloe, A.E., Pike, L.: Monitoring distributed real-time systems: a survey and future directions. Technical report, NASA Langley Research Center (2010)
12. Gorostiaga, F., Sánchez, C.: Striver: stream runtime verification for real-time event-streams. In: Colombo, C., Leucker, M. (eds.) RV 2018. LNCS, vol. 11237, pp. 282–298. Springer, Cham (2018). https://doi.org/10.1007/978-3-030-03769-7_16
13. Gorostiaga, F., Sánchez, C.: HLola: a very functional tool for extensible stream runtime verification. In: TACAS 2021. LNCS, vol. 12652, pp. 349–356. Springer, Cham (2021). https://doi.org/10.1007/978-3-030-72013-1_18

14. Gorostiaga, F., Sánchez, C.: Nested monitors: monitors as expressions to build monitors. In: Feng, L., Fisman, D. (eds.) RV 2021. LNCS, vol. 12974, pp. 164–183. Springer, Cham (2021). https://doi.org/10.1007/978-3-030-88494-9_9

15. Gorostiaga, F., Sánchez, C.: Stream runtime verification of real-time event streams with the Striver language. Int. J. Softw. Tools Technol. Transfer **23**, 157–183 (2021)

16. Gorostiaga, F., Sánchez, C.: Monitorability of expressive verdicts. In: Deshmukh, J.V., Havelund, K., Perez, I. (eds.) NASA Formal Methods, pp. 693–712. Springer, Cham (2022). https://doi.org/10.1007/978-3-031-06773-0_37

17. Leucker, M., Sánchez, C., Scheffel, T., Schmitz, M., Schramm, A.: Tessla: runtime verification of non-synchronized real-time streams. In: Proceedings of the 33rd ACM/SIGAPP Symposium on Applied Computing (SAC 2017), pp. 1925–1933. ACM Press (2018). https://doi.org/10.1145/3167132.3167338. https://dl.acm.org/doi/10.1145/3167132.3167338. Track on Software Verification and Testing Track (SVT)

18. Leucker, M., Schallhart, C.: A brief account of runtime verification. J. Logic Algebr. Progr. **78**(5), 293–303 (2009)

19. Manna, Z., Pnueli, A.: The Temporal Logic of Reactive and Concurrent Systems. Springer, New York (1992). https://doi.org/10.1007/978-1-4612-0931-7

20. Pedregal, P., Gorostiaga, F., Sánchez, C.: Retroactive parametrized monitoring (2023). https://doi.org/10.48550/arXiv.2307.06763

21. Perez, I., Dedden, F., Goodloe, A.: Copilot 3. Technical Report. NASA/TM-2020-220587, NASA Langley Research Center (2020)

22. Pike, L., Goodloe, A., Morisset, R., Niller, S.: Copilot: a hard real-time runtime monitor. In: Barringer, H., et al. (eds.) RV 2010. LNCS, vol. 6418, pp. 345–359. Springer, Heidelberg (2010). https://doi.org/10.1007/978-3-642-16612-9_26

23. Pnueli, A.: The temporal logic of programs. In: Proceedings of the 18th IEEE Symposium on Foundations of Computer Science (FOCS 1977), pp. 46–67. IEEE CS Press (1977)

24. Pnueli, A., Zaks, A.: PSL model checking and run-time verification via testers. In: Misra, J., Nipkow, T., Sekerinski, E. (eds.) FM 2006. LNCS, vol. 4085, pp. 573–586. Springer, Heidelberg (2006). https://doi.org/10.1007/11813040_38

EMOP: A Maven Plugin
for Evolution-Aware Runtime Verification

Ayaka Yorihiro, Pengyue Jiang$^{(\boxtimes)}$, Valeria Marqués, Benjamin Carleton,
and Owolabi Legunsen

Cornell University, Ithaca, USA
{ay436,pj257,vmm49,bc534,legunsen}@cornell.edu

Abstract. We present EMOP, a tool for incremental runtime verification (RV) of test executions during software evolution. We previously used
RV to find hundreds of bugs in open-source projects by monitoring passing tests against formal specifications of Java APIs. We also proposed
evolution-aware techniques to reduce RV's runtime overhead and human
time to inspect specification violations. EMOP brings these benefits to
developers in a tool that seamlessly integrates with the Maven build system. We describe EMOP's design, implementation, and usage. We evaluate EMOP on 676 versions of 21 projects, including those from our earlier prototypes' evaluation. EMOP is up to 8.4× faster and shows up to
31.3× fewer violations, compared to running RV from scratch after each
code change. EMOP also does not miss new violations in our evaluation,
and it is open-sourced at https://github.com/SoftEngResearch/emop.

1 Introduction

The prevalence of costly and harmful bugs in deployed software underscores the
need for techniques to help find more bugs during testing. Runtime verification
(RV) [3,13,14,26,30,38,44] is such a technique; it monitors executions against
formal specifications and produces violations if a specification is not satisfied.

We previously used RV to amplify the bug-finding ability of tests [32,34,40].
We found hundreds of bugs by monitoring passing tests in hundreds of open-
source projects against Java API behavioral specifications [31]. Such specifications should not change as client programs evolve. For example, monitoring
the `Collections_SynchronizedCollection` specification [7] revealed several bugs,
e.g., [8,9]: possible "non-deterministic behavior" caused by not synchronizing
on iterators over `Collection.synchronizedCollection()`'s output [27]. Developers confirmed and fixed these and many other bugs that RV helped us find.

We also found that RV incurs runtime overhead and requires a lot of human
time to inspect violations. To reduce RV costs, we proposed three evolution-aware
techniques that focus RV and its users on code affected by changes [35,37]:

(1) **Regression Property Selection (RPS)** re-checks, in a new code version,
    a subset of specifications that may be violated in code affected by changes.
(2) **Violation Message Suppression (VMS)** displays new violations—users
    are more likely to deal with violations that are related to their changes [41].

© The Author(s), under exclusive license to Springer Nature Switzerland AG 2023
P. Katsaros and L. Nenzi (Eds.): RV 2023, LNCS 14245, pp. 363–375, 2023.
https://doi.org/10.1007/978-3-031-44267-4_20

(3) **Regression Property Prioritization (RPP)** monitors important specifications on developers' critical path; others are monitored in the background.

These evolution-aware techniques reduce RV costs, but our proof-of-concept prototypes are hard to integrate with open-source projects. Also, these techniques can be used together but our prototypes do not allow users to easily do so.

We present EMOP, a Maven plugin for incremental RV of tests during software evolution. Maven is a popular build system, so EMOP can bring the benefits of RV to a wider audience of developers. EMOP improves RPS and RPP, re-implements VMS, and allows users to easily combine RPS, VMS, or RPP.

Components in EMOP's architecture (1) extend Maven's surefire plugin [48] to perform analysis before and after monitoring tests; (2) use STARTS [36] to reason about code changes and find classes affected by changes; (3) re-configure a JavaMOP [29] Java agent *on the fly* to select which specifications to monitor and where to instrument them; and (4) get fine-grained change information from Git for computing new violations. Once installed, users only need to change few Maven configuration lines to start using RPS, VMS, RPP, or their combination.

We evaluate EMOP on 676 versions of 21 projects. On the subset of projects and their versions that we previously used to evaluate our prototypes, EMOP produces similar results. Overall, on average, EMOP is up to 8.4× faster (average: 4.0×) and shows up to 31.3× fewer violations (average: 11.8×), compared to using JavaMOP to perform RV from scratch after each code change.

We defined an evolution-aware RV technique as *safe* if it finds all new violations after a change, and *precise* if it finds only new violations [37]. Also, we proposed two sets of RPS variants: two variants that are *theoretically safe* and ten variants that are not, under the assumptions that we make.

Our prior evaluation [37] showed that all RPS variants (including theoretically unsafe ones) were *empirically safe*. But, on projects that we did not previously evaluate, we initially find that our theoretically unsafe RPS variants are not empirically safe if 3rd-party libraries change. So, to improve RPS safety, we rerun RV from scratch when libraries change. We find that RPS with EMOP is empirically safe in all projects and versions that we evaluate in this paper.

Table 1. EMOP vs. our early prototypes [37].

Feature	Prototype	EMOP
Maven integration	✗	✓
Single-module projects	✓	✓
Multi-module projects	✗	✓/✗
RPS	✓	✓
VMS	✓	✓
RPP	✓	✓
RPS + VMS	✗	✓
RPP + VMS	✗	✓
RPS + RPP	6 variants	12 variants
RPS + RPP + VMS	✗	✓
Safe w.r.t. CUT	✓	✓
Safe w.r.t. 3rd-party lib	✗	✓
Version comparison	jDiff	jGit
Ease of configuration	low	high

Comparison with our Previous Prototypes. Table 1 compares EMOP with our original prototypes [37]. ✓ means "supported"; ✗ means "not supported", and ✓/✗ means "partially supported". Unlike EMOP, our prototypes (1) do not integrate with Maven or work on multi-module projects; (2) partially support combining RPS and RPP, but do not combine RPS or RPP with VMS;

(3) are less safe when 3rd-party libraries change; (4) use an external tool to re-obtain change information that is already in Git; and (5) are hard to configure. EMOP will aid future evolution-aware RV research; it is on GitHub [12], as are our artifacts [11].

2   EMOP

We summarize evolution-aware RV, and our EMOP implementation. Our original paper [37] has theoretical background, examples, definitions, diagrams, etc.

2.1   Evolution-Aware RV Techniques

Regression Property Selection (RPS). The inputs to RPS are the old and new program versions, and the set of Java API specifications. The outputs are *affected* specifications that may be violated in code affected by changes. RPS uses class-level static change-impact analysis [36] to find *impacted* classes that transitively depend on changed code. Then, RPS analyzes impacted classes together with all available specifications, and outputs specifications involving API methods that are called in impacted classes.

There are 12 RPS variants that differ in how impacted classes are computed (three options), and where affected specifications are instrumented (four options) [37]. Let Δ be the set of changed classes. Impacted classes are computed in three ways—(a) ps_3: Δ and its *dependents*—classes that use or extend those in Δ; (b) ps_2: classes in (a) plus *dependees*—classes that those in Δ use or extend; and (c) ps_1: classes in (b) plus *dependees of Δ's dependents*. Impacted classes are always instrumented, but there are two Boolean options (and four ways to combine them) for whether to instrument unimpacted classes or 3rd-party libraries. Theoretically, these variants differ in how much safety they trade off for efficiency. But, all variants were empirically safe in our original evaluation [37].

Violation Message Suppression (VMS). To reduce human time for inspecting specification violations, VMS aims to show only new violations after code changes. VMS does not reduce RV runtime overhead. The rationale behind VMS is that developers are more likely to look at and debug new violations, compared to looking at all old and new violations at the same time [41]. VMS takes the set of all violations in the new version, filters out those for which there is evidence that they are old violations, and presents the rest to the user as new violations.

Regression Property Prioritization (RPP). The goal is to reduce the time to see important violations, so users may react faster. RPP splits RV into two phases. Important specifications, defined by the user, are monitored in the *critical phase* and any violations of those specifications are reported immediately. The other specifications are monitored in a *background phase* that users do not have to wait for. Users can decide when and how violations from the background phase are presented or when specifications should be automatically promoted (demoted) from (to) the background phase.

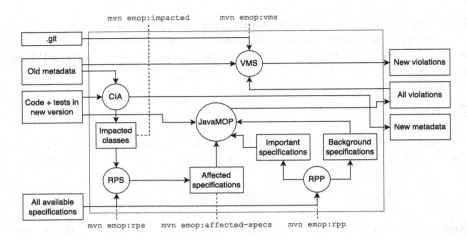

Fig. 1. EMOP's architecture.

2.2 Implementation

We implement 12 RPS variants, VMS, and RPP in our EMOP Maven plugin. We choose Maven (1) so users can more easily integrate evolution-aware RV, (2) to ease evolution-aware RV usage during testing, and (3) because we built Maven plugins before [21,36]. Future work can add EMOP to other build systems.

Figure 1 shows EMOP's architecture, and how components map to some available user commands (see Sect. 3). There, ovals show processes and rectangles show data. "Old Metadata" and "New Metadata" contain a per-class mapping from non-debug related bytecode to checksums computed from the old and new code versions, respectively, the classpath, and checksums for the jars on the classpath. EMOP uses STARTS [36] to compute these mappings and classpath information is used to detect changes in 3rd-party libraries. Also ".git" is Git's internal database of changes, which EMOP uses to find which violations are likely new. "CIA" represents our modified change impact analysis in STARTS; EMOP uses "CIA" to compute impacted classes in three ways (Sect. 2.1). Lastly, EMOP invokes "JavaMOP" to monitor test executions.

RPS. We invoke the AspectJ compiler, ajc [1], to statically analyze which specifications are related to impacted classes. JavaMOP specifications are written in an AspectJ dialect, so our static analysis outputs, as affected, specifications that ajc compiles into any impacted class. To reduce analysis cost, EMOP invokes ajc on stripped-down specifications that contain only method-related information. Finally, based on ajc's output, EMOP modifies a JavaMOP agent on the fly to only monitor affected specifications and instrument them in locations required by the RPS variant.

VMS. We re-implement VMS on top of JGit [28] (instead of jDiff). JGit provides an API for extracting fine-grained information from ".git". By default, EMOP takes the most recent Git commit as the old version and the current working tree as the new version. So, VMS users can check if code changes introduce new violations before making a commit. Users can also specify what commit to compare the working tree against, or the ID of any two commits.

In the first VMS run, all violations are new. Subsequently, VMS analyzes all violations from the old version against the code change. If a specification is violated in the same class and on a line that is mapped to the same location in both versions, VMS filters it out as old; the rest are presented as new violations. VMS users can choose to write new or old violations to the console, a file on disk, or both.

RPP. Users can provide a file containing important specifications for RPP to monitor in the critical phase; the rest are monitored in the background. Users can also provide a file containing important specifications and a file containing a disjoint set of specifications to be monitored in the background phase. If users do not provide a file, RPP uses the following default scheme. The first time, RPP monitors all specifications in the critical phase. Only specifications that are violated in the first run are monitored in the critical phase in the second run; the rest are monitored in the background. Subsequently, a specification that is violated in the background phase is promoted to the critical phase in the next run. Users can manually demote specifications from the critical phase. Future work can add options to let users specify when a specification should be automatically promoted to or demoted from the critical phase. RPP currently does not support multi-module projects.

Combinations. EMOP users can combine RPS, VMS, and RPP. When using all three together, RPS first finds affected specifications, then RPP splits the monitoring of affected specifications into critical and background phases before VMS shows new violations from RPP's critical phase. When using VMS with RPS or RPP, the other techniques are run first, then VMS shows new violations. Running RPS with RPP works in the same order as when combining all three.

3   Installation and Usage

Installing EMOP. EMOP can be installed by following the directions in the "Installation" section of the README.md file on EMOP's GitHub page [12]. Note that installing EMOP from sources requires satisfying all prerequisites that are listed on that GitHub page.

Integrating EMOP. To use EMOP in a Maven project, modify that project's configuration file—typically called pom.xml—to add the latest version of EMOP and the JavaMOP agent argument to the configuration of the Maven surefire plugin (which runs tests) file. The current way to add the EMOP to a project is to modify the pom.xml file like so:

```
1   <build><plugins>
2   ...
3     <plugin>
4       <groupId>org.apache.maven.plugins</groupId>
5       <artifactId>maven−surefire−plugin</artifactId>
6       <version>2.20−or−greater</version>
7       <configuration> <argLine>−javaagent:${JavaMOPAgent.jar}</argLine>
8     </configuration>
9     </plugin>
10    <plugin>
11      <groupId>edu.cornell</groupId>
12      <artifactId>emop−maven−plugin</artifactId>
13      <version>${latest_EMOP_version}</version>
14    </plugin>
15    ...
16  </plugins></build>
```

Using EMOP. These commands allow users to: (1) list impacted classes or affected specifications, or (2) run RPS, VMS, RPP, and their combinations:

```
1   $ mvn emop:help # list all goals (commands)
2   $ mvn emop:impacted # list impacted classes
3   $ mvn emop:affected−specs # list affected specifications
4   $ mvn emop:rps # run RPS
5   $ mvn emop:rpp # run RPP
6   $ mvn emop:vms # run VMS
7   $ mvn emop:rps−rpp # run RPS+RPP
8   $ mvn emop:rpp−vms # run RPP+VMS
9   $ mvn emop:rps−vms # run RPS+VMS
10  $ mvn emop:rps−rpp−vms # run RPS+RPP+VMS
11  $ mvn emop:clean # delete all metadata
```

The `emop:help` command lists all EMOP commands and what they do; the others are related to evolution-aware RV. Next, we describe some configuration options.

Running RPS. Three flags choose among RPS variants: (1) `closureOption` specifies how to compute impacted classes: `PS1`, `PS2`, or `PS3` (the default: `PS3`); (2) `includeLibraries` controls whether to instrument 3rd-party libraries (default: `true`); and (3) `includeNonAffected` controls whether non-impacted classes are instrumented (default: `true`). For example, this command runs RPS and instruments neither classes that are not impacted nor 3rd-party libraries:

```
1   $ mvn emop:rps −DincludeLibraries=false −DincludeNonAffected=false
```

Running VMS. Users can see violations on the console or in a `violation-counts` file. By default, only new violations are shown. But, users can view all violations in the console or in the file via Boolean `showAllInConsole` and `showAllInFile` options, respectively (default: `false`). Users can specify commit IDs using `lastSha` and `newSha`. For example, this command shows new violations relative to commit ID `abc123` in the console but it still outputs all violations to file:

```
1   $ mvn emop:vms −DlastSha=abc123 −DshowAllInFile=true
```

Running RPP. Users can provide specifications to RPP using two options named `criticalSpecsFile` and `backgroundSpecsFile`. If only `criticalSpecsFile` is provided, then all other specifications will be monitored in the background. By

default, RPP tracks metadata for critical and background phase specifications
as described in Sect. 2.1. But RPP also has a `demoteCritical` option (default:
`false`) for demoting previously important specifications that are not violated in
the critical phase of the current run to the background phase for the next run. For
example, this command monitors specifications in `critical.txt` (respectively,
`background.txt`) in the critical (respectively, background) phase:

```
1   $ mvn emop:rpp −DcriticalSpecsFile=critical.txt −DbackgroundSpecsFile=background.txt
```

Running Combinations. Options in the union of those from combined techniques can be used, e.g., this command runs RPS+RPP using the RPS variant
that instruments neither classes that are not impacted nor 3rd-party libraries,
while also demoting specifications during RPP:

```
1  $ mvn emop:rps−rpp −DincludeLibraries=false −DincludeNonAffected=false −DdemoteCritical=true
```

4   Evaluation

Setup. We evaluate EMOP on 21 Maven projects from our previous and ongoing
work on RV and regression testing. They are all single-module Maven projects
(RPP does not yet support multi-module projects). We use between 11 and
50 versions per project, for a total of 676 versions. Table 2 shows project names
(click or hover to see GitHub URL), number of versions that we evaluate (sha#),
sizes (KLOC), number of test classes in the first version (TC), average test time
(test[s]), and average JavaMOP overhead for these versions (mop).

Table 2. Projects that we evaluate.

Project	sha#	KLOC	TC	test[s]	mop
jgroups-aws	11	0.3	1	3.3	12.5
Yank	17	0.6	18	3.1	7.2
java-configuration-impl	24	1.7	5	3.9	7.0
embedded-jmxtrans	50	3.1	15	4.1	12.3
jbehave-junit-runner	50	1.5	17	4.7	15.2
compile-testing	50	7.0	25	6.2	6.0
javapoet	20	8.1	18	9.1	6.6
exp4j	50	3.5	5	9.3	3.8
joda-time	50	93.3	158	10.8	3.9
jnr-posix	50	11.8	24	11.9	11.9
imglib2	20	33.0	81	13.0	2.5
HTTP-Proxy-Servlet	50	1.0	1	13.3	3.2
smartsheet-java-sdk	21	7.9	51	13.5	4.5
zt-exec	15	2.6	24	14.6	1.9
commons-imaging	20	44.5	107	18.4	4.9
jscep	50	3.2	50	18.9	3.7
commons-lang	20	80.7	172	21.5	3.1
datasketches-java	48	41.9	178	35.8	2.3
commons-dbcp	20	11.4	43	53.0	1.8
stream-lib	20	4.7	28	91.0	6.9
commons-io	20	32.7	114	102.1	4.1

We use the same versions for
projects that we evaluated in our
original paper [37]. To choose
versions for the other projects,
we iterate over the 500 most
recent versions in each project
(most recent first) and terminate
when we have tried all 500 or
found 50 versions that change
at least one Java file, compile,
tests pass, JavaMOP does not
fail, and JavaMOP time is at
least 20 s. The versions that we
evaluate per project are in our
artifact repository [11].

For RPS, we measure the
time and the number of unique
violations per variant. For VMS,
we measure the number of new
and total violations per version.

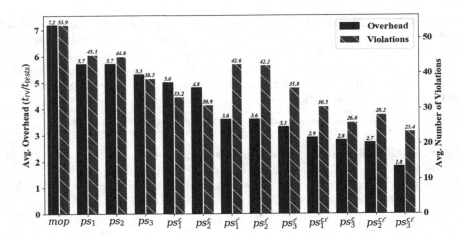

Fig. 2. Runtime overheads of, and violations from, JavaMOP and RPS variants in EMOP for projects and versions in our original evolution-aware RV paper [37].

For RPP, we measure the critical and background phase times. All overheads for RPS are computed from end-to-end times including time for compilation, analysis, running tests, and monitoring. RPP overhead is only for the critical phase. We run EMOP on 193 revisions (7 no longer compile) of 10 projects from our original paper [37], using the same experimental settings as before. We also run all EMOP variants on all 21 projects using Amazon EC2 C5.4xlarge instances.

Results: Comparing with Prior Evaluation. Solid bars in Fig. 2 show average overheads of JavaMOP and RPS variants for the 10 projects in our prior evaluation [37]. RV overhead is t_{rv}/t_{test}; t_{rv} and t_{test} are times with and without JavaMOP, respectively. Sect. 2 describes ps_1, ps_2, and ps_3; "ℓ" and "c" mean 3rd-party libraries and non-impacted classes, respectively, are not instrumented.

In Fig. 2, all RPS variants reduce the average JavaMOP overhead, which is 7.2× when our evolution-aware techniques are not applied. As expected, based on how we designed these variants, ps_1 incurs the most RPS overhead (5.7×), while $ps_3^{c\ell}$ incurs the least overhead (1.8×).

In general, excluding 3rd-party libraries has a significant effect on reducing RPS overhead, as seen for example in the difference between ps_1 (5.7×) and ps_1^{ℓ} (3.6×) in Fig. 2. For libraries that do not depend on 3rd-party libraries, or those that depend on libraries that do not use API methods related to monitored specifications, library exclusion has negligible effect.

Striped bars in Fig. 2 show average numbers of unique violations per version across these projects. RPS reduces the number of violations reported, but in the best case ($ps_3^{c\ell}$) it still shows an average of 23.4 violations—most of which are old—after every code change. So, a technique like VMS is needed that reports only the few new violations. The overheads and violations in Figs. 2 follow the same trends across RPS variants as in our original paper [37]. So, we are more

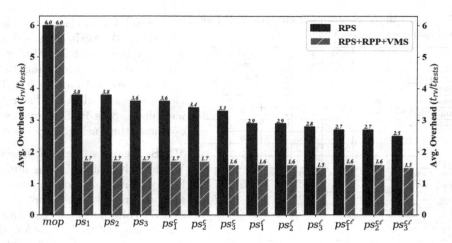

Fig. 3. Average runtime overheads of all RPS variants in EMOP when run alone, and when each RPS variant is combined with RPP and VMS.

confident in how we implemented evolution-aware RV in EMOP. Tooling and Maven overheads likely explain any differences with our old results.

Results on More Subjects and Versions than Prior Work. We discuss details about how EMOP performs when all three evolution-aware RV techniques are combined, and then discuss the contribution of each technique.

Striped bars in Fig. 3 show average overheads per project when all RPS variants are combined with RPP and VMS. The projects in Fig. 3 include some that were not in Fig. 2, and some in Fig. 2 are not in the figure because of dependency issues when we moved experiments to the cloud. We show the RPS variants in Fig. 3 in decreasing order of average overheads.

In terms of total time incurred (not shown in Fig. 3), the best-performing variant in RPS+RPP+VMS is $ps_3^{c\ell}$ (it does not instrument 3rd-party libraries or classes that are not impacted by changes). Comparing the striped mop and $ps_3^{c\ell}$ bars shows that, on average across these projects and versions, $ps_3^{c\ell}$ reduces RV overhead by roughly 4.0× (a very rough estimate, since we take a mean of means). The project with the biggest speedup saw a 8.4× reduction in overhead, from 15.2× with JavaMOP to 1.8× with $ps_3^{c\ell}$.

RPP Contributions to the Combination. Solid bars in Fig. 3 show how well RPS performs on its own. Comparing the mop and $ps_3^{c\ell}$ bars shows that RPS reduces RV overhead by 2.4× when used alone. We elide per-project details for lack of space, but we discuss two observations. First, the project that benefits the most from using only RPS had a 4.9× overhead reduction (from 6.9× to 1.4×).

Table 3. Unique violations from JavaMOP (not evolution-aware), and VMS.

Project	sha#	mop (sum)	VMS (sum)	mop (avg)	VMS (avg)
jgroups-aws	11	12	12	1.1	1.1
Yank	17	22	8	1.3	0.5
java-configuration	24	68	8	2.8	0.3
embedded-jmxtrans	50	627	19	12.5	0.4
jbehave-junit-runner	50	248	9	5.0	0.1
compile-testing	50	541	48	10.8	1
javapoet	20	180	9	9	0.5
exp4j	50	0	0	0	0
joda-time	50	1100	43	22	0.9
jnr-posix	50	1659	72	33.2	1.4
imglib2	20	1540	78	77	3.9
HTTP-Proxy-Servlet	50	929	66	11.6	1.3
smartsheet-java-sdk	21	598	300	28.5	14.3
zt-exec	15	15	2	1	0.1
commons-imaging	20	1064	57	53.2	2.9
jscep	50	1706	213	34.1	4.3
commons-lang	20	1220	61	61.0	3.0
datasketches-java	48	96	34	2	0.7
commons-dbcp	20	40	2	2	0.1
stream-lib	20	300	16	15	0.8
commons-io	20	1795	94	89.8	4.7
Across projects	676	13760	1151	20.2	1.7

Second, the further reduction of average RV overhead resulting from combining RPP with RPS can be seen by comparing the solid and striped bars in Fig. 3. Doing so shows that RPP's critical phase, plus RPS incurs less overhead than using RPS alone.

VMS Results. Table 3 shows VMS results; "sha#" is the number of versions that we evaluate per project, the "mop" and "VMS" columns show the sum and average of violations found per version. Recall that VMS does not reduce RV runtime overhead; rather, it aims to show only new violations. We find that using VMS shows much fewer violations than RPS or JavaMOP. Specifically, across all evaluated projects (see "Across projects" row), VMS shows only 1.7 violations per version, compared to 20.2 violations with JavaMOP—an average reduction of 11.8×. The project with the most average reduction—31.3×—is embedded-jmxtrans. Fractional values that are less than 1.0 in the per project average rows show the number of violations shown every ten versions, on average. For example, in jbehave-junit-runner, VMS shows an average of one violation in every ten versions, but JavaMOP shows five violations per version.

Our manual analysis shows that all RPS variants are safe—they do not miss any new violation that VMS reports. (Like in our original paper, we assume that VMS reports all new violations.) These results on VMS and safety are in line with findings from our original paper. So, users will likely feel less swamped by a deluge of violations that RV shows if run from scratch after every change.

Limitations. EMOP only supports JUnit; it does not yet work for other testing frameworks, e.g., TestNG. EMOP's bytecode instrumentation sometimes clashes with the instrumentation that open-source projects already use for non-RV reasons. Non-trivial engineering is needed to make instrumentation compatible. We evaluated EMOP on 161 Java API specifications that are commonly used in RV research. As more specifications are added, more optimizations will likely be needed. EMOP uses JGit to map lines from old to new versions, so a few old violations can still be presented as new. More precise change-impact analyses, such as semantic differencing [20] can be investigated and added as an option in the future. EMOP's use of a static change-impact analysis leads to two limitations. First, EMOP may be unsafe if it does not find classes that are impacted by the changes due to the use of dynamic features like reflection. Second, it is possible that the set of impacted classes would be more precise if analysis is done at the method-level instead. EMOP may not work as-is for other kinds of specifications than the kinds of API-level specifications that we check. Lastly, EMOP does not yet control for test flakiness [5,42,45,47] or non-determinism.

Related Work. Researchers proposed many other RV tools other than Java-MOP, e.g., [10,22–25,43]. EMOP is the first to integrate evolution-aware RV techniques into a popular build system. Evolution-awareness is not unique to JavaMOP; future work can make other tools evolution aware. Tools for offline RV exist, e.g., [4]. It is not yet clear how to make offline RV evolution aware. Plugins helped make non-RV techniques easier to use. For example, Evosuite [15,16] is a test generation technique that seemed to gain more popularity after plugins for Maven, Eclipse, and IntelliJ were developed [2]. Also, after decades of research on regression test selection (RTS) [6,18,19,33,39,46], RTS plugins that are integrated with Maven or Ant [17,36] led to recent adoption of RTS tools among developers and renaissance in RTS research.

5   Conclusions and Future Work

EMOP brings the benefits of evolution-aware RV to Maven. We find that EMOP reduces RV costs and makes it easier to use RV during regression testing. We plan to evaluate EMOP on more projects, address some of its limitations, and implement more features. EMOP is open-sourced; we hope that it will provide a platform for advancing the research on integrating software testing and RV.

Acknowledgements. We thank the anonymous reviewers for their comments on an earlier draft of this paper. This work was partially supported by funds from the Google Cyber NYC Institutional Research Program and the US National Science Foundation under Grant Nos. 2019277 and 2045596.

References

1. ajc. https://www.eclipse.org/aspectj/doc/next/devguide/ajc-ref.html
2. Arcuri, A., Campos, J., Fraser, J.: Unit test generation during software development: Evosuite plugins for Maven, IntelliJ, and Jenkins. In: ICST, pp. 401–408 (2016)
3. Bartocci, E., Falcone, Y., Francalanza, A., Reger, G.: Introduction to runtime verification. In: Bartocci, E., Falcone, Y. (eds.) Lectures on Runtime Verification. LNCS, vol. 10457, pp. 1–33. Springer, Cham (2018). https://doi.org/10.1007/978-3-319-75632-5_1
4. Basin, D., Harvan, M., Klaedtke, F., Zălinescu, E.: MONPOLY: monitoring usage-control policies. In: Khurshid, S., Sen, K. (eds.) RV 2011. LNCS, vol. 7186, pp. 360–364. Springer, Heidelberg (2012). https://doi.org/10.1007/978-3-642-29860-8_27
5. Bell, J., Legunsen, O., Hilton, M., Eloussi, L., Yung, T., Marinov, D.: DeFlaker: automatically detecting flaky tests. In: ICSE, pp. 433–444 (2018)

6. Biswas, S., Mall, R., Satpathy, M., Sukumaran, S.: Regression test selection techniques: a survey. Informatica 35(3), 289–321 (2011)
7. Collections_SynchronizedCollection Specification. https://github.com/owolabileg/property-db/blob/master/annotated-java-api/java/util/Collections_SynchronizedCollection.mop
8. SuiteHTMLReporter does not synchronize iteration on a synchronized list. https://github.com/testng-team/testng/pull/931
9. JUnitXMLReporter does not synchronize the two synchronized collections when iterating. https://github.com/testng-team/testng/pull/830
10. Ellul, J., Pace, G.J.: Runtime verification of ethereum smart contracts. In: EDCC, pp. 158–163 (2018)
11. eMOP Artifacts. https://github.com/SoftEngResearch/emop-artifacts
12. eMOP GitHub Page. https://github.com/SoftEngResearch/emop
13. Falcone, Y., Havelund, K., Reger, G.: A tutorial on runtime verification. In: EDSS, pp. 141–175 (2013)
14. Falcone, Y., Krstić, S., Reger, G., Traytel, D.: A taxonomy for classifying runtime verification tools. In: Colombo, C., Leucker, M. (eds.) RV 2018. LNCS, vol. 11237, pp. 241–262. Springer, Cham (2018). https://doi.org/10.1007/978-3-030-03769-7_14
15. Fraser, G., Arcuri, A.: Evosuite: automatic test suite generation for object-oriented software. In: FSE, pp. 416–419 (2011)
16. Fraser, G., Arcuri, A.: A large-scale evaluation of automated unit test generation using Evosuite. TOSEM 24(2), 1–42 (2014)
17. Gligoric, M., Eloussi, L., Marinov, D.: Ekstazi: lightweight test selection. In: ICSE Demo, pp. 713–716 (2015)
18. Gligoric, M., Eloussi, L., Marinov, D.: Practical regression test selection with dynamic file dependencies. In: ISSTA, pp. 211–222 (2015)
19. Graves, T.L., Harrold, M.J., Kim, J.-M., Porter, A., Rothermel, G.: An empirical study of regression test selection techniques. TOSEM 10(2), 184–208 (2001)
20. Gyori, A., Lahiri, S.K., Partush, N.: Refining interprocedural change-impact analysis using equivalence relations. In: ISSTA, pp. 318–328 (2017)
21. Gyori, A., Lambeth, B., Shi, A., Legunsen, O., Marinov, D.: NonDex: a tool for detecting and debugging wrong assumptions on Java API specifications. In: FSE Demo, pp. 993–997 (2016)
22. Hallé, S., Khoury, R.: Event stream processing with BeepBeep 3. In: RV-CuBES, pp. 81–88 (2017)
23. Havelund, K.: Rule-based runtime verification revisited. STTT 17, 143–170 (2015)
24. Havelund, K., Peled, D.: Efficient runtime verification of first-order temporal properties. In: Gallardo, M.M., Merino, P. (eds.) SPIN 2018. LNCS, vol. 10869, pp. 26–47. Springer, Cham (2018). https://doi.org/10.1007/978-3-319-94111-0_2
25. Havelund, K., Peled, D., Ulus, D.: First-order temporal logic monitoring with BDDs. FMSD 56(1–3), 1–21 (2020)
26. Havelund, K., Roşu, G.: Monitoring programs using rewriting. In: ASE, pp. 135–143 (2001)
27. java.util.Collections. https://docs.oracle.com/javase/8/docs/api/java/util/Collections.html
28. JGit. http://www.eclipse.org/jgit
29. Jin, D., Meredith, P.O., Lee, C., Roşu, G.: JavaMOP: efficient parametric runtime monitoring framework. In: ICSE Demo, pp. 1427–1430 (2012)
30. Kim, M., Kannan, S., Lee, I., Sokolsky, O., Viswanathan, M.: Java-MaC: a run-time assurance tool for Java programs. In: RV, pp. 218–235 (2001)

31. Lee, C., Jin, D., Meredith, P.O., Roşu, G.: Towards categorizing and formalizing the JDK API. Computer Science Dept., UIUC, Technical report (2012)
32. Legunsen, O., Al Awar, N., Xu, X., Hassan, W.U., Roşu, G., Marinov, D.: How effective are existing Java API specifications for finding bugs during runtime verification? ASEJ **26**(4), 795–837 (2019)
33. Legunsen, O., Hariri, F., Shi, A., Lu, Y., Zhang, L., Marinov, D.: An extensive study of static regression test selection in modern software evolution. In: FSE, pp. 583–594 (2016)
34. Legunsen, O., Hassan, W.U., Xu, X., Roşu, G., Marinov, D.: How good are the specs? A study of the bug-finding effectiveness of existing Java API specifications. In: ASE, pp. 602–613 (2016)
35. Legunsen, O., Marinov, D., Rosu, G.: Evolution-aware monitoring-oriented programming. In: ICSE NIER, pp. 615–618 (2015)
36. Legunsen, O., Shi, A., Marinov, D.: STARTS: STAtic regression test selection. In: ASE Demo, pp. 949–954 (2017)
37. Legunsen, O., Zhang, Y., Hadzi-Tanovic, M., Rosu, G., Marinov, D.: Techniques for evolution-aware runtime verification. In: ICST, pp. 300–311 (2019)
38. Leucker, M., Schallhart, C.: A brief account of runtime verification. In: Formal Languages and Analysis of Contract-Oriented Software, pp. 293–303 (2007)
39. Liu, Y., Zhang, J., Nie, P., Gligoric, M., Legunsen, O.: More precise regression test selection via reasoning about semantics-modifying changes. In: ISSTA, pp. 664–676 (2023)
40. Miranda, B., Lima, I., Legunsen, O., d'Amorim, M.: Prioritizing runtime verification violations. In: ICST, pp. 297–308 (2020)
41. O'Hearn, P.W.: Continuous reasoning: scaling the impact of formal methods. In: LICS, pp. 13–25 (2018)
42. Palomba, F., Zaidman, A.: Does refactoring of test smells induce fixing flaky tests? In: ICSME, pp. 1–12 (2017)
43. Reger, G., Cruz, H.C., Rydeheard, D.: MARQ: monitoring at runtime with QEA. In: Baier, C., Tinelli, C. (eds.) TACAS 2015. LNCS, vol. 9035, pp. 596–610. Springer, Heidelberg (2015). https://doi.org/10.1007/978-3-662-46681-0_55
44. Schneider, F.B.: Enforceable security policies. TISSEC **3**(1), 30–50 (2000)
45. Shi, A., Gyori, A., Legunsen, O., Marinov, D.: Detecting assumptions on deterministic implementations of non-deterministic specifications. In: ICST, pp. 80–90 (2016)
46. Shi, A., Hadzi-Tanovic, M., Zhang, L., Marinov, D., Legunsen, O.: Reflection-aware static regression test selection. PACML, **3**(OOPSLA), 1–29 (2019)
47. Shi, A., Lam, W., Oei, R., Xie, T., Marinov, D.: iFixFlakies: a framework for automatically fixing order-dependent flaky tests. In: FSE, pp. 545–555 (2019)
48. About surefire. https://maven.apache.org/surefire

Runtime Monitoring of Accidents in Driving Recordings with Multi-type Logic in Empirical Models

Ziyan An, Xia Wang, Taylor T. Johnson, Jonathan Sprinkle, and Meiyi Ma

Department of Computer Science, Vanderbilt University, Nashville,
TN 37235, USA
{Ziyan.an,meiyi.ma}@vanderbilt.edu
Ziyan.an@vanderbilt.edu, meiyi.ma@vanderbilt.edu

Abstract. Video capturing devices with limited storage capacity have become increasingly common in recent years. As a result, there is a growing demand for techniques that can effectively analyze and understand these videos. While existing approaches based on data-driven methods have shown promise, they are often constrained by the availability of training data. In this paper, we focus on dashboard camera videos and propose a novel technique for recognizing important events, detecting traffic accidents, and trimming accident video evidence based on anomaly detection results. By leveraging meaningful high-level time-series abstraction and logical reasoning methods with state-of-the-art data-driven techniques, we aim to pinpoint critical evidence of traffic accidents in driving videos captured under various traffic conditions with promising accuracy, continuity, and integrity. Our approach highlights the importance of utilizing a formal system of logic specifications to deduce the relational features extracted from a sequence of video frames and meets the practical limitations of real-time deployment.

Keywords: Logic Specifications for Images and Videos · Systems with Learning-Enabled Components · Runtime Assurance

1 Introduction

Dashboard cameras that are designed to continuously record video footage have become increasingly popular among vehicle owners [24,25]. However, this design faces inherent limitations, particularly due to limited device storage capacity. For example, critical video evidence can be overwritten by continuous loop recording dashcams. Thus, there is a growing need for automated accident detection mechanisms that can identify relevant incidents captured in these recordings,

---

Z. An and X. Wang—These authors made equal contributions to the work, and their order is based on the alphabetical order of their last names.

© The Author(s), under exclusive license to Springer Nature Switzerland AG 2023
P. Katsaros and L. Nenzi (Eds.): RV 2023, LNCS 14245, pp. 376–388, 2023.
https://doi.org/10.1007/978-3-031-44267-4_21

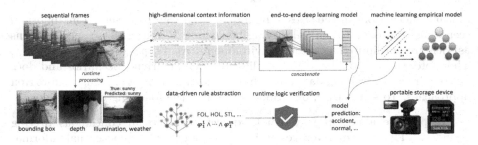

Fig. 1. Our approach leverages runtime logic verification, data-driven detection, and contextual information to accurately identify dangerous scenes in driving videos.

such that important evidence can be preserved, while irrelevant sections of longer recordings can be trimmed and discarded on the fly.

Training a neural network to directly predict the anomaly label of each frame for accident detection is a potential approach (e.g. [8,16]). However, this method typically demands a substantial amount of hand-annotated data, which may not always be practical or feasible to obtain [30]. Furthermore, ensuring that the dataset is diverse enough to capture the range of accident scenarios adds another layer of complexity [28].

An additional concern arises when data-driven models produce unrealistic labels while they are deployed online. For example, the labels may exhibit discontinuous behavior, jumping back and forth across consecutive frames. Such predictions contradict the continuous nature of accidents, which have clear starting and ending points. Ideally, the algorithm should produce consistent and continuous predictions in line with our understanding of accidents in reality.

Targeting these challenges, we propose a new framework for detecting driving accidents from dashboard camera recordings that address various accident scenarios without requiring access to additional privacy-sensitive information. Our approach is a lightweight framework that combines data-driven techniques with different types of logical properties, allowing for easy adaptation to different scenarios during deployment.

More specifically, we first demonstrate that high-level time-series features exhibit strong associativity with the occurrence of traffic accidents through supervised learning methods. Additionally, under other conditions being equal, the extensional experiment exhibits that the vision-based deep learning model incorporated with the interpretive time-series abstraction could exceed the pure vision model. From this, we give solid proof that the extracted interpretive contextual features have high discriminability for accident detection indeed. To further improve the accuracy and usability of the detection results, our proposed framework incorporates multiple types of logic properties for verification at runtime. Figure 1 depicts an overview of our proposed approach.

This integration allows our proposed method to demonstrate more stable and robust performance, based on essential patterns captured from not only pure vision data but also interpretive time-series abstraction. For example, significant fluctuations in the sizes of bounding boxes can be observed in abnormal scenes, as compared to normal driving behaviors. Moreover, logic specifications as such are not limited to specific environments, road types, or times of the day. Therefore, the proposed method applies to different driving scenarios and does not require extra training data for each scenario, unlike most existing data-driven approaches. To summarize, our framework offers the following contributions:

- We propose a two-step system to detect accidents in continuous driving videos. The system leverages vision-based algorithms, contextual information, and runtime supervision with higher-order logic to improve predictions.
- We extract interpretive high-level time-series features which capture important patterns and characteristics of abnormal scenes, enabling accurate and reliable accident detection.
- We further ensure the continuity, robustness, and generalizability of our framework under various driving scenarios by utilizing knowledge refined from the abstraction of high-level logic properties.

2   Related Work

Previously, data-driven approaches have demonstrated remarkable performance in detecting dangerous driving scenes and traffic accidents by leveraging offline-trained deep models (e.g., Zhao et al. [34], Doshi et al. [14]). However, data-driven methods for video-based accident detection face the inherent issue of dataset scarcity [4]. While large-scale vision datasets exist (e.g., Geiger et al. [17]), publicly available traffic anomaly datasets specifically designed for every detection algorithm's objective are limited. On the other hand, formal logic has found widespread application in image-related tasks. For example, Dokhanchi et al. [12] propose Timed Quality Temporal Logic to assess the quality of object detection algorithms in terms of spatio-temporal logical relations. Additionally, Balakrishnan et al. [2,3] extend this work, enabling the specification and monitoring of logic to evaluate the results of object detection algorithms with objects appearing at different times.

In recent years, the integration of rules into empirical methods has gained traction as a strategy to enhance the robustness of data-driven research [15,22,27]. This approach enables researchers to apply well-established theoretical constructs and expert specifications to observational or empirical models, thereby improving the reliability and validity of their findings [33]. Notable examples of this research direction include Bakar et al.'s Tsetlin Machine [1], a lightweight automata learning algorithm utilizing propositional logic, and a recent work by Hashemi et al. [18] exploring the integration of temporal logic into control systems, allowing for the leveraging of a more diverse range of domain knowledge. To the best of our knowledge, this work represents the first investigation into the utilization of logical reasoning as a verification strategy to enhance overall detection performance on video-based driving datasets.

3   Motivating Study

To examine the difficulties of real-time accident detection in long driving videos, we present two motivating studies in this section. Firstly, we find that time-series features exhibit a promising ability for anomaly differentiation. Thus, we incorporate this implicit contextual knowledge into empirical models to enhance their performance. Secondly, we observe discontinuity issues in the predictions made by end-to-end algorithms. As a solution, we emphasize the importance of incorporating logic verification to address this practical concern.

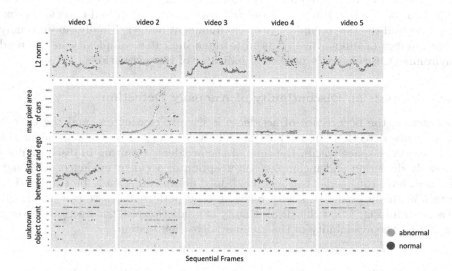

Fig. 2. Each column represents a randomly chosen video, while each row represents a meaningful high-level time-series feature, displayed sequentially. In row 1, a larger discrepancy in the L2 norm distance between two adjacent frames indicates an increased risk. In row 2, a larger pixel area of the car object's bounding box implies a higher level of risk. Row 3 shows a shorter distance (the distance feature is extracted from a thermal map, thus larger value implies a shorter distance) between the detected car object and the ego vehicle signifies a higher level of risk. Lastly, row 4 shows risky situations are usually accompanied by a higher number of unknown detected objects.

3.1   Analysis on High-Level Time-Series Abstraction

To demonstrate the distinguishing feature patterns between accident and non-accident driving video frames, we focus on four crucial high-level time series features. These features have been identified based on the feature importance factor of a trained Random Forest (RF) [5] model, as illustrated in Fig. 2.

By combining these observations, we gain a more insightful understanding of how accident frames can be distinguished from normal scenes. In the figure above, we randomly select five videos as columns, where the orange points represent abnormal (accident) frames, and the blue points represent normal (non-accident) frames in the driving video sequence. In particular, the first row demonstrates that large gaps between adjacent frames indicate an elevated risk factor. Considering an accident as an out-of-control scenario, it is easy to correlate these large gaps with reasons such as driving too fast or encountering sudden unexpected situations. The second row shows that a large pixel area of the car object in a frame, signifying the ego car's proximity to the leading car, indicates potential risk. This can be considered in conjunction with the third feature. As depicted in the third row of the figure, it is evident that a small distance from the car object to the ego in a frame is associated with a risk factor, and this close proximity beyond the safe boundary projects imminent danger. Finally, an unusually large number of unknown objects in a frame indicates complexity in the road environment, serving as a predictive indicator of risky situations.

3.2 Analysis on Discontinuity of Anomaly Detection

In practice, the occurrence of accidents is usually continuous, and the output of anomaly detection should not jump between normal and abnormal in the time sequence space within the time of the accident, resulting in discontinuous anomaly detection and incomplete interception of accident evidence. Although the high-level time-series features mentioned above can already be employed to obtain anomaly predictions with relevant good performance, we can intuitively observe from Fig. 3 that this discontinuity of prediction still has a serious adverse impact on the availability of the anomaly detection system.

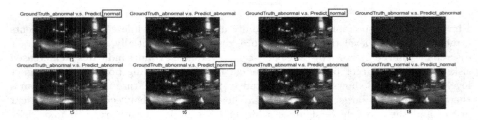

Fig. 3. Discontinious anomaly prediction provided by Random Forest via high-level time-series abstraction of an accident example video.

4   Proposed Method

Targeting the challenges identified above, our proposed framework (Fig. 1) begins by capturing frames from each first-person video stream using the small storage device. We employ pre-trained state-of-the-art vision models to extract multi-modality scene statistics and gain the differential features between two adjacent frames. Simultaneously, our second module extracts environmental features as time-series data, such as weather and illumination conditions. These two sets of time-series data are concatenated to generate a high-level time-series abstraction. The downstream decision-making component provides anomaly prediction by either utilizing only the abstraction via multiple machine learning models or by combining the abstraction with pure vision information via deep learning models. Finally, the decision is calibrated and enhanced by multiple types of logic specifications and properties.

4.1   High-Level Time-Series Feature Extraction

Object Detection Feature Extraction. As the contextual and surrounding data of the ego, we extract the following information from each video:

- Object count: We detect 12 transportation-related classes using YOLOv3 and aggregate the total count for each class in each frame.
- Detection confidence: We gather statistics for the minimum, maximum, and mean confidence scores associated with each object bounding box.
- Object distance: We measure the distance between the ego vehicle and the center of each detected bounding box, then record statistics for minimum, maximum, and mean distances.
- Object size: By calculating the pixel area of each object's bounding box, we determine the minimum, maximum, and mean sizes for each class.

Frame Difference Feature Extraction. The frame difference feature is a commonly used technique in video processing and analysis to detect motion in a sequence of frames. It involves computing the difference between two adjacent frames and using this difference as a feature for further analysis. Therefore, in this work, we incorporate the following frame-by-frame difference features:

- L-2 norm is a common method used to measure the difference between two frames. It quantifies the average squared difference between the pixel values of the two frames. Mathematically, the L-2 norm is defined as $L_2(x_1, x_2) = \|x_1 - x_2\|_2^2$. A lower L-2 distance indicates two more similar frames.
- We compute the top 10 eigenvalues of the absolute difference matrix, implying the most striking features of the difference between two consecutive frames.

Illumination and Weather Feature Extraction. For illumination and weather prediction tasks, we first perform model selection on part of the labeled dataset using several deep learning models, including ResNet-50 [19], MobileNet [20], VGG-19 [29], Xception [9], and DenseNet-201 [21]. For both prediction tasks, DenseNet-201 performs the best. For illumination prediction tasks, we train the model on a two-class dataset that contains day and night images, and for weather prediction tasks, we train the model on a hybrid five-class image dataset containing sunny, cloudy, rainy, snowy, and foggy weather [31]. Further, we use pre-trained models to predict illumination and weather labels for dash-cam driving frames. Finally, we assign the majority of predictions of the entire driving video as the final illumination and weather label for all frames in a video.

4.2 Empirical Model for Accident Classification

We show that our framework, incorporating a machine learning model based on only high-level time-series features, together with a deep learning model utilizing both vision information and high-level time-series abstraction, can provide feasible anomaly predictions.

As there are multiple time-series features extracted from driving dash cam video frames, we employ basic machine learning algorithms to examine the correlation between these features and the accident classes. The abstraction comprises 13 dimensions of frame difference features, 120 dimensions of object detection features, and 2 dimensions of illumination and weather label features, with the dependent variable being the binary label.

We then design a deep neural network architecture that leverages pre-trained ResNet-18 weights as the feature extractor and fully connected layers that process high-level contextual information to detect the occurrence of accidents. The structure consists of the following components. Firstly, raw frames from driving videos are passed through the pre-trained ResNet-18 feature extractor, which outputs learned image representations from the complex model. After that, a linear layer is utilized to reduce the dimension of the learned representation. Then, an additional linear layer equipped with batch normalization and ReLU activation is employed to learn representations from high-level contextual information. The outputs from both the pre-trained ResNet-18 feature extractor and the additional linear layer with contextual information are concatenated into a one-dimensional tensor. The concatenated tensor is then fed into a final linear layer with a Sigmoid activation function that maps the output to a probability range between 0 and 1. The output from the Sigmoid activation is rounded to obtain the final class label.

4.3 Logic Calibration and Verification

FOL and HOL Specifications. During the process of deploying machine learning models with high-level time-series features, we have observed that the path logic of the decision tree could provide usable anomaly predictions to some extent. It is familiar that a tree structure could be represented as a tree graph and several mutually exclusive rules, which could be considered as First Order Logic (FOL) for further applications. In this case, each rule has a probability associated with the class based on the majority of labels. However, as discussed above, this data-driven FOL cannot ensure the accuracy, continuity, and integrity of the anomaly detection task. Thus, we propose employing Higher Order Logic (HOL) generated from the FOL.

The design of HOL stems from an idea of simplicity. As mentioned above, each sample (frame) of the dataset will be assigned to a leaf node of the decision tree, thus each sample could apply to one rule, which is the path the sample goes through from the root node to the leaf node. Plus, this sample could inherit the probability associated with the leaf node. It is assumed that the final decision could rely on continuous observation of the sequential frames. Assuming the observation window size is k, the **abnormal impulse**, denoted as **odds**, up to the current frame i can be defined by dividing the combination of probabilities that these frames are abnormal by the combination of probabilities that the frames are normal, as (1). Note the probability of each frame normal is p_0^j, and the probability of abnormal is p_1^j, $p_0^j + p_1^j = 1$. Then, when the odds signal is strong enough, the system recognizes it as the starting point of an accident; when the odds signal is weak enough, the system recognizes it as the ending point of an accident, and all continuous frames between the starting point and the ending point will be judged as abnormal continuously, the process is shown in Fig. 4. Moreover, the threshold value of the odds signals for the starting and ending points can be obtained by data-driven method or annotated by experts.

$$\text{odds}^i = \frac{\prod_{j=i-(k-1)}^{i} p_1^j}{\prod_{j=i-(k-1)}^{i} p_0^j} \tag{1}$$

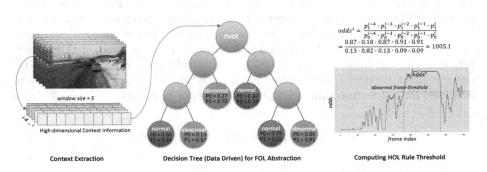

Context Extraction   Decision Tree (Data Driven) for FOL Abstraction   Computing HOL Rule Threshold

Fig. 4. Process of FOL and HOL calibration. In this example, we set the window size to 5, and we employ an array with dimension 122 to represent context information.

Temporal Logic Specifications. Temporal logic is a powerful tool for expressing specifications on time-series data, offering formal symbolism, evaluation mechanisms, and semantics [13]. In our proposed framework, we utilize Signal Temporal Logic (STL) to establish verification criteria [23]. This allows us to consider a range of signal types, such as raw images, extracted time-series features, and factorized data. These verification criteria can either be provided by an expert, derived from empirical observations, or learned from data-driven algorithms. In STL, we represent the temporal range as $[a, b] \in \mathbb{R}_{\geq 0}$, where $a \leq b$. We use the function $\mu : \mathbb{R}^n \to \{\top, \bot\}$ to denote a signal predicate, such as $f(x) \geq 0$, where $x \in \mathcal{X}$ is the signal variable. The temporal operator "always" is denoted by $\square$, and the temporal operator "eventually" is denoted by $\Diamond$. More specifically, $\square_{[a,b]}\varphi$ indicates that φ should hold at every future time step within the interval $[a,b]$. $\Diamond_{[a,b]}\varphi$ indicates that φ should hold at some future time step within $[a,b]$. In our framework, specifications such as "the accident frame should satisfy the property that its maximum bounding box sizes of the previous and following three frames are greater than 60% of the maximum bounding box size across all n frames" can be easily specified with the STL formula $\square_{[1,n]}(\square_{[t-3,t+3]}max(\mathbf{bbox}) \geq 0.6 \cdot \mathbf{mbox})$, where t specifies the current timestamp, n denotes the total number of frames, "bbox" denotes the bounding box areas of the current frame, and "mbox" denotes the maximum bounding box size across the video.

5   Evaluation Results

5.1   Evaluation Setup

In this work, we utilized real traffic accident frames obtained from user-uploaded YouTube videos for our evaluations [32]. To be more specific, we downloaded a total of 627 lengthy videos from the internet, each of which could be processed into several hundred frames with corresponding annotations. From these videos, we selected 29 videos (approximately 5%) to form our testing dataset, with each video containing complete sequential frames. Out of the remaining 598 videos, which encompassed a total of 64,563 individual frames, we divided the frames randomly into a training dataset (80%) and a validation dataset (20%). The percentage of accident frames in the dataset was 33.89%. The validation dataset was used for model fine-tuning and model selection processes.

Table 1. Comparison of model performance.

Methods	Testing Performance			
	Accuracy	Recall	F1	Runtime (s)
XGB [7]	76.36%	37.46%	47.78%	0.012
LR [11]	69.88%	0.44%	0.84%	0.003
DT [6]	63.43%	51.05%	44.64%	**0.002**
RF [5]	74.98%	44.64%	50.75%	0.071
SVM [10]	70.64%	1.22%	2.34%	12.99
NB [26]	70.64%	1.22%	2.34%	13.12
RF-HOL (Ours)	**85.74%**	**68.29%**	**73.44%**	3.197
ResNet-ft [19]	60.94%	47.73%	41.38%	2.155
ResNet-ts (Ours)	**73.48%**	50.61%	**52.43%**	2.125
ResNet-ts-STL (Ours)	67.80%	**59.12%**	51.47%	**0.017**

5.2   Baselines

In this work, all deep learning models were implemented and trained using PyTorch framework, utilizing an NVIDIA RTX-3070 GPU. We experimented with two optimization algorithms, namely Stochastic Gradient Descent (SGD) and Adam, with different learning rates of 1e-2, 1e-3, and 1e-4. The models with the best performance during the evaluation process were reported. More specifically, we consider the methods listed below.

1. ResNet18-ft: We employ a pre-trained ResNet18 on ImageNet and freeze the last two layers for fine-tuning, which solely relies on vision information.
2. ResNet18-ts: This model is proposed in this work, which incorporates both raw images and contextual information into the accident detection process.
3. Supervised ML models: We implement multiple machine learning models, such as XGBoost (XGB), Logistic Regression (LR), Decision Tree (DT), Random Forest (RF), SVM, and Naive Bayes (NB).

5.3   Evaluation of Model Performance

To evaluate the performance of our proposed algorithm, we consider the following metrics: accuracy, recall rate, F1 score, and runtime. More specifically, accuracy is defined as the ratio of correct predictions to the total number of instances. Recall Rate is defined as the ratio of true positives (TP) to the sum of TP and false negatives (FN). F1 Score is the harmonic mean of precision and recall. And precision is the ratio of TP to the sum of TP and false positives (FP). The performance of our accident detection module is demonstrated in Table 1.

With HOL calibration, the Random Forest model outperforms other models in terms of accuracy, recall rate, and F1 score. The accuracy of the ResNet finetuning model, which solely relies on vision information, was enhanced from 60.94% to 73.48% by incorporating the concatenated features of image representation and high-level time-series features proposed in this work. Moreover, when additionally equipped with Signal Temporal Logic (STL), the recall performance of ResNet also improved from 50.61% to 59.13%. It is worth noting that the post-hoc verification process only required 0.017 s. Additionally, the decision tree (DT) model demonstrates exceptional runtime effectiveness. In scenarios where real-time requirements are extremely demanding, the decision tree model demonstrated acceptable anomaly detection effectiveness.

6   Conclusion

In this paper, we investigate runtime verification for detecting accidents in driving footage with contextual information and raw dash cam videos. Moreover, we demonstrate that by integrating the abstraction of high-level time-series features, which exhibit distinguishable patterns under supervised learning methods, the performance of image-based deep learning models for accident detection can be significantly enhanced. Additionally, our proposed model leverages multiple logic specifications to verify and calibrate anomaly predictions. This approach ensures that the predicted accident labels maintain exceptional accuracy, continuity, and integrity, while also guaranteeing a stable and robust system across various accident scenarios.

Acknowledgment. This work was supported, in part, by the National Science Foundation under Grant 2151500, 2028001, and 2220401.

References

1. Bakar, A., Rahman, T., Shafik, R., Kawsar, F., Montanari, A.: Adaptive intelligence for batteryless sensors using software-accelerated tsetlin machines. In: Proceedings of SenSys (2022)
2. Balakrishnan, A., Deshmukh, J., Hoxha, B., Yamaguchi, T., Fainekos, G.: PerceMon: online monitoring for perception systems. In: Feng, L., Fisman, D. (eds.) RV 2021. LNCS, vol. 12974, pp. 297–308. Springer, Cham (2021). https://doi.org/10.1007/978-3-030-88494-9_18
3. Balakrishnan, A., et al.: Specifying and evaluating quality metrics for vision-based perception systems. In: 2019 Design, Automation & Test in Europe Conference & Exhibition (DATE), pp. 1433–1438. IEEE (2019)
4. Bashetty, S.K., Amor, H.B., Fainekos, G.: Deepcrashtest: turning dashcam videos into virtual crash tests for automated driving systems. In: 2020 IEEE International Conference on Robotics and Automation (ICRA), pp. 11353–11360. IEEE (2020)
5. Breiman, L.: Random forests. Mach. Learn. **45**, 5–32 (2001)
6. Breiman, L.: Classification and Regression Trees. Routledge, Milton Park (2017)
7. Chen, T., Guestrin, C.: Xgboost: a scalable tree boosting system. In: Proceedings of the 22nd ACM SIGKDD International Conference on Knowledge Discovery and Data Mining, pp. 785–794 (2016)
8. Choi, J.G., Kong, C.W., Kim, G., Lim, S.: Car crash detection using ensemble deep learning and multimodal data from dashboard cameras. Expert Syst. Appl. **183**, 115400 (2021)
9. Chollet, F.: Xception: deep learning with depthwise separable convolutions (2017)
10. Cortes, C., Vapnik, V.: Support-vector networks. Mach. Learn. **20**, 273–297 (1995)
11. Cox, D.R.: The regression analysis of binary sequences. J. Roy. Stat. Soc. Ser. B: Stat. Methodol. **20**(2), 215–232 (1958)
12. Dokhanchi, A., Amor, H.B., Deshmukh, J.V., Fainekos, G.: Evaluating perception systems for autonomous vehicles using quality temporal logic. In: Colombo, C., Leucker, M. (eds.) RV 2018. LNCS, vol. 11237, pp. 409–416. Springer, Cham (2018). https://doi.org/10.1007/978-3-030-03769-7_23
13. Donzé, A., Maler, O.: Robust satisfaction of temporal logic over real-valued signals. In: Chatterjee, K., Henzinger, T.A. (eds.) FORMATS 2010. LNCS, vol. 6246, pp. 92–106. Springer, Heidelberg (2010). https://doi.org/10.1007/978-3-642-15297-9_9
14. Doshi, K., Yilmaz, Y.: An efficient approach for anomaly detection in traffic videos. In: Proceedings of the IEEE/CVF Conference on Computer Vision and Pattern Recognition, pp. 4236–4244 (2021)

15. Dreossi, T., et al.: VERIFAI: a toolkit for the formal design and analysis of artificial intelligence-based systems. In: Dillig, I., Tasiran, S. (eds.) CAV 2019. LNCS, vol. 11561, pp. 432–442. Springer, Cham (2019). https://doi.org/10.1007/978-3-030-25540-4_25

16. Du, Y., Qin, B., Zhao, C., Zhu, Y., Cao, J., Ji, Y.: A novel spatio-temporal synchronization method of roadside asynchronous MMW radar-camera for sensor fusion. IEEE Trans. Intell. Transp. Syst. **23**(11), 22278–22289 (2021)

17. Geiger, A., Lenz, P., Stiller, C., Urtasun, R.: Vision meets robotics: the kitti dataset. Int. J. Rob. Res. **32**(11), 1231–1237 (2013)

18. Hashemi, N., Hoxha, B., Yamaguchi, T., Prokhorov, D., Fainekos, G., Deshmukh, J.: A neurosymbolic approach to the verification of temporal logic properties of learning-enabled control systems. In: Proceedings of the ACM/IEEE 14th International Conference on Cyber-Physical Systems (with CPS-IoT Week 2023), pp. 98–109 (2023)

19. He, K., Zhang, X., Ren, S., Sun, J.: Deep residual learning for image recognition (2015)

20. Howard, A.G., et al.: MobileNets: Efficient convolutional neural networks for mobile vision applications (2017)

21. Huang, G., Liu, Z., van der Maaten, L., Weinberger, K.Q.: Densely connected convolutional networks (2018)

22. Ma, M., Gao, J., Feng, L., Stankovic, J.: STLnet: signal temporal logic enforced multivariate recurrent neural networks. Adv. Neural. Inf. Process. Syst. **33**, 14604–14614 (2020)

23. Maler, O., Nickovic, D.: Monitoring temporal properties of continuous signals. In: Lakhnech, Y., Yovine, S. (eds.) FORMATS/FTRTFT -2004. LNCS, vol. 3253, pp. 152–166. Springer, Heidelberg (2004). https://doi.org/10.1007/978-3-540-30206-3_12

24. Rea, R.V., Johnson, C.J., Aitken, D.A., Child, K.N., Hesse, G.: Dash cam videos on Youtube offer insights into factors related to moose-vehicle collisions. Accid. Anal. Prevent. **118**, 207–213 (2018). https://doi.org/10.1016/j.aap.2018.02.020, www.sciencedirect.com/science/article/pii/S0001457518300824

25. Richardson, A., Sanborn, K., Sprinkle, J.: Intelligent structuring and semantic mapping of dash camera footage and can bus data. In: 2022 2nd Workshop on Data-Driven and Intelligent Cyber-Physical Systems for Smart Cities Workshop (DI-CPS), pp. 24–30 (2022). https://doi.org/10.1109/DI-CPS56137.2022.00010

26. Rish, I., et al.: An empirical study of the Naive Bayes classifier. In: IJCAI 2001 Workshop on Empirical Methods in Artificial Intelligence, vol. 3, pp. 41–46 (2001)

27. Seshia, S.A., Sadigh, D., Sastry, S.S.: Towards verified artificial intelligence. arXiv preprint arXiv:1606.08514 (2016)

28. Shah, A.P., Lamare, J.B., Nguyen-Anh, T., Hauptmann, A.: CADP: a novel dataset for CCTV traffic camera based accident analysis. In: 2018 15th IEEE International Conference on Advanced Video and Signal Based Surveillance (AVSS), pp. 1–9. IEEE (2018)

29. Simonyan, K., Zisserman, A.: Very deep convolutional networks for large-scale image recognition (2015)

30. Štitilis, D., Laurinaitis, M.: Legal regulation of the use of dashboard cameras: aspects of privacy protection. Comput. Law Secur. Rev. **32**(2), 316–326 (2016)

31. Xiao, H., Zhang, F., Shen, Z., Wu, K., Zhang, J.: Classification of weather phenomenon from images by using deep convolutional neural network. Earth Space Sci. **8**(5), e2020EA001604 (2021)

32. Yao, Y., Wang, X., Xu, M., Pu, Z., Atkins, E., Crandall, D.: When, where, and what? a new dataset for anomaly detection in driving videos (2020)
33. Zhao, Y., An, Z., Gao, X., Mukhopadhyay, A., Ma, M.: Fairguard: Harness logic-based fairness rules in smart cities. arXiv preprint arXiv:2302.11137 (2023)
34. Zhao, Y., Wu, W., He, Y., Li, Y., Tan, X., Chen, S.: Good practices and a strong baseline for traffic anomaly detection. In: Proceedings of the IEEE/CVF Conference on Computer Vision and Pattern Recognition, pp. 3993–4001 (2021)

Safety Monitoring for Pedestrian Detection in Adverse Conditions

Swapnil Mallick, Shuvam Ghosal$^{(\boxtimes)}$, Anand Balakrishnan,
and Jyotirmoy Deshmukh

University of Southern California, Los Angeles, CA 90007, USA
{smallick,sghosal,anandbal,jdeshmuk}@usc.edu

Abstract. Pedestrian detection is an important part of the perception system of autonomous vehicles. Foggy and low-light conditions are quite challenging for pedestrian detection, and several models have been proposed to increase the robustness of detections under such challenging conditions. Checking if such a model performs well is largely evaluated by manually inspecting the results of object detection. We propose a monitoring technique that uses Timed Quality Temporal Logic (TQTL) to do differential testing: we first check when an object detector (such as vanilla YOLO) fails to accurately detect pedestrians using a suitable TQTL formula on a sequence of images. We then apply a model specialized to adverse weather conditions to perform object detection on the same image sequence. We use Image-Adaptive YOLO (IA-YOLO) for this purpose. We then check if the new model satisfies the previously failing specifications. Our method shows the feasibility of using such a differential testing approach to measure the improvement in quality of detections when specialized models are used for object detection.

Keywords: Pedestrian Detection · Autonomous Driving · Temporal Logic

1 Introduction

Convolutional Neural Network (CNN) based models [5,10,14,25,28] have become widespread in the field of pedestrian detection and have been able to achieve impressive results when tested on benchmark driving datasets. Some of these models have also been deployed in autonomous vehicles [29].

According to the California DMV statistics, 627 autonomous vehicle collision have been reported as of July 25, 2023 despite numerous object detection models faring well when tested on high-quality images captured in clear weather conditions [1]. An important question is how these models fare under challenging lighting conditions such as when it is foggy or dark. Beyond the obvious issues presented by images being out-of-distribution with respect to the lighting conditions, this problem becomes harder when pedestrians wear black or dark colored clothes at night.

S. Mallick and S. Ghosal—These authors contributed equally to this work.

© The Author(s), under exclusive license to Springer Nature Switzerland AG 2023
P. Katsaros and L. Nenzi (Eds.): RV 2023, LNCS 14245, pp. 389–399, 2023.
https://doi.org/10.1007/978-3-031-44267-4_22

In this case study paper, we have two main objectives. First, we wish to demonstrate a logic-based metric that can show that pedestrian detection in low-light conditions suffers in quality *without the use of ground-truth annotations*. Towards this end, we use the YOLO object detection model [24] trained on a standard driving dataset, and apply it to videos containing poor lighting conditions. Our technical idea is to use the quality metric of Timed Quality Temporal Logic TQTL [4,7]. We show that we can express object consistency properties in TQTL, and use the PerceMon tool [3] to monitor violations of the given TQTL specification by the sequence of detections output by YOLO.

We then use a modified object detection framework called IA-YOLO [17]. IA-YOLO has a component that predicts parameters to be used for a differentiable image processing (DIP) module. The DIP module can be thought of as a way to implement a number of image filters to improve performance of object detection. We then monitor the detections by IA-YOLO against the same TQTL specification.

The main conclusions of this study are as follows: (1) The quality of a TQTL specification on detections using vanilla is poor when pre-trained YOLO is used on videos with low-light conditions. (2) The quality of TQTL specifications is significantly improved when IA-YOLO is used for detections.

Related Work. Significant research has been conducted for general pedestrian detection. However, only a few efforts have been made to detect pedestrians successfully in adverse lighting and weather conditions. Works like IA-YOLO [17] and DENet [22] use filters implementing ideas similar to those used in image processing to preprocess images for object detectors like YOLO, and thereby improving process. Other works, like the CycleGAN framework presented in [27] augment existing datasets with generative images that simulate adverse weather conditions to improve the robustness of an object detector. In a similar light, the authors of [18] present datasets synthetically generated images that simulate adverse weather conditions.

Evaluation of multi-object detection models have predominantly used the *mean average precision* (mAP) metric, popularized by the PASCAL-VOC dataset [8]. This metric evaluates the accuracy of object detectors by estimating the area under the curve of the precision-recall relationship with respect to a given dataset. Mean average precision(mAP) is the average of the Average precision(AP) values for each output object class. While other metrics have been proposed in literature, these aren't as popular as the mAP evaluation metric [20,21].

The above approaches rely on either augmenting existing datasets to improve robustness of object detectors, or comparing against ground truth to evaluate the accuracy of a model. To this light, recent literature has proposed the use of temporal logics to evaluate perception systems without access to groundtruth data [4,6,12]. These use TQTL (and its extension Spatio-temporal Quality Logic) to monitor for incorrect behavior of object detector models. Similarly, the works in [3] and [2] propose the use of online monitoring techniques to perform fault detection at runtime.

2   Preliminaries

Object detection is a computer vision task to check the presence of objects of a certain class in an image and also obtain a bounding box (in image coordinates) indicating the location of the object within the image. Object detection algorithms can be broadly categorized into two groups based on how they operate. Some algorithms propose regions of interest (RoIs) in the image space [9] and then classify the regions by training neural networks. These algorithms are called the region proposal-based methods. The other class of algorithms comprises single-stage regression based methods [15,16], such as the YOLO series [23] of algorithms. In algorithms like YOLO, the result of applying object detection to an image is a list of bounding boxes in image coordinates, and for each bounding box in this list, we obtain a class label (for the purported object in the box), and a number in $[0, 1]$ that indicates the confidence of the detector in the class label. In autonomous driving applications, class labels may include *bicycles, cars, pedestrians, traffic lights*, etc.

Usually, images captured in adverse weather or during low-light conditions do not have the same distribution of low-level features, which leads to poor detection of some kinds of object classes. Some weather effects like rain or fog can obscure key features or have the effect of adding noise to the image. In traditional image processing literature, custom image filters can be designed to denoise images [30], remove the effects of certain weather phenomena [19,26], or enhance features required for detection. However, designing custom image filters is a manual and tedious process. An approach to overcome this problem is to use an adaptive detection model such as IA-YOLO. Such a model can filter out weather-specific information and highlight latent information to make detection easier. We discuss IA-YOLO next.

2.1   IA-YOLO

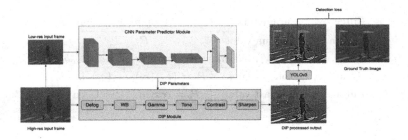

Fig. 1. The training pipeline of the IA-YOLO framework.

The IA-YOLO pipeline consists of (1) a parameter predictor based on a convolutional neural network (CNN), (2) a differentiable image processing module (DIP), and a (3) detection network. Before applying the IA-YOLO pipeline, we resize a given image to have 256 × 256 resolution, and then feed to the CNN parameter predictor. The CNN parameter predictor then tries to predict the parameters of DIP. Following that, the image filtered by the DIP module is fed as input to the YOLOv3 [24] detector for the pedestrian detection task.

CNN-Based Parameter Predictor. As shown in Fig. 1, the CNN parameter predictor module consists of five convolutional blocks followed by two fully-connected layers. Each convolutional block contains a 3 × 3 convolutional layer with stride 2 and a leaky ReLU activation layer. The module tries to understand the global content of the image, such as brightness, color and tone and the degree of fog in order to predict the parameters required by the DIP module. In order to save computation cost, the input images are downsampled to a lower resolution of 256 × 256 using bilinear interpolation. The output channels of the five convolutional layers are 16, 32, 32, 32 and 32, respectively. The output of this module is fed into the DIP module.

DIP Module. The DIP module consists of six differentiable filters with adjustable hyperparameters, namely Defog, White Balance (WB), Gamma, Contrast, Tone and Sharpen. According to Hu et al. [13], the standard color and tone operators, such as White Balance, Gamma, Contrast and Tone, can be expressed as pixel-wise filters. Therefore, the filters can be classified into three categories namely, Pixel-wise, Defog and Sharpen Filters. The Defog filter has been designed for foggy scenes only.

Pixel-Wise Filters. In pixel-wise filters, an input pixel value $P_i = (r_i, g_i, b_i)$ is mapped into an output pixel value $P_o = (r_o, g_o, b_o)$ where (r, g, b) represent the values of the red, green and blue color channels, respectively. The mapping functions of the pixel-wise filters have been shown in Table 1.

Table 1. Mapping functions of pixel wise filters.

Filter	Parameters	Mapping Function
Gamma	G: gamma value	$P_o = P_i^G$
WB	W_r, W_g, W_b: factors	$P_o = (W_r.r_i, W_g.g_i, W_b.b_i)$
Tone	t_i: tone params	$P_o = (L_{t_r}(r_i), L_{t_g}(g_i), L_{t_b}(b_i))$
Filter	α: contrast value	$P_o = \alpha.En(P_i) + (1-\alpha).P_i$

Defog Filter. We used a defog filter designed using the *dark channel prior method* by He *et al.* [11]. The formation of a hazy image can be formulated as follows:

$$I(x) = J(x)t(x) + A(1 - t(x)) \tag{1}$$

where $I(x)$ is the foggy image, $J(x)$ represents the scene radiance (clean image), A is the global atmospheric light, and $t(x)$ is the medium transmission map. The atmospheric light A and the transmission map $t(x)$ need to be obtained to recover the clean image $J(x)$. At first, the dark channel map of the haze image $I(x)$ has been computed and the top 1000 brightest pixels have been picked. Then, the average of those 1000 pixels of the corresponding position of the haze image $I(x)$ has been taken to estimate the value of A.

Sharpen Filter. We use the sharpen filter to enhance the image details. For sharpening the images, the following equation describes the process:

$$F(x, \lambda) = I(x) + \lambda(I(x) - Gau(I(x))) \tag{2}$$

where $I(x)$ is the input image, $Gau(I(x))$ denotes Gaussian filter, and λ is a positive scaling factor.

Detection Module. We use the single-stage YOLOv3 detection network, with the same network architecture and loss function as the original YOLOv3 [24]. YOLOv3 contains darknet-53 which has successive 3×3 and 1×1 convolutional layers based on the idea of ResNet.

2.2 Timed Quality Temporal Logic (TQTL)

Timed Quality Temporal Logic (TQTL) [6,12] is an extension of Timed Propositional Temporal Logic (TPTL) which incorporates syntax and semantics for reasoning about data from perception systems specifically. The syntax defines operators to reason about classes of detected objects and the confidence associated with the detection outputted by perception systems.

TQTL Syntax. A TQTL formula φ over a finite set of predicates $\mathcal{P}$, a finite set of frame number variables (ν_t), and a finite set of object ID variables (ν_{i_d}) can be defined according to the following grammar:

$$\begin{aligned} \varphi::&= \top \mid \mu \mid t.\varphi \mid \exists id@t, \varphi \mid \forall id@t, \varphi \mid \\ & t \leq u + n \mid \neg\varphi \mid \varphi_1 \wedge \varphi_2 \mid \varphi_1 \cup \varphi_2 \end{aligned} \tag{3}$$

The time constraint is $t \leq u + n$, which implies the timespan starting from u and spanning across n consecutive frames.

TQTL Semantics. The semantics of TQTL maps a data stream $\mathcal{D}$, which is a sequence of video frames containing multiple candidate objects in each frame, a frame number $\top$ and a valuation function ν to a real-valued entity. A valuation function in this context is a function that assigns some values to frames and objects present in the corresponding frames. TQTL mainly deals with the task that if a particular object is tracked across multiple frames of a video, the probability of detecting it does not fall below a certain threshold across a certain number of consecutive frames. The function $[\![\cdot]\!]$ can be defined recursively as follows:

$$[\![\top]\!](\mathcal{D}, \tau, \nu) = +\infty$$
$$[\![\mu]\!](\mathcal{D}, \tau, \nu) = \theta(\nu(f_\mu(t_1, ..., t_{n_1}, id_1, ..., id_{n_2})), c)$$
$$[\![t.\varphi]\!](\mathcal{D}, \tau, \nu) = [\![\varphi]\!](\mathcal{D}, \tau, \nu[t \leftarrow \tau])$$
$$[\![\exists id@t, \varphi]\!](\mathcal{D}, \tau, \nu) = \max_{k \epsilon \mathcal{S}(\mathcal{D}_{v(t)})} [\![\varphi]\!](\mathcal{D}, \tau, \nu[id \leftarrow k])$$
$$[\![t \leq u + n]\!](\mathcal{D}, \tau, \nu) = \begin{cases} +\infty, & \text{if } \nu(t) \leq \nu(u) + n, \\ -\infty, & \text{otherwise.} \end{cases}$$
$$[\![\neg\varphi]\!](\mathcal{D}, \tau, \nu) = -[\![\varphi]\!](\mathcal{D}, \tau, \nu)$$
$$[\![\varphi_1 \wedge \varphi_2]\!](\mathcal{D}, \tau, \nu) = \min([\![\varphi_1]\!], [\![\varphi_2]\!](\mathcal{D}, \tau, \nu))$$
$$[\![\varphi_1 \cup \varphi_2]\!](\mathcal{D}, \tau, \nu) = \max_{\tau' \geq \tau} \min \left(\begin{matrix} [\![\varphi_2]\!](\mathcal{D}, \tau', \nu), \\ \min_{\tau'' \in [\tau, \tau')} [\![\varphi_1]\!](\mathcal{D}, \tau'', \nu) \end{matrix} \right)$$

3   Our Approach

The pipeline consists of the IA-YOLO model for processing the input frame and detecting pedestrians along with a TQTL monitor for verifying a given specification under adverse weather conditions. The CNN parameter predictor module of the IA-YOLO takes an input frame and outputs the parameters for the different filters of the DIP module which then generates an enhanced image containing the latent information. In the second step, a TQTL monitor for a given specification φ monitors the output of the IA-YOLO model, reporting whether the specification has been satisfied or violated (Fig. 2).

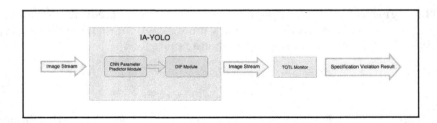

Fig. 2. TQTL Monitoring Pipeline for IA-YOLO

4   Experimental Analysis

In our case, we focus on detecting pedestrians in foggy and night conditions. We aim to validate the following specification: "If a person is detected with a confidence score greater than or equal to 0.3 in a particular frame, then in the next 4 frames, the probability of detecting the same person should never drop below 0.25." This specification is represented by the following TQTL expression:

$$\varphi = \Box(x.\forall id_1 @ x, (C(x, id_1) = Pedestrian \land P(x, id_1) \geq 0.3)$$
$$\rightarrow \Box(y.((x \leq y \land y \leq x + 4)$$
$$\rightarrow C(y, id_1) = Pedestrian \land P(y, id_1) > 0.25))$$

We have chosen the confidence scores to be 0.3 and 0.25 respectively to account for the comparatively poorer performance of detection models in adverse conditions as compared to clear weather conditions and to aid the comparison task between IA-YOLO and vanilla YOLO.

For the purpose of our experimentation, we have created a custom evaluation dataset containing night and foggy driving videos from dash-cam driving videos that are publically available on YouTube. In order to create our dataset, we have taken small clips from these videos where a pedestrian is found be crossing the road front of the car. Note that while these video clips do not contain any ground truth annotations, our evaluation metric is based on the quantitative semantics of TQTL, which do not rely on groundtruth.

To evaluate the models, we compute the robustness of both vanilla YOLO and IA-YOLO on the videos contained the dataset, with respect to the above specification φ. The results are shown in Table 2, and Fig. 3 and Fig. 4 show some examples of sequences of images that satisfy or violate the specification φ. We

Table 2. Robustness values achieved on custom dataset using Vanilla YOLO and IA-YOLO models against φ.

Weather Condition	Robustness φ	
	Vanilla YOLO	IA-YOLO
Foggy	−0.25	0.31
	−0.25	0.36
	−0.25	0.29
	−0.25	0.51
Night	0.28	0.54
	0.10	0.22
	−0.25	0.22
	0.07	0.3
	0.29	0.58
	−0.25	0.18

(a) vanilla YOLO: Pedestrian detected and TQTL formula satisfied.

(b) IA-YOLO: Pedestrian detected and TQTL formula satisfied.

Fig. 3. Monitoring results in night conditions.

(a) vanilla YOLO: Pedestrian detected but TQTL formula violated.

(b) IA-YOLO: Pedestrian detected and TQTL formula satisfied.

Fig. 4. Monitoring results in foggy conditions.

find that vanilla YOLO does not sufficiently satisfy the TQTL specification in foggy conditions, but detects pedestrians reasonably well night-time conditions. On the other hand, the IA-YOLO model is found to be able to detect pedestrians succesfully in both foggy and night conditions.

5 Conclusion

The IA-YOLO model has been able to detect pedestrians satisfactorily in foggy and night conditions. IA-YOLO performs better as compared to vanilla YOLO in adverse conditions. However, we found some cases where it fails to detect pedestrians in one of the consecutive frames with the desired level of confidence. The robustness of this model has been estimated using TQTL which has been able to correctly verify the required specification. This quality metric will help in debugging or improving the existing model and lead to better detection results in foggy and night conditions in a safety-critical context.

We plan to develop a more robust YOLO model for object detection in low-light conditions by fine-tuning the current model. We also aim to reduce the runtime of the entire monitoring process by only applying the DIP module on the frames where the TQTL monitor fails instead of all the frames. Moreover, we hope to create a training dataset which will be used to train the CNN-PP module more efficiently with the images which are flagged as "violated" by the TQTL monitor.

Acknowledgement. The authors would like to thank the anonymous reviewers for their feedback. This work was supported by the National Science Foundation through the following grants: CAREER award (SHF-2048094), CNS-1932620, CNS-2039087, FMitF-1837131, CCF-SHF-1932620, the Airbus Institute for Engineering Research, and funding by Toyota R&D and Siemens Corporate Research through the USC Center for Autonomy and AI.

References

1. Autonomous Vehicle Collision Reports. Technical report, California Department of Motor Vehicles (2023). www.dmv.ca.gov/portal/vehicle-industry-services/autonomous-vehicles/autonomous-vehicle-collision-reports/
2. Antonante, P., Spivak, D.I., Carlone, L.: Monitoring and Diagnosability of Perception Systems. arXiv:2005.11816 [cs] (2020)
3. Balakrishnan, A., Deshmukh, J., Hoxha, B., Yamaguchi, T., Fainekos, G.: PerceMon: online monitoring for perception systems. In: Feng, L., Fisman, D. (eds.) RV 2021. LNCS, vol. 12974, pp. 297–308. Springer, Cham (2021). https://doi.org/10.1007/978-3-030-88494-9_18
4. Balakrishnan, A., et al.: Specifying and evaluating quality metrics for vision-based perception systems. In: 2019 Design, Automation Test in Europe Conference Exhibition (DATE), pp. 1433–1438 (2019). https://doi.org/10.23919/DATE.2019.8715114
5. Dai, J., Li, Y., He, K., Sun, J.: R-FCN: object detection via region-based fully convolutional networks. In: Advances in Neural Information Processing Systems, vol. 29 (2016)
6. Dokhanchi, A., Amor, H.B., Deshmukh, J.V., Fainekos, G.: Evaluating perception systems for autonomous vehicles using quality temporal logic. In: Colombo, C., Leucker, M. (eds.) RV 2018. LNCS, vol. 11237, pp. 409–416. Springer, Cham (2018). https://doi.org/10.1007/978-3-030-03769-7_23

7. Dokhanchi, A., Hoxha, B., Tuncali, C.E., Fainekos, G.: An efficient algorithm for monitoring practical TPTL specifications. In: 2016 ACM/IEEE International Conference on Formal Methods and Models for System Design (MEMOCODE), pp. 184–193. IEEE (2016)

8. Everingham, M., Eslami, S.M.A., Van Gool, L., Williams, C.K.I., Winn, J., Zisserman, A.: The pascal visual object classes challenge: a retrospective. Int. J. Comput. Vision **111**(1), 98–136 (2015). https://doi.org/10.1007/s11263-014-0733-5

9. Girshick, R.: Fast R-CNN. In: 2015 IEEE International Conference on Computer Vision (ICCV), pp. 1440–1448 (2015). https://doi.org/10.1109/ICCV.2015.169

10. He, K., Gkioxari, G., Dollár, P., Girshick, R.: Mask R-CNN. In: Proceedings of the IEEE International Conference on Computer Vision, pp. 2961–2969 (2017)

11. He, K., Sun, J., Tang, X.: Single image haze removal using dark channel prior. IEEE Trans. Pattern Anal. Mach. Intell. **33**(12), 2341–2353 (2010)

12. Hekmatnejad, M.: Formalizing Safety, Perception, and Mission Requirements for Testing and Planning in Autonomous Vehicles. Ph.D. thesis, Arizona State University (2021)

13. Hu, Y., He, H., Xu, C., Wang, B., Lin, S.: Exposure: a white-box photo postprocessing framework. ACM Trans. Graph. (TOG) **37**(2), 1–17 (2018)

14. Lin, T.Y., Dollár, P., Girshick, R., He, K., Hariharan, B., Belongie, S.: Feature pyramid networks for object detection. In: Proceedings of the IEEE Conference on Computer Vision and Pattern Recognition, pp. 2117–2125 (2017)

15. Lin, T.Y., Goyal, P., Girshick, R., He, K., Dollár, P.: Focal loss for dense object detection. In: Proceedings of the IEEE International Conference on Computer Vision, pp. 2980–2988 (2017)

16. Liu, W., et al.: SSD: single shot multibox detector. In: Leibe, B., Matas, J., Sebe, N., Welling, M. (eds.) ECCV 2016. LNCS, vol. 9905, pp. 21–37. Springer, Cham (2016). https://doi.org/10.1007/978-3-319-46448-0_2

17. Liu, W., Ren, G., Yu, R., Guo, S., Zhu, J., Zhang, L.: Image-adaptive YOLO for object detection in adverse weather conditions. In: Proceedings of the AAAI Conference on Artificial Intelligence (2022)

18. Michaelis, C., et al.: Benchmarking Robustness in Object Detection: Autonomous Driving when Winter is Coming (2020). arXiv:1907.07484 [cs, stat]

19. Narasimhan, S.G., Nayar, S.K.: Chromatic framework for vision in bad weather. In: Proceedings IEEE Conference on Computer Vision and Pattern Recognition. CVPR 2000 (Cat. No. PR00662), vol. 1, pp. 598–605. IEEE (2000)

20. Padilla, R., Netto, S.L., da Silva, E.A.B.: A survey on performance metrics for object-detection algorithms. In: 2020 International Conference on Systems, Signals and Image Processing (IWSSIP), pp. 237–242 (2020). https://doi.org/10.1109/IWSSIP48289.2020.9145130, iSSN: 2157-8702

21. Padilla, R., Passos, W.L., Dias, T.L.B., Netto, S.L., da Silva, E.A.B.: A comparative analysis of object detection metrics with a companion open-source toolkit. Electronics **10**(3), 279 (2021). https://doi.org/10.3390/electronics10030279

22. Qin, Q., Chang, K., Huang, M., Li, G.: DENet: detection-driven enhancement network for object detection under adverse weather conditions. In: Proceedings of the Asian Conference on Computer Vision, pp. 2813–2829 (2022)

23. Redmon, J., Divvala, S., Girshick, R., Farhadi, A.: You only look once: unified, real-time object detection. In: Proceedings of the IEEE Conference on Computer Vision and Pattern Recognition, pp. 779–788 (2016)

24. Redmon, J., Farhadi, A.: YOLOv3: an incremental improvement. arXiv preprint arXiv:1804.02767 (2018)

25. Ren, S., He, K., Girshick, R., Sun, J.: Faster R-CNN: towards real-time object detection with region proposal networks. In: Advances in Neural Information Processing Systems, vol. 28 (2015)
26. Schechner, Y.Y., Narasimhan, S.G., Nayar, S.K.: Instant dehazing of images using polarization. In: Proceedings of the 2001 IEEE Computer Society Conference on Computer Vision and Pattern Recognition. CVPR 2001, vol. 1, pp. I–I. IEEE (2001)
27. Teeti, I., Musat, V., Khan, S., Rast, A., Cuzzolin, F., Bradley, A.: Vision in adverse weather: Augmentation using CycleGANs with various object detectors for robust perception in autonomous racing (2023). arXiv:2201.03246 [cs]
28. Wu, B., Iandola, F., Jin, P.H., Keutzer, K.: SqueezeDet: unified, small, low power fully convolutional neural networks for real-time object detection for autonomous driving. In: Proceedings of the IEEE Conference on Computer Vision and Pattern Recognition Workshops, pp. 129–137 (2017)
29. Xu, H., Gao, Y., Yu, F., Darrell, T.: End-to-end learning of driving models from large-scale video datasets. In: Proceedings of the IEEE Conference on Computer Vision and Pattern Recognition, pp. 2174–2182 (2017)
30. Xu, Y., Weaver, J.B., Healy, D.M., Lu, J.: Wavelet transform domain filters: a spatially selective noise filtration technique. IEEE Trans. Image Process. $3(6)$, 747–758 (1994)

Tutorials

Instrumentation for RV: From Basic Monitoring to Advanced Use Cases

Chukri Soueidi[✉][iD] and Yliès Falcone[✉][iD]

Univ. Grenoble Alpes, CNRS, Inria, Grenoble INP, LIG, 38000 Grenoble, France
{chukri.soueidi,ylies.falcone}@univ-grenoble-alpes.fr

Abstract. Instrumentation is crucial in Runtime Verification because it should ensure that monitors are fed with relevant and accurate information about the executing program under monitoring. While expressive instrumentation is desirable to handle any possible monitoring scenario, instrumentation should also efficiently capture the just-needed information and impact the monitoring program as least as possible. This tutorial comprehensively overviews the instrumentation process and considerations for single and multithreaded programs. We discuss often overlooked aspects in instrumenting multithreaded programs. We also cover metrics for evaluating the efficiency and effectiveness of instrumentation. We use four hands-on use cases to apply the introduced concepts and provide practical guidance on choosing and applying instrumentation for runtime verification.

1 Introduction

Ensuring software correctness often necessitates abstracting its behavior into suitable models and subsequently verifying whether these models adhere to properties. The predominant approach to modeling software behavior in monitoring and runtime verification involves observing the software execution and abstracting it into a *trace of events*. Extracting these events frequently relies on *instrumentation*, a technique that entails transforming the base program. Instrumentation consists of two main steps: 1) identifying the program points corresponding to the events of interest, 2) inserting additional code into the base program to extract information.

Choosing an instrumentation framework is a critical step in the runtime verification process. For example, bytecode manipulation libraries such as ASM [16], BCEL [9], and Soot [49] allow for extensive low-level coverage and bytecode transformations. However, implementing basic instrumentation for runtime verification with these can be quite verbose and demands a certain level of expertise from the user. On the other hand, aspect-oriented programming frameworks like AspectJ [29] provide a high-level language for specifying instrumentation. However, these frameworks have limited capabilities and introduce significant overhead. One main limitation is not being able to instrument at the bytecode

P. Katsaros and L. Nenzi (Eds.): RV 2023, LNCS 14245, pp. 403–427, 2023.
https://doi.org/10.1007/978-3-031-44267-4_23

level hindering their applicability in multithreaded programs and low-level monitoring scenarios. Other tools offer a balance between abstraction and expressiveness. For example, DiSL [35] offers advanced features targeting profiling, while BISM [46], which is tailored towards runtime verification, reduces overhead on execution and allows for arbitrary code insertion, which is needed for inlining code.

We cover several factors that influence the selection of an instrumentation technique in runtime verification encompassing multiple factors such as monitoring goals, observation granularity, specification, and trace semantics [24]. For instance, control-flow integrity monitoring requires low-level details [27], while typestate property monitoring focuses on high-level values [15,22,27]. Users can choose appropriate techniques by considering these parameters and others related to monitoring concurrent programs. Monitoring single-threaded programs relies on accurate instrumentation, while concurrent systems face challenges with event collection from multiple threads and components [12,23]. Ensuring correct event order is vital but may incur overhead. Various tradeoffs and optimizations help reduce the overhead associated with these challenges. Furthermore, the specification and parallelism in the monitored program determine a specific abstraction of the program execution. For single-threaded programs, a linear trace with totally ordered events suffices. In contrast, multithreaded programs often require a partial order of events, necessitating low-level instrumentation to capture synchronization [45]. Alternative approaches, such as Opportunistic Monitoring [43], define a 2-level specification of monitors, requiring a different execution abstraction that includes certain assumptions.

We present four use cases demonstrating different instrumentation requirements. The first use case, Instrumentation at the Control Flow Level, focuses on low-level program instrumentation in monitoring the control flow integrity. The second use case, Residual Runtime Verification, employs static verification to identify safe execution paths and perform residual runtime verification for unproven parts. This approach is valuable when seeking to optimize monitoring overhead and reduce resource consumption. The third use case, Concurrent Traces for Online Monitoring, tackles concurrent program monitoring challenges with real-time trace collection. This case is essential for efficient monitoring in multithreaded applications that require a partial order of events and low-level instrumentation to capture synchronization. Finally, Opportunistic Monitoring deploys monitors to specific threads that exchange information only at designated synchronization points. This use case requires specific execution abstractions and assumptions aiming to reduce overhead and minimize interference with verdict delay.

2   Understanding Instrumentation

Dynamic analysis and verification techniques such as testing, profiling, and runtime verification involve examining a program while it's running. These techniques analyze a behavioral model extracted from the program in order to identify errors, bugs, or unusual behaviors. In this section, we provide an overview of a crucial component of these techniques: *instrumentation*. We discuss various considerations that affect the choice of instrumentation technique. Specifically, we focus on managed languages, with a particular emphasis on JVM languages.

2.1 Unveiling the Complete Picture

Verification and analysis techniques are designed to focus on certain behavioral aspects of the system under study. Consequently, they require distinct behavioral *models* that accurately encapsulate the specific aspects of the system that are relevant to their intended reasoning. These models represent the *actual* behavior of the system suppressing irrelevant details and enabling the application of automated analysis. The term model is extended here to include any artifact generated to represent the system's behavior including logs, traces, automata, etc. Figure 1 illustrates the typical steps involved in the process of generating such models.

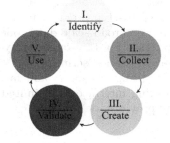

Fig. 1. Cyclic process of model generation.

The model generation process begins by **identifying elements of interest** within the program. This step involves recognizing relevant elements based on user observation or a systematic analysis, which could include structural components or specific actions. Following this, the process involves **collecting information** from these identified elements. Depending on the data required, this could be done statically or at runtime, especially when certain required information, such as the values of variables or program input, is only available during runtime. Once the necessary information has been gathered, along with any other assumptions, the next step is **creating the model**. Typically, the model is a mathematical object or a structured log, designed to be suitable for the analysis task. To ensure its accuracy and suitability for the intended analysis, the model may then undergo a **validation process**. Finally, the **model is used for the intended analysis**. It can serve various purposes, such as being compared with another model in processes like model checking [21] or runtime verification [12], or it can be used to generate test cases, thereby achieving the desired analysis results. While steps I and II assume a white-box approach to model generation, some processes start with execution traces, such as specification mining [13,31,38]. Moreover, these steps can overlap, and the cycle can be reiterated for refinement.

2.2   Observing the Execution

Observation is crucial for the completion of steps I, II, and III of the model generation process for dynamic techniques. Different methods can be utilized for observing an executing program, each offering unique capabilities. Some are beyond the scope of this discussion, such as hardware performance counters and operating system tracing.

Debugging Interfaces. Managed languages usually feature built-in debugging interfaces, such as the Java Debug Interface (JDI). Debuggers can use these interfaces to manage a range of events, including setting breakpoints and watchpoints, performing step-by-step execution, controlling threads, handling exceptions, and inspecting or modifying variables and fields. However, while these debugging interfaces are powerful for step-by-step program inspection, they are not inherently designed for automated or broad-scale data collection. Manual setting of breakpoints and data extraction for thousands of events can be impractical, often leading users to resort to ad-hoc scripting for automation. This requires proficiency in compatible scripting languages and familiarity with the debugger's API. Moreover, debugging interfaces are limited to the event types and information they inherently provide.

Execution Callbacks. Managed languages like Java provide capabilities to register callbacks for specific execution events via the Java Virtual Machine Tool Interface (JVMTI). This native interface allows interaction with the JVM's internal events, including thread start and end, method entry and exit, field access and alteration, exception handling, and more. This level of coverage offers detailed JVM activity monitoring, including monitoring internal environment events not directly linked to specific program instructions. Nevertheless, JVMTI presents limitations. Its scope of observation is confined to the event types and data it provides. Should custom events or additional context information be needed, the process can be complex and demand substantial platform knowledge.

Instrumentation. Instrumentation involves augmenting a program with additional code to collect data during its execution, often automated with the help of instrumentation languages. Unlike other observation techniques, instrumentation lets the user define events by identifying arbitrary sequences of instructions in the program, capturing a wide variety of behavioral aspects from fine-grained events such as local variable assignments to coarse-grained ones like method executions. While it's possible to perform instrumentation manually, it becomes significantly complex and prone to errors for large programs or when only a compiled version of the code is accessible. Compared to other observation methods, instrumentation is usually more portable, simpler, and performs better. In JVM, for instance, this added code can be optimized by the JIT compiler, which can significantly reduce the instrumentation overhead. However, it can't observe internal environment-executed events not directly linked to specific program instructions, such as Java's garbage collection. Also, injecting code can modify program behavior, which can cause issues if the program is already in production.

2.3   Instrumentation for Runtime Verification

Runtime verification is a field focused on analyzing system executions, typically to verify if they satisfy or violate a particular property. A property under verification represents a set of constraints or behaviors that the system is expected to adhere to, formalized in terms of abstract events drawn from an alphabet denoted as Σ_a. This process usually encompasses three stages. First, a monitor is created from the property, referred to as *monitor synthesis*. This monitor interprets events from a system and gives outcomes based on the property's current satisfaction. Next, the program is instrumented to generate relevant events for the monitor, known as system *instrumentation*. Seen as a generator of concrete events, denoted as Σ_c, the system's execution should be mapped into a trace of abstract events, rendering it suitable for runtime analysis. Instrumentation plays a key role in capturing these concrete events and mapping them into corresponding abstract ones to construct the suitable trace which is the model needed by the monitor. These concrete events correspond to locations in the program source code we refer to as *shadows* and execute at specific points the in the program we refer to as *joinpoints*, and the instrumentation process consists of adding extra code at these locations to capture the concrete events, we refer to this extra code as *advice*. Lastly, the system's execution is analyzed by the monitor, either in real-time or post-execution from logged events, a phase termed *execution analysis*. Instrumentation is particularly suitable for runtime verification. It provides flexibility in capturing concrete events by pinpointing arbitrary locations in the source code, as opposed to being limited to specific events provided by the execution environment.

2.4   Instrumentation Considerations for Runtime Verification

In this section, we go through various considerations for various applications of instrumentation for runtime verification, depicted in Fig. 2. We will go through some of these in the following sections and others will be covered in the rest of the tutorial.

The Program. Various aspects of the program must be taken into consideration when selecting an instrumentation language. Figure 3 depicts some of these considerations. For **concurrent** programs, instrumentation should be capable

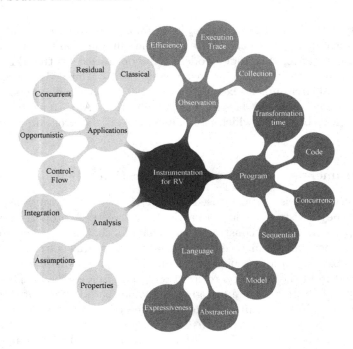

Fig. 2. Considerations for RV Instrumentation

of identifying and capturing the program's synchronization actions. These may be specified using both low-level concurrency **primitives** (such as synchronized blocks, volatile variables, lock interfaces, and atomic classes) and high-level abstractions (such as the fork-join framework and software transactional memory [26,32]). Other applications may be implemented using message-passing frameworks such as Akka [3]. Instrumentation may be needed at different stages of the program deployment. At the **source** level, it often necessitates compilation facilities and requires access to the application's source code. Weaving at the **bytecode** has several advantages. It is often high-level enough to easily recognize constructs of the original language, even without direct access to the source code. Moreover, it is portable across different languages as many languages compile to the same bytecode such as Java, Scala, Kotlin, and Groovy. Program **transformation** (weaving of instrumented code) can occur at different stages as well. **Independent** instrumentation is possible anytime resulting in a new statically instrumented program. However, it is limited to the code packaged within the application itself and may not extend to instrumenting Java class libraries used by the application. **Load-time** instrumentation intercepts class loading and performs instrumentation before a class is linked in the Java Virtual Machine (JVM). This allows also for targeting the libraries used by the application.

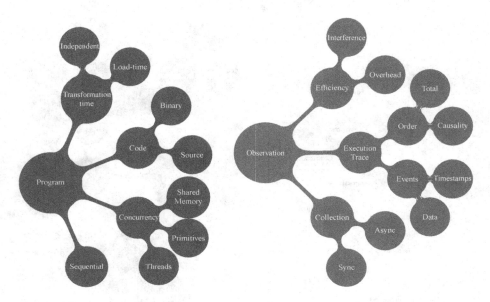

Fig. 3. Program Considerations   **Fig. 4.** Observation Considerations

Observation. In runtime verification, event **traces** serve as models for property-based detection and prediction techniques. An **event** typically captures an important action or a change in the system's state that is under observation. They may represent the program's state at a specific execution point, or they can be triggered by a program action. Depending on the analysis aim, **data** accompanying events may incorporate values from the program's memory, and various **time** representations like current time. Moreover, if events are tracking state changes, the observation should retain some memory instead of having to extract all the values of pertinent variables at each event. Figure 4 depicts some of the program observation considerations at runtime.

When properties necessitate reasoning about program concurrency, establishing **causality** between events is essential during trace collection. Causality is best represented as a partial order over events, compatible with various formalisms for the behavior of concurrent programs like weak memory consistency models [4,6,34] and Mazurkiewicz traces [25,37]. Collecting the trace of events can be done either **synchronously** or **asynchronously**. Synchronous refers to processing data simultaneously with its collection, whereas asynchronous involves receiving events and processing them at a later time. Asynchronous trace collection is ideal for scenarios where the monitoring overhead cannot be afforded and a small delay in the verdict can be tolerated. For instance, in real-time systems where the system is expected to produce a result within a defined strict deadline [42].

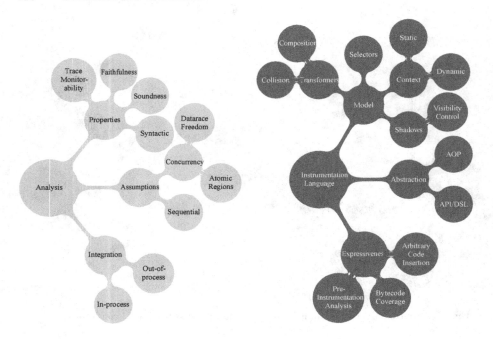

Fig. 5. Analysis Considerations   **Fig. 6.** Language Considerations

The Analysis. The execution analysis considerations are depicted in Fig. 5. Depending on the analysis different **properties** may be desired. For example, if the analysis is to check for the occurrence of a specific event, then the instrumentation should be able to capture the event. Other concurrency-related properties that are concerned with event ordering may be desired such as **soundness**, **faithfulness**, and **trace monitorability** [45] (see Sect. 7.3). These properties are affected by the completeness and correctness of the instrumentation. Monitoring techniques generally operate with the **assumption** of instrumentation completeness and correctness. Other approaches such as [48] address runtime verification with incomplete or uncertain information. Some approaches assume certain concurrency-related properties such as **data-race freedom** and **atomic regions** [43] to reduce the instrumentation points hence overhead and complexity. Moreover, the analysis integration with the program has a direct effect on the instrumentation. For instance, for **out-of-process** analysis, the instrumentation should extract all the necessary information to perform the analysis. Whereas in **in-process** analysis, the analysis typically has access to the program's state and can extract the necessary information itself.

The Instrumentation Language. An instrumentation language should equip users to handle three key considerations: identifying relevant program execution points (*joinpoints*), where events are extracted, which correspond to program code elements; specifying the necessary contextual information to be extracted with these events; and defining the destination of these events, detailing how and where they will be consumed. The instrumentation language considerations are depicted in Fig. 6. The usability of an instrumentation language is further characterized by two critical aspects: its **expressiveness** and the level of **abstraction**. Expressiveness refers to the language's ability to extract substantial information from the bytecode and modify the program's execution. On the other hand, abstraction relates to the complexity of low-level details that users must deal with in order to specify instrumentation.

Identifying joinpoints can be at the bytecode level or the source code level. At these joinpoints, a language should facilitate the extraction of either **static** information (compile-time information) or **dynamic** information (runtime information). Static information refers to information that is available at compile time, such as the name of a method or the type of a variable. Dynamic information refers to information that is only available at runtime, such as the value of a variable or the current thread. Finally, the instrumentation language should provide means to consume the extracted information. This can be done by either adding a hook to a monitor class passing this information or by weaving code to the program itself. As for the implementation, these languages are typically provided either as **external** domain-specific languages or as **internal** API-Based languages. External DSLs are often more accessible to domain experts due to the syntax's inherent focus on domain-specific concerns. In contrast, internal DSLs are implemented within a host language and integrate more seamlessly with it, and are more accessible to developers familiar with the host language.

Applications. In this paper, we examine five use cases that demonstrate different applications of instrumentation, which we will discuss further in Sect. 7. Here, we focus on the considerations relevant to selecting an instrumentation language for each of these use cases. In control-flow integrity monitoring, the program's control flow must not be altered, necessitating the reevaluation of conditional jumps by a monitor. This use case requires **bytecode coverage** to extract low-level details and control flow information. For concurrent and opportunistic monitoring, the instrumentation should be able to capture synchronization events in the program, which often result from low-level instructions. This also requires bytecode visibility. Additionally, in some cases, instrumentation advice may need to be inserted across nonadjacent bytecode instructions, necessitating **arbitrary code insertion**. In residual runtime verification, a pre-instrumentation static analysis is used to identify safe execution paths. The instrumentation must then extract the results of this analysis to guide its own process. This scenario calls for **pre-instrumentation analysis** to pinpoint safe paths. Additionally, it requires **visibility control**, which ensures the information is properly relayed to the instrumentation.

3   Instrumentation Requirements

Correctness and Completeness. Monitoring techniques assume the completeness and correctness of instrumentation in capturing events [12], however, this assumption is not always valid. For manual instrumentation, it is easy to miss identifying some locations of interest. Also, automated instrumentation can miss some events at runtime due to errors and exceptions raised by the runtime. Some instrumentation techniques wrap the advice with try-catch blocks to avoid system crashes. Although this guarantees the stability of the system, it can lead to missing events without being noticed. It is recommended to disable exception handling when instrumenting the program for the first time.

Non-interference. Ensuring non-interference is crucial to prevent disturbing the program's critical behaviors. Instrumentation should avoid altering aspects such as parallelism, event order, variable values, control flow, and thread scheduling. In a study by [28], the authors identify several interference problems, including deadlocks, state corruption, and JVM crashes, which can be unintended byproducts of instrumentation.

Memory Depletion. In-process monitoring makes memory management crucial. Large data storage for analysis risks depleting memory and potentially crashing the application. Hence, an effective data management strategy should be integral to information extraction with instrumentation. Efficient data structures can optimize memory use and prevent interference with memory management. For example, using integer identifiers for event types instead of string descriptions, or extracting unique hash IDs rather than retaining full object references, can be beneficial when applicable.

Environment Compatibility. Bytecode verification failures can occur in the JVM for instance due to issues such as incorrect bytecode manipulation, invalid stack or local variable states, control flow problems, or incompatible bytecode versions. In some cases, turning off bytecode verification can be a viable option, but it is not recommended as it can lead to unexpected behavior and crashes. Moreover, Java enforces a 64 KB maximum limit per method, and extensive instrumentation can exceed this limit, leading to compilation errors. These errors can sometimes be avoided by deferring the event construction to a separate method and passing the required object references to it.

4   How to Evaluate Instrumentation

Overhead. Evaluating the impact of instrumentation on a program often involves measuring execution time and memory consumption overheads. For precise measurements, using a dedicated machine and repeating the process multiple times is recommended. Profilers like [1,2] can yield the most accurate measurements. Below, we detail some techniques for measuring these overheads. To measure execution time overhead, compare the execution time of the instrumented program with the original one. One method involves inserting timers (via instrumentation) to capture timestamps at the program's entry and exit points. A nonobtrusive alternative is using a command-line benchmarking tool such as [41], offering features like warmup runs and statistical analysis of results. Memory consumption in the JVM is influenced by multiple factors, including the JVM internals and garbage collection. A good estimate of memory consumption can be obtained by calculating the heap and non-heap memory usage after forcing a garbage collection cycle, measured before the program's exit point. A specialized memory measurement virtual machine like [33] can also be employed.

Instrumentation Intensity. This synthetic metric provides an understanding of the extent of the code that has been instrumented. It is a measure of the number of code instructions that have been adjusted for instrumentation purposes, as a proportion of total code instructions. If a larger part of the code has been modified, the instrumentation intensity is higher. This metric is useful for evaluating the overall coverage of the instrumentation process and its impact on the codebase. For instance, when capturing method calls, consider all method calls invoked at runtime and compare this to the number of those method calls that have been instrumented.

Instrumentation Code Latency. Instrumentation code latency measures exactly the time taken for the execution of the added instrumentation code only. Here the time before and after the advice executes is measured or both timestamps are extracted with the event and the difference is calculated at the monitor side. In concurrent programs, this metric provides insight into the extent to which instrumentation is interfering and affecting the parallelism of the program when compared to the original program and the overall overhead mentioned above provided that it also includes extracting such timestamps.

5   Existing Instrumentation Frameworks

5.1   Bytecode Manipulation Libraries

We discuss some bytecode manipulation libraries that have been used in runtime verification tools. These libraries offer highly expressive languages for bytecode manipulation and can perform any instrumentation scenario. However, they require a good understanding of bytecode semantics. They typically provide mechanisms for program traversal, bytecode manipulation, and bytecode generation with varying levels of abstraction. *ASM* [16] for instance is a lightweight framework that provides two APIs: a visitor-based API that allows efficient traversal and manipulation of bytecode, and a tree-based API that provides a higher level of abstraction. *BCEL* [9] contains various tools like the JustIce byte code verifier and has been used successfully in numerous applications including compilers, optimizers, and code analysis tools. *Javassist* [20] provides two levels of API: source level and bytecode level. The former does not require the developer to understand Java bytecode, making it a suitable choice for those who prefer working at a higher level of abstraction. *CGLIB* [40] is a bytecode generation library that allows developers to extend Java classes and create new ones at runtime. *Soot* [49] is a framework for analyzing and transforming Java and Android applications. It generates several intermediate representations (IRs) of the program, including Jimple, a Java-specific IR. It provides several built-in static analyses such as call-graph construction, data-flow analysis, taint analysis, and points-to analysis.

5.2 Aspect Oriented Languages

AspectJ [29] is a standard aspect-oriented programming (AOP) [30] framework that is widely used for runtime verification, debugging, and logging. AspectJ offers a rich pointcut expression language for selecting and capturing joinpoints including dynamic pointcuts which are runtime conditional expressions that selectively apply advice based on the state or context of the executing program. However, AspectJ cannot capture bytecode instructions and basic block joinpoints, which limits its usefulness in many instrumentation tasks. *DiSL* [35] is a more feature-rich tool covering bytecode-level instrumentation framework and also following an aspect-oriented approach. DiSL offers an extensible joinpoint model and provides various advanced features such as dynamic dispatch for interference avoidance among multiple instrumentations. It is a suitable framework for instrumentation-heavy dynamic analysis such as profiling.

Both AspectJ and DiSL follow the pointcut/advice model. In this approach, users can specify advice (actions meant to be executed at joinpoints) using standard Java syntax. While AspectJ wraps these actions within methods triggered at the joinpoint, DiSL weaves the advice right into the application, ensuring it's directly inlined at the joinpoint. The limitation, however, is that users can only provide code to be inserted at these joinpoints. They cannot execute or assess this code during the instrumentation phase.

5.3 The Gap Between Bytecode Libraries and AOP Frameworks

Choosing an appropriate instrumentation language largely depends on the specifics of each use case, with each requiring a unique set of features. Existing AOP languages, such as AspectJ and DiSL, simplify the specification of instrumentation. However, they also limit the user's control over the traversal of a program's bytecode. AspectJ restricts the ability to manipulate code beyond predefined join points. Consequently, performing tasks like pre-instrumentation analysis or arbitrary code insertion, that may be needed for performing an instrumentation task, can be challenging with AOP languages. They typically require ad-hoc customizations or a fallback to bytecode manipulation libraries. On the other hand, most bytecode manipulation libraries provide full control over program traversal and allow various manipulations. However, these libraries are verbose and require a high degree of expertise to use effectively. Therefore, there is a pressing need for a more comprehensive approach to instrumentation. Ideally, this approach would combine the simplicity of the point-cut/advice model from AOP languages with the flexibility and control of bytecode manipulation libraries. In the following section, we will introduce BISM (Bytecode-Level Instrumentation for Software Monitoring) an instrumentation framework that addresses such a need.

6   A Comprehensive Instrumentation Approach: BISM

BISM [46,47], short for Bytecode-Level Instrumentation for Software Monitoring, is a lightweight Java instrumentation tool created for runtime verification and enforcement. Its design takes inspiration from aspect-oriented programming, but instead of following the common pointcut/advice model used by tools like AspectJ and DiSL, BISM introduces its own approach. In BISM, the instrumentation requirements are defined using *transformers*. These transformers are dedicated classes that handle both the selection of joinpoints and the inlining of advice. Unlike AspectJ and DiSL where only the advice can be specified and in plain Java, BISM requires advice to be defined using its instrumentation language. Notably, within these transformers, users have the flexibility to execute code at the time of instrumentation.

6.1   Instrumentation Model

A *joinpoint* in BISM refers to a specific configuration of the base program during its execution, characterized by both static and dynamic context information. *Shadows*, on the other hand, are used to demarcate specific bytecode regions in the program. They are defined as pairs that fundamentally include a bytecode instruction identifier and a direction, either *before* or *after* the instruction. These shadows are used to specify the precise regions in the bytecode where user-specified advice will be woven. In essence, joinpoints captured by BISM correspond to these bytecode regions given by shadows. BISM selectors are designed to match specific subsets of these shadows, enabling users to select desired segments of the code for instrumentation.

6.2   Instrumentation Language

BISM provides a high-level instrumentation language that allows users to specify instrumentation directives concisely. *Selectors* are used to select and capture joinpoints from the program execution. BISM provides selectors at the instruction, basic block, method, and class levels. Moreover, it provides control-flow selectors that allow users to select joinpoints based on the control-flow graph of the program. This variety of selectors allows users to specify instrumentation directives at different levels of granularity. Listing 1.1 shows the main available selectors.

```
Before/AfterInstruction          OnBasicBlockEnter/Exit
Before/AfterMethodCall           OnTrue/FalseBranchEnter
OnFieldSet/Get                   OnMethodEnter/Exit
```
Listing 1.1. BISM selectors

Within these selectors, filtering the joinpoints can be achieved with the help of guards and type patterns that support wildcard matching (see example below). Moreover, pointcuts allow users to combine multiple selectors under a single name. For contextual information extraction, BISM provides a set of *context objects* that can be used to extract the full static and dynamic information from the program. Moreover, it performs lightweight analysis on the program bytecode to provide additional out-of-the-box information about the program methods such as control-flow information and the states of the stack frames. Additionally, BISM provides *advice* methods such as method invocation `invoke` and `print` that allow the extraction of this information from the running program and also an `insert` method that allows users to inline arbitrary code at the joinpoints.

   BISM provides two distinct approaches for implementing transformers: an API-based and an external DSL approach. With the API approach, users define transformers in Java classes. This approach provides users with a high degree of control over the instrumentation process. The DSL approach, on the other hand, provides a declarative way of specifying instrumentation directives. It provides a subset of the language constructs available in the API approach, but it is more concise and easier to use. The tool offers two instrumentation modes: *build-time* mode, which allows for instrumenting the compiled classes of the program, and *load-time* mode, which acts as a Java Agent that intercepts and instruments classes before linking, including some of those from the Java class library. It also includes a visualization module that displays the control-flow graphs and code changes within instrumented methods.

7   Insrumentation Use Cases

In this section, we present different use cases of instrumentation for runtime verification, some that require considerations that are often beyond the scope of existing instrumentation frameworks. We discuss limitations in addressing these use cases with well-adopted tools and how BISM can be used to address these challenges.

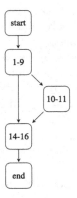

Fig. 7. A method using Iterators in Java, and its CFG.

7.1   Classical Example

Figure 7, shows a Java method along with its control-flow graph (CFG). We are interested to monitor the **SafeIterator** property which specifies that a `Collection` should not be updated when an iterator associated with it is created and being used. This scenario can be effectively handled by all instrumentation frameworks we discuss in this paper. Listing 1.2 shows a fragment of a transformer that can be used in a parametric monitoring setup [10,19] to instrument the program for the **SafeIterator** property. The BISM transformer, written in Java, uses the selector `afterMethodCall` to capture the return of an `Iterator` created from a `List.iterator()` method call. It uses the dynamic context object provided to retrieve the associated objects with the event, and pushes them into a list. Then, invokes a monitor passing the extracted information. Listing 1.3 shows an equivalent transformer written with the DSL.

```
public class IteratorTransformer extends Transformer {
    public void afterMethodCall(MethodCall mc, DynamicContext dc){
        // Filter to only method of interest
        if (mc.methodName.equals("iterator") && mc.methodOwner.endsWith("List")) {
            // Access to dynamic data
            DynamicValue list = dc.getMethodReceiver();
            DynamicValue iterator = dc.getMethodResult();
            // Create an ArrayList in the target method
            LocalArray la = dc.createLocalArray(mc.method, Object.class);
            dc.addToLocalArray(la,list);
            dc.addToLocalArray(la,iterator);
            // Invoke the monitor after passing arguments
            StaticInvocation sti =
                new StaticInvocation("monitors.SafeListMonitor", "receive");
            sti.addParameter("create");
            sti.addParameter(la);
            invoke(sti);
        }
    }
}
```

Listing 1.2. A BISM transformer written in Java that intercepts the creation of an iterator

```
pointcut pc1 after MethodCall(* *.List.iterator())

event e1(["create",[getMethodReceiver,getMethodResult]]) on pc1

monitor m1{
    class: monitors.SafeListMonitor
    events: [e1 to receive(String, List)]
}
```

Listing 1.3. A BISM transformer that intercepts the creation of an iterator.

7.2   Residual Runtime Verification

This use case demonstrates a traditional case of integrating static and runtime verification, to mitigate the runtime monitoring overhead during the verification of safety and co-safety properties. Through static verification, the goal of *residual analysis* [22] is to identify program elements or paths that always preserve the desired property. Consequently, these paths can be ignored during runtime verification and the residual parts are then subjected to runtime verification. The residual analysis detects a set of program instructions, represented as $\mathcal{S}_P$, that can be safely excluded from runtime observation without disrupting the verification process. The aim, thus, is to define a new instrumentation function residual : instrs* $\rightarrow$ ($\mathcal{S}_P \rightarrow \Sigma^*$). Let *Runs* $\subseteq$ instrs* denote the set of all possible runs of the program. The program instrumented with residual should ideally produce shorter traces than instrument (the regular instrumentation function), but the monitoring results should remain consistent for both. The condition that the residual analysis should fulfill can be expressed as follows:

$$\forall r \in \textit{Runs} : |\text{residual}(r)| \leq |\text{instrument}(r)|$$
$$\wedge \text{ residual}(r) \models \varphi \iff \text{instrument}(r) \models \varphi$$

Hence, here the instrumentation tool must incorporate the residual analysis outcomes when mapping program locations in the program; and this can be accomplished in various ways. For example, in [15], the AspectJ compiler ajc was customized to execute a similar static analysis and merge its results with the AspectJ instrumentation. However, this method requires deep knowledge of the ajc compiler for customization. In [44], the residual analysis was conducted entirely by writing BISM transformers. BISM transformers allow for writing custom logic in Java, thus, a static analyzer can be implemented as a transformer. This transformer while traversing the program and utilizes BISM control flow features to construct the control flow graph for each method. Then, it constructs a CFG automaton that abstracts the method behavior. This constructed model is needed to over-approximate the set of traces that the method might produce at runtime. The transformer then conducts a reachability analysis with a property specified as an automaton and marks the states of the CFG automaton that are safe to overlook. This first transformer performing the analysis does not instrument the base program; however, flags the safe shadows as invisible for other transformers. A second transformer then passes over the program and instruments the visible shadows that are matched by the specified selector by the user. Hence for each property, two transformers are written. Figure 8 showcases a CFG automaton, constructed from Fig. 7. In this figure, the transitions are labeled with c which denotes the creation of a list-associated iterator by calling list.iterator(), u denotes an update to the list via list.add(..), and event n denotes a call to the iterator.next() method on an iterator. States marked in red correspond to shadows that will remain visible for the instrumenting transformer.

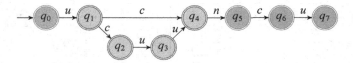

Fig. 8. Property-violating paths are marked in red, and safe ones are in green. (Color figure online)

Discussion. This scenario highlights the importance of being able to integrate static analyzers with instrumentation. Writing static analyzers with AspectJ for instance is infeasible and requires customizing the compiler such as in [8,14,15]. With DiSL it might be feasible, however, such analysis must be written manually using a bytecode manipulation library such as ASM in a pre-instrumentation step that does not support DiSL language. Moreover, without being able to relay the analysis results to the instrumentation, the user may need to annotate the unsafe instructions and then write custom markers within DiSL to capture those annotated shadows. This is not only tedious but also error-prone. BISM's ability to have a **composition of transformers** where transformers can **control the visibility** of shadows relaying such analysis results to the instrumentation makes such analysis feasible.

7.3 Runtime Verification of Concurrent Programs

In this scenario, we focus on the runtime verification of concurrent programs. In these programs, events may be produced by different execution flows and the order by which events are captured may not reflect the order by which they are produced. This is a challenge for runtime verification as it may lead to unsound monitoring results as shown in [23]. Suppose we want to monitor a precedence property, which specifies that a resource can only be granted (event g) in response to a request (event r), and can be expressed in LTL as $\neg g \ \mathbf{W} \ r$. Suppose these events are being produced by two threads, t_0 and t_1, and the program is not correctly synchronized to preserve this property.

To handle concurrency, frameworks such as Java-MOP [18], Tracematches [7], and others [11] have a feature to synchronize the monitor protecting it from concurrent access and data races. However, a challenge arises when events are produced in concurrent regions as advice may not always execute atomically with their actions. Consider the example in Fig. 9a, where the code in yellow depicts the instrumented advice that notifies the monitor, a context switch might occur leading to an unsound verdict. There is a need to ensure atomicity between all executing program actions and their advice.

One way to solve the lack of advice atomicity is to force it by instrumenting synchronization blocks that wrap the program actions with their advice in mutually exclusive regions. Figure 9b shows a depiction of such instrumentation. The code in Listing 1.4 shows a BISM transformer that forces atomicity between a method call and its advice. The transformer first inserts a call to a static method

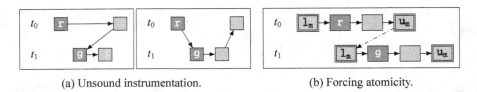

(a) Unsound instrumentation.   (b) Forcing atomicity.

Fig. 9. Instrumenting concurrent events.

getLock() in the class Monitor which returns an object that will be as a lock.
Then it duplicates the object on the stack and stores it in a local variable. Then
it inserts a call to MONITORENTER which starts a synchronized block in Java.
After the method call, the transformer inserts the code to emit the event and
then loads the object from the local variable and calls MONITOREXIT to release
the lock. This transformer can be used to instrument the example in Fig. 9b to
force atomicity between the method call and its advice.

```
public class ForcingAtomicityTransformer extends Transformer {
int lv; // local variable index
public void beforeMethodCall(MethodCall mc, DynamicContext dc) {
    lv = ...; // the index in the method can be max local variables + 1
    insert(new MethodInsnNode(Opcodes.INVOKESTATIC, "Monitor", "getLock",
           "()Ljava/lang/Object;", false)); // retrieve the lock object

    insert(new InsnNode(Opcodes.DUP)); // duplicate the lock object on the
        stack
    insert(new VarInsnNode(Opcodes.ASTORE, lv)); // store one copy in a local
        variable
    insert(new InsnNode(Opcodes.MONITORENTER)); // start synchronized block
}
public void afterMethodCall(MethodCall mc, DynamicContext dc) {

    // ADVICE TO EXTRACT EVENT GOES HERE

    insert(new VarInsnNode(Opcodes.ALOAD, lv)); // load the lock object
    insert(new InsnNode(Opcodes.MONITOREXIT)); // end synchronized block
}
}
```

Listing 1.4. A BISM transformer that forces atomicity between a method call and its
advice.

Discussion. An instrumentation language often aims to target specific locations
within a program, to insert code either before or after a particular instruction. It
is important to note that this kind of instrumentation necessitates the capability
for **arbitrary code insertion**. This is because there is a need to insert related

code at nonadjacent locations, both before and after the method call instruction. However, runtime verification (RV) tools that rely on AspectJ are not suitable for instrumenting such synchronization blocks. For instance, in the case discussed in [39], the bytecode manipulation library BCEL was utilized. On the other hand, BISM offers a straightforward API to insert arbitrary instructions at any point within the program, using the ASM syntax. This unique feature allows for a hybrid approach to specifying advice. With BISM within the same transformer, the event can be extracted using abstractions, as shown in Listing 1.2, while synchronization blocks can be inserted using the ASM syntax.

Concurrent Traces. Forcing atomicity introduces new problems. First, it forces a total order between concurrent program actions; interfering with the parallelism of the program and changing its behavior. One needs to avoid coarse-grained synchronization. From the monitor side, the verdict will be dependent on the specific scheduling of the execution. Second, any information about parallel actions in the program is lost and one can no longer determine whether two actions execute concurrently initially in the non-instrumented program. In that case, it becomes impossible to express properties on the concurrent parts of the execution. To preserve the inherent concurrency in programs one needs to collect partial order traces instead of total order ones, capturing the "happens-before" relation among the events produced by the program. This provides a more precise representation of the program's behavior and enables a richer set of properties to be specified and checked. Two properties can be used to determine if a trace is a good representative of an execution: **soundness** and **faithfulness** [45]. Soundness holds when the trace does not provide false information about the order of events. Faithfulness holds when the trace contains all the information about the order of events.

As the process of observation is sequential with events being passed to a central observer reestablishing the causality between events is crucial to have trace soundness. This necessitates additional instrumentation to capture the synchronization actions from the program. These are actions that synchronize threads such as `fork(t,u)` and `begin(u)` for the initiation of thread u by thread t, `unlock(t,l)` and `lock(t,l)` for the release/acquisition of lock l, and `write(t,x,v)` and `read(t,x,v)` for operations on shared variable x. Then upon receiving these events inferring the order of events can be done with the help of a vector clock algorithm such as in [5,17,36,39,45]. To ensure faithfulness, the instrumentation must be complete in capturing all synchronization actions, preventing any loss of ordering information from the trace.

However, it's worth noting that collecting all this information to build a representative trace can be quite resource-intensive in terms of time and memory, especially in an online setup. Therefore, it might be feasible to construct this representative trace off the critical path of program execution. In [45], a concurrent trace collection mechanism that does not block the execution of the program was presented demonstrating a reduced performance impact on the running program while still capturing a representative concurrent trace.

Discussion. This scenario requires instrumentation to be capable of identifying various concurrency constructs in the program, hence **bytecode coverage**. In our implementation experience, we identified a need to adapt to the diverse JVM languages, especially when considering higher-level concurrency primitives. Each JVM language, while converting to bytecode, possesses unique features and structures. This variance poses challenges for tools primarily designed for Java, such as AspectJ. Languages like Scala, Clojure, or Kotlin produce bytecode that reflects their distinct features, from functional programming constructs and object-oriented variations to pattern matching, destructuring, static method handling, implicit parameters, and advanced concurrency constructs like coroutines. Their specialized naming conventions further add to the complexity. Consequently, this intricacy in bytecode complicates the task for Java-centric instrumentation tools requiring more specialized instrumentation tools.

7.4   Opportunistic Monitoring

We proceed in our discourse on instrumentation in the context of concurrent programs and introduce opportunistic monitoring [43] which is tailored for multithreaded programs. Monitoring here is deployed at two levels. At the first level, thread-local monitors are employed to monitor the execution of individual threads. The second level introduces *scope* monitors which monitor global properties shared accross threads. This approach introduces a novel way of instrumenting multithreaded programs taking advantage of existing synchronization points in a program to monitor it, rather than introducing additional synchronization points, which might interfere with the program's behavior and introduce additional overhead. Scope monitors are evaluated at the end of scope regions which are assumed to be atomically executing. Hence by assuming the atomicity of scope regions, we can ensure that the thread-local monitors can accurately observe and report the state of the thread within the region.

Discussion. The same discussion as in the previous section applies here. Also, additional work needs to be invested to complete the automatic instrumentation and integration with monitors. So far, splitting the property over local and scope monitors is achieved manually. Analyzing the program pre-instrumentation to find and suggest scopes suitable for splitting and monitoring a given property is an interesting challenge that can be achieved within BISM.

7.5   Control Flow Integrity

In addition to capturing high-level events like method calls and executions, which are fundamental for many runtime verification tasks, instrumentation may also be needed to capture low-level events like bytecode instructions and contexts, like values on the stack and control flow. This scenario demonstrates the application of runtime verification to detect a type of control flow integrity violations namely test inversion attacks, where an attacker modifies the program's control flow by inverting conditional tests. By monitoring the execution flow of a program and logging stack values before conditional jumps, we can spot these attacks.

```
pointcut pc0 before Instruction(* *.*(..)) with (
   isConditionalJump = true)
pointcut pc1 on TrueBranchEnter(* *.*(..))
pointcut pc2 on FalseBranchEnter(* *.*(..))

event e0([opcode,getStackValues]) on pc0 to Mon.recieve(List)
event e1("tt")  on pc1 to Mon.recieve(String)
event e2("ff")  on pc2 to Mon.recieve(String)
```

Listing 1.5. A BISM spec that intercepts the creation of an iterator.

Here, a monitor can be created to check the evaluation of the stack values with the opcode of the conditional jump to detect test inversion attacks [27]. Moreover, as mitigation for this type of attack, one can inline a small monitor at each branch of the conditional statement that rechecks the evaluation of the stack values and throws an exception if the evaluation results in a different value than the one logged by the entered branch. Here the instrumentation is required to duplicate the stack values and then insert conditional instructions within each branch.

Discussion. To handle such instrumentation requirements, the instrumentation tool must first have **bytecode coverage** to capture low-level events like execution of bytecode instructions and contexts, like values on the stack and control flow. Moreover, the instrumentation should be able to identify branching locations which requires constructing the control flow graph of the program. Finally, to inline monitors, instrumentation needs to duplicate the stack values and the conditional statements within each branch. This requires the ability to insert **arbitrary bytecode instructions**. Tools like AspectJ and DiSL are incapable of inserting arbitrary bytecode instructions and thus cannot be used.

Table 1. Comparison of the tools. ✓ - Tool provides the feature, ✗ - Tool does not provide the feature, ✓ - Tool partially provides the feature

Feature	BCEL [9]	ASM [16]	CGLIB [40]	Javassist [20]	Soot [49]	DiSL [35]	AspectJ [29]	BISM [46]
Bytecode Coverage	✓	✓	✓	✓	✓	✓	✗	✓
Bytecode Insertion	✓	✓	✓	✓	✓	✗	✗	✓
No Bytecode Proficiency	✗	✗	✓	✓	✓	✓	✓	✓
Pre-Instrumentation Analysis	✓	✓	✓	✓	✓	✓	✗	✓
High-Level Abstraction	✗	✓	✓	✓	✓	✓	✓	✓
AOP Paradigm	✗	✗	✗	✗	✗	✓	✓	✓

8 Conclusion

In this tutorial, we presented an overview of instrumentation for runtime verification. We discussed the main considerations that should be taken into account when instrumenting a program for runtime verification. We also presented the main instrumentation techniques and tools that can be used for runtime verification. Table 1 shows a comparison between them. We also discussed the main challenges and pitfalls that can be encountered during the instrumentation process. We hope that this tutorial will help researchers and practitioners to better understand the instrumentation process and to choose the most suitable instrumentation technique and tool for their needs.

References

1. JProfiler. www.ej-technologies.com/products/jprofiler/overview.html. Accessed 01 June 2023
2. VisualVM: All-in-one Java troubleshooting tool. www.visualvm.github.io/. Accessed 30 May 2023
3. Akka documentation (2022). www.akka.io/docs/
4. Adve, S.V., Gharachorloo, K.: Shared memory consistency models: a tutorial. Computer **29**(12), 66–76 (1996). https://doi.org/10.1109/2.546611
5. Agarwal, A., Garg, V.K.: Efficient dependency tracking for relevant events in shared-memory systems. In: Proceedings of the Twenty-Fourth Annual ACM Symposium on Principles of Distributed Computing, pp. 19–28. PODC 2005, Association for Computing Machinery, New York, NY, USA (2005). https://doi.org/10.1145/1073814.1073818
6. Ahamad, M., Neiger, G., Burns, J.E., Kohli, P., Hutto, P.W.: Causal memory: definitions, implementation, and programming. Distrib. Comput. **9**(1), 37–49 (1995). https://doi.org/10.1007/BF01784241
7. Allan, C., et al.: Adding trace matching with free variables to AspectJ. In: Proceedings of the 20th Annual ACM SIGPLAN Conference on Object-oriented Programming, Systems, Languages, and Applications, pp. 345–364. OOPSLA 2005, ACM (2005). https://doi.org/10.1145/1094811.1094839
8. Aotani, T., Masuhara, H.: SCoPE: an AspectJ compiler for supporting user-defined analysis-based pointcuts. In: Proceedings of the 6th International Conference on Aspect-Oriented Software Development, pp. 161–172. AOSD 2007, Association for Computing Machinery, New York, NY, USA (2007). https://doi.org/10.1145/1218563.1218582
9. Apache Commons: BCEL (byte code engineering library). www.commons.apache.org/proper/commons-bcel. Accessed 18 June 2020
10. Barringer, H., Falcone, Y., Havelund, K., Reger, G., Rydeheard, D.: Quantified event automata: towards expressive and efficient runtime monitors. In: Giannakopoulou, D., Méry, D. (eds.) FM 2012. LNCS, vol. 7436, pp. 68–84. Springer, Heidelberg (2012). https://doi.org/10.1007/978-3-642-32759-9_9
11. Bartocci, E., Falcone, Y., Bonakdarpour, B., Colombo, C., Decker, N., Havelund, K., Joshi, Y., Klaedtke, F., Milewicz, R., Reger, G., Rosu, G., Signoles, J., Thoma, D., Zalinescu, E., Zhang, Y.: First international competition on runtime verification: rules, benchmarks, tools, and final results of CRV 2014. Int. J. Softw. Tools Technol. Transfer (2017). https://doi.org/10.1007/s10009-017-0454-5
12. Bartocci, E., Falcone, Y., Francalanza, A., Reger, G.: Introduction to runtime verification. In: Bartocci, E., Falcone, Y. (eds.) Lectures on Runtime Verification. LNCS, vol. 10457, pp. 1–33. Springer, Cham (2018). https://doi.org/10.1007/978-3-319-75632-5_1

13. Biermann, A.W., Feldman, J.A.: On the synthesis of finite-state machines from samples of their behavior. IEEE Trans. Comput. **21**(6), 592–597 (1972). https://doi.org/10.1109/TC.1972.5009015
14. Bodden, E., Havelund, K.: Racer: effective race detection using AspectJ. In: Proceedings of the 2008 International Symposium on Software Testing and Analysis, pp. 155–166. ISSTA 2008, Association for Computing Machinery, New York, NY, USA (2008). https://doi.org/10.1145/1390630.1390650
15. Bodden, E., Lam, P., Hendren, L.: Clara: a framework for partially evaluating finite-state runtime monitors ahead of time. In: Barringer, H., et al. (eds.) RV 2010. LNCS, vol. 6418, pp. 183–197. Springer, Heidelberg (2010). https://doi.org/10.1007/978-3-642-16612-9_15
16. Bruneton, E., Lenglet, R., Coupaye, T.: ASM: a code manipulation tool to implement adaptable systems. In: Adaptable and Extensible Component Systems (2002). http://www.asm.ow2.io/
17. Cain, H.W., Lipasti, M.H.: Verifying sequential consistency using vector clocks. In: Proceedings of the Fourteenth Annual ACM Symposium on Parallel Algorithms and Architectures. p. 153–154. SPAA 2002, Association for Computing Machinery, New York, NY, USA (2002). https://doi.org/10.1145/564870.564897
18. Chen, F., Roşu, G.: Java-MOP: a monitoring oriented programming environment for java. In: Halbwachs, N., Zuck, L.D. (eds.) TACAS 2005. LNCS, vol. 3440, pp. 546–550. Springer, Heidelberg (2005). https://doi.org/10.1007/978-3-540-31980-1_36
19. Chen, F., Roşu, G.: Parametric trace slicing and monitoring. In: Kowalewski, S., Philippou, A. (eds.) TACAS 2009. LNCS, vol. 5505, pp. 246–261. Springer, Heidelberg (2009). https://doi.org/10.1007/978-3-642-00768-2_23
20. Chiba, S.: Load-time structural reflection in java. In: Bertino, E. (ed.) ECOOP 2000. LNCS, vol. 1850, pp. 313–336. Springer, Heidelberg (2000). https://doi.org/10.1007/3-540-45102-1_16
21. Clarke, E.M., Henzinger, T.A., Veith, H., Bloem, R.: Handbook of Model Checking, 1st edn. Springer, Cham (2018). https://doi.org/10.1007/978-3-319-10575-8
22. Dwyer, M.B., Purandare, R.: Residual dynamic typestate analysis exploiting static analysis, p. 124 (2007)
23. El-Hokayem, A., Falcone, Y.: Can we monitor all multithreaded programs? In: Colombo, C., Leucker, M. (eds.) RV 2018. LNCS, vol. 11237, pp. 64–89. Springer, Cham (2018). https://doi.org/10.1007/978-3-030-03769-7_6
24. Falcone, Y., Krstić, S., Reger, G., Traytel, D.: A taxonomy for classifying runtime verification tools. In: Colombo, C., Leucker, M. (eds.) RV 2018. LNCS, vol. 11237, pp. 241–262. Springer, Cham (2018). https://doi.org/10.1007/978-3-030-03769-7_14
25. Gastin, P., Kuske, D.: Uniform satisfiability problem for local temporal logics over Mazurkiewicz traces. Inf. Comput. **208**(7), 797–816 (2010). https://doi.org/10.1016/j.ic.2009.12.003
26. Harris, T., Marlow, S., Peyton-Jones, S., Herlihy, M.: Composable memory transactions. In: Proceedings of the Tenth ACM SIGPLAN Symposium on Principles and Practice of Parallel Programming, pp. 48–60. PPoPP 2005, Association for Computing Machinery, New York, NY, USA (2005). https://doi.org/10.1145/1065944.1065952
27. Kassem, A., Falcone, Y.: Detecting fault injection attacks with runtime verification. In: Proceedings of the 3rd ACM Workshop on Software Protection, pp. 65–76. SPRO 2019, Association for Computing Machinery, New York, NY, USA (2019). https://doi.org/10.1145/3338503.3357724

28. Kell, S., Ansaloni, D., Binder, W., Marek, L.: The JVM is not observable enough (and what to do about it). In: Proceedings of the Sixth ACM Workshop on Virtual Machines and Intermediate Languages, pp. 33–38. VMIL 2012, Association for Computing Machinery, New York, NY, USA (2012). https://doi.org/10.1145/2414740.2414747

29. Kiczales, G., Hilsdale, E., Hugunin, J., Kersten, M., Palm, J., Griswold, W.G.: Getting started with AspectJ. Commun. ACM **44**(10), 59–65 (2001)

30. Kiczales, G., et al.: Aspect-oriented programming. In: Akşit, M., Matsuoka, S. (eds.) ECOOP 1997. LNCS, vol. 1241, pp. 220–242. Springer, Heidelberg (1997). https://doi.org/10.1007/BFb0053381

31. Krka, I., Brun, Y., Medvidovic, N.: Automatic mining of specifications from invocation traces and method invariants. In: Proceedings of the 22nd ACM SIGSOFT International Symposium on Foundations of Software Engineering, pp. 178–189. FSE 2014, Association for Computing Machinery, New York, NY, USA (2014). https://doi.org/10.1145/2635868.2635890

32. Lea, D.: A java fork/join framework. In: Proceedings of the ACM 2000 Java Grande Conference, San Francisco, CA, USA, June 3–5, 2000, pp. 36–43 (2000). https://doi.org/10.1145/337449.337465

33. Lengauer, P., Bitto, V., Mössenböck, H.: Accurate and efficient object tracing for java applications. In: Proceedings of the 6th ACM/SPEC International Conference on Performance Engineering, pp. 51–62. ICPE 2015, Association for Computing Machinery, New York, NY, USA (2015). https://doi.org/10.1145/2668930.2688037

34. Manson, J., Pugh, W., Adve, S.V.: The java memory model. In: Proceedings of the 32nd ACM SIGPLAN-SIGACT Symposium on Principles of Programming Languages, pp. 378–391. POPL 2005, ACM (2005). https://doi.org/10.1145/1040305.1040336

35. Marek, L., Villazón, A., Zheng, Y., Ansaloni, D., Binder, W., Qi, Z.: DiSL: a domain-specific language for bytecode instrumentation. In: Hirschfeld, R., Tanter, É., Sullivan, K.J., Gabriel, R.P. (eds.) Proceedings of the 11th International Conference on Aspect-oriented Software Development, AOSD, Potsdam, Germany, pp. 239–250. ACM (2012)

36. Mathur, U., Viswanathan, M.: Atomicity checking in linear time using vector clocks, p. 183–199. Association for Computing Machinery, New York, NY, USA (2020). https://doi.org/10.1145/3373376.3378475

37. Mazurkiewicz, A.: Trace theory. In: Brauer, W., Reisig, W., Rozenberg, G. (eds.) ACPN 1986. LNCS, vol. 255, pp. 278–324. Springer, Heidelberg (1987). https://doi.org/10.1007/3-540-17906-2_30

38. Ohmann, T., et al.: Behavioral resource-aware model inference. In: Proceedings of the 29th ACM/IEEE International Conference on Automated Software Engineering, pp. 19–30. ASE 2014, Association for Computing Machinery, New York, NY, USA (2014). https://doi.org/10.1145/2642937.2642988

39. Rosu, G., Sen, K.: An instrumentation technique for online analysis of multithreaded programs. In: 18th International Parallel and Distributed Processing Symposium, 2004. Proceedings, pp. 268- (2004). https://doi.org/10.1109/IPDPS.2004.1303344

40. Berlin, S., et al.: CGLIB (byte code generation library). www.github.com/cglib/cglib. Accessed 21 May 2021

41. Sharkdp, Contributors: Hyperfine. www.github.com/sharkdp/hyperfine. Accessed 01 June 2023

42. Shin, K., Ramanathan, P.: Real-time computing: a new discipline of computer science and engineering. Proc. IEEE **82**(1), 6–24 (1994). https://doi.org/10.1109/5.259423
43. Soueidi, C., El-Hokayem, A., Falcone, Y.: Opportunistic monitoring of multi-threaded programs. In: Lambers, L., Uchitel, S. (eds.) ETAPS 2023. LNCS, vol. 13991, pp. 173–194. Springer, Cham (2023). https://doi.org/10.1007/978-3-031-30826-0_10
44. Soueidi, C., Falcone, Y.: Residual runtime verification via reachability analysis. In: Lal, A., Tonetta, S. (eds.) VSTTE 2022. LNCS, vol. 13800, pp. 148–166. Springer, Cham (2022). https://doi.org/10.1007/978-3-031-25803-9_9
45. Soueidi, C., Falcone, Y.: Sound concurrent traces for online monitoring. In: Caltais, G., Schilling, C. (eds.) SPIN 2023. LNCS, vol. 13872, pp. 59–80. Springer, Cham (2023). https://doi.org/10.1007/978-3-031-32157-3_4
46. Soueidi, C., Kassem, A., Falcone, Y.: BISM: bytecode-level instrumentation for software monitoring (2020). https://doi.org/10.1007/978-3-030-60508-7_18. www.gitlab.inria.fr/bism/bism-public/
47. Soueidi, C., Monnier, M., Falcone, Y.: International Journal on Software Tools for Technology Transfer, pp. 1–27 (2023). https://doi.org/10.1007/s10009-023-00708-z. www.link.springer.com/article/10.1007/s10009-023-00708-z
48. Taleb, R., Khoury, R., Halle, S.: Runtime verification under access restrictions. In: 2021 IEEE/ACM 9th International Conference on Formal Methods in Software Engineering (FormaliSE), pp. 31–41 (2021). DOI: https://doi.org/10.1109/FormaliSE52586.2021.00010
49. Vallée-Rai, R. Co, P., Gagnon, E., Hendren, L., Lam, P., Sundaresan, V.: Soot - a java bytecode optimization framework. In: Proceedings of the 1999 Conference of the Centre for Advanced Studies on Collaborative Research, pp. 13. CASCON 1999, IBM Press, USA (1999). https://doi.org/10.1145/1925805.1925818

Runtime Monitoring DNN-Based Perception
(via the Lens of Formal Methods)

Chih-Hong Cheng[1]([✉]), Michael Luttenberger[1], and Rongjie Yan[2]

[1] Technical University of Munich, Munich, Germany
`chih-hong.cheng@tum.de`, `luttenbe@in.tum.de`
[2] Institute of Software, Chinese Academy of Sciences, Beijing, China
`yrj@ios.ac.cn`

Abstract. Deep neural networks (DNNs) are instrumental in realizing complex perception systems. As many of these applications are safety-critical by design, engineering rigor is required to ensure that the functional insufficiency of the DNN-based perception is not the source of harm. In addition to conventional static verification and testing techniques employed during the design phase, there is a need for runtime verification techniques that can detect critical events, diagnose issues, and even enforce requirements. This tutorial aims to provide readers with a glimpse of techniques proposed in the literature. We start with classical methods proposed in the machine learning community, then highlight a few techniques proposed by the formal methods community. While we surely can observe similarities in the design of monitors, how the decision boundaries are created vary between the two communities. We conclude by highlighting the need to rigorously design monitors, where data availability outside the operational domain plays an important role.

Keywords: deep neural networks · perception · runtime verification

1 Introduction

Deep neural networks (DNNs) play a pivotal role in realizing perception, revolutionizing our understanding of how machines can interpret and interact with the world. DNNs have transformed various fields, including computer vision, natural language processing, and audio recognition, by learning and extracting meaningful patterns from vast amounts of data. Apart from applications such as urban autonomous driving, it is now gaining attention in other domains such as railways and avionics. For example, the safe.trAIn project[1] considered how DNN-based perception can be used in creating driverless autonomous trains for regional transportation. Given the input represented in digital formats (RGB images or lidar point clouds), one can easily apply DNN to perform various tasks

---

[1] https://safetrain-projekt.de/en/.

P. Katsaros and L. Nenzi (Eds.): RV 2023, LNCS 14245, pp. 428–446, 2023.
https://doi.org/10.1007/978-3-031-44267-4_24

such as classification, 2D or 3D object detection, and semantic segmentation, to name a few applications.

Nevertheless, the use of DNNs in safety-critical applications such as autonomous driving necessitates additional care and precautionary measures, given the potential risks associated with incorrect or unreliable decisions made by these networks. In such applications, where human lives or important infrastructure are at stake, the robustness and reliability of deep neural networks become paramount. One prominent technique to address these concerns is *runtime monitoring*, which involves continuously monitoring the behavior and outputs of the network during its operation. Alongside runtime monitoring, other techniques like formal verification and thorough testing are also employed to ensure the safety and reliability of deep neural networks in critical domains. Combining these techniques enhances the trustworthiness and dependability of deep neural networks in safety-critical applications, providing a vital layer of assurance and mitigating potential risks.

This tutorial[2] aims to offer readers a glimpse into the complex topic of runtime monitoring DNN-based perception systems, where active research has been conducted in the machine learning community and has been receiving attention in the formal methods community. As the topic is very broad, we would like to constrain the scope by considering the simplified perception system pipeline illustrated in Fig. 1. The perception system first performs image formation and stores the image in a digital format. Then pre-processing methods can be applied before feeding into neural networks. Commonly used pre-processing methods include denoising or quantization. Post-processing refers to algorithms such as polishing the result of the DNN. For example, in object detection, *non-max suppression* is used to remove spatially overlapping objects whose output probability is lower. The tutorial emphasizes the runtime monitoring of DNN and may partly include the pre-and post-processing. Regarding the monitoring of hardware platforms, although there exists some confirmation on the hardware faults influencing the result of prediction [21], in this tutorial, we have decided to neglect them and relegate the monitoring activities to classical safety engineering paradigms such as ISO 26262 for dealing with hardware faults.

2   Challenges in Monitoring Perception Systems

Monitoring perception systems poses some unique challenges in contrast to the standard runtime verification paradigm, which we detail in the following sections.

Specification. In runtime verification, the type of formal specifications of interest can be state properties (invariance), temporal properties characterizing trace behaviors utilizing temporal logics, like qualitative linear temporal logic (LTL) [20] or extensions thereof like signal temporal logic (STL) [7] or

---

[2] All materials for the tutorial are made available at https://sites.google.com/site/chengchihhong/home/teaching/rv23.

metric temporal logic (MTL) [12], and hyper-properties comparing behaviors of multiple traces. The definition of states is application-specific.

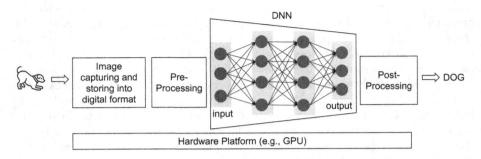

Fig. 1. A typical DNN-based perception system

For learning-based perception systems such as object detection with input from images (pedestrian, car, bicycle), the undesired situation for the perception, when considering only the single input than a sequence of inputs, can be separated into two parts:

- The output can be incorrect in one of the following ways, namely
  1. object not detected,
  2. detecting ghost objects,
  3. incorrect object classification (a pedestrian is detected as a car), or
  4. incorrect object size (too big or too small).
- The input can also be "strange" due to not resembling what is commonly expected as input (e.g., random noise rather than highway road scenes).

In many systems, during the runtime verification process, one can access the state information and know if a state property is satisfied. The measured state information offers the "ground truth". For perception, however, the *ground truth (i.e., whether an object exists) is unavailable for comparison during run-time.* Therefore, the above-mentioned error types can not be directly detected. This ultimately leads to *indirect* methods for error detection, with methods including the following types:

- error detection via *redundancy* (e.g., comparing the prediction based on additional sensor modalities),
- error detection via *domain knowledge* (e.g., utilizing Newton's law or classical computer vision methods to filter problematic situations),
- error detection via *temporal consistency* (e.g., comparing the result of prediction over time), and
- error detection via *monitoring the decision mechanism of the DNN*.

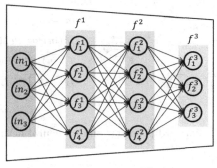

$$f(in) = f^3(f^2(f^1(\vec{in})))$$

Fig. 2. An example of multi-layer perceptron

While the first three methods (redundancy, domain knowledge, temporal consistency) can also be applied in any non-learning-based algorithms (e.g., algorithms utilizing classical computer vision algorithms), the latter is unique for deep neural networks.

Finally, we must admit that a formal specification is usually incomplete. Thus, only some important and necessary safety aspects might be formalized. For complex autonomous systems, the "operational design domain (ODD)", i.e., the input domain that the system is expected to operate, is often incompletely formalized and only implicitly given by means of the collected data set.

Reaction Time. The reaction time between the occurrence of a prediction error and the error being detected by the monitor is crucial. As a realistic example, consider a perception module for autonomous driving operated at 10 FPS. Assume that the object is continuously not perceived starting at time t, and the perception error is only detected at time $t + \Delta$ where the car performs a full break. As the vehicle can at least travel during the time interval $[t, t + \Delta]$, it may create dangerous scenarios when Δ is too large where applying maximum break is insufficient to avoid a collision.

3   Formulation

Throughout the text, for a vector $\vec{v}$, we refer $\vec{v}_i$ as its i-th component. We create the simplest formulation of neural networks using *multi-layer perceptron*. In our formulation, we also assume that the neural network has been trained, i.e., the parameters of the network are fixed. The concepts can also be applied in convolutional neural networks, residual networks, or transformers.

A neural network f is a composition of functions $f^L \circ f^{L-1} \circ \cdots \circ f^2 \circ f^1$, where for $l \in \{1, \ldots, L\}$, $f^l : \mathbb{R}^{d_{l-1}} \rightarrow \mathbb{R}^{d_l}$ is the computational function of the l-th layer. We refer to d_0 as the input dimension and d_L as the output

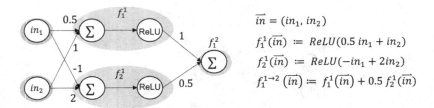

Fig. 3. Forward propagation of a neural network

dimension. At layer l, there are d_l neurons, with each neuron indexed i being a function that takes the output from the previous layer and produces the i-th output of f^l. In other words, $f_i^l : \mathbb{R}^{d_{l-1}} \to \mathbb{R}$. Given an input $\vec{in} \in \mathbb{R}^{d_0}$, the output of the neural network equals $f^L(f^{L-1}(\ldots(f^2(f^1(\vec{in})))))$. Finally, we use $f^{1 \to l}(\vec{in})$ to abbreviate $f^l(f^{l-1}(\ldots(f^2(f^1(\vec{in})))))$, i.e., the computation of value with input being $\vec{in}$, and use $f_i^{1 \to l}(\vec{in})$ to extract the i-th neuron value. Figure 2 illustrates an example of a neural network of 3 layers, taking a vector (in_1, in_2, in_3) of 3 numerical values as input and producing 3 outputs. The computation of a neuron in a multi-layer perception is done by performing a weighted sum, followed by a non-linear activation function. Figure 3 shows an example of how the computation is defined, where the *ReLU activation function* (also simply *ramp function*) is defined as follows:

$$ReLU(x) \overset{\text{def}}{:=} \max(0, x) = H(x) \cdot x = \begin{cases} x & \text{if x} > 0 \\ 0 & \text{otherwise} \end{cases}$$

with H the *Heaviside step function*. Fixed-point systesm $x_1 = f_1(x) \wedge \ldots \wedge x_n = f_n(x)$ $(x = (x_1, \ldots, x_n) \in \mathbb{R}^n, f_i : \mathbb{R}^n \to \mathbb{R})$ where f_i is a composition of linear forms, max and min have been studied also as abstractions of dynamic systems before, e.g. as abstractions of programs or turn-based two-player games (see e.g. [8]).

Finally, let $\mathcal{D} \overset{\text{def}}{:=} \{(\vec{in}, \vec{label})\}$ be the data set collected from the human-specified operational domain for training the neural network f, where $\vec{in} \in \mathbb{R}^{d_0}$ and $\vec{label} \in \mathbb{R}^{d_L}$. Let $\mathcal{D}^{train}, \mathcal{D}^{val}, \mathcal{D}^{test} \subseteq \mathcal{D}$ be the training, validation, and test set. Commonly, $\mathcal{D}^{train} \cap \mathcal{D}^{val} = \mathcal{D}^{train} \cap \mathcal{D}^{test} = \mathcal{D}^{test} \cap \mathcal{D}^{val} = \emptyset$.

4   Techniques

4.1   DNN Monitoring Techniques from the ML Community

This section gives insight into some renowned approaches proposed by the ML community, intending to identify inputs that are **out-of-distribution** (OoD), i.e., input data that are not similar to the data used in training[3]. We start with

---

[3] This concept is ambiguously defined in the field of machine learning.

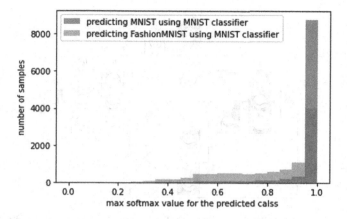

Fig. 4. Using an MNIST classifier to predict the output from images in the MNIST and Fashion-MNIST data set.

the work of Hendrycks and Gimpel that introduces extra components (with a reconstruction component) and softmax decision [10], followed by the work of Liang, Li, and Srikant that uses temperature scaling and positively perturbed examples [15], and conclude the section with the work from Lee et al. utilizing Mahalanobis distance [14].

Limitations of the Softmax Output. In the case of classification, the final layer consists of the application of the so-called *softmax function* which use the isomorphism from $\mathbb{R}$ to $\mathbb{R}_{>0}$ given by the exponentiation followed by the standard mean to normalize the output to a distribution over the possible classes. Formally, the i-th output of applying softmax is defined as follows.

$$\sigma(\vec{x})_i \overset{\text{def}}{:=} \frac{e^{\vec{x}_i}}{\sum_{i=1}^{d_L} e^{\vec{x}_i}}$$

In probability theory, the output of the softmax function can be used to represent a categorical distribution, i.e., a probability distribution over d_L different possible outcomes.

Unfortunately, the work from Hendrycks and Gimpel [10] discovered that pre-trained neural networks could be overconfident to out-of-distribution examples, thereby limiting the usefulness of directly using softmax as the output. To understand this concept, we have trained multiple neural networks on the MNIST data set [13] for digit recognition. Subsequently, we use the trained neural network to classify clothing types for the Fashion-MNIST data set [25]. Ideally, we hope that the output of the softmax function should not generate values close to 1. Unfortunately, as illustrated in Fig. 4, one can observe that among 10000 images from the Fashion-MNIST data set, around 4000 examples are predicted by the MNIST-classifier with a probability between 0.95 and 1.

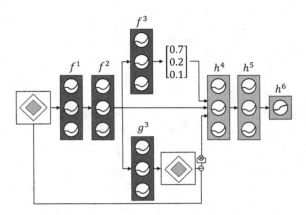

Fig. 5. The architectural diagram for the OoD detector by Hendrycks and Gimpel [10]. The blue layers (f^1, f^2, f^3, g^3) are trained with in-distribution data, and the yellow layers (h^4, f^5, h^6) are trained with both in-distribution and out-of-distribution data.

Consequently, the authors in [10] trained an additional classifier to detect if an input is out-of-distribution via the architecture as illustrated in Fig. 5.

– First, train a standard classifier $(f \overset{\text{def}}{:=} f^3 \circ f^2 \circ f^1)$ with in-distribution data.
– Next, use the feature extractors of the predictor (f^1, f^2) to train another image reconstructor g^3, also with in-distribution data.
– Finally, train the OoD detector $h^6 \circ h^5 \circ h^4$ with both in-distribution and out-of-distribution data, based on three types of inputs, namely
  • output of features f^2,
  • the softmax prediction from the standard classifier f^3, and
  • the quantity of the reconstruction error.

Intuitively, if an input is out-of-distribution, it may have different features, or it may not be reconstructed, thereby hinting at the usefulness of these types of inputs for h^4 in Fig. 5.

Temperature Scaling and Gradient Ascent. While the first method is based on the observation where softmax output can not be directly used as a means to detect out-of-distribution inputs, the immediate question turns to be if there exist lightweight methods to avoid training additional components. The ODIN approach by Liang, Li, Srikant [15] used temperature scaling and gradient ascent on inputs in-distribution to create better *separators* between in-distribution and out-of-distribution input. Temperature scaling, as defined in Eq. 1, uniformly divide each dimension of $\vec{x}$ with a positive constant T whose value is larger than 1, before performing the standard softmax function. Intuitively, it smooths out the large values caused by applying an exponential function. Figure 6 shows the result of applying the temperature scaling (with different T values) on the same predictor used in Fig. 4. When $T = 3$, when we set the

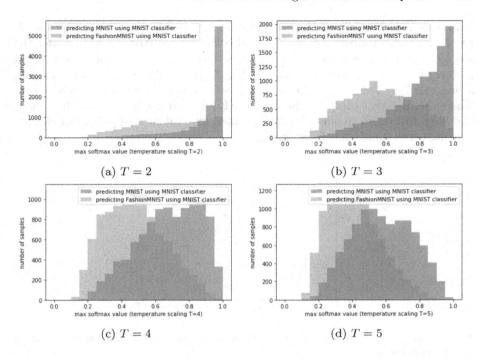

Fig. 6. Applying temperature scaling on the same predictor for creating Fig. 4

OoD cutoff threshold to be 0.6 (i.e., if the largest output value is below 0.6, report OoD; otherwise, return the class that has the largest output value), we can filter a great part of out-of-distribution samples while maintaining the performance for in-distribution samples.

$$\sigma(\vec{x}, T)_i \overset{\text{def}}{:=} \frac{e^{\vec{x}_i/T}}{\sum_{i=1}^{d_L} e^{\vec{x}_i/T}} \tag{1}$$

The second step of the ODIN approach is to create a modified input $\vec{in}'$ which perturbs the input $\vec{in}$ to increase the prediction score of the largest class. The intuition is that any input in-distribution is more likely to be perturbed to increase the maximum output probability. This technique needs to compute the gradient of the largest output over the input (i.e., $\frac{\partial f_i(\vec{in})}{\partial \vec{in}}$), and take a small step in the direction suggested by the gradient (thereby calling gradient ascent). This technique is the *dual of adversarial perturbation*, which tries to decrease the prediction score of the largest class.

Mahalanobis Distance. Provided that an input $\vec{in}$ is drawn from a probability distribution, the value of $f_i^{1\rightarrow l}(\vec{in})$ also follows a distribution. Consider the *imaginary scenario* where $f_i^{1\rightarrow l}(\vec{in})$ has the Gaussian distribution with mean μ and variance σ^2, as demonstrated in Fig. 7. Based on the interval estimate, around 99.7% of the values lie within three standard deviations of the mean. Therefore, one can compute the Z-score (Eq. 2) and use a simple containment checking if the Z-score falls within a specified interval such as $[-3, 3]$ for characterizing three standards of deviation.

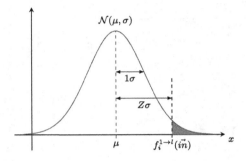

Fig. 7. Using Z-score as a method for rejecting inputs with neuron values deviating largely from the mean

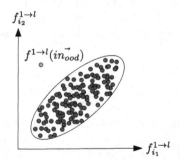

Fig. 8. A situation where looking at each neuron in isolation is insufficient

$$z \overset{\text{def}}{:=} \frac{f_i^{1\rightarrow l}(\vec{in}) - \mu}{\sigma} \tag{2}$$

Nevertheless, the method of using Z-values does not capture the interrelations among neurons. An example can be observed in Fig. 8, where for the value $f^{1\rightarrow l}(\vec{in_{ood}})$ is projected onto the plane with the axis on the i_1 and i_2

neuron values, correspondingly. If we only look at the Gaussian distribution in each dimension, then both $f_1^{1 \rightarrow l}(\vec{in_{ood}})$ and $f_2^{1 \rightarrow l}(\vec{in_{ood}})$ are considered to be in the decision boundary, as their values are within the minimum and maximum possible values when projecting the eclipse to the axis. However, it should be considered as OoD. The authors in [14] thus considered *Mahalanobis distance* (i.e., the distance is measured wrt. the scalar product induced by the *inverse* of the positive-definite covariance matrix of the multi-variate Gaussian distribution, which transforms the covariance ellipsoid back into an unbiased sphere), the generalization of the Z-score in the multi-variate Gaussian distribution setup, to characterize the distance measure for rejecting an input.

4.2   DNN Monitoring Techniques from the FM Community

We now detail some of the monitoring techniques rooted in the formal methods community, where the key differences compared to the work from the ML community can be understood in one of the following dimensions.

- Use *abstraction* to decide the decision boundary, to ensure that all encountered data points within the data set are considered as in-distribution.
- Move beyond convex decision boundaries and embrace *non-convex decision boundaries* (via disjunction of sets), to allow more effective filtering of inputs being out-of-distribution.

Abstraction-Based Monitoring Using Binary Neuron Activation Patterns. In 2018, Cheng, Nührenberg, and Yasuoka considered the monitoring problem for detecting abnormal inputs via activation pattern [6]. The motivation is that abnormal inputs shall enable DNN to create abnormal decisions, and one natural way of understanding the decision mechanisms is to view the activation of neurons in a layer as a binary word (feature activation), with each bit characterizing a particular neuron's binary *on-off activation*. Conceptually, during run-time, when encountering an unseen feature activation pattern, one may reasonably doubt if the data collection has been insufficient or the input is OoD.

Precisely, for $x \in \mathbb{R}$, define the binary abstraction function $b_\alpha(x)$ as follows. One natural selection of α value is considering $\alpha = 0$, which matches how a ReLU activation function performs suppression of its input.

$$b_\alpha(x) = \begin{cases} 1 & \text{if } x > \alpha \\ 0 & \text{otherwise} \end{cases} \tag{3}$$

Then given the vector $f^{1 \rightarrow l}(\vec{in})$, the *binary word vector* $bv_\alpha(f^{1 \rightarrow l}(\vec{in}))$ is defined by element-wise application of $b_\alpha(\cdot)$ over $f^{1 \rightarrow l}(\vec{in})$, i.e.,

$$bv_\alpha(f^{1 \rightarrow l}(\vec{in})) \overset{\text{def}}{=} (b_\alpha(f_1^{1 \rightarrow l}(\vec{in})), b_\alpha(f_2^{1 \rightarrow l}(\vec{in})), \ldots, b_\alpha(f_{d_l}^{1 \rightarrow l}(\vec{in})))$$

Given $\mathcal{D}$, the monitor $\mathcal{M}^{bv}$ is simply the set of all binary word vectors as detailed in Eq. 4. The decision mechanism of the monitor is simple: If there is an input $\vec{in} \in \mathbb{R}^{d_0}$ such that $bv_\alpha(f^{1 \rightarrow l}(\vec{in})) \notin \mathcal{M}^{bv}$, then consider $\vec{in}$ as OoD.

$$\mathcal{M}^{bv} \overset{\text{def}}{:=} \{ bv_\alpha(f^{1 \rightarrow l}(\vec{in})) \mid (\vec{in}, \vec{label}) \in \mathcal{D} \} \qquad (4)$$

The question that immediately arises is how the containment checking (i.e., whether $bv_\alpha(f^{1 \rightarrow l}(\vec{in})) \in \mathcal{M}^{bv}$ holds) can be made time-efficient. The authors in [6] represent the set $\mathcal{M}^{bv}$ using *binary decision diagrams* (BDDs) [2]. The containment checking can be done in time *linear* to the number of monitored neurons. In order to reduce the size of the BDD and thus the memory footprint, various heuristics for variable re-ordering[4] can be applied before deploying the monitor.

The second issue is to consider some slight variations in the created binary word, i.e., instead of rejecting every word not in $\mathcal{M}^{bv}$, one may relax the constraint only to reject if $bv_\alpha(f^{1 \rightarrow l}(\vec{in}))$ has a Hamming distance greater than κ to every word in $\mathcal{M}^{bv}$. This can be easily realized in BDD by directly building the set of all words with Hamming distance to any word in $\mathcal{M}^{bv}$ being less or equal to κ [6].

Finally, one can also create more fine-grained decisions, using two binary variables to characterize four intervals rather than using one variable that can only split the domain into two, as detailed in an extension [4]. One limitation of using more variables for encoding one neuron is that the concept of Hamming distance can no longer be mapped with physical interpretations.

Binary Word Monitoring Without BDD, and Abstraction on Convolutional Layers. The above basic principle on binary word encoding has been extended, where within the ML community, a joint team of academia and industry recently uses binary word monitoring to create the state-of-the-art OoD detectors against other techniques [19]. The key innovation in [19] is to utilize hardware accelerators such as GPU, where instead of building a BDD that compactly represents the set of binary words, simply store all binary words as 2D arrays/tensors (via libraries such as `np.ndarray` for numpy or `tf.tensor` for tensorflow). Then the containment checking is done by a hardware-assisted parallelized checking if one of the binary vectors in the tensor matches $bv_\alpha(f^{1 \rightarrow l}(\vec{in}))$. Computing the Hamming distance can be implemented with these libraries by first applying an XOR operation, followed by counting the number of discrepancies. Another innovation is that the authors apply the binary word generation on convolutional layers, each of which may contain multiple channels. For example, we have one channel for a grayscale image and three channels for a color image, respectively. The work adopts adaptive pooling for every channel to select

---

[4] BDDs are minimal acyclic finite automata that accept the fixed-length binary representation of some finite set wrt. a fixed order on the bits; finding an optimal order is NP-complete in general.

the most critical features and obtains a vector for all the channels in the convolutional layer. Finally, the vector is converted into a binary pattern with an adaptive activation function, using p-percentile values for the threshold.

Abstraction-Based Monitoring Using the Range of Neuron Values. Another idea of abstraction-based monitoring is to use the range of each neuron. This idea occurred independently in two papers around the same time [5,11], where we detail the underlying idea in [5]. In [5], the boxed abstraction monitor is introduced due to the need to perform *assume-guarantee-based formal verification*. For formal verification of perception-based deep neural networks where the input dimension is extremely high (e.g., images or lidar point clouds), one encounters both scalability and specification challenges. The network can be too large to be verified. At the same time, we may not be interested in every input $\vec{in} \in \mathbb{R}^{d_0}$ but rather the set of inputs characterizing the human-specified operational domain. As illustrated in Fig. 9, the authors in [5] thus considered building an *abstraction-based monitor* $\mathcal{M}^{box}$ using layer l that ensures to include all input $\vec{in}$ with $(\vec{in}, \vec{label}) \in \mathcal{D}$, the decision mechanism of $\mathcal{M}^{box}$ shall not view $\vec{in}$ as OoD.

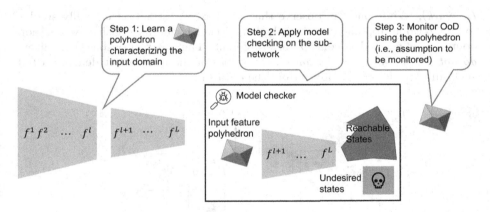

Fig. 9. The role of box abstraction monitors in assume-guarantee-based verification of neural networks

Precisely, the monitor $\mathcal{M}^{box} \stackrel{\text{def}}{=} ([m_1, M_1], \ldots, [m_{d_l}, M_{d_l}])$, where for $i \in \{1, \ldots, d_l\}$, m_i and M_i are defined using Eq. 5, with δ being a small positive constant that can be tuned.

$$m_i \stackrel{\text{def}}{=} \min(\{f_i^{1 \to l}(\vec{in}) \mid (\vec{in}, \vec{label}) \in \mathcal{D}\}) - \delta$$
$$M_i \stackrel{\text{def}}{=} \max(\{f_i^{1 \to l}(\vec{in}) \mid (\vec{in}, \vec{label}) \in \mathcal{D}\}) + \delta$$

(5)

Then $\mathcal{M}^{box}$ considers $\vec{in}$ to be OoD if $\exists i$ such that $f_i^{1\to l}(\vec{in}) \notin [m_i, M_i]$. In layman's words, the monitor is constructed by recording, for each neuron, the largest and smallest possible valuation (plus adding some buffers) that one can obtain when using the data set $\mathcal{D}$.

The creation of the monitor $\mathcal{M}^{box}$ can be used in the assume-guarantee-based formal neural network verification as follows. Given a set of unsafe output states $\mathcal{S}_{risk} \subseteq \mathbb{R}^L$, the assume-guarantee-based formal verification first poses the following safety verification problem:

$$\exists \vec{v} = (v_1, \ldots, v_{d_l}) \in \mathbb{R}^{d_l} \text{ s.t. } v_1 \in [m_1, M_1] \wedge \ldots \wedge v_l \in [m_l, M_l]$$
$$\wedge f^L(f^{L-1}(\ldots f^{l+1}(\vec{v}))) \in \mathcal{S}_{risk} \quad (6)$$

The verification problem is *substantially simpler* than a standard DNN formal verification problem, as it only takes part of the DNN into analysis without considering high-dimensional inputs and layers f_1 to f_l. However, the safety guarantee of no input $\vec{in} \in \mathbb{R}^{d_0}$ generating an unsafe output is only conditional to the assumption where $\forall i : f_i^{1\to l}(\vec{in}) \in [m_i, M_i]$, which is monitored during runtime.

(Remark). While one can observe that the boxed-abstraction is highly similar to the Z-value approach as described in Sect. 4.1, the approach how decision boundary is created is conceptually different. The abstraction-based monitors *do not assume any distribution* on the values of the neuron but demand a full enclosure for all neuron values from the data set.

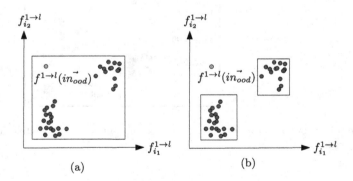

Fig. 10. An example where using two boxes is more appropriate

Extensions of Boxed Monitors. In the following, we highlight a few extensions that researchers in the formal method community created.

Boxed abstraction also suffers from the precision problem. Illustrated in Fig. 10(a), by only recording the minimum and maximum of each neuron value,

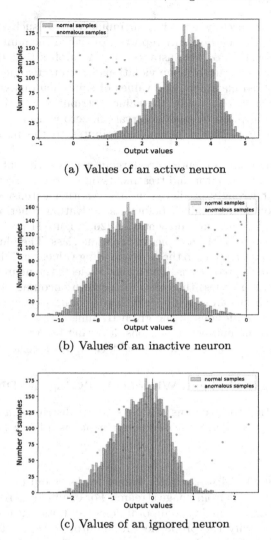

(a) Values of an active neuron

(b) Values of an inactive neuron

(c) Values of an ignored neuron

Fig. 11. Neuron value distribution before ReLU with data in the same class [26]

using only one box leads to including $f^{1 \to l}(\vec{in}_{ood})$. The authors in [24] thus consider an extension where unsupervised learning is first applied to perform clustering, followed by building boxed abstraction monitors for every cluster, as illustrated in Fig. 10(b). The extension thus allows the set of points in the feature space to be considered as "in-distribution" to be a non-convex set, similar to the capabilities of using binary neuron activation patterns.

Towards the concept of non-convex set, the work by Hashemi et al. [9] also starts with a concept similar to that of the Z-value as specified in Sect. 4.1.

However, instead of directly rejecting an input $\vec{in}$ if $\exists i$ such that $f_i^{1 \to l}(\vec{in}) \notin [\mu_i - \kappa\sigma_i, \mu_i + \kappa\sigma_i]$, the method only reports OoD when the number of violations is larger than a constant α. For instance, $\alpha = 2$ implies that the monitor can tolerate the number of neuron range violations by up to two neurons.

In the DNN-based classifiers, the values of some neurons with a class may always be greater than zero, while the value distribution of other neurons may be quite different. Inspired by such observation, zero is usually regarded as the threshold to decide whether a neuron contributes to the pattern of a given class [27].

Finally, the methods presented are largely generic without detailing what layer is appropriate to monitor and treatments on neuron activation patterns on in-distribution but wrongly predicted inputs. Another extension is to consider the distribution of neuron values before its activation function to select the candidate neurons for pattern representation [26]. Figure 11 provides three types of neuron distributions for the samples in the same class. The blue column shows the number of samples leading to the corresponding values, and the red dot shows the values from wrong predictions. The method selects the neurons whose values are always larger than or less than zero for pattern encoding. The pattern of a class consists of neurons and the upper or lower bound to avoid the influence of values from wrong predictions in the given training set. Given an input during run-time, it counts the number of neurons deviating from the specified bounds. If the number is larger than a given threshold, the input is regarded as abnormal.

4.3 Monitoring Techniques Without Analyzing the DNN

Except for extracting the patterns of DNNs or the distribution of output confidence, some works consider ML-based components as a black box and monitor abnormal outputs.

Consistency-Based Monitoring. Some works monitor the consistency between detected objects from image streams. For example, PerceMon [1] adopts specifications in timed quality temporal logic and its extensions with spatial operators to specify the properties. It monitors whether the data stream extracted from the ML-based component satisfies the specified property. The data stream includes the positions, classification, and detection confidence of objects. The structure of the monitor is similar to an existing online monitoring tool RTAMT [18] for STL specifications. The performance of the monitor decreases rapidly with the increasing number of objects in a frame.

Another work considers the consistency in image streams and the consistency with the training data sets [3]. Given the training data set and the associated labels, it divides an image into various regions, collects the attributes of objects for every region, and constructs the dictionary. During runtime, if the location or the size of an object detected in a frame is not in the dictionary, the alarm is triggered. The consistency between various image frames (temporal relation) helps to locate abnormalities such as label flips and object loss.

Learning and Monitoring Operational Design Domains (ODD). Using the training set to estimate the expected distribution of the inputs and/or the outputs is one form of defining (some aspect of) the *operational design domain* the ML-based component is supposed to operate in. A formal description (i.e., a specification in some logic) ϕ' of the complete (human-defined) ODD is often not available or infeasible, or only implicitly given by means of the training set (e.g. pre-classified by a human). That is, in general, we only have an incomplete specification ϕ of the ODD, which is an over-approximation (or relaxation) with $\models (\phi' \rightarrow \phi)$ (as a special case, we have $\phi = \mathsf{true}$); further ϕ might refer to properties (events) which are not observable in the actual implementation. Different variants of refining such an initial incomplete specification ϕ' using the training set or the ML-based component have been proposed recently:

For instance, in [22] the authors treat the already trained ML-based system (e.g. a controller) as a black box containing the ODD specification. By interacting with the black box in an simulated environment (using https://github.com/BerkeleyLearnVerify/VerifAI), a monitor (in case of [22] a decision tree) for detecting OoD-behavior is learned. Conformance testing is used to discover counterexamples which trigger additional simulations. A specification in MTL *for the simulation* (which can thus refer to events that are not observable to the black box and/or which are supposed to be inferred by it) allows to guide the generation of the traces used for training and checking the monitor.

The authors in [16] propose to train e.g. an LSTM (long short-term memory) to predict the future extension of the current run (trajectory) up to some finite horizon, and derive bounds (based on the training and calibration set) on the *quantitative semantics* to decide whether a given specification ϕ will be satisfied by the future run at least with probability $1 - \delta$ as long as the prediction is within the computed bounds. The specification is assumed to be given in bounded STL whose quantitative semantics returns a real number measuring how "robust" the satisfaction is wrt. small changes of the prediction. The requirement that the specification has to be bounded translates into the existence of a finite horizon up to which it suffices to predict future behavior.

Somewhat related is the idea to use the human-specified ODD already during the actual training. E.g. the authors in [23] study how to avoid in reinforcement learning (RL) that the agent is trained on unsafe or unwanted behavior: here, one usually unknown part of the ODD is the environment with which the agent is supposed to interact. The authors therefore use a specification of central safety aspects to not only *shield* the agent from being trained on unsafe behavior, but also to learn an approximate model of the environment to guide the exploration of the environment during RL and further improve the shield. The approximate model itself is obtained by combining learning algorithms for formal languages and computing optimal strategies for two-player games, similar to the approach used in formal synthesis. The computed strategy translates into a Mealy machine, which is then used for shielding the RL.

Entropy-Based Monitoring. As the probabilities provided by the softmax function may be overconfident to out-of-distribution data, some works analyze the distribution of the probabilities from the softmax layer to separate out-of-distribution data from in-distribution data. Entropy-based techniques aim to measure the uncertainty of the probabilities for all the classes. The larger entropy indicates higher uncertainty. For example, one can compute Shannon entropy (Eq. 7) to decide whether the prediction is acceptable, where **p** is the predictive distribution of the softmax layer.

$$H(\mathbf{p}) = -\sum_j p_j \log p_j \tag{7}$$

In addition to Shannon entropy, the generalized entropy can also be applied to measure the uncertainty of the prediction (Eq. 8) [17].

$$G_\gamma(\mathbf{p}) = \sum_j p_j^\gamma (1 - p_j)^\gamma \tag{8}$$

where $\gamma \in (0, 1)$. Lower values of γ are more sensitive to uncertainties in the predictive distribution. The intuition of the generalized entropy is to amplify minor derivations of a predictive distribution from the ideal one-hot encoding.

Facing applications with many classifications, the large fraction of very small predictive probabilities may have a significant impact on the generalized entropy. In such a case, one can consider the top-M classes to capture small entropy variations in the top-M classes.

Finally, the score from entropy can be combined with statistics from training data to improve the performance of out-of-distribution data detection. However, the performance from the combination of various techniques may not always be the best due to the variety of data and model architecture.

5   Challenges Ahead

There is no doubt that monitors are instrumental in realizing safety-critical perception systems. This tutorial outlined the special challenges in monitoring perception systems, followed by a sketch of some notable monitoring techniques proposed by the machine learning community and developments from the formal methods community.

Despite many fruitful results with ongoing technical innovations for DNN-based perception monitoring, we observe the absence of a rigorous design approach for developing, verifying, and validating OoD detectors. Such design principles must be carefully tailored to match the intended functionality and the specific operational domain they are meant to serve. This includes dimensions such as principled data collection (a counterexample is the evaluation conducted in this tutorial; we use Fashion-MNIST as the only OoD examples for MNIST), using reasonable assumptions (e.g., instead of arbitrarily assuming the neuron values have a Gaussian distribution and apply the 3σ rule for characterizing

99.7% of the data, use the more conservative Chebyshev's inequality that is applicable for arbitrary distribution), or the rigorous design of decision boundaries (e.g., consider the joint distribution of the output neurons, use better statistical methods for estimating their joint distribution; use higher moments than expected value and variance).

References

1. Balakrishnan, A., Deshmukh, J., Hoxha, B., Yamaguchi, T., Fainekos, G.: Percemon: online monitoring for perception systems. In: International Conference on Runtime Verification (RV), pp. 297–308 (2021)
2. Bryant, R.E.: Symbolic boolean manipulation with ordered binary-decision diagrams. ACM Comput. Surv. (CSUR) **24**(3), 293–318 (1992)
3. Chen, Y., Cheng, C.-H., Yan, J., Yan, R.: Monitoring object detection abnormalities via data-label and post-algorithm abstractions. In: IEEE/RSJ International Conference on Intelligent Robots and Systems (IROS), pp. 6688–6693 (2021)
4. Cheng, C.-H.: Provably-robust runtime monitoring of neuron activation patterns. In: Design, Automation & Test in Europe Conference & Exhibition (DATE), pp. 1310–1313 (2021)
5. Cheng, C.-H., Huang, C.-H., Brunner, T., Hashemi, V.: Towards safety verification of direct perception neural networks. In: Design, Automation & Test in Europe Conference & Exhibition (DATE), pp. 1640–1643 (2020)
6. Cheng, C.-H., Nührenberg, G., Yasuoka, H.: Runtime monitoring neuron activation patterns. In: Design, Automation & Test in Europe Conference & Exhibition (DATE), pp. 300–303 (2019)
7. Donzé, A., Maler, O.: Robust satisfaction of temporal logic over real-valued signals. In: International Conference on Formal Modeling and Analysis of Timed Systems (FORMATS), pp. 92–106 (2010)
8. Gawlitza, T.M., Seidl, H.: Solving systems of rational equations through strategy iteration. ACM Trans. Program. Lang. Syst. (TOPLAS) **33**(3), 11:1–11:48 (2011)
9. Hashemi, V., Křetínský, J., Mohr, S., Seferis, E.: Gaussian-based runtime detection of out-of-distribution inputs for neural networks. In: Feng, L., Fisman, D. (eds.) RV 2021. LNCS, vol. 12974, pp. 254–264. Springer, Cham (2021). https://doi.org/10.1007/978-3-030-88494-9_14
10. Hendrycks, D.,, Gimpel, K.: A baseline for detecting misclassified and out-of-distribution examples in neural networks. In: International Conference on Learning Representations (ICLR) (2017)
11. Henzinger, T.A., Lukina, A., Schilling, C.: Outside the box: abstraction-based monitoring of neural networks. arXiv preprint arXiv:1911.09032 (2019)
12. Koymans, R.: Specifying real-time properties with metric temporal logic. Real-Time Syst. **2**(4), 255–299 (1990)
13. LeCun, Y.: The MNIST database of handwritten digits. http://yann.lecun.com/exdb/most/ (1998)
14. Lee, K., Lee, K., Lee, H., Shin, J.: A simple unified framework for detecting out-of-distribution samples and adversarial attacks. In: Conference on Neural Information Processing Systems (NeurIPS), vol. 31 (2018)
15. Liang, S., Li, Y., Srikant, R.: Enhancing the reliability of out-of-distribution image detection in neural networks. In: International Conference on Learning Representations (ICLP) (2018)

16. Lindemann, L., Qin, X., Deshmukh, J. V., Pappas, G.J.: Conformal prediction for STL runtime verification. In: International Conference on Cyber-Physical Systems (ICCPS), pp. 142–153 (2023)
17. Liu, X., Lochman, Y., Zach, C.: Gen: pushing the limits of softmax-based out-of-distribution detection. In: IEEE/CVF Conference on Computer Vision and Pattern Recognition (CVPR), pp. 23946–23955 (2023)
18. Ničković, D., Yamaguchi, T.: RTAMT: online robustness monitors from STL. In: International Symposium on Automated Technology for Verification and Analysis (ATVA), pp. 564–571 (2020)
19. Olber, B., Radlak, K., Popowicz, A., Szczepankiewicz, M., Chachuła, K.: Detection of out-of-distribution samples using binary neuron activation patterns. In: IEEE/CVF Conference on Computer Vision and Pattern Recognition (CVPR), pp. 3378–3387 (2023)
20. Pnueli, A.: The temporal logic of programs. In: Annual Symposium on Foundations of Computer Science (FOCS), pp. 46–57 (1977)
21. Qutub, S., et al.: Hardware faults that matter: understanding and estimating the safety impact of hardware faults on object detection dnns. In: International Conference on Computer Safety, Reliability, and Security (SafeComp), pp. 298–318 (2022)
22. Torfah, H., Xie, C., Junges, S., Vazquez-Chanlatte, M., Seshia, S.A.: Learning monitorable operational design domains for assured autonomy. In: International Symposium on Automated Technology for Verification and Analysis (ATVA), pp. 3–22 (2022)
23. Waga, M., Castellano, E., Pruekprasert, S., Klikovits, S., Takisaka, T., Hasuo, I.: Dynamic shielding for reinforcement learning in black-box environments. In: International Symposium on Automated Technology for Verification and Analysis (ATVA), pp. 25–41 (2022)
24. Wu, C., Falcone, Y., Bensalem, S.: Customizable reference runtime monitoring of neural networks using resolution boxes. arXiv preprint arXiv:2104.14435 (2021)
25. Xiao, H., Rasul, K., Vollgraf, R.: Fashion-MNIST: a novel image dataset for benchmarking machine learning algorithms. arXiv preprint arXiv:1708.07747 (2017)
26. Yan, R., Chen, Y., Gao, H., Yan, J.: Test case prioritization with neuron valuation based pattern. Sci. Comput. Program. (SCP) **215**, 102761 (2022)
27. Zhang, K., Zhang, Y., Zhang, L., Gao, H., Yan, R., Yan, J.: Neuron activation frequency based test case prioritization. In: International Symposium on Theoretical Aspects of Software Engineering (TASE), pp. 81–88 (2020)

Monitorability for Runtime Verification

Klaud Havelund[1] and Doron Peled[2(✉)]

[1] Laboratory for Reliable Software, Jet Propulsion Laboratory,
California Institute of Technology, Pasadena, USA
[2] Department of Computer Science, Bar Ilan University, Ramat Gan, Israel
doron.peled@gmail.com

Abstract. Runtime verification (RV) facilitates the formal analysis of execution traces. In particular, it permits monitoring the execution of a system and checking it against a temporal specification. Online RV observes, at any moment, a prefix of the complete monitored execution and is required to provide a verdict whether *all* the complete executions that share that prefix satisfy or falsify the specification. Not every property (and for every kind of verdict) lends itself to obtaining such an early verdict. Monitorability of a temporal property is defined as the ability to provide positive (success) or negative (failure) verdicts after observing a finite prefix of the execution. We classify temporal properties based on their monitorability and present related monitoring algorithms. A common practice in runtime verification is to concentrate on the class of *safety* properties, where a failure to satisfy the specification can always be detected in finite time. In the second part of the paper we concentrate on monitoring safety properties and their place among the other classes of properties in terms of algorithms and complexity.

1 Introduction

Runtime verification (RV) allows monitoring executions of a system, either online or offline, checking them against a formal specification. It can be applied to improve the reliability of critical systems, including safety as well as security aspects, and can more generally be applied for processing streaming information. RV is not a comprehensive verification method such as model checking [7,9,23], as it is applied separately to executions of the system one at a time. On the other hand, due to its more modest goal, RV lacks of some of the restrictions of more comprehensive formal methods related to complexity and applicability.

The specifications, against which the system is checked during RV, are often expressed in *linear temporal logic* (LTL) [19]. These properties are traditionally interpreted over infinite execution sequences. This corresponds to the case where the number

---

[1] One can of course distinguish the case of terminating executions, or assume some indefinite padding by an *end-of-execution* event.

The research performed by Klaus Havelund was carried out at Jet Propulsion Laboratory, California Institute of Technology, under a contract with the National Aeronautics and Space Administration. The research performed by Doron Peled was partially funded by Israeli Science Foundation grant 1464/18: "Efficient Runtime Verification for Systems with Lots of Data and its Applications".

P. Katsaros and L. Nenzi (Eds.): RV 2023, LNCS 14245, pp. 447–460, 2023.
https://doi.org/10.1007/978-3-031-44267-4_25

of events that the monitored system can emit is unbounded[1]. Indeed, the input trace is often a priori not limited to a specific length, and checking it against a given specification is supposed to follow it for as long as the monitored system is running. At any time, only a finite prefix of the system is observed. For runtime verification to be useful, it is necessary to be able to provide a verdict after observing a finite prefix of an execution sequence (also referred to as just a *prefix*).

For example, consider the property $\Box p$ (for some atomic proposition p), which asserts that p always holds throughout the execution. A prefix of an execution can be *refuted* by a runtime monitor, i.e., demonstrating a *failure* to satisfy $\Box p$, if p does not hold in some observed event. At this point, no matter how the execution is extended, the property fail to hold. On the other hand, no finite prefix of an execution can guarantee a positive verdict that $\Box p$ holds, since no matter how long we have observed that p has been holding, it may still stop holding in some future. In a similar way, the property $\Diamond p$, which asserts that p will eventually happen, cannot be refuted, since even if p has not happened yet, it may hold at any time in the future; on the other hand, once p holds, we have established that the property is satisfied, independent on any continuation, and we can issue a positive (*success*) verdict. For the property $\Box \Diamond p$ we can never provide a verdict in finite time, since for a finite prefix p can hold only finitely many times.

The *monitorability problem* of a temporal property was studied in [5,10,22]. Accordingly, a specification property is considered to be monitorable if after monitoring any finite prefix, we still have a possibility to obtain a positive or a negative verdict in a finite number of steps. Nevertheless, it is possible that a priori, or after some prefix, only one type of verdicts is possible.

We follow [21] in classifying temporal properties as an extension of Lamport's *safety* and *liveness* properties. The class *Guarantee* was defined to be the dual of *safety* in [19], i.e., the negation of a safety property is a guarantee property and vice versa. We then defined *morbidity* as the dual of *liveness*. To complete this classification to cover all possible temporal specification we added another class that we termed *quaestio*. In particular the *safety* class includes the properties whose failure can be detected after a finite prefix, and the *liveness* properties are those where one can never conclude a failure after a finite prefix.

The second part of the paper focuses on safety properties. In RV, one often expresses safety properties in the form $\Box \varphi$, where φ is a past LTL formula. Furthermore, it is often only the past property φ that is monitored, returning a *yes/no* verdict for the currently observed prefix. We describe the algorithms for monitoring such safety properties and compare them to the future LTL monitoring algorithm in terms of complexity. Monitoring propositional past formulas was extended to first order safety properties [3,13]. In particular, this was focused on monitoring past-time first order LTL properties against traces that contain data. Although this resulted in quite efficient monitors, we show some theoretical limitations on monitoring first order LTL properties.

2 Preliminaries

2.1 Runtime Verification

Runtime verification [2,14] refers to the use of rigorous (formal) techniques for *processing* execution traces emitted by a system being observed. In general, the purpose of RV is to evaluate the state of the observed system. Since only single executions (or collections thereof) are analyzed, RV is devoid of some of the complexity and computational restrictions that some of the more comprehensive formal methods have. But on the other hand, RV does not provide a comprehensive coverage.

An execution trace is generated by the observed executing system, typically by instrumenting the system to generate events when important transitions take place. Instrumentation can be manual, by inserting logging statements in the code, or it can be automated using instrumentation software, such as aspect-oriented programming frameworks. Processing of RV can take place online, as the system executes, or offline, by processing log files produced by the system. In the case of online processing, observations can be used to control (shield) the monitored system [6].

In specification-based runtime verification, an execution trace is checked against a property expressed in a formal (often temporal) logic or using automata notation. More formally, assume a finite prefix of an execution of an observed system up to a certain point is captured as an execution trace $\sigma = e_1.e_2. \ldots .e_n$, which is a sequence of observed events. Then the RV problem can be formulated as constructing a program, which when applied to the trace σ, returns some data value in a domain of interest D. In specification-based RV, the monitor is generated from a formal specification, given e.g. as a temporal logic formula, a state machine, or a regular expression. The domain of interest D is often the Boolean domain or some extension of it [4] (in particular adding a third value "?" for *yet unknown*) indicating whether the execution trace conforms to the specification.

The input trace for RV is typically observed one event at a time and the monitoring algorithm updates a *summary* that contains enough information to provide given verdicts without observing the previous events. This summary can be, e.g., a state in an automaton that implements the monitor, or a vector of Boolean values representing the subformulas of the specification that hold given the observed prefix. Updating the summary upon seeing a new event needs to be performed efficiently, in particular in online RV, to keep up with the speed of reported events. The complexity of updating the summary is called the *incremental complexity* and needs to be kept minimal. In particular, this complexity need not depend on the length of the prefixed observed so far, which can grow arbitrarily.

Monitored execution traces are often unbounded in length, representing the fact that the observed system "keeps running", without a known termination point. Hence it is important that the monitoring program is capable of producing verdicts based on finite prefixes of the execution trace observed so far. Monitorability focuses on the kind of verdicts that can be produced based finite prefixes given a specific property.

2.2 Linear Temporal Logic

The classical definition of (future) linear temporal logic is based on future modal operators [19] with the following syntax:

$$\varphi ::= true \mid p \mid (\varphi \wedge \varphi) \mid \neg \varphi \mid (\varphi \, \mathcal{U} \, \varphi) \mid \bigcirc \varphi$$

where p is a proposition from a finite set of propositions P, with $\mathcal{U}$ standing for *until*, and $\bigcirc$ standing for *next-time*. One can also write *false* $= \neg true$, $(\varphi \vee \psi) = \neg(\neg \varphi \wedge \neg \psi)$,

$(\varphi \to \psi) = (\neg \varphi \vee \psi)$, $\Diamond \varphi = (true\; \mathcal{U} \varphi)$ (for *eventually* φ) and $\Box \varphi = \neg \Diamond \neg \varphi$ (for *always* φ).

An event e consists of a subset of the propositions in P. These are the propositions that were observed to *hold* or to be *true* during that event. A *trace* $\sigma = e_1.e_2.e_3 \ldots$ is an infinite sequence of events. We denote the event e_i in σ by $\sigma(i)$. LTL formulas are interpreted over an infinite sequence of events. LTL semantics is defined as follows:

- $\sigma, i \models true$.
- $\sigma, i \models p$ iff $p \in \sigma(i)$.
- $\sigma, i \models \neg \varphi$ iff not $\sigma, i \models \varphi$.
- $\sigma, i \models (\varphi \wedge \psi)$ iff $\sigma, i \models \varphi$ and $\sigma, i \models \psi$.
- $\sigma, i \models \bigcirc \varphi$ iff $\sigma, i+1 \models \varphi$.
- $\sigma, i \models (\varphi \mathcal{U} \psi)$ iff for some $j \geq i$, $\sigma, j \models \psi$, and for each k such that $i \leq k < j$, $\sigma, k \models \varphi$.

Then define $\sigma \models \varphi$ when $\sigma, 1 \models \varphi$.

3 Monitorability

Online runtime verification observes at each point a prefix of the monitored execution sequence and provides a verdict against a specification. There are three kinds of verdicts:

- *failed* (or *refuted* or *negative*) when the current prefix cannot be extended in any way into an infinite execution that satisfies the specification. Then the current prefix is called a *bad* prefix [5].
- *satisfied* (or *established* or *positive*) when any infinite extension of the current prefix satisfies the specification. Then the current prefix is called a *good* prefix [5].
- *undecided* when the current prefix can be extended into an infinite execution that satisfies the specification but also extended into an infinite execution that satisfies its negation.

Undecided prefixes that cannot be extended to either a good or a bad prefix are called *ugly* [5], as no further monitoring information will be obtained by continuing the monitoring. As will be shown in Sect. 3.2, at the expense of a more complex algorithm, one can also decide and report when the current prefix is ugly.

Monitorability of a property φ is defined in [5] as the lack of *ugly* prefixes for the property φ. This requirement means that during monitoring, we never "lose hope" to obtain a verdict. This definition is consistent with an early definition in [22]. The definition of monitorability is a bit crude in the sense that it only distinguish between specifications for which during monitoring one can always still expect a verdict, and those for which this is not the case. But it lumps together specifications where only a positive verdict or only a negative verdict can be expected. We study here monitorability in a wider context, classifying the temporal properties into families according to the ability to produce particular verdicts.

3.1   Characterizing Temporal Properties According to Monitorability

Safety and *liveness* temporal properties were defined informally on infinite execution sequences by Lamport [18] as *something bad cannot happen* and *something* good *will happen*. These informal definitions were later formalized by Alpern and Schneider [1]. *Guarantee* properties where defined by Manna and Pnueli [19]. We add to this classes the *morbidity* properties, which is the dual class of *liveness* properties. This leads us to the following classical way of describing these four classes of properties.

- *safety*: A property φ is a *safety* property, if for every execution that does not satisfy it, there is a finite prefix such that completing it in any possible way into an infinite sequence would violate φ.
- *guarantee* (co-*safety*): A property φ is a *guarantee* property if for every execution satisfying it, there is a finite prefix such that completing it in any possible way into an infinite sequence satisfies φ.
- *liveness*: A property φ is a *liveness* property if every finite sequence of events can be extended into an execution that satisfies φ.
- *morbidity* (co-*liveness*): A property φ is a *morbidity* property if every finite sequence of events can be extended to an execution that violates φ.

Safety, guarantee, liveness and *morbidity* can be seen as characterizing different cases related to the monitorability of temporal properties: if a *safety* property is violated, there will be a finite *bad* prefix witnessing it; on the other hand, for a *liveness* property, one can never provide such a finite negative evidence. We suggest the following alternative definitions of classes of temporal properties, given in terms of the verdicts available for the different classes. The adverbs *always* and *never* in the definitions of the classes below correspond to *for all the executions* and *for none of the executions*, correspondingly. The four classes of properties mentioned above, however, do not cover the entire set of possible temporal properties, and we need to add two more classes to complete the classification.

- AFR (*safety*): Always Finitely Refutable: for each execution where the property *does not hold*, refutation can be identified after a finite (*bad*) prefix, which cannot be extended to an (infinite) execution that satisfies the property.
- AFS (*guarantee*): Always Finitely Satisfiable: For each execution in which the property is satisfied, satisfaction can be identified after a finite (*good*) prefix, where each extension of it will satisfy the property.
- NFR (*liveness*): Never Finitely Refutable: For no execution, can a *bad* prefix be identified after a finite prefix. That is, every finite prefix can be extended into an (infinite) execution that satisfies the property.
- NFS (*morbidity*): Never Finitely Satisfiable: For no execution can a *good* prefix be identified after a finite prefix. That is, every finite prefix can be extended into an (infinite) execution that does not satisfy the property.
- SFR: Sometimes Finitely Refutable: for some infinite executions that violate the property, refutation can be identified after a finite (*bad*) prefix; for other infinite executions violating the property, this is not the case.

- SFS: Sometimes Finitely Satisfiable: for some infinite executions that satisfy the property, satisfaction can be identified after a finite (*good*) prefix; for other infinite executions satisfying the property, this is not the case.

Let φ be any property expressible in LTL. Then φ represents the set of executions satisfying it. It is clear by definition that φ must be either in AFR, SFR or in NFR (since this covers all possibilities). It also holds that φ must be in either AFS, SFS or in NFS. Every temporal property must belong then to one class of the form XFR, where X stands for A, S or N, and also to one class of the form XFS, again with X is A, S or N. The possible intersections between classes is shown in Fig. 1. Below we give examples for the nine combinations of XFR and XFS, appearing in clockwise order according to Fig. 1, ending with the intersection SFR $\cap$ SFS, termed *Quaetio* that appears in the middle.

- SFR $\cap$ NFS: $(\Diamond p \wedge \Box q)$
- AFR $\cap$ NFS: $\Box p$
- AFR $\cap$ SFS: $(p \vee \Box q)$
- AFR $\cap$ AFS: $\bigcirc p$
- SFR $\cap$ AFS: $(p \wedge \Diamond q)$
- NFR $\cap$ AFS: $\Diamond p$
- NFR $\cap$ SFS: $(\Box p \vee \Diamond q)$
- NFR $\cap$ NFS: $\Box \Diamond p$
- SFR $\cap$ SFS: $((p \vee \Box \Diamond p) \wedge \bigcirc q)$

Another way to cover all the temporal properties is as the union of *safety* (AFR), *guarantee* (AFS), *liveness* (NFR), *morbidity* (NFS) and *quaestio* (SFR $\cap$ SFS). Every *safety* property is monitorable. Because *guarantee* properties are the negations of *safety* properties, one obtains using a symmetric argument that every *guarantee* property is also monitorable.

The shadowed areas in Fig. 1 in the intersections between the classes of properties NFS, SFS and the classes NFR, SFR correspond to the cases where monitorability is not guaranteed. While in NFR $\cap$ NFS there are no monitorable properties, in the other three intersections there are both monitorable and nonmonitorable properties. Examples for these cases appear in the following table.

Class	monitorable example	non-monitorable example
SFR $\cap$ SFS	$((\Diamond r \vee \Box \Diamond p) \wedge \bigcirc q)$	$((p \vee \Box \Diamond p) \wedge \bigcirc q)$
SFR $\cap$ NFS	$(\Diamond p \wedge \Box q)$	$(\Box \Diamond p \wedge \bigcirc q)$
NFR $\cap$ SFS	$(\Box p \vee \Diamond q)$	$((\neg p \, \mathcal{U} \Diamond (p \wedge \bigcirc \neg p)) \vee \Box \Diamond p)$

3.2   Runtime Verification Algorithms for Monitorability

The following algorithm [8, 17] monitors executions and provides *success* (positive) or *fail* (negative) verdict of the checked property whenever a minimal *good* or a *bad* prefix is detected, respectively.

A procedure for detecting the minimal *good* prefix when monitoring an execution against the specification φ is as follows:

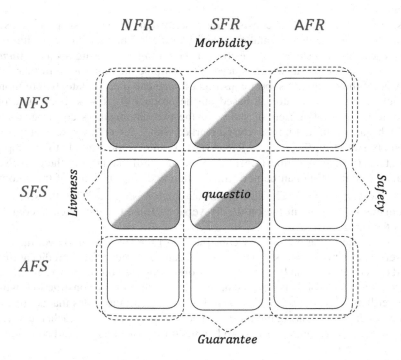

Fig. 1. Classification of properties according to monitorability: filled space correspond to non-monitorable properties.

1. Construct a Büchi automaton $\mathcal{A}_{\neg\varphi}$ for $\neg\varphi$, e.g., using the translation in [12]. This automaton is not necessarily deterministic [25].
2. Using DFS, find the states of $\mathcal{A}_{\neg\varphi}$ from which one *cannot* reach a cycle that contains an accepting state and *remove* these states.
3. *On-the-fly subset construction:* While monitoring input events, maintain the current subset of states that the automaton $\mathcal{A}_{\neg\varphi}$ reaches after observing the current input as follows:
   - Start with the set of initial states of the automaton $\mathcal{A}_{\neg\varphi}$.
   - Given the current set of successors S and a newly occurring event $e \in 2^P$ that extends the monitored prefix, the set of successors S' contains the successors of the states in S according to the transition relation Δ of $\mathcal{A}_{\neg\varphi}$. That is, $S' = \{s' \mid s \in S \wedge (s, e, s') \in \Delta\}$.
   - Reaching the empty set of states, the monitored sequence is *good* and a positive verdict is issued. This is because the empty subset of states means that following the current inputs, the automaton $\mathcal{A}_{\neg\varphi}$ cannot complete the input into an accepting execution.

A symmetric procedure constructs $\mathcal{A}_{\varphi}$ for detecting minimal *bad* prefixes. One can monitor using both $\mathcal{A}_{\neg\varphi}$ and $\mathcal{A}_{\varphi}$ at the same time, providing both failure and success verdicts. Translating the formula φ into a Büchi automaton can result in an automaton

$\mathcal{A}_\varphi$ of size $O(2^{|\varphi|})$. The subset construction described above has to keep in each state a set of states. Thus, the incremental complexity of the RV monitoring algorithm is also $O(2^{|\varphi|})$. The subsets of states that are constructed during monitoring form the *summary* of the trace observed so far, which is needed to continue the monitoring further.

Instead of the on-the-fly subset construction, one can precalculate, before monitoring, a deterministic automaton $\mathcal{B}$ based on the product $\mathcal{A}_\varphi \times \mathcal{A}_{\neg\varphi}$. Each state of the automaton is a pair of subsets of states, of the two automata, as constructed above. Then, each state of this automaton can be marked with $\bot$, $\top$ or ?, where $\bot$ corresponds to an empty subset of $\mathcal{A}_\varphi$ states (a *failed* verdict) and $\top$ corresponds to an empty set of $\mathcal{A}_{\neg\varphi}$ states (a *success* verdict). Instead of the on-the-fly updates in the above subset construction, monitoring can be performed while updating the state of the automaton based on the automaton $\mathcal{B}$. The size of this automaton is $O(2^{2^{|\varphi|}})$, but the size of each state remains $O(2^{|\varphi|})$, as in the on-the-fly version. Thus, the incremental complexity remains the same.

An advantage of the preliminary construction of the automaton $\mathcal{B}$ over the on-the-fly subset construction described above is that it can be further used to predict at runtime the kind of verdicts that can be expected after observing the current prefix. To allow this prediction, each state of $\mathcal{B}$ is annotated, during the preliminary construction, with the kind of verdicts, $\top$ (*success*), $\bot$ (*failed*) or both, that mark the nodes that are reachable from the current state. During monitoring, when neither verdicts is reachable anymore, the current prefix is identified as *ugly*. When the initial state of $\mathcal{B}$ is marked as *ugly*, the property is nonmonitorable.

3.3   A Lower Bound Example for LTL Monitoring

We present an example, following [17], to show that monitoring an LTL specification requires a summary of size exponential in the length of the property.

The specification is a safety property. It asserts about a nonempty and finite sequence of blocks of 0 and 1 bits of length n. Each block starts with the symbol #. Then, a final block, separated from the previous one by $ follows. After the last block, the symbol & repeats indefinitely. The property asserts that if the trace has the above structure, the last block (the one after the $) is identical to one of the blocks that appeared before. We denote by $\bigcirc^i$ a sequence of i occurrences of $\bigcirc$ in an LTL formula. The formula has length quadratic in n.

$$(\# \wedge \Box(((\# \vee \$) \rightarrow \wedge_{1 \le i \le n} \bigcirc^i(0 \vee 1)) \wedge (\# \rightarrow \bigcirc^{n+1}(\# \vee \$)) \wedge (\$ \rightarrow \bigcirc^{n+1}\Box\&))) \rightarrow$$
$$\Diamond(\# \wedge \wedge_{1 \le i \le n}((\bigcirc^i 0 \wedge \Box(\$ \rightarrow \bigcirc^i 0)) \vee (\bigcirc^i 1 \wedge \Box(\$ \rightarrow \bigcirc^i 1)))))$$

With n bits, one can encode 2^n different blocks. During the monitoring, the summary must remember which subset of blocks we have seen before inspecting the last block that appears after the $. Encoding the set of blocks that were observed requires space of size $O(2^n)$. With less memory, there will be two prefixes with different sets of occurring blocks, which have the same memory representation; this means that runtime verification will not be able to check the execution correctly.

4   Monitoring *Safety* Properties

4.1   Past Propositional Temporal Logic

Safety properties are a subset of the (future) LTL properties. One can apply a decision procedure [24] to check whether an LTL property forms a safety property. However, there is an alternative way of expressing LTL safety properties, which guarantees syntactically that the given property is safety. This is based on using *past* operators for LTL, symmetric to the future operators. Let P be a finite set of *propositions*. The syntax of *past-time propositional linear time temporal logic* PLTL is defined as follows.

$$\varphi :: = true \mid p \mid (\varphi \wedge \varphi) \mid \neg \varphi \mid (\varphi \mathcal{S} \varphi) \mid \ominus \varphi$$

where $p \in P$.

The operator $\ominus$ (for *previous-time*) is the past mirror of the $\bigcirc$ operator, $\diamondsuit$ is the past mirror of $\diamond$, $\boxminus$ is the past mirror of $\square$ and $\mathcal{S}$ (for *Since*) is the past mirror of $\mathcal{U}$. We can use the following additional operators: $false = \neg true$, $(\varphi \vee \psi) = \neg(\neg \varphi \wedge \neg \psi)$, $(\varphi \rightarrow \psi) = (\neg \varphi \vee \psi)$, $\diamondsuit \varphi = (true \, \mathcal{S} \, \varphi)$, $\boxminus \varphi = \neg \diamondsuit \neg \varphi$.

Let $\sigma = e_1 \ldots e_n$ be a finite sequence of events, consisting each of a subset of the propositions P. We denote the

Semantics. The semantics of a PLTL formula φ with respect to a finite trace σ is defined as follows:

- $\sigma, i \models true$.
- $\sigma, i \models p$ iff $p \in \sigma(i)$.
- $\sigma, i \models (\varphi \wedge \psi)$ iff $\sigma, i \models \varphi$ and $\sigma, i \models \psi$.
- $\sigma, i \models \neg \varphi$ iff not $\sigma, i \models \varphi$.
- $\sigma, i \models \ominus \varphi$ iff $|\sigma| > 1$ and $\sigma, i - 1 \models \varphi$.
- $\sigma, i \models (\varphi \mathcal{S} \psi)$ iff for some $j \leq i$, $\sigma, j \models \psi$, and for each k such that $j < k \leq i$, $\sigma, k \models \varphi$.

We can combine the past and future definitions of LTL. However, adding the past operators does not increase the expressive power of (future) LTL [11]. Based on the combined logic, we define four extensions of PLTL, which consist of a past property prefixed with one or two future operators from $\{\diamond, \square\}$. All extensions are interpreted over infinite sequences:

- $\square$PLTL, which consists of PLTL formulas prefixed with the future $\square$ operator.
- $\diamond$PLTL, which is, similarly, PLTL formulas prefixed by the $\diamond$ operator.
- $\square\diamond$PLTL, which consists of PLTL formulas prefixed with $\square\diamond$.
- $\diamond\square$PLTL, which consists of PLTL formulas prefixed with $\diamond\square$.

Note the duality between the first two classes, $\square$PLTL and $\diamond$PLTL: for every formula φ, $\neg \square \varphi = \diamond \neg \varphi$. Thus, the negation of a $\square$PLTL property is a $\diamond$PLTL property and vice versa. Similarly, for every φ, $\neg \square \diamond \varphi = \diamond \square \neg \varphi$, making the latter two classes also dual. Thus, the negation of a $\square\diamond$PLTL property is a $\diamond\square$PLTL property.

Manna and Pnueli [19] identified the LTL *safety* properties with $\square$PLTL and the *guarantee* properties with $\diamond$PLTL. They have also called the properties of $\square\diamond$PLTL and

$\Diamond\Box$PLTL *recurrence* and *obligation*, respectively. The entire set of LTL properties can be expressed as Boolean combination of recurrence and obligation properties. Except for safety and liveness properties, the Manna and Pnueli classification is orthogonal to the one that we explored here.

4.2   RV for Propositional Past Time LTL

Past properties play an important role in RV. Runtime verification of temporal specifications concentrates in many cases on the class of properties $\Box$PLTL. Further, instead of checking a property of the form $\Box\varphi$, one often checks whether φ holds for the trace observed so far, returning *true/false* output. When the current trace violates φ, then the fact that $\Box\varphi$ fails can be concluded.

The RV algorithm for past LTL, presented in [15] is based on the observation that the semantics of the past time formulas $\ominus\varphi$ and $(\varphi S \psi)$ in the current state i is defined in terms of the semantics of its subformula(s) in the previous state $i-1$. This becomes clearer when we rewrite the semantic definition of the S operator to a form that is more applicable for runtime verification.

– $(\sigma,i) \models (\varphi S \psi)$ if $(\sigma,i) \models \psi$, or $i > 1$ and both $(\sigma,i) \models \varphi$ and $(\sigma,i-1) \models (\varphi S \psi)$.

The semantic definition of past LTL is recursive in both the length of the prefix and the structure of the property. Thus, subformulas are evaluated based on smaller subformulas, and the evaluation of subformulas in the previous state. The algorithm shown below monitors a trace against a past temporal property η. It uses two vectors of values indexed by subformulas: pre, which summarizes the truth values of the subformulas for the observed prefix *without* its last event and now, for the observed prefix *including* its last event.

1. Initially, for each subformula φ of η, now$(\varphi) := false$.
2. Observe a new event e (as a set of propositions) as input.
3. Let pre $:=$ now.
4. Make the following updates for each subformula. If φ is a subformula of ψ then now(φ) is updated before now(ψ).
   – now$(p) := p \in e$.
   – now$(true) := true$.
   – now$((\varphi \wedge \psi)) :=$ now(φ) *and* now(ψ).
   – now$(\neg\varphi) := not$ now(φ).
   – now$((\varphi S \psi)) :=$ now(ψ) *or* (now(φ) *and* pre$((\varphi S \psi)))$.
   – now$(\ominus \varphi) :=$ pre(φ).
5. If now$(\eta) = false$ then report a violation, otherwise goto step 2.

As opposed to the monitoring algorithm for future LTL, presented in Sect. 3.2, which uses a summary exponential in the size of the monitored property, this algorithm has a summary and an incremental complexity that is linear in the length of the specification.

4.3   From Monitoring Past Property φ to Monitoring $\square\varphi$

We present an algorithm for specifications of the form $\square$PLTL. Recall the algorithm for future propositional LTL presented in Sect. 3.2. It identifies minimal good and bad prefixes hence provides a *success/failed* verdicts for the monitored input trace with respect to the specification.

For the case of $\square$PLTL, a simpler construction can be used. A single *deterministic* automaton $\mathcal{D}_{\square\varphi}$ can be constructed for the specification $\square\varphi$. Each state s of this automaton corresponds to the set of subformulas $sf(s)$ of φ that hold after a trace that is consistent with the inputs on any path that leads from the initial state to s. Calculating the transition relation is similar to updating the summary in the RV algorithm for past propositional LTL, as shown at the beginning of Sect. 4.2, using the two vectors pre and now. Let $s \xrightarrow{Q} s'$, where Q is the currently inspected set of propositions. Define pre as follows: for a subformula η of the given specification, $\text{pre}(\eta) = \textit{true}$ iff $\eta \in sf(s)$. For a propositional letter p, set $\text{now}(p) = \textit{true}$ iff $p \in Q$. Now, for the subformulas in $sub(\varphi)$ that do not consist solely of a proposition, calculate now as in Step 4 in the algorithm in Sect. 4.2. Then, for $\eta \in sub(\varphi)$, $\eta \in sf(s')$ iff $\text{now}(\eta) = \textit{true}$. The initial state consists of the empty set of subformulas. A state of $\mathcal{D}_{\square\varphi}$ is *accepting* if it contains the formula φ itself.

One can use $\mathcal{D}_{\square\varphi}$ to decide on verdicts when monitoring against the specification $\square\varphi$. An (infinite) execution satisfies $\square\varphi$ if it runs only through accepting states. Note that the number of states is $O(2^{|\varphi|})$, but each state can be represented using space linear of $|\varphi|$. We mark the states from which all the future successors are accepting by $\top$. Initially, mark every accepting node by $\top$. Then, repeatedly remove the $\top$ marking from nodes that have a successor that is *not* marked by $\top$. Keep doing that until there is no $\top$ marking that can be removed[2]. We mark states where there are no infinite accepting continuations $\bot$. To do that, start by marking the non accepting nodes by $\bot$. Repeatedly, mark by $\bot$ nodes whose entire set of successors are already marked by $\bot$. Keep doing this until no new node can be marked[3]. Finally, nodes that are not marked by $\top$ or $\bot$ are marked by ?.

Marking the states of the automaton $\mathcal{D}_{\square\varphi}$ is done as a preliminary step. Runtime verification uses the marked automaton $\mathcal{D}_{\square\varphi}$ to monitor input traces and return the corresponding verdict. The RV algorithm then needs to keep the current state, and can figure out the successor state based on the two-vector update. Consequently, the size of the summary, and the incremental complexity are linear in the size of φ. This can be compared to the automaton-based RV algorithm for future LTL from Sect. 3.2, which needs to keep a set of states of the constructed automata, hence requiring exponential space and time for each update.

We need to take the fact that the algorithm for $\square$PLTL has a linear incremental complexity and a linear summary in the size of the specification with a grain of salt. The example in Sect. 3.3 shows that the summary for the presented property needs to be exponential in n. This (safety) property is presented in future LTL with a formula whose

---

[2] This is similar to the model checking algorithm for the CTL property $AG\top$ [7].

[3] This is similar to the model checking algorithm for the CTL property $AF\bot$.

size is quadratic in n. But for $\Box\varphi$ with a past property φ, a summary that is only linear in $|\varphi|$ is sufficient. Unfortunately, this implies that expressing this property in the form $\Box\varphi$ requires a formula whose length is exponential in n. A similar reasoning implies that for a reversed property, where the block of length n that needs to repeat appears at the *beginning* rather at the end, the property can be written with past LTL formula of quadratic size in n, but the future LTL property needs to be of length exponential in n.

Monitoring with respect to a past property φ, rather than $\Box\varphi$, the verdict can change between *true* and *false* multiple times. However, for safety properties we may be mostly interested in finding the case where the current prefix fails to satisfy φ. When the verdict for the current prefix is *false*, we can issue a *fail* verdict for $\Box\varphi$. However, it is possible that a prefix σ satisfies φ, while $\Box\varphi$ does not hold for all extensions of this prefix to an infinite execution. Consider as an example the property $\Box(\ominus\ominus false \vee \ominus\ominus p)$, which becomes *false* only two events after the first event where $\neg p$ holds (the disjunct $\ominus\ominus false$ is used to rule out failure due to fact that the failing prefix is shorter than two events). Thus, although $\Box\varphi$ should return a *fail* verdict, performing RV on the past property φ will only reveal that two events later than on the minimal trace. Monitoring $\Box\varphi$ using $\mathcal{D}_{\Box\varphi}$ would provide the *fail* verdict at the minimal trace that cannot be extended to satisfy $\Box\varphi$.

If φ holds for some observed prefix σ but $\Box\varphi$ fails on every infinite extension of σ, then we will eventually observe an extension $\sigma.\rho$ of σ, where $|\rho|$ *depends on the size of* φ and where φ does not hold. Thus, if we do not want to use the automaton $\mathcal{D}_{\Box\varphi}$ to decide when $\Box\varphi$ already holds, but instead check φ after each new event, then there is a limit to the number of steps that we need to wait until $\neg\varphi$ will fail to hold that depends on $|\varphi|$. To see this, consider a finite trace σ where φ holds and where all the infinite extensions of σ have some finite prefix that does not satisfy φ. Let n be the number of states of $\mathcal{D}_{\Box\varphi}$, which is known to be bounded by $O(2^{|\varphi|})$ [16]. Running the deterministic automaton $\mathcal{D}_{\Box\varphi}$ on σ, we end up in some state s. Suppose, for the contradiction, that there is a path ρ from s with $|\rho| > n$, where all of its prefixes satisfy φ. Then running $\mathcal{D}_{\Box\varphi}$ on the input ρ from the state s, one must pass through at least one state of $\mathcal{D}_{\Box\varphi}$ more than once. This allows constructing ("pumping") an infinite path on $\mathcal{D}_{\Box\varphi}$, where all of its states indicate that the prefix so far satisfies φ, a contradiction.

4.4   From Monitoring Propositional to First Order Temporal Logic

Runtime verification was extended to specifications that contain data. In particular, the tools DejaVu and MonPoly[4] allow specification that is based on first-order past LTL. An *event* in this case consists of predicates with parameters, i.e., in the form $q(3)$. DejaVu algorithm is restricted to checking a first order past property φ, rather than checking $\Box\varphi$.

For first order RV, the problem of discovering that a finite trace σ cannot be extended to satisfy $\Box\varphi$, although the trace itself still satisfies φ intensifies: in some cases, the

---

[4] MonPoly allows a limited use of *finite* future, but the monitoring is then actually resolved when that future is reached.

maximal number of events that are required to extend σ depends to the trace σ itself, and is not a function of the specification φ. Consider the following specification φ:

$$\forall x((q(x) \rightarrow \neg\ominus \diamond q(0) \vee q(x)) \wedge (r(x) \rightarrow (\ominus \diamond q(x) \wedge \neg\ominus \diamond r(x))))$$

This property asserts that events of the form $q(x)$ or $r(x)$ can appear only once with the same parameter each. Further, an $r(x)$ event can occur only if a $q(x)$ event happened with the same parameter x. Moreover, after a $q(0)$ event, no event of the form $q(x)$ can happen. Consequently, if the event $q(0)$ has happened, no further $q(x)$ events can occur, and the only events that can occur are of the form $r(x)$, where $q(x)$ has already occurred (with the same value x). Therefore, the maximal number of events that can extend the trace until φ becomes *false* is the number of $q(x)$ events that occurred for which a matching $r(x)$ event has not happened yet. Thus, once the event $q(0)$ has occurred, the verdict of $\Box\varphi$ is *fail*, although φ may still be calculated to *true* for a long while.

In [20], an algorithm that calculates the possible values of φ for extensions up to a given fixed size k is presented. However, it is shown, by a reduction from the Post Correspondence Problem decision problem, that checking $\Box\varphi$ for a first order past property φ is undecidable.

References

1. Alpern, B., Schneider, F.B.: Recognizing safety and liveness. Distrib. Comput. **2**(3), 117–126 (1987)
2. Bartocci, E., Falcone, Y., Francalanza, A., Reger, G.: Introduction to runtime verification. In: Bartocci, E., Falcone, Y. (eds.) Lectures on Runtime Verification. LNCS, vol. 10457, pp. 1–33. Springer, Cham (2018). https://doi.org/10.1007/978-3-319-75632-5_1
3. Basin, D.A., Jiménez, C.C., Klaedtke, F., Zalinescu, E.: Deciding safety and liveness in TPTL. Inf. Process. Lett. **114**(12), 680–688 (2014)
4. Bauer, A., Leucker, M., Schallhart, C.: The good, the bad, and the ugly, but how ugly is ugly? In: Sokolsky, O., Taşiran, S. (eds.) RV 2007. LNCS, vol. 4839, pp. 126–138. Springer, Heidelberg (2007). https://doi.org/10.1007/978-3-540-77395-5_11
5. Bauer, A., Leucker, M., Schallhart, C.: Runtime verification for LTL and TLTL. ACM Trans. Softw. Eng. Methodol. **20**(4): 14:1–14:64 (2011)
6. Bloem, R., Könighofer, B., Könighofer, R., Wang, C.: Shield synthesis: runtime enforcement for reactive systems. In: Baier, C., Tinelli, C. (eds.) TACAS 2015. LNCS, vol. 9035, pp. 533–548. Springer, Heidelberg (2015). https://doi.org/10.1007/978-3-662-46681-0_51
7. Clarke, E.M., Emerson, E.A.: Design and synthesis of synchronization skeletons using branching time temporal logic. In: Kozen, D. (ed.) Logics of Programs Logic of Programs. LNCS, vol. 131, pp. 52–71. Springer, Heidelberg (1982). https://doi.org/10.1007/BFb0025774
8. Tabakov, D., Rozier, K.Y., Vardi, M.Y.: Optimized temporal monitors for SystemC. Formal Methods Syst. Des. **41**(3), 236–268 (2012)
9. Emerson, E.A., Clarke, E.M.: Characterizing correctness properties of parallel programs using fixpoints. In: de Bakker, J., van Leeuwen, J. (eds.) ICALP 1980. LNCS, vol. 85, pp. 169–181. Springer, Heidelberg (1980). https://doi.org/10.1007/3-540-10003-2_69
10. Falcone, Y., Fernandez, J.-C., Mounier, L.: What can you verify and enforce at runtime? STTT **14**(3), 349–382 (2012)

11. Gabbay, D.M., Pnueli, A., Shelah, S., Stavi, J.: On the temporal analysis of fairness. In: POPL 1980, pp. 163–173 (1980)

12. Gerth, R., Peled, D., Vardi, M.Y., Wolper, P.: Simple on-the-fly automatic verification of linear temporal logic. In: Dembiński, P., Średniawa, M. (eds.) PSTV 1995. IAICT, pp. 3–18. Springer, Boston, MA (1996). https://doi.org/10.1007/978-0-387-34892-6_1

13. Havelund, K., Peled, D., Ulus, D.: First-order temporal logic monitoring with BDDs. In: FMCAD 2017, pp. 116–123 (2017)

14. Havelund, K., Reger, G., Thoma, D., Zălinescu, E.: Monitoring events that carry data. In: Bartocci, E., Falcone, Y. (eds.) Lectures on Runtime Verification. LNCS, vol. 10457, pp. 61–102. Springer, Cham (2018). https://doi.org/10.1007/978-3-319-75632-5_3

15. Havelund, K., Roşu, G.: Synthesizing monitors for safety properties. In: Katoen, J.-P., Stevens, P. (eds.) TACAS 2002. LNCS, vol. 2280, pp. 342–356. Springer, Heidelberg (2002). https://doi.org/10.1007/3-540-46002-0_24

16. Kesten, Y., Manna, Z., McGuire, H., Pnueli, A.: A decision algorithm for full propositional temporal logic. In: Courcoubetis, C. (ed.) CAV 1993. LNCS, vol. 697, pp. 97–109. Springer, Heidelberg (1993). https://doi.org/10.1007/3-540-56922-7_9

17. Kupferman, O., Vardi, M.Y.: Model checking of safety properties. Formal Methods Syst. Des. **19**(3), 291–314 (2001)

18. Lamport, L.: Proving the correctness of multiprocess programs. IEEE Trans. Softw. Eng. **3**(2), 125–143 (1977)

19. Manna, Z., Pnueli, A.: The Temporal Logic of Reactive and Concurrent Systems - Specification. Springer, Heidelberg (1992). https://doi.org/10.1007/978-1-4612-0931-7

20. Omer, M., Peled, D.: Runtime Verification Prediction for Traces with Data, RV 2023. Springer, Thessaloniki (2023)

21. Peled, D., Havelund, K.: Refining the safety–liveness classification of temporal properties according to monitorability. In: Margaria, T., Graf, S., Larsen, K.G. (eds.) Models, Mindsets, Meta: The What, the How, and the Why Not? LNCS, vol. 11200, pp. 218–234. Springer, Cham (2019). https://doi.org/10.1007/978-3-030-22348-9_14

22. Pnueli, A., Zaks, A.: PSL model checking and run-time verification via testers. In: Misra, J., Nipkow, T., Sekerinski, E. (eds.) FM 2006. LNCS, vol. 4085, pp. 573–586. Springer, Heidelberg (2006). https://doi.org/10.1007/11813040_38

23. Queille, J.P., Sifakis, J.: Interactive methods for the analysis of Petri nets. In: Girault, C., Reisig, W. (eds.) Application and Theory of Petri Nets Informatik-Fachberichte, vol. 52, pp. 161–167. Springer, Heidelberg (1982). https://doi.org/10.1007/978-3-642-68353-4_27

24. Sistla, A.P.: Safety, liveness and fairness in temporal logic. Formal Aspects Comput. **6**(5), 495–512 (1994)

25. Thomas, W.: Automata on Infinite Objects, Handbook of Theoretical Computer Science. Volume B: Formal Models and Semantics, pp. 133–192 (1990)

Learning-Based Approaches to Predictive Monitoring with Conformal Statistical Guarantees

Francesca Cairoli[1]([✉]) [iD], Luca Bortolussi[1] [iD], and Nicola Paoletti[2] [iD]

[1] University of Trieste, Trieste, Italy
FRANCESCA.CAIROLI@UNITS.IT
[2] King's College London, London, UK

Abstract. This tutorial focuses on efficient methods to predictive monitoring (PM), the problem of detecting at runtime future violations of a given requirement from the current state of a system. While performing model checking at runtime would offer a precise solution to the PM problem, it is generally computationally expensive. To address this scalability issue, several lightweight approaches based on machine learning have recently been proposed. These approaches work by learning an approximate yet efficient surrogate (deep learning) model of the expensive model checker. A key challenge remains to ensure reliable predictions, especially in safety-critical applications.

We review our recent work on predictive monitoring, one of the first to propose learning-based approximations for CPS verification of temporal logic specifications and the first in this context to apply conformal prediction (CP) for rigorous uncertainty quantification. These CP-based uncertainty estimators offer statistical guarantees regarding the generalization error of the learning model, and they can be used to determine unreliable predictions that should be rejected. In this tutorial, we present a general and comprehensive framework summarizing our approach to the predictive monitoring of CPSs, examining in detail several variants determined by three main dimensions: system dynamics (deterministic, non-deterministic, stochastic), state observability, and semantics of requirements' satisfaction (Boolean or quantitative).

1 Introduction

Verification of temporal properties for a cyber-physical systems (CPS) is of paramount importance, especially with CPSs having become ubiquitous in safety-critical domains, from autonomous vehicles to medical devices [1]. We focus on *predictive monitoring* (PM), that is, the problem of predicting, at runtime, if a safety violation is imminent from the current CPS state. In this context, PM has the advantage, compared to traditional monitoring [9], of detecting potential safety violations before they occur, in this way enabling preemptive countermeasures to steer the system back to safety (e.g. switching to a failsafe mode as done in the Simplex architecture [37]). Thus, effective PM must balance between prediction accuracy, to avoid errors that can jeopardize safety, and computational efficiency, to support fast execution at runtime.

© The Author(s), under exclusive license to Springer Nature Switzerland AG 2023
P. Katsaros and L. Nenzi (Eds.): RV 2023, LNCS 14245, pp. 461–487, 2023.
https://doi.org/10.1007/978-3-031-44267-4_26

We focus on correctness specifications given in Signal Temporal Logic (STL) [29,42], a popular language for formal reasoning about CPS. An advantage of STL is that it admits two semantics, the usual Boolean semantics and a quantitative (robust) semantics, which quantifies the degree of satisfaction of a property. When using the latter, we speak of *quantitative PM (QPM)*.

Performing model checking of STL requirements at run-time would provide a precise solution to the PM problem (precise up to the accuracy of the system's model), but such a solution is computationally expensive in general, and thus infeasible for real-world applications. For this reason, a number of approximate PM techniques based on machine learning have been recently proposed (see e.g. [14,17,19,40,43]).

In this paper, we review our work on learning-based methods for PM, developed under the name of *Neural Predictive Monitoring* [13]. The core idea is that when a satisfaction (SAT) oracle is at our disposal, we can approximate it using deep learning models trained using a set of oracle-labeled examples. The resulting learning-based model overcomes the scalability issues faced by the original oracle: a forward pass of a (reasonably sized) neural network is most often more efficient than computing satisfaction of an STL property, especially if the underlying system is non-deterministic or stochastic. However, such a solution is inherently approximate, and so it becomes essential – especially in safety-critical domains – to offer assurances regarding the generalization performance of our approximation. To this purpose, we rely on *conformal prediction (CP)* [61], a technique that allows us to complement model predictions with uncertainty estimates that enjoy (finite-sample, i.e., non-asymptotic) statistical guarantees on the model's generalization error. CP requires only very mild assumptions on the data[1] and it is flexible enough to be applied on top of most predictors. Furthermore, computing CP-based uncertainty estimates is highly efficient, meaning that our approach can offer statistical guarantees on the PM predictions without affecting performance and runtime applicability.

In this tutorial, we present a general and comprehensive framework summarizing several variants of the neural predictive monitoring approach, variants determined by the following three dimensions:

1. *Dynamics*: The CPS dynamics can be either deterministic, non-deterministic, or stochastic, depending on whether the future behavior of the system is uniquely determined by its current state, is uncertain or exhibits randomness.
2. *State Observability*: The current CPS state can be fully observable, or we may only have access to partial and noisy measurements of the state, making it more challenging to obtain accurate predictions of the CPS evolution.
3. *Satisfaction*: The type of property satisfaction can be either Boolean or quantitative. In the former case, the PM outcome is a "yes" or "no" answer (the CPS either satisfies the property or does not). In the latter case, the outcome is a quantitative degree of satisfaction, which quantifies the robustness of STL (Boolean) satisfaction to perturbations (in space or time) of the CPS trajectories.

---

[1] The only assumption is exchangeability, a weaker version of the independent and identically distributed assumption. A collection of N values is exchangeable if the $N!$ different orderings are equally likely, i.e. have the same joint probability.

By considering the above dimensions, we can design accurate and reliable PM solutions in a variety of scenarios accounting for a vast majority of CPS models.

Overview of the Paper. This paper is structured as follows. We start by presenting the background theory in Sect. 2. Section 3 states rigorous formalizations of the predictive monitoring problems. Section 4 provides background on methods used to estimate predictive uncertainty and obtain statistical guarantees. Section 5 defines the different declinations of learning-based PM approaches. Related works are discussed in Sect. 6. Conclusions are drawn in Sect. 7.

2 Background

A cyber-physical system (CPS) is a system combining physical and digital components. Hybrid systems (HS), whose dynamics exhibit both continuous and discrete dynamics, can well capture the mixed continuous and discrete behaviour of a CPS. An HS has both flows, described by differential equations, and jumps, described by a state machine or an automaton. The continuous behaviour depends on the discrete state and discrete jumps are similarly determined by the continuous state. The state of an HS is defined by the values of the continuous variables and by a discrete mode. The continuous flow is permitted as long as a so-called invariant holds, while discrete transitions can occur as soon as given jump conditions are satisfied.

Remark 1. The approaches proposed in this paper are applicable to any blackbox system for which a satisfaction (SAT) oracle is available. That said, HS represent a very useful and expressive class of models for which several SAT oracles (model checkers) have been developed. Therefore, we will focus on this class of models for the rest of the paper.

A hybrid automaton (HA) is a formal model that mathematically describes the evolution in time of an HS.

Definition 1 (Hybrid automaton). *A hybrid automaton (HA) is a tuple $\mathcal{M} = (Loc, Var, Init, Flow, Trans, Inv)$, where Loc is a finite set of discrete locations (or modes); $Var = \{v_1, \ldots, v_n\}$ is a set of continuous variables, evaluated over a continuous domain $Var \subseteq \mathbb{R}^n$; $Init \subseteq S(\mathcal{M})$ is the set of initial states, where $S(\mathcal{M}) = Loc \times Var$ is the state space of $\mathcal{M}$; $Flow : Loc \rightarrow (Var \rightarrow Var)$ is the flow function, defining the continuous dynamics at each location; Trans is the transition relation, consisting of tuples of the form (l, g, r, l'), where $l, l' \in Loc$ are source and target locations, respectively, $g \subseteq Var$ is the guard, and $r : Var \rightarrow Var$ is the reset; $Inv : Loc \rightarrow 2^{Var}$ is the invariant at each location.*

In general, HA dynamics can be either deterministic, non-deterministic, or stochastic. *Deterministic* HAs are a special case where the transition relation is a function of the source location. On the other hand, when the continuous flow or the discrete transitions happen according to a certain probability distribution, we have a *stochastic* HA. In this case, the dynamics is represented as the combination of continuous stochastic flows probability $Flow : (Loc \times Var) \rightarrow$

($Var \rightarrow [0,1]$) and discrete jump probability $Trans : (Loc \times 2^{Var}) \rightarrow ((Loc \times (Var \times Var)) \rightarrow [0,1])$. In particular, $Flow(v' \mid l, v)$ denotes the probability of a change rate of v' when in state (l, v) and $Trans(r, l' \mid l, g)$ is the probability of applying reset r and jumping into l' through a transition starting from l with guard g. We often prefer to avoid transitions with both non-determinism and stochasticity and so, for each stochastic HA location, we define its invariant and guards so that they form a partition of Var.

We define a *signal* as a function $\vec{s} : \mathbb{T} \rightarrow \mathbb{V}$, where $\mathbb{T} \subset \mathbb{R}^+$ is the time domain, whereas $\mathbb{V}$ determines the nature of the signal. If $\mathbb{V} = \mathbb{B} := \{true, false\}$, we have a *Boolean signal*. If $\mathbb{V} = \mathbb{R}$, we have a *real-valued signal*. We consider signals that are solutions of a given HA. Let $\tau = \{[t_i, t_{i+1}] \mid t_i \leq t_{i+1}, i = 1, 2, \ldots\}$ be a hybrid time trajectory. If τ is infinite the last interval may be open on the right. Let $\mathbb{T}$ denote the set of hybrid time trajectories. Then, for a given $\tau \in \mathbb{T}$, a *hybrid signal* $\vec{s} : \tau \rightarrow S(\mathcal{M})$ defined on τ with values in a generic hybrid space $S(\mathcal{M})$ is a sequence of functions

$$\vec{s} = \{\vec{s}_i : [t_i, t_{i+1}] \rightarrow S(\mathcal{M}) \mid [t_i, t_{i+1}] \in \tau\}.$$

In practice, it can be seen as a pair of hybrid signals $\vec{v} : \tau \rightarrow Var$ and $\vec{l} : \tau \rightarrow Loc$ with $\tau \in \mathbb{T}$, such that $(\vec{l}_1(t_1), \vec{v}_1(t_1)) \in Init$, and for any $[t_i, t_{i+1}] \in \tau$, $\vec{l}_i$ is constant and there exist g and r such that $(l_i, g, r, l_{i+1}) \in Trans$, $\vec{v}_i(t_{i+1}^-) \in g$, and $\vec{v}_{i+1}(t_{i+1}) = r(\vec{v}_i(t_{i+1}^-))$. Moreover, for every $t \in [t_i, t_{i+1}]$, it must hold that $\vec{v}_i(t) \in Inv(l_i)$ and

$$\vec{v}_i(t) = \vec{v}_i(t_i) + \int_{t_i}^{t} Flow\left(\vec{l}_i(t'), \vec{v}_i(t')\right) dt'.$$

When the HA is stochastic, hybrid signals must have a non-zero probability, that is, for every piece i of the signal, there exists g, r such that $Trans(r, l_{i+1} \mid l_i, g) > 0$, $\vec{v}_i(t_{i+1}^-) \in g$, and $\vec{v}_{i+1}(t_{i+1}) = r(\vec{v}_i(t_{i+1}^-))$. Moreover, for every $t \in [t_i, t_{i+1})$, it must hold that $Flow(\dot{\vec{v}}_i(t) \mid l_i, \vec{v}_i(t)) > 0$, where $\dot{\vec{v}}_i(t) = \lim_{dt \to 0}(\vec{v}_i(t + dt) - \vec{v}_i(t))/\vec{v}_i(t)$.

Remark 2. We note that HA induces Markovian dynamics, that is, the evolution of the HA depends only on the current state. We do not see this as a restriction as most systems of interest are Markovian or can be made so by augmenting the state space.

2.1   Signal Temporal Logic (STL)

Signal temporal logic (STL) [42] was originally developed in order to specify and monitor the behaviour of physical systems, including temporal constraints between events. STL allows the specification of properties of dense-time, real-valued signals, and the automatic generation of monitors for testing these properties on individual simulation traces. The rationale of STL is to transform hybrid signals into Boolean ones, using predicates built on the following *STL syntax*:

$$\varphi := true \mid \mu_\ell \mid \mu_g \mid \neg\varphi \mid \varphi \wedge \varphi \mid \varphi\, \mathcal{U}_{[a,b]}\varphi, \tag{1}$$

where $[a, b] \subseteq \mathbb{T}$ is a bounded temporal interval. For a hybrid signal $\vec{s}[t]$, μ_g denotes atomic predicates over continuous variables, with $g : Var \to \mathbb{R}$, whereas μ_ℓ denotes atomic predicates over discrete variables, with $\ell \in Loc$. From this essential syntax, it is easy to define other operators, used to abbreviate the syntax in a STL formula: $false := \neg true$, $\varphi \vee \psi := \neg(\neg\varphi \wedge \neg\psi)$, $\Diamond_{[a,b]}\varphi := true\, \mathcal{U}_{[a,b]}\varphi$ and $\Box_{[a,b]}\varphi := \neg\Diamond_{[a,b]}\neg\varphi$.

Boolean semantics. The satisfaction of a formula φ by a signal $\vec{s}$ at time t is defined as:

- $(\vec{s}, t) \models \mu_g \iff g(\vec{v}[t]) > 0$;
- $(\vec{s}, t) \models \mu_\ell \iff \vec{l}[t] = \ell$;
- $(\vec{s}, t) \models \varphi_1 \wedge \varphi_2 \iff (\vec{s}, t) \models \varphi_1 \wedge (\vec{s}, t) \models \varphi_2$;
- $(\vec{s}, t) \models \neg\varphi \iff \neg((\vec{s}, t) \models \varphi))$;
- $(\vec{s}, t) \models \varphi_1 \mathcal{U}_{[a,b]}\varphi_2 \iff \exists t' \in [t+a, t+b]$ s.t. $(\vec{s}, t') \models \varphi_2 \wedge \forall t'' \in [t, t'), (\vec{s}, t'') \models \varphi_1$.
- Eventually: $(\vec{s}, t) \models \Diamond_{[a,b]}\varphi \iff \exists t' \in [t+a, t+b]$ s.t. $(\vec{s}, t') \models \varphi$;
- Always: $(\vec{s}, t) \models \Box_{[a,b]}\varphi \iff \forall t' \in [t+a, t+b] \quad (\vec{s}, t') \models \varphi$.

Given formula φ and a signal $\vec{s}$ over a bounded time interval, we can define the Boolean satisfaction signal as $\chi^\varphi(\vec{s}, t) = 1$ if $(\vec{s}, t) \models \varphi$ and $\chi^\varphi(\vec{s}, t) = 0$ otherwise. Monitoring the satisfaction of a formula is done recursively, by computing $\chi^{\varphi_i}(\vec{s}, \cdot)$ for each sub-formula φ_i of φ. The recursion is performed by leveraging the tree structure of the STL formula, where each node represents a sub-formula, in an incremental fashion, so that the leaves are the atomic propositions and the root represents the whole formula. Thus the procedure goes bottom-up from atomic predicated to the top formula.

Quantitative Semantics. The main kind of quantitative STL semantics is *space robustness*, which quantifies how much a signal can be perturbed with additive noise before changing the truth value of a given property φ [29]. It is defined as a function R_φ such that:

- $R_{\mu_g}(\vec{s}, t) = g(\vec{v}[t])$;
- $R_{\neg\varphi}(\vec{s}, t) = -R_\varphi(\vec{s}, t)$;
- $R_{\varphi_1 \wedge \varphi_2}(\vec{s}, t) = \min(R_{\varphi_1}(\vec{s}, t), R_{\varphi_2}(\vec{s}, t))$;
- $R_{\varphi_1 \mathcal{U}_{[a,b]}\varphi_2}(\vec{s}, t) = \sup_{t' \in [t+a, t+b]} \left(\min \left(R_{\varphi_2}(\vec{s}, t'), \inf_{t'' \in [t,t']} R_{\varphi_1}(\vec{s}, t'') \right) \right)$.

The sign of R_φ indicates the satisfaction status: $R_\varphi(\vec{s}, t) > 0 \Rightarrow (\vec{s}, t) \models \varphi$ and $R_\varphi(\vec{s}, t) < 0 \Rightarrow (\vec{s}, t) \not\models \varphi$. The definition of R_{μ_ℓ}, i.e., the robustness of discrete atoms, is arbitrary as long as it returns a non-negative value when μ_ℓ is true and non-positive when μ_ℓ is false (a common choice is returning $+\infty$ and $-\infty$, respectively). As for the Boolean semantics, it is possible to automatically generate monitors for the quantitative semantics as well. The algorithm follows a similar bottom-up approach over the syntax tree of the formula.

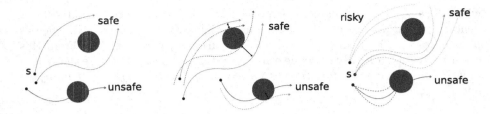

Fig. 1. Example of predictive monitoring of a safety property for a deterministic system (left) and a stochastic system (right). Blue circles denote the obstacles to avoid. (middle) shows the space robustness over the deterministic system. (Color figure online)

Similarly, *time robustness* capture the effect on the satisfaction of shifting events in time. The left and right time robustness of an STL formula φ with respect to a trace $\vec{s}$ at time t are defined inductively by letting:

$$Q_\varphi^-(\vec{s}, t) = \chi^\varphi(\vec{s}, t) \cdot \max\{d \geq 0 \ s.t. \ \forall t' \in [t - dt], \ \chi^\varphi(\vec{s}, t') = \chi^\varphi(\vec{s}, t)\}$$
$$Q_\varphi^+(\vec{s}, t) = \chi^\varphi(\vec{s}, t) \cdot \max\{d \geq 0 \ s.t. \ \forall t' \in [t, t + d], \ \chi^\varphi(\vec{s}, t') = \chi^\varphi(\vec{s}, t)\}.$$

While space and robustness are most common, our PM approach can support any other kind of STL quantitative semantics, e.g., based on a combined space-time robustness [29] or resiliency [22]. Hereafter, we represent a generic STL monitor, encompassing either Boolean or quantitative (spatial or temporal) satisfaction, as $C_\varphi \in \{\chi_\varphi, R_\varphi, Q_\varphi\}$.

Running Example. Let's consider, as a running example, a point moving at a constant velocity on a two-dimensional plane (see Fig. 1). Given the system's current state s, a controller regulates the yawn angle to avoid obstacles (D_1 and D_2 in our example). The avoid property can be easily expressed as an STL formula: $\varphi := G(\ (d(s, o_1) > r_1) \land (d(s, o_2) > r_2)\ )$, where o_i, r_i denote respectively the centre and the radius of obstacle $i \in \{1, 2\}$. Figure 1 (left) shows the deterministic evolution for three randomly chosen initial states. Figure 1 (middle) shows, for the same deterministic scenario, an intuition of the concept of spatial STL robustness, i.e. how much we can perturb a trajectory with additive noise before changing its truth value. Figure 1 (right) shows the evolution of a stochastic dynamics for three randomly initial states. The dashed lines denote the upper and lower quantiles of the distribution over the trajectory space.

3 Predictive Monitoring

Predictive monitoring of an HA is concerned with establishing whether given an initial state s and a desired property φ – e.g. always avoid a set of unsafe states D – the HA admits a trajectory starting from s that violates φ. We express such properties by means of time-bounded STL formulas, e.g. $\varphi_D := G_{[0, H_f]}(s \notin D)$. STL monitors automatically check whether an HA signal satisfies an STL property φ over a bounded temporal horizon (Boolean semantics) and possibly how robust is the satisfaction (quantitative semantics).

SAT Oracles. Given an HA $\mathcal{M}$ with state space $S(\mathcal{M})$, and an STL requirement φ over a time bound H_f, SAT oracles decide whether a state $s \in S(\mathcal{M})$ satisfies φ. This means that, when the system is *deterministic*, the SAT oracle decides whether the unique trajectory $\vec{s}$ starting from $s \in S(\mathcal{M})$ satisfies φ, i.e. decide whether $(\vec{s}, 0) \models \varphi$. This information can be retrieved from STL monitors by checking whether $\chi^{\varphi}(\vec{s}, 0) = 1$ or equivalently whether $R_{\varphi}(\vec{s}, 0) > 0$. On the other hand, when the system is *nondeterministic*, a state s satisfies φ if all trajectories starting from s satisfy φ. Similarly, a quantitative SAT oracle returns the minimal STL robustness value of all trajectories starting from s. For non-stochastic systems, the SAT oracle can thus be represented as a map Sat : $S(\mathcal{M}) \rightarrow \mathsf{B}$, where the output space B is either $\mathbb{B}$ in the Boolean scenario or $\mathbb{R}$ in the quantitative scenario. On the other hand, oracles for stochastic systems require a different treatment and we define them later in this section.

SAT Tools. Several tools have been developed for the automated verification of CPS properties and can thus be used as SAT oracles. The choice of the best tool depends on the problem at hand. STL monitors such as Breach [28] and RTAMT [44] allow to automatically check whether realizations of the system satisfy an STL property. When the system is nondeterministic we need tools that perform reachability analysis or falsification. Due to the well-known unde-cidability of HA model checking problem [16,35], none of existing tools are both sound and complete. Falsification tools like Breach [28], S-Taliro [2], C2E2 [30], and HyLAA [6] search for counter-example trajectories, i.e., for violations to the property of interest. A failure in finding a counter-example does not imply that the property is satisfied (i.e., the outcome is unknown). Conversely, HA reachability tools like PHAVer [31], SpaceEx [32], Flow*, HyPro/HyDra [56], Ariadne [10] and JuliaReach [11] rely on computing an over-approximation of the reachable set, meaning that the outcome is unknown when the computed reachable set intersects the target set. In order to be conservative, we treat unknown verdicts in a pessimistic way.

On the other hand, *stochastic* systems require the use of probabilistic model checking techniques implemented in tools like PRISM [39] or STORM [34]. Such tools provide precise numerical/symbolic techniques to determine the satisfaction probability of a formula, but only for a restricted class of systems and with significant scalability issues. Statistical model checking (SMC) techniques overcomes these limitations by solving the problem as one of hypothesis testing given a sample of system trajectories (at the cost of admitting some a priori statistical errors).

The above list of tools is far from being exhaustive, and we refer the interested reader to the ARCH-COMP competitions[2], where state-of-the-art verification tools are compared on a set of well-known benchmarks.

In the following, we formulate the predictive monitoring problem for non-stochastic systems (Problem 1), for partially observable systems (Problem 2),

---

[2] https://cps-vo.org/group/ARCH/FriendlyCompetition.

and for stochastic systems (Problem 3). We conclude by characterizing the probabilistic guarantees sought for our learning-based monitors (Problem 4).

We aim at deriving a predictive monitor for HA time-bounded satisfaction, i.e., a function that can predict whether or not the property φ is satisfied by the future evolutions of the system (bounded by time H_f) starting from the system's current state. In solving this problem, we assume a distribution $\mathcal{S}$ of HA states and seek the monitor that predicts HA reachability with minimal error probability w.r.t. $\mathcal{S}$. The choice of $\mathcal{S}$ depends on the application at hand and can include a uniform distribution on a bounded state space or a distribution reflecting the density of visited states in some HA executions [48].

Problem 1 (Predictive monitoring for HA). *Given an HA $\mathcal{M}$ with state space $S(\mathcal{M})$, a distribution $\mathcal{S}$ over $S(\mathcal{M})$, a time bound H_f and STL property φ, inducing the satisfaction function* Sat, *find a function $h^* : S(\mathcal{M}) \to$ B that minimizes the probability*

$$Pr_{s \sim \mathcal{S}} \left(h^*(s) \neq \mathsf{Sat}(s) \right).$$

A state $s \in S(\mathcal{M})$ is called positive *w.r.t. a predictor $h : S(\mathcal{M}) \to$ B if $h(s) > 0$. Otherwise, s is called* negative.

Any practical solution to the above PM problem must also assume a space of functions within which to restrict the search for the optimal predictive monitor h^*, for instance, one can consider functions described by deep neural networks (DNNs). Finding h^*, i.e., finding a function approximation with minimal error probability, is indeed a classical *supervised learning* problem. In particular, in the Boolean scenario, h^* is a classifier, i.e., a function mapping HA state inputs s into one of two classes: 1 (x is positive, property φ is satisfied) and 0 (s is negative, property φ is violated). On the other hand, in the quantitative scenario, h^* is a regressor aiming at reconstructing the robustness of satisfaction for a state s.

Dataset Generation. In supervised learning, one minimizes a measure of the empirical prediction error w.r.t. a *training set*. In our case, the training set Z' is obtained from a finite sample S' of $\mathcal{S}$ by labelling the training inputs $s \in S'$ using some SAT oracle, that is computing the true value for Sat(s). Hence, given a sample S' of $\mathcal{S}$, the training set is defined by $Z' = \{(s, \mathsf{Sat}(s)) \mid s \in S'\}$ (see Fig. 2).

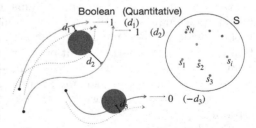

Fig. 2. Generation of the dataset to learn a PM (Boolean or quantitative) for deterministic HS.

Partial Observability. Problem 1 relies on the full observability (FO) assumption, i.e. the assumption of possessing full knowledge about the system's state. However, in most practical applications, state information is partial and noisy. Consider a discrete-time deterministic HS[3] modeled as a HA $\mathcal{M}$. The discrete-time deterministic dynamics of the system can be expressed by $v_{i+1} = Flow(l_i)(v_i)$, where $s_i = (l_i, v_i) = (l(t_i), v(t_i))$ and $t_i = t_0 + i \cdot \Delta t$. The measurement process can be modeled as

$$y_i = \pi(s_i) + w_i, \tag{2}$$

which produces partial and noisy observations $y_i \in Y$ by means of an *observation function* $\pi : S(\mathcal{M}) \to Y$ and additive noise $w_i \sim \mathcal{W}$. Under *partial observability* (PO), we only have access to a sequence of past observations $\mathbf{y}_t = (y_{t-H_p}, \ldots, y_t)$ of the *unknown* state sequence $\mathbf{s}_t = (s_{t-H_p}, \ldots, s_t)$ (as per (2)). Let $\mathcal{Y}$ denote the distribution over Y^{H_p}, the space of sequences of observations $\mathbf{y}_t$ induced by the sequence of states $\mathbf{s}_t \sim \mathcal{S}^{H_p}$ and a sequence of i.i.d. noise vectors $\mathbf{w}_t = (w_{t-H_p}, \ldots, w_t) \sim \mathcal{W}^{H_p}$.

Problem 2 (PM for HS under noise and partial observability). *Given the HA and reachability specification of Problem 1, find a function $h_{po}^* : Y^{H_p} \to \mathsf{B}$ that minimizes*

$$Pr_{s_t \sim \mathcal{S}, \mathbf{y}_t \sim \mathcal{Y}}\left(h_{po}^*(\mathbf{y}_t) \neq \mathsf{Sat}(s_t))\right).$$

In other words, h_{po}^* should predict the satisfaction values given in input only a sequence of past observations, instead of the true HA state. In particular, we require a sequence of observations (as opposed to one observation only) for the sake of identifiability. Indeed, for general non-linear systems, a single observation does not contain enough information to infer the HS state[4]. Problem 2 considers only deterministic systems. Dealing with partial observability and noise in nondeterministic systems remains an open problem as state identifiability is a non-trivial issue.

There are two natural learning-based approaches to tackle Problem 2 (Fig. 3):

1. an **end-to-end** solution that learns a direct mapping from the sequence of past measurements $\mathbf{y}_t$ to the satisfaction value in B.
2. a **two-step** solution that combines steps (a) and (b) below:
   (a) learns a *state estimator* able to reconstruct the history of full states $\mathbf{s}_t = (s_{t-H_p}, \ldots, s_t)$ from the sequence of measurements $\mathbf{y}_t = (y_{t-H_p}, \ldots, y_t)$;
   (b) learns a *state classifier/regressor* mapping the sequence of states $\mathbf{s}_t$ to the satisfaction value in B;

Dataset Generation. Given that we consider deterministic dynamics, we can use simulation, rather than model checking, to label the states as safe (positive), if $\mathsf{Sat}(s) > 0$, or unsafe (negative) otherwise. Because of the deterministic and Markovian (see Remark 2) nature of the system, one could retrieve the future satisfaction of a property at time t from the state of the system at time t alone. However, one can decide to exploit more information and make a prediction

---

[3] In case of partial observability we restrict our analysis to deterministic systems.
[4] Feasibility of state reconstruction is affected by the time lag and the sequence length. Our focus is to derive the best predictions for fixed lag and sequence length, not to fine-tune these to improve identifiability.

based on the previous H_p states. Formally, the generated dataset under FO can be expressed as $Z' = \{(\mathbf{s}_t^i, \mathsf{Sat}(s_t^i))\}_{i=1}^{N}$, where $\mathbf{s}_t^i = (s_{t-H_p}^i, s_{t-H_p+1}^i, \ldots, s_t^i)$. Under PO, we use the (known) observation function $\pi : S(\mathcal{M}) \to Y$ to build a dataset Z'' made of tuples $(\mathbf{y}_t, \mathbf{s}_t, l_t)$, where $\mathbf{y}_t$ is a sequence of noisy observations for $\mathbf{s}_t$, i.e., such that $\forall j \in \{t - H_p, \ldots, t\}$ $y_j = \pi(s_j) + w_j$ and $w_j \sim \mathcal{W}$.

The distribution of $\mathbf{s}_t$ and $\mathbf{y}_t$ is determined by the distribution S of the initial state of the sequences, s_{t-H_p}. We consider two different distributions: *independent*, where the initial states s_{t-H_p} are sampled independently, thus resulting in independent state/observation sequences; and *sequential*, where states come from temporally correlated trajectories in a sliding-window fashion. The latter is more

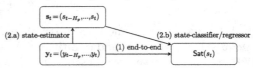

Fig. 3. Diagram of the learning steps under noise and partial observability.

suitable for real-world runtime applications, where observations are received in a sequential manner. On the other hand, temporal dependency violates the exchangeability property, which affects the theoretical validity guarantees of CP, as we will soon discuss.

Stochastic Dynamics. If the system evolves stochastically, we have a distribution over the trajectory space rather than a single trajectory that either satisfies of violates the property. Some realizations will satisfy the property, some others will not. Therefore, reasoning about satisfaction gets more complicated. Let $\mathbb{T} = \{0, 1, \ldots\}$ denote a discrete set of time instants and let $\mathcal{M}$ be a discrete-time stochastic HA over state space $S(\mathcal{M})$ and $\mathbb{T}$. Given that the system is in state $s \sim S$ at time $t \in \mathbb{T}$, the stochastic evolution (bounded by horizon H_f) of the system starting at s can be described by the conditional distribution $p(\vec{s} \mid \vec{s}(t) = s)$, where $\vec{s} = (\vec{s}(t), \ldots, \vec{s}(t + H_f)) \in S^H$ is the random trajectory of length H_f starting at time t. We thus introduce a satisfaction function SSat that inherits the stochasticity of the system's dynamics. For an STL property φ, we define SSat as a function mapping a state $s \in S(\mathcal{M})$ into a random variable $\mathsf{SSat}(s)$ denoting the distribution of satisfaction values over $\mathbb{B}$. In other words, the satisfaction function transforms the distribution over trajectories into the distribution over satisfaction values.

The predictive monitoring problem under stochastic dynamics can be framed as estimating one or more functionals of $\mathsf{SSat}(s)$ (e.g., mean, variance, quantiles). A formal statement of the problem is given below.

Problem 3 (PM for Stochastic HS). *Given a discrete-time stochastic HA $\mathcal{M}$ over a state space $S(\mathcal{M})$, temporal horizon H_f, and an STL formula φ, we aim at approximating a functional q of the distributions induced by SSat. We thus aim at deriving a monitoring function h_q^* that maps any state $s \sim S$ into the functional $\mathsf{q}[\mathsf{SSat}(s)]$ such that*

$$Pr_{s \sim S}\left(h_\mathsf{q}^*(s) \neq \mathsf{q}\big[\mathsf{SSat}(s)\big]\right). \tag{3}$$

We will focus on the case where q is a quantile function, making Problem 3 equivalent to a conditional quantile regression (QR) problem. This boils down to learning for a generic state s a quantile of the random variable $\mathsf{SSat}(s)$.

Dataset Generation. We perform Monte-Carlo simulations of the process in order to obtain empirical approximations of SSat. In particular, we randomly sample N states $s_1, \ldots, s_N \sim \mathcal{S}$. Then, for each state s_i, we simulate M trajectories of length H_f, $\vec{s}_i^1, \ldots, \vec{s}_i^M$ where $\vec{s}_i^j$ is a realization of $p(\vec{s} \mid \vec{s}(t) = s_i)$, and compute the satisfaction value $C_\varphi(\vec{s}_i^j)$ of each of these trajectories ($C_\varphi \in \{\chi_\varphi, R_\varphi, Q_\varphi\}$). Note how $\{C_\varphi(\vec{s}_i^j)\}_{j=1}^M$ is an empirical approximation of $\mathsf{SSat}(s_i)$. The dataset is thus defined as

$$Z' = \left\{ \left(s_i, \left(C_\varphi(\vec{s}_i^1), \ldots, C_\varphi(\vec{s}_i^M) \right) \right), i = 1, \ldots, N \right\}. \quad (4)$$

Figure 4 shows an overview of the steps needed to generate the dataset. The generation of the test set Z'_{test} is very similar to that of Z'. The main difference is in that the number of trajectories that we simulate from each state s is much larger than M. This allows us to obtain a highly accurate empirical approximation of the distribution induced by SSat, which we use as the ground-truth baseline in our experimental evaluation[5]. Moreover, since functionals of $\mathsf{SSat}(s)$ can not in general be computed exactly, for a choice of $\epsilon \in (0, 1)$, we derive the empirical quantile $\hat{q}_\epsilon^{s_i}$ from samples $C_\varphi(\vec{s}_i^1), \ldots, C_\varphi(\vec{s}_i^M)$ and use the generated training set Z' to train the QR h_q that learns how to map states s into $\hat{q}_\epsilon^s$.

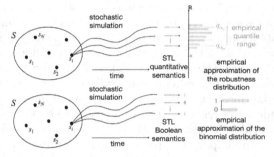

Fig. 4. Generation of the dataset to learn a PM for stochastic HS.

The predictors, either h, h_{po} or h_q, are approximate solutions and, as such, they can commit safety-critical prediction errors. The general goal of Problems 1, 2 and 3 is to minimize the risk of making mistakes in predicting the satisfaction of a property. We are also interested in establishing probabilistic guarantees on the expected error rate of an *unseen (test) state*, in the form of prediction regions guaranteed to include the true satisfaction value with arbitrary probability. We now introduce some notation to capture all three previously stated scenarios. Let f be the predictor (either h of Problem 1, h_{po} of Problem 2 or h_q of Problem 3) and let $x \in X$ be the input of predictor f (either a state s or a sequence of past measurements $\mathbf{y}$). The distribution over the generic input space X is denoted by $\mathcal{X}$.

---

[5] In the limit of infinite sample size, the empirical approximation approaches the true distribution.

Problem 4 (Probabilistic guarantees). *Given a system and property φ as in Problems 1, 2 and 3, find a function $\Gamma^\varepsilon : X \to 2^B$, mapping every input x into a prediction region for the corresponding satisfaction value, i.e., a region that satisfies, for any error probability level $\varepsilon \in (0,1)$, the validity property below*

$$Pr_{x \sim \mathcal{X}}\Big(\mathsf{SAT}(x) \in \Gamma^\varepsilon(x)\Big) \geq 1 - \varepsilon,$$

where $\mathsf{SAT}(\cdot)$ corresponds to $\mathsf{Sat}(\cdot)$ in Problems 1 and 2, and to $\mathsf{q}[\mathsf{SSat}(\cdot)]$ in Problem 3.

Among the maps that satisfy validity, we seek the most *efficient* one, meaning the one with the smallest, i.e. less conservative, prediction regions.

4 Uncertainty Estimation and Statistical Guarantees

The learning-based solutions of Problems 1, 2 and 3 are approximate and, even when extremely high accuracies are reached, offer no guarantees over the reliability of the learned predictor, and thus are not applicable in safety-critical scenarios. In this section, we present techniques for uncertainty estimation, techniques that overcome the above limitation by providing point-wise information about the reliability of the predictions. In particular, we examine two uncertainty quantification techniques, based on conformal prediction (CP) and Bayesian inference, respectively. We focus more on CP as, unlike Bayesian inference, can provide the desired statistical guarantees stated in Problem 4.

To simplify the presentation, we illustrate the techniques by considering a generic supervised learning model, as follows. Let X be the input space, T be the target (output) space, and define $Z = X \times T$. Let $\mathcal{Z}$ be the data-generating distribution, i.e., the distribution of the points $(x,t) \in Z$. We assume that the target t of a point $(x,t) \in Z$ is the result of the application of a function $f^* : X \to T$, typically unknown or very expensive to evaluate. Using a finite set of observations, the goal of a supervised learning algorithm is to find a function $f : X \to T$ that accurately approximates f^* over the entire input space. For a generic input $x \in X$, we denote with t the true target value of x and with $\hat{t}$ the prediction by f, i.e. $\hat{t} = f(x)$. Test inputs, whose unknown true target values we aim to predict, are denoted by x_*.

4.1 Conformal Inference

Conformal Prediction (CP) associates measures of reliability to any traditional supervised learning problem. It is a very general approach that can be applied across all existing deterministic classifiers and regressors [8,61]. CP produces *prediction regions with guaranteed validity*.

Definition 2 (Prediction region). *For significance level $\varepsilon \in (0,1)$ and test input x_*, the ε-prediction region for x_*, $\Gamma_*^\varepsilon \subseteq T$, is a set of target values s.t.*

$$\Pr_{(x_*,t_*) \sim \mathcal{Z}}\big(t_* \in \Gamma_*^\varepsilon\big) = 1 - \varepsilon. \tag{5}$$

The idea of CP is to construct the prediction region by "inverting" a suitable hypothesis test: given a test point x_* and a tentative target value t', we *exclude* t' from the prediction region only if it is unlikely that t' is the true value for x_*. The test statistic is given by a so-called *nonconformity function (NCF)* $\delta : Z \to \mathbb{R}$, which, given a predictor f and a point $z = (x, t)$, measures the deviation between the true value t and the corresponding prediction $f(x)$. In this sense, δ can be viewed as a generalized residual function. In other words, CP builds the prediction region Γ_*^ε for a test point x_* by excluding all targets t' whose NCF values are unlikely to follow the NCF distribution of the true targets:

$$\Gamma_*^\varepsilon = \left\{ t' \in T \mid Pr_{(x,t)\sim\mathcal{Z}}\left(\delta(x_*, t') \geq \delta(x, t)\right) > \varepsilon \right\}. \qquad (6)$$

The probability term in Eq. 6 is often called the p-value. From a practical viewpoint, the NCF distribution $Pr_{(x,t)\sim\mathcal{Z}}(\delta(x,t))$ cannot be derived in an analytical form, and thus we use an empirical approximation derived using a sample Z_c of $\mathcal{Z}$. This approach is called *inductive* (or split) CP [45] and Z_c is referred to as *calibration set*.

Validity and Efficiency. CP performance is measured via two quantities: 1) *validity* (or *coverage*), i.e. the empirical error rate observed on a test sample, which should be as close as possible to the significance level ε, and 2) *efficiency*, i.e. the size of the prediction regions, which should be small. CP-based prediction regions are automatically valid, whereas the efficiency depends on the size of the calibration set (leading to high uncertainty when data is scarce), the quality of the underlying model and the chosen nonconformity function.

Remark 3 (Assumptions and guarantees of inductive CP). Importantly, CP prediction regions have *finite-sample validity* [8], i.e., they satisfy (5) for any sample of $\mathcal{Z}$ (of reasonable size), and not just asymptotically. On the other hand, CP's theoretical guarantees hold under the *exchangeability* assumption (a "relaxed" version of iid) by which the joint probability of any sample of $\mathcal{Z}$ is invariant to permutations of the sampled points. Independent observations are exchangeable but sequential ones are not (due to the temporal dependency). In such scenarios, some adaptations to conformal inference (see [58,66]) are needed to recover and preserve validity guarantees.

CP for Classification. In classification, the target space is a discrete set of possible labels (or classes) $T = \{t^1, \ldots, t^c\}$. We represent the classification model as a function $f_d : X \to [0,1]^c$ mapping inputs into a vector of class likelihoods, such that the predicted class is the one with the highest likelihood[6].

The inductive CP algorithm for classification is divided into an offline phase, executed only once, and an online phase, executed for every test point x_*. In the offline phase (steps 1–3 below), we train the classifier f and construct the calibration distribution, i.e., the empirical approximation of the NCF distribution. In the online phase (steps 4–5), we derive the prediction region for x_* using the computed classifier and distribution.

---

[6] Ties can be resolved by imposing an ordering over the classes.

1. Draw sample Z' of $\mathcal{Z}$. Split Z' into training set Z_t and calibration set Z_c.
2. Train classifier f using Z_t. Use f_d to define an NCF δ.
3. Construct the calibration distribution by computing, for each $z_i \in Z_c$, the NCF score $\alpha_i = \delta(z_i)$.
4. For each label $t^j \in T$, compute $\alpha_*^j = \delta(x_*, t^j)$, i.e., the NCF score for x_* and t^j, and the associated p-value p_*^j:

$$p_*^j = \frac{|\{z_i \in Z_c \mid \alpha_i > \alpha_*^j\}|}{|Z_c| + 1} + \theta \frac{|\{z_i \in Z_c \mid \alpha_i = \alpha_*^j\}| + 1}{|Z_c| + 1}, \qquad (7)$$

where $\theta \in \mathcal{U}[0, 1]$ is a tie-breaking random variable.
5. Return the prediction region

$$\Gamma_*^\varepsilon = \{t^j \in T \mid p_*^j > \varepsilon\}. \qquad (8)$$

In defining the NCF δ, we should aim to obtain high δ values for wrong predictions and low δ values for correct ones. Thus, a natural choice in classification is to define

$$\delta(x, t^j) = 1 - f_d^j(x), \qquad (9)$$

where $f_d^j(x)$ is the likelihood predicted by f_d for class t_j. Indeed, if t^j is the true target for x and f correctly predicts t^j, then $f_d^j(x)$ is high (the highest among all classes) and $\delta(x, t^j)$ is low; the opposite holds if f does not predict t^j.

Prediction Uncertainty. A CP-based prediction region provides a set of plausible predictions with statistical guarantees, and as such, also captures the uncertainty about the prediction. Indeed, if CP produces a region Γ_*^ε with more than one class, then the prediction for x_* is *ambiguous* (i.e., multiple predictions are plausible), and thus, potentially erroneous. Similarly, if Γ_*^ε is empty, then there are no plausible predictions at all, and thus, none can be trusted. The only reliable prediction is the one where Γ_*^ε contains only one class. In this case, $\Gamma_*^\varepsilon = \{\hat{t}_*\}$, i.e., the region only contains the predicted class, as stated in the following proposition.

Proposition 1. *For the NCF function* (9), *if* $\Gamma_*^\varepsilon = \{t^{j_1}\}$, *then* $t^{j_1} = f(x_*)$.

The size of the prediction region is determined by the chosen significance level ε and by the p-values derived via CP. Specifically, from Equation (8) we can see that, for levels $\varepsilon_1 \geq \varepsilon_2$, the corresponding prediction regions are such that $\Gamma_*^{\varepsilon_1} \subseteq \Gamma_*^{\varepsilon_2}$. It follows that, given a test input x_*, if ε is lower than all its p-values, i.e. if $\varepsilon < \min_{j=1,\ldots,c} p_*^j$, then the region Γ_*^ε contains all the classes, and Γ_*^ε shrinks as ε increases. In particular, Γ_*^ε is empty when $\varepsilon \geq \max_{j=1,\ldots,c} p_*^j$.

In the classification scenario, CP introduces two additional point-wise measures of uncertainty, called confidence and credibility, defined in terms of two p-values, independently of the significance level ε. The intuition is that these two p-values identify the range of ε values for which the prediction is reliable, i.e., $|\Gamma_*^\varepsilon| = 1$.

Definition 3 (Confidence and credibility). *Given a predictor F, the confidence of a point $x_* \in X$, denoted by $1-\gamma_*$, is defined as $1-\gamma_* = \sup\{1-\varepsilon : |\Gamma_*^\varepsilon| = 1\}$, and the credibility of x_*, denoted by κ_*, is defined as $\kappa_* = \inf\{\varepsilon : |\Gamma_*^\varepsilon| = 0\}$. The so-called confidence-credibility interval $[\gamma_*, \kappa_*)$ contains all the values of ε such that $|\Gamma_*^\varepsilon| = 1$.*

The confidence $1 - \gamma_*$ is the highest probability value for which the corresponding prediction region contains only $\hat{t}_*$, and thus it measures how likely (according to the calibration set) our prediction for x_* is. In particular, γ_* corresponds to the second largest p-value. The credibility κ_* is the smallest level for which the prediction region is empty, i.e., no plausible prediction is found by CP. It corresponds to the highest p-value, i.e., the p-value of the predicted class.

Figure 5 illustrates CP p-values and corresponding prediction region sizes. In binary classification problems, each point x_* has only two p-values: κ_* (p-value of the predicted class) and γ_* (p-value of the other class). It follows that the higher $1 - \gamma_*$ and κ_* are, the more reliable the prediction $\hat{t}_*$ is, because we have an expanded range $[\gamma_*, \kappa_*)$ of ε values by which $|\Gamma_*^\varepsilon| = 1$. Indeed, in the degenerate case where $\kappa_* = 1$ and $\gamma_* = 0$, then $|\Gamma_*^\varepsilon| = 1$ for any value of $\varepsilon < 1$. This is why, as we will explain in the

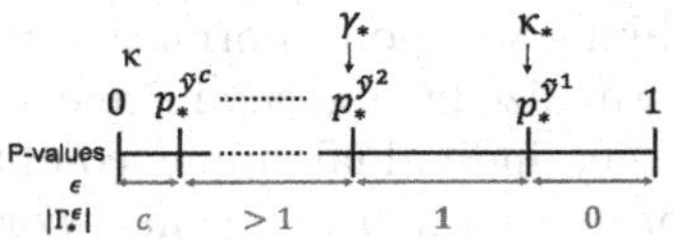

Fig. 5. CP p-values and corresponding sizes of prediction interval. $\tilde{y}^i$ is the class with the i-th largest p-value, so $p_*^{\tilde{\ell}^1} = \kappa_*$ and $p_*^{\tilde{\ell}^2} = \gamma_*$.

next section, we do not trust predictions with low values of $1-\gamma_*$ and κ_*. Hence, our CP-based uncertainty measure associates with each input its confidence and credibility values.

Label-Conditional Approach. The validity property, as stated above, guarantees an error rate over all possible labels, not on a per-label basis. The latter can be achieved with a CP variant, called *label-conditional CP* [33,57,60]. In this variant, the p-value associated with class t^j on a test point x_* is defined in a conditional manner as follows:

$$p_*^j = \frac{|\{z_i \in Z_c : t_i = t^j, \alpha_i > \alpha_*^j\}|}{|\{z_i \in Z_c : t_i = t^j\}| + 1} + \theta \frac{|\{z_i \in Z_c : t_i = t^j, \alpha_i = \alpha_*^j\}| + 1}{|\{z_i \in Z_c : t_i = t^j\}| + 1}. \quad (10)$$

In other words, we consider only the α_i corresponding to examples with the same label t^j as the hypothetical label that we are assigning at the test point.

Label-conditional validity is very important when CP is applied to an unbalanced dataset, whereby CP regions tend to have larger error rates with the minority class than with the majority one. The label-conditional approach ensures that, even for the minority class, the expected error rate will tend to the chosen significance level ε.

CP for Regression. In regression, we have a continuous target space $T \subseteq \mathbb{R}^n$. The CP algorithm for regression is similar to the classification one. In particular, the offline phase of steps 1–3, i.e., training of regression model f and definition of NCF δ, is the same (with obviously a different kind of f and δ).

The online phase changes though, because T is a continuous space and thus, it is not possible to enumerate the target values and compute for each a p-value. Instead, we proceed in an equivalent manner, that is, identify the critical value $\alpha_{(\varepsilon)}$ of the calibration distribution, i.e., the NCF score corresponding to a p-value of ε. The resulting ε-prediction region is given by $\Gamma_*^\varepsilon = f(x_*) \pm \alpha_{(\varepsilon)}$, where $\alpha_{(\varepsilon)}$ is the $(1 - \varepsilon)$-quantile of the calibration distribution, i.e., the $\lfloor \varepsilon \cdot (|Z_c| + 1) \rfloor$-th largest calibration score. A natural NCF in regression, and the one used in our experiments, is the norm of the difference between the real and the predicted target value, i.e., $\delta(x, t) = ||t - f(x)||$.

Normalized CP. The main limitation of CP for regression, presented above, is that the size of prediction intervals is identical $(2\alpha_{(\varepsilon)})$ for all test inputs, making CP non-informative to check how the uncertainty distributes over X. Normalized Conformal Predictions (NCP) [46,47] tackle this limitation. In order to get individual, input-conditional bounds for each point x_i, we can define normalized nonconformity scores as follows

$$\tilde{\alpha}_c = \left\{ \frac{\delta(x_i, t_i)}{u(x_i)} \ \middle| \ (x_i, t_i) \in Z_c \right\}, \tag{11}$$

where $u(x_i)$ estimates the difficulty of predicting $f(x_i)$. The rationale is that if two points have the same nonconformity scores using δ, the one expected to be more accurate, should be stranger (more nonconforming) than the other one. Hence, we aim at error bounds that are tighter for inputs x that are deemed easy to predict and vice-versa. Even for locally-weighted residuals, as in (11), the validity of the conformal methods carries over. As before we compute $\tilde{\alpha}_{(\varepsilon)}$ as the $(1 - \varepsilon)$-quantile of the scores $\tilde{\alpha}_c$ and the coverage guarantees over the error become:

$$Pr_{(x,t) \sim Z}\Big(\delta(x, t) \leq \tilde{\alpha}_{(\varepsilon)} \cdot u(x) \Big) \geq 1 - \varepsilon. \tag{12}$$

Conformalized Quantile Regression. The goal of conformalized quantile regression (CQR) [53] is to adjust the QR prediction interval (i.e. the interval obtained by the prediction of two quantiles as in Problem 3) so that it is guaranteed to contain the $(1 - \varepsilon)$ mass of probability. As for CP, we divide the dataset Z' in a training set Z_t and a calibration set Z_c. We train the QR f over Z_t and on Z_c we compute the nonconformity scores as

$$\alpha_c := \max\{\hat{q}_{\varepsilon_{lo}}(x_i) - t_i, t_i - \hat{q}_{\varepsilon_{hi}}(x_i) \mid (x_i, t_i) \in Z_c\}. \tag{13}$$

In our notation, $\hat{q}_{\varepsilon_{lo}}(x)$ and $\hat{q}_{\varepsilon_{hi}}(x)$ denotes the two outputs of the pretrained predictor f evaluated over x[7]. The conformalized prediction interval is thus defined as

$$CPI(x_*) = [\hat{q}_{\varepsilon_{lo}}(x_*) - \alpha_{(\varepsilon)}, \hat{q}_{\varepsilon_{hi}}(x_*) + \alpha_{(\varepsilon)}],$$

---

[7] If f outputs more than two quantiles, $\hat{q}_{\varepsilon_{lo}}(x)$ and $\hat{q}_{\varepsilon_{hi}}(x)$ denote the predicted quantiles associated respectively with the lowest and highest associated significance level.

where $\alpha_{(\varepsilon)}$ is the $\lfloor (1-\varepsilon)(1+1/|Z_c|)\rfloor$-th empirical quantile of α_c. In the following, we will abbreviate with PI a (non-calibrated) QR prediction interval and with CPI a (calibrated) conformalized prediction interval.

Similarly to normalized CP, the above-defined CPI provides individual uncertainty estimates as the size of the interval changes according to the (input-conditional) quantile predictions.

Remark 4. This nonconformity function, and thus $\alpha_{(\varepsilon)}$, can be negative and thus the conformalized prediction interval can be tighter than the original prediction interval. This means that the CPI can be more efficient than the PI, where the efficiency is the average width of the prediction intervals over a test set. The CPI has guaranteed coverage (the PI does not), i.e. $\mathbb{P}_{(x_*,t_*)\sim\mathcal{Z}}(t_* \in CPI(x_*)) \geq 1-\varepsilon$.

CP Under Covariate Shift. CP guarantees hold under the assumption that training, calibration and test data come from the same data distribution $\mathcal{Z}$. However, there exist CP extensions [20,59] that provide statistical guarantees even in the presence of covariate shift at test time, meaning that the distribution $\mathcal{X}$ over inputs changes. The core concept is to reweight the nonconformity scores of the calibration set to account for the distribution shift. Such weights are defined using the density ratio between the shifted and original distribution, to quantify the probability of observing a particular calibration input relative to the shifted distribution.

4.2 Bayesian Inference

In general, a Bayesian inference problem aims at inferring an accurate probabilistic estimate of the unknown function from X to T (as before). In the following, let $f : X \rightarrow T$. The main ingredients of a Bayesian approach are the following:

1. Choose a *prior* distribution, $p(f)$, over a suitable function space, encapsulating the beliefs about function f prior to any observations being taken.
2. Determine the functional form of the observation process by defining a suitable *likelihood* function $p(Z'|f)$ that effectively models how the observations depend on the input.
3. Leverage Bayes' theorem to define the *posterior* distribution over functions given the observations $p(f|Z') = p(Z'|f)p(f)/p(Z')$. Computing $p(Z') = \int p(Z'|f)p(f)df$ is almost always computationally intractable as we have non-conjugate prior-likelihood distributions. Therefore, we need algorithms to accurately approximate such posterior distribution.
4. Evaluate such posterior at points x_*, resulting in a predictive distribution $p(f_*|x_*, Z')$, whose statistics are used to obtain the desired estimate of the satisfaction probability together with the respective credible interval.

Predictive Uncertainty. Once the empirical approximation of the predictive distribution $p(f_*|x_*, Z')$ is derived, one can extract statistics from it to characterize predictive uncertainty. We stress that the predictive distribution, and hence its statistics, effectively capture prediction uncertainty. For instance, the empirical mean and variance of the predictive distribution can be used as measures for Bayesian predictive uncertainty.

Remark 5. The Bayesian quantification of uncertainty, despite being based on statistically sound operations, offers no guarantees per se as it strongly depends on the chosen prior and typically relies on approximate inference. However, we can make predictions based on a functional of the predictive distribution and exploit the provided quantification of uncertainty as the normalizing function of an NCP approach, that in turn will provide us with point-specific statistical guarantees over the error coverage.

In a Bayesian framework two main ingredients are essential to define the solution strategy to a Bayesian inference problem define above: (*i*) the probabilistic model chosen to describe the distribution over functions f and (*ii*) the approximate inference strategy. We refer to Appendix A of [12] for details on the possible approaches to Bayesian inference. In particular, we present Gaussian Processes and Bayesian Neural Nets, as alternatives for ingredient (*i*), and Variational Inference (VI) and Hamilton Monte Carlo (HMC), as alternatives for ingredient (*ii*).

5   Learning-Based PM with Statistical Guarantees

5.1   Monitoring Under Full Observability

Given a fully observable Markovian system with a known SAT oracle, the system's current state s_t at time t is sufficient information to predict the future satisfaction of a requirement φ. The input space of the Sat function is thus $S(\mathcal{M})$.

When the system evolves *deterministically* each state $s \in S(\mathcal{M})$ is associated with a unique satisfaction value (as in Problem 1). If we are interested in the Boolean satisfaction the output space B of the Sat function is $\{0, 1\}$ and the learning problem is a classical binary classification problem, i.e. inferring a function $h : S(\mathcal{M}) \rightarrow \{0, 1\}$ that classify a state as positive (if it satisfies the requirement) or negative (if it violates the requirement). Analogously, if we want to better quantify how robust is the satisfaction we can leverage the quantitative STL semantics, either spatial or temporal. In this scenario, the output space B of the Sat function is $\mathbb{R}$ and the learning problem becomes a regression task, i.e. inferring a function $h : S(\mathcal{M}) \rightarrow \mathbb{R}$ that estimates the level of satisfaction of φ for each state in $S(\mathcal{M})$.

The function h, introduced in its general form in Problem 1, can be inferred either using a deterministic neural network or one of the proposed Bayesian approaches. CP can be used on top of both approaches to meet the validity guarantees of Problem 4. In the CP-based version, we apply either CP for classification or CP for regression to obtain prediction regions with guaranteed coverage over the entire state space (see [13] for details). On the other, we can design either a Bayesian classifier (with Bernoulli likelihood for the Boolean semantics) or a Bayesian regressor (Gaussian likelihood for quantitative semantics). See [14] for details. In order to meet the desired statistical guarantees we could use CP. Since Bayesian predictions are probabilistic, whereas CP is defined for deterministic predictors, we apply CP to the expectation over the predictive distribution. Nonetheless, the variance of the latter can be exploited as normalizing constant in a NCP framework so to obtain state-specific prediction intervals while preserving the statistical guarantees. Similar reasoning is applied to *nondeterministic systems.*

Otherwise, when the system evolves *stochastically*, each state $s \in S(\mathcal{M})$ is associated with a distribution over the satisfaction values $\mathsf{SSat}(s)$ (as discussed in Problem 3 in Sect. 3). We are not able to extract an analytic expression for this distribution but we can empirically approximate it via sampling. If we consider the Boolean semantics, $\mathsf{SSat}(s)$ is a Binomial distribution centred around the satisfaction probability in the interval $[0, 1]$. In such a scenario, we could either train a deterministic neural regressor that infers the satisfaction probability in $[0, 1]$ or design a Bayesian framework with Binomial likelihood (see [12] for details). In order to meet the desired statistical guarantees we could use CP for regression. Once again, in the Bayesian scenario, CP is applied to the expectation over the predictive distribution. However, the variance of the latter can be used as normalizing constant in a NCP framework so to obtain state-specific prediction intervals. On the other hand, the quantitative STL semantics, either spatial or temporal, results in a distribution over $\mathbb{R}$. We can train neural quantile regression (QR) that, given a desired confidence level ε, infers some quantiles of this distribution (e.g. $q_{\frac{\varepsilon}{2}}$, $q_{0.5}$ and $q_{\frac{\varepsilon}{2}}$). A typical loss for the regression of a quantile q_α is the pinball loss $\mathcal{L}_\alpha(t, \hat{q}_\alpha) = \alpha \cdot \max(t - \hat{q}_\alpha, 0) + (1 - \alpha) \cdot \max(\hat{q}_\alpha - t, 0)$, where $\hat{q}_\alpha$ is the predicted quantile and $t \in \mathbb{R}$ denotes an observed output. Once the QR is trained we can resort to CQR (see Fig. 6) to meet the probabilistic guarantees, in that the conformal intervals cover with probability at least $1 - \varepsilon$ the STL robustness values relative to the stochastic evolution of the system. The rationale is to evaluate the nonconformity scores of the interval $\left[\hat{q}_{\frac{\varepsilon}{2}}(s), \hat{q}_{1 - \frac{\varepsilon}{2}}(s)\right]$ over the calibration set and extract τ, the $\lfloor (1 - \varepsilon)(1 + 1/|Z_c|)\rfloor$-th empirical quantile of α_c, to recalibrate the prediction interval (see [19] for details).

5.2 Monitoring Under Partial Observability

For ease of discussion, in the PO scenario (outlined in Problem 2), we discuss only the CP-based setting and not the Bayesian one (see [17] for details). The *end-to-*

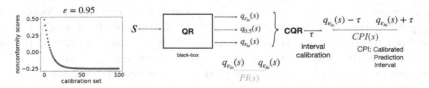

Fig. 6. Overview of conformalized quantile regression.

end approach is very similar to the FO deterministic one. The main difference is that instead of the state at time t we map the history of past measurements $\mathbf{y}_t$ to the satisfaction value in B, i.e. we infer a function $h_{po} : Y^{H_p} \to$ B. As before, the output can be either Boolean B = $\{0, 1\}$ (binary classification task), or quantitative B = $\mathbb{R}$ (regression task). The sequence of past observations is mapped to a unique satisfaction value in B and CP can be used to enrich the predictions with guaranteed validity. On the other hand, if we consider a *two-step* approach we first estimate the sequence of states $\mathbf{s}_t$ (regression task) and then we estimate the satisfaction value associated with each sequence which is either a classification or a regression task (as in the end-to-end approach). The two steps can be fine-tuned together and conformal inference can be applied to both steps to obtain statistical guarantees.

5.3   Uncertainty-Aware Error Detection and Active Learning

It is well known that neural networks are universal approximators. However, such methods cannot completely avoid prediction errors (no supervised learning method can). Therefore, we have to deal with predictive monitors f that are prone to prediction errors: when, for a state $s \in S(\mathcal{M})$, $f(x) \neq \mathsf{Sat}(x)$. These errors are respectively denoted by predicates $pe(s)$.

Problem 5 (Uncertainty-based error detection). *Given a reachability predictor f, a distribution $\mathcal{X}$ over HA states X, a predictive uncertainty measure $u_f : X \to U$ over some uncertainty domain U, and a kind of error pe find an optimal error detection rule $G^*_{f,pe} : U \to \{0, 1\}$, i.e., a function that minimizes the probability*

$$Pr_{x \sim \mathcal{X}} \left(pe(x) \neq G^*_{f,pe}(u_f(x)) \right).$$

In the above problem, we consider all kinds of prediction errors, but the definition and approach could be easily adapted to focus on the detection of only e.g., false positives (the most problematic errors from a safety-critical viewpoint).

In the CP-based setting, a meaningful measure of predictive uncertainty is given by confidence and credibility. In the Bayesian framework, we can consider the mean and the variance of the predictive distribution.

As for Problem 1, 2 and 3, we can obtain a sub-optimal solution $G_{f,pe}$ to Problem 5 by expressing the latter as a supervised learning problem, where the inputs are, once again, sampled according to $\mathcal{X}$ and labelled using a SAT oracle. We call *validation set* the set of labelled observations used to learn $G_{f,pe}$. These observation need to be independent from the above introduced training set Z', i.e., those used to learn the reachability predictor f. The final rejection rule $\mathsf{Rej}_{f,pe}$ for detecting HA states where the satisfaction prediction (given by f) should not be trusted, and thus rejected, is readily obtained by the composition of the uncertainty measure and the error detection rule $\mathsf{Rej}_{f,pe} = G_{f,e} \circ u_f : X \to \{0, 1\}$, where $\mathsf{Rej}_{f,pe}(x) = 1$ if the prediction on x is rejected and $\mathsf{Rej}_{f,pe}(x) = 0$ otherwise.

This error-detection criterion can be also used as a query strategy in an uncertainty-aware *active learning* setting. Active learning should reduce the overall number of erroneous predictions because it improves the predictor on the inputs where it is most uncertain.

6   Related Work

A number of methods have been proposed for online reachability analysis that rely on separating the reachability computation into distinct offline and online phases. However, these methods are limited to restricted classes of models [23,63], or require handcrafted optimization of the HA's derivatives [7], or are efficient only for low-dimensional systems and simple dynamics [55]. In contrast, the approaches presented in this paper are based on learning DNN-based predictors, are fully automated and have negligible computational cost at runtime. In [26,54], similar techniques are introduced for neural approximation of Hamilton-Jacobi (HJ) reachability. However, our methods for prediction rejection and active learning are independent of the class of systems and the machine-learning approximation of reachability, and thus can also be applied to neural approximations of HJ reachability. In [62], Yel and others present a runtime monitoring framework that has similarities with our approach, in that they also learn neural network-based reachability monitors (for UAV planning applications), but instead of using, like we do, uncertainty measures to pin down potentially erroneous predictions, they apply NN verification techniques [36] to identify input regions that might produce false negatives. Thus, their approach is complementary to our uncertainty-based error detection, but, due to the limitations of the underlying verification algorithms, they can only support deterministic neural networks with sigmoid activations. On the contrary, our techniques support any kind of ML-based monitors, including probabilistic ones. The work of [3,4] addresses the predictive monitoring problem for stochastic black-box systems, where a Markov model is inferred offline from observed traces and used to construct a predictive runtime monitor for probabilistic reachability checking. In contrast to our method, this method focuses on discrete-space models, which allows the predictor to be represented as a look-up table, as opposed to a neural network. In [49], a method is presented for predictive monitoring of STL specifications with probabilistic guarantees. These guarantees derive from computing prediction intervals of ARMA/ARIMA models learned from observed traces. Similarly, we use CP which also can derive prediction intervals with probabilistic guarantees, with the difference that CP supports any class of prediction models (including auto-regressive ones). In [27], model predictions are used to forecast future robustness values of MTL specifications for runtime monitoring. However, no guarantee, statistical or otherwise, is provided for the predicted robustness. Deshmukh and others [25] have proposed an interval semantics for STL over partial traces, where such intervals are guaranteed to include the true STL robustness value for any bounded continuation of the trace. This approach can be used in the context of predictive monitoring but tends to produce over-conservative intervals. Another related approach is smoothed model checking [15], where Gaussian processes [51] are used to approximate the satisfaction function of stochastic models, i.e., mapping model parameters into the satisfaction probability of a specification. Smoothed model checking leverages Bayesian statistics to quantify prediction uncertainty, but faces scalability issues as the dimension of the system increases. These scalability issues are alleviated in [12] using stochastic variational inference. In contrast, computing our conformal measure of prediction reliability is very efficient, because it is nearly equivalent to executing the underlying predictor.

This tutorial builds on the methods presented in [12–14, 17–19, 48]. In NPM [13, 14], neural networks are used to infer the Boolean satisfaction of a reachability property and conformal prediction (CP) are used to provide statistical guarantees. NPM has been extended to support some source of stochasticity in the system: in [17] they allow partial observability and noisy observations, in [18] the system dynamics are stochastic but the monitor only evaluates the Boolean satisfaction of some quantile trajectories, providing a limited understanding of the safety level of the current state. Finally in [19] a conformal quantitative predictive monitor to reliably check the satisfaction of STL requirements over evolutions of a stochastic system at runtime is presented. Predictive monitoring under partial observability is also analysed in [24], where the authors combine Bayesian state estimation with pre-computed reach sets to reduce the runtime overhead. While their reachability bounds are certified, no correctness guarantees can be established for the estimation step.

Various learning-based PM approaches for temporal logic properties [41, 43, 50, 52, 64, 65] have been recently proposed. In particular, Ma et al. [41] use uncertainty quantification with Bayesian RNNs to provide confidence guarantees. However, these models are, by nature, not well-calibrated (i.e., the model uncertainty does not reflect the observed one [38]), making the resulting guarantees not theoretically valid. In [5] the parameter space of a parametric CTMC is explicitly explored, while [21] assumes a probability distribution over the parameters and proposes a sampling-based approach. In [40] conformal predictions are used over the expected value of the stochastic process rather than its distribution.

We contribute to the state of the art by presenting a wide variety of learning-based predictive monitors that offer good scalability, provide statistical guarantees, and support partial observability, stochasticity and rich STL-based requirements.

7   Conclusions

We have presented an overview of various learning-based approaches to reliably monitor the evolution of a CPS at runtime. The proposed methods complement predictions over the satisfaction of an STL specification with principled estimates of the prediction uncertainty. These estimates can be used to derive optimal rejection criteria that identify potentially erroneous predictions without knowing the true satisfaction values. The latter can be exploited as an active learning strategy increasing the accuracy of the satisfaction predictor. The strength is given by high-reliability and high computational efficiency of our predicitons. The efficiency is not directly affected by the complexity of the system under analysis but only by the complexity of the learned predictor. Our approach overcomes the computational footprint of model checking (infeasible at runtime) while improving on traditional runtime verification by being able to detect future violations in a preemptive way. We have devised two alternative solution methods: a frequentist and a Bayesian approach. Conformal predictions are used on top of both methods to obtain statistical guarantees.

In future work, we will investigate dynamics-aware approaches to inference. The aim is to improve the performances by limiting inference only to an estimate of the system manifold, i.e. the region of the state space that is likely to be visited by the evolving stochastic process.

Acknowledgments. This work has been partially supported by the PRIN project "SEDUCE" n. 2017TWRCNB, by the "REXASI-PRO" H-EU project, call HORIZON-CL4-2021-HUMAN-01-01, Grant agreement ID: 101070028 and by the PNRR project iNEST (Interconnected North-Est Innovation Ecosystem) funded by the European Union Next-GenerationEU (Piano Nazionale di Ripresa e Resilienza (PNRR) - Missione 4 Componente 2, Investimento 1.5 - D.D. 1058 23/06/2022, ECS_00000043).

References

1. Alur, R.: Principles of Cyber-Physical Systems. MIT Press, Cambridge (2015)
2. Annpureddy, Y., Liu, C., Fainekos, G., Sankaranarayanan, S.: S-TALiRo: a tool for temporal logic falsification for hybrid systems. In: Abdulla, P.A., Leino, K.R.M. (eds.) TACAS 2011. LNCS, vol. 6605, pp. 254–257. Springer, Heidelberg (2011). https://doi.org/10.1007/978-3-642-19835-9_21
3. Babaee, R., Ganesh, V., Sedwards, S.: Accelerated learning of predictive runtime monitors for rare failure. In: Finkbeiner, B., Mariani, L. (eds.) RV 2019. LNCS, vol. 11757, pp. 111–128. Springer, Cham (2019). https://doi.org/10.1007/978-3-030-32079-9_7
4. Babaee, R., Gurfinkel, A., Fischmeister, S.: Predictive run-time verification of discrete-time reachability properties in black-box systems using trace-level abstraction and statistical learning. In: Colombo, C., Leucker, M. (eds.) RV 2018. LNCS, vol. 11237, pp. 187–204. Springer, Cham (2018). https://doi.org/10.1007/978-3-030-03769-7_11
5. Badings, T.S., Jansen, N., Junges, S., Stoelinga, M., Volk, M.: Sampling-based verification of CTMCs with uncertain rates. In: Shoham, S., Vizel, Y. (eds.) CAV 2022. LNCS, vol. 13372, pp. 26–47. Springer, Cham (2022). https://doi.org/10.1007/978-3-031-13188-2_2
6. Bak, S., Duggirala, P.S.: HyLAA: a tool for computing simulation-equivalent reachability for linear systems. In: Proceedings of the 20th International Conference on Hybrid Systems: Computation and Control, pp. 173–178 (2017)
7. Bak, S., Johnson, T.T., Caccamo, M., Sha, L.: Real-time reachability for verified simplex design. In: Real-Time Systems Symposium (RTSS), 2014 IEEE, pp. 138–148. IEEE (2014)

8. Balasubramanian, V., Ho, S.S., Vovk, V.: Conformal Prediction for Reliable Machine Learning: Theory, Adaptations and Applications. Newnes, Oxford (2014)

9. Bartocci, E., et al.: Specification-based monitoring of cyber-physical systems: a survey on theory, tools and applications. In: Bartocci, E., Falcone, Y. (eds.) Lectures on Runtime Verification. LNCS, vol. 10457, pp. 135–175. Springer, Cham (2018). https://doi.org/10.1007/978-3-319-75632-5_5

10. Benvenuti, L., et al.: Reachability computation for hybrid systems with Ariadne. IFAC Proc. Volumes **41**(2), 8960–8965 (2008)

11. Bogomolov, S., Forets, M., Frehse, G., Potomkin, K., Schilling, C.: JuliaReach: a toolbox for set-based reachability. In: Proceedings of the 22nd ACM International Conference on Hybrid Systems: Computation and Control, pp. 39–44 (2019)

12. Bortolussi, L., Cairoli, F., Carbone, G., Pulcini, P.: Stochastic variational smoothed model checking. arXiv preprint arXiv:2205.05398 (2022)

13. Bortolussi, L., Cairoli, F., Paoletti, N., Smolka, S.A., Stoller, S.D.: Neural predictive monitoring. In: Finkbeiner, B., Mariani, L. (eds.) RV 2019. LNCS, vol. 11757, pp. 129–147. Springer, Cham (2019). https://doi.org/10.1007/978-3-030-32079-9_8

14. Bortolussi, L., Cairoli, F., Paoletti, N., Smolka, S.A., Stoller, S.D.: Neural predictive monitoring and a comparison of frequentist and Bayesian approaches. Int. J. Softw. Tools Technol. Transfer **23**(4), 615–640 (2021)

15. Bortolussi, L., Milios, D., Sanguinetti, G.: Smoothed model checking for uncertain continuous-time Markov chains. Inf. Comput. **247**, 235–253 (2016)

16. Brihaye, T., Doyen, L., Geeraerts, G., Ouaknine, J., Raskin, J.-F., Worrell, J.: On reachability for hybrid automata over bounded time. In: Aceto, L., Henzinger, M., Sgall, J. (eds.) ICALP 2011. LNCS, vol. 6756, pp. 416–427. Springer, Heidelberg (2011). https://doi.org/10.1007/978-3-642-22012-8_33

17. Cairoli, F., Bortolussi, L., Paoletti, N.: Neural predictive monitoring under partial observability. In: Feng, L., Fisman, D. (eds.) RV 2021. LNCS, vol. 12974, pp. 121–141. Springer, Cham (2021). https://doi.org/10.1007/978-3-030-88494-9_7

18. Cairoli, F., Paoletti, N., Bortolussi, L.: Neural predictive monitoring for collective adaptive systems. In: Margaria, T., Steffen, B. (eds.) ISoLA 2022. LNCS, vol. 13703, pp. 30–46. Springer, Cham (2022). https://doi.org/10.1007/978-3-031-19759-8_3

19. Cairoli, F., Paoletti, N., Bortolussi, L.: Conformal quantitative predictive monitoring of STL requirements for stochastic processes. In: Proceedings of the 26th ACM International Conference on Hybrid Systems: Computation and Control, pp. 1–11 (2023)

20. Cauchois, M., Gupta, S., Ali, A., Duchi, J.C.: Robust validation: confident predictions even when distributions shift. arXiv preprint arXiv:2008.04267 (2020)

21. Češka, M., Dannenberg, F., Paoletti, N., Kwiatkowska, M., Brim, L.: Precise parameter synthesis for stochastic biochemical systems. Acta Informatica **54**, 589–623 (2017)

22. Chen, H., Lin, S., Smolka, S.A., Paoletti, N.: An STL-based formulation of resilience in cyber-physical systems. In: Bogomolov, S., Parker, D. (eds.) FORMATS 2022. LNCS, vol. 13465, pp. 117–135. Springer, Cham (2022). https://doi.org/10.1007/978-3-031-15839-1_7

23. Chen, X., Sankaranarayanan, S.: Model predictive real-time monitoring of linear systems. In: Real-Time Systems Symposium (RTSS), 2017 IEEE, pp. 297–306. IEEE (2017)

24. Chou, Y., Yoon, H., Sankaranarayanan, S.: Predictive runtime monitoring of vehicle models using Bayesian estimation and reachability analysis. In: International Conference on Intelligent Robots and Systems (IROS) (2020)

25. Deshmukh, J.V., Donzé, A., Ghosh, S., Jin, X., Juniwal, G., Seshia, S.A.: Robust online monitoring of signal temporal logic. Formal Meth. Syst. Des. **51**(1), 5–30 (2017)
26. Djeridane, B., Lygeros, J.: Neural approximation of PDE solutions: an application to reachability computations. In: Proceedings of the 45th IEEE Conference on Decision and Control, pp. 3034–3039. IEEE (2006)
27. Dokhanchi, A., Hoxha, B., Fainekos, G.: On-line monitoring for temporal logic robustness. In: Bonakdarpour, B., Smolka, S.A. (eds.) RV 2014. LNCS, vol. 8734, pp. 231–246. Springer, Cham (2014). https://doi.org/10.1007/978-3-319-11164-3_19
28. Donzé, A.: Breach, a toolbox for verification and parameter synthesis of hybrid systems. In: Touili, T., Cook, B., Jackson, P. (eds.) CAV 2010. LNCS, vol. 6174, pp. 167–170. Springer, Heidelberg (2010). https://doi.org/10.1007/978-3-642-14295-6_17
29. Donzé, A., Maler, O.: Robust satisfaction of temporal logic over real-valued signals. In: Chatterjee, K., Henzinger, T.A. (eds.) FORMATS 2010. LNCS, vol. 6246, pp. 92–106. Springer, Heidelberg (2010). https://doi.org/10.1007/978-3-642-15297-9_9
30. Duggirala, P.S., Mitra, S., Viswanathan, M., Potok, M.: C2E2: a verification tool for stateflow models. In: Baier, C., Tinelli, C. (eds.) TACAS 2015. LNCS, vol. 9035, pp. 68–82. Springer, Heidelberg (2015). https://doi.org/10.1007/978-3-662-46681-0_5
31. Frehse, G.: PHAVer: algorithmic verification of hybrid systems past HyTech. In: Morari, M., Thiele, L. (eds.) HSCC 2005. LNCS, vol. 3414, pp. 258–273. Springer, Heidelberg (2005). https://doi.org/10.1007/978-3-540-31954-2_17
32. Frehse, G., et al.: SpaceEx: scalable verification of hybrid systems. In: Gopalakrishnan, G., Qadeer, S. (eds.) CAV 2011. LNCS, vol. 6806, pp. 379–395. Springer, Heidelberg (2011). https://doi.org/10.1007/978-3-642-22110-1_30
33. Gammerman, A., Vovk, V.: Hedging predictions in machine learning. Comput. J. **50**(2), 151–163 (2007)
34. Hensel, C., Junges, S., Katoen, J.P., Quatmann, T., Volk, M.: The probabilistic model checker storm. Int. J. Softw. Tools Technol. Transfer **24**, 589–610 (2021)
35. Henzinger, T.A., Kopke, P.W., Puri, A., Varaiya, P.: What's decidable about hybrid automata? In: Proceedings of the Twenty-Seventh Annual ACM Symposium on Theory of Computing, pp. 373–382 (1995)
36. Ivanov, R., Weimer, J., Alur, R., Pappas, G.J., Lee, I.: Verisig: verifying safety properties of hybrid systems with neural network controllers. In: Proceedings of the 22nd ACM International Conference on Hybrid Systems: Computation and Control, pp. 169–178 (2019)
37. Johnson, T.T., Bak, S., Caccamo, M., Sha, L.: Real-time reachability for verified simplex design. ACM Trans. Embed. Comput. Syst. (TECS) **15**(2), 1–27 (2016)
38. Kuleshov, V., Fenner, N., Ermon, S.: Accurate uncertainties for deep learning using calibrated regression. In: International Conference on Machine Learning, pp. 2796–2804. PMLR (2018)
39. Kwiatkowska, M., Norman, G., Parker, D.: PRISM 4.0: verification of probabilistic real-time systems. In: Gopalakrishnan, G., Qadeer, S. (eds.) CAV 2011. LNCS, vol. 6806, pp. 585–591. Springer, Heidelberg (2011). https://doi.org/10.1007/978-3-642-22110-1_47
40. Lindemann, L., Qin, X., Deshmukh, J.V., Pappas, G.J.: Conformal prediction for STL runtime verification. In: Proceedings of the ACM/IEEE 14th International Conference on Cyber-Physical Systems (with CPS-IoT Week 2023), pp. 142–153 (2023)

41. Ma, M., Stankovic, J., Bartocci, E., Feng, L.: Predictive monitoring with logic-calibrated uncertainty for cyber-physical systems. ACM Trans. Embed. Comput. Syst. (TECS) **20**(5s), 1–25 (2021)
42. Maler, O., Nickovic, D.: Monitoring temporal properties of continuous signals. In: Lakhnech, Y., Yovine, S. (eds.) FORMATS/FTRTFT -2004. LNCS, vol. 3253, pp. 152–166. Springer, Heidelberg (2004). https://doi.org/10.1007/978-3-540-30206-3_12
43. Muthali, A., et al.: Multi-agent reachability calibration with conformal prediction. arXiv preprint arXiv:2304.00432 (2023)
44. Ničković, D., Yamaguchi, T.: RTAMT: online robustness monitors from STL. In: Hung, D.V., Sokolsky, O. (eds.) ATVA 2020. LNCS, vol. 12302, pp. 564–571. Springer, Cham (2020). https://doi.org/10.1007/978-3-030-59152-6_34
45. Papadopoulos, H.: Inductive conformal prediction: theory and application to neural networks. In: Tools in Artificial Intelligence. InTech (2008)
46. Papadopoulos, H., Haralambous, H.: Reliable prediction intervals with regression neural networks. Neural Netw.: J. Int. Neural Net. Soc. **24**(8), 842–51 (2011)
47. Papadopoulos, H., Vovk, V., Gammerman, A.: Regression conformal prediction with nearest neighbours. J. Artif. Intell. Res. **40**, 815–840 (2014)
48. Phan, D., Paoletti, N., Zhang, T., Grosu, R., Smolka, S.A., Stoller, S.D.: Neural state classification for hybrid systems. In: Lahiri, S.K., Wang, C. (eds.) ATVA 2018. LNCS, vol. 11138, pp. 422–440. Springer, Cham (2018). https://doi.org/10.1007/978-3-030-01090-4_25
49. Qin, X., Deshmukh, J.V.: Predictive monitoring for signal temporal logic with probabilistic guarantees. In: Proceedings of the 22nd ACM International Conference on Hybrid Systems: Computation and Control, pp. 266–267. ACM (2019)
50. Qin, X., Deshmukh, J.V.: Clairvoyant monitoring for signal temporal logic. In: Bertrand, N., Jansen, N. (eds.) FORMATS 2020. LNCS, vol. 12288, pp. 178–195. Springer, Cham (2020). https://doi.org/10.1007/978-3-030-57628-8_11
51. Rasmussen, C.E., Williams, C.K.: Gaussian Processes for Machine Learning. vol. 1. MIT Press, Cambridge (2006)
52. Rodionova, A., Lindemann, L., Morari, M., Pappas, G.J.: Time-robust control for STL specifications. In: 2021 60th IEEE Conference on Decision and Control (CDC), pp. 572–579. IEEE (2021)
53. Romano, Y., Patterson, E., Candes, E.: Conformalized quantile regression. In: Advances in Neural Information Processing Systems, vol. 32 (2019)
54. Royo, V.R., Fridovich-Keil, D., Herbert, S., Tomlin, C.J.: Classification-based approximate reachability with guarantees applied to safe trajectory tracking. arXiv preprint arXiv:1803.03237 (2018)
55. Sauter, G., Dierks, H., Fränzle, M., Hansen, M.R.: Lightweight hybrid model checking facilitating online prediction of temporal properties. In: Proceedings of the 21st Nordic Workshop on Programming Theory, pp. 20–22 (2009)
56. Schupp, S., Ábrahám, E., Makhlouf, I.B., Kowalewski, S.: HyPro: A C++ Library of state set representations for hybrid systems reachability analysis. In: Barrett, C., Davies, M., Kahsai, T. (eds.) NFM 2017. LNCS, vol. 10227, pp. 288–294. Springer, Cham (2017). https://doi.org/10.1007/978-3-319-57288-8_20
57. Shafer, G., Vovk, V.: A tutorial on conformal prediction. J. Mach. Learn. Res. **9**, 371–421 (2008)
58. Stankeviciute, K., Alaa, A.M., van der Schaar, M.: Conformal time-series forecasting. In: Advances in Neural Information Processing Systems, vol. 34, pp. 6216–6228 (2021)

59. Tibshirani, R.J., Foygel Barber, R., Candes, E., Ramdas, A.: Conformal prediction under covariate shift. In: Advances in Neural Information Processing Systems, vol. 32 (2019)
60. Toccaceli, P., Gammerman, A.: Combination of inductive Mondrian conformal predictors. Mach. Learn. **108**(3), 489–510 (2019)
61. Vovk, V., Gammerman, A., Shafer, G.: Algorithmic Learning in a Random World. Springer, Cham (2005). https://doi.org/10.1007/978-3-031-06649-8
62. Yel, E., et al.: Assured runtime monitoring and planning: toward verification of neural networks for safe autonomous operations. IEEE Robot. Autom. Mag. **27**(2), 102–116 (2020)
63. Yoon, H., Chou, Y., Chen, X., Frew, E., Sankaranarayanan, S.: Predictive runtime monitoring for linear stochastic systems and applications to geofence enforcement for UAVs. In: Finkbeiner, B., Mariani, L. (eds.) RV 2019. LNCS, vol. 11757, pp. 349–367. Springer, Cham (2019). https://doi.org/10.1007/978-3-030-32079-9_20
64. Yoon, H., Sankaranarayanan, S.: Predictive runtime monitoring for mobile robots using logic-based Bayesian intent inference. In: 2021 IEEE International Conference on Robotics and Automation (ICRA), pp. 8565–8571. IEEE (2021)
65. Yu, X., Dong, W., Yin, X., Li, S.: Model predictive monitoring of dynamic systems for signal temporal logic specifications. arXiv preprint arXiv:2209.12493 (2022)
66. Zaffran, M., Féron, O., Goude, Y., Josse, J., Dieuleveut, A.: Adaptive conformal predictions for time series. In: International Conference on Machine Learning, pp. 25834–25866. PMLR (2022)

Author Index

P. Katsaros and L. Nenzi (Eds.): RV 2023, LNCS 14245, pp. 489–490, 2023.
https://doi.org/10.1007/978-3-031-44267-4

Printed in the United States
by Baker & Taylor Publisher Services